And others

The History of Indian Literature

And others

The History of Indian Literature

ISBN/EAN: 9783337059811

Printed in Europe, USA, Canada, Australia, Japan

Cover: Foto ©ninafisch / pixelio.de

More available books at **www.hansebooks.com**

THE HISTORY

OF

INDIAN LITERATURE.

BY

ALBRECHT WEBER.

Translated from the Second German Edition

BY

JOHN MANN, M.A.,

AND

THEODOR ZACHARIAE, PH.D.,

With the Sanction of the Author.

Nil desperari—
Auch hier wird es tagen.

THIRD EDITION.

LONDON:
KEGAN PAUL, TRENCH, TRÜBNER, & CO. LTD
PATERNOSTER HOUSE, CHARING CROSS ROAD.
1892.

TRANSLATORS' NOTE.

ACCORDING to the original intention, the English translation of this work was to have appeared shortly after the second German edition, which came out in the end of 1875, and which, as mentioned by the author in his preface, was in part prepared with a view to this translation. In consequence, however, of the death of Professor Childers, under whose direction it was in the first instance begun, and of whose aid and supervision it would, had he lived, have had the benefit, the work came to a stand-still, and some time elapsed before the task of continuing and completing it was entrusted to those whose names appear on the title-page. The manuscript of the translation thus interrupted embraced a considerable part of the text of the first division of the work (Vedic Literature). It had not undergone any revision by Professor Childers, and was found to be in a somewhat imperfect state, and to require very material modification. Upon Mr. Zachariae devolved the labour of correcting it, of completing it as far as the close of the Vedic Period, and of adding the notes to this First Part, none of which had been translated. From the number of changes introduced in the course of revision, the portion of the work comprised in the manuscript in question has virtually been re-translated. The rendering of the second division of the volume (Sanskṛit Literature) is entirely and exclusively the work of Mr. Mann.

The circumstances under which the translation has been

produced have greatly delayed its appearance. But for this delay some compensation is afforded by the Supplementary Notes which Professor Weber has written for incorporation in the volume (p. 311 ff.), and which supply information regarding the latest researches and the newest publications bearing upon the subjects discussed in the work. Professor Weber has also been good enough to read the sheets as they came from the press, and the translators are indebted to him for a number of suggestions.

A few of the abbreviations made use of in the titles of works which are frequently quoted perhaps require explanation: *e.g.*, *I. St.* for Weber's *Indische Studien*; *I. Str.* for his *Indische Streifen*; *I. AK.* for Lassen's *Indische Alterthumskunde*; *Z. D. M. G.* for *Zeitschrift der deutschen morgenländischen Gesellschaft*, &c.

The system of transliteration is in the main identical with that followed in the German original; as, however, it varies in a few particulars, it is given here instead of in the Author's Preface. It is as follows:—

a	á	i	í	u	ú	ṛi	ṛí
ḷi	ḷí	e	ai	o	au;		
k	kh	g	gh	ṅ;			
ch	chh	j	jh	ñ;			
ṭ	ṭh	ḍ	ḍh	ṇ;			
t	th	d	dh	n;			
p	ph	b	bh	m;			
y	r	l	v;				
ś	sh	s	h;				

Anusvára ṃ, in the middle of a word before sibilants ṅ; Visarga ḥ.

July, 1878.

PREFACE TO THE SECOND EDITION.

The work of my youth, which here appears in a new edition, had been several years out of print. To have republished it without alteration would scarcely have done; and, owing to the pressure of other labours, it was impossible for me, from lack of time, to subject it to a complete and systematic remodelling. So the matter rested. At last, to meet the urgent wish of the publisher, I resolved upon the present edition, which indeed leaves the original text unchanged, but at the same time seeks, by means of the newly added notes, to accommodate itself to the actual position of knowledge. In thus finally deciding, I was influenced by the belief that in no other way could the great advances made in this field of learning since the first appearance of this work be more clearly exhibited than precisely in this way, and that, consequently, this edition might at the same time serve in some measure to present, *in nuce*, a history of Sanskṛit studies during the last four-and-twenty years. Another consideration was, that only by so doing could I furnish a critically secured basis for the English translation contemplated by Messrs. Trübner & Co., which could not possibly now give the original text alone, as was done in the French translation,* which appeared at Paris in 1859. It was, indeed, while going over the work with the view of preparing it for this English translation, that the hope, nay, the conviction, grew upon me, that, although a complete reconstruction of it was out of the question, still an edition like the present might advantageously appear in a German dress also. I rejoiced to see that this labour of my youth was standing well the test of time. I found in it little that was absolutely erroneous, although much even now remains as uncertain and unsettled as formerly; while, on the other hand, many things already stand clear and sure which I then only doubtfully conjectured, or which were at that time still completely enveloped in obscurity.

The obtaining of critical data from the contents of Indian literature, with a view to the establishment of its internal chronology and history—not the setting forth in detail of the subject-matter of the different works—was, from the beginning, the object I had before me in these lectures; and this object, together with that of specifying the publications which have seen the light in the interval, has continued to be my leading point of view in the present annotation of them. To mark off the new matter, square brackets are used.† . . . . .

The number of fellow-workers has greatly increased during the last twenty-four years. Instead of here running over their names, I have preferred—in order thus to faci-

* *Histoire de la Littérature Indienne, trad. de l'Allemand par Alfred Sadous.* Paris: A. Durand. 1859.

† In the translation, these brackets are only retained to mark new matter added in the second edition to the original notes of the first; the notes which in the second edition were entirely new are here simply indicated by numbers.—Tr.

litate a general view of this part of the subject—to add to the Index, which in other respects also has been considerably enlarged, a new section, showing where I have availed myself of the writings of each, or have at least referred to them. One work there is, however, which, as it underlies all recent labours in this field, and cannot possibly be cited on every occasion when it is made use of, calls for special mention in this place—I mean the Sanskṛit Dictionary of Böhtlingk and Roth, which was completed in the course of last summer.* The carrying through of this great work, which we owe to the patronage of the St. Petersburg Academy of Sciences, over a period of a quarter of a century, will reflect lasting honour upon that body as well as upon the two editors.

A. W.

BERLIN, *November*, 1875.

---

* The second edition bears the inscription : 'Dedicated to my friends, Böhtlingk and Roth, on the completion of the Sanskṛit Dictionary.'—TR.

PREFACE TO THE FIRST EDITION.

The lectures herewith presented to the narrow circle of my fellows in this field of study, and also, it is hoped, to the wider circle of those interested in researches into the history of literature generally, are a first attempt, and as such, naturally, defective and capable of being in many respects supplemented and improved. The material they deal with is too vast, and the means of mastering it in general too inaccessible, not to have for a lengthened period completely checked inquiry into its *internal relative* chronology—the only chronology that is possible. Nor could I ever have ventured upon such a labour, had not the Berlin Royal Library had the good fortune to possess the fine collection of Sanskṛit MSS. formed by Sir R. Chambers, the acquisition of which some ten years ago, through the liberality of his Majesty, Frederick William IV., and by the agency of his Excellency Baron Bunsen, opened up to Sanskṛit philology a fresh path, upon which it has already made vigorous progress. In the course of last year, commissioned by the Royal Library, I undertook the work of cataloguing this collection, and as the result a detailed catalogue will appear about simultaneously with these lectures, which may in some sense be regarded as a commentary upon it. Imperfect as, from the absolute point of view, both works must appear, I yet cherish the hope that they may render good service to learning.

How great my obligations are, in the special investigations, to the writings of Colebrooke, Wilson, Lassen, Burnouf, Roth, Reinaud, Stenzler, and Holtzmann, I only mention here generally, as I have uniformly given ample references to these authorities in the proper place.

The form in which these lectures appear is essentially the same in which they were delivered,* with the exception of a few modifications of style: thus, in particular, the transitions and recapitulations belonging to oral delivery have been either curtailed or omitted; while, on the other hand, to the incidental remarks—here given as foot-notes—much new matter has been added.

A. W.

BERLIN, *July*, 1852.

* In the Winter-Semester of 1851–52.

TABLE OF CONTENTS.

INTRODUCTION, ... 1-7

Antiquity of Indian literature, 2; proved by geographical evidence, 3-4; by internal evidence from the history of the Hindú religion, 5; by evidence drawn from the language, 6; want of external chronology, 7.

FIRST PERIOD—VEDIC LITERATURE.

PRELIMINARY SURVEY, ... 8-30

(1.) *The Saṃhitás*, 8-11.

Saṃhitás of the three older Vedas, 8-9; mutual relation of these three Vedas, 9-10; period of their final compilation, 10; Saṃhitá of the Atharvan, 11.

(2.) *The Bráhmaṇas*, 11-15.

Their character, 12, and origin, 13; mutual relation of the Bráhmaṇas of the several Vedas, 14; their common name Śruti, 15.

(3.) *The Sútras*, &c.

Their character and origin, 16; Śrauta-Sútras, 17; Gṛihya- or Smárta-Sútras, 17; gradual transformation of the original Smṛiti (Custom and Law), 17, 18; origin of caste, 18; connection between the Gṛihya-Sútras and the legal literature, 19-20; linguistic Sútras, their origin, 20, 21; character of the time in question, 21, 22; Prátiśákhya-Sútras, 23; metric, 23; Anukramaṇís, 24; tradition—Bṛihaddevatá, 24; Nighaṇṭu, Nirukti, the Vedáñgas, 25; science of grammar, 26; philosophical speculation, 26 ff.; names applied to the early sages, 28; Upanishads, Áraṇyakas, 28, 29; astronomy and medicine, 29, 30.

A.—ṚIGVEDA, ... 31-62

(*a*) *Saṃhitá*, 31-44.

Its divisions, 31, 32; Śákala and Váshkala recensions.

32; Várkali, the school of the Śunakas, 33; Śaunaka, Pañchála Bábhravya, 34; mythology of the primitive Indo-Germanic time, 35; Persian and Indian cycles of legend, 36, 37; mode of life of the Indians in their ancient home, 37, 38; reasons why they left their ancient homes, 38, 39; different constituents of Ṛigveda-Saṃhitá, 39; gods to whom the hymns are addressed, 40; exegetic literature connected with the Saṃhitá: Yáska, 41; Sáyaṇa, 41, 42; editions, translations, &c., 43, 44.

(b) *Bráhmaṇas*, 44–52.

Aitareya- and Śáṅkháyana-Bráhmaṇas, 44; data therein bearing on time of their composition, 45; they presuppose earlier compositions with similar contents, 45–47; fables and legends contained in these two Bráhmaṇas, 47; the Áraṇyakas of the Ṛik: Aitareya-Áraṇyaka, 48 ff.; Kaushítakáraṇyaka, Kaushítakopanishad, 50, 51; Śaṃkara's commentaries on the Upanishads, 51; Váshkala-Upanishad, 52.

(c) *Sútras*, 52, 62.

The Śrauta-Sútras of Áśvaláyana and Śáṅkháyana, 52 ff.; commentaries thereon, 54, 55; the Gṛihya-Sútras of Áśvaláyana and Śáṅkháyana, 55 ff.; the literature presupposed in these, 56, 57; Ṛik-Prátiśákhya, Upalekha, 59, 60; Śikshá, Chhandas, Jyotisha, 60, 61; Anukramaṇís, 61; Bṛihaddevatá, Ṛigvidhána, Pariśishṭas, 62.

B.—SÁMAVEDA, ... 63–85

(a) *Saṃhitá*, 63–66.

Its arrangement, 63; the Gánas, 64; antiquity of the readings of the Sáma-Saṃhitá, 64, 65; recensions, 65; editions, &c., 65, 66.

(b) *Bráhmaṇas*, 66–75.

The Táṇḍya-Pañchaviṅśa-Bráhmaṇa, 66 ff.; geographical and other data contained therein, 67–68; Shaḍviṅśa-Bráhmaṇa, 69; Chhándogyopanishad, its relation to the Vṛihad-Áraṇyaka, 70, 71; literary and other data in the Chhándogyop., 71, 72; Kenopanishad, 73; the smaller Bráhmaṇas of the Sáman.—Sámavidhána, &c., 74, 75.

(c) *Sútras*, 75–85.

Śrauta-Sútras: the Kalpa-Sútra of Maśaka, 75–76; Láṭyáyana-Sútra, 76 ff.; literature therein presupposed, 76, 77; position of non-Brahmaṇical tribes in this work, 77; existence of Buddhism presupposed, 78; Sútra of Dráhyáyaṇa, 79; its relation to the Sútras of the other

Vedas, 80; Anupada-Sútra, 80, 81; Nidána-Sútra, 81, 82; the Pushpa-Sútra of Gobhila, 82; Sáma-Tantra, Pañchavidhi-, Pratihára-, Taṇḍúlakshaṇa-, and Upagrantha-Sútras, 83; the Gṛihya-Sútra of Gobhila, 84; the Karma-pradípa of Kátyáyana, 84; Paddhatis and Pariśishṭas, 85.

C.—YAJURVEDA, ... 85-145

I.—The Black Yajus, ... 85-103

(a) *Saṃhitás*, 85-91.

Difference between the Black and the White Yajus, 86; names of the Black Yajus, 86 ff.; Charaka, Taittiríya, and Kháṇḍikíya, 87, 88; schools of the Black Yajus: Taittiríya-Saṃhitá (Ápastamba), the Káṭhaka, and the Átreyí Śákhá, 88; Saṃhitás of the Ápastamba and Átreya schools, and the Káṭhaka, 89; data contained therein, 90; Yáska's connection with the arrangement of the Saṃhitá of the Black Yajus, 91; the Mánava and the Maitra, 91.

(b) *Bráhmaṇas*, 92-99.

The Bráhmaṇas of the Ápastamba and Átreya schools; the Káṭhaka portion of the Taitt. Bráhmaṇa, 92; Taittiríya-Áraṇyaka, 93; Upanishads of the Taitt. Ár., 93, 94; schools of the Bhállavins, Śáṭyáyanins, Śákáyanins, &c., 95; Śvetáśvataropanishad, 96; Maitráyaṇa-Upanishad, its modern date, 97; the planets, &c., in the Maitr. Up., 98; possible relation of the work to Buddha, 99.

(c) *Sútras*, 99-103.

Śrauta-Sútras, 99-101; Gṛihya-Sútras, 101, 102; Prátiśákhya-Sútra, 102; Anukramaṇís, 103.

II.—The White Yajus, ... 103-145

The name explained, 103 f.; the name 'Vájasaneya,' 104 f.; the two schools of the Káṇvas and Mádhyaṃdinas, 105; possible connection of the Mádhyaṃdinas with the *Μαδιανδινοί*, 106.

(a) *Saṃhitá*, 107-116.

Division of the Vájasaneyi-Saṃhitá, 107; later origin of the last fifteen *adhyáyas*, 108; relation of the several parts of the Váj. S. to the Black Yajus, 108; to its own Bráhmaṇa, and to each other, 109-110; probable date of the Rudra-book, 110; the mixed castes, 111; position of the Mágadha, 111; his position in the Atharva-Veda, 112; astronomical and other data in the Váj. S., 113; position of the Kurus and Pañchálas, the names Subhadrá and Kámpíla, 114; Arjuna and

Phalguna as (secret) names of Indra, 115; the *richas* incorporated in the Yajus, 115, 116; editions, commentaries, 116.

(*b*) *Bráhmaṇa*, 116–139.

The Śatapatha-Bráhmaṇa, 116; its name and extent, 117; relation of the Bráhmaṇa of the Káṇva school to that of the Mádhyaṃdinas, 117, 118; relation of the several *káṇḍas* to the Saṃhitá and to each other, 118, 119; posteriority of the last five *káṇḍas*, 120; Agnirahasya-káṇḍa, 120, 121; Ashṭádhyáyí-káṇḍa, 121; subjects of study named therein, 121, 122; other data, 122, 123; Aśvamedha-káṇḍa, 124 ff.; Gáthás, 124, 125; position of Janamejaya, 125; of the Párikshitíyas, 126; the Áraṇyaka-káṇḍa, 126; the Vṛihad-Áraṇyaka:—Madhu-káṇḍa, 127; its name and list of teachers, 128; Yájnavalkíya-káṇḍa, 129; Khila-káṇḍa, 130; the concluding *vaṅśa* of the Śatapatha-Bráhmaṇa, 131; probable north-western origin of *káṇḍas* vi.–x. of the Śatap. Br., 132; the whole blended together by one arranging hand, 133; teachers mentioned in the Śatap. Br., 133, 134; legends, 134 ff.; relation of these to the Epic legends, 135; position of the Kuru-Pañchálas compared with that of the Párikshitas, 136; the Páṇḍavas not mentioned, 137; points of contact with the Sáṃkhya tradition, 137; with Buddhist legend, 138; commentaries on the Śatap. Br., editions, &c., 139.

(*c*) *Sútras*, 139–145.

The Śrauta-Sútra of Kátyáyana, teachers mentioned therein, 139; other data, 140; commentaries, 141; Paddhatis and Pariśishṭas: Nigama-Pariśishṭa, Pravarádhyáya, Charaṇa-vyúha; the Vaijavápa-Sútra, 142; the Kátíya-Gṛihya-Sútra of Páraskara, 142, 143; the Prátiśákhya-Sútra of the Vájasaneyi-Saṃh., 143, 144; Anukramaṇí, 144, 145.

D.—ATHARVAVEDA, ... 145–171

(*a*) *Saṃhitá*, 145–150.

Extent and division of Atharvaveda-Saṃhitá, 145, 146; its contents and arrangement, 146; it probably originated in part with the unbráhmanised Aryans of the West, 147; data furnished by the Ath. S., the name 'Atharvan,' 148; earliest mention of this name, 149; the name 'Brahmaveda,' its meaning, 149, 150; editions, &c., of the Ath. S., 150.

(b) *Bráhmaṇa.*

The Gopatha-Bráhmaṇa, 150–151.

(c) *Sútras*, 151–153.

The Śaunakíyá Chaturadhyáyiká, 151; Anukramaṇí, 152; the Kauśika-Sútra, 152; Kalpas and Pariśishṭas, 153.

UPANISHADS, 153–171.

Number of the Upanishads, 154, 155; Upanishads belonging to the three older Vedas, 155, 156; special division of the Atharvopanishads into three groups: Vedánta, Yoga, and Sectarian Upanishads, 156; Atharvan recension of Upanishads borrowed from the other Vedas, 157. THE ATHARVOPANISHADS PROPER: (1.) *those of the Vedánta class*—the Muṇḍakopanishad, 158, 159; Praśnopanishad, 159, 160; Garbhopanishad, 160; Brahmopanishad, 160, 161; Máṇḍúkyopanishad, 161; remaining Upanishads of the Vedánta class: Práṇágnihotrop., Árshikop., 161, 162; (2) *Atharvopanishads of the Yoga class:* Jábála, Kaṭhaśruti, Áruṇika, Bhállavi, and others, 163; range of ideas and style in this class of Upanishads, 165; (3) *the Sectarian Upanishads*, 165 ff.; (a) those in which worship of Vishṇu (under the names Náráyaṇa, &c.) is inculcated, 166; Nṛisiṅhatápaníyopanishad, 167; Rámatápaníyopanishad, 168; Gopálatápaníyopanishad, 169; (β) Upanishads of the Śiva sects: Śatarudriya, Kaivalyopanishad, 169; Atharvaśiras, 169, 170; remaining Upanishads of the Śiva sects, 170, 171.

SECOND PERIOD—SANSKRIT LITERATURE.

WHEREIN DISTINGUISHED FROM FIRST PERIOD, . . . 175–183

Distinction in respect of language, 175; gradual development of Indo-Aryan *Bháshá*, 176; influence of Indian aborigines thereon, 177; separation of written language from popular dialects—ancient dialectic differences, 178; rock-inscriptions in popular dialects, 179; internal evidence for posteriority of second period, 180; critical condition of texts in this period—age of MSS., 181; distinction as regards subject-matter, 182; classification of Sanskṛit literature, 183.

A.—WORKS OF POETRY, ... 183–215

1. EPIC POETRY, 183–196.

(a) *Itihása*, 183–189: forerunners of Epic poetry in Vedic

period, 183; the Mahá-Bhárata, 184; existence of a work resembling it in first century A.D., 186; legend of Mahá-Bhárata, its relation to Śatapatha-Bráhmaṇa, &c., 186; text of Mahá-Bhárata, non-epic constituents, 187; Kavi translation; Jaimini-Bhárata, 189; (*b*) *Puráṇas*: their general character—ancient Puráṇas lost—absence of epic and prominence of ritual element in existing Puráṇas and Upa-puráṇas, 190, 191; (*c*) *Kávyas*, 191–196: the Rámáyaṇa, 191; its allegorical character, 192; colonisation of Southern India, 193; Rámáyaṇa the work of a single author, 193; different recensions of the text, 194; remaining Kávyas, artificial Epic, 195.

2. DRAMATIC POETRY, 196–208.

Origin of Drama from dancing, 196; Naṭa-Sútras mentioned in Páṇini, 197; dancing at the great sacrificial festivals, 198; alleged mention of dramas in oldest (?) Buddhistic writings, 199; age of surviving dramas, 200; no foundation for the view which places Kálidása in the first century B.C., 201, 202; internal evidence from Kálidása's dramas themselves on this point, 203; authenticity of the Málavikágnimitra, 204; age of Śúdraka's Mṛichhakaṭí, 205; subject-matter and special peculiarities of the Hindú drama, 206; possibility of Greek influence on its development, 207.

3. LYRICAL POETRY, 208–210.

Religious lyric, 208; Erotic lyric: Megha-dúta, &c., 209; mystical character of some of these poems—the Gíta-govinda, 210.

4. ETHICO-DIDACTIC POETRY, 210–213.

Níti-śástras, 210; 'Beast-Fable,' 211; Pañcha-tantra, Hitopadeśa, 212; popular tales and romances, 213.

5. HISTORY AND GEOGRAPHY, 213–215.

Rája-taraṃgiṇí, 213; inscriptions, grants, and coins, 215.

B.—WORKS OF SCIENCE AND ART, ... 215–276

1. SCIENCE OF LANGUAGE, 216–232.

(*a*) *Grammar*, 216–225: Páṇini's Grammar, its peculiar terminology, 216; Páṇini's date—statements of the Chinese traveller Hiuan Thsang, 217; weakness of the evidence on which Böhtlingk's view rests, 218; existence of Mahábháshya in the time of Abhimanyu, 219; acquaintance with Greeks presupposed in Páṇini, 220; 'Yavanání,' 221; commentaries on Páṇini—Paribhásháš,

Várttikas, Maháblháshya, 222; date of Kátyáyana, 222; of the Mahábhéshya, 223; critical condition of the text of Páṇini, 224; Gaṇa-páṭha, &c., 225; other grammatical systems, 226. (b) *Lexicography*, 227–230: Amara-kosha, no foundation for the view which places it in the first century B.C., 228; internal evidence against this view, 229; age of the work still uncertain, 230; Dhátu-páṭhas, 230. (c) *Metric, Poetics, Rhetoric*, 231, 232: Chhandaḥ-śástra of Piṅgala, Alaṃkára-śástra of Bharata, Sáhitya-darpaṇa, 231.

2. PHILOSOPHY, 232–246.

High antiquity of philosophical speculation among the Hindús, 232; 'Development,' 'Arrangement,' 'Creation' theories of the world, 233; gradual growth of these theories into philosophical systems, 234; the Sáṃkhya-system, 235, 236; the Yoga-system, 237; Deistic sects, 238; influence of Sáṃkhya-Yoga on development of Gnosticism and Śúfism, 239; the two Mímáṅsás, 239; Karma-Mímáṅsá-Sútra of Jaimini, 240; Brahma-Mímáṅsá-Sútra of Bádaráyaṇa, 242; age of Bádaráyaṇa, 243; the two logical systems, Nyáya and Vaiśeshika, 244; Heterodox systems, 246.

3. ASTRONOMY AND AUXILIARY SCIENCES, 246–264.

Antiquity of astronomy, 246; solar year, quinquennial cycle, Yugas, 247; the lunar asterisms, 247; mention of these in Ṛik-Saṃhitá, 248; Jyotisha, 249; the planets, 249; their peculiar Indian names and number, 250; importance of Greek influence here, 251; relations of Greeks with India, 251; the Yavanas, teachers of the ancient Indian astronomers, 252; 'Ptolemaios,' 'Asura-Maya,' 253; Romaka-Siddhánta, Pauliśa-Siddhánta, 253; Greek terms in Varáha-Mihira, 254, 255; further development of Indian astronomy: Hindús the teachers of the Arabs, 255 (also in algebra and arithmetic,—the arithmetical figures, 256), and through the Arabs, of European mediæval astronomers, 257; Áryabhaṭa, 257; the five Siddhántas, 258; Brahmagupta, Varáha-Mihira, 259; date of Varáha-Mihira, Śatánanda, and Bháskara, 260, 261; Albírúní's statements regarding Bháskara (?), 262. Later period: Arabs in turn the teachers of the Hindús in astrology, 263; Arabic technical terms in Indian and European astrological works, 263, 264; lore of omens and portents, 264; magic, &c., 264.

4. Medical Science, 265–271.

Its earliest representatives, 265; Charaka, Suśruta, Dhanvantari, 266; Śálihotra, Vátsyáyana, 267; uncertain date of extant medical works, 268; Hindú medicine apparently an independent development, 269; questionable authenticity of existing texts, 269; importance of Indian medicine, 269; its influence on Arabs, 270.

5. Art of War, Music, Formative and Technical Arts, 271–276.

Art of war (Dhanur-veda): Viśvámitra, Bharadvája, 271; music (Gándharva-veda), 271 (musical notation, 272); Artha-śástra, 273: painting and sculpture, 273; architecture, 274; technical arts, 275.

C.—WORKS ON LAW, CUSTOM, AND RELIGIOUS WORSHIP, ... 276–283

The Dharma-Śástras, 276; Code of Manu, Brahmanical organisation as here presented, 276; highly developed judicial procedure here exhibited, 277; connection of Dharma-Śástras with Gṛihya-Sútras, 277, 278; critical questions connected with existing text of Manu, 279; different redactions of Manu and the other Dharma-Śástras, number of these, 280; relation of Manu's Code to that of Yájnavalkya, date of the latter, 280, 281; Epic poetry and Puráṇas also sources for Hindú law, 282; modern jurisprudence, 282; Dekhan the chief seat of literary activity after eleventh century, 283.

D.—BUDDHISTIC SANSKṚIT LITERATURE, ... 283–310

Buddhism, its origin from Sáṃkhya doctrine, 284; relation of Buddhist legend to the later portions of Vedic literature, 285; princes of same name in Buddhist legend and Śatapatha-Bráhmaṇa, 286; position in former of Kuru-Pañchálas, Páṇḍavas, Mágadhas, 286, 287; Buddhist eras, 287; discordance of these with other historical evidence, 287; earliest demonstrable use of these eras, 288; Buddha's doctrine, 288; his novel way of promulgating it, and opposition to Brahmanical hierarchy, 289; tradition as to redaction of Buddhistic sacred scriptures, Northern and Southern, 290; mutual relation of the two collections, 292; Páli historical literature, 293; scriptures of Northern Buddhists, their gradual origin, 294; language in which Southern scriptures were at first preserved different from that in which the Northern scriptures were recorded at third council, 295, 296 (Jaina-literature, 296); data furnished by Buddhistic Sanskṛit literature of doubtful authority for Buddha's age, 297.

(*a*) The *Sútra-Piṭaka:* distinction between the *simple* and the Mahávaipulya-Sútras, 298; poetical pieces in latter, Gáthá-dialect, 299; contents of the *simple* Sútras: Ityukta, Vyákaraṇa, Avadána, Adbhuta-dharma, Geya, Gáthá, Upadeśa, Nidána, Játaka, 300, 301; their Pantheon different from that of the Bráhmaṇa-texts, 301; but identical with that of the Epic poetry, 303; other chronological data in the Sútras, 304.—(*b*) The *Vinaya-Piṭaka:* discipline of clergy, system of mendicancy, 305; Buddhistic hierarchy as distinguished from the Brahmanical, Buddhist cult, 306; points of connection with Christian ritual, 307.—(*c*) The *Abhidharma-Piṭaka,* 307; schools of Buddhist philosophy, 308; relation to the Sáṃkhya-system, 308; and to Gnosticism, 309.—Commentaries on the sacred scriptures, 309; Tantras, 310.

SUPPLEMENTARY NOTES, ... 311

INDICES:

SANSKRIT INDEX, ... 329

INDEX OF MATTERS, &c., ... 353

INDEX OF AUTHORS, ... 358

LECTURES

ON THE

HISTORY OF INDIAN LITERATURE.

At the very outset of these lectures I find myself in a certain degree of perplexity, being rather at a loss how best to entitle them. I cannot say that they are to treat of the history of "Indian Literature;" for then I should have to consider the whole body of Indian languages, including those of non-Aryan origin. Nor can I say that their subject is the history of "Indo-Aryan Literature;" for then I should have to discuss the modern languages of India also, which form a third period in the development of Indo-Aryan speech. Nor, lastly, can I say that they are to present a history of "Sanskṛit Literature;" for the Indo-Aryan language is not in its first period "Sanskṛit," *i.e.*, the language of the educated, but is still a popular dialect; while in its second period the people spoke not Sanskṛit, but Prákṛitic dialects, which arose simultaneously with Sanskṛit out of the ancient Indo-Aryan vernacular. In order, however, to relieve you from any doubt as to what you have to expect from me here, I may at once remark that it is only the literature of the first and second periods of the Indo-Aryan language with which we have to do. For the sake of brevity I retain the name "Indian Literature."

I shall frequently in the course of these lectures be forced to draw upon your forbearance. The subject they discuss may be compared to a yet uncultivated tract of country, of which only a few spots have here and there been cleared, while the greater part of it remains covered with dense forest, impenetrable to the eye, and obstructing the prospect. A clearance is indeed now by degrees being made, but slowly, more especially because in addition to the natural obstacles which impede investigation, there still prevails a dense mist of prejudice and preconceived opinions hovering over the land, and enfolding it as with a veil.

The literature of India passes generally for the most ancient literature of which we possess written records, and justly so.[1] But the reasons which have hitherto been thought sufficient to establish this fact are not the correct ones; and it is indeed a matter for wonder that people should have been so long contented with them. In the first place, Indian tradition itself has been adduced in support of this fact, and for a very long time this was considered sufficient. It is, I think, needless for me to waste words upon the futile nature of such evidence. In the next place, astronomical data have been appealed to, according to which the Vedas would date from about 1400 B.C. But these data are given in writings, which are evidently of very modern origin, and they might consequently be the result of calculations[2] instituted for the express purpose. Fur-

---

[1] In so far as this claim may not now be disputed by the Egyptian monumental records and papyrus rolls, or even by the Assyrian literature which has but recently been brought to light.

[2] Besides, these calculations are of a very vague character, and do not yield any such definite date as that given above, but only some epoch lying between 1820-860 B.C., see *I. St.*, x. 236; Whitney in *Journ. R. A. S.*, i. 317, ff. (1864). True, the circumstance that the oldest records begin the series of *nakshatras* with the sign *Krittikâ*, carries us back to a considerably earlier period even than these dates, derived from the so-called Vedic Calendar, viz., to a period between 2780-1820 B.C., since the vernal equinox coincided with *η Tauri* (*Krittikâ*), in round numbers, about the year 2300 B.C., see *I. St.*, x. 234 236. But, on the other hand, the opinion expressed in the first edition of this work (1852), to the effect that the Indians may either have brought the knowledge of these lunar mansions, headed by *Krittikâ*, with them into India, or else have obtained it at a later period through the commercial relations of the Phoenicians with the Panjâb, has recently gained considerably in probability; and therewith the suggestion of Babylon as the mother country of the observations on which this date is established. See the second of my two treatises, *Die vedischen Nachrichten von den Nakshatra* (Berlin, 1862), pp. 362-400; my paper, *Ueber den Veda-kalender Namens Jyotisha* (1862), p. 15; *I. St.*, x. 429. ix. 241, ff.; Whitney, *Oriental and Linguistic Studies* (1874), ii. 418.—Indeed a direct reference to Babylon and its sea trade, in which the exportation of peacocks is mentioned, has lately come to light

ther, one of the Buddhist eras has been relied upon, according to which a reformer is supposed to have arisen in the sixth century B.C., in opposition to the Brahmanical hierarchy; but the authenticity of this particular era is still extremely questionable. Lastly, the period when Páṇini, the first systematic grammarian, flourished, has been referred to the fourth century B.C., and from this, as a starting-point, conclusions as to the period of literary development which preceded him have been deduced. But the arguments in favour of Páṇini's having lived at that time[3] are altogether weak and hypothetical, and in no case can they furnish us with any sort of solid basis.

The reasons, however, by which we are fully justified in regarding the literature of India as the most ancient literature of which written records on an extensive scale have been handed down to us, are these:—

In the more ancient parts of the Ṛigveda-Saṃhitá, we find the Indian race settled on the north-western borders of India, in the Panjáb, and even beyond the Panjáb, on the Kubhá, or **Κωφήν**, in Kabul.[4] The gradual spread of

---

in an Indian text, the Báverujátaka, see Minayeff in the *Mélanges Asiatiques* (Imperial Russian Academy), vi. 577, ff. (1871), and *Monatsberichte* of the Berlin Academy, p. 622 (1871). As, however, this testimony belongs to a comparatively late period, no great importance can be attached to it.—Direct evidence of ancient commercial relations between India and the West has recently been found in hieroglyphic texts of the seventeenth century, at which time the Áryas would appear to have been already settled on the Indus. For the word *kapi*, 'ape,' which occurs in 1 Kings x. 22, in the form *qôf*, Gr. *κῆπος*, is found in these Egyptian texts in the form *kafu*, see Joh. Dümichen, *Die Flotte einer egypt. Königin aus dem 17. Jahrh.* (Leipzig, 1868), table ii. p. 17. Lastly, *tukhiîm*, the Hebrew name for peacocks (1 Kings x. 22, 2 Chron. ix. 21) necessarily implies that already in Solomon's time the Phœnician ophir-merchants "ont eu affaire soit au pays même des Abhira soit sur un autre point de la côte de l'Inde avec des peuplades dravidiennes," Julien Vinson, *Revue de Linguistique*, vi. 120, ff. (1873). See also Burnell, *Elements of South Indian Palæography*, p. 5 (Mangalore, 1874).

[3] Or even, as Goldstücker supposes, earlier than Buddha.

[4] One of the Vedic Ṛishis, asserted to be Vatsa, of the family of Kaṇva, extols, Ṛik, viii. 6. 46–48, the splendid presents, consisting of horses, cattle, and *ushṭras* yoked four together—(Roth in the St. Petersburg Dict. explains *ushṭra* as 'buffalo, humped bull;' generally it means 'camel')—which, to the glory of the Yádvas, he received whilst residing with Tirimdira and Parśu. Or have we here only a single person, Tirimdira Parśu? In the Śáñkháyana Śrauta-Sútra, xvi. 11. 20, at least, he is understood as Tirimdira Páraśavya. These names suggest Tiridates and the Persians; see *I. St.*, iv. 379, n., but compare Girard de Rialle, *Revue de Linguist.*, iv. 227 (1872). Of course, we must not think of the

the race from these seats towards the east, beyond the Sarasvatí and over Hindustán as far as the Ganges, can be traced in the later portions of the Vedic writings almost step by step. The writings of the following period, that of the epic, consist of accounts of the internal conflicts among the conquerors of Hindustán themselves, as, for instance, the Mahá-Bhárata; or of the farther spread of Brahmanism towards the south, as, for instance, the Rámáyaṇa. If we connect with this the first fairly accurate information about India which we have from a Greek source, viz., from Megasthenes,* it becomes clear that at the time of this writer the Brahmanising of Hindustán was already completed, while at the time of the Periplus (see Lassen, *I. AK.*, ii. 150, n.; *I. St.*, ii. 192) the very southernmost point of the Dekhan had already become a seat of the worship of the wife of Śiva. What a series of years, of centuries, must necessarily have elapsed before this boundless tract of country, inhabited by wild and vigorous tribes, could have been brought over to Brahmanism!! It may perhaps here be objected that the races and tribes found by Alexander on the banks of the Indus appear to stand entirely on a Vedic, and not on a Brahmanical footing. As a matter of fact this is true; but we should not be justified in drawing from this any conclusion whatever with regard to India itself. For these peoples of the Panjáb never submitted to the Brahmanical order of things, but always retained their ancient Vedic standpoint, free and independent, without either priestly domination or system of caste. For this reason, too, they were the objects of a cordial hatred on the part of their kinsmen, who had wandered farther on, and on this account also Buddhism gained an easy entrance among them.

Persians after Cyrus: that would bring us too far down. But the Persians were so called, and had their own princes, even before the time of Cyrus. Or ought we rather, as suggested by Olshausen in the *Berliner Monatsberichte* (1874), p. 708, to think of the Parthavas, *i.e.*, Parthians, who as well as Párśas are mentioned in the time of the Achæmenidæ? The derivation, hitherto current, of the word Tiri in Tiridates, &c., from the Pahlavi *tîr* = Zend *tistrya* (given, *e.g.*, by M. Bréal, *De Persicis nominibus* (1863), pp. 9, 10), is hardly justified.

* Who as ambassador of Seleucus resided for some time at the court of Chandragupta. His reports are preserved to us chiefly in the 'Ινδικά of Arrian, who lived in the second century A.D.

And while the claims of the written records of Indian literature to a high antiquity—its beginnings may perhaps be traced back even to the time when the Indo-Aryans still dwelt together with the Persa-Aryans—are thus indisputably proved by external, geographical testimony, the internal evidence in the same direction which may be gathered from their contents, is no less conclusive. In the songs of the Ṛik, the robust spirit of the people gives expression to the feeling of its relation to nature, with a spontaneous freshness and simplicity; the powers of nature are worshipped as superior beings, and their kindly aid besought within their several spheres. Beginning with this nature-worship, which everywhere recognises only the individual phenomena of nature, and these in the first instance as superhuman, we trace in Indian literature the progress of the Hindú people through almost all the phases of religious development through which the human mind generally has passed. The individual phenomena of nature, which at first impress the imagination as being superhuman, are gradually classified within their different spheres; and a certain unity is discovered among them. Thus we arrive at a number of divine beings, each exercising supreme sway within its particular province, whose influence is in course of time further extended to the corresponding events of human life, while at the same time they are endowed with human attributes and organs. The number—already considerable—of these natural deities, these regents of the powers of nature, is further increased by the addition of abstractions, taken from ethical relations; and to these as to the other deities divine powers, personal existence, and activity are ascribed. Into this multitude of divine figures, the spirit of inquiry seeks at a later stage to introduce order, by classifying and co-ordinating them according to their principal bearings. The principle followed in this distribution is, like the conception of the deities themselves, entirely borrowed from the contemplation of nature. We have the gods who act in the heavens, in the air, upon the earth; and of these the sun, the wind, and fire are recognised as the main representatives and rulers respectively. These three gradually obtain precedence over all the other gods, who are only looked upon as their creatures and servants. Strengthened by these classifications, speculation presses on and seeks to establish the relative position of these three deities, and to arrive at unity for the supreme Being. This is accomplished either speculatively, by actually assuming such a supreme and purely absolute Being, viz., "Brahman" (neut.), to whom these three in their turn stand in the relation of creatures, of servants only; or arbitrarily, according as one or other of the three is worshipped as the supreme god. The sun-god seems in the first instance to have been promoted to this honour; the Persa-Aryans at all events retained this standpoint, of course extending it still further; and in the older parts of the Bráhmaṇas also—to which rather than to the Samhitás the Avesta is related in respect of age and contents—we find the sun-god here and there exalted far above the other deities (*prasavitá devánám*). We also find ample traces of this in the forms of worship, which so often preserve relics of antiquity.[5] Nay, as "Brahman" (masc.), he has in theory retained this position, down even to the latest times, although in a very colourless manner. His colleagues, the air and fire gods, in consequence of their much more direct and sensible influence, by degrees obtained complete possession of the supreme power, though constantly in conflict with each other. Their worship has passed through a long series of different phases, and it is evidently the same which Megasthenes found in Hindustán,* and which at the time of the Periplus had penetrated, though in a form already very corrupt, as far as the southernmost point of the Dekhan.

But while we are thus justified in assuming a high antiquity for Indian literature, on external geographical grounds, as well as on internal evidence, connected with the history of the Hindú religion,[6] the case is sufficiently unsatisfactory, when we come to look for definite chrono-

[5] Cf. my paper. *Zwei vedische Texte über Omina und Portenta* (1859), pp. 392–393.

[6] To these, thirdly, we have to add evidence derived from the language. The edicts of Piyadasi, whose date is fixed by the mention therein of Greek kings, and even of Alexander himself, are written in popular dialects, for whose gradual development out of the language of the Vedic hymns into this form it is absolutely necessary to postulate the lapse of a series of centuries.

* According to Strabo, p. 117, Διόνυσος (Rudra, Soma, Śiva) was worshipped in the mountains, Ἡρακλῆς (Indra, Vishṇu) in the plain.

logical dates. We must reconcile ourselves to the fact that any such search will, as a general rule, be absolutely fruitless. It is only in the case of those branches of literature which also became known abroad, and also in regard to the last few centuries, when either the dates of manuscripts, or the data given in the introductions or closing observations of the works themselves, furnish us some guidance, that we can expect any result. Apart from this, an internal chronology based on the character of the works themselves, and on the quotations, &c., therein contained, is the only one possible.

Indian literature divides itself into two great periods, the Vedic and the Sanskṛit. Turning now to the former, or Vedic period, I proceed to give a preliminary general outline of it before entering into the details.

FIRST PERIOD.

VEDIC LITERATURE.

WE have to distinguish four Vedas—the Ṛig-Veda, the Sáma-Veda, the Yajur-Veda, which is in a double form, and the Atharva-Veda. Each of these is again subdivided into three distinct parts—Saṃhitá, Bráhmaṇa, and Sútra.

Their relation to each other is as follows:—

The Saṃhitá * of the Ṛik is purely a lyrical collection, comprising the store of song which the Hindús brought with them from their ancient homes on the banks of the Indus, and which they had there used for "invoking prosperity on themselves and their flocks, in their adoration of the dawn, in celebration of the struggle between the god who wields the lightning and the power of darkness, and in rendering thanks to the heavenly beings for preservation in battle." † The songs are here classified according to the families of poets to which they are ascribed. The principle of classification is consequently, so to speak, a purely scientific one. It is therefore possible, though more cannot be said, that the redaction of the text may be of later date than that of the two Saṃhitás which

---

* The name Saṃhitá (collection) first occurs in the so-called Áraṇyakas, or latest supplements to the Bráhmaṇas, and in the Sútras; but whether in the above meaning, is not as yet certain. The names by which the Saṃhitás are designated in the Bráhmaṇas are—either *richaḥ*, *sámáni*, *yajúṅshi*,—or Ṛigveda, Sámaveda, Yajurveda,—or Bahvṛichas, Chhandogas, Adhvaryus,—or *trayí vidyá*, *svádhyáya*, *adhyayana*, also 'Veda' alone. It is in the Sútras that we first find the term Chhandas specially applied to the Saṃhitás, and more particularly in Páṇini, by whom Ṛishi, Nigama, Mantra (?) are also employed in the same manner.

† See Roth, *Zur Litteratur und Geschichte des Weda*, p. 8 (Stuttgart, 1846).

will come next under our consideration, and which, providing as they do for a practical want, became necessary immediately upon the institution of a worship with a fixed ritual. For the Saṃhitá of the Sáman, and both the Saṃhitás of the Yajus, consist only of such *ṛichas* (verses) and sacrificial formulas as had to be recited at the ceremonies of the Soma offering and other sacrifices, and in the same order in which they were practically used; at least, we know for certain, that this is the case in the Yajus. The Saṃhitá of the Sáman contains nothing but verses (*ṛichas*); those of the Yajus, sentences in prose also. The former, the *ṛichas*, all recur, with a few exceptions, in the Ṛik-Saṃhitá, so that the Sáma-Saṃhitá is nothing more than an extract from the songs of the latter, of the verses applied to the Soma offering. Now the *ṛichas* found in the Sáma-Saṃhitá and Yajuḥ-Saṃhitá appear in part in a very altered form, deviating considerably from the text of the Ṛik, the Ṛik-Saṃhitá. Of this a triple explanation is possible. First, these readings may be earlier and more original than those of the Ṛik, liturgical use having protected them from alteration, while the simple song, not being immediately connected with the sacred rite, was less scrupulously preserved. Or, secondly, they may be later than those of the Ṛik, and may have arisen from the necessity of precisely adapting the text to the meaning attributed to the verse in its application to the ceremony. Or, lastly, they may be of equal authority with those of the Ṛik, the discrepancies being merely occasioned by the variety of districts and families in which they were used, the text being most authentic in the district and family in which it originated, and less so in those to which it subsequently passed. All three methods of explanation are alike correct, and in each particular case they must all be kept in view. But if we look more closely at the relation of these verses, it may be stated thus: The *ṛichas* occurring in the Sáma-Saṃhitá generally stamp themselves as older and more original by the greater antiquity of their grammatical forms; those in the two Saṃhitás of the Yajus, on the contrary, generally give the impression of having undergone a secondary alteration. Instances which come under the third method of explanation are found in equal numbers, both in the Sáma-Saṃhitá and the Yajuḥ-Saṃhitá. Altogether, too much stress cannot be laid on this point, namely, that the alterations which the songs and hymns underwent in the popular mouth during their oral transmission, must in any case be regarded as very considerable; since preservation by means of writing is not to be thought of for this period. Indeed we can hardly admit it for the time of the Bráhmaṇas either, otherwise it would be difficult to account for the numerous deviations of the various schools with regard to the text of these works also, as well as for the great number of different schools (Śákhás) generally.

But although the songs of the Ṛik, or the majority of them, were composed on the banks of the Indus, their final compilation and arrangement can only have taken place in India proper; at what time, however, it is difficult to say. Some portions come down to an age so recent, that the system of caste had already been organised; and tradition itself, in ascribing to Śákalya and Pañchála Bábhravya a leading part in the arrangement of the Ṛik-Saṃhitá, points us to the flourishing epoch of the Videhas and Pañchálas, as I shall show hereafter. The Saṃhitá of the Sáman, being entirely borrowed from the Ṛik, gives no clue to the period of its origin; only, in the fact that it contains no extracts from any of the later portions of the Ṛik, we have perhaps an indication that these were not then in existence. This, however, is a point not yet investigated. As for the two Saṃhitás of the Yajus, we have in the prose portions peculiar to them, most distinct proofs that both originated in the eastern parts of Hindustán,[7] in the country of the Kurupañchálas, and that they belong to a period when the Brahmanical element had already gained the supremacy, although it had still to encounter many a hard struggle, and when at all events the hierarchy of the Brahmans, and the system of caste, were completely organised. Nay, it may be that we have even external grounds for supposing that the present redaction of the Saṃhitá of the White Yajus dates from the third century B.C. For Megasthenes mentions a people called *Μαδιανδινοί*, and this name recurs in the Má-

[7] Or rather to the east of the Indus, in Hindustán.

dhyaṃdinas, the principal school of the White Yajus. More of this later on.

The origin of the Atharva-Saṃhitá dates also from the period when Brahmanism had become dominant. It is in other respects perfectly analogous to the Ṛik-Saṃhitá, and contains the store of song of this Brahmanical epoch. Many of these songs are to be found also in the last, that is, the least ancient book of the Ṛik-Saṃhitá. In the latter they are the latest additions made at the time of its compilation; in the Atharvan they are the proper and natural utterance of the present. The spirit of the two collections is indeed entirely different. In the Ṛik there breathes a lively natural feeling a warm love for nature; while in the Atharvan there prevails, on the contrary, only an anxious dread of her evil spirits, and their magical powers. In the Ṛik we find the people in a state of free activity and independence; in the Atharvan we see it bound in the fetters of the hierarchy and of superstition. But the Atharva-Saṃhitá likewise contains pieces of great antiquity, which may perhaps have belonged more to the people proper, to its lower grades; whereas the songs of the Ṛik appear rather to have been the especial property of the higher families.* It was not without a long struggle that the songs of the Atharvan were permitted to take their place as a fourth Veda. There is no mention made of them in the more ancient portions of the Bráhmaṇas of the Ṛik, Sáman, and Yajus; indeed they only originated simultaneously with these Bráhmaṇas, and are therefore only alluded to in their later portions.

We now come to the second part of Vedic literature, the Bráhmaṇas.

The character of the Bráhmaṇas † may be thus gene-

---

* This surmise, based upon certain passages in the Atharvan, would certainly be at variance with the name 'Atharváñgirasas,' borne by this Saṃhitá; according to which it would belong, on the contrary, to the most ancient and noble Brahman families. But I have elsewhere advanced the conjecture, that this name was simply assumed in order to impart a greater sanctity to the contents, see *I. St.*, i. 295. [*Zwei vedische Texte über Omina und Portenta*, pp. 346–348.]

† This term signifies 'that which relates to prayer, *brahman*.' *Brahman* itself means 'drawing forth,' as well in a physical sense 'producing,' 'creating,' as in a spiritual one 'lifting up,' 'elevating,' 'strengthening.' The first mention of the name Bráhmaṇa, in the above sense, is found in the Bráhmaṇa of the White Yajus, and especially in its thir-

rally defined: Their object is to connect the sacrificial songs and formulas with the sacrificial rite, by pointing out, on the one hand, their direct mutual relation; and, on the other, their symbolical connection with each other. In setting forth the former, they give the particular ritual in its details: in illustrating the latter, they are either directly explanatory and analytic, dividing each formula into its constituent parts, or else they establish that connection dogmatically by the aid of tradition or speculation. We thus find in them the oldest rituals we have, the oldest linguistic explanations, the oldest traditional narratives, and the oldest philosophical speculations. This peculiar character is common generally to all works of this class, yet they differ widely in details, according to their individual tendency, and according as they belong to this or that particular Veda. With respect to age they all date from the period of the transition from Vedic civilisation and culture to the Brahmanic mode of thought and social order. Nay, they help to bring about this very transition, and some of them belong rather to the time of its commencement, others rather to that of its termination.* The Bráhmaṇas originated from the opinions of individual sages, imparted by oral tradition, and preserved as well as supplemented in their families and by their disciples. The more numerous these separate traditions became, the more urgent became the necessity for bringing them into harmony with each other. To this end, as time went on, compilations, comprising a variety of these materials, and in which the different opinions on each subject were uniformly traced to their original represen-

---

teenth book. In cases where the dogmatical explanation of a ceremonial or other precept has already been given, we there find the expression *tasyoktam bráhmaṇam*, 'of this the Bráhmaṇa has already been stated;' whereas in the books preceding the thirteenth, we find in such cases *tasyokto bandhuḥ* 'its connection has already been set forth.' [*I. St.*, v. 60, ix. 351.]—Besides Bráhmaṇa, Pravachana is also used in the Sáma-Sútras, according to the commentary, in the same sense; they also mention Anubráhmaṇa, a term which does not occur elsewhere except in Páṇini.

* Páṇini, iv. 3. 105, directly mentions 'older (*purâṇaprokta*) Bráhmaṇas;' and in contradistinction to these there must, of course, have been in existence in his day 'more modern (or as the scholiast says, *tulyakála*) Bráhmaṇas.' [See on this Goldstücker, *Páṇini*, p. 132, ff., and my rejoinder in *I. St.*, v. 64, ff.]

tatives, were made in different districts by individuals peculiarly qualified for the task. But whether these compilations or digests were now actually written down, or were still transmitted orally only, remains uncertain. The latter supposition would seem probable from the fact that of the same work we here and there find two texts entirely differing in their details. Nothing definite, however, can be said on the subject, for in these cases there may possibly have been some fundamental difference in the original, or even a fresh treatment of the materials. It was, moreover, but natural that these compilers should frequently come into collision and conflict with each other. Hence we have now and then to remark the exhibition of strong animosity against those who in the author's opinion are heterodox. The preponderant influence gradually gained by some of these works over the rest—whether by reason of their intrinsic value, or of the fact that their author appealed more to the hierarchical spirit*—has resulted, unfortunately for us, in the preservation of these only, while works representative of the disputed opinions have for the most part disappeared. Here and there perhaps in India some fragments may still be found; in general, however, here as everywhere in Indian literature, we encounter the lamentable fact that the works which, in the end, came off victorious, have almost entirely supplanted and effaced their predecessors. After all, a comparatively large number of Bráhmaṇas is still extant—a circumstance which is evidently owing to their being each annexed to a particular Veda, as well as to the fact that a sort of petty jealousy had always prevailed among the families in which the study of the different Vedas was hereditarily transmitted. Thus in the case of each Veda, such works at least as had come to be considered of the highest authority have been preserved, although the practical significance of the Bráhmaṇas was

---

* The difficulty of their preservation is also an important factor in the case, as at that time writing either did not exist at all, or at any rate was but seldom employed. ["In considering the question of the age and extent of the use of writing in India, it is important to point out that the want of suitable materials, in the North at least, before the introduction of paper, must have been a great obstacle to its general use."—Burnell, *Elements of South Indian Palæography*, p. 10.]

gradually more and more lost, and passed over to the Sútras, &c. To the number of the Bráhmaṇas, or recensions of the Saṃhitás, which were thus lost, belong those of the Váshkalas, Paiñgins, Bhállavins, Śáṭyáyanins, Kálabavins, Lámakáyanins, Śámbuvis, Khádáyanins, and Śálañkáyanins, which we find quoted on various occasions in writings of this class; besides all the Chhandas works (Saṃhitás) specified in the *gaṇa* 'Śaunaka' (Páṇ., iv. 3. 106), whose names are not so much as mentioned elsewhere.

The difference between the Bráhmaṇas of the several Vedas as to subject-matter is essentially this: The Bráhmaṇas of the Ṛik, in their exposition of the ritual, generally specify those duties only which fell to the Hotar, or reciter of the *richas*, whose office it was to collect from the various hymns the verses suited to each particular occasion, as its *śastra* (canon). The Bráhmaṇas of the Sáman confine themselves to the duties of the Udgátar, or singer of the *sámans;* the Bráhmaṇas of the Yajus, to the duties of the Adhvaryu, or actual performer of the sacrifice. In the Bráhmaṇas of the Ṛik, the order of the sacrificial performance is on the whole preserved, whereas the sequence of the hymns as they occur in the Ṛik-Saṃhitá is not attended to at all. But in the Bráhmaṇas of the Sáman and Yajus, we find a difference corresponding to the fact that their Saṃhitás are already adapted to the proper order of the ritual. The Bráhmaṇa of the Sáman enters but seldom into the explanation of individual verses; the Bráhmaṇa of the White Yajus, on the contrary, may be almost considered as a running dogmatic commentary on its Saṃhitá, to the order of which it adheres so strictly, that in the case of its omitting one or more verses, we might perhaps be justified in concluding that they did not then form part of the Saṃhitá. A supplement also has been added to this Bráhmaṇa for some of those books of the Saṃhitá which were incorporated with it at a period subsequent to its original compilation, so that the Bráhmaṇa comprises 100 *adhyáyas* instead of 60, as formerly seems to have been the case. The Bráhmaṇa of the Black Yajus does not, as we shall see further on, differ in its contents, but only in point of time, from its Saṃhitá. It is, in fact, a supplement to it. The Bráhmaṇa of the

Atharvan is up to the present time unknown, though there are manuscripts of it in England.[8]

The common name for the Bráhmaṇa literature is *Śruti*, 'hearing,' *i.e.*, that which is subject of hearing, subject of exposition, of teaching, by which name their learned, and consequently exclusive, character is sufficiently intimated. In accordance with this we find in the works themselves frequent warnings against intrusting the knowledge contained in them to any profane person. The name Śruti is not indeed mentioned in them, but only in the Sútras, though it is perfectly justified by the corresponding use of the verb *śru* which occurs in them frequently.

The third stage in Vedic literature is represented by the Sútras.* These are, upon the whole, essentially founded

---

[8] It has since been published, see below. It presents no sort of direct internal relation to the Ath. Saṃhitá.

* The word Sútra in the above sense occurs first in the Madhukáṇḍa, one of the latest supplements to the Bráhmaṇa of the White Yajus, next in the two Gṛihya-Sútras of the Ṛik, and finally in Páṇini. It means 'thread,' 'band,' cf. Lat. *suere*. Would it be correct to regard it as an expression analogous to the German *band* (volume)? If so, the term would have to be understood of the fastening together of the leaves, and would necessarily presuppose the existence of writing (in the same way, perhaps, as *grantha* does, a term first occurring in Páṇini?). Inquiry into the origin of Indian writing has not, unfortunately, led to much result as yet. The oldest inscriptions, according to Wilson, date no earlier than the third century B.C. Nearchus, however, as is well known, mentions writing, and his time corresponds very well upon the whole to the period to which we must refer the origin of the Sútras. But as these were composed chiefly with a view to their being committed to memory—a fact which follows from their form, and partly accounts for it—there might be good grounds for taking exception to the etymology just proposed, and for regarding the signification 'guiding-line,' 'clue,' as the original one. [This is the meaning given in the St. Petersburg Dictionary.—The writing of the Indians is of Semitic origin: see Benfey, *Indien* (in *Ersch and Gruber's Encyclopædia*, 1840), p. 254; my *Indische Skizzen* (1856), p. 127, ff.; Burnell, *Elem. of South Indian Pal.*, p. 3, ff. Probably it served in the first instance merely for secular purposes, and was only applied subsequently to literature. See Müller, *Anc. S. Lit.*, p. 507; *I. St.*, v. 20, ff.; *I. Str.*, ii. 339. Goldstücker (*Páṇini*, 1860, p. 26, ff.) contends that the words *sútra* and *grantha* must absolutely be connected with writing. See, however, *I. St.*, v. 24, ff.; xiii. 476.]—Nor does etymology lead us to a more certain result in the case of another word found in this connection, viz., *akshara*, 'syllable.' This word does not seem to occur in this sense in the Saṃhitá of the Ṛik (or Sáman); it there rather signifies 'imperishable.' The connecting link between this primary signification and the meaning 'syllable,' which is first met with in the Saṃhitá of the Yajus, might perhaps be the idea of writing, the latter being the making imperishable, as it were, of otherwise

on the Bráhmaṇas, and must be considered as their necessary supplement, as a further advance in the path struck out by the latter in the direction of more rigid system and formalism.[9] While the Bráhmaṇas, with the view of explaining the sacrifice and supporting it by authority, &c., uniformly confine themselves to individual instances of ritual, interpretation, tradition, and speculation, subjecting these to copious dogmatic treatment, the object of the Sútras is to comprehend everything that had any reference whatever to these subjects. The mass of matter became too great; there was risk of the tenor of the whole being lost in the details; and it gradually became impossible to discuss all the different particulars consecutively. Diffuse discussion of the details had to be replaced by concise collective summaries of them. The utmost brevity was, however, requisite in condensing this great mass, in order to avoid overburdening the memory; and this brevity ultimately led to a remarkably compressed and enigmatical style, which was more and more cultivated as the literature of the Sútras became more independent, and in proportion as the resulting advantages became apparent. Thus the more ancient a Sútra, the more intelligible it is; the more enigmatical it is, the more modern will it prove.*

But the literature of the Sútras can by no means be said to rest entirely upon the Bráhmaṇas, for these, as a rule, give too exclusive a prominence to the ritual of the sacrifice. Indeed, it is only one particular division of the Sútras—viz., the Kalpa-Sútras, aphorisms exclusively devoted to the consideration of this ritual[10]—which bears

---

fleeting and evanescent words and syllables (?). Or is the notion of the imperishable λόγος at the root of this signification? [In the *Errata* to the first German edition it was pointed out, on the authority of a communication received from Professor Aufrecht, that *akshara* is twice used in the Ṛik of the 'measuring of speech,' viz., i. 164. 24 (47), and ix. 13. 3, and consequently may there mean 'syllable.' According to the St. Petersburg Dictionary, this latter meaning is to be derived from the idea of 'the constant, simple' element in language.]

[9] On the mutual relations of the Bráhmaṇas and Sútras, see also *I. St.*, viii. 76, 77; ix. 353, 354.

* Precisely as in the case of the Bráhmaṇas, so also in the case of the Kalpas, *i.e.*, Kalpa-Sútras, Páṇini, iv. 3. 105, distinguishes those composed by the ancients from those that are nearer to his own time.

[10] On the sacrifice and sacrificial implements of the Śrauta-Sútras, see M. Müller in *Z. D. M. G.*, IX. xxxvi.–lxxxii.; Haug's notes to his translation of the Aitareya-Bráhmaṇa; and my paper, *Zur Kenntniss des vedischen Opferrituals*, *I. St.*, x. xiii.

the special name of Śrauta-Sútras, *i.e.*, "Sútras founded on the Śruti." The sources of the other Sútras must be sought elsewhere.

Side by side with the Śrauta-Sútras we are met by a second family of ritual Sútras, the so-called Gṛihya-Sútras, which treat of domestic ceremonies, those celebrated at birth and before it, at marriage, as well as at death and after it. The origin of these works is sufficiently indicated by their title, since, in addition to the name of Gṛihya-Sútras, they also bear that of Smárta-Sútras, *i.e.*, "Sútras founded on the *Smṛiti*." *Smṛiti*, 'memory,' *i.e.*, that which is the subject of memory, can evidently only be distinguished from *Śruti*, 'hearing,' *i.e.*, that which is the subject of hearing, in so far as the former impresses itself on the memory directly, without special instruction and provision for the purpose. It belongs to all, it is the property of the whole people, it is supported by the consciousness of all, and does not therefore need to be specially inculcated. Custom and law are common property and accessible to all; ritual, on the contrary, though in like manner arising originally from the common consciousness, is developed in its details by the speculations and suggestions of individuals, and remains so far the property of the few, who, favoured by external circumstances, understand how to inspire the people with a due awe of the importance and sanctity of their institutions. It is not, however, to be assumed from this that Smṛiti, custom and law, did not also undergo considerable alterations in the course of time. The mass of the immigrants had a great deal too much on their hands in the subjugation of the aborigines to be in a position to occupy themselves with other matters. Their whole energies had, in the first instance, to be concentrated upon the necessity of holding their own against the enemy. When this had been effected, and resistance was broken down, they awoke suddenly to find themselves bound and shackled in the hands of other and far more powerful enemies; or rather, they did not awake at all; their physical powers had been so long and so exclusively exercised and expended to the detriment of their intellectual energy, that the latter had gradually dwindled away altogether. The history of these new enemies was this: The knowledge of the ancient songs with which, in their ancient homes, the Indians had worshipped the powers of nature, and the knowledge of the ritual connected with these songs, became more and more the exclusive property of those whose ancestors perhaps composed them, and in whose families this knowledge had been hereditary. These same families remained in the possession of the traditions connected with them, and which were necessary to their explanation. To strangers in a foreign country, anything brought with them from home becomes invested with a halo of sacredness; and thus it came about that these families of singers became families of priests, whose influence was more and more consolidated in proportion as the distance between the people and their former home increased, and the more their ancient institutions were banished from their minds by external struggles. The guardians of the ancestral customs, of the primitive forms of worship, took an increasingly prominent position, became the representatives of these, and, finally, the representatives of the Divine itself. For so ably had they used their opportunities, that they succeeded in founding a hierarchy the like of which the world has never seen. To this position it would have been scarcely possible for them to attain but for the enervating climate of Hindustán, and the mode of life induced by it, which exercised a deteriorating influence upon a race unaccustomed to it. The families also of the petty kings who had formerly reigned over individual tribes, held a more prominent position in the larger kingdoms which were of necessity founded in Hindustán; and thus arose the military caste. Lastly, the people proper, the *Viśas*, or settlers, united to form a third caste, and they in their turn naturally reserved to themselves prerogatives over the fourth caste, or Śúdras. This last was composed of various mixed elements, partly, perhaps, of an Aryan race which had settled earlier in India, partly of the aborigines themselves, and partly again of those among the immigrants, or their Western kinsmen, who refused adherence to the new Brahmanical order. The royal

* Who were distinguished by their very colour from the three other castes; hence the name *varṇa*, i.e. colour, for caste. [See *I. St.*, x. 4, 10.]

families, the warriors, who, it may be supposed, strenuously supported the priesthood so long as it was a question of robbing the people of their rights, now that this was effected turned against their former allies, and sought to throw off the yoke that was likewise laid upon them. These efforts were, however, unavailing; the colossus was too firmly established. Obscure legends and isolated allusions are the only records left to us in the later writings, of the sacrilegious hands which ventured to attack the sacred and divinely consecrated majesty of the Brahmans; and these are careful to note, at the same time, the terrible punishments which befell those impious offenders. The fame of many a Barbarossa has here passed away and been forgotten!

The Smárta-Sútras, which led to this digression, generally exhibit the complete standpoint of Brahmanism. Whether in the form of actual records or of compositions orally transmitted, they in any case date from a period when more than men cared to lose of the Smriti—that precious tradition passed on from generation to generation—was in danger of perishing. Though, as we have just seen, it had undergone considerable modifications, even in the families who guarded it, through the influence of the Brahmans, yet this influence was chiefly exercised with reference to its political bearings, leaving domestic manners and customs[11] untouched in their ancient form; so that these works cover a rich treasure of ideas and conceptions of extreme antiquity. It is in them also that we have to look for the beginnings of the Hindú legal literature,[12] whose subject-matter, indeed, in part corresponds exactly to theirs, and whose authors bear for the most part the same names as those of the Gṛihya-Sútras. With the strictly legal portions of the law-books, those dealing with

---

[11] For the ritual relating to birth see Speijer's book on the *Játakarma* (Leyden, 1872)—for the marriage ceremonies, Haas's paper, *Ueber die Heirathsgebräuche der alten Inder*, with additions by myself in *I. St.*, v. 267, ff.; also my paper *Vedische Hochzeitssprüche*, *ibid.*, p. 177, ff. (1862)—on the burial of the dead, Roth in *Z. D. M. G.*, viii. 487, ff. (1854), and M. Müller, *ibid.*, IX. i.–xxxvi. (1855); and lastly, O. Donner's *Pindapitriyajna* (1870).

[12] Besides the Gṛihya-Sútras we find some texts directly called Dharma-Sútras, or Sámayácharika-Sútras, which are specified as portions of Śrauta-Sútras, but which were no doubt subsequently inserted into these.

civil law, criminal law, and political law, we do not, it is true, find more than a few points of connection in these Sútras; but probably these branches were not codified at all until the pressure of actual imminent danger made it necessary to establish them on a secure foundation. The risk of their gradually dying out was, owing to the constant operation of the factors involved, not so great as in the case of domestic customs. But a far more real peril threatened them in the fierce assaults directed against the Brahmanical polity by the gradually increasing power of Buddhism. Buddhism originally proceeded purely from theoretical heterodoxy regarding the relation of matter to spirit, and similar questions; but in course of time it addressed itself to practical points of religion and worship, and thenceforth it imperilled the very existence of Brahmanism, since the military caste and the oppressed classes of the people generally availed themselves of its aid in order to throw off the overwhelming yoke of priestly domination. The statement of Megasthenes, that the Indians in his time administered law only ἀπὸ μνήμης, 'from memory,' I hold therefore to be perfectly correct, and I can see no grounds for the view that μνήμη is but a mistranslation of Smṛiti in the sense of Smṛiti-Śástra, 'a treatise on Smṛiti.'* For the above-mentioned reason, however—in consequence of the development of Buddhism into an anti-Brahmanical religion—the case may have altered soon afterwards, and a code, that of Manu, for example (founded on the Mánava Gṛihya-Sútra), may have been drawn up. But this work belongs not to the close of the Vedic, but to the beginning of the following period.

As we have found, in the Smṛiti, an independent basis for the Gṛihya-Sútras—in addition to the Bráhmaṇas, where but few points of contact with these Sútras can be traced—so too shall we find an independent basis for those Sútras the contents of which relate to language. In this case it is in the recitation of the songs and formulas at the sacrifice that we shall find it. Although, accordingly, these

* This latter view has been best set forth by Schwanbeck, *Megasthenes*, pp. 50, 51. [But see also Burnell, *Elements of S. Ind. Palæogr.*, p. 4.]

Sútras stand on a level with the Bráhmaṇas, which owe their origin to the same source, yet this must be understood as applying only to those views on linguistic relations which, being presupposed in the Sútras, must be long anterior to them. It must not be taken as applying to the works themselves, inasmuch as they present the results of these antecedent investigations in a collected and systematic form. Obviously also, it was a much more natural thing to attempt, in the first instance, to elucidate the relation of the prayer to the sacrifice, than to make the form in which the prayer itself was drawn up a subject of investigation. The more sacred the sacrificial performance grew, and the more fixed the form of worship gradually became, the greater became the importance of the prayers belonging to it, and the stronger their claim to the utmost possible purity and safety. To effect this, it was necessary, first, to fix the text of the prayers; secondly, to establish a correct pronunciation and recitation; and, lastly, to preserve the tradition of their origin. It was only after the lapse of time, and when by degrees their literal sense had become foreign to the phase into which the language had passed—and this was of course much later the case with the priests, who were familiar with them, than with the people at large—that it became necessary to take precautions for securing and establishing the sense also. To attain all these objects, those most conversant with the subject were obliged to give instruction to the ignorant, and circles were thus formed around them of travelling scholars, who made pilgrimages from one teacher to another according as they were attracted by the fame of special learning. These researches were naturally not confined to questions of language, but embraced the whole range of Brahmanical theology, extending in like manner to questions of worship, dogma, and speculation, all of which, indeed, were closely interwoven with each other. We must, at any rate, assume among the Brahmans of this period a very stirring intellectual life, in which even the women took an active part, and which accounts still further for the superiority maintained and exercised by the Brahmans over the rest of the people. Nor did the military caste hold aloof from these inquiries, especially after they had succeeded in securing a time of repose from external warfare. We have here a faithful copy of the scholastic period of the Middle Ages; sovereigns whose courts form the centres of intellectual life; Brahmans who with lively emulation carry on their inquiries into the highest questions the human mind can propound; women who with enthusiastic ardour plunge into the mysteries of speculation, impressing and astonishing men by the depth and loftiness of their opinions, and who—while in a state which, judging from description, seems to have been a kind of somnambulism—solve the questions proposed to them on sacred subjects. As to the quality of their solutions, and the value of all these inquiries generally, that is another matter. But neither have the scholastic subtleties any absolute worth in themselves; it is only the striving and the effort which ennobles the character of any such period.

The advance made by linguistic research during this epoch was very considerable. It was then that the text of the prayers was fixed, that the redaction of the various Saṃhitás took place. By degrees, very extensive precautions were taken for this purpose. For their study (Páṭha), as well as for the different methods of preserving them—whether by writing or by memory, for either is possible[13]—such special injunctions are given, that it seems

---

[13] All the technical terms, however, which occur for study of the Veda and the like, uniformly refer to speaking and reciting only, and thereby point to exclusively oral tradition. The writing down of the Vedic texts seems indeed not to have taken place until a comparatively late period. See *I. St.*, v. 18, ff. (1861). Müller, *Anc. S. Lit.*, p. 507, ff. (1859); Westergaard, *Ueber den ältesten Zeitraum der indischen Geschichte* (1860, German translation 1862, p. 42, ff.); and Haug, *Ueber das Wesen des vedischen Accents* (1873, p. 16, ff.), have declared themselves in favour of this theory. Haug thinks that these Brahmans who were converted to Buddhism were the first who consigned the Veda to writing—for polemical purposes—and that they were followed by the rest of the Brahmans. On the other hand, Goldstücker, Böhtlingk, Whitney, and Roth (*Der Atharvaveda in Kashmir*, p. 10), are of the opposite opinion, holding, in particular, that the authors of the Prátiśákhyas must have had written texts before them. Benfey also formerly shared this view, but recently (*Einleitung in die Grammatik der ved. Sprache*, p. 31), he has expressed the belief that the Vedic texts were only committed to writing at a late date, long subsequent to their '*diaskeuasis.*' Burnell also, *l. c.*, p. 10, is of opinion that, amongst other things, the very scarcity of the material for writing in ancient times "almost precludes the existence of MSS. of books or long documents."

all but impossible that any alteration in the text, except in the form of interpolation, can have taken place since. These directions, as well as those relating to the pronunciation and recitation of the words, are laid down in the Prátiśákhya-Sútras, writings with which we have but recently been made acquainted.* Such a Prátiśákhya-Sútra uniformly attaches itself to the Saṃhitá of a single Veda only, but it embraces all the schools belonging to it; it gives the general regulations as to the nature of the sounds employed, the euphonic rules observed, the accent and its modifications, the modulation of the voice, &c. Further, all the individual cases in which peculiar phonetic or other changes are observed are specially pointed out;[14] and we are in this way supplied with an excellent critical means of arriving at the form of the text of each Saṃhitá at the time when its Prátiśákhya was composed. If we find in any part of the Saṃhitá phonetic peculiarities which we are unable to trace in its Prátiśákhya, we may rest assured that at that period this part did not yet belong to the Saṃhitá. The directions as to the recital of the Veda, *i.e.*, of its Saṃhitá,† in the schools—each individual word being repeated in a variety of connections—present a very lively picture of the care with which these studies were pursued.

For the knowledge of metre also, rich materials have been handed down to us in the Sútras. The singers of the hymns themselves must naturally have been cognisant of the metrical laws observed in them. But we also find the technical names of some metres now and then mentioned in the later songs of the Ṛik. In the Bráhmaṇas the oddest tricks are played with them, and their harmony is in some mystical fashion brought into connection with the harmony of the world, in fact stated to be its funda-

---

* By Roth in his essays, *Zur Litteratur und Geschichte des Weda*, p. 53, ff. (translated in *Journ. As. Soc. Bengal*, January 1848, p. 6, ff.).

[14] This indeed is the real purpose of the Prátiśákhyas, namely, to show how the continuous Saṃhitá text is to be reconstructed out of the Pada text, in which the individual words of the text are given separately in their original form, unaffected by *saṃdhi*, *i.e.*, the influence of the words which immediately precede and follow. Whatever else, over and above this, is found in the Prátiśákhyas is merely accessory matter. See Whitney in *Journal Am. Or. Soc.*, iv. 259 (1853).

† Strictly speaking, only these (the Saṃhitás) are Veda.

mental cause. The simple minds of these thinkers were too much charmed by their rhythm not to be led into these and similar symbolisings. The further development of metre afterwards led to special inquiries into its laws. Such investigations have been preserved to us, both in Sútras [15] treating directly of metre, *e.g.*, the Nidána-Sútra, and in the Anukramaṇís, a peculiar class of works, which, adhering to the order of each Saṃhitá, assign a poet, a metre, and a deity to each song or prayer. They may, therefore, perhaps belong to a later period than most of the Sútras, to a time when the text of each Saṃhitá was already extant in its final form, and distributed as we there find it into larger and smaller sections for the better regulation of its study. One of the smallest sections formed the pupil's task on each occasion.—The preservation of the tradition concerning the authors and the origin of the prayers is too intimately connected herewith to be dissociated from the linguistic Sútras, although the class of works to which it gave rise is of an entirely different character. The most ancient of such traditions are to be found, as above stated, in the Bráhmaṇas themselves. These latter also contain legends regarding the origin and the author of this or that particular form of worship; and on such occasions the Bráhmaṇa frequently appeals to Gáthás, or stanzas, preserved by oral transmission among the people. It is evidently in these legends that we must look for the origin of the more extensive Itihásas and Puráṇas, works which but enlarged the range of their subject, but which in every other respect proceeded after the same fashion, as is shown by several of the earlier fragments preserved, *e.g.*, in the Mahá-Bhárata. The most ancient work of the kind hitherto known is the Bṛihad-devatá by Śaunaka, in *ślokas*, which, however, strictly follows the order of the Ṛik-Saṃhitá, and proves by its very title that it has only an accidental connection with this class of works. Its object properly is to specify the deity for each verse of the Ṛik-Saṃhitá. But in so doing, it supports its views with so many legends, that we are fully justified in classing it here. It, however, like the other Anukramaṇís, belongs to a much later period than most

[15] See Part i. of my paper on Indian Prosody, *I. St.*, viii. 1, ff. (1863).

of the Sútras, since it presupposes Yáska, the author of the Nirukti, of whom I have to speak presently; it is, in fact, essentially based upon his work. [See Adalb. Kuhn in *I. St.*, i. 101–120.]

It was remarked above, that the investigations into the literal sense of the prayers only began when this sense had gradually become somewhat obscure, and that, as this could not be the case among the priests, who were familiar with it, so soon as amongst the rest of the people, the language of the latter may at that time have undergone considerable modifications. The first step taken to render the prayers intelligible was to make a collection of synonyms, which, by virtue of their very arrangement, explained themselves, and of specially obsolete words, of which separate interpretations were then given orally. These collected words were called, from their being "ranked," "strung together," *Nigranthu*, corrupted into *Nighaṇṭu*,* and those occupied with them *Naighaṇṭukas*. One work of this kind has been actually preserved to us.[16] It is in five books, of which the three first contain synonyms; the fourth, a list of specially difficult Vedic words; and the fifth, a classification of the various divine personages who figure in the Veda. We also possess one of the ancient expositions of this work, a commentary on it, called *Nirukti*, "interpretation," of which Yáska is said to be the author. It consists of twelve books, to which two others having no proper connection with them were afterwards added. It is reckoned by the Indians among the so-called Vedáṅgas, together with Śikshá, Chhandas, and Jyotisha—three very late treatises on phonetics, metre, and astronomical calculations—and also with Kalpa and Vyákaraṇa, *i.e.*, ceremonial and grammar, two general categories of literary works. The four first names likewise originally signified the class in general,[17] and it was only later that they were applied to the four individual works

* See Roth, Introduction to the Nirukti, p. xii.

[16] To this place belong, further, the Nighaṇṭu to the Atharva-S., mentioned by Haug (cf. *I. St.*, ix. 175, 176,) and the Nigama-Pariśishṭa of the White Yajus.

[17] Śikshá still continues to be the name of a species. A considerable number of treatises so entitled have recently been found, and more are constantly being brought to light. Cf. Kielhorn, *I. St.*, xiv. 160.

now specially designated by those titles. It is in Yáska's work, the Nirukti, that we find the first general notions of grammar. Starting from the phonetic rules, the observance of which the Prátiśákhya-Sútras had already established with so much minuteness—but only for each of the Veda-Saṃhitás—advance was no doubt gradually made, in the first place, to a general view of the subject of phonetics, and thence to the remaining portions of the domain of language. Inflection, derivation, and composition were recognised and distinguished, and manifold reflections were made upon the modifications thereby occasioned in the meaning of the root. Yáska mentions a considerable number of grammatical teachers who preceded him, some by name individually, others generally under the name of Nairuktas, Vaiyákaraṇas, from which we may gather that a very brisk activity prevailed in this branch of study. To judge from a passage in the Kaushítaki-Bráhmaṇa, linguistic research must have been carried on with peculiar enthusiasm in the North of India; and accordingly, it is the northern, or rather the north-western district of India that gave birth to the grammarian who is to be looked upon as the father of Sanskrit grammar, Páṇini. Now, if Yáska himself must be considered as belonging only to the last stages of the Vedic period, Páṇini—from Yáska to whom is a great leap—must have lived at the very close of it, or even at the beginning of the next period. Advance from the simple designation of grammatical words by means of terms corresponding to them in sense, which we find in Yáska, to the algebraic symbols of Páṇini, implies a great amount of study in the interval. Besides, Páṇini himself presupposes some such symbols as already known; he cannot therefore be regarded as having invented, but only as having consistently carried out a method which is certainly in a most eminent degree suited to its purpose.

Lastly, Philosophical Speculation also had its peculiar development contemporaneously with, and subsequently to, the Bráhmaṇas. It is in this field and in that of grammar that the Indian mind attained the highest pitch of its marvellous fertility in subtle distinctions, however abstruse or naïve, on the other hand, the method may occasionally be.

Several hymns of a speculative purport in the last book of the Ṛik-Saṃhitá testify to a great depth and concentration of reflection upon the fundamental cause of things, necessarily implying a long period of philosophical research in a preceding age. This is borne out by the old renown of Indian wisdom, by the reports of the companions of Alexander as to the Indian gymnosophists, &c.

It was inevitable that at an early stage, and as soon as speculation had acquired some vigour, different opinions and starting-points should assert themselves, more especially regarding the origin of creation; for this, the most mysterious and difficult problem of all, was at the same time the favourite one. Accordingly, in each of the Bráhmaṇas, one at least, or it may be more, accounts on the subject may be met with; while in the more extensive works of this class we find a great number of different conjectures with regard to cosmogony. One of the principal points of difference naturally was whether indiscrete matter or spirit was to be assumed as the First Cause. The latter theory became gradually the orthodox one, and is therefore the one most frequently, and indeed almost exclusively, represented in the Bráhmaṇas. From among the adherents of the former view, which came by degrees to be regarded as heterodox, there arose, as thought developed, enemies still more dangerous to orthodoxy, who, although they confined themselves in the first place solely to the province of theory, before long threw themselves into practical questions also, and eventually became the founders of the form of belief known to us as Buddhism. The word *buddha*, "awakened, enlightened," was originally a name of honour given to all sages, including the orthodox. This is shown by the use both of the root *budh* in the Bráhmaṇas, and of the word *buddha* itself in even the most recent of the Vedántic writings. The technical application of the word is as much the secondary one as it is in the case also of another word of the kind, *śramaṇa*, which was in later times appropriated by the Buddhists as peculiarly their own. Here not merely the corresponding use of the root *śram*, but also the word *śramaṇa* itself, as a title of honour, may be pointed out in several passages in the Bráhmaṇas. Though Megasthenes, in a passage quoted by Strabo, draws a distinct line between two sects of philosophers, the *Βραχμᾶνες* and the *Σαρμάναι*, yet we should hardly be justified in identifying the latter with the Buddhist mendicants, at least, not exclusively; for he expressly mentions the *ὑλόβιοι—i.e.*, the Brahmachárins and Vánaprasthas, the first and third of the stages into which a Brahman's life is distributed—as forming part of the *Σαρμάναι*. The distinction between the two sects probably consisted in this, that the *Βραχμᾶνες* were the "philosophers" by birth, also those who lived as householders (Gṛihasthas); the *Σαρμάναι*, on the contrary, those who gave themselves up to special mortifications, and who might belong also to other castes. The *Πράμναι*, mentioned by Strabo in another passage (see Lassen, *I. AK.* i. 836), whom, following the accounts of Alexander's time, he describes as accomplished polemical dialecticians, in contradistinction to the *Βραχμᾶνες*, whom he represents as chiefly devoted to physiology and astronomy, appear either to be identical with the *Σαρμάναι*—a supposition favoured by the fact that precisely the same things are asserted of both—or else, with Lassen, they may be regarded as Prámáṇas, *i.e.*, founding their belief on *pramáṇa*, logical proof, instead of revelation. As, however, the word is not known in the writings of that period, we should in this case hardly be justified in accepting Strabo's report as true of Alexander's time, but only of a later age. Philosophical systems are not to be spoken of in connection with this period; only isolated views and speculations are to be met with in those portions of the Bráhmaṇas here concerned, viz., the so-called Upanishads (*upanishad*, a session, a lecture). Although there prevails in these a very marked tendency to systematise and subdivide, the investigations still move within a very narrow and limited range. Considerable progress towards systematising and expansion is visible in the Upanishads found in the Áraṇyakas,* *i.e.*, writings supplementary to the Bráhmaṇas, and specially designed for the *ὑλόβιοι*; and still greater progress in those Upanishads which stand by themselves, *i.e.*,

* The name Áraṇyaka occurs first in the *várttika* to Páṇ. iv. 2. 129 [see on this, *I. St.*, v. 49], then in Manu, iv. 123; Yájnavalkya, i. 145 (in both passages in contradistinction to 'Veda'), iii. 110, 309; and in the Atharvopanishads (see *I. St.*, ii. 179).

those which, although perhaps originally annexed to a Bráhmaṇa or an Áraṇyaka of one of the three older Vedas, have come down to us at the same time—or, it may be, have come down to us only—in an Atharvan recension. Finally, those Upanishads which are directly attached to the Atharva-Veda are complete vehicles of developed philosophical systems; they are to some extent sectarian in their contents, in which respect they reach down to the time of the Puráṇas. That, however, the fundamental works now extant of the philosophical systems, viz., their Sútras, were composed much later than has hitherto been supposed, is conclusively proved by the following considerations. In the first place, the names of their authors are either not mentioned at all in the most modern Bráhmaṇas and Áraṇyakas, or, if they are, it is under a different form and in other relations—in such a way, however, that their later acceptation is already foreshadowed and exhibited in the germ. Secondly, the names of the sages mentioned in the more ancient of them are only in part identical with those mentioned in the latest liturgical Sútras. And, thirdly, in all of them the Veda is expressly presupposed as a whole, and direct reference is also made to those Upanishads which we are warranted in recognising as the latest real Upanishads; nay, even to such as are only found attached to the Atharvan. The style, too, the enigmatical conciseness, the mass of technical terms—although these are not yet endowed with an algebraic force—imply a long previous period of special study to account for such precision and perfection. The philosophical Sútras, as well as the grammatical Sútra, should therefore be considered as dating from the beginning of the next period, within which both are recognised as of predominant authority.

In closing this survey of Vedic literature, I have lastly to call attention to two other branches of science, which, though they do not appear to have attained in this period to the possession of a literature—at least, not one of which direct relics and records have reached us—must yet have enjoyed considerable cultivation—I mean Astronomy and Medicine. Both received their first impulse from the exigencies of religious worship. Astronomical observations—though at first, of course, these were only of the rudest description—were necessarily required for the regulation of the solemn sacrifices; in the first place, of those offered in the morning and evening, then of those at the new and full moon, and finally of those at the commencement of each of the three seasons. Anatomical observations, again, were certain to be brought about by the dissection of the victim at the sacrifice, and the dedication of its different parts to different deities. The Indo-Germanic mind, too, being so peculiarly susceptible to the influences of nature, and nature in India more than anywhere else inviting observation, particular attention could not fail to be early devoted to it. Thus we find in the later portions of the Vájasaneyi-Saṃhitá and in the Chhándogyopanishad express mention made of "observers of the stars" and "the science of astronomy;" and, in particular, the knowledge of the twenty-seven (twenty-eight) lunar mansions was early diffused. They are enumerated singly in the Taittiríya-Saṃhitá, and the order in which they there occur is one that must necessarily* have been established somewhere between 1472 and 536 B.C. Strabo, in the above-mentioned passage, expressly assigns ἀστρονομία as a favourite occupation of the Βραχμᾶνες. Nevertheless, they had not yet made great progress at this period; their observations were chiefly confined to the course of the moon, to the solstice, to a few fixed stars, and more particularly to astrology.

As regards Medicine, we find, especially in the Saṃhitá of the Atharvan, a number of songs addressed to illnesses and healing herbs, from which, however, there is not much to be gathered. Animal anatomy was evidently thoroughly understood, as each separate part had its own distinctive name. Alexander's companions, too, extol the Indian physicians, especially for their treatment of snake-bite.

---

* See *I. St.*, ii. 240, note. [The correct numbers are rather 2780–1820 B.C., see *I. St.*, x. 234–236 (1866); and for the *bharaṇi* series, which seems to be that contained in the Jyotisha, we obtain the years 1820–860, *ibid.* p. 236, ff. See further the remarks in note 2 above.]

From this preliminary survey of Vedic literature we now pass to the details. Adhering strictly to the Indian classification, we shall consider each of the four Vedas by itself, and deal with the writings belonging to them in their proper order, in connection with each Veda separately.

And first of the *Ṛigveda*. The *Ṛigveda-Saṃhitá* presents a twofold subdivision—the one purely external, having regard merely to the compass of the work, and evidently the more recent; the other more ancient, and based on internal grounds. The former distribution is that into eight *ashṭakas* (eighths), nearly equal in length, each of which is again subdivided into as many *adhyáyas* (lectures), and each of these again into about 33 (2006 in all) *vargas* (sections), usually consisting of five verses.[18] The latter is that into ten *maṇḍalas* (circles), 85 *anuvákas* (chapters), 1017 *súktas* (hymns), and 10,580 *ṛichas* (verses); it rests on the variety of authors to whom the hymns are ascribed. Thus the first and tenth *maṇḍalas* contain songs by Ṛishis of different families; the second *maṇḍala*, on the contrary (*ashṭ.* ii. 71–113), contains songs belonging to Gṛitsamada; the third (*ashṭ.* ii. 114–119, iii. 1–56) belongs to Viśvámitra; the fourth (*ashṭ.* iii. 57–114) to Vámadeva; the fifth (*ashṭ.* iii. 115–122, iv. 1–79) to Atri; the sixth (*ashṭ.* iv. 80–140, v. 1–14) to Bharadvája; the seventh (*ashṭ.* v. 15–118) to Vasishṭha; the eighth (*ashṭ.* v. 119–129, vi. 1–81) to Kaṇva; and the ninth (*ashṭ.* vi. 82–124, vii. 1–71) to Añgiras.[19] By the names of these Ṛishis we must understand not merely the individuals, but also their families. The hymns in each separate *maṇḍala* are arranged in the order of the deities addressed.[19b] Those addressed to Agni occupy the first place, next come those

---

[18] For particulars see *I. St.*, iii. 255; Müller, *Anc. S. Lit.*, p. 220.

[19] The first *maṇḍala* contains 24 *anuvákas* and 191 *súktas*; the second 4 *an.* 43 *s.*; the third 5 *an.* 62 *s.*; the fourth 5 *an.* 58 *s.*; the fifth 6 *an.* 87 *s.*; the sixth 6 *an.* 75 *s.*; the seventh 6 *an.* 104 *s.*; the eighth 10 *an.* 92 *s.* (besides 11 *válakhilya-súktas*); the ninth 7 *an.* 114 *s.*; and the tenth 12 *an.* 191 *s.*

[19b] Delbrück, in his review of *Siebenzig Lieder des Ṛigveda* (cf. note 32) in the *Jenaer Literaturzeitung* (1875, p. 867), points out that in books 2–7 the hymns to Agni and Indra are arranged in a descending gradation as regards the number of verses.

to Indra, and then those to other gods. This, at least, is the order in the first eight *maṇḍalas*. The ninth is addressed solely to Soma, and stands in the closest connection with the Sáma-Saṃhitá, one-third of which is borrowed from it; whereas the tenth *maṇḍala* stands in a very special relation to the Atharva-Saṃhitá. The earliest mention of this order of the *maṇḍalas* occurs in the Aitareya-Áraṇyaka, and in the two Gṛihya-Sútras of Áśvaláyana and Śáñkháyana. The Prátiśákhyas and Yáska recognise no other division, and therefore give to the Ṛik-Saṃhitá the name of *daśatayyas*, *i.e.*, the songs "in ten divisions," a name also occurring in the Sáma-Sútras. The Anukramaṇí of Kátyáyana, on the contrary, follows the division into *ashṭakas* and *adhyáyas*. The name *súkta*, as denoting hymn, appears for the first time in the second part of the Bráhmaṇa of the White Yajus; the Ṛig-Bráhmaṇas do not seem to be acquainted with it,[20] but we find it in the Aitareya-Áraṇyaka, &c. The extant recension of the Ṛik-Saṃhitá is that of the Śákalas, and belongs specially, it would seem, to that branch of this school which bears the name of the Śaiśiríyas. Of another recension, that of the Váshkalas, we have but occasional notices, but the difference between the two does not seem to have been considerable. One main distinction, at all events, is that its eighth *maṇḍala* contains eight additional hymns, making 100 in all, and that, consequently, its sixth *ashṭaka* consists of 132 hymns.[21] The name of the Śákalas is evidently related to Śákalya, a sage often mentioned in the Bráhmaṇas and Sútras, who is

---

[20] This is a mistake. They know the word not only in the above, but also in a technical sense, viz., as a designation of one of the six parts of the *śastra* ('canon'), more especially of the main substance of it; when thus applied, *súkta* appears in a collective meaning, comprising several *súktas*. Cf. Śáñkh. Bráhm., xiv. 1.

[21] I am at present unable to corroborate this statement in detail. I can only show, from Śaunaka's Anuvákánukramaṇí, that the recension of the Váshkalas had eight hymns more than that of the Śákalas, but not that these eight hymns formed part of the eighth *maṇḍula*. When I wrote the above I was probably thinking of the Válakhilyas, whose number is given by Sáyaṇa, in his commentary on the Ait. Br., as eight (cf. Roth, *Zur Litt. und Gesch. des Weda*, p. 35; Haug on Ait. Br., 6. 24, p. 416), whereas the editions of Müller and Aufrecht have eleven. But as to whether these eight or eleven Válakhilyas belong specially to the Váshkalas, I cannot at present produce any direct evidence. On other differences of the Váshkala school, &c., see Adalb. Kuhn, in *I. St.*, i. 108, ff.

stated by Yáska[22] to be the author of the Padapáṭha * of the Ṛik-Saṃhitá.† According to the accounts in the Bráhmaṇa of the White Yajus (the Śatapatha-Bráhmaṇa), a Śákalya, surnamed Vidagdha (the cunning?), lived contemporaneously with Yájnavalkya as a teacher at the court of Janaka, King of Videha, and that as the declared adversary and rival of Yájnavalkya. He was vanquished and cursed by the latter, his head dropped off, and his bones were stolen by robbers.—Várkali also (a local form of Váshkali) is the name of one of the teachers mentioned in the second part of the Śatapatha-Bráhmaṇa.[23]

The Śákalas appear in tradition as intimately connected with the Śunakas, and to Śaunaka in particular a number of writings are attributed,‡ which he is said to have composed with a view to secure the preservation of the text (*rigvedaguptaye*), as, for instance, an Anukramaṇí of the Ṛishis, of the metres, of the deities, of the *anuvákas*, of the hymns, an arrangement (? Vidhána) of the verses and their constituent parts,[24] the above-mentioned Bṛihaddevatá,

[22] Or rather Durga, in his comm. on Nir. iv. 4; see Roth, p. 39, introduction, p. lxviii.

* This is the designation of that peculiar method of reciting the Veda in which each word of the text stands by itself, unmodified by the euphonic changes it has to undergo when connected with the preceding and following words. [See above, p. 23.]

† His name seems to point to the north-west (?). The scholiast on Páṇini [iv. 2. 117], at least, probably following the Mahábháshya, cites Śákala in connection with the Báhíkas; see also Burnouf, *Introduction à l'Hist. du Buddh.*, p. 620, ff. The passage in the *sútra* of Páṇini, iv. 3. 128, has no local reference [on the data from the Mahábháshya bearing on this point, see *I. St.*, xiii. 366, 372, 409, 428, 445]. On the other hand, we find Śákyas also in the Kosala country in Kapilavastu, of whom, however, as of the Śákáyanins in the Yajus, we do not exactly know what to make (see below). [The earliest mention of the word Śákala, in immediate reference to the Ṛik, occurs in a memorial verse, *yajnagáthá*, quoted in the Ait. Bráhm., iii. 43 (see *I. St.*, ix. 277).—For the name Śaiśiríya I can only cite the *pravara* section added at the close of the Áśvaláyana-Śrauta-Sútra, in which the Śaiśiris are mentioned several times, partly by themselves, partly beside and in association with the Śuṅgas.]

[23] This form of name, which might be traced to *vṛikala*, occurs also in the Śáṅkháyana Áraṇyaka, viii. 2: "*aśítisahasraṃ Várkalino bṛihatír ahar abhisampádayanti;*" though the parallel passage in the Aitar. Áraṇy., iii. 8, otherwise similarly worded, reads instead of "*Várkalino,*" "*vá (i.e., vai) Arkalino!*"

‡ By Shaḍguruśishya, in the introduction to his commentary on the Ṛig-Anukramaṇí of Kátyáyana.

[24] Rather *two* Vidhána texts (see below), the one of which has for its object the application of particular *ṛichas*, the other probably that of particular *pádas*, to superstitious purposes, after the manner of the Sámavidhána-Bráhmaṇa.

the Prátiśákhya of the Ṛik, a Smárta-Sútra,* and also a Kalpa-Sútra referring specially to the Aitareyaka, which, however, he destroyed after one had been composed by his pupil, Áśvaláyana. It is not perhaps, on the face of it, impossible that all these writings might be the work of one individual Śaunaka; still they probably, nay, in part certainly, belong only to the school which bears his name. But, in addition to this, we find that the second *maṇḍala* of the Saṃhitá itself is attributed to him; and that, on the other hand, he is identified with the Śaunaka at whose sacrificial feast Sauti, the son of Vaiśampáyana, is said to have repeated the Mahá-Bhárata, recited by the latter on an earlier occasion to Janamejaya (the second), together with the Harivaṅśa. The former of these assertions must, of course, only be understood in the sense that the family of the Śunakas both belonged to the old Ṛishi families of the Ṛik, and continued still later to hold one of the foremost places in the learned world of the Brahmans. Against the second statement, on the contrary, no direct objection can be urged; and it is at least not impossible that the teacher of Áśvaláyana and the sacrificer in the Naimisha† forest are identical.—In the Bráhmaṇa of the White Yajus we have, further, two distinct Śaunakas mentioned; the one, Indrota, as sacrificial priest of the prince who, in the Mahá-Bhárata, appears as the first Janamejaya (Párikshita, so also in M.-Bh. xii. 5595, ff.), the other, Svaidáyana, as Audíchya, dwelling in the north.

As author of the Krama-pátha of the Ṛik-Saṃhitá a Pañchála Bábhravya[25] is mentioned. Thus we see that to the Kuru-Pañchálas and the Kosala-Videhas (to whom Śákalya belongs) appertains the chief merit of having fixed and arranged the text of the Ṛik, as well as that of the Yajus;

---

* On the Gṛihya of Śaunaka, see Stenzler, *I. St.*, i. 243.

† The sacrifice conducted by this Śaunaka in the Naimisha forest would, in any case, have to be distinguished from the great sacrificial festival of the Naimishíyas, so often mentioned in the Bráhmaṇas.

[25] In the Ṛik-Prát., xi. 33, merely Bábhravya; only in Uaṭa's scholium is he designated as a Pañchála. As, however, the Pañchálas are twice quoted as an authority in the text of the Ṛik-Prátiśákhya itself, viz., ii. 12, 44, and that beside the Práchyas (people of the east), the above conclusions still hold good. See Regnier on Ṛik-Pr., ii. 12, p. 113. Compare also Śáñkh. Śr., xii. 13. 6 (*pañchálapadavṛittiḥ*), and Saṃhitopanishad-Bráhmaṇa, § 2 (*sarvatra Práchya-Páñchálishu muktam, sarvatrá 'muktam*).

and this was probably accomplished, in the case of both Vedas, during the most flourishing period of these tribes.

For the origin of the songs themselves we must go back, as I have already repeatedly stated, to a far earlier period. This is most clearly shown by the mythological and geographical data contained in them.

The former, the mythological relations, represented in the older hymns of the Ṛik, in part carry us back to the primitive Indo-Germanic time. They contain relics of the childlike and naïve conceptions then prevailing, such as may also be traced among the Teutons and Greeks. So, for instance, the idea of the change of the departed spirit into air, which is conducted by the winged wind, as by a faithful dog, to its place of destination, as is shown by the identity of Sárameya and *Ἑρμείας*,* of Śabala and *Κέρβερος*.† Further, the idea of the celestial sea, Varuṇa, *Οὐρανός*, encompassing the world; of the Father-Heaven, Dyaushpitar, *Ζεύς*, Diespiter; of the Mother-Earth, *Δημήτηρ*; of the waters of the sky as shining nymphs; of the sun's rays as cows at pasture; of the dark cloud-god as the robber who carries off these maidens and cows; and of the mighty god who wields the lightning and thunderbolt, and who chastises and strikes down the ravisher; and other such notions.‡ Only the faintest outlines of this comparative mythology are as yet discernible; it will unquestionably, however, by degrees claim and obtain, in relation to classical mythology, a position exactly analogous to that which has already, in fact, been secured by comparative Indo-Germanic grammar in relation to classical grammar. The ground on which that mythology has hitherto stood trembles beneath it, and the new light about to be shed upon it we owe to the hymns of the Ṛigveda, which enable us to glance, as it were, into the workshop whence it originally proceeded.§

---

* See Kuhn, in Haupt's *Deutsche Zeitschrift*, vi. 125, ff.

† *I. St.*, ii. 297, ff. [and, still earlier, Max Müller; see his *Chips from a German Workshop*, ii. 182].

‡ See Kuhn, *l. c.*, and repeatedly in the *Zeitschrift für vergleichende Sprachforschung*, edited by him jointly with Aufrecht (vol. i., 1851).

§ See *Z. D. M. G.*, v. 112. [Since I wrote the above, comparative mythology has been enriched with much valuable matter, but much also that is crude and fanciful has been advanced. Deserving of special mention, besides various papers by Adalb. Kuhn in his *Zeitschrift*, are two papers by the same author, entitled,

Again, secondly, the hymns of the Ṛik contain sufficient evidence of their antiquity in the invaluable information which they furnish regarding the origin and gradual development of two cycles of epic legend, the Persian and the Indian. In both of these the simple allegories of natural phenomena were afterwards arrayed in an historic garb. In the songs of the Ṛik we find a description, embellished with poetical colours, of the celestial contest between light and darkness, which are depicted either quite simply and naturally, or else in symbolical guise as divine beings. In the Persian Veda, the Avesta, on the other hand, "the contest* descends from heaven to earth, from the province of natural phenomena into the moral sphere. The champion is a son, born to his father, and given as a saviour to earth, as a reward for the pious exercise of the Soma worship. The dragon slain by him is a creation of the Power of Evil, armed with demoniacal might, for the destruction of purity in the world. Lastly, the Persian epic enters upon the ground of history. The battle is fought in the Aryan land; the serpent, Aji Dahaka in Zend, Ahi [Dásaka] in the Veda, is transformed into Zohak the tyrant on the throne of Irán; and the blessings achieved for the oppressed people by the warlike Ferédún—Traitana in the Veda, Thraétaonó in Zend—are freedom and contentment in life on the paternal soil." Persian legend traversed these phases in the course of perhaps 2000 years, passing from the domain of nature into that of the epic, and thence into the field of history. A succession of phases, corresponding to those of Ferédún, may be traced also in the case of Jemshíd (Yama, Yima); a similar series in the case of Kaikavús (Kávya Uśanas, Kava Uś); and probably also in the case of Kai Khosrú (Suśravas, Husravaṅh). Indian legend in its development is the counterpart of the Persian myth. Even in the time of the Yajurveda the natural significance

Die Herabkunft des Feuers und des Göttertranks (1859), and *Ueber Entwicklungsstufen der Mythenbildung* (1874); further, Max Müller's '*Comparative Mythology*,' in the *Oxford Essays* (1856), reprinted in the *Chips*, vol. ii.; M. Bréal, *Hercule et Cacus* (1863); Cox, *Mythology of the Aryan Nations* (1870, 2 vols.); A. de Gubernatis, *Zoological Mythology* (1872, 2 vols.); and *Mitologia Vedica* (1874).]

* See Roth, in *Z. D. M. G.*, ii. 216, ff.

of the myth had become entirely obliterated. Indra is there but the quarrelsome and jealous god, who subdues the unwieldy giant by low cunning; and in the Indian epic the myth either still retains the same form, or else Indra is represented by a human hero, Arjuna, an incarnation of himself, who makes short work of the giant, and the kings who pass for the incarnations of the latter. The principal figures of the Mahá-Bhárata and Rámáyaṇa fall away like the kings of Firdúsí, and there remain for history only those general events in the story of the people to which the ancient myths about the gods have been applied. The personages fade into the background, and in this representation are only recognisable as poetic creations.

Thirdly, the songs of the Ṛik unfold to us particulars as to the time, place, and conditions of their origin and growth. In the more ancient of them the Indian people appear to us settled on the banks of the Indus, divided into a number of small tribes, in a state of mutual hostility, leading a patriarchal life as husbandmen and nomads; living separately or in small communities, and represented by their kings, in the eyes of each other by the wars they wage, and in presence of the gods by the common sacrifices they perform. Each father of a family acts as priest in his own house, himself kindling the sacred fire, performing the domestic ceremonies, and offering up praise and prayer to the gods. Only for the great common sacrifices—a sort of tribe-festivals, celebrated by the king—are special priests appointed, who distinguish themselves by their comprehensive knowledge of the requisite rites and by their learning, and amongst whom a sort of rivalry is gradually developed, according as one tribe or another is considered to have more or less prospered by its sacrifices. Especially prominent here is the enmity between the families of Vaśishṭha and Viśvámitra, which runs through all Vedic antiquity, continues to play an important part in the epic, and is kept up even to the latest times; so that, for example, a commentator of the Veda who claims to be descended from Vaśishṭha leaves passages unexpounded in which the latter is stated to have had a curse imprecated upon him. This implacable hatred owes its origin to the trifling circumstance of Vaśishṭha having once been appointed chief sacrificial priest instead of Viśvámitra by one of the petty kings of these early times.—The influence of these royal priests does not, however, at this early period, extend beyond the sacrifice; there are no castes as yet; the people is still one united whole, and bears but one name, that of *viśas*, settlers. The prince, who was probably elected, is called Viśpati, a title still preserved in Lithuanian. The free position held by women at this time is remarkable. We find songs of the most exquisite kind attributed to poetesses and queens, among whom the daughter of Atri appears in the foremost rank. As regards love, its tender, ideal element is not very conspicuous; it rather bears throughout the stamp of an undisguised natural sensuality. Marriage is, however, held sacred; husband and wife are both rulers of the house (*dampatí*), and approach the gods in united prayer. The religious sense expresses itself in the recognition of man's dependence on natural phenomena, and the beings supposed to rule over them; but it is at the same time claimed that these latter are, in their turn, dependent upon human aid, and thus a sort of equilibrium is established. The religious notion of sin is consequently wanting altogether, and submissive gratitude to the gods is as yet quite foreign[26] to the Indian. 'Give me, and I will render to thee,' he says,[27] claiming therewith a right on his part to divine help, which is an exchange, no grace. In this free strength, this vigorous self-consciousness, a very different, and a far more manly and noble, picture of the Indian is presented to us than that to which we are accustomed from later times. I have already endeavoured above to show how this state of things became gradually altered, how the fresh energy was broken, and by degrees disappeared, through the dispersion over Hindustán, and the enervating influence of the new climate. But what it was that led to the emigration of the people in such masses from the Indus across the Sarasvatí towards the Ganges,

---

[26] 'Quite foreign' is rather too strong an expression. See Roth's paper, *Die höchsten Götter der arischen Völker*, in *Z. D. M. G.*, vi. 72 (1851). There are different phases to be distinguished.

[27] Váj. S., iii. 50; or, "Kill him, then will I sacrifice to thee," Taitt. S., vi. 4. 5. 6.

what was its principal cause, is still uncertain. Was it the pressure brought about by the arrival of new settlers? Was it excess of population? Or was it only the longing for the beautiful tracts of Hindustán? Or perhaps all these causes combined? According to a legend preserved in the Bráhmaṇa of the White Yajus, the priests were in a great measure the cause of this movement, by urging it upon the kings, even against their will [*I. St.*, i. 178]. The connection with the ancestral home on the Indus remained, of course, at first a very close one; later on, however, when the new Brahmanical organisation was completely consolidated in Hindustán, a strong element of bitterness was infused into it, since the Brahmans looked upon their old kinsmen who had remained true to the customs of their forefathers as apostates and unbelievers.

But while the origin of the songs of the Ṛik dates from this primitive time, the redaction of the Ṛik-Saṃhitá only took place, as we observed, at a period when the Brahmanical hierarchy was fully developed, and when the Kosala-Videhas and Kuru-Pañchálas,* who are to be regarded as having been specially instrumental in effecting it, were in their prime. It is also certain that not a few of the songs were composed either at the time of the emigration into Hindustán, or at the time of the compilation itself. Such songs are to be found in the last book especially, a comparatively large portion of which, as I have already remarked, recurs in the Atharvaveda-Saṃhitá. It is for the critic to determine approximately in the case of each individual song, having regard to its con-

* *Maṇḍa'a* x. 98 is a dialogue between Devápi and Śaṃtanu, the two '*Kauravyau*,' as Yáska calls them. In the Mahá-Bhárata Śaṃtanu is the name of the father of Bhíshma and Vichitravírya, by whose two wives, Ambiká and Ambáliká, Vyása became the father of Dhṛitaráshṭra and Páṇḍu. This Śaṃtanu is, therefore, the grandfather of these latter, or the great-grandfather of the Kauravas and Páṇḍavas, the belligerents in the Mahá-Bhárata. We should thus have to suppose that the feud described in this epic had been fought out long before the final arrangement of the Ṛik-Saṃhitá! It is, however, questionable whether the Śaṃtanu of the Mahá-Bhárata is identical with the Śaṃtanu mentioned in the Ṛik; or, even if we take this for granted, whether he may not merely have been associated with the epic legend *in majorem rei gloriam.* Devápi, at least, who, according to Yáska, is his brother, has in the Ṛik a different father from the one given in the epic. See *I. St.*, i. 203.

tents, its ideas, its language, and the traditions connected with it, to what period it ought possibly to be ascribed. But as yet this task is only set; its solution has not yet even begun.[28]

The deities to whom the songs are for the most part addressed are the following:—First, Agni, the god of fire. The songs dedicated to him are the most numerous of all—a fact sufficiently indicative of the character and import of these sacrificial hymns. He is the messenger from men to the gods, the mediator between them, who with his far-shining flame summons the gods to the sacrifice, however distant they may be. He is for the rest adored essentially as earthly sacrificial fire, and not as an elemental force. The latter is rather pre-eminently the attribute of the god to whom, next to Agni, the greatest number of songs is dedicated, viz., Indra. Indra is the mighty lord of the thunderbolt, with which he rends asunder the dark clouds, so that the heavenly rays and waters may descend to bless and fertilise the earth. A great number of the hymns, and amongst them some of the most beautiful, are devoted to the battle that is fought because the malicious demon will not give up his booty; to the description of the thunderstorm generally, which, with its flashing lightnings, its rolling thunders, and its furious blasts, made a tremendous impression upon the simple mind of the people. The break of day, too, is greeted; the dawns are praised as bright, beautiful maidens; and deep reverence is paid to the flaming orb of the mighty sun, as he steps forth vanquishing the darkness of night, and dissipating it to all the quarters of the heavens. The brilliant sun-god is besought for light and warmth, that seeds and flocks may thrive in gladsome prosperity.

Besides the three principal gods, Agni, Indra, and Súrya, we meet with a great number of other divine personages, prominent amongst whom are the Maruts, or winds, the faithful comrades of Indra in his battle; and Rudra, the howling, terrible god, who rules the furious tempest. It is not, however, my present task to discuss the whole of the Vedic Olympus; I had only to sketch generally

---

[28] See now Pertsch, *Upalekha*, p. 57 (1854; compare *Literarisches Centralblatt*, 1875, p. 522); *I. St.*, ix. 299, xiii. 279, 280; *I. Str.*, i. 19.

the groundwork and the outlines of this ancient edifice.[29] Besides the powers of nature, we find, as development progresses, personifications also of spiritual conceptions, of ethical import; but the adoration of these, as compared with the former, is of later origin.

I have already discussed the precautions taken to secure the text of the Ṛik-Saṃhitá, *i.e.*, the question of its authenticity, and I have likewise alluded to the aids to its explanation furnished by the remaining Vedic literature. These latter reduce themselves chiefly to the Nighaṇṭus, and the Nirukta of Yáska.[30] Both works, in their turn, found their commentators in course of time. For the Nighaṇṭus, we have the commentary of Devarájayajvan, who belongs to about the fifteenth or sixteenth century. In the introduction he enlarges upon the history of their study, from which they appear to have found only one other complete commentator since Yáska, viz., Skandasvámin. For Yáska's Nirukta a commentary has been handed down to us dating from about the thirteenth century, that of Durga. Both works, moreover, the Nighaṇṭus as well as the Nirukta, exist in two different recensions. These do not materially differ from one another, and chiefly in respect of arrangement only; but the very fact of their existence leads us to suppose that these works were originally transmitted orally rather than in writing. A commentary, properly so called, on the Ṛik-Saṃhitá, has come down to us, but it dates only from the fourteenth century, that of Sáyaṇáchárya.* "From the long series of

---

[29] Muir's *Original Sanskrit Texts*, vol. v. (1870), is the best source of information for Vedic mythology.

[30] This name appears both in the Vaṅśas in the last book of the Śatap. Br., and in the Káṇḍánukrama of the Átreyí school, where he is called Paiṅgi, and described as the pupil of Vaiśampáyana, and teacher of Tittiri. From Páṇ., ii. 4. 63, it follows that Páṇini was cognisant of the name Yáska, for he there teaches the plural *Yaskás* for the patronymic *Yáska*. Compare on this the *pravara* section in the Áśvaláyana-Śrauta-Sútra. The *Yaská Gairikshitáḥ* are mentioned in the Káṭhaka, which again is quoted by Páṇini; see *I. St.*, iii. 475. A direct reference to Yáska is made in the Ṛik-Prát. and in the Bṛihaddevatá; see also *I. St.*, viii. 96, 245, 246.

* The circumstance that commentaries on almost all branches of the Vedas, and on various other important and extensive works as well, are ascribed to Sáyaṇa and his brother Mádhava, is to be explained by the practice prevailing in India by which works composed by order of some distinguished person bear his name as the author. So in the present day the Paṇḍits work for the person who pays them, and leave

centuries* between Yáska and Sáyaṇa but scanty remains of an exegetic literature connected with the Ṛik-Saṃhitá are left to us, or, at any rate, have as yet been discovered. Śaṃkara and the Vedántic school turned their attention chiefly to the Upanishads. Nevertheless, a gloss upon a portion at least of the Ṛik-Saṃhitá was drawn up by Ánandatírtha, a pupil of Śaṃkara, of which there is an exposition by Jayatírtha, comprising the second and third *adhyáyas* of the first *ashṭaka*, in the Library of the India House in London." Sáyaṇa himself, in addition to Durga's commentary on the Nirukti, only quotes Bhaṭṭa Bháskara Miśra and Bharatasvámin as expositors of the Vedas.[31] The former wrote a commentary upon the Taitt. Yajus, not the Ṛik-Saṃhitá, in which he refers to Káśakṛitsna, Ekachúrṇi, and Yáska as his predecessors in the work. For Bharatasvámin we have no further data than that his name is also cited by Deváraja (on the Nighaṇṭus), who further mentions Bhaṭṭa Bháskara Miśra, Mádhavadeva, Bhavasvámin, Guhadeva, Śrínivása, and Uvaṭṭa. The latter, otherwise called Úaṭa, wrote a commentary on the

---

the fruit of their labour to him as his property. Mádhava, and probably also Sáyaṇa, were ministers at the court of King Bukka at Vijayanagara, and took advantage of their position to give a fresh impulse to the study of the Veda. The writings attributed to them point, by the very difference of their contents and style, to a variety of authorship. [According to A. C. Burnell, in the preface to his edition of the Vaṅśa-Bráhmaṇa, p. viii., ff. (1873), the two names denote one person only. Sáyaṇa, he says, is "the Bhoganátha, or mortal body, of Mádhava, the soul identified with Vishṇu." Burnell is further of opinion that the twenty-nine writings current under the name of Mádhava all proceed from Mádhava himself, unassisted to any large extent by others, and that they were composed by him during a period of about thirty of the fifty-five years between 1331–1386 A.D., which he spent as abbot of the monastery at Śṛiñgeri, under the name Vidyáraṇyasvámin. See my remarks to the contrary in *Literarisches Centralblatt* (1873), p. 1421. Burnell prefers the form Vidyánagara to Vijayanagara. Cowell, in his note on Colebr., *Misc. Ess.*, i. 235, has Vidyá° and Vijaya° side by side.]

* See Roth, *Zur Litt.*, p. 22.

31 To these have to be added Skandasvámin (see p. 41) and Kapardin (see below); and as anterior to Sáyaṇa we must probably regard the works of Átmánanda, Rávaṇa, and Kauśika (or is the latter identical with Bhaṭṭa Kauśika Bháskara Miśra? cf. Burnell, *Catalogue of Vedic MSS.*, p. 12), and the Gúḍhártharatnamálá; Burnell, *Vaṅśabr.*, p. xxvi., ff.; Müller, in the preface to his large edition of the Ṛik-Saṃhitá, vol. vi. p. xxvii., ff. Some extracts from Rávaṇa's commentary have been published by Fitz-Edward Hall in *Journal As. Soc. Beng.*, 1862, pp. 129–134.

Saṃhitá of the White Yajus, not the Ṛik-Saṃhitá, as well as commentaries on the two Prátiśákhyas of the Ṛik and the White Yajus.

As regards European researches, the Ṛik-Saṃhitá, as well as the other Vedas, first became known to us through Colebrooke's excellent paper "On the Vedas," in the *As. Res.* vol. viii. (Calc. 1805). To Rosen we are indebted for the first text, as given partly in his *Ṛigvedæ Specimen* (London, 1830), partly in the edition of the first *ashṭaka*, with Latin translation, which only appeared after the early death of the lamented author (*ibid.* 1838). Since then, some other smaller portions of the text of the Ṛik-Saṃhitá have here and there been communicated to us in text or translation, especially in Roth's already often quoted and excellent *Abhandlungen zur Litteratur und Geschichte des Weda* (Stuttgart, 1846). The entire Saṃhitá, together with the commentary of Sáyaṇa, is now being published, edited by Dr. M. Müller of Oxford, at the expense of the East India Company; the first *ashṭaka* appeared in 1849. At the same time an edition of the text, with extracts from the commentary, is in course of publication in India. From Dr. M. Müller, too, we may expect detailed prolegomena to his edition, which are to treat in particular of the position held by the songs of the Ṛik in the history of civilisation. A French translation by Langlois comprises the entire Saṃhitá (1848–1851); it is, of course, in many respects highly useful, although in using it great caution is necessary. An English translation by Wilson is also begun, of which the first *ashṭaka* only has as yet appeared.[32]

[32] Müller's edition of the text, together with the commentary of Sáyaṇa, a complete index of words, and list of *pratíkas*, is now complete in six vols., 1849–1875. He has also published separately the text of the first *maṇḍala*, in *saṃhitá*- and *pada-páṭha* (Leipzig, 1856–69), as also the whole 10 maṇḍalas, likewise in double form (London, 1873). The first complete edition of the text was published, in Roman transliteration, by Aufrecht, in vols. vi. and vii. of the *Indische Studien* (1861–63). Roer's edition of text and commentary, in the *Bibliotheca Indica*, Nos. 1–4 (Calc. 1849), only reaches to the end of the second *adhyáya*. A fragment of the text, edited by Stevenson so long ago as 1833, extends but a little farther (i. 1–35).—Of Wilson's translation, five volumes have appeared; the last, in 1866, under the editorship of Cowell, brings it up to *maṇḍ.* viii. 20. Benfey published in his *Orient und Occident* (1860–68) a critical translation of *maṇḍ.* i. 1–118. Twelve hymns to the Maruts are translated and furnished with a detailed commentary in vol. i. of Max Müller's *Ṛigveda Saṃhitá, trans-*

We now turn to the *Bráhmaṇas* of the Ṛik.

Of these, we have two, the *Aitareya-Bráhmaṇa* and the *Śáñkháyana-* (or *Kaushítaki-*) *Bráhmaṇa*. They are closely connected with one another,* treat essentially of the same matter, not unfrequently, however, taking opposite views of the same question. It is in the distribution of their matter that they chiefly differ. In the Śáñkháyana-Bráhmaṇa we have a perfectly arranged work, embracing on a definite plan the entire sacrificial procedure; but this does not seem to be the case in an equal degree in the Aitareya-Bráhmaṇa. The latter, moreover, appears to treat exclusively of the Soma sacrifice; whereas in the former it merely occupies the principal place. In the Śáñkháyana-Bráhmaṇa we meet with nothing at all corresponding to the last ten *adhyáyas* of the Aitareya-Bráhmaṇa, a gap which is only filled up by the Śáñkháyana-Sútra; and for this reason, as well as from internal evidence, it may perhaps be assumed that the *adhyáyas* in question are but a later addition to the Aitareya-Bráhmaṇa. In the extant text, the Aitareya-Bráhmaṇa contains 40 *adhyáyas* (divided into eight *pañchikás*, or pen-

---

lated and explained (London, 1869). But the scholar who has done most by far for the right understanding of the Ṛik is Roth; both in the commentary added to his edition of Yáska's Nirukta (Göttingen, 1848–52), and in the great St. Petersburg Sanskrit Dictionary (seven vols., 1853–75), edited by Böhtlingk and him. Here we may also mention the following works:—Grassmann, *Wörterbuch zum Ṛigveda* (1873, ff.); Delbrück, *Das altindische Verbum* (1874); Benfey, *Einleitung in die Grammatik der vedischen Sprache* (1874), and *Die Quantitätsverschiedenheiten in den Saṃhitá- und Paḍa-Texten der Veden*; Bollensen, *Die Lieder des Paráśara*, in *Z. D. M. G.* xxii. (1868); *Siebenzig Lieder des Ṛigveda, übersetzt von* Karl Geldner *und* Adolf Kaegi, *mit Beiträgen von* R. Roth (Tübingen, 1875)—reviewed by Abel Bergaigne in the *Revue Critique*, Dec. 11 and 18, 1875; Alfred Ludwig, *Die Nachrichten des Ṛig- und Atharvaveda über Geographie, Geschichte und Verfassung des alten Indiens* (the identification here mentioned, p. 13, of the Vedic Sarasvatí with the Indus, was first made by myself; cf. *Váj. S. Spec.*, ii. 80 n., 1847), and *Die philosophischen und religiösen Anschauungen des Veda* (Prag, 1875); Alfred Hillebrandt, *Ueber die Göttin Aditi* (Breslau, 1876); H. Zimmer, *Parjanya Fiörgyn Váta Wodan* in *Zeitschrift für Deutsches Alterthum*, New Series, vii. 164, ff. Lastly, we have to draw attention specially to Muir's *Original Sanskrit Texts* (5 vols., second edit., London, 1868, ff.), in which the antiquarian information contained in the Ṛik-Saṃhitá on the different stages and phases of Indian life at that early period is clearly and comprehensively grouped: translations of numerous Vedic passages and pieces are given.

* See on this *I. St.*, ii. 289, ff. [and ix. 377].

tails), while the Śáñkháyana-Bráhmaṇa contains 30; and it is perhaps allowable to refer to them the rule in Páṇini v. 1. 62, which states how the name of a Bráhmaṇa is to be formed if it contain 30 or 40 *adhyáyas,*—a view which would afford external warrant also of the fact of their existence in this form in Páṇini's time, at all events. Geographical or similar data, from which a conclusion might be drawn as to the time of their composition, are of very rare occurrence. Most of these, together with really historical statements, are to be found in the last books of the Aitareya-Bráhmaṇa (see *I. St.*, i. 199, ff.), from which it at any rate specially follows that their scene is the country of the Kuru-Pañchálas and Vaśa-Uśínaras (see viii. 14). In the Śáñkháyana-Bráhmaṇa mention is made of a great sacrifice in the Naimisha forest; but this can hardly be identified with the one at which, according to the accounts of the Mahá-Bhárata, the second recitation of this epic took place. Another passage implies a very special prominence amongst the other gods of the deity who is afterwards known to us exclusively by the name of Śiva. He here receives, among other titles, those of Íśána and Mahádeva, and we might perhaps venture to conclude from this that he was already the object of a very special worship. We are at any rate justified in inferring, unless the passage is an interpolation, that the Śáñkháyana-Bráhmaṇa ranks chronologically with the last books of the Saṃhitá of the White Yajus, and with those portions of its Bráhmaṇa and of the Atharva-Saṃhitá in which this nomenclature is likewise found. Lastly, a third passage of the Śáñkháyana-Bráhmaṇa implies, as already hinted, a special cultivation of the field of language in the northern parts of India. People resorted thither in order to become acquainted with the language, and on their return enjoyed a special authority on questions connected with it. [*I. St.*, ii. 309.]

Both Bráhmaṇas presuppose literary compositions of some extent as having preceded them. Thus mention is made of the *ákhyánavidas, i.e.,* "those versed in tradition;" and *gáthás, abhiyajna-gáthás,* a sort of memorial verses (*kárikás*), are also frequently referred to and quoted. The names Ṛigveda, Sámaveda, and Yajurveda, as well as *trayí vidyá,* a term used to express them collectively, repeatedly occur. In the Śáṅkháyana-Bráhmaṇa, however, special regard is had to the Paiṅgya and Kaushítaka, whose views are very frequently quoted side by side, that of the Kaushítaka being always recognised as final. The question now arises what we are to understand by these expressions, whether works of the Bráhmaṇa order already extant in a written form, or still handed down orally only—or merely the inherited tradition of individual doctrines. Mention of the Kaushítaka and the Paiṅgya occurs in the Aitareya-Bráhmaṇa only in a single passage—and that perhaps an interpolated one—in the latter part of the work. This at all events proves, what already seemed probable from its more methodical arrangement, that the Śáṅkháyana-Bráhmaṇa is to be considered a later production than the Aitareya-Bráhmaṇa, since it appears to be a recast of two sets of views of similar tenor already extant under distinct names, while the Aitareya-Bráhmaṇa presents itself as a more independent effort. The name Paiṅgya belongs to one of the sages mentioned in the Bráhmaṇa of the White Yajus and elsewhere, from whose family Yáska Paiṅgi* was descended, and probably also Piṅgala, the author of a treatise on metre. The *Paiṅgí Kalpaḥ* is expressly included by the commentator of Páṇini, probably following the Mahábháshya, among the ancient Kalpa-Sútras, in contradistinction to the *Áśmarathaḥ Kalpaḥ*, with which we shall presently become acquainted as an authority of the Áśvaláyana-Sútra. The Paiṅgins are, besides, frequently mentioned in early writings, and a Paiṅgi-Bráhmaṇa must still have been in existence even in Sáyaṇa's time, for he repeatedly refers to it. The case stands similarly as regards the name Kaushítaka, which, is, moreover, used directly in the majority of passages where it is quoted for the Śáṅkháyana-Bráhmaṇa itself—a fact easy of explanation, as in the latter the view represented by the Kaushítaka is invariably upheld as the authoritative one, and we have in this Bráhmaṇa but a remoulding by Śáṅkháyana of the stock of dogma peculiarly the property of the Kaushítakins. Further, in its commentary, which, it may be remarked,

* The quotations from Bráhmaṇas in Yáska, therefore, belong in part perhaps to the Paiṅgya (?). [On the *Paiṅgí Kalpaḥ* in the Mahábháshya, see *I. St.*, xiii. 455.]

interprets the work under the sole title of the "Kaushítaki-Bráhmaṇa," passages are frequently quoted from a Mahá-Kaushítaki-Bráhmaṇa, so that we have to infer the existence of a still larger work of similar contents,—probably a later handling of the same subject (?). This commentary further connects the Kaushítaki-Bráhmaṇa with the school of the Kauthumas—a school which otherwise belongs only to the Sámaveda: this, however, is a relation which has not as yet been cleared up.—The name Śáṅkháyana-Bráhmaṇa interchanges occasionally with the form Śáṅkhyáyana-Bráhmaṇa, but the former would seem to deserve the preference; its earliest occurrence is probably in the Prátiśákhya-Sútra of the Black Yajus.

The great number of myths and legends contained in both these Bráhmaṇas of the Ṛik invests them with a peculiar interest. These are not indeed introduced for their own sake, but merely with a view to explain the origin of some hymn; but this, of course, does not detract from their value. One of them, the legend of Śunaḥśepa, which is found in the second part of the Aitareya-Bráhmaṇa, is translated by Roth in the *Indische Studien*, i. 458–464, and discussed in detail, *ibid.*, ii. 112–123. According to him, it follows a more ancient metrical version. We must indeed assume generally, with regard to many of these legends, that they had already gained a rounded, independent shape in tradition before they were incorporated into the Bráhmaṇa, and of this we have frequent evidence in the distinctly archaic character of their language, compared with that of the rest of the text. Now these legends possess great value for us from two points of view: first, because they contain, to some extent at least, directly or indirectly, historical data, often stated in a plain and artless manner, but at other times disguised and only perceptible to the eye of criticism; and, secondly, because they present connecting links with the legends of later times, the origin of which would otherwise have remained almost entirely obscure.

On the Aitareya-Bráhmaṇa we have a commentary by Sáyaṇa, and on the Kaushítaki-Bráhmaṇa one by Vináyaka, a son of Mádhava.[33]

[33] The Aitareya-Bráhmaṇa has been edited, text with translation, by Martin Haug, 2 vols., Bombay, 1863, see *I. St.*, ix. 177–380 (1865).

To each of these Bráhmaṇas is also annexed an Áraṇyaka, or 'forest-portion,' that is, the portion to be studied in the forest by the sages known to us through Megasthenes as ὑλόβιοι, and also by their disciples. This forest-life is evidently only a later stage of development in Brahmanical contemplation, and it is to it that we must chiefly ascribe the depth of speculation, the complete absorption in mystic devotion by which the Hindús are so eminently distinguished. Accordingly, the writings directly designated as Áraṇyakas bear this character impressed upon them in a very marked degree; they consist in great part of Upanishads only, in which, generally speaking, a bold and vigorous faculty of thought cannot fail to be recognised, however much of the bizarre they may at the same time contain.

The *Aitareya-Áraṇyaka*[33b] consists of five books, each of which again is called Áraṇyaka. The second and third books* form a separate Upanishad; and a still further subdivision here takes place, inasmuch as the four last sections of the second book, which are particularly consonant with the doctrines of the Vedánta system, pass κατ' ἐξοχὴν as the *Aitareyopanishad*.[34] Of these two books Mahidása Aitareya is the reputed author; he is supposed to be the son of Viśála and Itará, and from the latter his name Aitareya is derived. This name is indeed several times quoted in the course of the work itself as a final authority, a circumstance which conclusively proves the correctness of tracing to him the views therein propounded. For we must divest ourselves of the notion that a teacher of this period ever put his ideas into writing; oral delivery was his only method of imparting them to his pupils; the knowledge of them was transmitted by tradition, until it became fixed in

---

The legend of Śunaḥśepa (vii. 13–18), had been discussed by Roth; see also M. Müller, *Hist. of A. S. L.*, p. 573, ff. Another section of it (viii. 5–20), treating of royal inaugurations, had previously been edited by Schönborn (Berlin, 1862).

33b The first fasciculus of an edition, together with Sáyaṇa's commentary, of the Aitareya-Áraṇyaka, by Rájendra Lála Mitra, has just come to hand (Nov. 30, 1875), see *Bibliotheca Indica*, New Series, No. 325; the text reaches as far as i. 4. 1.

* See *I. St.*, i. 388, ff.

34 This Aitareyopanishad, amongst others, has been edited (with Śaṃkara's commentary) and translated by Roer, *Bibl. Ind.*, vii. 143, ff. (Calc. 1850), xv. 28, ff. (1853).

some definite form or other, always however retaining his name. It is in this way that we have to account for the fact of our finding the authors of works that have been handed down to us, mentioned in these works themselves. For the rest, the doctrines of Aitareya must have found especial favour, and his pupils have been especially numerous; for we find his name attached to the Bráhmaṇa as well as the Áraṇyaka. With respect to the former, however, no reasons can for the present be assigned, while for the fourth book of the Áraṇyaka we have the direct information that it belongs to Áśvaláyana,* the pupil of Śaunaka; nay, this Śaunaka himself appears to have passed for the author of the fifth book, according to Colebrooke's statements on the subject, *Misc. Ess.*, i. 47, n. The name of Aitareya is not traceable anywhere in the Bráhmaṇas; he is first mentioned in the Chhándogyopanishad. The earliest allusion to the school of the Aitareyins is in the Sáma-Sútras.—To judge from the repeated mention of them in the third book, the family of the Maṇḍúkas, or Máṇḍúkeyas, must also have been particularly active in the development of the views there represented. Indeed, we find them specified later as one of the five schools of the Ṛigveda; yet nothing bearing their name has been preserved except an extremely abstruse Upanishad, and the Máṇḍúkí-Śikshá, a grammatical treatise. The former, however, apparently only belongs to the Atharvan, and exhibits completely the standpoint of a rigid system. The latter might possibly be traced back to the Máṇḍúkeya who is named here as well as in the Ṛik-Prátiśákhya.

The contents of the Aitareya-Áraṇyaka, as we now have it,[35] supply no direct clue to the time of its composi-

---

* I find an Áśvaláyana-Bráhmaṇa also quoted, but am unable to give any particulars regarding it. [In a MS. of the Ait. Ár., India Office Library, 986, the entire work is described at the end as *Áśvaláyanoktam Áraṇyakam.*]

[35] See *I. St.*, i. 387–392. I am now in possession of the complete text, but have nothing material to add to the above remarks. Great stress is laid upon keeping the particular doctrines secret, and upon the high importance of those familiar with them. Among the names mentioned in the course of the work, Ágniveśyáyana is of significance on account of its formation. The interesting passages on the three *páṭhas* of the Veda, *nirbhuja* = *saṃhitápáṭha*, *pratṛiṇṇa* = *padapáṭha*, and *ubhayamantareṇa* = *kramapáṭha*, are discussed by M. Müller on Ṛik-Prát., i. 2–4 (see also *ibid.*, *Nachträge*, p. 11).

tion, other than the one already noticed, namely, that in the second chapter of the second book the extant arrangement of the Ṛik-Saṃhitá is given. Again, the number of teachers individually mentioned is very great, particularly in the third book—among them are two Śákalyas, a Kṛishṇa Háríta, a Pañchálachaṇḍa—and this may be considered as an additional proof of its more recent origin, a conclusion already implied by the spirit and form of the opinions enunciated.[36]

The Kaushítakáraṇyaka, in its present form, consists of three books; but it is uncertain whether it is complete.[37] It was only recently that I lighted upon the two first books.* These deal rather with ritual than with speculation. The third book is the so-called *Kaushítaky-Upanishad*,† a work of the highest interest and importance. Its first *adhyáya* gives us an extremely important account of the ideas held with regard to the path to, and arrival in, the world of the blessed, the significance of which in relation to similar ideas of other races is not yet quite apparent, but it promises to prove very rich in information. The second *adhyáya* gives us in the ceremonies which it describes, amongst other things, a very pleasing picture of the warmth and tenderness of family ties at that period. The third *adhyáya* is of inestimable value in connection with the history and development of the epic myth, inasmuch as it represents Indra battling with the same powers of nature that Arjuna in the epic subdues as evil demons. Lastly, the fourth *adhyáya* contains the second recension of a legend which also appears, under a somewhat different

---

[36] The circumstance here emphasised may be used to support the very opposite view; indeed I have so represented it in the similar case of the Láṭyáyana-Sútra (see below). This latter view now appears to me to have more in its favour.

[37] A manuscript sent to Berlin by Bühler (*MS. Or. fol.* 630) of the 'Śáñkháyana-Áraṇyaka' (as it is there called) presents it in 15 *adhyáyas*; the first two correspond to Ait. Ár. i., v.; *adhy.* 3–6 are made up of the Kaush. Up.; *adhy.* 7, 8 correspond to Ait. Ár. iii.; *adhy.* 9 gives the rivalry of the senses (like Śatap. Br. 14. 9. 2).

* See Catalogue of the Berlin Skr. MSS., p. 19, n. 82.

† See *I. St.*, i. 392–420. It would be very desirable to know on what Poley's assertion is founded, "that the Kaushítaki-Bráhmaṇa consists of nine *adhyáyas*, the first, seventh, eighth, and ninth of which form the Kaushítaki-Bráhmaṇa-Upanishad." I have not succeeded in finding any statement to this effect elsewhere. [See now Cowell's Preface, p. vii., to his edition of the Kaush. Up. in the *Bibl. Ind.*]

form, in the Áraṇyaka of the White Yajus, the legend, namely, of the instruction of a Brahman, who is very wise in his own esteem, by a warrior called Ajátaśatru, king of Káśi. This Upanishad is also peculiarly rich in geographical data, throwing light upon its origin. Thus the name of Chitra Gáñgyáyani, the wise king in the first *adhyáya* who instructs Áruṇi, clearly points to the Gaṅgá. According to ii. 10, the northern and southern mountains, *i.e.*, Himavant and Vindhya, enclose in the eyes of the author the whole of the known world, and the list of the neighbouring tribes in iv. 1 perfectly accords with this. That, moreover, this Upanishad is exactly contemporaneous with the Vṛihad-Áraṇyaka of the White Yajus is proved by the position of the names Áruṇi, Śvetaketu, Ajátaśatru, Gárgya Báláki, and by the identity of the legends about the latter. [See *I. St.*, i. 392–420.]

We have an interpretation of both Áraṇyakas, that is to say, of the second and third books of the Aitareya-Áraṇyaka, and of the third book of the Kaushítaki-Áraṇyaka in the commentary of Saṃkaráchárya, a teacher who lived about the eighth century A.D.,[38] and who was of the highest importance for the Vedánta school. For not only did he interpret all the Vedic texts, that is, all the Upanishads, upon which that school is founded, he also commented on the Vedánta-Sútra itself, besides composing a number of smaller works with a view to elucidate and establish the Vedánta doctrine. His explanations, it is true, are often forced, from the fact of their having to accommodate themselves to the Vedánta system; still they are of high importance for us. Pupils of his, Ánandajnána, Ánandagiri, Ánandatírtha, and others, in their turn composed glosses on his commentaries. Of most of these commentaries and glosses we are now in possession, as they have been recently edited, together with their Upanishads, by Dr. Roer, Secretary to the Asiatic Society of Bengal, in the *Bibliotheca Indica*, a periodical appearing under the auspices of that Society, and devoted exclusively

---

[38] Śaṃkara's date has not, unfortunately, been more accurately determined as yet. He passes at the same time for a zealous adversary of the Buddhists, and is therefore called a Śaiva, or follower of Siva. In his works, however, he appears as a worshipper of Vásudeva, whom he puts forward as the real incarnation or representative of *brahman*.

to the publication of texts. Unfortunately the Kaushítaki-Upanishad is not yet among the number, neither is the Maitráyaṇy-Upanishad, of which we have to speak in the sequel. It is, however, to be hoped that we shall yet receive both.[39]—And may yet a third, the Váshkala-Upanishad, be recovered and added to the list of these Upanishads of the Ṛik! It is at present only known to us through Anquetil Duperron's *Oupnekhat*, ii. 366–371; the original must therefore have been extant at the time of the Persian translation (rendered into Latin by Anquetil) of the principal Upanishads (1656). The Váshkala-Śruti is repeatedly mentioned by Sáyaṇa. We have seen above that a particular recension of the Ṛik-Saṃhitá, which has likewise been lost, is attributed to the Váshkalas. This Upanishad is therefore the one sorry relic left to us of an extensive cycle of literature. It rests upon a legend repeatedly mentioned in the Bráhmaṇas, which in substance, and one might almost say in name also, corresponds to the Greek legend of Gany-Medes. Medhátithi, the son of Kaṇva, is carried up to heaven by Indra, who has assumed the form of a ram, and during their flight he inquires of Indra who he is. Indra, in reply, smilingly declares himself to be the All-god, identifying himself with the universe. As to the cause of the abduction, he goes on to say that, delighted with Medhátithi's penance, he desired to conduct him into the right path leading to truth; he must therefore have no further misgiving. With regard to the date of this Upanishad, nothing more definite can of course at present be said than that its general tenor points to a tolerably high antiquity.[40]

We now descend to the last stage in the literature of the Rigveda, viz., to its *Sútras*.

First, of the *Śrauta-Sútras*, or text-books of the sacrificial rite. Of these we possess two, the Sútra of Áśvaláyana in 12 *adhyáyas*, and that of Śáṅkháyana in 18

[39] Both have now been published and translated by Cowell in the *Bibliotheca Indica*. The Kaush.-Up. (Calc. 1861) is accompanied with the comm. of Saṃkaránanda, the Maitri-Up. with that of Rámatírtha (1863-69).

[40] See now my special paper on the subject in *I. St.*, ix. 38–42; the original text has not yet been met with.

adhyayas. The former connects itself with the Aitareya-Bráhmaṇa, the latter with the Śáṅkháyana-Bráhmaṇa, and from these two works frequent literal quotations are respectively borrowed. From this circumstance alone, as well as from the general handling of the subject, we might infer that these Sútras are of comparatively recent origin; and direct testimony is not wanting to establish the fact. Thus the name Áśvaláyana is probably to be traced back to Aśvala, whom we find mentioned in the Áraṇyaka of the White Yajus as the Hotar of Janaka, king of Videha (see *I. St.*, i. 441). Again, the formation of the word by the affix *áyana*,* probably leads us to the time of established schools (*ayana*)? However this may be, names formed in this way occur but seldom in the Bráhmaṇas themselves, and only in their latest portions; in general, therefore, they always betoken a late period. We find corroboration of this in the data supplied by the contents of the Áśvaláyana-Sútra. Among the teachers there quoted is an Áśmarathya, whose *kalpa* (doctrine) is considered by the scholiast on Páṇini, iv. 3. 105, probably following the Mahábháshya,[41] as belonging to the new *kalpas* implied in this rule, in contradistinction to the old *kalpas*. If, then, the authorities quoted by Áśvaláyana were regarded as recent, Áśvaláyana himself must of course have been still more modern; and therefore we conclude, assuming this statement to originate from the Mahábháshya,[41] that Áśvaláyana was nearly contemporaneous with Páṇini. Another teacher quoted by Áśvaláyana, Taulvali, is expressly mentioned by Páṇini (ii. 4. 61) as belonging to the *práñchas*, or "dwellers in the east."—At the end there is a specially interesting enumeration of the various Bráhmaṇa-families, and their distribution among the family stems of Bhṛigu, Aṅgiras, Atri, Viśvámitra, Kaśyapa, Vasishṭha, and Agastya.—The sacrifices on the Sarasvatí, of which I shall treat in the sequel, are here only briefly touched upon, and this with some differences in the

---

* As in the case of Ágniveśyáyana, Álambáyana, Aitiśáyana, Audumbaráyaṇa, Káṇḍamáyana, Kátyáyana, Kháḍáyana, Dráhyáyaṇa, Pákshayaṇa, Bádaráyaṇa, Máṇḍúkáyana, Ráṇáyana, Láṭyáyana, Lábukáyana (?), Lámakáyana, Várshyáyaṇi, Sákaṭáyana, Śáṅkháyana, Śáṭyáyana, Śáṇḍilyáyana, Śálaṃkáyana, Saityáyana, Śaulváyana, &c.

[41] The name is not known in the Mahábháshya, see *I. St.*, xiii. 455.

names, which may well be considered as later corruptions. We have also already seen that Áśvaláyana is the author of the fourth book of the Aitareya-Áraṇyaka, as also that he was the pupil of Śaunaka, who is stated to have destroyed his own Sútra in favour of his pupil's work.

The Sútra of Śáñkháyana wears in general a somewhat more ancient aspect, particularly in the fifteenth and sixteenth books, where it assumes the appearance of a Bráhmaṇa. The seventeenth and eighteenth books are a later addition, and are also ranked independently, and separately commented upon. They correspond to the first two books of the Kaushítaki-Áraṇyaka.

From my but superficial acquaintance with them, I am not at present in a position to give more detailed information as to the contents and mutual relation of these two Sútras.[42] My conjecture would be that their differences may rest upon local grounds also, and that the Sútra of Áśvaláyana, as well as the Aitareya-Bráhmaṇa, may belong to the eastern part of Hindustán; the Sútra of Śáñkháyana, on the contrary, like his Bráhmaṇa, rather to the western.* The order of the ceremonial is pretty much the same in both, though the great sacrifices of the kings, &c., viz., *vájapeya* (sacrifice for the prospering of the means of subsistence), *rájasúya* (consecration of the king), *aśvamedha* (horse sacrifice), *purushamedha* (human sacrifice), *sarvamedha* (universal sacrifice), are handled by Śáñkháyana with far more minuteness.

For Áśvaláyana I find mention made of a commentary by Náráyaṇa,[43] the son of Kṛishṇajit, a grandson of Śrípati. A namesake of his, but son of Paśupatiśarman,

[42] The Áśvaláyana-Sútra has since been printed, *Bibl. Ind.* (Calc. 1864–74), accompanied with the comm. of Náráyaṇa Gárgya, edited by Ráma-Náráyaṇa and Ánandachandra. A special comparison of it with the Śáñkháyana-Sútra is still wanting. Bühler, *Catalogue of MSS. from Gujarát*, i. 154 (1871), cites a commentary by Devatráta on the Áśv. Śr. S., likewise a partial one by Vidyáraṇya.

* Perhaps to the Naimisha forest (?). See below, p. 59.

[43] This is a confusion. The abovenamed Náráyaṇa wrote a commentary upon the Śáñkháyana-Gṛihya; but the one who commented the Áśvaláyana-Śrauta-Sútra calls himself in the introduction a son of Narasiñha, just as Náráyaṇa, the commentator of the Uttara-Naishadhíya, does, who, according to tradition (Roer, Pref., p. viii., 1855), lived some five hundred years ago. Are these two to be regarded as one and the same person? See *I. Str.*, 2, 298 (1869).

composed a *paddhati* ('outlines') to Śáṅkháyana, after the example of one Brahmadatta. When he lived is uncertain, but we may with some probability assign him to the sixteenth century. According to his own statements he was a native of Malayadeśa. Further, for the Sútra of Śáṅkháyana we have the commentary of Varadattasuta Ánarttíya. Three of its *adhyáyas* were lost, and have been supplied by Dásaśarman Muñjasúnu, viz., the ninth, tenth, and eleventh.[44] On the last two *adhyáyas*, xvii., xviii., there is a commentary by Govinda. That these commentaries were preceded by others, which, however, have since been lost, is obvious, and is besides expressly stated by Ánarttíya.

Of the *Gṛihya-Sútras* of the Ṛigveda we likewise only possess two, those of Áśvaláyana (in four *adhyáyas*) and of Śáṅkháyana (in six *adhyáyas*). That of Śaunaka is indeed repeatedly mentioned, but it does not seem to be any longer in existence.

However widely they may differ as to details, the contents of the two works are essentially identical, especially as regards the order and distribution of the matter. They treat mainly, as I have already stated (p. 17), of the ceremonies to be performed in the various stages of conjugal and family life, before and after a birth, at marriage, at the time of and after a death. Besides these, however, manners and customs of the most diverse character are depicted, and "in particular, the sayings and formulas to be uttered on different occasions bear the impress of a very high antiquity, and frequently carry us back into the time when Brahmanism had not yet been developed" (see Stenzler in *I. St.*, ii. 159). It is principally popular and superstitious notions that are found in them; thus, we are pointed to star-worship, to astrology, portents, and witchcraft, and more especially to the adoration and propitiation of the evil powers in nature, the averting of their malign influence, &c. It is especially in the *pitṛitarpaṇa*, or oblation to the Manes, that we find a decisive proof of

---

[44] Sections 3-5 of the fourth book have been published by Donner in his *Piṇḍapitṛiyajna* (Berlin, 1870), and the section relating to the legend of Śunaḥśepa (xv. 17-27) by Streiter (1861); the variants presented therein to the parallel passage in the Ait. Bráhm. had already been given by M. Müller, *A. S. L.*, p. 573, ff.

the modern composition of these works, as the forefathers are there enumerated individually by name—a custom which, although in itself it may be very ancient (as we find a perfect analogy to it in the Yeshts and Nerengs of the Parsís), yet in this particular application belongs to a very recent period, as is apparent from the names themselves. For not only are the Ṛishis of the Ṛik-Saṃhitá cited in their extant order, but all those names are likewise mentioned which we encounter as particularly significant in the formation of the different schools of the Ṛik, as well as in connection with its Bráhmaṇas and Sútras; for example, Váshkala, Śákalya, Máṇḍúkeya, Aitareya, Paiñgya, Kaushítaka, Śaunaka, Áśvaláyana, and Śáñkháyana themselves, &c. Joined to these, we find other names with which we are not yet otherwise acquainted, as also the names of three female sages, one of whom, Gárgí Váchaknaví, meets us repeatedly in the Vṛihad-Áraṇyaka of the White Yajus, as residing at the court of Janaka. The second[45] is unknown; but the name of the third, Sulabhá Maitreyí, is both connected with this very Janaka in the legends of the Mahá-Bhárata,* and also points us to the *Saulabháni Bráhmaṇáni*, quoted by the scholiast on Páṇini, iv. 3. 105, probably on the authority of the Mahábháshya,[46] as an instance of the 'modern' Bráhmaṇas implied by this rule. Immediately after the Ṛishis of the Ṛik-Saṃhitá, we find mention of other names and works which have not yet been met with in any other part of Vedic literature. In the Śáñkháyana-Gṛihya we have these: *Sumantu-Jaimini-Vaiśampáyana-Paila-sútra-bháshya* [*-Gárgya-Babhru*] . . .; and in the Áśvaláyana-Gṛihya these: *Sumantu-Jaimini-Vaiśampáyana-Paila-sútra-bhárata-mahábhárata-dharmácháryáḥ*.[47] The latter

[45] Her name is Vaḍavá Prátitheyí; a teacher called Prátithi is mentioned in the Vaṅśa-Bráhmaṇa of the Sámaveda.

* [Cf. Śaṃkara's statements as to this in Ved. Sútrabh. to iii. 3. 32, p. 915, ed. Ráma Náráyaṇa.] Buddha's uncle is called by the Buddhists Sulabha; see Schiefner, *Leben des Sákyamuni*, p. 6.

[46] See on this *I. St.*, xiii. 429. They are there cited a second time also, to Páṇ., iv. 2. 68, and are explained by Kaiyaṭa as *Sulabhena proktáni*.

[47] The word *bháshya* is to be inserted above between *sútra* and *bhárata;* though wanting in the MS. used by me at the time when I wrote, it is found in all the other MSS.

passage is evidently the more modern, and although we must not suppose that the Mahá-Bhárata in its present form is here referred to, still, in the expression "*Vaiśampáyano mahábhháratácháryaḥ,*" apparently indicated by this passage, there must at all events be implied a work of some compass, treating of the same legend, and therefore forming the basis of our extant text. The passage seems also to indicate that the same material had already been handled a second time by Jaimini, whose work, however, can have borne but a distant resemblance to the Jaimini-Bhárata of the present day. We shall find in the sequel frequent confirmation of the fact that the origin of the epic and the systematic development of Vedic literature in its different schools belong to the same period. Of a Sútra by Sumantu, and a Dharma by Paila, we have no knowledge whatever. It is only in more modern times, in the Puráṇas and in the legal literature proper, that I find a work attributed to Sumantu, namely, a Smṛiti-Śástra; while to Paila (whose name appears from Páṇ. iv. 1. 118) is ascribed the revelation of the Ṛigveda—a circumstance which at least justifies the inference that he played a special part in the definitive completion of its school development.—It is, however, possible to give a wholly different interpretation of the passage from Áśvaláyana; and in my opinion it would be preferable to do so. We may divest the four proper names of any special relation to the names of the four works, and regard the two groups as independent,[48] as we must evidently assume them to be in the Śáṅkháyana-Gṛihya.* If this be done, then what most readily suggests itself in connection with the passage is the manner in which the Puráṇas apportion

---

[48] This interpretation becomes imperative after the rectification of the text (see the previous note), according to which no longer four, but five names of works are in question.

* What is meant in the latter [and cf. note 47 in the Áśv. Gṛih. too] by the word *bháshya,* appears from the Prátiśákhya of the White Yajus, where (i. 1. 19, 20) *vedeshu* and *bháshyeshu* are found in contradistinction to one another, just as in the Prátiśákhya of the Black Yajus (ii. 12) we find *chhandas* and *bháshá,* and in Yáska *anvadhyáya* and *bháshá.* We must therefore understand by it 'works in *bháshá,*' though the meaning of the word is here more developed than in the works just mentioned, and approaches the sense in which Páṇini uses it. I shall return to the subject further on.

the revelation of the several Vedas; inasmuch as they assign the Atharvaveda to Sumantu, the Sámaveda to Jaimini, the Yajurveda to Vaiśampáyana, and the Ṛigveda to Paila. But in either case we must assume with Roth, who first pointed out the passage in Áśvaláyana (*op. c.*, p. 27), that this passage, as well as the one in Śáñkháyana, has been touched up by later interpolation;[49] otherwise the dates of these two Gṛihya-Sútras would be brought down too far! For although, from the whole tenor of both passages, that in the Áśvaláyana-Gṛihya, as well as that in the Śáñkháyana-Gṛihya—which for the rest present other material discrepancies of detail—it is sufficiently clear that they presuppose the literature of the Ṛigveda as entirely closed, still the general attitude of both works shows their comparatively ancient origin.—The question whether any connection exists between the Smṛiti-Śástra of Śañkha and the Gṛihya-Sútra of Śáñkháyana, remains still unanswered.

For both Gṛihya-Sútras there are commentaries by the same Náráyaṇa who commented the Śrauta-Sútra of Áśvaláyana.[50] They probably belong to the fifteenth century.* There are, besides, as in the case of the Śrauta-Sútras,

---

[49] We find the *Sumantu-Jaimini-Vaiśampáyana - Pailádyá áchâryáḥ* quoted a second time in the Śáñkh. G., in its last section (vi. 6), which is probably of later origin; and here, without any doubt, the reference is to the same distribution of the four Vedas among the above-named personages which occurs in the Vishṇu-Puráṇa, iii. 4. 8, 9. Both times the representative of the Atharvan comes first, that of the Ṛik last, which in a Ṛik text serves as a clear proof that we have here to do with later appendages. A similar precedence is given to the Atharvaveda in the Mahábháshya; cf. *I. St.*, xiii. 431.

[50] This is a mistake, see note 43; all three Náráyaṇas must be kept distinct. The commentator of the Áśval. Śr. S. calls himself a Gárgya, and son of Narasiñha; the comm. of the Áśval. Gṛihya, a Naidhruva, and son of Divákara; the comm. of the Śáñkh. Gṛihya, son of Krishṇajit, and grandson of Śrîpati. (This third Nár. lived A.D. 1538; see Catalogue of the Berlin MSS., p. 354, sub No. 1282.)—The text of the Áśval. Gṛihya has been edited by Stenzler, with a translation (*Indische Hausregeln*, 1864-65); the text, with Náráyaṇa's comm., by Rámanáráyaṇa and Ánandachandra, in *Bibl. Ind.* (1866-69). The sections relating to marriage ceremonies have been edited by Haas, *I. St.*, v. 283, ff.; those relating to funeral rites, by Müller, *Z. D. M. G.*, ix.

* Two glosses on Śaṃkara's commentary on the Praśnopanishad and the Muṇḍakopanishad bear the same name, so that possibly the author of them is identical with the above-named Náráyaṇa. Acc. to what has just been remarked in note 50, this must appear *à priori* very doubtful, since a considerable number of other

many small treatises in connection with the Gṛihya-Sútras, some of them being summaries, in which the larger works are reduced to system. Among them is a Paddhati to the Śáñkháyana-Gṛihya by Rámachandra, who lived in the Naimisha forest in the middle of the fifteenth century; and I am inclined to think that this Naimisha forest was the birthplace of the Sútra itself. It is perhaps for this reason that the tradition connected with it was so well preserved in that district.

The extant *Prátiśákhya-Sútra* of the Ṛik-Saṃhitá is ascribed to Śaunaka, who has been repeatedly mentioned already, and who was the teacher of Áśvaláyana. This extensive work is a metrical composition, divided into three *káṇḍas*, of six *paṭalas* each, and containing 103 *kaṇḍikás* in all. The first information regarding it was given by Roth, *op. c.*, p. 53, ff. According to tradition, it is of more ancient origin than the Sútras of Áśvaláyana just mentioned, which only purport to be written by the pupil of this Śaunaka; but whether it really was composed by the latter, or whether it is not much more probably merely the work of his school, must for the present remain undecided. The names quoted in it are in part identical with those met with in Yáska's Nirukti and in the Sútra of Páṇini. The contents of the work itself are, however, as yet but little known[61] in their details. Of special interest are those passages which treat of the correct and incorrect pronunciation of words in general. There is an excellent commentary on it by Uaṭa, which professes in the introduction to be a remodelling of an earlier commentary by Vishṇuputra.—The *Upalekha* is to be con-

---

authors bear the same name. But in this particular case we are able to bring forward definite reasons against this identification. The glossarist of the Praśnop. was called *Náráyaṇendra* according to *I. St.*, i. 470; according to the note, *ibid.*, i. 439, *Náráyaṇa Sarasvatí*; according to Aufrecht, Catalogue of the Oxford MSS., p. 366 (1859–64), rather *Ráyaṇendrasarasvatí* (!). The glossarist of the Muṇḍakop., on the other hand, was, according to *I. St.*, i. 470, called *Náráyaṇabhaṭṭa*; and he is probably identical with the author of the *dípiká* on the small Atharvopanishads published in the *Bibl. Ind.* in 1872, who (*ibid.*, p. 393) is called *Bhaṭṭa Náráyaṇa*, and son of Bhaṭṭa Ratnákara.]

[61] We are now in possession of two editions of this most important work, text and translation, with elucidatory notes, by Ad. Regnier (Paris, 1857–58), and M. Müller (Leipzig, 1856–69); see *I. Str.*, ii. 94, ff., 127, ff., 159, ff.; *Lit. Centralblatt*, 1870, p. 530.

sidered as an epitome of the Prátiśákhya-Sútra, and to some extent as a supplement to it [specially to chapters x. xi.]. It is a short treatise, numbered among the Pariśishṭas (supplements); and it has in its turn been repeatedly commented upon.[52]

A few other treatises have still to be noticed here, which, although they bear the high-sounding name of *Vedáṅgas*, or 'members of the Veda,' are yet, as above stated (p. 25), only to be looked upon as later supplements to the literature of the Ṛigveda: the *Śikshá*, the *Chhandas*, and the *Jyotisha*. All three exist in a double recension according as they profess to belong to the Ṛigveda or to the Yajurveda. The Chhandas is essentially alike in both recensions, and we have to recognise in it the Sútra on prosody ascribed to Piṅgala.[53] It is, moreover, like both the other treatises, of very recent origin. We have a proof of this, for instance, in the fact that, in the manner peculiar to the Indians, it expresses numbers by words,[54] and feet by letters, and that it treats of the highly elaborated metres, which are only found in modern poetry.[55] The part dealing with Vedic metres may perhaps be more ancient. The teachers quoted in it bear in part comparatively ancient

---

[52] Edited by W. Pertsch (Berlin, 1854); this tract treats of the *krama-páṭha*, an extended form of the *padapáṭha*, which at the same time gives the text in the *saṃhitá* form, namely, each word twice, first joined with the preceding, and then with the following word (thus: *ab, bc, cd, de* . . .). There are also other still more complicated modes of reciting the Veda, as to which cf. Thibaut in his edition of the Jaṭápaṭala (1870), p. 36, ff. The next step, called *jaṭá*, exhibits the text in the following manner: *ab ba ab, bc cb bc*, and MSS. of this kind have actually been preserved, *e.g.*, in the case of the Vájas. Saṃh. The following step, called *ghana*, is said to be still in use; cf. Bhaṇḍarkar, *Indian Antiquary*, iii. 133; Haug, *Ueber das Wesen des vedischen Accents*, p. 58; it runs: *ab ba abc cba abc, bc cb bc bcd dcb bcd.*

[53] Edited and commented by myself in *I. St.*, viii. (1863); the text, together with the commentary of Halâyudha, edited by Viśvanátha-śástrin in *Bibl. Indica* (1871–74).

[54] See Albírúní's account in Woepcke's *Mémoire sur la propagation des chiffres indiens*, p. 102, ff. (1863). Burnell, *Elem. of S. I. Palæogr.*, p. 58.

[55] On the other hand, there are metres taught in this work which but rarely occur in modern literature, and which must be looked upon as obsolete and out of fashion. Therefore, in spite of what has been said above, we must carry back the date of its composition to a period about simultaneous with the close of the Vedic Sútra literature, or the commencement of the astronomical and algebraical literatures; see *I. St.*, viii. 173, 178.

names. These are: Kraushṭuki, Táṇḍin, Yáska, Saitava, Ráta, and Máṇḍavya. The recensions most at variance with each other are those of the Śikshá and Jyotisha respectively. The former work is in both recensions directly traced to Páṇini, the latter to Lagadha, or Lagata, an otherwise unknown name in Indian literature.*—Besides the Páṇiníyá Śikshá, there is another bearing the name of the Máṇḍúkas, which therefore may more directly follow the Ṛik, and which is at any rate a more important work than the former. As a proof of the antiquity of the name 'Śikshá' for phonetic investigations, we may adduce the circumstance that in the Taitt. Áraṇy., vii. 1, we find a section beginning thus: "we will explain the Śikshá;" whereupon it gives the titles of the topics of the oral exposition which we may suppose to have been connected therewith (*I. St.*, ii. 211), and which, to judge by these titles, must have embraced letters, accents, quantity, articulation, and the rules of euphony, that is to say, the same subjects discussed in the two existing Śikshás.[56]

Of the writings called *Anukramaṇí*, in which the metre, the deity, and the author of each song are given in their proper order, several have come down to us for the Ṛik-Saṃhitá, including an *Anuvákánukramaṇí* by Śaunaka, and a *Sarvánukramaṇí* by Kátyáyana.[57] For both of these we have an excellent commentary by Shaḍguru-

* Reinaud in his *Mémoire sur l'Inde*, pp. 331, 332, adduces from Albírúní a Láta, who passed for the author of the old Súrya-Siddhánta; might he not be identical with this Lagadha, Lagata? According to Colebr., *Ess.*, ii. 409, Brahmagupta quotes a Láḍháchárya; this name also could be traced to Lagadha. [By Súryadeva, a scholiast of Áryabhaṭa, the author of the Jyotisha is cited under the name of Lagaḍácharya; see Kern, Preface to the Áryabhaṭíya, p. ix., 1874. An edition of the text of the Jyotisha, together with extracts from Somákara's commentary and explanatory notes, was published by me in 1862 under the title: *Ueber den Vedakalender, Namens Jyotisham.*]

[56] The Páṇiníyá Śikshá has been printed with a translation in *I. St.*, iv. 345–371 (1858); on the numerous other treatises bearing the same name, see Rájendra Lála Mitra, *Notices of Sanskrit MSS.*, i. 71, ff. (1870), Burnell, *Catalogue of Vedic MSS.*, pp. 8, 42 (1870), my essay on the Pratijnásútra (1872), pp. 70–74; specially on the Máṇḍúkí Śikshá, pp. 106–112; Haug, *Ueber das Wesen des vedischen Accents*, p. 53, ff. (1873), on the Nárada-Śikshá, *ibid.*, 57, ff., and lastly Kielhorn, *I. St.*, xiv. 160.

[57] In substance published by Müller in the sixth volume of his large edition of the Ṛik, pp. 621–671.

śishya, whose time is unknown,[58] as also his real name. The names of the six teachers from whom he took this surname are enumerated by himself; they are Vináyaka, Triśúláñka, Govinda, Súrya, Vyása, and Śivayogin, and he connects their names with those of the corresponding deities.—Another work belonging to this place, the Bṛihaddevatá, has been already mentioned (p. 24), as attributed to Śaunaka, and as being of great importance, containing as it does a rich store of mythical fables and legends. From Kuhn's communications on the subject (*I. St.*, i. 101–120), it appears that this work is of tolerably late origin, as it chiefly follows Yáska's Nirukta, and probably therefore only belongs to Śaunaka in the sense of having proceeded from his school. It mentions a few more teachers in addition to those quoted by Yáska, as Bháguri and Áśvaláyana; and it also presupposes, by frequently quoting them, the existence of the Aitareyaka, Bhállavi-Bráhmaṇa, and Nidána-Sútra. As the author strictly adheres to the order of the hymns observed in the Saṃhitá, it results that in the recension of the text used by him there were a few deviations from that of the Śákalas which has been handed down to us. In fact, he here and there makes direct reference to the text of the Váshkalas, to which, consequently, he must also have had access.—Lastly, we have to mention the writings called *Ṛigvidhána*, &c., which, although some of them bear the name of Śaunaka, probably belong only to the time of the Puráṇas. They treat of the mystic and magic efficacy of the recitation of the hymns of the Ṛik, or even of single verses of it, and the like. There are, likewise, a number of other similar Pariśishṭas (supplements) under various names; for instance, a Bahvṛicha-Pariśishṭa, Śáñkháyana-P., Áśvaláyana-Gṛihya-P., &c.

---

[58] His work was composed towards the close of the twelfth century, about 1187 A.D.; cf. *I. St.*, viii. 160, n. (1863).

I now turn to the *Sámaveda.**

The *Samhitá* of the Sámaveda is an anthology taken from the Ṛik-Saṃhitá, comprising those of its verses which were intended to be chanted at the ceremonies of the Soma sacrifice. Its arrangement would seem to be guided by the order of the Ṛik-Saṃhitá; but here, as in the case of the two Saṃhitás of the Yajus, we must not think to find any continuous connection. Properly speaking, each verse is to be considered as standing by itself: it only receives its real sense when taken in connection with the particular ceremony to which it belongs. So stands the case at least in the first part of the Sáma-Saṃhitá. This is divided into six *prapáṭhakas*, each of which † consists of ten *daśats* or decades, of ten verses each, a division which existed as early as the time of the second part of the Śatapatha-Bráhmaṇa, and within which the separate verses are distributed according to the deities to whom they are addressed. The first twelve decades contain invocations of Agni, the last eleven invocations of Soma, while the thirty-six intermediate ones are for the most part addressed to Indra. The second part of the Sáma-Saṃhitá, on the contrary, which is divided into nine *prapáṭhakas*, each of which again is subdivided into two or occasionally three sections, invariably presents several, usually three, verses closely connected with one another, and forming an independent group, the first of them having generally appeared already in the first part. The principle of distribution here is as yet obscure.[59] In the Saṃhitá these verses are still exhibited in their *ṛich*-form, although with the *sáman*-accents; but in addition to this we have four *gánas*, or song-books, in which they appear in their *sáman*-form. For, in singing they were consider-

* See *I. St.*, i. 28–66.

† Except the last, which contains only nine decades.

[59] The first part of the Saṃhitá is referred to under the names *árchika*, *chhandas*, *chhandasiká*, the second as *uttarárchika* or *uttará*; the designation of the latter as *staubhika* (see *I. St.*, i. 29, 30, 66), into the use of which my example has misled Müller also, *History of A. S. L.*, p. 473, n., is wrong, see *Monatsberichte der Berl. Acad.*, 1868, p. 238. According to Durga, the author of the *padapáṭha* of the Sáma-Saṃhitá was a Gárgya; see Roth, Comm., p. 39 (respecting this family, see *I. St.*, xiii. 411).

ably altered by the prolongation and repetition of the syllables, by the insertion of additional syllables, serving as a rest for the chanting, and so forth; and only thus were they transformed into *sámans*. Two of these song-books, the *Grámageya-gána* (erroneously called *Veya-gána*), in seventeen *prapáṭhakas*, and the *Áraṇya-gána*, in six *prapáṭhakas*, follow the order of the *ṛichas* contained in the first part of the Saṃhitá; the former being intended for chanting in the *grámas*, or inhabited places, the latter for chanting in the forest. Their order is fixed in a comparatively very ancient Anukramaṇí, which even bears the name of Bráhmaṇa, viz., *Ṛishi-Bráhmaṇa*. The other two *gánas*, the *Úha-gána*, in twenty-three *prapáṭhakas*, and the *Úhya-gána*, in six *prapáṭhakas*, follow the order of the *ṛichas* contained in the second part of the Saṃhitá. Their mutual relation here still requires closer investigation. Each such *sáman* evolved out of a *ṛich* has a special technical name, which probably in most cases originated from the first inventor of the form in question, is often, however, borrowed from other considerations, and is usually placed in the manuscripts before the text itself. As each *ṛich* can be chanted in a great variety of ways, in each of which it bears a particular name, the number of *sámans*, strictly speaking, is quite unlimited, and is of course far greater than that of the *ṛichas* contained in the Saṃhitá. Of these latter there are 1549,* of which all but seventy-eight have been traced in the Ṛik-Saṃhitá. Most of them are taken from its eighth and ninth *maṇḍalas*.

I have already remarked (p. 9) upon the antiquity of the readings of the Sáma-Saṃhitá as compared with those of the Ṛik-Saṃhitá. It follows from this almost with

* Benfey [*Einleitung*, p. xix.] erroneously states the number as 1472, which I copied from him, *I. St.*, i. 29, 30. The above number is borrowed from a paper by Whitney, which will probably find a place in the *Indische Studien*. The total number of the *ṛichas* contained in the Sáma-Saṃhitá is 1810 (585 in the first, 1225 in the second part), from which, however, 261 are to be deducted as mere repetitions, inasmuch as 249 of those occurring in the first part are repeated in the second, three of them twice, while nine of the *ṛichas* which occur in the second part only, appear twice. [See on this Whitney's detailed table at the end of his *Tabellarische Darstellung der gegenseitigen Verhältnisse der Saṃhitás des Ṛik, Sáman, Weissen Yajus, und Atharvan*, *I. St.*, ii. 321, ff., 363 (1853)].

certainty that the *richas* constituting the former were borrowed from the songs of the latter at a remote period, before their formation into a Ṛik-Saṃhitá had as yet taken place; so that in the interval they suffered a good deal of wearing down in the mouth of the people, which was avoided in the case of the *richas* applied as *sámans*, and so protected by being used in worship. The fact has also already been stated that no verses have been received into the Sáma-Saṃhitá from those songs of the Ṛik-Saṃhitá which must be considered as the most modern. Thus we find no *sámans* borrowed from the Purusha-Súkta, in the ordinary recensions at least, for the school of the Naigeyas has, in fact, incorporated the first five verses of it into the seventh *prapáṭhaka* of the first part—a section which is peculiar to this school. The Sáma-Saṃhitá, being a purely derivative production, gives us no clue towards the determination of its date. It has come down to us in two recensions, on the whole differing but little from each other, one of which belongs to the school of the Ráṇáyaníyas, the other to that of the Kauthumas. Of this latter the school of the Negas, or Naigeyas, alluded to above, is a subdivision, of which two Anukramaṇís at least, one of the deities and one of the Ṛishis of the several verses, have been preserved to us.[60] Not one of these three names has as yet been traced in Vedic literature; it is only in the Sútras of the Sámaveda itself that the first and second at least are mentioned, but even here the name of the Negas does not appear.—The text of the Ráṇáyaníyas was edited and translated, with strict reference to Sáyaṇa's commentary, by the missionary Stevenson in 1842; since 1848 we have been in possession of another edition, furnished with a complete glossary and much

[60] The seventh *prapáṭhaka*, which is peculiar to it, has since been discovered. It bears the title Áraṇyaka-Saṃhitá, and has been edited by Siegfried Goldschmidt in *Monatsberichte der Berl. Acad.* 1868, pp. 228–248. The editor points out that the Áraṇya-gána is based upon the *árchika* of the Naigeya text (*l. c.*, p. 238), and that MSS. have probably been preserved of its *uttarárchika* also (p. 241).—A London MS. of Bharatasvámin's Sámavedavivaraṇa specially refers to the Áraṇyaka-Saṃhitá, see Burnell, *Catalogue of Vedic MSS.* (1870), p. 39.—Of the Áraṇyaka-gána as well as of the Grámageya-gána we find, *ibid.*, p. 49, a text in the Jaimini-Śákhá also. According to Rájendra Lála Mitra (Preface to Translation of Chhánd. Up., p. 4), 'the Kauthuma (-Śákhá) is current in Guzerat, the Jaiminíya in Karṇáṭaka, and the Ráṇáyaníya in Maháráshṭra.'

additional material, together with translation, which we owe to Professor Benfey, of Göttingen.[61]

Although, from its very nature, the Saṃhitá of the Sámaveda is poor in data throwing light upon the time of its origin, yet its remaining literature contains an abundance of these; and first of all, the *Bráhmaṇas*.

The first and most important of these is the *Táṇḍya Bráhmaṇa*, also called *Pañchaviṅśa*, from its containing twenty-five books. Its contents, it is true, are in the main of a very dry and unprofitable character; for in mystic trifling it often exceeds all bounds, as indeed it was the adherents of the Sámaveda generally who carried matters furthest in this direction. Nevertheless, from its great extent, this work contains a mass of highly interesting legends, as well as of information generally. It refers solely to the celebration of the Soma sacrifices, and to the chanting of the *sámans* accompanying it, which are quoted by their technical names. These sacrifices were celebrated in a great variety of ways; there is one special classification of them according as they extended over one day or several, or finally over more than twelve days.[62] The latter, called *sattras*, or sessions, could only be performed by Brahmans, and that in considerable numbers, and might last 100 days, or even several years. In consequence of the great variety of ceremonies thus involved, each bears its own name, which is borrowed either from the object of its celebration, or the sage who was the first to celebrate it, or from other considerations. How far the order of the Saṃhitá is here observed has not yet been investigated,

---

[61] Recently a new edition, likewise very meritorious, of the first two books, the *ágneyam* and the *aindram parva*, of the *árchika* (up to i. 5. 2. 3. 10), has been published by Satyavrata Sámaśramin, in the *Bibliotheca Indica* (1871–74), accompanied by the corresponding portions (*prapáṭhakas* 1–12) of the Geyagána, and the complete commentary of Sáyaṇa, and other illustrative matter.—The division of the *sámans* into *parvans* is first mentioned by Páraskara, ii. 10 (*adhyáyádín prabrúyád, ṛishimukháni bahvṛichánám, parváṇi chhandogánám*). A Rávaṇabháshya on the Sámaveda is said to be still in existence in Malabar; see Rost, *I. St.*, ix. 176.

[62] To each Soma sacrifice belong several (four at least) preparatory days; these are not here taken into account. The above division refers only to those days when Soma juice is expressed, that is, to the *sutyá* days. Soma sacrifices having only one such day are called *ekáha*; those with from two to twelve, *ahína*. *Sattras* lasting a whole year, or even longer, are called *ayana*. For the *sutyá* festival there are seven fundamental forms, called *saṃsthá*; *I. St.*, x. 352–355.

but in any case it would be a mistake to suppose that for all the different sacrifices enumerated in the Bráhmaṇa corresponding prayers exist in the Saṃhitá. On the contrary, the latter probably only exhibits the verses to be chanted generally at all the Soma sacrifices; and the Bráhmaṇa must be regarded as the supplement in which the modifications for the separate sacrifices are given, and also for those which arose later. While, as we saw above (p. 14), a combination of verses of the Ṛik for the purpose of recitation bears the name *śastra*, a similar selection of different *sámans* united into a whole is usually called *uktha* (√*vach*, to speak), *stoma* (√*stu*, to praise), or *pṛishṭha* (√*prachh*, to ask); and these in their turn, like the *śastras*, receive different appellations.[63]

Of special significance for the time of the composition of the Táṇḍya Bráhmaṇa are, on the one hand, the very minute descriptions of the sacrifices on the Sarasvatí and Dṛishadvatí; and, on the other, the Vrátyastomas, or sacrifices by which Indians of Aryan origin, but not living according to the Brahmanical system, obtained admission to the Brahman community. The accounts of these latter sacrifices are preceded by a description of the dress and mode of life of those who are to offer them. "They drive in open chariots of war, carry bows and lances, wear turbans, robes bordered with red and having fluttering ends, shoes, and sheepskins folded double; their leaders are distinguished by brown robes and silver neck-ornaments; they pursue neither agriculture nor commerce; their laws are in a constant state of confusion; they speak the same language as those who have received Brahmanical consecration, but nevertheless call what is easily spoken hard to pronounce." This last statement probably refers to

[63] The term directly opposed to *śastra* is, rather, *stotra*. *Pṛishṭha* specially designates several *stotras* belonging to the mid-day sacrifice, and forming, as it is expressed, its "back;" *uktha* is originally employed as a synonym of *śastra*, and only at a later period in the meaning of *sáman* (*I. St.*, xiii. 447); *stoma*, lastly, is the name for the six, seven, or more ground-forms of the *stotras*, after which these latter are formed for the purposes of chanting. The simple recitation of the *śastras* by the Hotar and his companions always comes after the chanting recitation of the same verses by the Udgátar and his assistants (*graháya gṛihítáya stuvate 'tha śaṅsati*, Śat. viii. 1. 3. 3). The differences of the seven *saṃsthás*, or fundamental types of the Soma sacrifice, rest mainly upon the varying number of the *śastras* and *stotras* belonging to their *sutyá* days. See *I. St.*, x. 353, ff., ix. 229.

prákritic, dialectic differences, to the assimilation of groups of consonants, and similar changes peculiar to the Prákrit vernaculars. The great sacrifice of the Naimishíya-Rishis is also mentioned, and the river Sudáman. Although we have to conclude from these statements that communication with the west, particularly with the non-Brahmanic Aryans there, was still very active, and that therefore the locality of the composition must be laid more towards the west,[64] still data are not wanting which point us to the east. Thus, there is mention of Para Áṭṇára, king of the Kosalas; of Trasadasyu Purukutsa, who is also named in the Rik-Saṃhitá; further of Namin Sápya, king of the Videhas (the Nimi of the epic); of Kurukshetra, Yamuná, &c. The absence, however, of any allusion in the Táṇḍya-Bráhmaṇa either to the Kuru-Pañchálas or to the names of their princes, as well as of any mention of Janaka, is best accounted for by supposing a difference of locality. Another possible, though less likely, explanation of the fact would be to assume that this work was contemporary with, or even anterior to, the flourishing epoch of the kingdom of the Kuru-Pañchálas. The other names quoted therein seem also to belong to an earlier age than those of the other Bráhmaṇas, and to be associated, rather, with the Rishi period. It is, moreover, a very significant fact that scarcely any differences of opinion are stated to exist amongst the various teachers. It is only against the Kaushítakis that the field is taken with some acrimony; they are denoted as *vrátyas* (apostates) and as *yajnávakírṇa* (unfit to sacrifice). Lastly, the name attached to this Bráhmaṇa,* viz., Táṇḍya, is mentioned in the Bráhmaṇa of the White Yajus as that of a teacher; so that, combining all this, we may at least safely infer its priority to the latter work.[65]

---

[64] The fact that the name of Chitraratha (*etena vai Chitraratham Kápeyá ayájayan . . . tasmách Chaitrarathínám ekaḥ kshatrapatir jáyate 'nulamba iva dvitíyaḥ*, xx. 12, 5) occurs in the *gaṇa* '*Rájadanta*' to Páṇ., ii. 2. 31, joined with the name Báhlika in a compound (*Chitraratha-Báhlíkam*), is perhaps also to be taken in this connection.

* The first use of this designation, it is true, only occurs in Láṭyáyana, the other Sútras invariably quoting it by '*iti śruteḥ*.'

[65] The Táṇḍya-Bráhmaṇa has been edited, together with Sáyaṇa's commentary, in the *Bibl. Ind.* (1869–74), by Ánandachandra Vedántavágíśa. At the time of the Bháshika-Sútra (see Kielhorn, *I. St.*, x. 421) it must still have been accentuated, and that in the same manner as the Śatapatha; in Kumárilabhaṭṭa's time, on the contrary (the last half of the

The *Shaḍviṅśa-Bráhmaṇa* by its very name proclaims itself a supplement to the Pañchaviṅśa-Bráhmaṇa. It forms, as it were, its twenty-sixth book, although itself consisting of several books. Sáyaṇa, when giving a summary of its contents at the commencement of his here excellent commentary, says that it both treats of such ceremonies as are not contained in the Pañchaviṅśa-Bráhmaṇa, and also gives points of divergence from the latter. It is chiefly expiatory sacrifices and ceremonies of imprecation that we find in it, as also short, comprehensive general rules. The fifth book (or sixth *adhyáya*) has quite a peculiar character of its own, and is also found as a separate Bráhmaṇa under the name of *Adbhuta-Bráhmaṇa;* in the latter form, however, with some additions at the end. It enumerates untoward occurrences of daily life, omens and portents, along with the rites to be performed to avert their evil consequences. These afford us a deep insight into the condition of civilisation of the period, which, as might have been expected, exhibits a very advanced phase. The ceremonies first given are those to be observed on the occurrence of vexatious events generally; then come those for cases of sickness among men and cattle, of damaged crops, losses of precious things, &c.; those to be performed in the event of earthquakes, of phenomena in the air and in the heavens, &c., of marvellous appearances on altars and on the images of the gods, of electric phenomena and the like, and of miscarriages.[66] This sort of superstition is elsewhere only treated of in the Gṛihya-Sútras, or in the Pariśishṭas (supplements); and this imparts to the last *adhyáya* of the Shaḍviṅśa-Bráhmaṇa—as the remaining contents do to the work generally—the appearance of belonging to a very modern period. And, in accordance with this, we find mention here made of Uddálaka Áruṇi, and other teachers, whose names are altogether unknown to the Pañchaviṅśa-Bráhmaṇa.—A *śloka* is cited in the course of

---

seventh century, according to Burnell), it was already being handed down without accents, as in the present day. See Müller, *A. S. L.*, p. 348; Burnell, Sámavidhána-Bráhmaṇa, Preface, p. vi.

[66] The Adbhuta-Bráhmaṇa has been published by myself, text with translation, and explanatory notes, in *Zwei vedische Texte über Omina und Portenta* (1859).

the work, in which the four *yugas* are still designated by their more ancient names, and are connected with the four lunar phases, to which they evidently owe their origin, although all recollection of the fact had in later times died out.[67] This *śloka* itself we are perhaps justified in assigning to an earlier time than that of Megasthenes, who informs us of a fabulous division of the mundane ages analogous to that given in the epic. But it does not by any means follow that the Shaḍviṅśa-Bráhmaṇa, in which the *śloka* is quoted, itself dates earlier than the time of Megasthenes.

The third Bráhmaṇa of the Sámaveda bears the special title of *Chhándogya-Bráhmaṇa*, although Chhándogya is the common name for all Sáman theologians. We, however, also find it quoted, by Śaṁkara, in his commentary on the Brahma-Sútra, as "*Táṇḍinám śruti*," that is to say, under the same name that is given to the Pañchaviṅśa-Bráhmaṇa. The two first *adhyáyas* of this Bráhmaṇa are still missing, and the last eight only are preserved, which also bear the special title of *Chhándogyopanishad*. This Bráhmaṇa is particularly distinguished by its rich store of legends regarding the gradual development of Brahmanical theology, and stands on much the same level as the Vṛihad-Áraṇyaka of the White Yajus with respect to opinions, as well as date, place, and the individuals mentioned. The absence in the Vṛihad-Áraṇyaka, as in the Bráhmaṇa of the White Yajus generally, of any reference to the Naimiṣíya-Ṛishis, might lead us to argue the priority of the Chhándogyopanishad to the Vṛihad-Áraṇyaka. Still, the mention in the Chhándogyopanishad of these, as well as of the Maháveṛishas and the Gandháras—the latter, it is true, are set down as distant—ought perhaps only to be taken as proof of a somewhat more western origin; whereas the Vṛihad-Áraṇyaka belongs, as we shall hereafter see, to quite the eastern part of Hindustán. The numerous animal fables, on the contrary, and the mention of Mahidása Aitareya, would sooner incline me to suppose that the Chhándogyopanishad is more modern than the Vṛihad-Áraṇyaka. With regard to another allusion, in

---

[67] Differently Roth in his essay *Die Lehre von den vier Weltaltern* (Tübingen, 1860).

itself of the greatest significance, it is more hazardous to venture a conjecture: I mean the mention of Kṛishṇa Devakíputra, who is instructed by Ghora Áñgirasa. The latter, and besides him (though not in connection with him) Kṛishṇa Áñgirasa, are also mentioned in the Kaushítaki-Bráhmaṇa; and supposing this Kṛishṇa Áñgirasa to be identical with Kṛishṇa Devakíputra, the allusion to him might perhaps rather be considered as a sign of priority to the Vṛihad-Áraṇyaka. Still, assuming this identification to be correct, due weight must be given to the fact that the name has been altered here: instead of Áñgirasa, he is called Devakíputra, a form of name for which we find no analogy in any other Vedic writing excepting the Vaṅśas (genealogical tables) of the Vṛihad-Áraṇyaka, and which therefore belongs, at all events, to a tolerably late period.* The significance of this allusion for the understanding of the position of Kṛishṇa at a later period is obvious. Here he is yet but a scholar, eager in the pursuit of knowledge, belonging perhaps to the military caste. He certainly must have distinguished himself in some way or other, however little we know of it, otherwise his elevation to the rank of deity, brought about by external circumstances, would be inexplicable.[68]

The fact of the Chhándogyopanishad and the Vṛihad-Áraṇyaka having in common the names Praváhaṇa Jaivali, Ushasti Chákráyaṇa, Śáṇḍilya, Satyakáma Jábála, Uddálaka Áruṇi, Śvetaketu, and Aśvapati, makes it clear that they were as nearly as possible contemporary works; and this appears also from the generally complete identity of the seventh book of the former with the corresponding passages of the Vṛihad-Áraṇyaka. What, however, is of most significance, as tending to establish a late date for

* Compare also Páṇ., iv. 1. 159, and the names Śaṃbúputra, Ráṇáyaníputra, in the Sáma-Sútras; as also Kátyáyaníputra, Maitráyaṇíputra, Vátsíputra, &c., among the Buddhists. [On these metronymic names in *putra* see *I. St.*, iii. 157, 485, 486; iv. 380, 435; v. 63, 64.]

[68] By what circumstances the elevation of Kṛishṇa to the rank of deity was brought about is as yet obscure; though unquestionably mythical relations to Indra, &c., are at the root of it; see *I. St.*, xiii. 349, ff. The whole question, however, is altogether vague. Kṛishṇa-worship proper, *i.e.*, the sectarian worship of Kṛishṇa as the one God, probably attained its perfection through the influence of Christianity. See my paper, *Kṛishṇa's Geburtsfest*, p. 316, ff. (where also are further particulars as to the name Devakí).

the Chhándogyopanishad, is the voluminous literature, the existence of which is presupposed by the enumeration at the beginning of the ninth book. Even supposing this ninth book to be a sort of supplement (the names of Sanatkumára and Skanda are not found elsewhere in Vedic literature; Nárada also is otherwise only mentioned in the second part of the Aitareya-Bráhmaṇa[69]), there still remains the mention of the 'Atharváñgirasas,' as well as of the Itihásas and Puráṇas in the fifth book. Though we are not at liberty here, any more than in the corresponding passages of the Vṛihad-Áraṇyaka, to understand by these last the Itihásas and Puráṇas which have actually come down to us, still we must look upon them as the forerunners of these works, which, originating in the legends and traditions connected with the songs of the Ṛik, and with the forms of worship, gradually extended their range, and embraced other subjects also, whether drawn from real life, or of a mythical and legendary character. Originally they found a place in the Bráhmaṇas, as well as in the other expository literature of the Vedas; but at the time of this passage of the Chhándogyopanishad they had possibly already in part attained an independent form, although the commentaries,* as a rule, only refer such expressions to passages in the Bráhmaṇas themselves. The Mahá-Bhárata contains, especially in the first book, a few such Itihásas, still in a prose form; nevertheless, even these fragments so preserved to us belong, in respect both of style and of the conceptions they embody, to a much later period than the similar passages of the Bráhmaṇas. They however suffice, together with the *ślokas*, *gáthás*, &c., quoted in the Bráhmaṇas themselves, and with such works as the Bárhaddaivata, to bridge over for us the period of transition from legend to epic poetry.

We meet, moreover, in the Chhándogyopanishad with one of those legal cases which are so seldom mentioned in Vedic literature, viz., the infliction of capital punishment for (denied) theft, exactly corresponding to the severe

---

[69] And a few times in the Atharva-Saṃhitá, as also in the Vaṅśa of the Sámavidhána-Bráhmaṇa.

* Not Śaṃkara, it is true, in this case, but Sáyaṇa, Harisvámin, and Dvivedagañga in similar passages of the Śatapatha-Bráhmaṇa and Taittiríya-Áraṇyaka.

enactments regarding it in Manu's code. Guilt or innocence is determined by an ordeal, the carrying of a red-hot axe; this also is analogous to the decrees in Manu. We find yet another connecting link with the state of culture in Manu's time in a passage occurring also in the Vṛihad-Áraṇyaka, viz., the doctrine of the transmigration of souls. We here meet with this doctrine for the first time, and that in a tolerably complete form; in itself, however, it must certainly be regarded as much more ancient. The circumstance that the myth of the creation in the fifth book is on the whole identical with that found at the beginning of Manu, is perhaps to be explained by regarding the latter as simply a direct imitation of the former. The tenth book, the subject of which is the soul, its seat in the body and its condition on leaving it, *i.e.*, its migration to the realm of Brahman, contains much that is of interest in this respect in connection with the above-mentioned parallel passage of the Kaushítaky-Upanishad, from which it differs in some particulars. Here also for the first time in the field of Vedic literature occurs the name Ráhu, which we may reckon among the proofs of the comparatively recent date of the Chhándogyopanishad.

Of expressions for philosophical doctrines we find only *Upanishad*, *Ádeśa*, *Guhya Ádeśa* (the keeping secret of doctrine is repeatedly and urgently inculcated), *Upákhyána* (explanation). The teacher is called *áchárya* [as he is also in the Śat. Br.]; for "inhabited place," *ardha* is used; single *ślokas* and *gáthás* are very often quoted.

The Chhándogyopanishad has been edited by Dr. Roer in the *Bibliotheca Indica*, vol. iii., along with Śaṃkara's commentary and a gloss on it.[70] Fr. Windischmann had previously given us several passages of it in the original, and several in translation; see also *I. St.*, i. 254–273.

The *Kenopanishad* has come down to us as the remnant of a fourth Bráhmaṇa of the Sámaveda, supposed to be its ninth book.* In the colophons and in the quotations found in the commentaries, it also bears the other-

[70] In this series (1854–62) a translation also has been published by Rájendra Lála Mitra.

* Regarding the contents of the first eight books, Śaṃkara furnishes us with information in the beginning of his commentary.

wise unknown name of the *Talavakáras.** It is divided into two parts: the first, composed in *ślokas*, treats of the being of the supreme Brahman, appealing in the fourth verse to the tradition of the "earlier sages who have taught us this" as its authority. The second part contains a legend in support of the supremacy of Brahman, and here we find Umá Haimavatí, later the spouse of Śiva, acting as mediatrix between Brahman and the other gods; probably because she is imagined to be identical with Sarasvatí, or Vách, the goddess of speech, of the creative word.†

These are the extant Bráhmaṇas of the Sámaveda. Sáyaṇa, indeed, in his commentary on the Sámavidhána enumerates eight (see Müller, Ṛik i. Pref. p. xxvii): the *Prauḍha-* or *Mahá-Bráhmaṇa* (*i.e.*, the *Pañchaviṅśa*), the *Shaḍviṅśa*, the *Sámavidhi*, the *Ársheya*, the *Devatádhyáya*, the *Upanishad*, the *Saṃhitopanishad*, and the *Vanśa*. The claims, however, of four of these works to the name of Bráhmaṇa, have no solid foundation. The Ársheya is, as already stated, merely an Anukramaṇí, and the Devatádhyáya can hardly be said to be anything else; the Vañśa elsewhere always constitutes a part of the Bráhmaṇas themselves: the two latter works, moreover, can scarcely be supposed to be still in existence, which, as far as the Vañśa is concerned, is certainly very much to be regretted. The Sámavidhána also, which probably treats, like the portion of the Láṭyáyana-Sútra bearing the same name, of the conversion of the *ṛichas* into *sámans*, can hardly pass for a Bráhmaṇa.[71] As to the Saṃhitopanishad, it appears

* Might not this name be traceable to the same root *táḍ*, *taṇḍ*, from which Táṇḍya is derived?

† On the literature, &c., of the Kenopanishad, see *I. St.*, ii. 181, ff. [We have to add Roer's edition with Saṃkara's commentary, in *Bibliotheca Indica*, vol. viii., and his translation, *ibid.*, vol. xv.]

[71] The above statements require to be corrected and supplemented in several particulars. The Vañśa-Bráhmaṇa was first edited by myself in *I. St.*, iv. 371, ff., afterwards by Burnell with Sáyaṇa's commentary (1873). The Devatádhyáya is not an Anukramaṇí, but only contains some information as to the deities of the different *sámans*, to which a few other short fragments are added. Finally, the Sámavidhána-Bráhmaṇa does not treat of the conversion of *ṛichas* into *sámans*; on the contrary, it is a work similar to the Ṛigvidhána, and relates to the employment of the *sámans* for all sorts of superstitious purposes. Both texts have likewise been edited by Burnell, with Sáyaṇa's commentaries (1873). By Kumárila, too, the number of the Bráhmaṇas of the Sámaveda is given as eight (Müller,

to me doubtful whether Sáyaṇa meant by it the Kenopanishad; for though the *saṃhitá* (universality) of the Supreme Being certainly is discussed in the latter, the subject is not handled under this name, as would seem to be demanded by the analogy of the title of the Saṃhitopanishad of the Aitareya-Áraṇyaka as well as of the Taittiríya-Áraṇyaka. My conjecture would be that he is far more likely to have intended a work[72] of the same title, of which there is a MS. in the British Museum (see *I. St.*, i. 42); and if so, all mention of the Kenopanishad has been omitted by him; possibly for the reason that it appears at the same time in an Atharvan-recension (differing but little, it is true), and may have been regarded by him as belonging to the Atharvan?

There is a far greater number of *Sútras* to the Sáma-veda than to any of the other Vedas. We have here three Śrauta-Sútras; a Sútra which forms a running commentary upon the Pañchaviṅśa-Bráhmaṇa; five Sútras on Metres and on the conversion of *ṛichas* into *sámans;* and a Gṛihya-Sútra. To these must further be added other similar works of which the titles only are known to us, as well as a great mass of different Pariśishṭas.

Of the *Śrauta-Sútras*, or Sútras treating of the sacrificial ritual, the first is that of *Maśaka*, which is cited in the other Sáma-Sútras, and even by the teachers mentioned in these, sometimes as *Ársheya-Kalpa*, sometimes as *Kalpa*, and once also by Láṭyáyana directly under the name of Maśaka.[73] In the colophons it bears the name of *Kalpa-Sútra*. This Sútra is but a tabular enumeration of the prayers belonging to the several ceremonies of the Soma sacrifice; and these are quoted partly by their technical Sáman names, partly by their opening words. The

A. S. L., p. 348); in his time all of them were already without accents. One fact deserves to be specially noticed here, namely, that several of the teachers mentioned in the Vaṅśa-Bráhmaṇa, by their very names, point us directly to the north-west of India, *e.g.*, Kámboja Aupamanyava, Madragára Śauṅgáyani, Sáti Aushṭrákshi, Sálaṃkáyana, and Kauhala; see *I. St.*, iv. 378–380.

[72] This is unquestionably correct, since this text appears there, as well as elsewhere, in connection with the Vaṅśa-Bráhmaṇa, &c. It is not much larger than the Devatádhyáya, but has not yet been published; see *I. St.*, iv. 375.

[73] Láṭyáyana designates Maśaka as Gárgya. Is this name connected with the Μάσσαγα of the Greeks? Lassen, *I. AK.*, i. 130; *I. St.*, iv 78.

order is exactly that of the Pañchaviṅśa-Bráhmaṇa; yet a few other ceremonies are inserted, including those added in the Shaḍviṅśa-Bráhmaṇa, as well as others. Among the latter the *Janakasaptarátra* deserves special notice, —a ceremony owing its origin to King Janaka,[74] of whom, as we saw above, no mention is yet made in the Pañchaviṅśa-Bráhmaṇa. His life and notoriety therefore evidently fall in the interval between the latter work and the Sútra of Maśaka.—The eleven *prapáṭhakas* of this Sútra are so distributed that the *ekáhas* (sacrifices of one day) are dealt with in the first five chapters; the *ahínas* (those lasting several days) in the following four; and the *sattras* (sacrifices lasting more than twelve days) in the last two. There is a commentary on it, composed by Varadarája, whom we shall meet with again as the commentator of another Sáma-Sútra.

The second Śrauta-Sútra is that of *Láṭyáyana*, which belongs to the school of the Kauthumas. This name appears to me to point to Láṭa, the *Λαρική* of Ptolemy,[75] to a country therefore lying quite in the west, directly south of Suráshṭra (*Συραστρηνή*). This would agree perfectly with the conjecture above stated, that the Pañchaviṅśa-Bráhmaṇa belongs more to the west of India; and is borne out by the data contained in the body of the Sútra itself, as we shall see presently.

This Sútra, like that of Maśaka, connects itself closely with the Pañchaviṅśa-Bráhmaṇa, and indeed often quotes passages of some length from it, generally introducing them by "*tad uktam bráhmaṇena*;" or, "*iti bráhmaṇam bhavati*;" once also by "*tathá purâṇam Táṇḍam.*" It usually gives at the same time the different interpretations which these passages received from various teachers. Śáṇḍilya, Dhánaṃjayya, and Śáṇḍilyáyana are most frequently mentioned in this manner, often together, or one after the other, as expounders of the Pañchaviṅśa-Bráhmaṇa. The first-named is already known to us through the Chhándogyopanishad, and he, as well as Śáṇḍilyáyana, is repeatedly

[74] Sáyaṇa, it is true, to Pañch. xxii. 9. 1, takes *janaka* as an appellative in the sense of *prajápati*, which is the reading of the Pañchaviṅśa-Bráhmaṇa.

[75] Láṭika as early as the edicts of Piyadasi; see Lassen, *I. AK.*, i. 108; ii. 793 n.

mentioned also in another Sútra, the Nidána-Sútra; the same is the case with Dhánaṃjayya. Besides these, however, Láṭyáyana mentions a number of other teachers and schools, as, for example, his own *áchâryas*, with especial frequency; the Ársheya-Kalpa, two different Gautamas, one being distinguished by the surname Sthavira (a technical title, especially with the Buddhists); further Śauchivṛikshi (a teacher known to Páṇini), Kshairakalambhi, Kautsa, Várshagaṇya, Bháṇḍitáyana, Lámakáyana, Ráṇáyaníputra, &c.; and in particular, the Śáṭyáyanins, and their work, the Sáṭyáyanaka, together with the Śálaṅkáyanins, the latter of whom are well known to belong to the western part of India. Such allusions occur in the Sútra of Láṭyáyana, as in the other Sútras of the Sámaveda, much more frequently than in the Sútras of the other Vedas, and are in my opinion evidence of their priority to the latter. At the time of the former there still existed manifold differences of opinion, while in that of the latter a greater unity and fixedness of exegesis, of dogma, and of worship had been attained. The remaining data appear also to point to such a priority, unless we have to explain them merely from the difference of locality. The condition of the Śúdras, as well as of the Nishádas, *i.e.*, the Indian aborigines, does not here appear to be one of such oppression and wretchedness as it afterwards became. It was permitted to sojourn with them (Śáṇḍilya, it is true, restricts this permission to "in the neighbourhood of their *grámas*"), and they themselves were allowed to attend in person at the ceremonies, although outside of the sacrificial ground. They are, moreover, now and then represented, though for the most part in a mean capacity, as taking an actual part on such occasions, which is not to be thought of in later times. Toleration was still a matter of necessity, for, as we likewise see, the strict Brahmanical principle was not yet recognised even among the neighbouring Aryan tribes. These, equally with the Brahmanical Indians, held in high esteem the songs and customs of their ancestors, and devoted to them quite as much study as the Brahmanical Indians did; nay, the latter now and then directly resorted to the former, and borrowed distinct ceremonies from them. This is sufficiently clear from the particulars of one ceremony of the kind, which is embodied, not indeed in the Pañchaviṅśa-Bráhmaṇa, but in the Shaḍviṅśa-Bráhmaṇa, and which is described at full length by Láṭyáyana. It is an imprecatory ceremony (called *śyena*, falcon); and this naturally suggests the idea that the ceremonial of the Atharvan, which is essentially based upon imprecations and magical expedients,—as well as the songs of the Atharvan itself,—may perhaps chiefly owe its cultivation to these western, non-Brahmanical, Aryan tribes. The general name given to these tribes by Láṭyáyana (and with this Páṇini v. 2. 21 agrees) is Vrátínas, and he further draws a distinction between their *yaudhas*, warriors, and their *arhants*, teachers. Their *anúchánas, i.e.*, those versed in Scripture, are to be chosen priests for the above-mentioned sacrifice. Śáṇḍilya limits this to the *arhants* alone, which latter word—subsequently, as is well known, employed exclusively as a Buddhistic title—is also used in the Bráhmaṇa of the White Yajus, and in the Áraṇyaka of the Black Yajus, to express a teacher in general. The turban and garments of these priests should be red (*lohita*) according to Shaḍviṅśa and Láṭyáyana; and we find the same colour assigned to the sacrificial robes of the priests of the Rákshasas in Lañká, in the Rámáyaṇa, vi. 19. 110, 51. 21; with which may be compared the light red, yellowish red (*kasháya*) garments of the Buddhists (see for instance Mṛichhakaṭ., pp. 112, 114, ed. Stenzler; M.-Bhár., xii. 566, 11898; Yájnav., i. 272), and the red (*rakta*) dress of the Sáṃkhyabhikshu * in the Laghujátaka of Varáha-Mihira. Now, that these western non-Brahmanical Vrátyas, Vrátínas, were put precisely upon a par with the eastern non-Brahmanical, *i.e.*, Buddhistic, teachers, appears from an addition which is given by Láṭyáyana to the description of the Vrátyastomas as found in the Pañchaviṅśa-Bráhmaṇa. We are there told that the converted Vrátyas, *i.e.*, those who have entered into the Brahman community, must, in order to cut off all connection with their past, hand over their wealth to those of their companions who still abide by the old mode of life—thereby transferring to these their own former impurity—or else, to a "Brahma-

* According to the commentary; or should this be *Sákyabhikshu*? See *I. St.*, ii. 287.

bandhu Mágadhadeśíya." This latter expression is only explicable if we assume that Buddhism, with its anti-Brahmanical tendencies, was at the time flourishing in Magadha; and the absence of any such allusion in the Pañchavinśa-Bráhmaṇa is significant as to the time which elapsed between this work and the Sútra of Láṭyáyana.*

The first seven *prapáṭhakas* of the Láṭyáyana-Sútra comprise the rules common to all Soma sacrifices; the eighth and part of the ninth book treat, on the contrary, of the separate *ekáhas;* the remainder of the ninth book, of the *ahínas;* and the tenth, of the *sattras.* We have an excellent commentary on it by Agnisvámin,[76] who belongs probably to the same period as the other commentators whose names terminate in *svámin*, as Bhavasvámin, Bharatasvámin, Dhúrtasvámin, Harisvámin, Khadirasvámin, Meghasvámin, Skandasvámin, Kshírasvámin, &c.; their time, however, is as yet undetermined.[77]

The third Sáma-Sútra, that of *Dráhyáyaṇa*, differs but slightly from the Láṭyáyana-Sútra. It belongs to the school of the Ráṇáyaníyas. We meet with the name of these latter in the Ráṇáyaníputra of Láṭyáyana; his family is descended from Vasishṭha, for which reason this Sutra is also directly called *Vásishṭha-Sútra.* For the name Dráhyáyaṇa nothing analogous can be adduced.[78] The difference between this Sútra and that of Láṭyáyana

---

* In the Ṛik-Saṃhitá, where the Kikaṭas—the ancient name of the people of Magadha—and their king Pramagaṃda are mentioned as hostile, we have probably to think of the aborigines of the country, and not of hostile Áryas (?). It seems not impossible that the native inhabitants, being particularly vigorous, retained more influence in Magadha than elsewhere, even after the country had been brahmanised,—a process which perhaps was never completely effected;—that they joined the community of the Brahmans as Kshatriyas, as happened elsewhere also; and that this is how we have to account for the special sympathy and success which Buddhism met with in Magadha, these native inhabitants regarding it as a means of recovering their old position though under a new form.

76 We now possess in the *Bibl. Indica* (1870–72) an edition of the Láṭyáyana-Sútra, with Agnisvámin's commentary, by Ánandachandra Vedántavágíśa.

77 We find quite a cluster of Brahman names in *-svámin* in an inscription dated Śáka 627 in *Journal Bombay Branch R. A. S.*, iii. 208 (1851), and in an undated inscription in *Journal Am. Or. Soc.*, vi. 589.

78 It first occurs in the Vanśa-Bráhmaṇa, whose first list of teachers probably refers to this very school; see *I. St.*, iv. 378: *draha* is said to be a Prákṛit corruption of *hrada*; see Hem. Prákr., ii. 80, 120.

is mainly confined to the different distribution of the matter, which is on the whole identical, and even expressed in the same words. I have not yet met with a complete codex of the whole work, but only with its beginning and its end, in two different commentaries, the date of which it is not yet possible to determine—the beginning, namely, in Maghasvámin's commentary, remodelled by Rudraskanda; the end in the excellent commentary of Dhanvin.

The only knowledge I have of a Śrauta-Sútra by Gobhila is derived from a notice of Roth's (*op. c.*, pp. 55, 56), according to which Kṛityachintámaṇi is said to have composed a commentary upon it.[79]

In a far more important degree than he differs from Dráhyáyaṇa does Láṭyáyana differ, on the one hand, from Kátyáyana, who in his Śrauta-Sútra, belonging to the White Yajus, treats in books 22–24 of the *ekáhas, ahínas,* and *sattras;* and on the other, from the Ṛik-Sútras of Áśvaláyana and Śáṅkháyana, which likewise deal with these subjects in their proper place. In these there is no longer any question of differences of opinion; the stricter view represented by Śáṇḍilya in the Láṭyáyana-Sútra has everywhere triumphed. The ceremonies on the Sarasvatí and the Vrátyastomas have also become, in a local sense too, further removed from actual life, as appears both from the slight consideration with which they are treated, and from modifications of names, &c., which show a forgetting of the original form. Many of the ceremonies discussed in the Sáma-Sútras are, moreover, entirely wanting in the Sútras of the other Vedas; and those which are found in the latter are enumerated in tabular fashion rather than fully discussed—a difference which naturally originated in the diversity of purpose, the subject of the Sútra of the Yajus being the duties of the Adhvaryu, and that of the Sútras of the Ṛik the duties of the Hotar.

A fourth Sáma-Sútra is the *Anupada-Sútra,* in ten *prapáṭhakas,* the work of an unknown author. It explains

---

[79] The name 'Kṛityachintámaṇi' probably belongs to the work itself; compare *I. St.*, i. 60, ii. 396; Aufrecht, *Catalogus*, p. 365ᵃ; but whether it really was a commentary on a Śrauta-Sútra of Gobhila remains doubtful in the meantime, since such a work is not mentioned elsewhere.

the obscure passages of the Pañchavinśa-Bráhmaṇa, and, it would appear, of the Shaḍvinśa-Bráhmaṇa also, accompanying the text step by step. It has not as yet been closely examined; but it promises to prove a rich mine of material for the history of Brahmanical theology, as it makes mention of, and appeals to, an extremely large number of different works. For example, of schools of the Ṛik, it cites the Aitareyins, the Paiṅgins, the Kaushítaka; of schools of the Yajus, the Adhvaryus in general; further, the Śáṭyáyanins, Khádáyanins, the Taittiríyas, the Káṭhaka, the Kálabavins, Bhállavins, Śámbuvis, Vájasaneyins; and frequently also *śruti, smṛiti, ácháryas,* &c. It is a work which deserves to be very thoroughly studied.[80]

While the above-named four Sútras of the Sámaveda specially attach themselves to the Pañchavinśa-Bráhmaṇa, the Sútras now to be mentioned stand out more independently beside the latter, although of course, in part at least, often referring to it. In the first place, we have to mention the *Nidána-Sútra,* which contains in ten *prapáṭhakas* metrical and other similar investigations on the different *ukthas, stomas,* and *gánas.* The name of the author is not given. The word *nidána,* 'root,' is used with reference to metre in the Bráhmaṇa of the White Yajus;[81] and though in the two instances where the Naidánas are mentioned by Yáska, their activity appears to have been directed less to the study of metre than to that of roots, etymology, still the Nidánasaṃjnaka Grantha is found cited in the Bṛihaddevatá, 5. 5, either directly as the Śruti of the Chhandogas, or at least as containing their Śruti.* This Sútra is especially remarkable for the great number of Vedic schools and teachers whose various opinions it adduces; and in this respect it stands on pretty much the same level as the Anupada-Sútra. It differs from it, however, by its particularly frequent quotation

[80] Unfortunately we do not even now know of more than one MS.; see *I. St.,* i. 43.

[81] This is wrong; on the contrary, the word has quite a general meaning in the passages in question (*e.g.,* in *gáyatrí vá eshá nidánena,* or *yo vá atrá 'gnir gáyatrí sa nidánena*).

* *Nidána,* in the sense of 'cause, foundation,' is a favourite word in the Buddhistic Sútras; see Burnouf, *Introd. à l'Histoire du Buddhisme Indien,* pp. 59, ff., 484, ff.

also of the views of the Sáman theologians named by Látyáyana and Dráhyáyaṇa, viz., Dhánaṃjayya, Śáṇḍilya, Śauchivṛikshi, &c.—a thing which seldom or never occurs in the former. The animosity to the Kaushítakis, with which we have already become acquainted in the Pañchaviṅśa-Bráhmaṇa, is here again exhibited most vividly in some words attributed to Dhánaṃjayya. With regard to the Ṛigveda, the *daśatayí* division into ten *maṇḍalas* is mentioned, as in Yáska. The allusion to the Átharvaṇikas, as well as to the Anubráhmaṇins, is particularly to be remarked; the latter peculiar name is not met with elsewhere, except in Páṇini. A special study of this Sútra is also much to be desired, as it likewise promises to open up a wealth of information regarding the condition of literature at that period.[82]

Not much information of this sort is to be expected from the *Pushpa-Sútra* of Gobhila,* which has to be named along with the Nidána-Sútra. The understanding of this Sútra is, moreover, obstructed by many difficulties. For not only does it cite the technical names of the *sámans*, as well as other words, in a very curtailed form, it also makes use of a number of grammatical and other technical terms, which, although often agreeing with the corresponding ones in the Prátiśákhya-Sútras, are yet also often formed in quite a peculiar fashion, here and there, indeed, quite after the algebraic type so favoured by Páṇini. This is particularly the case in the first four *prapáṭhakas;* and it is precisely for these that, up to the present time at least, no commentary has been found; whereas for the remaining six we possess a very good commentary by Upádhyáya Ajátaśatru.† The work treats of the modes in which the separate *ṛichas*, by various insertions, &c., are transformed into *sámans*, or "made to blossom," as it were, which is evidently the origin of the name Pushpa-Sútra, or "Flower-Sútra." In addition to

---

[82] See *I. St.*, i. 44, ff.; the first two *paṭalas*, which have special reference to metre, have been edited and translated by me in *I. St.*, viii. 85–124. For Anubráhmaṇin, °ṇa, see also Áśv. Śr., ii. 8. 11, and Schol. on T. S., i. 8. 1. 1.

* So, at least, the author is called in the colophons of two chapters in MS. Chambers 220 [Catalogue of the Berlin MSS., p. 76].

† Composed for his pupil, Vishṇuyaśas.

the Pravachana, *i.e.* (according to the commentary), Bráhmaṇa, of the Kálabavins and that of the Śáṭyáyanins, I found, on a cursory inspection, mention also of the Kauthumas. This is the first time that their name appears in a work connected with Vedic literature. Some portions of the work, particularly in the last books, are composed in *ślokas*, and we have, doubtless, to regard it as a compilation of pieces belonging to different periods.[83] In close connection with it stands the *Sáma-Tantra*, composed in the same manner, and equally unintelligible without a commentary. It treats, in thirteen *prapáṭhakas*, of accent and the accentuation of the separate verses. A commentary on it is indeed extant, but at present only in a fragmentary form. At its close the work is denoted as the *vyákaraṇa*, grammar, of the Sáman theologians.[84]

Several other Sútras also treat of the conversion of *ṛichas* into *sámans*, &c. One of these, the *Pañchavidhi-Sútra* (*Páñchavidhya, Pañchavidheya*), is only known to me from quotations, according to which, as well as from its name, it treats of the five different *vidhis* (modes) by which this process is effected. Upon a second, the *Pratihára-Sútra*, which is ascribed to Kátyáyana, a commentary called *Daśatayí* was composed by Varadarája, the abovementioned commentator of Maśaka. It treats of the aforesaid five *vidhis*, with particular regard to the one called *pratihára*. The *Taṇḍálakshaṇa-Sútra* is only known to me by name, as also the *Upagrantha-Sútra*,* both of which, with the two other works just named, are, according to the catalogue, found in the Fort-William

[83] In Dekhan MSS. the work is called *Phulla*-Sútra, and is ascribed to Vararuchi, not to Gobhila; see Burnell, *Catalogue*, pp. 45, 46. On this and other points of difference, see my paper, *Ueber das Saptaśatakam des Hála* (1870), pp. 258, 259. I now possess a copy of the text and commentary, but have nothing of consequence to add to the above remarks.

[84] See also Burnell, *Catalogue*, pp. 40, 41.—*Ibid.*, p. 44, we find a 'Svaraparibháshá, or Sámalakshaṇa,' specified. Kaiyaṭa also mentions a '*sámalakshaṇam prátiśákhyam śástram*,' by which he explains the word *ukthártha*, which, according to the Mahábháshya, is at the foundation of *aukthika*, whose formation is taught by Páṇini himself (iv. 2. 60); see *I. St.*, xiii. 447. According to this it certainly seems very doubtful whether the Sámalakshaṇa mentioned by Kaiyaṭa is to be identified with the extant work bearing the same name.

* Shaḍguruśishya, in the introduction to his commentary on the Anukramaṇí of the Ṛik, describes Kátyáyana as '*upagranthasya káraka*.'

collection of MSS. By the anonymous transcriber of the Berlin MS. of the Maśaka-Sútra, who is of course a very weak authority, ten Śrauta-Sútras for the Sámaveda are enumerated at the close of the MS., viz., besides Láṭyáyana, Anupada, Nidána, Kalpa, Taṇḍálakshaṇa, Pañchavidheya, and the Upagranthas, also the *Kalpánupada*, *Anustotra*, and the *Kshudras*. What is to be understood by the three last names must for the present remain undecided.[85]

The *Gṛihya-Sútra* of the Sámaveda belongs to *Gobhila*, the same to whom we also found a Śrauta-Sútra and the Pushpa-Sútra ascribed.[86] His name has a very unvedic ring, and nothing in any way coresponding to it appears in the rest of Vedic literature.[87] In what relation this work, drawn up in four *prapáṭhakas*, stands to the Gṛihya-Sútras of the remaining Vedas has not yet been investigated.[88] A supplement (*pariśishṭa*) to it is the *Karma-pradípa* of Kátyáyana. In its introductory words it expressly acknowledges itself to be such a supplement to Gobhila; but it has also been regarded both as a second Gṛihya-Sútra and as a Smṛiti-Śástra. According to the statement of Áśárka, the commentator of this Karma-pradípa, the Gṛihya-Sutra of Gobhila is authoritative for both the schools of the Sámaveda, the Kauthumas as well as the Ráṇáyaníyas.*—Is the *Khádira-Gṛihya*, which is now and then mentioned, also to be classed with the Sámaveda?[89]

---

[85] On the Pañchavidhi-Sútra and the Kalpánupada, each in two *prapáṭhakas*, and the Kshaudra, in three *prapáṭhakas*, see Müller, *A. S. L.*, p. 210; Aufrecht, *Catalogus*, p. 377[b]. The Upagrantha-Sútra treats of expiations, *práyaśchittas*, see Rájendra L. M., *Notices of Sanskṛit MSS.*, ii. 182.

[86] To him is also ascribed a Naigeya-Sútra, "a description of the Metres of the Sámaveda," see Colin Browning, *Catalogue of Sanskṛit MSS. existing in Oude* (1873), p. 4.

[87] A list of teachers belonging to the Gobhila school is contained in the Vaṁśa-Bráhmaṇa.

[88] An edition of the Gobhila-Gṛihya-Sútra, with a very diffuse commentary by the editor, Chandrakánta Tarkálaṃkára, has been commenced in the *Bibl. Indica* (1871); the fourth *fasciculus* (1873) reaches to ii. 8. 12. See the sections relating to nuptial ceremonies in Haas's paper, *I. St.*, v. 283, ff.

* Among the authors of the Smṛiti-Śástras a Kuṭhumi is also mentioned.

[89] Certainly. In Burnell's *Catalogue*, p. 56, the Dráhyáyaṇa-Gṛihya-Sútra (in four *paṭalas*) is attributed to Khádira. Rudraskandasvámin composed a *vṛitti* on this work also (see p. 80); and Vámana is named as the author of '*kárikás* to the Gṛihya-Sútras of Khádira,' Burnell, p. 57. To the Gṛihya-Sútras of the Sámaveda probably belong also Gautama's *Pitṛimedha-Sútra*

As representative of the last stage of the literature of the Sámaveda, we may specify, on the one hand, the various *Paddhatis* (outlines) and commentaries, &c., which connect themselves with the Sútras, and serve as an explanation and further development of them; and, on the other, that peculiar class of short treatises bearing the name of *Pariśishṭas*, which are of a somewhat more independent character than the former, and are to be looked upon more as supplements to the Sútras.* Among these, the already mentioned *Ársha* and *Daivata*—enumerations of the Ṛishis and deities—of the Saṃhitá in the Naigeya-Śákhá deserve prominent notice. Both of these treatises refer throughout to a comparatively ancient tradition; for example, to the Nairuktas, headed by Yáska and Śáka-púṇi, to the Naighaṇṭukas, to Śaunaka (*i.e.*, probably to his Anukramaṇí of the Ṛik), to their own Bráhmaṇa, to Aitareya and the Aitareyins, to the Śátapathikas, to the Pravachana Káṭhaka, and to Áśvaláyana. The *Dálbhya-Pariśishṭa* ought probably also to be mentioned here; it bears the name of an individual who appears several times in the Chhándogyopanishad, but particularly often in the Puráṇas, as one of the sages who conduct the dialogue.

The *Yajurveda*, to which we now turn, is distinguished above the other Vedas by the great number of different schools which belong to it. This is at once a consequence and a proof of the fact that it became pre-eminently the subject of study, inasmuch as it contains the formulas for the entire sacrificial ceremonial, and indeed forms its

(cf. Burnell, p. 57; the commentator Anantayajvan identifies the author with Akshapáda, the author of the Nyáya-Sútra), and the *Gautama-Dharma-Sútra*; see the section treating of the legal literature.

* Rámakṛishṇa, in his commentary on the Gṛihya-Sútra of the White Yajus, several times ascribes their authorship to a Kátyáyana (India Office Library, No. 440, fol. 52ᵃ, 56ᵃ, 58ᵃ, &c.); or do these quotations only refer to the above-named Karmapradípa?

proper foundation; whilst the Rigveda prominently, and the Sámaveda exclusively, devote themselves to a part of it only, viz., to the Soma sacrifice. The Yajurveda divides itself, in the first place, into two parts, the *Black* and the *White* Yajus. These, upon the whole, indeed, have their matter in common; but they differ fundamentally from each other as regards its arrangement. In the Saṃhitá of the Black Yajus the sacrificial formulas are for the most part immediately followed by their dogmatic explanation, &c., and by an account of the ceremonial belonging to them; the portion bearing the name of Bráhmaṇa differing only in point of time from this Saṃhitá, to which it must be viewed as a supplement. In the White Yajus, on the contrary, the sacrificial formulas, and their explanation and ritual, are entirely separated from one another, the first being assigned to the Saṃhitá, and their explanation and ritual to the Bráhmaṇa, as is also the case in the Ṛigveda and the Sámaveda. A further difference apparently consists in the fact that in the Black Yajus very great attention is paid to the Hotar and his duties, which in the White Yajus is of rare occurrence. By the nature of the case in such matters, what is undigested is to be regarded as the commencement, as the earlier stage, and what exhibits method as the later stage; and this view will be found to be correct in the present instance. As each Yajus possesses an entirely independent literature, we must deal with each separately.

First, of the *Black Yajus.* The data thus far known to us concerning it open up such extensive literary perspectives, but withal in such a meagre way, that investigation has, up to the present time, been less able to attain to approximately satisfactory results* than in any other field. In the first place, the name "Black Yajus" belongs only to a later period, and probably arose in contradistinction to that of the White Yajus. While the theologians of the Ṛik are called Bahvṛichas, and those of the Sáman Chhandogas, the old name for the theologians of the Yajus is Adhvaryus; and, indeed, these three names are already so

* See *I. St.*, i. 68, ff. [All the texts, with the exception of the Sútras relating to ritual, have now been published; see the ensuing notes.]

employed in the Saṃhitá of the Black Yajus and the Bráhmaṇa of the White Yajus. In the latter work the designation Adhvaryus is applied to its own adherents, and the Charakádhvaryus are denoted and censured as their adversaries—an enmity which is also apparent in a passage of the Saṃhitá of the White Yajus, where the Charakácharya, as one of the persons to be dedicated at the Purushamedha, is devoted to Dushkṛita, or "Ill deed." This is all the more strange, as the term *charaka* is otherwise always used in a good sense, for "travelling scholar;" as is also the root *char*, "to wander about for instruction." The explanation probably consists simply in the fact that the name Charakas is also, on the other hand, applied to one of the principal schools of the Black Yajus, whence we have to assume that there was a direct enmity between these and the adherents of the White Yajus who arose in opposition to them—a hostility similarly manifested in other cases of the kind. A second name for the Black Yajus is "Taittiríya," of which no earlier appearance can be traced than that in its own Prátiśákhya-Sútra, and in the Sáma-Sútras. Páṇini * connects this name with a Rishi called Tittiri, and so does the Anukramaṇí to the Átreya school, which we shall have frequent occasion to mention in the sequel. Later legends, on the contrary, refer it to the transformation of the pupils of Vaiśampáyana into partridges (*tittiri*), in order to pick up the *yajus*-verses disgorged by one of their companions who was wroth with his teacher. However absurd this legend may be, a certain amount of sense yet lurks beneath its surface. The Black Yajus is, in fact, a motley, undigested jumble of different pieces; and I am myself more inclined to derive the name Taittiríya from the variegated partridge (*tittiri*) than from the Ṛishi Tittiri; just as another name of one of the principal schools of the Black Yajus, that of the Khánḍikíyas, probably owes its formation to

* The rule referred to (iv. 3. 102) is, according to the statement of the Calcutta scholiast, not explained in Patamjali's Bháshya; possibly, therefore, it may not be Páṇini's at all, but may be later than Patamjali. [The name Taittiríya itself, however, is several times mentioned in the Bháshya, see *I. St.*, xiii. 442, which is also acquainted with '*Tittiriṇá proktáḥ ślokáḥ*,' *not* belonging to the Chhandas, see *I. St.*, v. 41; Goldstücker, *Páṇini*, p. 243.]

this very fact of the Black Yajus being made up of *khaṇḍas*, fragments, although Páṇini,* as in the case of Taittiríya, traces it to a Rishi of the name of Khaṇḍika, and although we do really meet with a Khaṇḍika (Audbhári) in the Bráhmaṇa of the White Yajus (xi. 8. 4. 1).

Of the many schools which are allotted to the Black Yajus, all probably did not extend to Saṃhitá and Bráhmaṇa; some probably embraced the Sútras only.† Thus far, at least, only three different recensions of the Saṃhitá are directly known to us, two of them in the text itself, the third merely from an Anukramaṇí of the text. The two first are the *Taittiríya-Saṃhitá*, κατ' ἐξοχὴν so called, which is ascribed to the school of Ápastamba, a subdivision of the Khánḍikíyas; and the *Káṭhaka*, which belongs to the school of the Charakas, and that particular subdivision of it which bears the name of Cháráyaṇíyas.‡ The Saṃhitá, &c., of the Átreya school, a subdivision of the Aukhíyas, is only known to us by its Anukramaṇí; it agrees in essentials with that of Ápastamba. This is not the case with the Káṭhaka, which stands on a more independent footing, and occupies a kind of intermediate position between the Black and the White Yajus, agreeing frequently with the latter as to the readings, and with the former in the arrangement of the matter. The Káṭhaka, together with the *Háridravika*—a lost work, which, however, likewise certainly belonged to the Black Yajus, viz., to the school of the Háridravíyas, a subdivision of the Maitráyaṇíyas—is the only work of the Bráhmaṇa order mentioned by name in Yáska's Nirukta. Páṇini, too, makes direct reference to it in a rule, and it is further alluded to in the Anupada-Sútra and Bṛihaddevatá. The name of the Kaṭhas does not appear in other Vedic writings, nor does that of Ápastamba.§

* The rule is the same as that for Tittiri. The remark in the previous note, therefore, applies here also.

† As is likewise the case with the other Vedas.

‡ Besides the text, we have also a Rishyanukramaṇí for it.

§ In later writings several Kaṭhas are distinguished, the Kaṭhas, the Práchya-Kaṭhas, and the Kapishṭhala-Kaṭhas; the epithet of these last is found in Páṇini (viii. 3. 91), and Megasthenes mentions the Καμβίσθολοι as a people in the Panjáb—In the Fort-William Catalogue a Kapishṭhala-Saṃhitá is mentioned [see *I. St.*, xiii. 375, 439.—At the time of the Mahábháshya the position of the Kaṭhas must have been one of great consideration, since

The Saṃhitá of the Ápastamba school consists of seven books (called *ashṭakas !*); these again are divided into 44 *praśnas*, 651 *anuvákas*, and 2198 *kaṇḍikás*, the latter being separated from one another on the principle of an equal number of syllables to each.[90] Nothing definite can be ascertained as to the extent of the Átreya recension; it is likewise divided into *káṇḍas*, *praśnas*, and *anuvákas*, the first words of which coincide mostly with those of the corresponding sections of the Ápastamba school. The Káṭhaka is quite differently divided, and consists of five parts, of which the three first are in their turn divided into forty *sthánakas*, and a multitude of small sections (also probably separated according to the number of words); while the fourth merely specifies the *ṛichas* to be sung by the Hotar, and the fifth contains the formulas belonging to the horse-sacrifice. In the colophons to the three first parts, the Charaka-Śákhá is called *Iṭhimiká*, *Madhyamiká*, and *Orimiká*, respectively: the first and last of these three appellations are still unexplained.[91] The Bráhmaṇa portion in these works is extremely meagre as regards the ritual, and gives but an imperfect picture of it; it is, however, peculiarly rich in legends of a mythological character. The sacrificial formulas themselves are on the whole the same as those contained in the Saṃhitá of the White Yajus; but the order is different, although the

---

they—and their text, the Káṭhaka—are repeatedly mentioned; see *I. St.*, xiii. 437, ff. The founder of their school, Kaṭha, appears in the Mahábháshya as Vaiśampáyana's pupil, and the Kaṭhas themselves appear in close connection with the Kálápas and Kauthumas, both schools of the Sáman. In the Rámáyaṇa, too, the Kaṭha-Kálápas are mentioned as being much esteemed in Ayodhyá (ii. 32. 18, Schlegel). Haradatta's statement, "*Bahvṛichánám apyasti Kaṭhaśákhá*" (Bhaṭṭoji's Siddh. Kaum. ed. Táránátha (1865), vol. ii. p. 524, on Páṇ., vii. 4. 38), probably rests upon some misunderstanding; see *I. St*, xiii. 438.]

[90] It is not the number of syllables, but the number of words, that constitutes the norm; fifty words, as a rule, form a *kaṇḍiká*; see *I. St.*, xi. 13, xii. 90, xiii. 97–99.—Instead of *ashṭaka*, we find also the more correct name *káṇḍa*, and instead of *praśna*, which is peculiar to the Taittiríya texts, the generally employed term, *prapáṭhaka*; see *I. St.*, xi. 13, 124.—The Taitt. Bráhm. and the Taitt. Ár., are also subdivided into *kaṇḍikás*, and these again into very small sections; but the principle of these divisions has not yet been clearly ascertained.

[91] Iṭhimiká is to be derived from *heṭṭhima* (from *heṭṭhá*, *i.e.*, *adhastát*), and Orimiká from *urarima* (from *upari*); see my paper, *Ueber die Bhagavatí der Jaina*, i. 404, n.

order of the ceremonial to which they belong is pretty much the same. There are also many discrepancies with regard to the words; we may instance, in particular, the expansion of the semi-vowels *v* and *y* after a consonant into *uv* and *iy*, which is peculiar to the Ápastamba school.[92] As to data, geographical or historical, &c. (here, of course, I can only speak of the Ápastamba school and the Káṭhaka), in consequence of the identity of matter these are essentially the same as those which meet us in the Saṃhitá of the White Yajus. (In the latter, however, they are more numerous, formulas being also found here for ceremonies which are not known in the former—the *purushamedha*, for instance.) Now these data—to which we must add some other scattered allusions * in the portions bearing the character of a Bráhmaṇa—carry us back, as we shall see, to the flourishing epoch of the kingdom of the Kuru-Pañchálas,[93] in which district we must therefore recognise the place of origin of both works. Whether this also holds good of their final redaction is another question, the answer to which, as far as the Ápastamba-Saṃhitá is concerned, naturally depends upon the amount of influence in its arrangement to be ascribed to Ápastamba, whose name it bears. The Káṭhaka, according to what has been stated above, appears to have existed as an entirely finished work even in Yáska's time, since he quotes it; the Anukramaṇí of the Átreya school, on the contrary, makes Yáska Paiṅgi[94] (as the pupil of Vaiśampáyana) the teacher of Tittiri, the latter again the in-

---

[92] For further particulars, see *I. St.*, xiii. 104-106.

* Amongst them, for example, the enumeration of the whole of the lunar asterisms in the Ápastamba-Saṃhitá, where they appear in an order deviating from that of the later series, which, as I have pointed out above (p. 30), must necessarily have been fixed between 1472 and 536 B.C. But all that follows from this, in regard to the passage in question, is that it is not earlier than 1472 B.C., which is a matter of course; it nowise follows that it may not be later than 536 B.C. So we obtain nothing definite here. [This remains correct, though the position of the case itself is somewhat different; see the notes above, p. 2 and p. 30. In connection with the enumeration of the Nakshatras, compare especially my essay, *Die vedischen Nachrichten von den Nakshatra*, ii. 299, ff.]

[93] Of peculiar interest is the mention of Dhṛitaráshṭra Vaichitravírya, as also of the contests between the Pañchálas and the Kuntis in the Káṭhaka; see *I. St.*, iii. 469-472.

[94] Bhaṭṭa Bháskara Miśra, on the contrary, gives Yájnavalka instead of Paiṅgi; see Burnell's *Catalogue*, p. 14.

structor of Ukha, and Ukha the preceptor of Átreya.* This at least clearly exhibits its author's view of the priority of Yáska to the schools and redactions of the Black Yajus bearing the names of Tittiri and Átreya; although the data necessary to prove the correctness of this view are wanting. That, however, some sort of influence in the arrangement of the Saṃhitá of the Black Yajus is certainly to be attributed to Yáska, is evident further from the fact that Bhaṭṭa Bháskara Miśra, in an extant fragment of his commentary on the Ápastamba-Saṃhitá,† quotes, side by side with the views of Káśakṛitsna and Ekachúrṇi regarding a division of the text, the opinion of Yáska also.

Along with the Káṭhaka, the *Mánava* and the *Maitra* are very frequently quoted in the commentaries on the Kátíya-Sútra of the White Yajus. We do not, it is true, find these names in the Sútras or similar works; but at all events they are meant for works resembling the Káṭhaka, as is shown by the quotations themselves, which are often of considerable length. Indeed, we also find, although only in later writings, the Maitráyaṇíyas, and, as a subdivision of these, the Mánavas, mentioned as schools of the Black Yajus. Possibly these works may still be in existence in India.‡

---

* Átreya was the *padakára* of his school; Kuṇḍina, on the contrary, the *vṛittikára*. The meaning of *vṛitti* is here obscure, as it is also in Schol. to Páṇ., iv. 3. 108 (*mádhurí vṛittiḥ*) [see *I. St.*, xiii. 381].

† We have, besides, a commentary by Sáyaṇa, though it is only fragmentary; another is ascribed to a Bálakṛishṇa. [In Burnell's Collection of MSS., see his *Catalogue*, pp. 12–14, is found the greater portion of Bhaṭṭa Kauśika Bháskara Miśra's commentary, under the name *Jnánayajna;* the author is said to have lived 400 years before Sáyaṇa; he quotes amongst others Bhavasvámin, and seems to stand in special connection with the Átreyí school. A *Paiśáchabháshya* on the Black Yajus is also mentioned; see *I. St.*, ix. 176.—An edition of the Taittiríya-Saṃhitá in the *Bibl. Indica*, with Sáyaṇa's complete commentary, was commenced by Roer (1854), continued by Cowell and Ráma Náráyaṇa, and is now in the hands of Maheśachandra Nyáyaratna (the last part, No. 28, 1874, reaches to iv. 3. 11); the complete text, in Roman transcript, has been published by myself in *I. St.*, xi., xii. (1871–72). On the Káṭhaka, see *I. St.*, iii. 451–479.]

‡ According to the Fort-William Catalogue, the 'Maitráyaṇí-Śákhá' is in existence there. [Other MSS. have since been found; see Haug in *I. St.*, ix. 175, and his essay *Brahma und die Brahmanen*, pp. 31–34 (1871), and Bühler's detailed survey of the works composing this Śákhá in *I. St.*, xiii. 103, 117–128. According to this, the Maitr. Saṃhitá consists at present of five *káṇḍas*, two of which, however, are but later ad-

Besides the Saṃhitá so called, there is a Bráhmaṇa recognised by the school of Ápastamba, and also by that of Átreya,* which, however, as I have already remarked, differs from the Saṃhitá, not as to the nature of its contents, but only in point of time; it is, in fact, to be regarded merely as a supplement to it. It either reproduces the formulas contained in the Saṃhitá, and connects them with their proper ritual, or it develops further the liturgical rules already given there; or again, it adds to these entirely new rules, as, for instance, those concerning the *purushamedha*, which is altogether wanting in the Saṃhitá, and those referring to the sacrifices to the lunar asterisms. Only the third and last book, in twelve *prapáṭhakas*, together with Sáyaṇa's commentary, is at present known.[95] The three last *prapáṭhakas*, which contain four different sections, relating to the manner of preparing certain peculiarly sacred sacrificial fires, are ascribed in the Anukramaṇí of the Átreya school (and this is also confirmed by Sáyaṇa in another place) to the sage Kaṭha. Two other sections also belong to it, which, it seems, are only found in the Átreya school, and not in that of Ápastamba; and also, lastly, the two first books of the Taittiríya-Áraṇyaka, to be mentioned presently. Together these eight sections evidently form a supplement to the Káṭhaka above discussed; they do not, however, appear to exist as an independent work, but only in connection with the Bráhmaṇa and Áraṇyaka of the Ápastamba- (and Átreya-) schools, from which, for the rest, they can be externally distinguished easily enough by the absence of the expansion of *v* and *y* into *uv* and *iy*. The legend quoted towards the end of the second of these sections (*prap.* xi. 8), as to the visit of Nachiketas, to the lower

---

ditions, viz., the Upanishad (see below), which passes as *káṇḍa* ii., and the last *káṇḍa*, called Khila.]

* At least as regards the fact, for the designation Saṃhitá or Bráhmaṇa does not occur in its Anukramaṇí. On the contrary, it passes without any break from the portions which belong in the Ápastamba school to the Saṃhitá, to those there belonging to the Bráhmaṇa.

[95] All three books have been edited, with Sáyaṇa's commentary, in the *Bibl. Ind.* (1855–70), by Rájendra Lála Mitra. The Hiraṇyakeśi-śákhíya-Bráhmaṇa quoted by Bühler, *Catalogue of Sanskṛit MSS. from Gujarát*, i. 38, is not likely to depart much from the ordinary Ápastamba text; the respective Srauta-Sútras at least agree almost literally with each other; see Bühler, *Ápastambíya-dharmasútra*, Preface, p. 6 (1868).

world, gave rise to an Upanishad of the Atharvan which bears the name of Káṭhakopanishad. Now, between this supplement to the Káṭhaka and the Káṭhaka itself a considerable space of time must have elapsed, as follows from the allusions made in the last sections to Mahá-Meru, Krauñcha, Mainága; to Vaiśampáyana, Vyása Páráśarya, &c.; as well as from the literature therein presupposed as existing, the 'Atharváñgirasas,' Bráhmaṇas, Itihásas, Puráṇas, Kalpas, Gáthás, and Náráśansís being enumerated as subjects of study (*svádhyáya*). Further, the last but one of these sections is ascribed to another author, viz., to the Aruṇas, or to Áruṇa, whom the scholiast on Páṇini[96] speaks of as a pupil of Vaiśampáyana, a statement with which its mention of the latter as an authority tallies excellently; this section is perhaps therefore only erroneously assigned to the school of the Kaṭhas.—The *Taittiríya-Áraṇyaka*, at the head of which that section stands (as already remarked), and which belongs both to the Ápastamba and Átreya schools, must at all events be regarded as only a later supplement to their Bráhmaṇa, and belongs, like most of the Áraṇyakas, to the extreme end of the Vedic period. It consists of ten books, the first six of which are of a liturgical character: the first and third books relate to the manner of preparing certain sacred sacrificial fires; the second to preparatives to the study of Scripture; and the fourth, fifth, and sixth to purificatory sacrifices and those to the Manes, corresponding to the last books of the Saṃhitá of the White Yajus. The last four books of the Áraṇyaka, on the contrary, contain two Upanishads; viz., the seventh, eighth, and ninth books, the *Taittiríyopanishad*, κατ' ἐξοχὴν so called, and the tenth, the *Yájniki-* or *Náráyaṇíyá-Upanishad*. The former, or Taittiríyopanishad, is in three parts. The first is the *Saṃhitopanishad*, or *Śikshávallí*,* which begins with a short grammatical disquisition,[97] and then turns to

---

[96] Kaiyaṭa on Páṇ., iv. 2. 104 (Mahábháshya, fol. 73ᵇ, ed. Benares); he calls him, however, Áruṇi instead of Áruṇa, and derives from him the school of the Áruṇins (cited in the Bháshya, *ibid.*); the Áruṇis are cited in the Káṭhaka itself; see *I. St.*, iii. 475.

* *Valli* means 'a creeper;' it is perhaps meant to describe these Upanishads as 'creepers,' which have attached themselves to the Veda-Śákhá.

[97] See above, p. 61; Müller, *A. S. L.*, p. 113, ff.; Haug, *Ueber das Wesen des vedischen Accents*, p. 54.

the question of the unity of the world-spirit. The second and third are the *Ánandavallí* and *Bhriguvallí*, which together also go by the name of *Váruṇí-Upanishad*, and treat of the bliss of entire absorption in meditation upon the Supreme Spirit, and its identity with the individual soul.* If in these we have already a thoroughly systematised form of speculation, we are carried even further in one portion of the Yájnikí-Upanishad, where we have to do with a kind of sectarian worship of Náráyaṇa: the remaining part contains ritual supplements. Now, interesting as this whole Áraṇyaka is from its motley contents and evident piecing together of collected fragments of all sorts, it is from another point of view also of special importance for us, from the fact that its tenth book is actually extant in a double recension, viz., in a text which, according to Sáyaṇa's statements, belongs to the Drávidas, and in another, bearing the name of the Ándhras, both names of peoples in the south-west of India. Besides these two texts, Sáyaṇa also mentions a recension belonging to the Karṇátakas, and another whose name he does not give. Lastly, this tenth book † exists also as an Atharvopanishad, and here again with many variations; so that there is here opened up to criticism an ample field for researches and conjectures. Such, certainly, have not been wanting in Indian literary history; it is seldom, however, that the facts lie so ready to hand as we have them in this case, and this we owe to Sáyaṇa's commentary, which is here really excellent.

When we look about us for the other Bráhmaṇas of the Black Yajus, we find, in the first place, among the schools

---

* See a translation, &c., of the Taitt. Upanishad in *I. St.*, ii. 207–235. It has been edited, with Śaṃkara's commentary, by Roer in *Bibl. Indica*, vol. vii. [; the text alone, as a portion of the Taitt. Ár., by Rájendra Lála Mitra also, see next note. Roer's translation appeared in vol. xv. of the *Bibliotheca Indica*].

† See a partial translation of it in *I. St.*, ii. 78–100. [It is published in the complete edition of the Taitt. Áraṇyaka, with Sáyaṇa's commentary thereon (excepting books vii.–ix., see the previous note), in *Bibl. Ind.* (1864–72), by Rájendra Lála Mitra; the text is the Dráviḍa text commented upon by Sáyaṇa, in sixty-four *anuvákas*, the various readings of the Ándhra text (in eighty *anuvákas*) being also added. In Burnell's collection there is also a commentary on the Taitt. Ár., by Bhaṭṭa Bháskara Miśra, which, like that on the Saṃhitá, is entitled Jnánayajna; see Burnell's *Catalogue*, pp. 16, 17.]

cited in the Sáma-Sútras two which must probably be considered as belonging to the Black Yajus, viz., the *Bhállavins* and the *Śáṭyáyanins.* The Bráhmaṇa of the *Bhállavins* is quoted by the scholiast on Páṇini, probably following the Mahábháshya,[98] as one of the 'old' Bráhmaṇas: we find it mentioned in the Brihaddevatá; Sureśvarácharya also, and even Sáyaṇa himself, quote passages from the Bhállaviśruti. A passage supposed to be borrowed from the Bhállavi-Upanishad is adduced by the sect of the Mádhavas in support of the correctness of their (Dvaita) belief (*As. Res.*, xvi. 104). That the Bhállavins belong to the Black Yajus is, however, still uncertain; I only conclude so at present from the fact that Bhállaveya is the name of a teacher specially attacked and censured in the Bráhmaṇa of the White Yajus. As to the *Śáṭyáyanins,* whose Bráhmaṇa is also reckoned among the 'old' ones by the scholiast on Páṇini,[99] and is frequently quoted, especially by Sáyaṇa, it is pretty certain that they belong to the Black Yajus, as it is so stated in the Charaṇavyúha, a modern index of the different schools of the Vedas, and, moreover, a teacher named Śáṭyáyani is twice mentioned in the Bráhmaṇa of the White Yajus. The special regard paid to them in the Sáma-Sútras, and which, to judge from the quotations, they themselves paid to the Sáman, is probably to be explained by the peculiar connection (itself still obscure) which we find elsewhere also between the schools of the Black Yajus and those of the Sáman.[100] Thus, the Kaṭhas are mentioned along with the Sáman schools

---

[98] This is not so, for in the Bháshya to the particular *sútra* of Páṇ. (iv. 3. 105), the Bhállavins are not mentioned. They are, however, mentioned elsewhere in the work, at iv. 2. 104 (here Kaiyaṭa derives them from a teacher Bhallu: *Bhallunâ proktam adhîyate*); as a *Bhállaveyo Matsyo rájaputraḥ* is cited in the Anupada, vi. 5, their home may have been in the country of the Matsyas; see *I. St.*, xiii. 441, 442. At the time of the Bháshika-Sútra their Bráhmaṇa text was still accentuated, in the same way as the Śatapatha; see Kielhorn, *I. St*, x. 421.

[99] The Mahábháshya is not his authority in this case either, for it does not mention the Śáṭyáyanins in its comment on the *sútra* in question (iv. 3. 105). But Kaiyaṭa cites the Bráhmaṇas proclaimed by Śáṭyáyana, &c., as contemporaneous with the *Yájnavalkáni Bráhmaṇáni* and *Saulabháni Br.*, which are mentioned in the Mahábháshya (see, however, *I. St.*, v. 67, 68); and the Mahábháshya itself cites the Śáṭyáyanins along with the Bhállavins (on iv. 2. 104); they belonged, it would seem, to the north; see *I. St.*, xiii. 442.

[100] See on this *I. St.*, iii. 473, xiii. 439.

of the Kálápas and Kauthumas; and along with the latter the Laukákshas also. As to the Śákáyanins,* Sáyakáyanins, Kálabavins, and Śálaṅkáyanins,[101] with whom, as with the Śáṭyáyanins, we are only acquainted through quotations, it is altogether uncertain whether they belong to the Black Yajus or not. The *Chhagalins*, whose name seems to be borne by a tolerably ancient Upanishad in Anquetil's *Oupnekhat*, are stated in the Charaṇavyúha[102] to form a school of the Black Yajus (according to Páṇini, iv. 3. 109, they are called Chhágaleyins): the same is there said of the *Śvetáśvataras*. The latter gave their name to an Upanishad composed in a metrical form, and called at its close the work of a Śvetáśvatara: in which the Sáṃkhya doctrine of the two primeval principles is mixed up with the Yoga doctrine of one Lord, a strange misuse being here made of wholly irrelevant passages of the Saṃhitá, &c., of the Yajus; and upon this rests its sole claim to be connected with the latter. Kapila, the originator of the Sáṃkhya system, appears in it raised to divine dignity itself, and it evidently belongs to a very late period; for though several passages from it are quoted in the Brahma-Sútra of Bádaráyaṇa (from which its priority to the latter at least would appear to follow), they may just as well have been borrowed from the common source, the Yajus. It is, at all events, a good deal older than Śaṃkara, since he regarded it as Śruti, and commented upon it. It has recently been published, together with this commentary,* by Dr. Roer, in the *Bibliotheca Indica*, vol. vii.; see also *Ind. Stud.*, i. 420, ff.—The *Maitráyaṇa Upanishad* at least bears a more ancient name, and might perhaps be connected

* They are mentioned in the tenth book of the Bráhmaṇa of the White Yajus [see also Káṭhaka 22. 7, *I. St.*, iii. 472]; as is also Sáyakáyana.

[101] The Śálaṅkáyanas are ranked as Bráhmaṇas among the Váhikas in the Calcutta scholium to Páṇ. v. 3. 114 (*bháshye na vyákhyátam*). Vyása's mother, Satyavatí, is called Śálaṅkáyanajá, and Páṇini himself Śálaṅki; see *I. St.*, xiii. 375, 395, 428, 429.

[102] This statement needs correction to this extent, that the Charaṇavyúha does not know the name Chhagalin at all (which is mentioned by Páṇini alone), but speaks only of Chhágeyas or Chhágaleyas; see *I. St.*, iii. 258; Müller, *A. S. L.*, p. 370. On Anquetil's 'Tschakli' Upanishad see now *I. St.*, ix. 42–46.

* Distinguished by a great number of sometimes tolerably long quotations from the Puráṇas, &c. [Roer's translation was published in the *Bibl. Ind.*, vol. xv.]

with the above-mentioned Maitra (Bráhmaṇa). Its text, however, both in language and contents, shows that, compared with the latter, it is of a very modern date. At present, unfortunately, I have at my command only the four first *prapáṭhakas*, and these in a very incorrect form,*—whereas in Anquetil's translation, the Upanishad consists of twenty chapters,—yet even these are sufficient clearly to determine the character of the work. King Bṛihadratha, who, penetrated by the nothingness of earthly things, resigned the sovereignty into the hands of his son, and devoted himself to contemplation, is there instructed by Śákáyanya (see *gaṇa* 'Kuñja') upon the relation of the *átman* (soul) to the world; Śákáyanya communicates to him what Maitreya had said upon this subject, who in his turn had only repeated the instruction given to the Bálakhilyas by Prajápati himself. The doctrine in question is thus derived at third hand only, and we have to recognise in this tradition a consciousness of the late origin of this form of it. This late origin manifests itself externally also in the fact that corresponding passages from other sources are quoted with exceeding frequency in support of the doctrine, introduced by "*athá 'nyatrá 'py uktam,*" "*etad apy uktam,*" "*atre 'me ślokà bhavanti,*" "*atha yathe 'yaṃ Kautsáyanastutiḥ.*" The ideas themselves are quite upon a level with those of the fully developed Sáṃkhya doctrine,† and the language is completely marked off from the

---

* I obtained them quite recently, in transcript, through the kindness of Baron d'Eckstein, of Paris, together with the tenth *adhyáya* of a metrical paraphrase, called *Anabhútiprakáśa*, of this Upanishad, extending, in 150 *ślokas*, over these four *prapáṭhakas*. The latter is copied from E. I. H., 693, and is probably identical with the work of Vidyáraṇya often mentioned by Colebrooke. [It is really so; and this portion has since been published, together with the Upanishad in full, by Cowell, in his edition of the Maitr. Upanishad, in seven *prapáṭhakas*, with Rámatírtha's commentary and an English translation, in the *Bibl. Ind.* (1862–70). According to the commentary, on the one hand, the two last books are to be considered as *khilas*, and on the other, the whole Upanishad belongs to a *púrvakáṇḍa*, in four books, of ritual purport, by which most likely is meant the Maitráyaṇí-Saṃhitá discussed by Bühler (see *I. St.*, xiii. 119, ff.), in which the Upanishad is quoted as the second (!) *káṇḍa*; see *l. c.*, p. 121. The transcript sent me by Eckstein shows manifold deviations from the other text; its original has unfortunately not been discovered yet.]

† Brahman, Rudra, and Vishṇu represent respectively the Sattva, the Tamas, and the Rajas elements of Prajápati.

prose of the Bráhmaṇas, both by extremely long compounds, and by words entirely foreign to these, and only belonging to the epic period (such as *sura*, *yaksha*, *uraga*, *bhútagaṇa*, &c.). The mention also of the *grahas*, planets, and of the motion of the polar star (*dhruvasya prachalanam*), supposes a period considerably posterior to the Bráhmaṇa.[103] The zodiacal signs are even mentioned in Anquetil's translation; the text to which I have access does not unfortunately extend so far.[104] That among the princes enumerated in the introduction as having met their downfall, notwithstanding all their greatness, not one name occurs belonging to the narrower legend of the Mahá-Bhárata or Rámáyaṇa, is no doubt simply owing to the circumstance that Bṛihadratha is regarded as the predecessor of the Páṇḍus. For we have probably to identify him with the Bṛihadratha, king of Magadha, who according to the Mahá-Bhárata (ii. 756) gave up the sovereignty to his son Jarásaṃdha, afterwards slain by the Páṇḍus, and retired to the wood of penance. I cannot forbear connecting with the instruction here stated to have been given to a king of Magadha by a *Śákáyanya* the fact that it was precisely in Magadha that Buddhism, the doctrine of *Śákyamuni*, found a welcome. I would even go so far as directly to conjecture that we have here a Brahmanical legend about Śákyamuni; whereas otherwise legends of this kind reach us only through the adherents of the Buddhist doctrine. Maitreya, it is well known, is, with the Buddhists, the name of the future Buddha, yet in their legends the name is also often directly connected with their Śákyamuni; a Púrṇa Maitráyaṇíputra, too, is given to the latter as a pupil. Indeed, as far as we can judge at

---

103 According to Cowell (p. 244), by *graha* we have here to understand, once at least (i. 4), not the planets but *bálagrahas* (children's diseases); "*Dhruvasya prachalanam* probably only refers to a *pralaya*; then even 'the never-ranging pole star' is forced to move." In a second passage, however (vi. 16, p. 124), the *grahas* appear along with the moon and the *ṛikshas*. Very peculiar, too, is the statement as to the stellar limits of the sun's two journeys (vi. 14; Cowell, pp. 119, 266); see on this *I. St.*, ix. 363.

104 The text has nothing of this (vii. 1, p. 198); but special mention is here made of Saturn, *śani* (p. 201), and where *śukra* occurs (p. 200), we might perhaps think of Venus. This last *adhyáya* throughout clearly betrays its later origin; of special interest is the bitter polemic against heretics and unbelievers (p. 206).

present, the doctrine of this Upanishad stands in close connection with the opinions of the Buddhists,[105] although from its Brahmanical origin it is naturally altogether free from the dogma and mythology peculiar to Buddhism. We may here also notice, especially, the contempt for writing (*grantha*) exhibited in one of the *ślokas* * quoted in corroboration.

Neither the Chhagalins, nor the Śvetáśvataras, nor the Maitráyaṇíyas are mentioned in the Sútras of the other Vedas, or in similar works, as schools of the Black Yajus; still, we must certainly ascribe to the last mentioned a very active share in its development, and the names Maitreya and Maitreyí at least are not unfrequently quoted in the Bráhmaṇas.

In the case of the *Sútras*, too, belonging to the Black Yajus, the large number of different schools is very striking. Although, as in the case of the Bráhmaṇas, we only know the greater part of them through quotations, there is reason to expect, not only that the remarkably rich collection of the India House (with which I am only very superficially acquainted) will be found to contain many treasures in this department, but also that many of them will yet be recovered in India itself. The Berlin collection does not contain a single one. In the first place, as to the *Śrauta-Sútras*, my only knowledge of the *Kaṭha-Sútra*,† the *Manu-Sútra*, the *Maitra-Sútra*, and the *Laugákshi-Sútra* is derived from the commentaries on the Kátíya-Sútra of the White Yajus; the second, however,[106] stands in the catalogue of the Fort-William col-

---

[105] Báṇa's Harshacharitra informs us of a Maitráyaṇíya Divákara who embraced the Buddhist creed; and Bháu Dáji (*Journal Bombay Branch R. A. S.*, x. 40) adds that even now Maitr. Brahmans live near Bhaḍgáon at the foot of the Vindhya, with whom other Brahmans do not eat in common; 'the reason may have been the early Buddhist tendencies of many of them.'

* Which, by the way, recurs together with some others in precisely the same form in the Amṛitavindu- (or Brahmavindu-) Upanishad. [Though it may be very doubtful whether the word *grantha* ought really *à priori* and for the earlier period to be understood of written texts (cf. *I. St.*, xiii. 476), yet in this verse, at any rate, a different interpretation is hardly possible; see below.]

† Laugákshi and the '*Lámakáyanínám Bráhmaṇam*' are said to be quoted therein.

[106] On this, as well as on the contents and the division of the work, see my remarks in *I. St.*, v. 13–16, in accordance with communications received from Professor Cowell; cf. also Haug, *ibid.*, ix. 175. A Mánava

lection, and of the last, whose author is cited in the Kaṭha-Sútra, as well as in the Kátíya-Sútra, there is, it appears, a copy in Vienna. Mahádeva, a commentator of the Kalpa-Sútra of Satyáshádha Hiraṇyakeśi, when enumerating the Taittiríya-Sútras in successive order in his introduction, leaves out these four altogether, and names at the head of his list the Sútra of *Baudháyana* as the oldest, then that of *Bháradvája*, next that of *Ápastamba*, next that of *Hiraṇyakeśi* himself, and finally two names not otherwise mentioned in this connection, *Vádhúna* and *Vaikhánasa*, the former of which is perhaps a corrupted form. Of these names, Bháradvája is the only one to be found in Vedic works; it appears in the Bráhmaṇa of the White Yajus, especially in the supplements to the Vṛihad-Áraṇyaka (where several persons of this name are mentioned), in the Kátíya-Sútra of the same Yajus, in the Prátiśákhya-Sútra of the Black Yajus, and in Páṇini. Though the name is a patronymic, yet it is possible that these last citations refer to one and the same person, in which case he must at the same time be regarded as the founder of a grammatical school, that of the Bháradvájíyas. As yet, I have seen nothing of his Sútra, and am acquainted with it only through quotations. According to a statement by the Mahádeva just mentioned, it treats of the oblation to the Manes, in two *praśnas*, and therefore shares with the rest of the Sútras this designation of the sections, which is peculiar to the Black Yajus.[107] The Sútra of Ápastamba* is found in the Library of the India House, and a part of it in Paris also. Commentaries on it by

---

Śrauta-Sútra is also cited in Bühler's *Catalogue of MSS. from Gujarát*, i. 188 (1871); it is in 322 foll. The manuscript edited in facsimile by Goldstücker under the title, '*Mánava Kalpa-Sútra, being a portion of this ancient work on Vaidik rites, together with the Commentary of Kumárilasvámin*' (1861), gives but little of the text, the commentary quoting only the first words of the passages commented upon; whether the concluding words, '*Kumáre'ablidshyam samáptam*,' really indicate that Kumárilasvámin was the author of the commentary seems still doubtful.

[107] The Bháradvájíya-Sútra has now been discovered by Bühler; see his *Catal. of MSS. from Guj.*, i. 186 (212 foll.); the Vaikhánasa-Sútra is also quoted, *ib.* i. 190 (292 foll.); see also Haug in *I. St.*, ix. 175.

* According to the quotations, the Vájasaneyaka, Bahvṛicha-Bráhmaṇa, and Śáṭyáyanaka are frequently mentioned therein.

Dhúrtasvámin and Tálavṛintanivásin are mentioned,[108] also one on the Sútra of Baudháyana by Kapardisvámin.[109] The work of Satyáshádha contains, according to Mahádeva's statement,[110] twenty-seven *praśnas*, whose contents agree pretty closely with the order followed in the Kátíya-Sútra; only the last nine form an exception, and are quite peculiar to it. The nineteenth and twentieth *praśnas* refer to domestic ceremonies, which usually find a place in the Gṛihya- and Smárta-Sútras. In the twenty-first, genealogical accounts and lists are contained; as also in a *praśna* of the Baudháyana-Sútra.*

Still scantier is the information we possess upon the *Gṛihya-Sútras* of the Black Yajus. The *Káṭhaka* Gṛihya-Sútra is known to me only through quotations, as are also the Sútras of *Baudháyana* (extant in the Fort-William

---

[108] On the Ápastamba-Śrauta-Sútra and the commentaries belonging to it, by Dhúrtasv., Kapardisvámin, Rudradatta, Gurudevasvámin, Karavindasvámin, Tálav., Ahobalasúri (Aḍabila in Bühler, *l. c.*, p. 150, who also mentions a Nṛisiṅha, p. 152), and others, see Burnell in his *Catalogue*, pp. 18–24, and in the *Indian Antiquary*, i. 5, 6. According to this the work consists of thirty *praśnas*; the first twenty-three treat of the sacrificial rites in essentially the same order (from *darśapúrṇamásau* to *sattráyaṇam*) as in Hiraṇyakeśi, whose Sútra generally is almost identical with that of Ápastamba; see Bühler's preface to the Áp. Dharma-Sútra, p. 6; the 24th *praśna* contains the general rules, *paribháshás*, edited by M. Müller in *Z. D. M. G.*, ix. (1855), a *pravarakhaṇḍa* and a *hautraka*; *praśnas* 25–27 contain the Gṛihya-Sútra; *praśnas* 28, 29, the Dharma-Sútra, edited by Bühler (1868); and finally, *praśna* 30, the Śulva-Sútra (*śulva*, 'measuring cord').

[109] On the Baudháyana-Sútra compare likewise Burnell's *Catalogue*, pp. 24–30. Bhavasvámin, who amongst others commented it, is mentioned by Bhaṭṭa Bháskara, and is consequently placed by Burnell (p. 26) in the eighth century. According to Kielhorn, *Catalogue of S. MSS. in the South Division of the Bombay Pres.*, p. 8, there exists a commentary on it by Sáyaṇa also, for whom, indeed, it constituted the special text-book of the Yajus school to which he belonged; see Burnell, *Vaṁśa-Bráhmaṇa*, pp. ix.–xix. In Bühler's *Catalogue of MSS. from Guj.*, i. 182, 184, Anantadeva, Navahasta, and Śesha are also quoted as scholiasts. The exact compass of the entire work is not yet ascertained; the Baudháyana-Dharma-Sútra, which, according to Bühler, *Digest of Hindu Law*, i. p. xxi. (1867), forms part of the Śrauta-Sútra, as in the case of Ápastamba and Hiraṇyakeśi, was commented by Govindasvámin: see Burnell, p. 35.

[110] Mátṛidatta and Váñcheśvara (?) are also mentioned as commentators; see Kielhorn, *l. c.*, p. 10.

* Such lists are also found in Áśvaláyana's work, at the end, though only in brief: for the Kátíya-Sútra, a Pariśishṭa comes in. [*Praśnas* 26, 27, of Hiraṇyakeśi treat of *dharmas*, so that here also, as in the case of Ápast. and Baudh., the Dharma-Sútra forms part of the Śrauta-Sútra.]

collection), of *Bháradvája*, and of *Satyáshádha*, or *Hiraṇyakeśi*, unless in this latter case only the corresponding *praśnas* of the Kalpa-Sútra are intended.[111] I have myself only glanced through a Paddhati of the Gṛihya-Sútra of the *Maitráyaṇíya* school, which treats of the usual subject (the sixteen *saṃskáras*, or sacraments). I conclude that there must also have been a Gṛihya-Sútra[112] of the *Mánava* school, from the existence of the Code bearing that name,[113] just as the Codes ascribed to Atri, Ápastamba, Chhágaleya, Baudháyana, Laugákshi, and Śáṭyáyana are probably to be traced to the schools of the same name belonging to the Black Yajus, that is to say, to their Gṛihya-Sútras.[114]

Lastly, the *Prátiśákhya-Sútra* has still to be mentioned as a Sútra of the Black Yajus. The only manuscript with which I am acquainted unfortunately only begins at the fourth section of the first of the two *praśnas*. This work is of special significance from the number of very peculiar names of teachers * mentioned in it: as Átreya, Kauṇḍinya (once by the title of Sthavira), and Bháradvája, whom we know already; also Válmíki, a name which in this connection is especially surprising; and further Ágniveśya, Ágniveśyáyana, Paushkarasádi, and others. The two last names, as well as that of Kauṇḍinya,† are mentioned in Buddhist writings as the names either of pupils or of contemporaries of Buddha, and Paushkarasádi is also cited in the *várttikas* to Páṇini by Kátyáyana, their author. Again, the allusion occurring here for the first time to the Mímáṅsakas and Taittiríyakas deserves to be remarked:

---

[111] This is really so. On Ápastamba- and Bháradvája-Gṛihya, see Burnell, *Catalogue*, pp. 30–33. The sections of two '*prayogas*,' of both texts, relating to birth ceremonial, have been edited by Speijer in his book *De Ceremonia apud Indos quæ vocatur játakarma* (Leyden, 1872).

[112] It is actually extant; see Bühler, *Catalogue*, i. 188 (80 foll.), and Kielhorn, *l. c.*, p. 10 (fragment).

[113] Johäntgen in his valuable tract *Ueber das Gesetzbuch des Manu* (1863), p. 109, ff., has, from the geographical data in Manu, ii. 17, ff., fixed the territory between the Dṛishadvatí and Sarasvatí as the proper home of the Mánavas. This appears somewhat too strict. At any rate, the statements as to the extent of the Madhyadeśa which are found in the Pratijñá-Pariśishṭa of the White Yajus point us for the latter more to the east; see my essay *Ueber das Pratijná-Sútra* (1872), pp. 101, 105.

[114] See Johäntgen, *l. c.*, p. 108, 109.

* Their number is twenty; see Roth, *Zur Litt. und Gesch.*, pp. 65, 66.

† See *I. St.*, i. 441 not. [xiii. 387, ff., 418].

also the contradistinction, found at the close of the work, of *Chhandas* and *Bháshá*, *i.e.*, of Vedic and ordinary language.[115] The work appears also to extend to a portion of the Áraṇyaka of the Black Yajus; whether to the whole cannot yet be ascertained, and is scarcely probable.[116]

In conclusion, I have to notice the two *Anukramaṇís* already mentioned, the one belonging to the Átreya school, the other to the Cháráyaṇíya school of the Káṭhaka. The former[117] deals almost exclusively with the contents of the several sections, which it gives in their order. It consists of two parts. The first, which is in prose, is a mere nomenclature; the second, in thirty-four *ślokas*, is little more. It, however, gives a few particulars besides as to the transmission of the text. To it is annexed a commentary upon both parts, which names each section, together with its opening words and extent. The Anukramaṇí of the Káṭhaka enters but little into the contents; it limits itself, on the contrary, to giving the Ṛishis of the various sections as well as of the separate verses; and here, in the case of the pieces taken from the Ṛik, it not unfrequently exhibits considerable divergence from the statements given in the Anukramaṇí of the latter, citing, in particular, a number of entirely new names. According to the concluding statement, it is the work of Atri, who imparted it to Laugákshi.

We now turn to the *White Yajus.*

With regard, in the first place, to the name itself, it probably refers, as has been already remarked, to the fact that the sacrificial formulas are here separated from their

---

[115] In the passage in question (xxiv. 5), '*chhandobháshá*' means rather 'the Veda language;' see Whitney, p. 417.

[116] We have now an excellent edition of the work by Whitney, *Journal Am. Or. Soc.*, ix. (1871), text, translation, and notes, together with a commentary called *Tribháshyaratna*, by an anonymous author (or is his name Kárttikeya?), a compilation from three older commentaries by Átreya, Máhisheya, and Vararuchi.—No reference to the Taitt. Ár. or Taitt. Bráhm. is made in the text itself; on the contrary, it confines itself exclusively to the Taitt. S. The commentary, however, in some few instances goes beyond the T. S.; see Whitney's special discussion of the points here involved, pp. 422–426; cf. also *I. St.*, iv. 76–79.

[117] See *I. St.*, iii. 373–401, xii. 350–357, and the similar statements from Bhaṭṭa Bháskara Miśra in Burnell's *Catalogue*, p. 14. The Átreyí text here appears in a special relation to a *sárasvata páṭha*.

ritual basis and dogmatical explanation, and that we have here a systematic and orderly distribution of the matter so confusedly mixed up in the Black Yajus. This is the way in which the expression *śukláni yajúṅshi* is explained by the commentator Dviveda Gaṅga, in the only passage where up till now it has been found in this sense, namely, in the last supplement added to the Vṛihad-Áraṇyaka of the White Yajus. I say in the only passage, for though it appears once under the form *śukrayajúṅshi*, in the Áraṇyaka of the Black Yajus (5. 10), it has hardly the same general meaning there, but probably refers, on the contrary, to the fourth and fifth books of that Áraṇyaka itself. For in the Anukramaṇí of the Átreya school these books bear the name *śukriyakáṇḍa*, because referring to expiatory ceremonies; and this name *śukriya*, 'expiating' [probably rather 'illuminating'?] belongs also to the corresponding parts of the Saṃhitá of the White Yajus, and even to the *sámans* employed at these particular sacrifices.

Another name of the White Yajus is derived from the surname Vájasaneya, which is given to Yájnavalkya, the teacher who is recognised as its author, in the supplement to the Vṛihad-Áraṇyaka, just mentioned. Mahídhara, at the commencement of his commentary on the Saṃhitá of the White Yajus, explains Vájasaneya as a patronymic, "the son of Vájasani." Whether this be correct, or whether the word *vájasani* is to be taken as an appellative, it at any rate signifies * "the giver of food," and refers to the chief object lying at the root of all sacrificial ceremonies, the obtaining of the necessary food from the gods whom the sacrifices are to propitiate. To this is also to be traced the name *vájin*, "having food," by which the theologians of the White Yajus are occasionally distinguished.[118] Now, from Vájasaneya are derived two forms of words by which the Saṃhitá and Bráhmaṇa of the White Yajus are found

* In Mahá-Bhárata, xii. 1507, the word is an epithet of Kṛishṇa. [Here also it is explained as above; for the Rik, however, according to the St. Petersburg Dictionary, we have to assign to it the meaning of 'procuring courage or strength, victorious, gaining booty or prize.' The explanation of the word *vája* by 'food' (*anna*) is probably purely a scholastic one.]

118 According to another explanation, this is because the Sun as Horse revealed to Yájnavalkya the *ayátayámasaṃjnáni yajúṅshi*; see Vishṇu-Puráṇa, iii. 5. 28; 'swift, courageous, horse,' are the fundamental meanings of the word.

cited, namely, *Vájasaneyaka*, first used in the Taittiríya-Sútra of Ápastamba and the Kátíya-Sútra of the White Yajus itself, and *Vájasaneyinas*,* *i.e.*, those who study the two works in question, first used in the Anupada-Sútra of the Sámaveda.

In the White Yajus we find, what does not occur in the case of any other Veda, that Saṃhitá and Bráhmaṇa have been handed down in their entirety in two distinct recensions; and thus we obtain a measure for the mutual relations of such schools generally. These two recensions agree almost entirely in their contents, as also in the distribution of them; in the latter respect, however, there are many, although slight, discrepancies. The chief difference consists partly in actual variants in the sacrificial formulas, as in the Bráhmaṇa, and partly in orthographic or orthoepic peculiarities. One of these recensions bears the name of the *Káṇvas*, the other that of the *Mádhyaṃdinas*, names which have not yet been found in the Sútras or similar writings. The only exception is the Prátiśákhya-Sútra of the White Yajus itself, where there is mention both of a Káṇva and of the Mádhyaṃdinas. In the supplement to the Vṛihad-Áraṇyaka again, in the lists of teachers, a Káṇvíputra (vi. 5 1) and a Mádhyaṃdináyana (iv. 6. 2) at least are mentioned, although only in the Káṇva recension, not in the other; the former being cited among the latest, the latter among the more recent members of the respective lists. The question now arises whether the two recensions are to be regarded as contemporary, or if one is older than the other. It is possible to adopt the latter view, and to consider the Káṇva school as the older one. For not only is Káṇva the name of one of the ancient Ṛishi families of the Ṛigveda—and with the Ṛigveda this recension agrees in the peculiar notation of the cerebral *ḍ* by *l*—but the remaining literature of the White Yajus appears to connect itself rather with the school of the Mádhyaṃdinas. However this may be,[119] we cannot, at

---

* Occurs in the *gaṇa* '*Śaunaka*.' [The Vájasaneyaka is also quoted by Látyáyana.]

[119] The Mádhyaṃdinas are not mentioned in Patañjali's Mahábháshya, but the Káṇvas, the Káṇvaka, a yellow (*piñgala*) Káṇva, and a Káṇvyáyana, and also their pupils, are mentioned; see *I. St.*, xiii. 417, 444. The school of the *Kaṇvás Sauśravasás* is mentioned in the Káṭhaka, see on this *I. St.*, iii. 475,

any rate, assume anything like a long interval between the two recensions; they resemble each other too closely for this, and we should perhaps do better to regard their distinction as a geographical one, orthoepic divergencies generally being best explained by geographical reasons. As to the exact date to be ascribed to these recensions, it may be, as has already been stated in our general survey (p. 10), that we have here historical ground to go upon—a thing which so seldom happens in this field. Arrian, quoting from Megasthenes, mentions a people called *Μαδιανδινοί*, "through whose country flows the river Andhomatí," and I have ventured to suggest that we should understand by these the Mádhyaṃdinas,[120] after whom one of these schools is named, and that therefore this school was either then already in existence, or else grew up at that time or soon afterwards.* The matter cannot indeed be looked upon as certain, for this reason, that *mádhyaṃdina*, 'southern,' might apply in general to any southern people or any southern school; and, as a matter of fact, we find mention of *mádhyaṃdina-Kauthumás*, 'southern Kauthumas.'† In the main, however, this date suits so perfectly that the conjecture is at least not to be rejected offhand. From this, of course, the question of the time of origin of the White Yajus must be strictly separated; it can only be solved from the evidence contained in the

---

and in the Ápastamba-Dharma-Sútra also, reference is sometimes made to a teacher Kaṇva or Káṇva. Kaṇva and Káṇva appear further in the *pravara* section of Áśvaláyana, and in Páṇini himself (iv. 2. 111), &c.

[120] The country of the *Μαδιανδινοί* is situate precisely in the middle of that 'Madhyadeśa' the limits of which are given in the Pratijná-Pariśishṭa; see my paper *Ueber das Pratijná-Sútra*, pp. 101–105.

* Whether, in that case, we may assume that all the works now comprised in the Mádhyaṃdina school had already a place in this redaction is a distinct question. [An interesting remark of Müller's, *Hist. A. S. L.*, p. 453, points out that the Gopatha-Bráhmaṇa, in citing the first words of the different Vedas (i. 29), quotes in the case of the Yajurveda the beginning of the Vájas. S., and not that of the Taitt. S. (or Káṭh.).]

† [Vináyaka designates his Kaushítaki-Bráhmaṇa-Bháshya as *Mádhyaṃdina-Kauthumánugam*; but does he not here mean the two schools so called (Mádhy. and Kauth.)? They appear, in like manner, side by side in an inscription published by Hall, *Journal Am. Or. Soc.*, vi. 539.] In the Káśiká (to Páṇ. vii. 1. 94) a grammarian, Mádhyaṃdini, is mentioned as a pupil of Vyághrapád (*Vyághrapadáṃ varishṭhaḥ*); see Böhtlingk, *Páṇini*, Introd., p. l. On this it is to be remarked, that in the Bráhmaṇa two Vaiyághrapadyas and one Vaiyághrapadíputra are mentioned.

work itself. Here our special task consists in separating the different portions of it, which in its present form are bound up in one whole. Fortunately we have still data enough here to enable us to determine the priority or posteriority of the several portions.

In the first place, as regards the Saṃhitá of the White Yajus, the *Vájasaneyi-Samhitá*, it is extant in both recensions in 40 *adhyáyas*. In the Mádhyaṃdina recension these are divided into 303 *anuvákas* and 1975 *kaṇḍikás*. The first 25 *adhyáyas* contain the formulas for the general sacrificial ceremonial;[121] first (i., ii.) for the new and full-moon sacrifice; then (iii.) for the morning and evening fire sacrifice, as well as for the sacrifices to be offered every four months at the commencement of the three seasons; next (iv.–viii.) for the Soma sacrifice in general, and (ix., x.) for two modifications of it; next (xi.–xviii.) for the construction of altars for sacred fires; next (xix.–xxi.) for the *sautrámaṇí*, a ceremony originally appointed to expiate the evil effects of too free indulgence in the Soma drink; and lastly (xxii.–xxv.) for the horse sacrifice. The last seven of these *adhyáyas* may possibly be regarded as a later addition to the first eighteen. At any rate it is certain that the last fifteen *adhyáyas* which follow them are of later, and possibly of considerably later, origin. In the Anukramaṇí of the White Yajus, which bears the name of Kátyáyana, as well as in a Pariśishṭa[122] to it, and subsequently also in Mahídhara's commentary on the Saṃhitá, xxvi.–xxxv. are expressly called a ***Khila***, or supplement, and xxxvi.–xl., *Śukriya*, a name above explained. This statement the commentary on the Code of Yájnavalkya (called Mitákshará) modifies to this effect, that the *Sukriya* begins at xxx. 3, and that xxxvi. 1 forms the beginning of an Áraṇyaka.* The first four of these later added *adhyáyas* (xxvi.–xxix.) contain sacrificial formulas which belong to the ceremonies treated of in the earlier *adhyáyas*, and

---

121 A comprehensive but condensed exposition of it has been commenced in my papers, *Zur Kenntniss des vedischen Opferrituals*, in *I. St.*, x. 321-396, xiii. 217-292.

122 See my paper, *Ueber das Pratijná-Sútra* (1872), pp. 102–105.

* That a portion of these last books is to be considered as an Áraṇyaka seems to be beyond doubt; for xxxvii.-xxxix., in particular, this is certain, as they are explained in the Áraṇyaka part of the Bráhmaṇa.

must be supplied thereto in the proper place. The ten following *adhyáyas* (xxx.–xxxix.) contain the formulas for entirely new sacrificial ceremonies, viz., the *purusha-medha* (human sacrifice),[123] the *sarva-medha* (universal sacrifice), the *pitṛi-medha* (oblation to the Manes), and the *pravargya* (purificatory sacrifice).[124] The last *adhyáya*, finally, has no sort of direct reference to the sacrificial ceremonial. It is also regarded as an Upanishad,* and is professedly designed to fix the proper mean between those exclusively engaged in sacrificial acts and those entirely neglecting them. It belongs, at all events, to a very advanced stage of speculation, as it assumes a Lord (*íś*) of the universe.†—Independently of the above-mentioned external testimony to the later origin of these fifteen *adhyáyas*, their posteriority is sufficiently proved by the relation in which they stand both to the Black Yajus and to their own Bráhmaṇa, as well as by the data they themselves contain. In the Taittiríya-Saṃhitá only those formulas appear which are found in the first eighteen *adhyáyas*, together with a few of the *mantras* belonging to the horse sacrifice; the remainder of the latter, together with the *mantras* belonging to the *sautrámaṇí* and the human sacrifice, are only treated of in the Taittiríya-Bráhmaṇa; and those for the universal and the purificatory sacrifices, as well as those for oblations to the Manes, only in the Taittiríya-Áraṇyaka. In like manner, the first eighteen *adhyáyas* are cited in full, and explained word by word in the first nine books of the Bráhmaṇa of the White Yajus; but only a few of the formulas for the *sautrámaṇí*, the horse sacrifice, human sacrifice, universal

---

123 See my essay, *Ueber Menschenopfer bei den Indern der vedischen Zeit*, in *I. Str.*, i. 54, ff.

124 This translation of the word *pravargya* is not a literal one (for this see the St. Petersburg Dict., under root *varj* with prep. *pra*), but is borrowed from the sense and purpose of the ceremony in question; the latter is, according to Haug on Ait. Bráhm., i. 18, p. 42, "a preparatory rite intended for providing the sacrificer with a heavenly body, with which alone he is permitted to enter the residence of the gods."

* Other parts, too, of the Vájas. S. have in later times been looked upon as Upanishads; for example, the sixteenth book (*Śatarudriya*), the thirty-first (*Purusha-súkta*), thirty-second (*Tadeva*), and the beginning of the thirty-fourth book (*Śivasaṃkalpa*).

† According to Mahídhara's commentary, its polemic is directed partially against the Bauddhas, that is, probably, against the doctrines which afterwards were called Sáṃkhya.

sacrifice, and oblation to the Manes (xix.–xxxv.) are cited in the twelfth and thirteenth books, and that for the most part only by their initial words, or even merely by the initial words of the *anuvákas,* without any sort of explanation; and it is only the three last *adhyáyas* but one (xxxvii.–xxxix.) which are again explained word by word, in the beginning of the fourteenth book. In the case of the *mantras,* but slightly referred to by their initial words, explanation seems to have been considered unnecessary, probably because they were still generally understood; we have, therefore, of course, no guarantee that the writer of the Bráhmana had them before him in the form which they bear at present. As to those *mantras,* on the contrary, which are not mentioned at all, the idea suggests itself that they may not yet have been incorporated into the Saṃhitá text extant when the Bráhmaṇa was composed. They are, roughly speaking, of two kinds. First, there are strophes borrowed from the Ṛik, and to be recited by the Hotar, which therefore, strictly speaking, ought not to be contained in the Yajus at all, and of which it is possible that the Bráhmaṇa may have taken no notice, for the reason that it has nothing to do with the special duties of the Hotar; *e.g.,* in the twentieth, thirty-third, and thirty-fourth *adhyáyas* especially. Secondly, there are passages of a Bráhmaṇa type, which are not, however, intended, as in the Black Yajus, to serve as an explanation of *mantras* preceding them, but stand independently by themselves; *e.g.,* in particular, several passages in the nineteenth *adhyáya,* and the enumeration, in the form of a list, of the animals to be dedicated at the horse sacrifice, in the twenty-fourth *adhyáya.* In the first eighteen *adhyáyas* also, there occur a few sacrificial formulas which the Bráhmaṇa either fails to mention (and which, therefore, at the time when it was composed, did not form part of the Saṃhitá), or else cites only by their initial words, or even merely by the initial words of the *anuvákas.* But this only happens in the sixteenth, seventeenth, and eighteenth *adhyáyas,* though here with tolerable frequency, evidently because these *adhyáyas* themselves bear more or less the character of a Bráhmaṇa.—With regard, lastly, to the data contained in the last *adhyáyas,* and testifying to their posteriority, these are to be sought more especially in the thirtieth and thirty-ninth *adhyáyas*, as compared with the sixteenth. It is, of course, only the Yajus portions proper which can here be adduced, and not the verses borrowed from the Rik-Saṃhitá, which naturally prove nothing in this connection. At most they can only yield a sort of measure for the time of their incorporation into the Yajus, in so far as they may be taken from the latest portions of the Rik, in which case the existence of these at that period would necessarily be presupposed. The data referred to consist in two facts. First, whereas in the sixteenth book Rudra, as the god of the blazing fire, is endowed with a large number of the epithets subsequently applied to Śiva, two very significant epithets are here wanting which are applied to him in the thirty-ninth book, viz., *íśána* and *mahádeva*, names probably indicating some kind of sectarian worship (see above, p. 45). Secondly, the number of the mixed castes given in the thirtieth is much higher than that given in the sixteenth book. Those mentioned in the former can hardly all have been in existence at the time of the latter, or we should surely have found others specified besides those that are actually mentioned.

Of the forty books of the Saṃhitá, the sixteenth and thirtieth are those which bear most distinctly the stamp of the time to which they belong. The sixteenth book, on which, in its Taittiríya form, the honour was afterwards bestowed of being regarded as an Upanishad, and as the principal book of the Śiva sects, treats of the propitiation of Rudra; and (see *I. St.*, ii. 22, 24–26) by its enumeration and distinction of the many different kinds of thieves, robbers, murderers, night-brawlers, and highwaymen, his supposed servants, reveals to us a time of insecurity and violence: its mention, too, of various mixed castes indicates that the Indian caste system and polity were already fully developed. Now as, in the nature of things, these were not established without vigorous opposition from those who were thrust down into the lower castes, and as this opposition must have manifested itself chiefly in feuds, open or secret, with their oppressors, I am inclined to suppose that this Rudra book dates from the time of these secret feuds on the part of the conquered aborigines, as well as of the Vrátyas or unbrahmanised Aryans, after their open resistance had been more or less crushed.[125] At such a time, the worship of a god who passes as the prototype of terror and fury is quite intelligible.—The thirtieth book, in enumerating the different classes of persons to be dedicated at the *purusha-medha*, gives the names of most of the Indian mixed castes, whence we may at any rate conclude that the complete consolidation of the Brahmanical polity had then been effected. Some of the names here given are of peculiar interest. So, for example, the *mágadha*, who is dedicated in v. 5 "*atikrushṭáya*." The question arises, What is to be understood by *mágadha?* If we take *atikrushṭa* in the sense of "great noise," the most obvious interpretation of *mágadha* is to understand it, with Mahídhara, in its epic sense, as signifying a minstrel,* son of a Vaiśya by a Kshatriyá. This agrees excellently with the dedications immediately following (in v. 6), of the *súta* to the dance, and of the *śailúsha* to song, though not so well, it must be admitted, with the dedications immediately preceding, of the *klíba* (eunuch), the *ayogú* (gambler?), and the *puńśchalú* (harlot). The *mágadha* again appears in their company in v. 22,† and they cannot be said to throw the best light upon his moral character, a circumstance which is certainly surprising, considering the position held by this caste in the epic; though, on the other hand, in India also, musicians, dancers, and singers (*śailúshas*) have not at any time enjoyed the best reputation. But another interpretation of the word *mágadha* is possible.‡ In the fifteenth, the

---

[125] By the Buddhist author Yaśomitra, scholiast of the Abhidharmakośa, the Śatarudriya is stated to be a work by Vyása against Buddhism, whence, however, we have probably to conclude only that it passed for, and was used as, a principal support for Śiva worship, especially in its detached form as a separate Upanishad; see Burnouf's *Introduction à l'Histoire du Buddhisme*, p. 568; *I. St.*, ii. 22.

* How he comes by this name is, it is true, not clear.

† Here, however, the *kitava* is put instead of the *ayogú*, and besides, an express condition is laid down that the four must belong neither to the Śúdra nor to the Bráhmaṇa caste. [By *ayogú* may also be meant an unchaste woman; see *I. Str.*, i. 76]

‡ Sáyaṇa, commenting on the corresponding passage of the Taitt. Bráhmaṇa (iii. 4. 1), explains the word *atikrushṭáya* by *atininditadeváya*, "dedicated to the very Blameworthy as his deity" [in Rájendra Lála Mitra's edition, p. 347]; this 'very Blameworthy,' it is true, might also refer to the bad moral reputation of the minstrels.

so-called Vrátya book* of the Atharva-Saṃhitá, the Vrátya (*i.e.*, the Indian living outside of the pale of Brahmanism) is brought into very special relation to the *puṅśchalí* and the *mágadha;* faith is called his harlot, the *mitra* (friend ?) his *mágadha;* and similarly the dawn, the earth (?), the lightning his harlots, the *mantra* (formula), *hasa* (scorn ?), the thunder his *mágadhas.* Owing to the obscurity of the Vrátya book, the proper meaning of this passage is not altogether clear, and it is possible, therefore, that here also the dissolute minstrel might be intended. Still the connection set forth in the Sáma-Sútras of Láṭyáyana and Dráhyáyaṇa, as well as in the corresponding passage of the Kátíya-Sútra between the Vrátyas and the *magadhadeśíya brahmabandhu,*[126] and the hatred with which the Magadhas are elsewhere (see Roth, p. 38) spoken of in the Atharva-Saṃhitá, both lead us to interpret the *mágadha* of the Vrátya book as an heretical teacher. For the passages, also, which we are more immediately discussing, this interpretation vies with the one already given; and it seems, in particular, to be favoured by the express direction in v. 22, that "the *mágadha,* the harlot, the gambler, and the eunuch" must neither be Śúdras nor Brahmans,—an injunction which would be entirely superfluous for the *mágadha* at least, supposing him to represent a mixed caste, but which is quite appropriate if the word signifies "a native of the country Magadha." If we adopt this latter interpretation, it follows that heretical (*i.e.*, Buddhist) opinions must have existed in Magadha at the time of the composition of this thirtieth *adhyáya.* Meanwhile, however, the question which of these two interpretations is the better one remains, of course, unsolved.—The mention of the *nakshatradarśa,* "star-gazer," in v. 10, and of the

* Translated by Aufrecht, *I. St.*, i. 130, ff. [The St. Petersburg Dict., *s. v.*, considers 'the praise of the Vrátya in Ath. xv. as an idealising of the devout vagrant or mendicant (*parivrájaka*, &c.);' the fact of his being specially connected with the *puṅśchalí* and the *mágadha* remains, nevertheless, very strange, and even with this interpretation leads us to surmise suggestions of Buddhism.]

[126] In the very same way, the *Mágadha*—explained by Sáyaṇa as *Magadhadeśotpanno brahmachárí*—is contemptuously introduced by the Sútrakára (probably Baudháyana ?) to T. S., vii. 5. 9. 4, in association with a *puṅśchalí;* see *I. St.*, xii. 330.—That there were good Brahmans also in Magadha appears from the name *Magadhavási*, which is given to Prátibodhíputra, the second son of Hrasva Máṇḍúkeya, in Śáṅkh. Ár., vii. 14.

gaṇaka, "calculator," in v. 20, permits us, at all events, to conclude that astronomical, *i.e.*, astrological, science was then actively pursued. It is to it that, according to Mahídhara at least, the "questions" repeatedly mentioned in v. 10 relate, although Sáyaṇa, perhaps more correctly, thinks that they refer to the usual disputations of the Brahmans. The existence, too, of the so-called Vedic quinquennial cycle is apparent from the fact that in v. 15 (only in xxvii. 45 besides) the five names of its years are enumerated; and this supposes no inconsiderable proficiency in astronomical observation.[127]—A barren wife is dedicated in v. 15 to the Atharvans, by which term Sáyaṇa understands the imprecatory and magical formulas bearing the name Atharvan; to which, therefore, one of their intended effects, barrenness, is here dedicated. If this be the correct explanation, it necessarily follows that Atharvan-songs existed at the time of the thirtieth book.—The names of the three dice in v. 18 (*krita*, *tretá*, and *dvápara*) are explained by Sáyaṇa, commenting on the corresponding passage of the Taittiríya-Bráhmaṇa, as the names of the epic *yugas*, which are identical with these—a supposition which will not hold good here, though it may, perhaps, in the case of the Taittiríya-Bráhmaṇa.*—The hostile reference to the Charakácharya in v. 18 has already been touched upon (p. 87).[128]

In the earlier books there are two passages in particular which give an indication of the period from which they date. The first of these exists only in the Káṇva recension, where it treats of the sacrifice at the consecration of the king. The text in the Mádhyaṃdina recension (ix. 40, x. 18) runs as follows: "This is your king, O ye So and So," where, instead of the name of the people, only the indefinite pronoun *amí* is used; whereas in the Káṇva

---

127 Since *saṃvatsara* is here mentioned twice, at the beginning and at the end, possibly we have here to do with a sexennial cycle even (cf. T. Br., iii. 10. 4. 1); see my paper, *Die vedischen Nachrichten von den Nakshatra*, ii. 298 (1862). The earliest allusion to the quinquennial *yuga* occurs in the Ṛik itself, iii. 55. 18 (i. 25. 8).

* Where, moreover, the fourth name, *kali*, is found, instead of the *áskanda* given here [see *I. Str.*, i. 82].

128 Sáyaṇa on T. Br., iii. 4. 16, p. 361, explains (!) the word by 'teacher of the art of dancing on the point of a bamboo;' but the *vaṃśanartin* is introduced separately in v. 21 (T. Br., iii. 4. 17).

recension we read (xi. 3. 3, 6. 3): "This is your king, O ye Kurus, O ye Pañchálas." * The second passage occurs in connection with the horse sacrifice (xxiii. 18). The *mahishí*, or principal wife of the king, performing this sacrifice, must, in order to obtain a son, pass the night by the side of the horse that has been immolated, placing its *śiśna* on her *upastha;* with her fellow-wives, who are forced to accompany her, she pours forth her sorrow in this lament: "O Ambá, O Ambiká, O Ambáliká, no one takes me (by force to the horse); (but if I go not of myself), the (spiteful) horse will lie with (another, as) the (wicked) Subhadrá who dwells in Kámpíla."† Kámpíla is a town in the country of the Pañchálas. Subhadrá, therefore, would seem to be the wife of the king of that district,‡ and the benefits of the *aśvamedha* sacrifice are supposed to accrue to them, unless the *mahishí* consents voluntarily to give herself up to this revolting ceremony. If we are justified in regarding the *mahishí* as the consort of a king of the Kurus,—and the names Ambiká and Ambáliká actually appear in this connection in the Mahá-Bhárata, to wit, as the names of the mothers of Dhṛitaráshṭra and Páṇḍu,—we might then with probability infer that there existed a hostile, jealous feeling on the part of the Kurus towards the Pañchálas, a feeling which was possibly at that time only smouldering, but which in the epic legend of the Mahá-Bhárata we find had burst out into the flame of open warfare. However this may be, the allusion to Kámpíla at all events betrays that the verse, or even the whole book (as well as the correspond-

---

* Sáyaṇa, on the corresponding passage of the Bráhmaṇa (v. 3. 3. 11), remarks that Baudháyana reads *esha vo Bharatá rájeti* [thus T. S., i. 8. 10. 2; T. Br., i. 7. 4. 2]. Ápastamba, on the contrary, lets us choose between *Bharatá, Kuravo, Pañchálá, Kurupáñchálá*, or *janá rájá*, according to the people to whom the king belongs. [The Káṭh., xv. 7, has *esha te janate rájá*.]

† The Bráhmaṇa of the White Yajus quotes only the beginning of this verse; consequently the words *subhadrikáṃ kámpílavásiním* are wanting in it.

‡ As a matter of fact, we find in the Mahá-Bhárata a Subhadrá as wife of Arjuna, the representative of the Pañchálas; on account of a Subhadrá (possibly on account of her abduction, related in the Mahá-Bhárata?) a great war seems to have arisen, as appears from some words quoted several times by the scholiast on Páṇini. Has he the authority of the Mahábháshya for this? [the Mahábháshya has nothing about it].

ing passages of the Taitt. Bráhmaṇa), originated in the region of the Pañchálas; and this inference holds good also for the eleventh book of the Káṇva recension.[129] We might further adduce in proof of it the use of the word *arjuna* in the Mádhyaṃdina, and of *phalguna* in the Káṇva recension, in a formula[130] relating to the sacrifice at the consecration of the king (x. 21): "To obtain intrepidity, to obtain food(, I, the offerer, ascend) thee(, O chariot,) I, the inviolate Arjuna (Phalguna)," *i.e.*, Indra, Indra-like. For although we must take both these words in this latter sense, and not as proper names (see *I. St.*, i. 190), yet, at any rate, some connection must be assumed between this use and the later one, where they appear as the appellation of the chief hero of the Páṇḍus (or Pañchálas?); and this connection consists in the fact that the legend specially applied these names of Indra* to that hero of the Páṇḍus (or Pañchálas?) who was pre-eminently regarded by it as an incarnation of Indra.

Lastly, as regards the critical relation of the *ṛichas* incorporated into the Yajus, I have to observe, that in general the two recensions of the Káṇvas and of the Mádhyaṃdinas always agree with each other in this particular, and that their differences refer, rather, to the Yajus-portions. One half of the Vájasaneyi-Saṃhitá consists of *ṛichas*, or verses; the other of *yajúṅshi*, *i.e.*, formulas in prose, a measured prose, too, which rises now and then to a true rhythmical swing. The greater number of these *ṛichas*

---

[129] In T. S., vii. 4. 19. 1, Káṭh. Áś., iv. 8, there are two vocatives instead of the two accusatives; besides, we have *subhage* for *subhadráṃ*. The vocative *kámpílavásini* is explained by Sáyaṇa, 'O thou that art veiled in a beautiful garment' (*kámpílaśabdena ślághyo vastraviśesha uchyate*; see *I. St.*, xii. 312). This explanation is hardly justifiable, and Mahídhara's reference of the word to the city of Kámpíla must be retained, at least for the wording of the text which we have in the V. S. In the Pratijñá-Pariśishṭa, Kámpílya is given as the eastern limit of Madhyadeśa; see my *Pratijñásútra*, pp. 101–105.

[130] See V. S., x. 21; the parallel passages in T. S., i. 8, 15, T. Br., i. 7. 9. 1, Káṭh., xv. 8, have nothing of this.

* The Bráhmaṇa, moreover, expressly designates *arjuna* as the 'secret name' (*guhyaṃ náma*) of Indra [ii. 1. 2. 11, v. 4. 3. 7]. How is this to be understood? The commentary remarks on it: *arjuna iti hindrasya rahasyaṃ náma | ata eva khalu tatputre Páṇḍavamadhyame pravṛittiḥ*. [What is the reading of the Káṇva recension in these passages? Has it, as in the Saṃhitá, so here also, not *arjuna*, but *phalguna*?]

recur in the Ṛik-Saṃhitá, and frequently with considerable variations, the origin and explanation of which I have already discussed in the introduction (see above, pp. 9, 10). Readings more ancient than those of the Ṛik are not found in the Yajus, or at least only once in a while, which results mainly from the fact that Ṛik and Yajus agree for the most part with each other, as opposed to the Sáman. We do, however, find that verses have undergone later alterations to adapt them to the sense of the ritual. And finally, we meet with a large number of readings which appear of equal authority with those of the Ṛik, especially in the verses which recur in those portions of the Ṛik-Saṃhitá that are to be regarded as the most modern.

The Vájasaneyi-Saṃhitá, in both recensions, has been edited by myself (Berlin, 1849–52), with the commentary of Mahídhara,[131] written towards the end of the sixteenth century; and in the course of next year a translation is intended to appear, which will give the ceremonial belonging to each verse, together with a full glossary.* Of the work of Uaṭa, a predecessor of Mahídhara, only fragments have been preserved, and the commentary of Mádhava, which related to the Káṇva recension,[132] appears to be entirely lost. Both were supplanted by Mahídhara's work, and consequently obliterated; an occurrence which has happened in a similar way in almost all branches of Indian literature, and is greatly to be regretted.

I now turn to the *Bráhmaṇa* of the White Yajus, the *Śatapatha-Bráhmaṇa*, which, from its compass and contents, undoubtedly occupies the most significant and important position of all the Bráhmaṇas. First, as to its

---

[131] For which, unfortunately, no sufficient manuscript materials were at my disposal; see Müller, Preface to vol. vi. of his large edition of the Ṛik, p. xlvi. sqq., and my reply in *Literarisches Centralblatt*, 1875, pp. 519, 520.

* [This promise has not been fulfilled, owing to the pressure of other labours.] The fortieth *adhyáya*, the Îśopanishad, is in the Káṇva recension commented by Śaṃkara; it has been translated and edited several times together with this commentary (lately again by Roer in the *Bibliotheca Indica*, vol. viii.) [and vol. xv.—A lithographed edition of the text of the Vájas. Saṃhitá, with a Hindí translation of Mahídhara's commentary, has been published by Giriprasádavarman, Rája of Besma, 1870-74, in Besma].

[132] Upon what this special statement is based I cannot at present show; but that Mádhava commented the V. S. also is shown, for example, by the quotation in Mahídhara to xiii. 45.

extent,—this is sufficiently denoted by its very name, which describes it as consisting of 100 *pathas* (paths), or sections. The earliest known occurrence of this name is in the ninth *várttika* to Páṇ. iv. 2. 60, and in the *gaṇa* to Páṇ. v. 3. 100, both authorities of very doubtful* antiquity. The same remark applies to the *Naigeya-daivata*, where the name also appears (see Benfey's *Sámaveda*, p. 277). With the single exception of a passage in the twelfth book of the Mahá-Bhárata, to which I shall revert in the sequel, I have only met with it, besides, in the commentaries and in the colophons of the MSS. of the work itself. In the Mádhyamdina school the Śatapatha-Bráhmaṇa consists of fourteen *káṇḍas*, each of which bears a special title in the commentaries and in the colophons: these titles are usually borrowed from the contents; ii. and vii. are, however, to me inexplicable.† The fourteen *káṇḍas* are together subdivided into 100 *adhyáyas* (or 68 *prapáṭhakas*), 438 *bráhmaṇas*, and 7624 *kaṇḍikás*.[133] In the Káṇva recension the work consists of seventeen *káṇḍas*, the first, fifth, and fourteenth books being each divided into two parts; the first book, moreover, has here changed places with the second, and forms, consequently, the second and third. The names of the books are the same, but the division into *prapáṭhakas* is altogether unknown: the *adhyáyas* in the thirteen and a half books that have thus far been recovered‡ number 85, the *bráhmaṇas* 360, the *kaṇḍikás* 4965. The total for the whole work amounts, according to a list accompanying one of the manuscripts, to 104 *adhyáyas*, 446 *bráhmaṇas*, 5866 *kaṇḍikás*. If from this the recension of the Káṇva school seems considerably

* The *gaṇa* is an *ákṛitigaṇa*, and the *sútra* to which it belongs is, according to the Calcutta edition, not explained in the Mahábháshya; possibly therefore it does not belong to the original text of Páṇini. [The *várttika* in question is, in point of fact, explained in the Mahábháshya (fol. 67ᵇ), and thus the existence of the name *śatapatha*, as well as *shashṭipatha* (see p. 119), is guaranteed, at least for the time when this work was composed; see *I. St.*, xiii. 443.]

† The name of the second book is *Ekapádiká*, that of the seventh *Hastighaṭa*.

[133] For statements disagreeing with this, which are found in the MSS., see note on pp. 119, 120.

‡ Of the fourth book there exists only the first half; and the third, thirteenth, and sixteenth books are wanting altogether. [It is much to be regretted that nothing has yet been done for the Káṇva recension, and that a complete copy has not yet been recovered.]

shorter than that of the Mádhyamdinas, it is so only in appearance; the disparity is probably rather to be explained by the greater length of the *kaṇḍikás* in the former. Omissions, it is true, not unfrequently occur. For the rest, I have no means of ascertaining with perfect accuracy the precise relation of the Bráhmaṇa of the Káṇva school to that of the Mádhyamdinas; and what I have to say in the sequel will therefore relate solely to the latter, unless I expressly mention the former.

As I have already remarked, when speaking of the Saṃhitá, the first nine *káṇḍas* of the Bráhmaṇa refer to the first eighteen books of the Saṃhitá; they quote the separate verses in the same order* word for word, explaining them dogmatically, and establishing their connection with the ritual. The tenth *káṇḍa*, which bears the name of *Agni-rahasya* ("the mystery of fire"), contains mystical legends and investigations as to the significance, &c., of the various ceremonies connected with the preparation of the sacred fires, without referring to any particular portions of the Saṃhitá. This is the case likewise in the eleventh *káṇḍa*, called from its extent *Ashṭádhyáyí*, which contains a recapitulation of the entire ritual already discussed, with supplements thereto, especially legends bearing upon it, together with special particulars concerning the study of the sacred works and the provisions made for this purpose. The twelfth *káṇḍa*, called *Madhyama*, "the middle one," treats of *práyaśchittas* or propitiatory ceremonies for untoward events, either previous to the sacrifice, during, or after it; and it is only in its last portion, where the Sautrámaṇí is discussed, that it refers to certain of the formulas contained in the Saṃhitá (xix.–xxi.) and relating to this ceremony. The thirteenth *káṇḍa*, called *Aśvamedha*, treats at some length of the horse sacrifice; and then with extreme brevity of the human sacrifice, the universal sacrifice, and the sacrifice to the Manes; touching upon the relative portions of the Saṃhitá (xxii.–xxxv.) but very seldom, and even then very slightly. The fourteenth *káṇḍa*, called *Áraṇyaka*, treats in its first three *adhyáyas*

* Only in the introduction does a variation occur, as the Bráhmaṇa treats first of the morning and evening sacrifices, and not till afterwards of the new moon and full moon sacrifices, which is evidently more correct systematically.

of the purification of the fire,[134] and here it quotes almost in their entirety the three last books but one of the Samhitá (xxxvii.–xxxix.); the last six *adhyáyas* are of a purely speculative and legendary character, and form by themselves a distinct work, or Upanishad, under the name of *Vṛihad-Áraṇyaka.* This general summary of the contents of the several *káṇḍas* of itself suggests the conjecture that the first nine constitute the most ancient part of the Bráhmaṇa, and that the last five, on the contrary, are of later origin,—a conjecture which closer investigation reduces to a certainty, both on external and internal evidence. With reference to the external evidence, in the first place, we find it distinctly stated in the passage of the Mahá-Bhárata above alluded to (xii. 11734) that the complete Śatapatha comprises a *Rahasya* (the tenth *káṇḍa*), a *Saṃgraha* (the eleventh *káṇḍa*), and a *Pariśesha* (the twelfth, thirteenth, and fourteenth *káṇḍas*). Further, in the *várttika* already quoted for the name Śatapatha, we also meet with the word *shashṭipatha*[135] as the name of a work; and I have no hesitation in referring this name to the first nine *káṇḍas*, which collectively number sixty *adhyáyas.* On the other hand, in support of the opinion that the last five *káṇḍas* are a later addition to the first nine, I have to adduce the term *Madhyama* ("the middle one"), the name of the twelfth *káṇḍa*, which can only be accounted for in this way, whether we refer it merely to the last three *káṇḍas* but one, or to all the five.*

---

[134] The *pravargya* concerns, rather, the lustration of the sacrificer himself; see above note 124, p. 108.

[135] It is found in the Pratijná-Pariśishṭa also, and along with it the name *aśítipatha* (!); *śatapatha*, on the contrary, is apparently wanting there; see my essay on the Pratijná-Sútra, pp. 104, 105.

* In the latter case a difficulty is caused by the Káṇva recension, which subdivides the last *káṇḍa* into two parts (xvi., xvii.); this division, however, seems not to have been generally received, since in the MSS. of Śaṃkara's commentary, at least, the Upanishad (xvii.) is reckoned throughout as beginning with the third *adhyáya* (viz., of the *káṇḍa*), so that xvi. and xvii. coincide.—[A highly remarkable statement is found in the MSS. of the Mádhyaṃdina recension at v. 3. 1. 14, to the effect that this point marks not only *káṇḍasyá 'rdham*, with 236 *kaṇḍikás*, but also, according to a marginal gloss, *śatapathasyá 'rdham*, with 3129 *kaṇḍikás*; see p. 497 of my edition. As a matter of fact, the preceding *kaṇḍikás* do amount to this latter number; but if we fix it as the norm for the second half, we are only brought down to xii. 7. 3. 18, that is, not even to the close of the twelfth book! The point which marks the exact half for the

Now these last five *káṇḍas* appear to stand in the same order in which they actually and successively originated; so that each succeeding one is to be regarded as less ancient than the one that precedes it. This conjecture is based on internal evidence drawn from the data therein contained,—evidence which at the same time decides the question of their being posterior to the first nine *káṇḍas.* In the first place, the tenth *káṇḍa* still connects itself pretty closely with the preceding books, especially in its great veneration for Śáṇḍilya, the principal authority upon the building of altars for the sacred fires. The following are the data which seem to me to favour the view that it belongs to a different period from the first nine books. In i. 5. 1, ff., all the sacrifices already discussed in the preceding books are enumerated in their proper order, and identified with the several ceremonies of the Agni-chayana, or preparation of the sacred fireplace.—Of the names of teachers here mentioned, several end in *-áyana,* a termination of which we find only one example in the seventh, eighth, and ninth *káṇḍas* respectively: thus we meet here with a Rauhiṇáyana, Sáyakáyana, Vámakakshâyana (also in vii.), Rájastambáyana, Śáṇḍilyáyana (also in ix.), Sáṭyáyani (also in viii.), and the Śákáyanins.—The Vaṅśa appended at the close (*i.e.*, the list of the teachers of this book) differs from the general Vaṅśa of the entire Bráhmaṇa (at the close of the fourteenth book) in not referring the work to Yájnavalkya, but to Śáṇḍilya, and also to Tura Kávasheya (whose ancestor Kavasha we find on the banks of the Sarasvatí in the Aitareya-Bráhmaṇa). The only tribes mentioned are the Salvas and Kekayas (especially their king, Aśvapati Kaikeya),—two western tribes not elsewhere alluded to in the Bráhmaṇas.—The

present extent of the work (3812 *k.*) is at vi. 7. 1. 19, where also the MSS. repeat the above statement (p. 555).—It deserves special mention that the notation of the accents operates beyond the limits of the individual *kaṇḍikás,* the accent at the end of a *kaṇḍiká* being modified by the accent of the first word of the next *kaṇḍiká.* From this we might perhaps conclude that the marking of the accents is earlier in date than the division of the text into *kaṇḍikás.* As, however, we find exactly the same state of things with regard to the final and initial words of the individual *bráhmaṇas* (see *Jenaer Literaturzeitung,* 1875, p. 314), we should also have to refer the *bráhmaṇa* division to a later date, and this is hardly possible].

legends here as well as in the four succeeding *káṇḍas* are mostly of an historical character, and are besides chiefly connected with individual teachers who cannot have lived at a time very distant from that of the legends themselves. In the earlier *káṇḍas*, on the contrary, the legends are mostly of a mythological character, or, if historical, refer principally to occurrences belonging to remote antiquity; so that here a distinct difference is evident.—The *trayí vidyá* (the three Vedas) is repeatedly discussed in a very special manner, and the number of the *ṛichas* is stated to be 12,000, that of the *yajus*-verses 8000, and that of the *sámans* 4000. Here also for the first time appear the names Adhvaryus, Bahvṛichas, and Chhandogas side by side;* here, too, we have the first occurrence of the words *upanishad* (as *sára* of the Veda), *upanishadám ádeśáḥ*, *mímáṅsá* (mentioned once before, it is true, in the first *káṇḍa*), *adhidevatam, adhiyajnam, adhyátmam*;[136] and lastly, here for the first time we have the form of address *bhaván* (instead of the earlier *bhagaván*). Now and then also a *śloka* is quoted in confirmation, a thing which occurs extremely seldom in the preceding books. Further, many of the technical names of the *sámans* and *śastras* are mentioned (this, however, has occurred before, and also in the tenth book of the Saṃhitá); and generally, frequent reference is made to the connection subsisting with the *ṛichas* and *sámans*, which harmonises with the peculiarly mystical and systematising character of the whole *káṇḍa*.

That the eleventh *káṇḍa* is a supplement to the first nine is sufficiently evident from its contents. The first two *adhyáyas* treat of the sacrifices at the new and full moon; the four following, of the morning and evening sacrificial fires, of the sacrifices at the three seasons of the year, of the inauguration of the pupil by the teacher (*áchárya*), of the proper study of the sacred doctrines, &c.; and the last two, of the sacrifices of animals. The *Ṛigveda, Yajurveda*, and *Sámaveda*, the *Atharváṅgirasas*, the *anuśásanas*, the *vidyás*, the *vákovákya*, the *itihaśapuráṇa*, the *náráśaṅsís*, and the *gáthás* are named as subjects of study. We have

* Along with the *yátuvidas* (those skilful in witchcraft), *sarpavidas* (serpent-charmers), *devajanavidas*, &c.

[136] *Mímáṅsá*, *adhidaivataṃ*, and *adhyátmaṃ* occur several times in the earlier books.

already met with this enumeration (see p. 93) in the second chapter of the Taitt. Áraṇyaka, although in a considerably later form,* and we find a similar one in the fourteenth *káṇḍa*. In all these passages, the commentaries,† probably with perfect justice, interpret these expressions in this way, viz., that first the Saṃhitás are specified, and then the different parts of the Bráhmaṇas; so that by the latter set of terms we should have to understand, not distinct species of works, but only the several portions respectively so designated which were blended together in the Bráhmaṇas, and out of which the various branches of literature were in course of time gradually developed. The terms *anuśásana* ("ritual precept" according to Sáyaṇa, but in Vṛihad-Ár., ii. 5. 19, iv. 3. 25, Kaṭhopan., 6. 15, "spiritual doctrine"), *vidyá*, "spiritual doctrine," and *gáthá*, "strophe of a song" (along with *śloka*), are in fact so used in a few passages (*gáthá* indeed pretty frequently) in these last five books, and in the Bráhmaṇas or Upanishads of the Ṛik and Sáman. Similarly *vákovákya* in the sense of "disputation" occurs in the seventh *káṇḍa*, and *itihása* at least once in the eleventh *káṇḍa* itself (i. 6. 9). It is only the expressions *puráṇa* and *náráśaṅsís* that do not thus occur; in their stead—in the sense of narrative, legend—we find, rather, the terms *ákhyána*, *vyákhyána*, *anvákhyána*, *upákhyána*. *Vyákhyána*, together with *anuvyákhyána* and *uparyákhyána*, also occurs in the sense of "explanation." In these expressions, accordingly, we have evidence that at the time of this eleventh *káṇḍa* certain Saṃhitás and Bráhmaṇas of the various Vedas, and even the Atharva-Saṃhitá itself, were in existence. But, further, as bearing upon this point, in addition to the single verses from the songs of the Ṛik, which are here, as in the earlier books, frequently cited (by "*tad etad ṛishiṇá 'bhyanúktam*"), we have in the eleventh *káṇḍa* one very special quotation, extending over an entire hymn, and introduced by the words "*tad etad uktapratyuktam pañchadaśarcham Bahvṛicháḥ práhuḥ*." It is an interesting fact for the critic that in our text of the Ṛik the hymn in question

* From it has evidently originated a passage in Yájnavalkya's Code (i. 45), which does not harmonise at all with the rest of that work.

† Here Sáyaṇa forms an exception, as he at least states the other explanation also.

(*maṇḍ.* x. 95) numbers not fifteen but eighteen *ṛichas.* Single *ślokas* are also frequently quoted as confirmation. From one of these it appears that the care taken of horses in the palace of Janamejaya had at that time passed into a proverb: this is also the first mention of this king. Rudra here for the first time receives the name of Mahádeva * (v. 3. 5).—In iii. 3. 1, ff., special rules are for the first time given concerning the begging (*bhikshá*) of the *brahmachárins,* &c., which custom is besides alluded to in the thirtieth book of the Saṃhitá [v. 18].—But what throws special light upon the date of the eleventh *káṇḍa* is the frequent mention here made, and for the first time, of Janaka, king (*samráj*) of Videha, as the patron of Yájnavalkya. The latter, the Kaurupañchála Uddálaka Áruṇi and his son Śvetaketu, are (as in the Vṛihad-Áraṇyaka) the chief figures in the legends.

The twelfth *káṇḍa* alludes to the destruction of the kingdom of the Sṛiñjayas, whom we find in the second *káṇḍa* at the height of their prosperity, and associated with the Kurus. This connection may still be traced here, for it seems as if the Kauravya Valhika Prátipíya wished to take their part against Chákra, their enemy, who was a native of the country south of the Revá, and priest of King Dushṭarítu of Daśapurushaṃrájya, but that his efforts failed.—The names Várkali (*i.e.,* Váshkali) and Náka Maudgalya probably also point to a later period of time; the latter does not occur elsewhere except in the Vṛihad-Áraṇyaka and the Taittiríyopanishad.—The Ṛigveda, the Yajurveda, and the Sámaveda are mentioned, and we find testimony to the existence of the Vedic literature generally in the statement that a ceremony once taught by Indra to Vasishṭha and formerly only known to the Vásishṭhas—whence in former times only a Vásishṭha could act as *brahman* (high priest) at its performance—might now be studied by any one who liked, and consequently that any one might officiate as *brahman* thereat.[137]—In iii. 4. 1 occurs the first mention of *purusha Náráyaṇa.*—The name of Proti Kauśámbeya Kausurubindi probably presupposes the existence of the Pañchála city Kauśámbí.

---

* In the sixth *káṇḍa* he is still called *mahán devaḥ.*

137 See on this *I. St.,* x. 34, 35.

The thirteenth *káṇḍa* repeatedly mentions *purusha Náráyaṇa.* Here also Kuvera Vaiśravaṇa, king of the Rakshasas, is named for the first time. So, too, we find here the first allusion to the *súktas* of the Ṛik, the *anuvákas** of the Yajus, the *daśats* of the Sáman, and the *parvans* of the Atharváṇas and Añgirasas, which division, however, does not appear in the extant text of the Atharvan. A division into *parvans* is also mentioned in connection with the Sarpavidyá and the Devajanavidyá, so that by these names at all events distinct works must be understood. Of Itihása and Puráṇa nothing but the name is given; they are not spoken of as divided into *parvans*, a clear proof that even at that time they were merely understood as isolated stories and legends, and not as works of any extent.[138]—While in the first nine books the statement that a subject has been fully treated of already is expressed by *tasyokto bandhuḥ* [or, *so 'sáv eva bandhuḥ*, and the like], the same is expressed here by *tasyoktam bráhmaṇam.*—The use in v. 1. 18 of the words *ekavachana* and *bahuvachana* exactly corresponds to their later grammatical signification.—This *káṇḍa* is, however, very specially distinguished by the number of *gáthás*, strophes of historical purport, which it quotes at the close of the account of the horse sacrifice, and in which are given the names of kings who celebrated it in earlier times. Only one of these *gáthás* appears in the Ṛik-Saṃhitá (*maṇḍ.* iv. 42. 8); the greater number of them recur in the last book of the Aitareya-Bráhmaṇa, and in the Mahá-Bhárata, xii. 910, ff., in both places with many variations.† The question here arises whether we have to regard these *gáthás* as fragments of more lengthy hymns, or if they must be looked upon merely as separate memorial verses. The fact that in connection with some of these names (if we take into account

* This term, however, occurs in the preceding *káṇḍas* also, *e.g.*, in ix. 1. 1. 15.

[138] This is favoured also by the fact that they are here attributed to fishermen and fowlers; with which may be compared the tale of the fishermaiden as mother of Vyása, in the Mahá-Bhárata. The whole statement recurs in almost identical terms in the Śáñkh. Śr., xvi. 2; Áśval. Śr., x. 7.

† The passages in the Mahá-Bhárata evidently connect themselves with the Śatapatha-Bráhmaṇa, to which, as well as to its author Yájnavalkya, and his patron Janaka, special regard is had in this book of the Mahá-Bhárata. [See also Śáñkh., xvi. 8. 25-29. 32.]

the Aitareya-Bráhmaṇa also) two, three, four, five, and even six verses are quoted, and always in the same metre, in *ślokas*, certainly favours the former view. Only one exception occurs where the first and fourth verses are *ślokas*, but the second *trishṭubh*, the third not being quoted at all; it is, however, according to the commentary, understood by implication, so that this instance tells, perhaps, with a very special force in favour of the view in question. The analogy of the *gáthás* or *ślokas* of non-historic purport quoted elsewhere cannot be brought forward in support either of the one view or of the other, for the very same uncertainty exists respecting them. Moreover, these verses repeatedly contain very old Vedic forms.* Again, their expressions of eulogy are for the most part very hyperbolical, and they might therefore perhaps be looked upon as the utterance of a still fresh feeling of gratitude; so that we should have to consider their origin as in part contemporary with the princes they extol: otherwise this circumstance does not readily admit of explanation.† A passage in the thirteenth *káṇḍa* itself directly favours this view (see *I. St.*, i. 187). Among the kings here named the following deserve special mention: Bharata, son of Duḥshanta and the Apsaras Śakuntalá, and descendant of Sudyumna—Śatáníka ‡ Sátrájita, king of the Bharatas, and enemy of Dhṛitaráshṭra, king of the Káśis—Purukutsa § Aikshváka—Para Áṭṇára Hairaṇyanábha Kausalya — but above all, Janamejaya Párikshita, with the Párikshitíyas (his three brothers), Bhímasena, Ugrasena, and Śrutasena, who by means of the horse sacrifice were absolved from "all guilt, all *brahmahatyá*." The time when these last four lived cannot be considered as very distant from that of the *káṇḍa* itself, since their sacrificial priest Indrota Daivápa Śaunaka (whom the Mahá-Bhárata, xii. 5595, also specifies as such) is once mentioned in it apparently as coming forward in opposi-

* And names too: thus, the king of the Pañchálas is called Kraivya, the explanation given by the Bráhmaṇa being that the Pañchálas were 'formerly' called Krivis.

† Unless these verses were merely invented by priests in order to stimulate kings to copy and emulate the liberality of their ancestors. Still this is both in itself a very forced explanation, and besides many of these verses are of purely historical purport, and contain no allusion to the presents given to the priests.

‡ See Váj. S., 34. 52 (not in the Ṛik).

§ See Ṛik, *maṇḍ.* iv. 42. 8.

tion to Bhállaveya; while his own opinion, differing from that of the latter, is in turn rejected by Yájnavalkya. On account of the interest of the subject I introduce here another passage from the fourteenth book, from which we may gather the same result. We there find a rival of Yájnavalkya testing him with a question, the solution of which the former had previously obtained from a Gandharva, who held in his possession the daughter of Kápya Patamchala of the country of the Madras;—the question, namely, "Whither have the Párikshitas gone?" the solution of which therefore appears to have been looked upon as extremely difficult. Yájnavalkya answers: "Thither where (all) *aśvamedha* sacrificers go." Consequently the Párikshitas must at that time have been altogether extinct. Yet their life and end must have been still fresh in the memory of the people, and a subject of general curiosity.* It almost seems as though their "guilt, their *brahmahatyá*," had been too great for people to believe that it could have been atoned for by sacrifices were they ever so holy; or that by such means the Párikshitas could have become partakers of the reward fixed for other less culpable evil-doers. It appears further as if the Brahmans had taken special pains to rehabilitate their memory, and in this undoubtedly they were completely successful. Or was it, on the contrary, that the majesty and power of the Párikshitas was so great and dazzling, and their end so surprising, that it was difficult to believe they had really passed away? I prefer, however, the former explanation.

The fourteenth *káṇḍa*, at the beginning of its first part (that relating to ritual), contains a legend of a contention among the gods, in which Vishṇu came off victorious, whence it became customary to say, "Vishṇu is the *śreshṭha* (luckiest?) of the gods." This is the first time that we find Vishṇu brought into such prominence; indeed, he otherwise only appears in the legend of the three strides, and as the representative of the sacrifice itself,—a position which is, in fact, ascribed to

* The country of the Madras lies in the north-west, and is therefore remote from the country of the Kurus. According to the Mahá-Bhárata, however, Mádrí, second wife of Páṇḍu and mother of the two youngest Páṇḍavas, Nakula and Sahadeva, was a native of this region, and Parikshit also had a Mádravatí to wife.

him here also. Indra, as here related, afterwards strikes off his head in jealousy.[139] The second part of this *káṇḍa*, the *Vṛihad-Áraṇyaka*, which consists of five *prapáṭhakas*, or six *adhyáyas*, is again divided into three *káṇḍas*, the *Madhukáṇḍa, adhy.* i. ii. (*prap.* i. 1–ii. 5); the *Yájnaval-kíya-káṇḍa, adhy.* iii. iv. (*prap.* ii. 6–iv. 3); and the *Khila-káṇḍa, adhy.* v. vi. (*prap.* iv. 4–v. 5). Of these three divisions, each succeeding one appears to be later than that which precedes it, and each closes with a Vaṅśa or statement of the line of teachers, carried back to Brahman, the primeval source. The third *bráhmaṇa* of the Madhu-káṇḍa is an explanation of three *ślokas* prefixed to it, a form of which we have no previous example. The fifth (*adhy.* ii. 1) contains, as has already been stated (p. 51), another recension of the legend related in the fourth *adhyáya* of the Kaushítaky-Upanishad, of Ajátaśatru, the king of Káśi, who was jealous of Janaka's fame as a patron of learning. The eighth (*adhy.* ii. 4) contains another recension of the closing legend in the Yájnavalkíya-káṇḍa, of Yájnavalkya's two wives, Maitreyí and Kátyáyaní,—this being the first mention we have of these names. Here, as also in the eleventh *kaṇḍa*, we find an enumeration of the subjects of Vedic study, namely, *Ṛigveda, Yajurveda, Sámaveda*, the *Atharváṅgirasas, itihása, puráṇa, vidyás, upanishads, ślokas, sútras, anuvyákhyánas, vyákhyánas.** The same enumeration recurs in the Yájnavalkíya-káṇḍa (*adhy.* vi. 10). Śaṃkara and Dvivedagaṅga, the commentators of the Vṛihad-Áraṇyaka, both, like Sáyaṇa (on the eleventh *káṇḍa*), take the expressions *itihása*, &c., to mean sections in the Bráhmaṇas. They are, in fact, as I have already pointed out (p. 122), used in

---

[139] This is wrong. The gods send forth ants to gnaw the bowstring of Vishṇu, who stands leaning on his bended bow; the string, snapping and springing upwards, severs his head from his body. The same legend recurs not only in the parallel passage of the Taitt. Ár. (v. 1), but also in the Pañch. Br., vii. 5. 6; but whilst in the Śat. Br. it is related of Vishṇu, the Taitt. Ár. tells it of Makha Vaishṇava, and the Pañch. Br. of Makha alone (cf. also T. S., iii. 2. 4. 1). In the Śatapatha, Makha is only mentioned among the gods who assembled, though, to be sure, he appears immediately before Vishṇu.

* The last five expressions take here the place of *anuśásana, váko-vákya, náráśaṅsís*, and *gáthás* in the eleventh book. The latter are clearly the more ancient.

this sense in the Bráhmaṇas themselves. It is only in regard to *sútra** that I am unable to prove a similar use (though Dvivedagaṅga pretty frequently calls certain sentences by the name of *sútra, e.g.*, i. 2. 18, 22, 3. 1, &c.); and this term raises a doubt whether the opinion of the commentators ought to hold good with reference to these passages also, and their time. The ninth (which is the last) *bráhmaṇa* is evidently the one from which the Madhu-káṇḍa received its name. It treats of the intimate relation existing between the four elements (earth, water, fire, air), the sun, the quarters of the heavens, the moon, lightning, thunder, *ákáśa* (ether), &c., on the one hand, and all beings on the other; this relation being set forth by representing the one as the *madhu* (honey) of the other. This doctrine is traced to Dadhyañch Átharvaṇa, as is also, in fact, done in the Ṛik-Saṃhitá itself (i. 116. 12, 117. 22). In the beginning of the fourth *káṇḍa* of the Śatap. Bráhmaṇa also (iv. 1. 5. 18) we find the *madhu náma bráhmaṇam* mentioned expressly in this connection; Sáyaṇa, too, quotes *Śáṭyáyana* (*-Vájasaneyau*) in support of it. A very early date is thus guaranteed for the name at least, and probably also for the contents of this chapter; though its form, of course, cannot make any pretension to high antiquity. The concluding Vaṅśa here, as elsewhere, varies very much in the two schools; that is, as regards the last twenty members or so back to Yáska and Ásuráyaṇa; but from these upwards to the mythical fountain-heads the two schools generally agree. Ásuráyaṇa himself (consequently, also Yáska, who is recorded as his contemporary) is here placed two stages after Ásuri; at the end of the Khila-káṇḍa he is even designated as his pupil; Ásuri, again, being set down as the pupil of Yájnavalkya. The list closes, therefore, with about the twenty-fifth member from the latter. It must consequently have been continued long after the Madhu-káṇḍa had been finally put into shape, since both the analogy of the Vaṅśa contained in the last *bráhmaṇa* but one of the Khila-káṇḍa and the very nature of the case forbid the

* The word *sútra* is found several times here, but in the sense of 'thread, band,' only, to denote the supreme Brahman itself, which, like a band, embraces and holds together everything.

conclusion that its redaction could have taken place so late as the twenty-fifth generation from Yájnavalkya. The commentators never enter into any explanation of these Vaṅśas; doubtless, therefore, they too regarded them as supplements. The names themselves are naturally highly interesting, and, as far at least as the later stages are concerned, are probably strictly authentic.—The aim of the *Yájnavalkíya-káṇḍa* is the glorification of Yájnavalkya, and it recounts how, at the court of his patron Janaka, king of Videha, he silenced all the Brahmans * of the Kurupañchálas, &c., and gained his patron's full confidence (like the corresponding legends in the twelfth book of the Mahá-Bhárata). The legend narrated in the eleventh *káṇḍa* (vi. 3. 1. ff.) may perhaps have been the model; at least the Yájnavalkíya here begins in exactly the same manner, and gives also, almost in the same words, the account of the discomfiture and punishment of Vidagdha Śákalya, which alone is given in the eleventh *káṇḍa*. It closes with a legend already given in the Madhu-káṇḍa, but with some deviations. The expressions *páṇḍitya*, *muni*, and *mauna*, occurring in this *káṇḍa*, are worthy of special notice as being new[140] (iii. 2. 1, iv. 2. 25); further, *ekahaṅsa*, *śramaṇa*, *tápasa* (iv. 1. 12, 22), *pravrájin* (iv. 2. 25, where *bhikshácharya* is recommended), and *pratibuddha* (iv. 2. 17; the verb *pratibudh* occurs in this sense i. 2. 21), and lastly, the names *cháṇḍála* and *paulkasa* (iv. 1. 22). I am now of opinion † that it is to this Yájnavalkíya-káṇḍa that the *várttika* to Páṇini iv. 3. 105 refers when it speaks of the *Yájnavalkáni bráhmaṇáni* as not *puráṇa-prokta*, but *tulyakála*, "contemporaneous," *i.e.*, with Páṇini. The wording of the *várttika* does not necessarily imply that

---

* Among them Aśvala, the king's Hotar, Vidagdha Śákalya, who lost his life for his impertinence, Kahola Kaushítakeya, and Gárgí Váchaknaví, who all four (the latter, at least, according to the Gṛihya-Sútra) may be looked upon as representatives of the Ṛik, towards which therefore a kind of jealousy is here unmistakably exhibited.

[140] "The word *muni* occurs in the later portions of the Ṛik-Saṃhitá, viz., viii. 17. 14, and x. 136. 2-5."—First German edition, Errata. Paulkasa is found also in V. S. 30. 17.

† Formerly I was of different opinion; see *I. St.*, i. 57. Many of the views there expressed—especially pp. 161–232—have here either been further developed or modified after careful consideration of the various passages, as may be perceived by comparison.

these Bráhmaṇas originated from Yájnavalkya himself; consequently they might bear his name simply because treating of him. I prefer the latter view, for it appears to me very hazardous to regard the entire Śatapatha-Bráhmaṇa, or even its last books only, as directly bearing the name of Yájnavalkya,—however fully it may embody his system,—or to set it down as contemporaneous with, or but little anterior to, Páṇini. In regard to the Yájnavalkíya-káṇḍa, however, I have not the slightest hesitation in doing the latter.[141]—Finally, the *Khila-káṇḍa*, or last *káṇḍa* of the Vṛihad-Áraṇyaka, is uniformly described by the commentators as such a *khila*, or supplement; and as a matter of fact it is clearly enough distinguished from the other *káṇḍas*. Its first *adhyáya*—the fifth of the Vṛihad-Áraṇyaka—is made up of a number of small fragments, which contain for the most part mystical plays upon words, of the most clumsy description. The second *adhyáya* contains two *bráhmaṇas*, parts of which, as I have already remarked (p. 71), recur in precisely the same form in the Chhándogyopanishad vii. 1, 3. Of the third *bráhmaṇa*, which contains ritual injunctions, we also find another recension, *ibid.* vii. 2. It concludes with a Vaṅśa, not, however, in the form of a list, but of a detailed account. According to it, the first author of the doctrine here taught was Uddálaka Áruṇi, who imparted it to Yájnavalkya, here for the first time called Vájasaneya;* his pupil was Madhuka Paiṅgya, from whom the doctrine was transmitted to Chúḍa Bhágavitti, then to Jánaki Ayaḥsthúṇa, and lastly to Satyakáma Jábála. The name of the latter (a teacher often alluded to in the Chhándogyopanishad) is in fact borne in later works by a school of the White Yajus, so

---

141 On this subject compare Goldstücker's detailed discussion in his *Páṇini*, p. 132–140, and my special rejoinder, *I. St.*, v. 65–74, xiii. 443, 444, *I. Str.*, ii. 214. According to these expositions, the author of the *várttikas* must, on the one hand, have considered the *Yájnavalkáni Bráhmaṇáni* as originally promulgated (*prokta*) by Yájnavalkya; but, on the other hand, he must also have looked upon the recension then extant as contemporaneous with Páṇini. Although he here counts Yájnavalkya among the *puráṇas*, 'ancients,'—and this interpretation is required by the wording of the *várttika*,—yet the Káśiká, on the contrary, expressly declares him to be "not *chirakála*."

* In the Yájnavalkíyakáṇḍa Uddálaka Áruṇi is, like the other Brahmans, silenced by Yájnavalkya, no mention being made of his being the preceptor of the latter.

that we might perhaps ascribe to him the final adjustment of this doctrine in its existing form. The fourth and last *bráhmaṇa* of this *adhyáya* is, like the third, surprising, from the nature of its contents, which, consisting as they do of the rites to be observed before, and at the time of, coitus, as well as after the birth of a son, more properly pertain to a Gṛihya-Sútra. It too closes with a Vaṅśa,* this time of quite unusual length, and distinguished, as far as the more recent members are concerned, by this peculiarity, that their names are formed by the addition of *putra* to the mother's name (see above p. 71), and that both parts of the names are accentuated. Ásuri is here called the pupil of Yájnavalkya, and the latter the pupil of Uddálaka. Then, having passed through ten more stages and arrived at Áditya, the sun-god, as the original author, we find the following words as the close of the whole Bráhmaṇa: *ádityání 'máni śukláni yajúṅshi Vájasaneyena Yájnavalkyená "khyáyante,* 'these White Yajus-texts originating † from Áditya are transmitted by Vájasaneya Yájnavalkya.' According to Śaṃkara and Dvivedagaṅga, this Vaṅśa does not refer to the Khila-káṇḍa, but to the entire Pravachana, the entire Veda (*i.e.*, the White Yajus). This view is at all events favoured by the fact that the Vaṅśa at the close of the tenth book (the only one which appears in the whole of the Śatapatha-Bráhmaṇa, besides those of the Madhu-káṇḍa, Yájnavalkíya-káṇḍa, and Khila-káṇḍa) ‡ evidently refers to this Vaṅśa, and presupposes its existence when at its commencement it says: *samánam á Sáṃjívíputrát,* 'up to Sáṃjívíputra the teachers are the same.' For, ascending from this Sáṃjívíputra, there are still in this Vaṅśa three steps up to Yájnavalkya, while in the tenth book, as before remarked, the doctrine is not traced up to the latter at all, but from Sáṃjívíputra through five steps to Śáṇḍilya, and through two more to Tura Kávasheya.§—This latter circumstance suggests to

---

* In the Káṇva recension the Vaṅśas invariably form separate chapters.

† Or: 'these White Yajus-texts are named by Vájasaneya Yájnavalkya as originating from Áditya' (?).

‡ The Káṇva recension adds this Vaṅśa here too at the close after the words: *Yájnavalkyená "khyáyante.*

§ Who is quoted in the Aitar. Bráhmaṇa as contemporaneous with Janamejaya (as his sacrificial priest); see *I. St.*, i. 203, note.

us, moreover, the possibility of yet another division of the Śatapatha-Bráhmaṇa with reference to the origin of the different *káṇḍas.* For in the first five and the last four *káṇḍas* the name of Yájnavalkya meets us exclusively, and very frequently, as that of the teacher whose opinion is appealed to as the decisive authority, whose system consequently is in any case there set forth.* Further, if we except the Yájnavalkíya-káṇḍa and the *gáthás* in the thirteenth *káṇḍa,* races settled in eastern or central Hindustán are the only ones mentioned in these *káṇḍas,* viz., the Kurupañchálas, Kosalavidehas, Śviknas, and Sṛiñjayas. Once only the Práchyas (eastern tribes) are opposed to the Váhíkas (western tribes); again there is once mention made of the Udíchyas (inhabitants of the north); and lastly, the (southern) Nishadhas are once alluded to in the name of their king, Nala Naishadha (or, as he is here called, Naishidha). From this the remaining *káṇḍas*—the sixth to the tenth—differ palpably enough. They recognise Śáṇḍilya as the final authority † instead of Yájnavalkya, whom they do not even name; neither do they mention any but north-western races, viz., the Gandháras with their king Nagnajit, the Salvas, and the Kekayas.‡ May not the above-mentioned Vaṅśa apply not only to the tenth book, but to these five *káṇḍas?* Since the latter treat specially of the fire-ritual, of the erection of the sacred fire-altars, their possible north-

* The fact that this is so clear may easily account for the circumstance that the Puráṇas have here for once a statement in conformity with fact, as they cite Yájnavalkya as the author of the White Yajus. We may here mention that the name of Yájnavalkya occurs nowhere else in Vedic literature, which might be explained partly by the difference of locality, partly by his having edited the White Yajus after the text of the other Vedas had been fixed; though the latter reason seems insufficient, since other teachers of the White Yajus are mentioned frequently in later Vedic literature, as, for instance, Áruṇi, Śvetaketu, Satyakáma Jábála, &c., who are either his contemporaries, or belong to even later times. Besides, his patron Janaka is mentioned at least in the Kaushítaky - Upanishad. [In two sections of the Kaushítaki-, or, Śáṅkháyana-Áraṇyaka, which, however, are clearly of very late origin, Yájnavalkya himself is actually cited (9. 7 and 13. 1); but these passages are themselves direct quotations from Śatap. Br. xiv.—In the Gopatha-Br., which shows so many special points of relationship to the Śatapatha, Yájnavalkya is never mentioned.]

† So do the Sáma-Sútras; Śáṇḍilya is mentioned besides in the Chhándogyop. only.

‡ The legend concerning these recurs in the Chhándogyop.

western origin might be explained by the fact that the doctrine upon this subject had, though differing from that of the Persa-Aryans, been kept particularly pure in the north-west owing to the proximity of this latter people.* However this may be, whether the north-western origin of the doctrine of these five *káṇḍas* be well founded or otherwise,[142] they at any rate belong, in their present form, to the same period as (the tenth possibly to a somewhat later period than) the first five *káṇḍas*. On this point the mention of Aruṇa Aupaveśi, Áruṇi, Śvetaketu Áruṇeya, and of Indradyumna (in the tenth book), as well as the frequent reprehension of the Charakádhvaryus, is decisive. That the various parts of the Bráhmaṇa were blended together by one arranging hand[143] is evident in particular from the repeated occurrence of phrases intimating that a subject has already been treated of in an earlier part, or is to be found presented more in detail in a later part. A closer investigation of the various instances where this occurs has not as yet been within my power.

The number of deviations in regard to ritual or readings cited in the Bráhmaṇa is very great. To these regard is had here and there even in the Saṃhitá itself, two different *mantras* being quoted side by side as equally good. Most frequently the citation of such variations in the Bráhmaṇa is introduced by the words *ity eke*, or *tad áhuḥ*; yet pretty often the names of individual teachers are also mentioned, who must here, in part at least, be looked upon as representing the schools which bear their names. Thus in addition to those already named we have: Asháḍha Sávayasa, Barku Várshṇa, Aupoditeya, Páñchi, Takshan, Jívala Chailaki, Ásuri, Mádhuki, Kahoḍa Kaushítaki, Várshṇya Sátyayajna, Sátyayajni, Táṇḍya, Buḍila Áśvataráśvi,

* Ought we to bring the Śákáyanins into direct connection with the latter? But then what would become of the connection between Śákáyanya (in the Maitráyaṇí-Upanishad) and the Śákyas? (!).

[142] See on this my detailed discussion in *I. St.*, xiii. 265–269, where I call special attention to various differences in point of language between books i.–v. and vi.–ix.

[143] The strong censure passed upon the residents on the seven western rivers in ix. 3. 1. 24 must be ascribed to this 'arranging hand;' see *I. St.*, xiii. 267.—That the White Yajus was arranged in eastern Hindustán, seems to be proved by the statements in the Pratijná-Pariśishṭa respecting the extent of the Madhyadeśa; see my essay on the Pratijná-Sútra, pp. 101, 105.

Ráma Aupatasvini, Kaukústa, Máhitthi, Muḍimbha* Auḍanya, Saumápau Mánutantavyau, Satyakáma Jábála, Śailáli, &c. Besides the Charakádhvaryus, Bhállaveya in particular is regularly censured, from which I conclude, as already stated (p. 95), that the Bhállavi-Bráhmaṇa should be reckoned among those of the Black Yajus. By the "*cke*," where these are found fault with, we should probably also understand (*e.g.*, once for certain in the first *káṇḍa*) the adherents of the Black Yajus. Once, however (in the eighth *káṇḍa*), a reading of the Káṇva school is quoted by "*cke*" and disputed. How the matter stands in the Bráhmaṇa of the latter as to this passage, whether it finds fault with the reading of the Mádhyaṃdina school, I am not able to say. A collection of passages of this kind would naturally be of peculiar interest.

The legends interspersed in such numbers throughout the Bráhmaṇa have a special significance. In some of them the language is extremely antiquated, and it is probable therefore that before their incorporation into it they possessed an independent form. The following deserve special mention from their being treated in detail, viz., the legends of the Deluge and the rescue of Manu; of the emigration of Videgha Máthava from the Sarasvatí to the Sadánírá in the country of the Kosala-Videhas; of the restoration to youth of Chyavana by the Aśvins at the request of his wife Sukanyá, the daughter of Śaryáta Mánava; of the contest between Kadrú and Suparṇí; of the love and separation of Purúravas and Urvaśí, and others. Many of them reappear as episodes in the epic, in a metrical garb, and often very much altered. It is obvious that we have here a much more intimate connection with the epic than exists in the other Bráhmaṇas. The names Valhika, Janamejaya, and Nagnajit have the most direct reference to the legend of the Mahá-Bhárata; as also the names already discussed above in connection with the Saṃhitá, Ambá, Ambiká, Ambáliká, Subhadrá, and the use there made of the words *arjuna* and *phalguna*. In any case, we must look for the explanation

* Compare the Muṭibhas in the Aitar. Br.—Of the above, only Buḍila, the Saumápau, Satyakáma, Mádhuki (or Paiñgya), and Kaushítaki are mentioned elsewhere.

of this in the circumstance, that this Bráhmaṇa substantially originated and attained its final shape among the tribes of the Kurupañchálas and the neighbouring Kosala-Videhas. The king of the latter, Janaka, who is represented in it as the chief patron of the sacred doctrine it embodies, bears the same name as the father of Sítá and father-in-law of Ráma, in the Rámáyaṇa. This is, however, the only point of contact with the Rámáyaṇa legend which can here be traced, and as the name Janaka seems to have belonged to the whole family, it also virtually disappears. Nevertheless I am inclined to identify the father of Sítá with this exceptionally holy Janaka, being of opinion that Sítá herself is a mere abstraction, and that consequently she had assigned to her the most renowned father possible. As regards the special relation in which the Bráhmaṇa stands to the legend of the Mahá-Bhárata, Lassen, it is well known, takes as the fundamental feature of the latter a conflict between the Kurus and the Pañchálas, ending in their mutual annihilation, the latter being led by the family of the Páṇḍus, who came from the west. Now at the time of the Bráhmaṇa, we find the Kurus and the Pañchálas still in full prosperity,* and also united in the closest bonds of friendship as one people.† Consequently this internecine strife cannot yet have taken place. On the other hand, in the latest portions of the Bráhmaṇa, we find the prosperity, the sin, the expiation, and the fall of Janamejaya Párikshita and his brothers Bhímasena, Ugrasena, and Śrutasena, and of the whole family of the Párikshitas, apparently still fresh in the memory of the people and discussed as a subject of controversy. In the Mahá-Bhárata boundless confusion prevails regarding these names. Janamejaya and his brothers, already mentioned, are represented either as great-grandsons of Kuru, or else as the great-grandsons of the Páṇḍuid Arjuna, at whose snake-sacrifice Vaiśampáyana related the history of the

* Though certainly in the last portions of the Br. the Kosala-Videhas seem to have a certain preponderance; and there had perhaps existed as early as the time of the Saṃhitá (see p. 114) a certain rivalry between the Kurus and Pañchálas.

† At least I am not able to offer another explanation of the word Kurupañchála; it is, moreover, noteworthy that no name of a king of the Kurupañchálas is ever mentioned. Such names are quoted only for Kauravya- or Páñchála-kings.

great struggle between the Kurus and the Páṇḍus. Adopting the latter view, which appears to be the better warranted, from the fact that the part of the Mahá-Bhárata which contains it is written in prose, and exhibits a peculiarly ancient garb, the supposed great internecine conflict between the Kurus and the Pañchálas, and the dominion of the Páṇḍavas, must have been long past at the time of the Bráhmaṇa. How is this contradiction to be explained? That something great and marvellous had happened in the family of the Párikshitas, and that their end still excited astonishment at the time of the Bráhmaṇa, has already been stated. But what it was we know not. After what has been said above, it can hardly have been the overthrow of the Kurus by the Pañchálas; but at any rate, it must have been deeds of guilt; and indeed I am inclined to regard this as yet unknown 'something' as the basis of the legend of the Mahá-Bhárata.[144] To me it appears absolutely necessary to assume, with Lassen, that the Páṇḍavas did not originally belong to the legend, but were only associated with it at a later time,[145] for not only is there no trace of them anywhere in the Bráhmaṇas or Sútras, but the name of their chief hero, Arjuna (Phalguna), is still employed here, in the Śatapatha-Bráhmaṇa (and in the Saṃhitá), as a name of Indra; indeed he is probably to be looked upon as originally identical with Indra, and therefore destitute of any real existence. Lassen further (*I. AK.*, i. 647, ff.) concludes, from what Megasthenes (in Arrian) reports of the Indian Heracles, his sons and his daughter *Πανδαία*, and also from other accounts in Curtius, Pliny, and Ptolemy,* that at the time when Megasthenes wrote, the mythical association of Kṛishṇa (?) with the Páṇḍavas already ex-

---

[144] See *Indian Antiquary*, ii. 58 (1873). I may add the following, as it possibly has a bearing here. Vṛiddhadyumna Ábhipratáriṇa (see Ait. Br., iii. 48) was cursed by a Brahman on account of improper sacrifice, to the effect that: *imam eva prati samaram Kuravaḥ Kurukshetrách chyoshyanta iti*, Śáñkh., xv. 16. 12 (and so it came to pass). For the glorification of the Kauravya king Parikshit the four verses, Śáñkh. Śr., xii. 17. 1–4 (Ath., xx. 127. 7–10), serve; although in Ait. Br., vi. 22 (Śáñkh. Br., xxx. 5), they are referred to 'fire' or 'year;' but see Gopatha-Br., xi. 12. Another legend respecting Janamejaya Párikshita is found in the Gopatha-Br., ii. 5.

[145] See my detailed discussion of this in *I. St.*, ii. 402–404.

* Curtius and Pliny wrote in the first, Arrian and Ptolemy in the second century A.D.

isted. But this conclusion, although perhaps in itself probable, is at least not certain;* and even if it were, it would not prove that the Páṇḍavas were at that time already associated with the legend of the Kurus. And if we have really to assign the arrangement of the Mádhyaṃdina recension (see p. 106) to about the time of Megasthenes, it may reasonably be inferred, from the lack of all mention of the Páṇḍavas in it, that their association with the Kurus had not then been established; although, strictly speaking, this conclusion has weight not so much for the period when the arrangement of the work actually took place, as for the time to which the pieces arranged belong.

As with the epic legends, so also do we find in the Śatapatha-Bráhmaṇa several points of contact with the legends of the Buddhists, on the one hand, and with the later tradition concerning the origin of the Sáṃkhya doctrine, on the other. First, as regards the latter. Ásuri, the name of one of its chief authorities, is at the same time the name of a teacher frequently mentioned in the Śatapatha-Bráhmaṇa. Again, though only in the Yájnavalkíya-káṇḍa, we have mention of a Kápya Pataṃchala of the country of the Madras as particularly distinguished by his exertions in the cause of Brahmanical theology; and in his name we cannot but see a reference to Kapila and Pataṃjali, the traditional founders of the Sáṃkhya and Yoga systems. As regards the Buddhist legends, the Śákyas of Kapilavastu (whose name may possibly be connected with the Śákáyanins of the tenth *káṇḍa*, and the Śákáyanya of the Maitráyaṇa-Upanishad) called themselves Gautamas, a family name which is particularly often represented among the teachers and in the lists of teachers of the Bráhmaṇa. It is, moreover, the country of the Kosalas and Videhas that is to be looked upon as the cradle of Buddhism.—Śvetaketu (son of Áruṇi), one of the teachers most frequently mentioned in the Śatapatha-Bráhmaṇa, is with the Buddhists the name of one of the earlier births of Śákyamuni

---

* The incest of Hercules with *Παvδala* must certainly be traced to the incest of Prajápati and his daughter, so often touched on in the Bráhmaṇas. [That Vásudeva and Arjuna occur together in Páṇ., iv. 3. 98, cannot be considered as a proof of their being connected with each other; see *I. St.*, xiii. 349, ff.]

(see *Ind. Stud.*, ii. 76, note).—That the *mágadha* of the Saṃhitá may perhaps also be adduced in this connection is a point that has already been discussed (pp. 111, 112).—The words *arhant* (iii. 4. 1. 3, ff.), *śramaṇa* (Vṛih. Ár., iv. 1. 22, as well as Taitt. Ár., ii. 7, beside *tápasa*), *mahábráhmaṇa* * (Vṛih. Ár., ii. 1. 19. 22), and *pratibuddha*, although by no means used in their Buddhistic technical sense, yet indicate how this gradually arose.—The name Chelaka also in the Bráhmaṇa may possibly have some connection with the peculiarly Buddhistic sense attached to the word *chela*. Ajátaśatru and Brahmadatta,† on the contrary, are probably but namesakes of the two persons designated by the Buddhists under these names as contemporaries of Buddha (?). The same probably also applies to the Vátsíputríyas of the Buddhists and the Vátsíputras of the Vṛih. Áraṇy. (v. 5. 31), although this form of name, being uncommon, perhaps implies a somewhat closer connection. It is, however, the family of the Kátyáyanas, Kátyáyaníputras, which we find represented with special frequency among the Buddhists as well as in the Bráhmaṇa (although only in its very latest portions). We find the first mention ‡ of this name in the person of one of the wives of Yájnavalkya, who is called Kátyáyaní, both in the Madhu-káṇḍa and the Yájnavalkíya-káṇḍa; it also appears frequently in the lists of teachers, and almost the whole of the Sútras belong-

---

* Beside *mahárája*, which is found even earlier, i. 5. 3. 21, ii. 5. 4. 9.

† With the surname Chaikitáneya Vṛih. Ár. Mádhy., i. 1. 26.—In Mahá-Bhárata, xii. 5136, 8603, a *Páñchálya rájá* named Brahmadatta is mentioned, who reigned in Kámpilya.—Chaikitáneya is to be distinguished from Chaikitáyana in the Chhándogyopan., iii. 8.—[On a curious coincidence of a legend in the Vṛihad-Ár. with a Buddhist legend, see *I. St.*, iii. 156, 157.]

‡ In the tenth book of the Taitt. Ár., Kátyáyana (instead of °ní) is a name of Durgá; on this use see *I. St.*, ii. 192 [xiii. 422].—In the *Gaṇa-páṭha* to Páṇini, Kátyáyana is wanting. [But Kátyáyaní is to be gathered from Páṇini himself, iv. 1. 18; see *I. St.*, v. 61, 63, 64. A Kátyáyaníputra Játúkarṇya is quoted in the Śánkh. Ár., viii. 10. Patamjali in the Mahábháshya mentions several Kátyas (*I. St.*, xiii. 399, 407), and indeed the *várttikakára* directly belongs to this family. In no other Vedic texts have I found either the Katas or the Kátyas, Kátyáyanas, excepting in the *pravara* section appended at the end of the Áśvaláyana-Śrauta-Sútra, xii. 13–15, in which the Katas and the patronymic, Kátya, are mentioned several times. The Kuru-Katas are cited in the *gaṇa* '*Garga*,' and the family of the Katas seems therefore to have been specially connected with the Kurus; see *I. St.*, i. 227, 228.]

ing to the White Yajus bear this name as that of their author.

The Śatapatha-Bráhmaṇa has been commented in the Mádhyamdina recension by Harisvámin and Sáyaṇa; but their commentaries are so far extant only in a fragmentary form.[146] The Vṛihad-Áraṇyaka has been explained by Dviveda Gañga (of Gujarát); and in the Káṇva recension by Śaṃkara, to whose commentary a number of other works by his pupils, &c., attach themselves. As yet only the first *káṇḍa*, with extracts from the commentaries, has been published, edited by myself. In the course of the next three years, however, the work will be printed in its entirety.[147] The Vṛihad-Áraṇyaka in the Káṇva recension has been edited by Poley, and recently by Roer, together with Śaṃkara's commentary and a gloss thereon.[148]

I now turn to the *Sútras* of the White Yajus. The first of these, the *Śrauta-Sútra* of *Kátyáyana*, consists of twenty-six *adhyáyas*, which on the whole strictly observe the order of the Bráhmaṇa. The first eighteen correspond to its first nine *káṇḍas;* the Sautrámaṇí is treated of in the nineteenth, the horse sacrifice in the twentieth *adhyáya;* the twenty-first contains the human, universal, and Manes sacrifices. The next three *adhyáyas* refer, as before stated (p. 80), to the ceremonial of the Sámaveda, to its several *ekáhas, ahínas,* and *sattras;* yet they rather specify these in the form of lists than present, as the other *adhyáyas* do, a clear picture of the whole sacrificial proceedings. The twenty-fifth *adhyáya* treats of the *práyaśchittas*, or expiatory ceremonies, corresponding to the first part of the twelfth *káṇḍa;* and lastly, the twenty-sixth *adhyáya* contains the *pravargya* sacrifice, corresponding to the first part of the fourteenth *káṇḍa.*—Only a few teachers are cited by name, and among these are two belonging to authors of Sútras of the Black Yajus, viz., Laugákshi and Bháradvája; besides whom, only Játúkarṇya, Vátsya, Bádari, Káśa-

---

146 And in very bad manuscripts.

147 The last fasciculus was published in 1855. A translation of the first book, and also of some legends specially mentioned above, is printed in vol. i. of my *Indische Streifen* (1868).

148 Roer's translation (1856) includes the commentary of the first *adhyáya;* he also gives several extracts from it in the subsequent chapters.

kṛitsni, and Kárshṇájini are named. We meet with the three last of these elsewhere only[149] in the Vedánta-Sútra of Bádaráyaṇa, Bádari excepted, who appears also in the Mímáńsá-Sútra of Jaimini. Vátsya is a name which occasionally occurs in the Vańśas of the Śatapatha-Bráhmaṇa;[150] and the same applies to Játúkarṇya, who appears in the Vańśa of the Madhu- and Yájnavalkíya-káṇḍas in the Káṇva recension as a pupil of Ásuráyaṇa and of Yáska. (In the Mádhyaṃdina recension, another teacher intervenes between the last-named and Játúkarṇya, viz., Bháradvája.) He is also mentioned in the Aitareya-Áraṇyaka, and repeatedly in the Prátiśákhya-Sútra of the White Yajus. Besides these, "*eke*" are frequently quoted, whereby reference is made to other Śákhás. One passage gives expression to a certain hostility towards the descendants of the daughter of Atri (the Háleyas, Váleyas, Kaudreyas, Śaubhreyas, Vámarathyas, Gopavanas); while the descendants of Atri himself are held in especial honour. A similar hostility is exhibited in other passages towards the descendants of Kaṇva, Kaśyapa, and Kautsa; yet these three words, according to the commentaries, may also be taken as appellatives, *kaṇva* as "deaf," *kaśyapa* as "having black teeth" (*śyávadanta*), and *kautsa* as "doing blamable things." The first *adhyáya* is of peculiar interest, as it gives the *paribháshás*, or general rules for the sacrificial ceremonial. Otherwise this work, being entirely based upon the Bráhmaṇa, and therefore in no way an independent production, contains but few data throwing light upon its probable age. Amongst such we may reckon in particular* the circumstance that the word *vijaya*, "conquest," *sc.* of the

---

[149] Káśakṛitsni appears as a grammarian also; he is possibly even earlier than Páṇini; see *I. St.*, xiii. 398, 413. On a Vedic commentator Káśakṛitsna, see above, pp. 42, 91.

[150] In addition to this there is quoted in ix. 5. 1. 62 the opinion of a teacher bearing this name; a Vátsa is mentioned in the Aitar. Ár. and Śáṅkh. Ár.

* The use of *maṇi*, xx. 7. 1, to denote 101, may also be instanced as pointing to later times; it belongs to the same class as *agni* = 3, *bhú* = 1, &c. [This is wrong; a little before, in xx. 5. 16, mention is made of 101 *maṇis*, and in xx. 7. 1 we have simply a reference back to this. We might rather cite *gáyatrísampanná*, &c., xx. 11. 21, ff., in the sense of 24 &c., but there is this material difference from the later use, that it is not *gáyatrí* alone which means 24, but *gáyatrísampanna*.]

points of the compass,* is once used in the sense of "the points of the compass" themselves (xx. 4. 26), which evidently presupposes the custom of the *dig-vijayas*—probably also poetical descriptions of them (?). The *adhyáyas* relating to the Sáman ceremonial (xxii.–xxiv.) are the richest in this kind of data. They treat, for instance, like the Sáma-Sútras, of the sacrifices on the Sarasvatí, and also of the Vrátya-sacrifices, at which we find the *Mágadhadeśíya brahmabandhu* (xxii. 4. 22) occupying the same position as in Láṭyáyana.

The Kátyáyana-Sútra has had many commentators, as Yaśoga,[151] Pitṛibhúti, Karka (quoted by Sáyaṇa, and therefore prior to him[152]), Bhartṛiyajna, Śrí-Ananta, Devayájnika (or Yájnikadeva), and Mahádeva. The works of the three last,† and that of Karka are, however, the only ones that seem to have been preserved. The text, with extracts from these commentaries, will form the third part of my edition of the White Yajus.[153]—To this Sútra a multitude

---

* See Lassen, *I. AK.*, i. 542. [According to the St. Petersburg Dictionary, the word in the above passage should only mean 'gain, the thing conquered, booty;' but a reference to locality is made certain by the parallel passage, Láṭy., ix. 10. 17: *vijitasya vá madhye yajet* (*yo yasya deśo vijitaḥ syát, sa tasya m. y.*); for the *digvijayas*, it is true, we do not gain anything by this passage.]

[151] This name must be read Yaśogopi; see my edition, Introd., p. vii.

[152] A *Dhúmráyaṇasagotra Karkádhyápaka* occurs in an inscription published by Dowson in *Journal R. A. S.*, i. 283 (1865), of Śrídattakuśalin (Praśántarága), dated *saṃ.* 380 (but of what era?).

† [They are, however, incomplete, in part exceedingly so.] The earliest MS. hitherto known of the *vyákhyá* of Yájnikadeva is dated *saṃvat* 1639.—I have given the names of these commentators in the order in which they are cited by one another; no doubt there were other commentators also preceding Yaśoga [Yaśogopi]. In the Fort William Catalogue, under No. 742, a commentary by Mahídhara is mentioned, but I question provisionally the correctness of this statement. [The correct order is: Karka, Pitṛibhúti, Yaśogopi, Bhartṛiyajna. They are so cited by Ananta, who himself seems to have lived in the first half of the sixteenth century, provided he be really identical with the Śrímadanantákhyacháturmásyayájin, whom Náráyaṇa, the author of the Muhúrtamártaṇḍa, mentions as his father; see my Catalogue of the Berlin MSS., No. 879. Deva on i. 10. 13 quotes a Náráyaṇabháshya; might not Ananta's son be its author?]

[153] This part was published 1856–59; Deva's Paddhati to books i.–v. is there given in full, also his commentary on book i.; the extracts from the scholia to books ii.–xi. are likewise taken from Deva's commentary: those to books ii.–v. there exhibit, as to style, some differences from the original wording, resulting from abbreviations; the extracts for books xii.–xxvi. come from the scholium of Karka and from an ano-

of Paddhatis (outlines), extracts, and similar works * attach themselves, and also a large number of Pariśishṭas (supplements), which are all attributed to Kátyáyana, and have found many commentators. Of these, we must specially draw attention to the *Nigama-Pariśishṭa*, a kind of synonymic glossary to the White Yajus; and to the *Pravarádhyáya*,† an enumeration of the different families of the Brahmans, with a view to the proper selection of the sacrificial priests, as well as for the regulation of the intermarriages forbidden or permissible among them. The *Charaṇa-vyúha*, an account of the schools belonging to the several Vedas, is of little value. Its statements may for the most part be correct, but it is extremely incomplete, and from beginning to end is evidently quite a modern compilation.[154]

The Sútra of *Vaijavápa*, to which I occasionally find allusion in the commentaries on the Kátíya-Sútra, I am inclined to class among the Sútras of the White Yajus, as I do not meet with this name anywhere else except in the Vaṅśas of the Śatap. Br. Here we have both a Vaijavápa and a Vaijavápáyana, both appearing among the most recent members of the lists (in the Káṇva recension I find only the latter, and he is here separated by five steps only from Yáska). A Gṛihya-Sútra of this name is also cited.

The *Kátíya Gṛihya-Sútra*,[155] in three *káṇḍas*, is attributed to Páraskara, from whom a school of the White

nymous epitome (*saṃkshiptasára*) of Deva, the MS. of which dates from *saṃvat* 1609. None of these commentaries is complete.

* By Gadádhara, Harisharamiśra, Reṇudíkshita, Gaṅgádhara, &c.

† Printed, but unfortunately from a very bad codex, in my Catalogue of the Berlin MSS., pp. 54–62. [See *I. St.*, x. 88, ff.]

[154] Edited in *I. St.*, iii. 247–283 (1854); see also Müller, *A. S. L.*, p. 368, ff., and Rájendra Lála Mitra in the preface to his translation of the Chhándogyopanishad, p. 3. The enumerations of the Vedic schools in the Vishṇu-Puráṇa, iii. 4, and especially in the Váyu-Puráṇa, chap. lx. (see Aufrecht's *Catalogus*, p. 54, ff.), contain by far richer material. If all these schools actually existed —but there is certainly a great deal of mere error and embellishment in these statements—then, in truth, lamentably little has been left to us!

[155] See Stenzler's account of its contents in *Z. D. M. G.*, vii. (1853). and his essay on the *arghádána* (Pár., i. 3, Breslau, 1855).—The sections on marriage ceremonial have been published by Haas, *I. St.*, v. 283, ff., whilst the sections on the *játakarman* have been edited by Speijer (1872), together with critical variants (pp. 17–23) to the MS. of the whole text which was used by Stenzler.

Yajus also (according to the Charaṇavyúha) derived its name. The word Páraskara is used as a *saṃjná*, or proper name—but, according to the *gaṇa*, to denote a district—in the Sútra of Páṇini; but I am unable to trace it in Vedic literature. To this Gṛihya-Sútra there are still extant a Paddhati by Vásudeva, a commentary by Jayaráma, and above all a most excellent commentary by Rámakṛishṇa under the title of *Saṃskára-gaṇapati*, which ranks above all similar works from its abundant quotations and its very detailed and exhaustive handling of the various subjects. In the introduction, which deals with the Veda in general and the Yajurveda in particular, Rámakṛishṇa declares that the Káṇva school is the best of those belonging to the Yajus.—Under the name of Páraskara there exists also a Smṛiti-Śástra, which is in all probability based upon this Gṛihya-Sútra. Among the remaining Smṛiti-Śástras, too, there are a considerable number whose names are connected with those of teachers of the White Yajus; for instance, Yájnavalkya, whose posteriority to Manu quite corresponds to the posteriority of the White Yajus to the Black Yajus—and no doubt also to that of the Kátíya-Sútra to the Mánava-Sútra;—further, Kátyáyana (whose work, however, as we saw, connects itself with the Sámaveda), Kaṇva, Gautama, Śáṇḍilya, Jábáli, and Paráśara. The last two names appear among the schools of the White Yajus specified in the Charaṇavyúha, and we also find members of their families named in the Vaṅśas of the Śatapatha-Bráhmaṇa, where the family of the Paráśaras is particularly often represented.*

The *Prátiśákhya-Sútra* of the White Yajus, as well as its Anukramaṇí, names at its close Kátyáyana as its author. In the body of the work there is mention, first, of three grammarians, whom we also find cited in the Prátiśákhya of the Ṛik, in Yáska, and in Páṇini, viz., Śákaṭáyana, Śákalya, and Gárgya; next, of Káśyapa, likewise mentioned by Páṇini; and, lastly, of Dálbhya, Játúkarṇya, Śaunaka (the author of the Ṛik-Prátiśákhya?), Aupaśivi,

* [See *I. St.*, i. 156.] Páṇini, iv. 3. 110 (a rule which possibly does not belong to him), attributes to a Páráśarya a Bhikshu-Sútra, *i.e.*, a compendium for religious mendicants. [The *Páráśariṇo bhikshavaḥ* are mentioned in the Mahábháshya also, and besides a Kalpa by Paráśara; see *I. St.*, xiii. 340, 445.]

Káṇva, and the Mádhyaṃdinas. The distinction in i. 1. 18, 19 between *veda* and *bháshya, i.e.*, works in *bháshá*,—which corresponds to the use of the latter word in Páṇini,—has already been mentioned (p. 57). The first of the eight *adhyáyas* contains the *saṃjnás* and *paribháshás, i.e.*, technical terms * and general preliminary remarks. The second *adhy.* treats of the accent; the third, fourth, and fifth of *saṃskára, i.e.*, of loss, addition, alteration, and constancy of the letters with reference to the laws of euphony; the sixth of the accent of the verb in the sentence, &c.; the eighth contains a table of the vowels and consonants, lays down rules on the manner of reading[156] (*svádhyáya*), and gives a division of words corresponding to that of Yáska. Here, too, several *ślokas* are quoted referring to the deities of the letters and words, so that I am almost inclined to consider this last *adhyáya* (which is, moreover, strictly speaking, contained in the first) as a later addition.† We have an excellent commentary on this work by Uvaṭa, who has been repeatedly mentioned, under the title of *Mátṛimodaka*.[157]

The *Anukramaṇí* of Kátyáyana contains, in the first place, in the first four *adhyáyas* (down to iv. 9), an index of the authors, deities, and metres of the several *śukláni yajúṇshi* "White Yajus-formulas" contained in the "*Mádhyaṃdiníye Vájasaneyake Yajurvedámnáye sarve* [?] *sakhile saśukriye*," which the saint Yájnavalkya received from Vivasvant, the sun-god. For their *viniyoga*, or liturgical use, we are referred to the Kalpakára. As regards the names of authors here mentioned, there is much to be remarked. The authors given for the *ṛichas* usually agree with those assigned to the same verses in the Ṛig-anukramaṇí; there are, however, many exceptions to this. Very often the particular name appears (as is also the case in

---

* Among them *tiṅ, kṛit, taddhita*, and *upadhá*, terms quite agreeing with Páṇini's terminology.

[156] Rather: 'reciting;' because here too we must dismiss all idea of writing and reading.

† In that case the mention of the Mádhyaṃdinas would go for nothing.

[157] In connection with my edition of this Prátiśákhya, text and translation, with critical introduction and explanatory notes, in *I. St.*, iv. 65–160, 177–331, Goldstücker in his *Páṇini*, pp. 186–207, started a special controversy, in which *inter alia* he attempts in particular to show that the author of this work is identical with the author of the *várttikas* to Páṇini; see my detailed rejoinder in *I. St.*, v. 91–124.

the Ṛig-anukramaṇí) to be borrowed from some word occurring in the verse. In the case where a passage is repeated elsewhere, as very often happens, it is frequently assigned to an author different from the one to whom it had previously been attributed. Many of the Ṛishis here mentioned do not occur among those of the Ṛik, and belong to a later stage than these; among them are several even of the teachers mentioned in the Śatapatha-Bráhmaṇa. The closing part of the fourth *adhyáya** contains the dedication of the verses to be recited at particular ceremonies to their respective Ṛishis, deities, and metres, together with other similar mystical distributions. Lastly, the fifth *adhyáya* gives a short analysis of the metres which occur. In the excellent but unfortunately not altogether complete Paddhati of Śríhala to this Anukramaṇí we find the liturgical use of each individual verse also given in detail.

The Yajus recension of the three works called Vedáñgas, viz., Śikshá, Chhandas, and Jyotisha, has already been discussed (p. 60).†

We come now to the *Atharvaveda*.

The *Saṃhitá* of the Atharvaveda contains in twenty *káṇḍas*[158] and thirty-eight *prapáṭhakas* nearly 760 hymns and about 6000 verses. Besides the division into *prapáṭhakas*, another into *anuvákas* is given, of which there are

---

* Published together with the fifth *adhyáya*, and the beginning of the work, in my edition of the Vája-saneyi-Saṃhitá, introduction, pp. lv.-lviii.

† For particulars I refer to my Catalogue of the Berlin MSS., pp. 96-100 [and to my editions, already mentioned, of these three tracts].

[158] This division of the Ath. S. into twenty books is attested for the period of the author of the *várttikas*, and also by the Gopatha-Bráhmaṇa i. 8; see *I. St.*, xiii. 433; whereas both the Ath. S. itself (19. 22, 23) and the Ath. Par. 48. 4-6 still contain the direct intimation that it formerly consisted of sixteen books only; see *I. St.*, iv. 432-434.

some ninety. The division into *parvans,* mentioned in the thirteenth book of the Śatapatha-Bráhmaṇa, does not appear in the manuscripts; neither do they state to what school the existing text belongs. As, however, in one of the Pariśishṭas to be mentioned hereafter (the seventh), the *ṛichas* belonging to the ceremony there in question are quoted as *Paippaládá mantráḥ,* it is at least certain that there was a Saṃhitá belonging to the Paippaláda school, and possibly this may be the Saṃhitá now extant.[159] Its contents and principle of division are at present unknown[160] in their details. We only know generally that "it principally contains formulas intended to protect against the baneful influences of the divine powers,* against diseases and noxious animals; cursings of enemies, invocations of healing herbs; together with formulas for all manner of occurrences in every-day life, prayers for protection on journeys, luck in gaming, and the like" †—all matters for which analogies enough are to be found in the hymns of the Ṛik-Saṃhitá. But in the Ṛik the instances are both less numerous, and, as already remarked in the introduction (p. 11), they are handled in an entirely different manner, although at the same time a not inconsiderable portion of these songs reappears directly in the Ṛik, particularly in the tenth *maṇḍala.** As to the ceremonial for which the hymns of the Atharvan were used, what corre-

[159] According to a tract recently published by Roth, *Der Atharvaveda in Kashmir* (1875), this is not the case; the extant Saṃhitá seems rather to belong to the school of the Śaunakas, whilst the Paippaláda-Saṃhitá has come down to us in a second recension, still preserved in Kashmir.

[160] The arrangement in books i.–vii. is according to the number of verses in the different pieces; these have, on an average, four verses in book i., five in ii., six in iii., seven in iv., eight to eighteen in v., three in vi., and only one in vii. Books viii.–xiii. contain longer pieces. As to the contents, they are indiscriminately mixed up. Books xiv.–xviii., on the contrary, have all a uniform subject-matter; xiv. treats of marriage, xv. of the glorification of Vrátya, xvi., xvii. of certain conjurations, xviii. of burial and the festival of the Manes. Book xix. is a mixture of supplementary pieces, part of its text being in a rather corrupt condition; book xx. contains,—with one peculiar exception, the so-called *kuntápasúkta,*—only complete hymns addressed to Indra, which are borrowed directly and without change from the Rigveda. Neither of these two last books is noticed in the Atharva-Prátiśákhya (see note 167), and therefore they did not belong to the original text at the time of this work.

* Of the stars, too, *i.e.,* of the lunar asterisms.

† See Roth, *Zur Litt. und Gesch. des Weda,* p. 12.

sponds to it in the other Vedas is found, not in the Śrauta-Sútras, but with few exceptions in the Gṛihya-Sútras only; and it appears therefore (as I have likewise already remarked) that this ceremonial in its origin belonged rather to the people proper than to the families of priests. As in the Shaḍviṅśa-Bráhmaṇa and in the Sáma-Sútras we actually meet with a case (see p. 78) where an imprecatory ceremony is borrowed from the Vrátínas, or Aryans who had not adopted the Brahmanical organisation, we may further reasonably conjecture that this was not a solitary instance; and thus the view naturally presents itself that, though the Atharva-Saṃhitá originated for the most part in the Brahmanical period, yet songs and formulas may also have been incorporated into it which properly belonged to these unbrahmanical Aryans of the west.* And as a matter of fact, a very peculiar relation to these tribes is unmistakably revealed in the fifteenth *káṇḍa*, where the Supreme Being is expressly called by the name of Vrátya,[161] and is at the same time associated with the attributes given in the Sámaveda as characteristics of the Vrátyas. In the same way, too, we find this word Vrátya employed in the Atharva-Upanishads in the sense of "pure in himself" to denote the Supreme Being. The mention of the *mágadha* in the Vrátya-book, and the possibility that this word may refer to anti-brahmanical Buddhist teachers, have already been discussed (p. 112). In a passage communicated by Roth, *op. c.* p. 38, special, and hostile, notice is taken of the Aṅgas and Magadhas in the East, as well as of the Gandháris, Mújavants, Śúdras, Maháyṛishas, and Valhikas in the North-West, between which tribes therefore the Brahmanical district was apparently shut in at the time of the composition of the song in question. Intercourse with the West appears to have been more active than with the East, five of the races settled in the West being mentioned, and two only of those belonging to the

* In the Vishṇu-Puráṇa the Saindhavas, Saindhaváyanas are mentioned as a school of the Atharvan.

[161] This explanation of the contents of this book and of the word *vrátya* is based upon its employment in the Praśnopanishad 2. 7, and in the Chúlikopanishad, v. 11 (see *I. St.*, i. 445, 446, ix. 15, 16). According to Roth, on the contrary (see above p. 112, note), the purpose of the book is rather "the idealising of the devout vagrant or mendicant (*parivrájaka*, &c.)."

East. In time it will certainly be possible, in the Atharva-Saṃhitá also, to distinguish between pieces that are older and pieces that are more modern, although upon the whole geographical data are of rare occurrence. Its language exhibits many very peculiar forms of words, often in a very antique although prákṛitized shape. It contains, in fact, a mass of words used by the people, which from lack of occasion found no place in the other branches of the literature. The enumeration of the lunar asterisms in the nineteenth *káṇḍa* begins with *kṛittiká*, just as in the Taittiríya-Saṃhitá, but otherwise it deviates considerably from the latter, and gives for the most part the forms of the names used in later times.[162] No direct determination of date, however, can be gathered from it, as Colebrooke imagined. Of special interest is the mention of the Asura Kṛishṇa * Keśin, from the slaying of whom Kṛishṇa (Áñgirasa ?, Devakíputra) receives the epithets of Keśihan, Keśisúdana in the Epic and in the Puráṇas. In those hymns which appear also in the Ṛik-Saṃhitá (mostly in its last *maṇḍala*), the variations are often very considerable, and these readings seem for the most part equally warranted with those of the Ṛik. There are also many points of contact with the Yajus.

The earliest mention of the Atharvan-songs occurs under the two names "Atharváṇas" and "Añgirasas," names which belong to the two most ancient Ṛishi-families, or to the common ancestors of the Indo-Aryans and the Persa-Aryans, and which are probably only given to these songs in order to lend all the greater authority and holiness to the incantations, &c., contained in them.† They are also often specially connected with the ancient family of the Bhṛigus.[163] Whether we have to take the "Athar-

---

[162] The piece in question proves, on special grounds, to be a later supplement; see *I. St.*, iv. 433, n.

* An Asura Kṛishṇa we find even in the Ṛik-Saṃhitá, and he plays a prominent part in the Buddhist legends (in which he seems to be identified with the Kṛishṇa of the epic (?)).

† See *I. St.*, i. 295, ff. That these names indicate any Persa-Aryan influence is not to be thought of; and if, according to the Bhavishya-Puráṇa (Wilson in Reinaud's *Mém. sur l'Inde*, p. 394), the Parsis (Magas) have four Vedas, the Vada (! Yaśna ?), Viśvavada (Viśpered), Vidut (Vendidad), and Āñgirasa, this is a purely Indian view, though indeed very remarkable.

[163] See my essay *Zwei vedische Texte über Omina und Portenta*, pp. 346-348.

vâṇas" in the thirtieth book of the Váj. Saṃhitá as Atharvan-songs is not yet certain; but for the period to which the eleventh, thirteenth, and fourteenth books of the Śatapatha-Bráhmaṇa, as well as the Chhándogyopanishad and the Taittiríya-Áraṇyaka (ii. and viii.), belong, the existence of the Atharvan-songs and of the Atharvaveda is fully established by the mention of them in these works. The thirteenth book of the Śatapatha-Bráhmaṇa even mentions a division into *parvans*,* which, as already remarked, no longer appears in the manuscripts. In the eighth book of the Taittiríya-Áraṇyaka, the *ádeśa*, *i.e.*, the Bráhmaṇa, is inserted between the three other Vedas and the "Atharváñgirasas." Besides these notices, I find the Atharvaveda, or more precisely the "Átharvaṇikas," only mentioned in the Nidána-Sútra of the Sámaveda (and in Páṇini). The names, too, which belong to the schools of the Atharvaveda appear nowhere in Vedic literature,† with the exception perhaps of Kauśika; still, this patronymic does not by any means involve a special reference to the Atharvan.‡ Another name, which is, however, only applied to the Atharvaveda in the later Atharvan-writings themselves, viz., in the Pariśishṭas, is "Brahma-veda." This is explained by the circumstance that it claims to be the Veda for the chief sacrificial priest, the Brahman,[164] while the other Vedas are represented as those of his assistants only, the Hotar, Udgátar, and Adhvaryu,

* Corresponding to the *súktas*, *anuvákas*, and *daśats* of the Ṛik, Yajus, and Sáman respectively.

† Members of the family of the Atharvans are now and then mentioned; thus especially Dadhyañch Áth., Kabandha Áth., whom the Vishṇu-Puráṇa designates as a pupil of Sumantu (the latter we met in the Gṛihya-Sútras of the Ṛik, see above, p. 57), and others.

‡ It seems that even in later times the claim of the Atharvan to rank as Veda was disputed. Yájnavalkya (i. 101) mentions the two separately, *vedátharva;* though in another passage (i. 44) the "Atharváñgirasas" occur along with Ṛich, Sáman, and Yajus. In Manu's Code we only once find the *śrutir atharváñgirasíḥ*, as magic formulas; in the Rámáyaṇa likewise only once ii. 26. 20 (Gorr.) the *mantráś chátharvaṇás* (the latter passage I overlooked in *I. St.*, i. 297). [In Patamjali's Mahábháshya, however, the Atharvan is cited at the head of the Vedas (as in the Ṛig-Gṛihyas, see above, p. 58), occasionally even as their only representative; see *I. St.*, xiii. 431–32.]

164 This explanation of the name, though the traditional one, is yet very likely erroneous; by Brahmaveda (a name which is first mentioned in the Śáñkh. Gṛihya, i. 16) we have rather to understand 'the Veda of *brahmáṇi*,' of prayers, *i.e.*, here in the narrower sense of 'incantations.' (St. Petersburg Dict.)

—a claim which has probably no other foundation than the circumstance, cleverly turned to account, that there was, in fact, no particular Veda for the Brahman, who was bound to know all three, as is expressly required in the Kaushítaki-Bráhmaṇa (see *I. St.*, ii. 305). Now the weaker these pretensions are, the more strongly are they put forward in the Atharvan-writings, which indeed display a very great animosity to the other Vedas. Towards one another, too, they show a hostile enough spirit; for instance, one of the Pariśishṭas considers a Bhárgava, Paippaláda, and Śaunaka alone worthy to act as priest to the king,* while a Mauda or Jalada as *purohita* would only bring misfortune.

The Atharva-Saṃhitá also, it seems, was commented upon by Sáyaṇa. Manuscripts of it are comparatively rare on the Continent. Most of them are distinguished by a peculiar mode of accentuation.† A piece of the Saṃhitá of some length has been made known to us in text and translation by Aufrecht (*I. St.*, i. 121–140); besides this, only some fragments have been published.[105]

The Bráhmaṇa-stage is but very feebly represented in the Atharvaveda, viz., by the *Gopatha-Bráhmaṇa*, which, in the manuscript with which I am acquainted (E. I. H., 2142), comprises a *púrva-* and an *uttara*-portion, each containing five *prapáṭhakas;* the MS., however, breaks off with the beginning of a sixth (*i.e.*, the eleventh) *prapá-*

* Yájnavalkya (i. 312) also requires that such an one be well versed *atharváñgirase*.

† Dots are here used instead of lines, and the *svarita* stands mostly beside, not above, the *akshara*.

[105] The whole text has been edited long since (1855-56) by Roth and Whitney. The first two books have been translated by me in *I. St.*, iv. 393-430, and xiii. 129-216, and the nuptial formulas contained in the fourteenth book, together with a great variety of love charms and similar formulas from the remaining books, *ibid.*, v. 204-266. For the criticism of the text see Roth's tracts, *Ueber den Atharvaveda* (1856), and *Der Atharvaveda in Kashmir* (1875). In the Gopatha-Bráhmaṇa (i. 29), and in Patamjali's Mahábháshya (see *I. St.*, xiii. 433; although, according to Burnell, Introd. to Vaṅśa-Bráhmaṇa, p. xxii., the South Indian MSS. omit the quotation from the Atharvaveda), the beginning of the Saṃhitá is given otherwise than in our text, as it commences with i. 6, instead of i. 1. It is similarly given by Bhaṇḍarkar, *Indian Antiquary*, iii. 132; and two MSS. in Haug's possession actually begin the text in this manner; see Haug's *Brahman und die Brahmanen*, p. 45.—Burnell (Introd. to Vaṅśa-Br., p. xxi.) doubts whether the Ath. S. was commented by Sáyaṇa.

ṭhaka. In one of the Pariśishṭas the work is stated to have originally contained 100 *prapáṭhakas*. The contents are entirely unknown to me. According to Colebrooke's remarks on the subject, Atharvan is here represented as a Prajápati who is appointed by Brahman as a Demiurge; and this is, in fact, the position which he occupies in the Pariśishṭas and some of the Upanishads. The division of the year into twelve (or thirteen) months consisting of 360 days, and of each day into thirty *muhúrtas*, which Colebrooke points out as remarkable, equally appears in the Bráhmaṇas of the Yajus, &c.[166]

Departing from the order hitherto followed I will add here what I have to say about the *Sútras* of the Atharva-veda, as these are the only other writings which have reference to the Saṃhitá, whereas the remaining parts of the Atharvan-literature, corresponding to the Áraṇyakas of the other Vedas, have no reference to it whatever.

In the first place, I have to mention the *Śaunakíyá chatur-adhyáyiká*,[166b] a kind of Prátiśákhya for the Atharva-Saṃhitá, in four *adhyáyas*, which might possibly go back to the author of the Ṛik-Prátiśákhya, who is also mentioned in the Prátiśákhya of the White Yajus. The Śaunakas are named in the Charaṇavyúha as a school of the Atharvan, and members of this school are repeatedly mentioned in the Upanishads. The work bears here and there a more generally grammatical character than is the case with the remaining Prátiśákhyas. Śáka-

[166] M. Müller first gave us some information as to the Gopatha-Bráhmaṇa in his *History of A. S. L.*, p. 445–455; and now the work itself has been published by Rájendra Lála Mitra and Harachandra Vidyábhúshaṇa in the *Bibl. Indica* (1870–72). According to this it consists of eleven (*i.e.*, 5+6) *prapáṭhakas* only. We do not discover in it any special relation to the Ath. S., apart from several references thereto under different names. The contents are a medley, to a large extent derived from other sources. The first half is essentially of speculative, cosmogonic import, and is particularly rich in legends, a good number of which appear in the same form as in the Śatapatha-Bráhmaṇa, xi. xii., and are therefore probably simply copied from it. The second half contains a brief exposition of a variety of points connected with the Śrauta ritual, specially adapted, as it seems, from the Aitar. Br. Very remarkable is the assumption in i. 28 of a *doshapati*, lord of evil (!?), who at the beginning of the Dvápara (-yuga) is supposed to have acted as '*rishíṇám ekadeśaḥ*.' This reminds us of, and doubtless rests upon, the Mára of the Buddhists.

[166b] The form of name in the MS. is: *chaturádhyáyiká*.

ṭáyana and other grammatical teachers are mentioned. In the Berlin MS.—the only one as yet known—each rule is followed by its commentary.[167]

An *Anukramaṇí* to the Atharva-Saṃhitá is also extant; it, however, specifies for the most part only divine beings, and seldom actual Ṛishis, as authors.

The *Kauśika-Sútra* is the sole existing ritual Sútra of the Atharvaveda, although I am acquainted with an Átharvaṇa-Gṛihya through quotations.[168] It consists of fourteen *adhyáyas*, and in the course of it the several doctrines are repeatedly ascribed to Kauśika. In the introduction it gives as its authorities the Mantras and the Bráhmaṇas, and failing these the *sampradáya*, *i.e.*, tradition, and in the body of the work the Bráhmaṇa is likewise frequently appealed to (by *iti br.*); whether by this the Gopatha-Bráhmaṇa is intended I am unable to say. The style of the work is in general less concise than that of the other Sútras, and more narrative. The contents are precisely those of a Gṛihya-Sútra. The third *adhyáya* treats of the ceremonial for Nirṛiti (the goddess of misfortune); the fourth gives *bhaishajyas*, healing remedies; the sixth, &c., imprecations, magical spells; the tenth treats of marriage; the eleventh of the Manes-sacrifice; the thirteenth and fourteenth of expiatory ceremonies for various omens and portents (like the Adbhuta-Bráhmaṇa of the Sámaveda).[169]

---

[167] Of this Prátiśákhya also Whitney has given us an excellent edition in *Journal Am. Or. Soc.*, vii. (1862), x. 156, ff. (1872, additions). See also my remarks in *I. St.*, iv. 79–82. According to Whitney, this work takes no notice of the two last books of the existing Ath. text, which it otherwise follows closely; since therefore the Atharva-Saṃhitá in Patamjali's time already comprised twenty books, we might from this directly infer the priority of the Saun. ohat.; unless Patamjali's statement refer not to our text at all, but rather to that of the Paippaláda school; see Roth, *Der Atharvaveda in Kashmir*, p. 15.—Bühler has discovered another quite different Ath. Prátiśákhya; see *Monatsber.* of the Berl. Acad. 1871, p. 77.

[168] By which is doubtless meant just this Kauśika-Sútra. A Śrauta-Sútra belonging to the Atharvaveda has recently come to light, under the name of Vaitána-Sútra; see Haug, *I. St.*, ix. 176; Bühler, *Cat. of MSS. from Gujarát*, i. 190, and *Monatsberichte* of the Berl. Acad. 1871, p. 76; and some fuller accounts in Roth's *Atharvaveda in Kashmir*, p. 22.

[169] These two sections are published, with translation and notes, in my essay, *Zwei vedische Texte über Omina und Portenta* (1859); the section relating to marriage ceremonies is communicated in a paper by Haas, *Ueber die Heirathsgebräuche der alten Inder* in *I. St.*, v. 378, ff.

To this Sútra belong further five so-called *Kalpas:* the *Nakshatra-Kalpa*, an astrological compendium relating to the lunar mansions, in fifty *kaṇḍikás*; the *Śánti-Kalpa*, in twenty-five *kaṇḍikás*, which treats likewise of the adoration of the lunar mansions,[170] and contains prayers addressed to them; the *Vitána-Kalpa*, the *Saṃhitá-Kalpa*, and the *Abhichára-Kalpa*. The Vishṇu-Puráṇa and the Charaṇavyúha, to be presently mentioned, name, instead of the last, the *Áṅgirasa-Kalpa*. Further, seventy-four smaller Pariśishṭas [171] also belong to it, mostly composed in *ślokas*, and in the form of dialogues, like the Puráṇas. The contents are Gṛihya-subjects of various kinds; astrology,[172] magic, and the doctrine concerning omens and portents are most largely represented. Some sections correspond almost literally to passages of a like nature in the astrological Saṃhitás. Among these Pariśishṭas, there is also a *Charaṇa-vyúha*, which states the number of the *ṛichas* in the Atharva-Saṃhitá at 12,380, that of the *paryáyas* (hymns) at 2000; but the number of the *Kauśikoktáni pariśishṭáni* only at 70. Of teachers who are mentioned the following are the chief: first, Bṛihaspati Atharvan, Bhagavant Atharvan himself, Bhṛigu, Bhárgava, Aṅgiras, Áṅgirasa, Kávya (or Kavi) Uśanas; then Śaunaka, Nárada, Gautama, Káṃkáyana, Karmagha, Pippaláda, Máhaki, Garga, Gárgya, Vṛiddhagarga, Átreya, Padmayoni, Kraushṭuki. We meet with many of these names again in the astrological literature proper.

I now turn to the most characteristic part of the literature of the Atharvan, viz., the *Upanishads*. Whilst the Upanishads κατ' ἐξοχὴν so called, of the remaining Vedas all belong to the later, or even the latest, portions of these

---

[170] An account of the contents of both texts is given in my second essay on the Nakshatras, pp. 390–393 (1862); Haug in *I. St.*, ix. 174, mentions an Áraṇyaka-Jyotisha, different from the Nakshatra-Kalpa.

[171] Haug, *l. c.*, speaks of 72; amongst them is found a Nighaṇṭu, which is wanting in the Berlin MS. Compare the Nigama-Pariśishṭa of the White Yajus.—Texts of this kind are quoted even in the Mahábháshya; see *I. St.*, xiii. 463.

[172] One of the Pariśishṭas relating to this subject has been communicated by me in *I. St.*, x. 317, ff.; it is the fifty-first of the series. The statements found therein concerning the planets presuppose the existence of Greek influence; cf. *ibid.*, p. 319, viii. 413.

Vedas, they at least observe a certain limit which they never transgress, that is to say, they keep within the range of inquiry into the nature of the Supreme Spirit, without serving sectarian purposes. The Atharvan Upanishads, on the contrary, come down as far as the time of the Puráṇas, and in their final phases they distinctly enter the lists in behalf of sectarian views. Their number is as yet undetermined. Usually only fifty-two are enumerated. But as among these there are several which are of quite modern date, I do not see why we should separate these fifty-two Upanishads from the remaining similar tracts which, although not contained in the usual list, nevertheless call themselves Upanishads, or Atharvopanishads; more especially as this list varies in part according to the different works where it is found, and as the manuscripts mix up these fifty-two with the remaining Upanishads indiscriminately. Indeed, with regard to the Upanishad literature we have this peculiar state of things, that it may extend down to very recent times, and consequently the number of writings to be reckoned as belonging to it is very considerable. Two years ago, in the second part of the *Indische Studien*, I stated the number at ninety-five, including the Upanishads contained in the older Vedas.* The researches instituted by Walter Elliot in Masulipatam among the Telingana Brahmans on this subject have, however, as Dr. Roer writes to me, yielded the result that among these Brahmans there are

* This number is wrong; it ought to be ninety-three. I there counted the Ánandavallí and Bhṛiguvallí twice, first among the twenty-three *Atharvopanishads* omitted by Anquetil, and then among the nine Upanishads borrowed from the other Vedas which are found in his work. The number would further have to be reduced to ninety-two, since I cite Colebrooke's Amṛitavindu and Anquetil's Amṛitanáda as distinct Upanishads, whereas in point of fact they are identical; but then, on the other hand, two Upanishads identified by me ought to be kept distinct, viz., Colebrooke's Práṇágnihotra and Anquetil's Pranou, the latter (Praṇavopanishad) being different from the former.—The number now here finally arrived at—ninety-six—is obtained (1) by the addition of six new Upanishads, viz., the Bhállavi-Upanishad, the Saṃvartop., the second Mahopanishad, and three of the Upanishads contained in the Atharvaśiras (Gaṇapati, Súrya, Deví); (2) by the omission of two, the Rudropanishad and the Átharvaṇíya-Rudropanishad, which are possibly identical with others of those cited; and (3) by counting the Mahánáráyaṇopanishad as only one, whereas Colebrooke counts it as two.

123 Upanishads actually extant; and if we include those which they do not possess, but which are contained in my list just referred to, the total is raised to 147.* A list of these 123 is given in two of them, viz., in the Mahávákyamuktávalí and in the Muktikopanishad, and is exactly the same in both. According to the statement given above, there must be among these 123 fifty-two † in all which are wanting in my own list, and these include the two names just mentioned.—A Persian translation made in 1656 of fifty Upanishads is extant in Anquetil du Perron's Latin rendering.

If now we attempt to classify the Upanishads so far known, the most ancient naturally are those (1–12) which are found in the three older Vedas only.‡ I have already remarked that these never pursue sectarian aims. A seeming—but only a seeming—exception to this is the *Śatarudriya;* for although the work has in fact been used for sectarian purposes, it had originally quite a different significance, which had nothing to do with the misapplication of it afterwards made; originally, indeed, it was not an Upanishad at all.§ A real exception, however, is the *Śvetáśvataropanishad* (13), which is in any case wrongly classed with the Black Yajus; it is only from its having incorporated many passages of the latter that it has been foisted in here. It belongs to about the same rank and date as the Kaivalyopanishad. Nor can the *Maitráyaṇa-Upanishad* (14) reasonably claim to be ranked with the Black

---

* According to the previous note, only 145.

† According to last note but one, only fifty. [In the list published by W. Elliot of the Upanishads in the Muktikopan., see *Journal As. Soc. Beng.*, 1851, p. 607, ff., 108 names are directly cited (and of these 98 are analysed singly in Taylor's *Catalogue* (1860) *of the Oriental MSS. of Fort St. George*, ii. 457–474). But to these other names have to be added which are there omitted; see *I. St.*, iii. 324–326. The alphabetical list published by M. Müller in *Z. D. M. G.*, xix. 137–158 (1865), brings the number up to 149 (170, Burnell, *Indian Antiquary*, ii. 267). Since then many new names have been brought to our knowledge by the Catalogues of MSS. published by Burnell, Bühler, Kielhorn, Rájendra Lála Mitra, Haug (*Brahman und die Brahmanen*, pp. 29–31), &c.; so that at present I count 235 Upanishads, many of which, however, are probably identical with others, as in many cases the names alone are at present known to us.]

‡ Namely, Aitareya, Kaushítaki, Váshkala, Chhándogya, Śatarudriya, Śikshávallí or Taitt. Saṃhitopanishad, Chhágaleya (?), Tadeva, Śiva-saṃkalpa, Purushasúkta, Íśá, Vṛihad-Áraṇyaka.

§ See on this *I. St.*, ii. 14–47.

Yajus; it belongs rather, like the Śvetáśvataropanishad, only to the Yoga period. Still it does not, at least in the part known to me,[173] pursue any sectarian aim (see pp. 96–99).

Apart from the two last-named Upanishads, the transition to the Atharvopanishads is formed on the one hand by those Upanishads which are found in one of the other three Vedas, as well as in a somewhat modified form in an Atharvan-recension, and on the other hand by those Upanishads of which the Atharvan-recension is the only one extant, although they may have formerly existed in the other Vedas as well. Of the latter we have only one instance, the *Káṭhaka-Upanishad* (15, 16); of the former, on the contrary, there are several instances (17–20), viz., *Kena* (from the Sámaveda), *Bhriguvallí*, *Ánandavallí*, and *Brihannáráyaṇa* (Taitt. Ár., viii.–ix.).

The Atharvopanishads, which are also distinguished externally by the fact that they are mostly composed in verse, may themselves be divided into three distinct classes, which in their beginnings follow the earlier Upanishads with about equal closeness. Those of the first class continue directly to investigate the nature of Atman, or the Supreme Spirit; those of the second deal with the subject of absorption (*yoga*) in meditation thereon, and give the means whereby, and the stages in which, men may even in this world attain complete union with Átman; and lastly, those of the third class substitute for Átman some one of the many forms under which Śiva and Vishṇu, the two principal gods, were in the course of time worshipped.

Before proceeding to discuss these three classes in their proper order, I have to make some observations on the Atharvan-recensions of those Upanishads which either belong at the same time to the other Vedas also, or at any rate originally did so.

The Atharvan-text of the Kenopanishad, in the first place, differs but very little from its Sáman-text. The reason why this Upanishad has been incorporated into the Atharvan collection seems to be the fact that Umá Haimavatí is here (and for the first time) mentioned, as she

---

[173] In the remaining parts also there is nothing of the kind to be found.

was probably understood in the sense of the Śiva sects. With the Atharvan-text both of the Ánandavallí and of the Bhṛiguvallí * I am unacquainted. Of the Brihannáráyaṇop. † also, which corresponds to the Náráyaṇíyop. of the Taitt. Áraṇyaka, only a few data are known to me; these, however, sufficiently show that the more ancient and obscure forms have here throughout been replaced by the corresponding later and regular ones.‡—The two *Kaṭhavallís*, for the most part in metrical form, are extant in the Atharvan-text only.§ The second is nothing but a supplement to the first, consisting as it does almost exclusively of quotations from the Vedas, intended to substantiate more fully the doctrines there set forth. The first is based upon a legend (see pp. 92, 93) related in the Taitt. Bráhmaṇa [iii. 11. 8]. Nachiketas, the son of Áruṇi,‖ asks Death for a solution of his doubt whether man exists after death or not. After much reluctance, and after holding out enticements of all kinds, which Nachiketas withstands, Death at length initiates him into the mystery of existence. Life and death, he says, are but two different phases of development; true wisdom consists in the perception of identity with the Supreme Spirit, whereby men are elevated above life and death. The exposition in this first part is really impressive: the diction, too, is for the most part antique. A few passages, which do not harmonise at all with the remainder, seem either to have been inserted at a later time, or else, on the contrary, to have been retained

* Two lists of the Atharvopanishads in Chambers's Collection (see my Catalogue, p. 95) cite after these two *vallís* (39, 40), also a *madhyavallí* and an *uttaravallí* (41, 42)!

† By Colebrooke it is reckoned as two Upanishads.

‡ Thus we have *visasarja* instead of *vya-cha-sarja*; *Kanyákumárím* instead of °*ri*; *Kátyáyanyai* instead of °*yandya*, &c.

§ See *I. St.*, ii. 195, ff., where the various translations and editions are cited. Since then this Upanishad has appeared in a new edition, with Śaṃkara's commentary, in the *Bibl. Indica*, vol. viii., edited by Dr. Röer [and translated in vol. xv.].

‖ Two other names, which are given to the father of Nachiketas, viz., Auddálaki and Vájaśravasa, conflict with the usual accounts. Vájaśravasa appears also in the passage above referred to of the Taittiríya-Bráhmaṇa; whether Auddálaki does so likewise I am unable to say. [Auddálaki is wanting in the T. Br., as also the whole passage itself.] Benfey (in the *Göttinger Gelehrte Anzeigen*, January 1852, p. 129) suggests that we should refer Auddálaki Áruṇi to Nachiketas; but the incompatibility of the two names is not thereby removed. Áruṇi is Uddálaka, and Auddálaki is Áruṇeya.

from a former exposition drawn up more for a liturgical purpose. Its polemics against those holding different opinions are very sharp and bitter. They are directed against *tarka*, "doubt," by which the Sáṃkhyas and Bauddhas are here probably intended. The sacredness of the word *om* as the expression for the eternal position of things is very specially emphasised, a thing which has not occurred before in the same way. The gradation of the primeval principles (in iii. 10, 11) exactly corresponds to the system of the deistical Yoga, whereas otherwise the exposition bears a purely Vedántic character.

Of the Atharvopanishads proper the *Muṇḍaka-* and *Praśna*-Upanishads (21, 22) connect themselves most closely with the Upanishads of the older Vedas and with the Vedánta doctrine;[174] indeed, in the Vedánta-Sútra of Bádaráyaṇa reference is made to them quite as often as to these others. The *Muṇḍaka-Upanishad*, mostly in verse, and so called because it "shears" away, or frees from, all error, is very like the Káṭhakop. with regard to doctrine and style; it has, in fact, several passages in common with it. At the outset it announces itself as an almost direct revelation of Brahman himself. For Aṅgiras, who communicates it to Śaunaka, has obtained it from Bháradvája Satyaváha, and the latter again from Aṅgir,* the pupil of Atharvan, to whom it was revealed by Brah-

---

[174] The list of the Atharvopanishads begins, as a rule, with the Muṇḍakopanishad; and, according to the statements in Náráyaṇabhaṭṭa's scholium on the smaller Ath. Upanishads now being edited (since 1872) in the *Bibl. Indica* by Ráma-maya Tarkaratna, a settled order of these Upanishads must still have been in existence in the time of Náráyaṇabhaṭṭa, since he denotes the individual Upanishads as, *e.g.*, the seventh, the eighth, &c., reckoning from the Muṇḍaka. This order is occasionally ascribed by him to the Śaunaka-school. Compare as to this the remarks of Colebrooke, *Misc. Ess.*, i. 93, according to which the first fifteen Upanishads only would belong to the Śaunakíyas, and the following Up. to other Śákhás. But Náráyaṇa, with whom, as regards the order of the first twenty-eight names, Colebrooke agrees in the main (from this point their statements differ), also quotes the *Śaunakagranthavistara* for the Brahmavindu No. 18, and the *śákhá Śaunakavartitá* for the Átmopanishad No. 28, as authority for these numbers, or places, of the two Upanishads. The Gopálatápani, however, is marked by him as the forty-sixth '*Atharva-Paippale*,' and the Vásudevopanishad as the forty-ninth '*kshudragranthagaṇe;*' see Rájendra Lála Mitra, *Notices of Sanskṛit MSS.*, i. 18 (1870).

* Aṅgir is a name which occurs nowhere else.

man himself. Shortly afterwards, Vedic literature is opposed, as the inferior science, to speculation. The former is stated to consist of the four Vedas, and of the six Vedáṅgas, which are singly enumerated. Some manuscripts here insert mention of the *itihása-purána-nyáya-mímáṅsá-dharmaśástráṇi;* but this is evidently a later addition. Such additions are also found in other passages of this Upanishad in the manuscripts. This enumeration (here occurring for the first time) of the different Vedáṅgas is of itself sufficient to show that at that time the whole material of the Vedas had been systematically digested, and that out of it a new literature had arisen, which no longer belongs to the Vedic, but to the following period. We may further conclude from the mention of the Tretá in the course of the work that the Yuga-system also had already attained its final form. On the other hand, we here find the words *kálí* (the dark one) and *karálí* (the terrible one) still reckoned among the seven tongues of fire, whereas in the time of the dramatic poet Bhavabhúti (eighth century A.D.) they are names of Durgá—the wife of Śiva, developed out of Agni (and Rudra)—who under these names was the object of a bloody sacrificial worship. Since evidently a considerable time is required for the transition from the former meaning to the latter, the Muṇḍakop. must be separated by a very wide interval from the date of Bhavabhúti,—a conclusion which follows besides from the circumstance that it is on several occasions turned to account in the Vedánta-Sútra, and that it has been commented by Śaṃkara.—The *Praśnopanishad,* in prose, seems to be borrowed from an Atharva-Bráhmaṇa, viz., that of the Pippaláda-school.* It contains the instruction by Pippaláda of six different teachers, amongst whom the following names are especially significant in regard to the date of the Upanishad: Kauśalya Áśvaláyana, Vaidarbhi Bhárgava, and Kabandhin Kátyáyana. In the course of

* In the colophons, at least, it is once so described; by Śaṃkara, too, at the beginning of his commentary, it is called *bráhmaṇa,* although this proves but little, since with him all the Upanishads he comments pass as *śruti* and *bráhmaṇa.*—The name Pippaláda is probably to be traced to the conception found in the first verse of the Muṇḍaka iii. 1 (taken from Ṛik *maṇḍ.* i. 164. 20) (?). The same verse recurs in the Śvetáśvataropanishad iv. 6 and in Nir xiv. 30.

the work Hiranyanábha, a prince of the Kośalas, is also mentioned,—the same doubtless who is specially extolled in the Purâṇas. As in the Muṇḍakopan., so here also some interpolated words are found which betray themselves as such by the fact that they are passed over by Śaṃkara in his commentary. They refer to Atharvan himself, and to the half *mátrá* (mora), to which the word *om*, here appearing in its full glory, is entitled in addition to its three moræ (*a*, *u*, *m*), and are evidently a later addition by some one who did not like to miss the mention of these two subjects in an Atharvopanishad, as in these they otherwise invariably occur. Both Muṇḍaka and Praśna have been several times edited and translated, see *I. St.*, i. 280, ff., 439, ff., again recently by Dr. Roer in vol. viii. of the *Bibliotheca Indica* together with Śaṃkara's commentary.[175]—The name of Pippaláda is borne by another Upanishad, the *Garbha-Upanishad* (23), which I add here for this reason, although in other respects this is not quite its proper place. Its contents differ from those of all the other Upanishads, and relate to the human body, to its formation as embryo and the various parts of which it is composed, and the number and weight of these. The whole is a commentary on a *trishṭubh* strophe prefixed to it, the words of which are passed in review singly and further remarks then subjoined. The mention of the names of the seven musical notes of the present day, as well as of the weights now in use (which are found besides in Varáha Mihira), brings us to a tolerably modern date; so also the use of Devadatta in the sense of *Caius*. A few passages in which, among other things, mention is made, for instance, of Náráyaṇa as Supreme Lord, and of the Sáṃkhya and Yoga as the means of attaining knowledge of him, reappear in the fourteenth book—a supplementary one—of Yáska's Nirukti. Whether Śaṃkara expounded this Upanishad is as yet uncertain. It is translated in *Ind. Stud.*, ii. 65–71.[176]—In the *Brahmopanishad* also (24), Pippaláda appears, here with the title *bhagaván Añgirás*; he is thus identified with the latter, as the authority for the particular

[175] Roer's translation is published in vol. xv. of the *Bibl. Indica* (1853).

[176] Edited with Náráyaṇa's commentary in the *Bibliotheca Indica*, 1872; in his introduction described as *pañchakhaṇḍá 'shṭamán* (read °*mi!*) *Muṇḍát Paippaládábhidhá tathá*.

doctrine here taught which he imparts to Śaunaka (*mahá-śála*), exactly as is the case in the Muṇḍakopanishad. There is, for the rest, a considerable difference between this Upanishad[177] and the Muṇḍaka and Praśna; it belongs more to the Yoga-Upanishads properly so called. It consists of two sections: the first, which is in prose, treats, in the first place, of the majesty of Átman; and later on, in its last portion, it alleges Brahman, Vishṇu, Rudra, and Akshara to be the four *pádas* (feet) of the *nirváṇam brahma;* the first eleven of the nineteen verses of the second section discuss the subject of the Yogin being allowed to lay aside his *yajnopavíta*, or sacred thread, as he stands in the most intimate relation to the *sútra*, or mundane thread; the whole therefore amounts to a mere play upon words. The last eight verses are borrowed from the Śvetáśvataropanishad, Muṇḍakopanishad, and similar Upanishads, and again describe the majesty of the One.—The *Máṇḍúkyopanishad* (25–28) is reckoned as consisting of four Upanishads, but only the prose portion of the first of these, which treats of the three and a half *mátrás* of the word *om*, is to be looked upon as the real Máṇḍúkyopanishad, all the rest is the work of Gauḍapáda,* whose pupil Govinda was the teacher of Śaṃkara; it dates therefore from about the seventh century A.D. Similarly, there are two works by Śaṃkara himself specified among the Upanishads, viz., the *Áptavajrasúchí* (29), in prose, and the *Tripurí* (30), likewise in prose; both composed in a Vedánta sense. The former treats at the outset of what makes a *Bráhmaṇa* a *Bráhmaṇa;* it is not *játi* (birth), *varṇa* (colour), *páṇḍitya* (learning); but the *Brahmavid* (he who knows *Brahman*) is alone a *Bráhmaṇa*.† Then it passes to the different definitions of *moksha* (liberation),

---

177 Edited with Náráyaṇa's comm. in *Bibl. Ind.* 1873; in the introduction described as *chatushkhaṇḍá daśamí;* the two sections of the text seem to have been transposed in some of the MSS.

* As such, it has been commented on by Śaṃkara under the title *ágama-śástra*. For particulars see *I. St.*, ii. 100–109. [Roer has published the entire Máṇḍúkyopanishad together with Śaṃkara's comm. in *Bibl. Ind.* vol. viii., also a translation of sect. 1 in vol. xv.]

† This portion has been used by a Buddhist (Aśvaghosha), almost literally, against the system of caste in general, in the tract of the same title which is given by Gildemeister, *Bibl. S.*, Praef. p. vi. not.; see also

stating the only correct one to be the perception of the oneness of *jíva* (the individual soul) and *parameśvara* (the All-Soul), and lastly, distinctly rejecting all sects, it expounds the two highly important words *tat* (the Absolute) and *tvam* (the Objective). The *Tripurí* treats of the relation of Átman to the world, and stands as fourth *prakaraṇa* in a series of seven little Vedánta writings attributed to Śaṃkara.[178] The *Sarvopanishatsáropanishad* (31), in prose, may be considered as a kind of catechism of these doctrines; its purpose is to answer several queries prefixed to it as an introduction.[179] The same is the case with the *Nirálambopanishad* (32),[180] which, however, exhibits essentially the Yoga standpoint. The *Átmopanishad* (33), in prose, contains an inquiry by Añgiras into the three factors (*purushas*), the body, the soul, and the All-Soul.* The *Práṇágnihotropanishad* (34), in prose, points out the relation of the parts and functions of the body to those of the sacrifice, whence by implication it follows that the latter is unnecessary. At its conclusion it promises to him who reads this Upanishad the same reward as he receives who expires in Váráṇasí, viz., deliverance from transmigration.[181] The *Árshikopanishad* (? 35) contains a dialogue on the nature of Átman between Viśvámitra, Jamadagni, Bharadvája, Gautama, and Vasishṭha, the last of whom, appealing to the opinion of "K'hak" (? another MS. in Anquetil has "Kapl" = Kapila ?), obtains the assent of the others.[182]

Burnouf, *Introd. à l'Hist. du Buddh. Ind.*, p. 215. [Text and translation see now in my essay *Die Vajrasúchí des Aśvaghosha* (1860). By Haug, *Brahman und die Brahmanen*, p. 29, the Upanishad is described as *sámavedoktá.*]

178 See my Catalogue of the Berlin MSS., p. 180. By Rájendra Lála Mitra, however (*Notices of Sanskṛit MSS.*, i. 10, 11), a different text is cited as the *śrímachchhaṃkarácháryaviracitá tripuryupanishad.*

179 See *I. St.*, i. 301; edited with Náráyaṇa's comm. in *Bibl. Ind.* 1874; described in the introd. as *Taittiríyake | sarvopanishadáṃ sáraḥ saptatriṅśe chaturdaśe* (! ?).

180 See Rájendra Lála Mitra, ii. 95. Taylor, *Catalogue of Oriental MSS. of the College Fort St. George*, ii. 462.

* Translated in *I. St.*, ii. 56, 57. [Text and Náráyaṇa's comm. in *Bibl. Ind.* 1873; described in the introd. as *khaṇḍatrayánvitá | ashṭáviṅśí granthasaṃghe śákhá Śaunakavartitá.*]

181 Text and Náráyaṇa's comm. in *Bibl. Ind.* 1873; described in the introd. as *ekádaśí Śaunakíye;* see Taylor, ii. 472. Rájendra L. M. i. 49. Burnell, *Catalogue*, p. 63.

182 See *I. St.*, ix. 48–52. The name of the Upanishad is not yet certain.

The second class of the Atharvopanishads, as above stated, is made up of those whose subject is Yoga, or absorption in Átman, the stages of this absorption, and the external means of attaining it. These last chiefly consist in the giving up of all earthly connections, and in the frequent repetition of the word *om*, which plays a most prominent part, and is itself therefore the subject of deep study. Yájnavalkya is repeatedly named in the Upanishads of this class as the teacher of the doctrines they set forth;* and indeed it would seem that we ought to look upon him as one of the chief promoters of the system of religious mendicancy so intimately associated with the Yoga-doctrine. Thus, in the *Tárakopanishad* (36) he instructs Bharadvája as to the saving and sin-dispelling efficacy of the word *om*,[183] and similarly in the *Śákalyopanishad* (37)* Śákalya as to true emancipation.[184] The one, however, in which he stands out most prominently is the *Jábálopanishad* (38), in prose, which, moreover, bears the name of a school of the White Yajus, although no doubt wrongly, as it must in any case be considered as merely an imitation of the Áraṇyaka of this Veda (see *I. St.*, ii. 72–77). Still, it must have been composed before the Bádaráyaṇa-Sútra, as several passages of it† seem to be given in the latter (unless these passages have been borrowed from a common source?). Of special importance with regard to the mode of life of the Paramahaṅsas, or religious mendicants, are also, in addition to the Upanishad just mentioned, the *Kaṭhaśruti* (39; Colebrooke gives the name incorrectly as *Kaṇṭhaśruti*), in prose, and the *Áruṇikopanishad* (40), likewise in prose; ‡ both are to be

---

[183] See *I. St.*, ix. 46–48.

* This name seems to result as the most probable one from comparison of the variants in Anquetil.

[184] See *I. St.*, ii. 170.

† They presuppose the name Váráṇasí for Benares. [The text of the *Jábálopanishad* with Náráyaṇa's comm. appeared in *Bibl. Ind.* 1874; it is described in the introd. as *yájushí* and *ekachatvárinśattamí* (the latter, however, is said of the *Kaivalyopanishad* also!); see also Burnell, p. 61, Taylor ii. 474, Rájendra L. M. i. 92 (Commentary by Śaṃkaránanda). There are, besides, quite a number of other Upanishads bearing the name of Jábála, viz., Bṛihajjábála, Mahájábála, Laghujábála, Bhasma°, Rudra°, Rudráksha°.]

‡ Translated in *I. St.*, ii. 176–181. [Text and Náráyaṇa's comm. in *Bibl. Ind.*, 1872; described in the introd. as *pañchavinśí*. There is also a commentary upon it by Śaṃkaránanda; see Rájendra L. M. i. 92.—The *Kaṭhaśruti*, also, is

regarded as supplements to the Áraṇyaka of the Black Yajus, as the Jábálopanishad is to that of the White Yajus. The *Bhállavi-Upanishad* (41) also belongs to this class, to judge by quotations from it, and so does the *Saṃvartaśruti* (42); similarly the *Saṃnyásopanishad* (43) and the *Paramahansopanishad* (44), both in prose.* The *Haṅsopanishad* (45) I have not yet met with; but from its name it probably also belongs to this place.[185] The *Áśramopanishad* (46), in prose, gives a classification of the four Indian orders—the Brahmachárins, Gṛihasthas, Vánaprasthas, and Parivrájakas. It is even quoted by Śaṃkara, and the names applied in it to the several classes are now obsolete. The *Śrímaddattopanishad* (47) consists of twelve *ślokas* put into the mouth of one of these religious mendicants, and uniformly concluding with the refrain: *tasyá 'haṃ pañchamáśramam*, "I am his, *i.e.*, *brahman's*, fifth *Áśrama*." Apart from the two Upanishads already mentioned, the Máṇḍúkya and the Táraka, the investigation of the sacred word *om* is principally conducted in the *Atharvaśikhá* (48), in prose (explained by Śaṃkara), in which instruction is given on this subject by Atharvan to Pippaláda, Sanatkumára, and Aṅgiras;† further, in the *Brahmavidyá* (49), in thirteen *ślokas*, now and then quoted by Śaṃkara;‡ and lastly, in the *Śaunaka*

---

edited in *Bibl. Ind.* (1873), with Náráyaṇa's commentary; although under the name Kaṇṭha°, it is clear from Náráyaṇa's words in his introduction, *Yajurvede tu Charaká dvádaśai 'shá kaṇṭháśrayaḥ* (!) | *saṃnyásopanishattulyá chatuḥkhaṇḍá kṛita*(!) *śrutiḥ* || that this mode of spelling here, as well as in Burnell's *Catalogue*, p. 60, is a mere mistake, and that Náráyaṇa himself connected the Upanishad with the Kaṭhas; see also Bühler, *Catalogue of MSS. from Guj.*, i. 58.]

* The *Paramahaṅsopanishad* is translated in *I. St.*, ii., 173-176. [Text with Nár.'s comm. in *Bibl. Ind.*, 1874; described in the introd. as *trikhaṇḍá 'tharvaśikhare chatváriṅśattamí*. —The *Saṃnyásopanishad*, too, is printed *ibid.*, 1872; we there find a direct reference made to four *anuvákas* of the Ath. S. (xviii.); their text is therefore given by the editor in the scholium, and that in a double form acc. to two MSS. (pp. 131-175); see also Rájendra L. M. i. 54, Taylor, ii. 469.]

[185] Text and Nár.'s comm. in *Bibl. Ind.*, 1874; described in the introd. as *ashṭatriṅśattamí* | *átharvaṇe*. By Rájendralál., i. 90, a comm. by Śaṃkaránanda is specified; see besides Burnell, p. 65.

† See *I. St.*, ii. 55.—Here, therefore, we have Pippaláda and Aṅgiras appearing side by side (see above, p. 160). [Text and Nár.'s comm. in *Bibl. Ind.*, 1873; described in the introd. as *saptamí muṇḍát*.]

‡ Translated in *I. St.*, ii. 58. [Text and Nár.'s comm. in *Bibl. Ind.*, 1873.]

(50) and the *Praṇava* (51). These two are found in Anquetil only.[186] The various stages of gradual absorption into Átman form the contents of the following Upanishads (52–59): *Haṅsanáda* (in prose), *Kshuriká* (24 *ślokas*), *Nádavindu* (20 *ślokas*), *Brahmavindu* (22 *ślokas*; also called *Amṛitavindu*), *Amṛitavindu* (38 *ślokas*; also called *Amṛitanáda*), *Dhyánavindu* (23 *ślokas*), *Yogaśikhá* (10 *ślokas*), and *Yogatattva* (15 *ślokas*); while the majesty of Átman himself is depicted in the *Chúliká* (60, in 21 *ślokas*) and *Tejovindu* (61, in 14 *ślokas*): * in the former direct reference is repeatedly made to the doctrine of the Atharvans. The range of ideas and the style are quite identical in all the Upanishads just enumerated. The latter frequently suffers from great obscurity, partly because there occur distinct grammatical inaccuracies, partly because the construction is often very broken and without unity. Many verses recur in several of them; many again are borrowed from the Śvetáśvataropanishad or Maitráyaṇopanishad. Contempt for caste as well as for writing (*grantha*) is a trait which appears again and again in almost all these Upanishads, and one might therefore be inclined to regard them as directly Buddhistic, were they not entirely free from all Buddhistic dogma. This agreement is to be explained simply by the fact that Buddhism itself must be considered as having been originally only a form of the Sáṃkhya-doctrine.

The sectarian Upanishads have been set down as forming the third class. They substitute for Átman one of the forms of Vishṇu or Śiva, the earlier ones following the Yoga-doctrine most closely, whilst in those of a modern date the personal element of the respective deities comes

---

[186] See *I. St.*, ix. 52-53 and 49-52; the *Praṇavopanishad* is mentioned by Taylor, ii. 328.

* For the *Haṅsanáda* see *I. St.*, i. 385-387; the *Kshuriká* is translated, *ib.*, ii. 171-173; likewise *Amṛitavindu*, ii. 59-62; *Tejovindu*, ii. 62-64; *Dhyánavindu*, ii. 1-5; *Yogaśikhá* [so we ought to read] and *Yogatattva*, ii. 47-50, [*Amṛitanáda*, ix. 23-28; *Chúliká*, ix. 10-21. All these Upanishads are now published in the *Bibliotheca Indica* with Náráyaṇa's comm. (1872-73), excepting the *Haṅsanádopanishad*, which, however, seems to be identical with the *Haṅsopanishad* printed *ibid.* In the Introductions to the comm. *Chúliká* is described as *pañchamí*; *Brahmavindu* as *ashṭádaśí Śaunakagranthavistare*; *Dhyánavindu* as *viṅśá* (*viṅśí*!); *Tejovindu* as *ekaviṅśam*; *Yogaśikhá* as *granthasandohe* (!) *dvátriṅśatitamí* (probably meant for *dvátriṅś°*!); *Yogatattva* as *trayoviṅśá* (*°śí*)].

more and more into the foreground. A special characteristic of this class are the unmeasured promises usually held out at the close of the work to him who reads and studies it, as also the quotation and veneration of sacred formulas containing the name of the particular deity.

First, as regards the Upanishads of the *Vishṇu*-sects,—the oldest form under which Vishṇu is worshipped is *Náráyaṇa*. We find this name for the first time in the second part of the Śatapatha-Bráhmaṇa, where, however, it is not in any way connected with Vishṇu; it rather stands, as at the commencement of Manu and the Vishṇu-Puráṇa, in the sense of Brahman (mascul.). This is also the case in the Náráyaṇíyopanishad of the Taittiríya-Áraṇyaka, and in its Atharvan-recension as Bṛihannárá-yaṇopanishad, although in the latter he is at least called Hari, and in one passage brought into direct relation to Vásudeva and Vishṇu. It is in the *Mahá-Upanishad* (62),—a prose tract, which* in its first part contains the emanation of the universe from Náráyaṇa, and in its second a paraphrase of the principal passage of the Náráyaṇíyopanishad,—that Náráyaṇa first distinctly appears as the representative of Vishṇu, since Śúlapáṇi (Śiva) and Brahman proceed from him, and Vishṇu is not mentioned at all. In the *Náráyaṇopanishad* (64, in prose),[187] on the contrary, Vishṇu also emanates from him, exactly as in the Náráyaṇa section † of the twelfth book of the Mahá-Bhárata (a book which in other respects also is of special significance in relation to the Sámkhya- and Yoga-doctrines). The sacred formula here taught is: *om namo Náráyaṇáya*. There exists of this Upanishad another, probably a later, recension which forms part of the Atharvaśiras to be mentioned hereafter, and in which Devakíputra Madhusúdana is mentioned as particularly *brahmaṇya*, pious, as is also the case in the *Átmaprabodha-Upanishad* (65), which like-

---

* Translated in *I. St.*, ii. 5-8 [see also Taylor, ii. 468, Rájendra L. M. i. 25]; besides it there must have existed another *Mahá-Upan.* (63), which is cited by the adherents of the Mádhava sect as a warrant for their belief in a personal soul of the universe, distinct from the soul of man.

[187] See also Rájendra L. M. i. 12, 91 (comm. by Saṃkaránanda).

† At the time of the (last?) arrangement of the present text of the Mahá-Bhárata, Náráyaṇa worship must have been particularly flourishing.

wise celebrates Náráyaṇa as the Supreme Lord;[188] see *I. St.*, ii. 8, 9. He (Náráyaṇa) is named, besides, in the same quality in the Garbhopanishad (in a passage recurring in the Nirukti, xiv.) and in the Śákalyopanishad.

The second form under which we find Vishṇu worshipped is *Nṛisiṅha*: The earliest mention of him hitherto known appears in the Taitt. Ár., x. 1. 8 (in the Náráyaṇíyop.), under the name of Nárasiṅha, and with the epithets *vajranakha* and *tíkshṇadaṅshṭra*. The only Upanishad in which he is worshipped is the *Nṛisiṅhatápaníyopanishad* (in prose). It is relatively of considerable extent, and is also counted as six separate Upanishads (66–71), as it consists of two parts,* the first of which is in turn subdivided into five distinct Upanishads. The first part treats of the Anushṭubh-formula † sacred to Nṛisiṅha, the *mantrarája nárasiṅha ánushṭubha*, with which the most wondrous tricks are played; wherein we have to recognise the first beginnings of the later Málámantras with their Tantra-ceremonial. A great portion of the Máṇḍúkyopanishad is incorporated into it, and the existence also of the Atharvaśikhá is presupposed, as it is directly quoted. The contents of the second part are of a more speculative character; but in respect of mystical trifling it does not yield to the first part. In both, the triad—Brahman, Vishṇu, and Śiva—is repeatedly mentioned. As regards language, the expression *buddha* for the supreme Átman, which occurs (along with *nitya*, *śuddha*, *satya*, *mukta*, &c.) in the second part, is of peculiar interest; and the expression is still retained in Gauḍapáda and Śaṃkara; originally it belongs evidently to the Sáṃkhya school (see above, pp. 27, 129).

This Upanishad has been interpreted by Gauḍapáda and Śaṃkara; and in addition to much that is quite modern, it presents a great deal that is ancient. It probably dates from about the fourth century A.D., as at that

---

[188] See also Rájendra L. M., iii. 36; Taylor, ii. 328.

* The above-mentioned lists of Upanishads in the Chambers collection admit a *Madhyatápini* also [see my Catalogue, p. 95].

† It runs *ugram víraṃ mahávishṇuṃ jvalantaṃ sarvatomukham | nṛisiṅhaṃ bhíshaṇaṃ bhadraṃ mṛityumṛityuṃ namámy aham.* || "I worship the terrible, powerful, mighty Vishṇu, the flaming, the omnipresent; Nṛisiṅha, the dread, the holy one, the death of death."

time the Nṛisiṅha worship flourished on the western coast of India, while otherwise we find no traces of it.[189]

The *Rámatápaníyopanishad* (72, 73), in which Ráma is worshipped as the Supreme God, shows a great resemblance to the Nṛisiṅhatápaníyop., especially in its second part. This second part, which is in prose, is, properly speaking, nothing but a collection of pieces from the Tárakopanishad, Máṇḍúkyopanishad, Jábálopanishad, and Nṛisiṅhopanishad, naturally with the necessary alterations. Yájnavalkya here appears as the proclaimer of the divine glory of Ráma. A London MS. adds at the close a long passage which is unknown to the commentator Ánandavana (a native of the town Kuṇḍina). The crowning touch of the sectarian element in this Upanishad is found in the circumstance that Ráma is implored by Śiva (Śaṃkara) himself to spare those a second birth who die in Maṇikarṇiká or in the Gaṅgá generally, the two principal seats of the Śiva worship. The first part, in ninety-five *ślokas*, contains at the beginning a short sketch of Ráma's life, which bears a great similarity to that at the beginning of the Adhyátmarámáyaṇa (in the Brahmáṇḍa-Puráṇa). The Mantrarája is next taught by the help of a mystical alphabet, specially invented for the purpose.* This Upanishad evidently belongs to the school of Rámánuja, possibly to Rámánuja himself, consequently its earliest date would be the eleventh century A.D.[190]

Under the names Vishṇu, Purushottama, and Vásudeva, Vishṇu is mentioned as the supreme Átman in several

---

[189] See text and translation of this Upanishad in *I. St.*, ix. 53–173; and specially on the chronological question, pp. 62, 63. In the *Bibl. Indica* also, this Upanishad has been published by Rámamaya Tarkaratna (1870–71), with Śaṃkara's commentary (it is, however, doubtful whether the commentary on the second part belongs to Śaṃkara), together with the small (*Nárasiṅha*) *shaṭchakropanishad* and Náráyaṇa's comm. on it.

* The Nárasiṅha- and a Váráha-Mantra are also mentioned.

[190] See text and translation in my essay *Die Ráma-Tápaníya-Upanishad* (1864); text and Náráy.'s comm. in *Bibl. Ind.* also (1873); in the introductions the two sections are called *pañchatriṅśattama* and *shaṭtriṅśa* respectively. The time of composition is probably even later than above supposed. In the first place, according to Nṛisiṅha's statements in his *Smṛityarthasára* (see Aufrecht, *Catalogus*, pp. 285[b], 286[a]), Rámánuja flourished as late as the twelfth century (*śake* 1049 = A.D. 1127). But further, the Rámatápaní displays still closer relations to Rámánanda, who is supposed to have lived towards the end of the fourteenth century; see my essay, p. 382.

Upanishads;* Kṛishṇa Devakíputra appears likewise in some of them (the Átmaprabodha and Náráyaṇa), not, however, as supreme Átman, but merely, as in the Chhándogyop., as a particularly pious sage. It is in the *Gopálatápaníyopanishad* (74, 75) that we first find him elevated to divine dignity. Of this Upanishad, the second part at least, in prose, is known to me.† It treats first of the *gopís* of Mathurá and Vraja, then it passes to the identification of Mathurá with Brahmapura, &c.; and it belongs without doubt to a very modern period, as it exhibits hardly any points of contact with other Upanishads in regard to contents and language.[191] The *Gopíchandanopanishad* (76) also probably belongs to this place:[192] I know it only by name.

At the head of the Upanishads belonging to the *Śiva*-sects stands, according to the use that has been made of it, the *Śatarudriya.* I have already remarked, however, that this is nothing but an abuse. In its germs the worship of Śiva may be traced even in the later portions of the Yajus.‡ He appears very prominently as Mahádeva in a portion of the Náráyaṇíyopanishad, and here he is already associated with his spouse. The Śvetáśvataropanishad also pays homage to him. Among the Atharvopanishads the most ancient in this regard is the *Kaivalyopanishad* (77), a mixture of prose and *ślokas*, in which *bhagaván mahádevaḥ* himself instructs Áśvaláyana concerning his own majesty; in a similar way he acts as his own herald § in the *Atharvaśiras* (78), in prose. The latter

---

* And also, in particular, under the name Vásudeva, in the writings ascribed to Śaṃkara.

† The lists in the Chambers collection specify a *Gopálatápiní. Madhyatápiní, Uttaratápiní*, and *Bṛihaduttaratápiní!*

[191] The text of this Upanishad, with Viśveśvara's commentary, is printed in the *Bibl. Indica* (1870), edited by Harachandra Vidyábhúshaṇa and Viśvanáthaśástrin. Occasionally extracts are added from the commentaries by Náráyaṇa and Jívagosvámin. According to Rájendral., i. 18, its first section is described in Náráyaṇa's introduction as *shaṭchatvárinśati cha púrṇá chá 'tharvapaippale.*—See an analysis of the second section in Taylor, ii. 472.

[192] So also according to Rájendral., i. 20 (comm. by Nár.), 60; it is specially "a treatise on the merits of putting on sectarial marks on the forehead with an ochrous earth, called *gopíchandana.*"

‡ As in the Atharva-Saṃhitá and in the Śáṅkháyana-Bráhmaṇa (see pp. 45, 110).

§ Like Kṛishṇa in the Bhagavadgítá. The *Kaivalyopanishad* is translated *I. St.*, ii. 9–14; on *Atharvaśiras* see *ibid.*, i. pp. 382–385. [Text of, and two commentaries on,

Upanishad has been expounded by Śaṃkara. Under the same title, "head of Atharvan,"—a name that is also borne by Brahman himself, although in a different relation,—there exists a second Upanishad, itself a conglomeration of five different Upanishads referring to the five principal deities, Gaṇapati (79), Náráyaṇa, Rudra, Súrya (80), and Deví (81).* Its Náráyaṇa-portion is a later recension of the Náráyaṇopanishad (64, see above, p. 166), and the Rudra-portion follows the first chapter of the Atharvaśiras proper. All five have been translated by Vans Kennedy. In the Mahá-Bhárata (i. 2882), and the Code of Vishṇu, where the Atharvaśiras is mentioned along with the *Bháruṇḍáni sámáni*, and in Vishṇu also, where it appears beside the Śatarudriya (as the principal means of expiation), the reference probably is to the Upanishad explained by Śamkara (?).—The *Rudrop.* and *Átharvaṇíya-Rudrop.* are known to me only through the Catalogue of the India Office Library. Possibly they are identical with those already named; I therefore exclude them from my list. The *Mṛityulaṅghanopanishad* (82)† is quite modern, and with it is wor-

---

the Kaivalyopanishad printed in *Bibl. Ind.*, 1874; the first commentary is that of Náráyaṇa; the second is described by the editor as that of Śaṃkara, in the colophon as that of Saṃkaránanda; it follows, however, from Rájendra Lála Mitra's *Catalogue*, i. 32, that it is different from the commentary written by the latter; and according to the same authority, ii. 247, it is identical rather with that of Vidyáraṇya. In Náráyaṇa's introduction this Upanishad is described (exactly like the Jábálop. !) as *ekachatvárinśattamí*. The *Śiras-* or *Atharvaśiras*-Upanishad is likewise printed in *Bibl. Ind.* (1872), with Náráyaṇa's comm., which describes it as *rudrádhyáyaḥ saptakhaṇḍaḥ*. See also Rájendral., i. 32 (comm. by Śaṃkaránanda), 48.]

* See *I. St.*, ii. 53, and Vans Kennedy, *Researches into the Nature and Affinity of Hindu and Ancient Mythology*, p. 442, &c. [Taylor, ii. 469-471. By Rájendral., i. 61, a *Gaṇapatyapúrvatápaníyopanishad* is mentioned; by Bühler, *Cat. of MSS. from Guj.*, i. 70, a *Gaṇapatipúrvatápiní* and a *Gaṇeśatápiní*; and by Kielhorn, *Sanskṛit MSS. in the Southern Division of the Bombay Pres.* (1869), p. 14, a *Gaṇapatipúrvatápaniyopanishad.*]

† So we have probably to understand Anquetil's *Amrat Lankoul*, since he has also another form, *Mrat Lankoun*; instead of, *id est* '*halitus mortis*,' we ought to read '*salitus mortis*.' [See now *I. St.*, ix. 21-23; according to this it is doubtful whether the name ought not to be written *Mṛityuláṅgúla* (?). An Upanishad named *Mṛityulaṅghana* is mentioned by Bühler, *Cat. of MSS. from Guj.*, i. 120; a Mṛityuláṅgúla, however, appears as 82d Upanishad in the Catalogue of Paṇḍit Rádhákṛishṇa's library. Finally, Burnell, in publishing the text in the *Indian Antiquary*, ii. 266, gives the form *Mṛityuláṅgala*.]

thily associated the *Kálágnirudropanishad* (83),[193] in prose, of which there are no less than three different recensions, one of which belongs to the Nandikeśvara-Upapuráṇa. The *Tripuropanishad* (84) also appears from its name—otherwise it is unknown to me—to belong to this division;[194] it has been interpreted by Bhaṭṭa Bháskara Miśra. The *Skandopanishad* (85), in fifteen *ślokas*, is also Śiva-itic[195] (likewise the *Amṛitanádopanishad*). The adoration of Śiva's spouse, his Śakti,—the origin of which may be traced back to the Kenopanishad and the Náráyaṇíyopanishad,—is the subject of the *Sundarítápaníyopanishad* (known to me by name only), in five parts (86–90), as well as of the *Deví-Upanishad* (79), which has already been mentioned. The *Kaulopanishad* (91), in prose, also belongs to a Śákta sectary.*

Lastly, a few Upanishads (92–95) have to be mentioned, which are known to me only by their names, names which do not enable us to draw any conclusion as to their contents, viz., the *Piṇḍopanishad*, *Nílaruhopanishad* (Colebrooke has *Nílarudra*), *Paiṅgalopanishad*, and *Darśanopanishad*.[196] The *Garuḍopanishad* (96), of which I know two totally different texts, celebrates the serpent-destroyer Garuḍa,† and is not without some antiquarian interest.

---

[193] It treats specially of the *tripuṇḍravidhi*; see Taylor, i. 461; Rájendr., i. 59; Burnell, p. 61.

[194] See on it Taylor, ii. 470; Burnell, p. 62.

[195] "Identifies Śiva with Vishṇu, and teaches the doctrines of the Advaita school." Taylor, ii. 467; Burnell, p. 65.

* In the Tejovindu (61) also, *brahman* is described as *áṇava*, *śámbhava*, *śákta*.

[196] The *Piṇḍop.* and the *Nilarudrop.*—this is its proper name—are now printed in *Bibl. Ind.* (1873), with Náráyaṇa's comm.; the former, which treats of the *piṇḍas* to the *pretas*, is described by Náráyaṇa as *saptaviṅśatipúraṇí*, the latter as *shoḍaśí*: it is addressed to Rudra (see also Rájendral., i. 51), and consists only of verses, which closely follow those contained in Váj. S. xvi. On the Paiṅgalop. and Darśanop., see Taylor, ii. 468–471.

† As is done in the *Náráyaṇíyopanishad* also, and more especially in the *Suparṇádhyáya*, which is considered to belong to the Ṛik [edited by Elimar Grube, 1875; see also *I. St.*, xiv. 1, ff.—The *Gáruḍopanishad* is now printed in *Bibl. Ind.* (1874), with Náráyaṇa's commentary; in the introduction it is described as *chatuśchatváriṅśattamí*.]

SECOND PERIOD.

SANSKṚIT LITERATURE.

SECOND PERIOD.

SANSKṚIT LITERATURE.

HAVING thus followed the first period of Indian literature, in its several divisions, down to its close, we now turn to its second period, the so-called Sanskṛit literature. Here, however, as our time is limited, we cannot enter so much into detail as we have hitherto done, and we must therefore content ourselves with a general survey. In the case of the Vedic literature, details were especially essential, both because no full account of it had yet been given, and because the various works still lie, for the most part, shut up in the manuscripts; whereas the Sanskṛit literature has already been repeatedly handled, partially at least, and the principal works belonging to it are generally accessible.

Our first task, naturally, is to fix the distinction between the second period and the first. This is, in part, one of age, in part, one of subject-matter. The former distinction is marked by the language and by direct data; the latter by the nature of the subject-matter itself, as well as by the method of treating it.

As regards the language, in the first place, in so far as it grounds a distinction in point of age between the two periods of Indian literature, its special characteristics in the second period, although apparently slight, are yet, in reality, so significant that it appropriately furnishes the name for the period; whereas the earlier one receives its designation from the works composing it.

Among the various dialects of the different Indo-Aryan tribes, a greater unity had in the course of time been established after their immigration into India, as the natural result of their intermingling in their new homes, and of their combination into larger communities. The grammatical * study, moreover, which by degrees became necessary for the interpretation of the ancient texts, and which grew up in connection therewith, had had the effect of substantially fixing the usage; so that a generally recognised language, known as the *bháshá*, had arisen, that, namely, in which the Bráhmaṇas and Sútras are composed.† Now the greater the advance made by the study of grammar, the more stringent and precise its precepts and rules became, and all the more difficult it was for those who did not occupy themselves specially therewith to keep in constant accord with grammatical accuracy. The more the language of the grammatically educated gained on the one hand in purity, and in being purged of everything not strictly regular, the more foreign did it become on the other hand to the usage of the majority of the people, who were without grammatical training. In this way a refined language gradually disconnected itself from the vernacular, as more and more the exclusive property of the higher classes of the people; ‡ the estrange-

* Respecting the use of the verb *vyákṛi* in a grammatical signification, Sáyaṇa in his introduction to the Ṛik (p. 35. 22 ed. Müller) adduces a legend from a Bráhmaṇa, which represents Indra as the oldest grammarian. (See Lassen, *I. AK.*, ii. 475.) [The legend is taken from the TS. vi. 4. 7. 3. All that is there stated, indeed, is that *vách* was *vyákṛitá* by Indra; manifestly, however, the later myths which do actually set up Indra as the oldest grammarian connect themselves with this passage.]

† *Bháshika-svara* in Kátyáyana, Srauta-Sútra, i. 8. 17, is expressly interpreted as *bráhmaṇa-svara*; see *Váj. Saṃh. Specimen*, ii. 196. 197. [*I. St.*, x. 428–429, 437.] Yáska repeatedly opposes *bháshá yám* and *anvadhyáyam* (*i.e.*, 'in the Veda reading,' 'in the text of the hymns') to each other; similarly, the Prátiśákhya-Sútras employ the words *bháshá* and *bháshya* as opposed to *chhandas* and *veda*, *i.e.*, *saṃhitá* (see above, pp. 57, 103, 144). The way in which the word *bháshya* is used in the Gṛihya-Sutra of Śáṅkháyana, namely, in contradistinction to *Sútra*, shows that its meaning had already by this time become essentially modified, and become restricted, precisely as it is in Páṇini, to the extra-Vedic, so to say, profane literature. (The Áśvaláyana-Gṛihya gives instead of *bháshya*, in the corresponding passage, *bhárata-mahábhárata-dharma*.) [This is incorrect; rather, in the passage in question, these words follow the word *bháshya*; see the note on this point at p. 56.] In the same way, in the Nir. xiii. 9, *mantra*, *kalpa*, *bráhmaṇa*, and the *vyávahárikí* (sc. *bháshá*) are opposed to each other (and also *Ṛik*, *Yajus*, *Sáman*, and the *vyávahárikí*).

‡ Ought the passage cited in Nir. xiii. 9 from a Bráhmaṇa [cf. Káṭh. xiv. 5], to the effect that the Brahmans spoke both tongues, that of the gods as well as that of men, to be taken in this connection? or has this reference merely to a conception resembling the Homeric one?

ment between the two growing more and more marked, as the popular dialect in its turn underwent further development. This took place mainly under the influence of those aboriginal inhabitants who had been received into the Brahmanic community; who, it is true, little by little exchanged their own language for that of their conquerors, but not without importing into the latter a large number of new words and of phonetic changes, and, in particular, very materially modifying the pronunciation. This last was all the more necessary, as the numerous accumulations of consonants in the Aryan *bháshá* presented exceeding difficulties to the natives; and it was all the easier, as there had evidently prevailed within the language itself from an early period a tendency to clear away these troublesome encumbrances of speech,—a tendency to which, indeed, the study of grammar imposed a limit, so far as the educated portion of the Aryans was concerned, but which certainly maintained itself, and by the very nature of the case continued to spread amongst the people at large. This tendency was naturally furthered by the native inhabitants, particularly as they acquired the language not from those who were conversant with grammar, but from intercourse and association with the general body of the people. In this way there gradually arose new vernaculars, proceeding directly from the common *bháshá*,* and distinguished from it mainly by the assimilation of consonants, and by

---

* And therefore specially so called down even to modern times; whereas the grammatically refined *bháshá* afterwards lost this title, and substituted for it the name *Saṃskṛita-bháshá*, 'the cultivated speech.' The name *Prákṛita-bháshá*, which was at the same time applied to the popular dialects, is derived from the word *prakṛiti*, 'nature,' 'origin,' and probably describes these as the 'natural,' 'original' continuations of the ancient *bháshá*: or does *prákṛita* here signify 'having a *prakṛiti* or origin,' *i.e.*, 'derived'? [Out of the signification 'original,' 'lying at the root of' (*prakṛiti-bhúta*), 'unmodified,' arose that of 'normal,' then that of 'ordinary,' '*communis*,' '*vulgaris*,' and lastly, that of 'proceeding in common from.' The term directly opposed to it is not *saṃskṛita*, but *vaikṛita*; see, *e.g.*, Ath. Pariś. 49. 1, "*varṇán púrvaṃ vyákhyásyámaḥ prákṛitá ye cha vaikṛitáḥ.*"] The earliest instances as yet known of the name *Saṃskṛit* as a designation of the language occur in the Mṛichhakaṭí (p. 44. 2, ed. Stenzler), and in Varáha-Mihira's Bṛihat-Saṃhitá, 85. 3. The following passages also of the Rámáyaṇa are doubtless to be understood in this sense, viz., v. 18. 19. 29. 17, 34 (82. 3), vi. 104. 2. Páṇini is familiar with the word *Saṃskṛita*, but does not use it in this sense; though the Páṇiníyá-Śikshá does so employ it (v. 3), in contradistinction to *prákṛita*.

the curtailment or loss of terminations. Not unfrequently, however, they present older forms of these than are found in the written language, partly because the latter has rigorously eliminated all forms in any way irregular or obsolete, but partly also, no doubt, from the circumstance that grammar was cultivated principally in the north or north-west of India, and consequently adapted itself specially to the usage there prevailing. And in some respects (*e.g.*, in the instr. plur. of words in *a* ?)[197] this usage may have attained a more developed phase than appears to have been the case in India Proper,* since the language was not there hampered in its independent growth by any external influence; whereas the Aryans who had passed into India maintained their speech upon the same internal level on which it stood at the time of the immigration,† how-

[197] This example is not quite pertinent, as the instr. plur. in *-ais* is of very ancient date, being reflected not only in Zend, but also in Slavonic and Lithuanian; see Bopp, *Vergl. Gram.*, i. 156[2] (159[3]).

* The difference in usage between the Eastern and Western forms of speech is once touched upon in the Bráhmaṇa of the White Yajus, where it is said that the Váhíkas style Agni *Bhava*, while the Práchyas, on the contrary, call him *Śarva*. Yáska (ii. 2) opposes the Kambojas (the Persa-Aryans?) to the Áryas (the Indo-Aryans?), stating that the latter, for instance, possess derivatives only of the root *śu*, whereas the Kambojas possess it also as a verb. (Grammarians of the Kambojas are hardly to be thought of here, as Roth, *Zur Lit.*, p. 67, supposes.) Yáska further opposes the Práchyas and the Udíchyas, and the same is done by Páṇini. According to the Bráhmaṇa, the Udíchyas were most conversant with grammar [see *I. St.*, i. 153, ii. 309, 310, xiii. 363, ff. Burnell's identification of the Kambojas here, and in the other earlier passages where they are mentioned, with Cambodia in Farther India, see his *Elements of South Indian Palæography*, pp. 31, 32, 94, is clearly a mistake. For the time of the Páli Abhidhánappadípiká (v. Childers, *Páli Dict.*) this identification may perhaps be correct; but the older Páli texts, and even the inscriptions of Piyadasi (*e.g.*, most distinctly the facsimile of the Khálsi inscription in Cunningham's *Archæological Survey*, i. 247, pl. xli., line 7), introduce the Kambojas in connection with the Yavanas; and this of itself determines that the two belonged geographically to the same region in the north-west of India; see *I. Str.*, ii. 321. In addition to this we have the name Kabujiya = Καμβύσης, and therewith all the various references to this latter name, which point to a very wide ramification of it throughout Irán; see *I. Str.*, ii. 493. To Farther India the name Kamboja evidently found its way only in later times, like the names Ayodhyá, Indraprastha, Irávatí, Champá; though it certainly remains strange that this lot should have fallen precisely to it. Perhaps causes connected with Buddhism may have helped to bring this about. See on this point the *Jenaer Literaturzeitung*, 1875, p. 418; *Indian Antiquary*, iv. 244.]

† Much as the Germans did, who in the middle ages emigrated to Transylvania.

ever considerable were the external modifications which it underwent.

The second period of Indian literature, then, commences with the epoch when the separation of the language of the educated classes—of the written language—from the popular dialects was an accomplished fact. It is in the former alone that the literature is presented to us. Not till after the lapse of time did the vernaculars also in their turn produce literatures of their own,—in the first instance under the influence of the Buddhist religion, which addressed itself to the people as such, and whose scriptures and records, therefore, were originally, as for the most part they still are, composed in the popular idiom. The epoch in question cannot at present be precisely determined; yet we may with reasonable certainty infer the existence of the written language also, at a time when we are in a position to point to the existence of popular dialects; and with respect to these we possess historical evidence of a rare order, in those rock-inscriptions, of identical purport, which have been discovered at Girnar in the Gujarát peninsula, at Dhauli in Orissa, and at Kapur di Giri[198] in Kabul. J. Prinsep, who was the first to decipher them, and Lassen, refer them to the time of the Buddhist king Aśoka, who reigned from B.C. 259; but, according to the most recent investigations on the subject—by Wilson, in the "Journal of the Royal Asiatic Society," xii., 1850 (p. 95 of the separate impression)—they were engraved "at some period subsequent to B.C. 205,"* and are are still, therefore, of uncertain date. However this question may be settled, it in any case results with tolerable certainty

[198] This name ought probably to be written *Kapardigiri*? See my paper on the Śatruṃjaya Máhátmya, p. 118. In these inscriptions, moreover, we have a text, similar in purport, presented to us in three distinct dialects. See further on this subject Burnouf's admirable discussion of these inscriptions in his *Lotus de la bonne Loi*, p. 652, ff. (1852); *I. St.*, iii. 467, ff. (1855); and Kern, *De Gedenkstukken van Aśoka den Buddhist* (1873, particularly p. 32 ff., 45 ff.).

* And that not much later; as is vouched for by the names of the Greek kings therein mentioned—Alexander, Antigonus, Magas, Ptolemy, Antiochus. These cannot, it is true, be regarded as contemporaneous with the inscriptions; but their notoriety in India can hardly have been of such long duration that the inscriptions can have been composed long after their time. See Wilson, *l. c.*

that these popular dialects were in existence in the third century B.C. But this is by no means to be set down as the limit for the commencement of their growth; on the contrary, the form in which they are presented to us sufficiently shows that a very considerable period must have elapsed since their separation from the ancient *bháshá*. This separation must therefore have taken place comparatively early, and indeed we find allusions to these vernaculars here and there in the Bráhmaṇas themselves.*

The direct data, attesting the posteriority of the second period of Indian literature, consist in these facts: first, that its opening phases everywhere presuppose the Vedic period as entirely closed; next, that its oldest portions are regularly based upon the Vedic literature; and, lastly, that the relations of life have now all arrived at a stage of development of which, in the first period, we can only trace the germs and beginning. Thus, in particular, divine worship is now centred on a triad of divinities, Brahman, Vishṇu, and Śiva; the two latter of whom, again, in course of time, have the supremacy severally allotted to them, under various forms, according to the different sects that grew up for this purpose. It is by no means implied that individual portions of the earlier period may not run on into the later; on the contrary, I have frequently endeavoured in the preceding pages to show that such is the case. For the rest, the connection between the two periods is, on the whole, somewhat loose: it is closest as regards those branches of literature which had already attained a definite stage of progress in the first period, and which merely continued to develop further in the second,—Grammar, namely, and Philosophy. In regard to those branches, on the contrary, which are a more independent

* Thus in the second part of the Aitareya-Bráhmaṇa the Śyáparṇas, a clan (?) of the western Salvas, are mentioned as "*pútáyai vácho vaditárah*," 'speaking a filthy tongue;' and in the Pañchaviṅśa-Bráhmaṇa, the Vrátyas are found fault with for their debased language. The Asuras are similarly censured in the Śatapatha-Bráhmaṇa (iii. 2. 1. 24), where, at the same time, the Bráhmans are warned against such forms of speech; "*tasmád bráhmaṇo na mlechhet.*"—I may remark here in passing that M. Müller, in his edition of the Ṛik, in Sáyaṇa's introduction, p. 36. 21, erroneously writes *helayo* as one word: it stands for *he 'lavo*,—the Asura corruption of the battle-cry *he 'rayo (arayo)*: according to the Śatapatha-Bráhmaṇa, it even took the form *he 'lavo.*

growth of the second period, the difficulty of connecting them with the earlier age is very great. We have here a distinct gap which it is altogether impossible to fill up. The reason of this lies simply in the fact, that owing to the difficulty of preserving literary works, the fortunate successor almost always wholly supplanted the predecessor it surpassed: the latter thus became superfluous, and was consequently put aside, no longer committed to memory, no longer copied. In all these branches therefore—unless some other influence has supervened—we are in possession only of those master-works in which each attained its culminating point, and which in later times served as the classical models upon which the modern literature was formed, itself more or less destitute of native productive energy. This fact has been already adduced as having proved equally fatal in the case of the more ancient Bráhmaṇa literature, &c.; there, much to the same extent as here, it exercised its lamentable, though natural influence. In the Vedic literature also, that is to say, in its Śákhás, we find the best analogy for another kindred point, namely, that some of the principal works of this period are extant in several—generally two—recensions. But along with this a further circumstance has to be noted, which, in consequence of the great care expended upon the sacred literature, has comparatively slight application to it, namely, that the mutual relation of the manuscripts is of itself such as to render any certain restoration of an original text for the most part hopeless. It is only in cases where ancient commentaries exist that the text is in some degree certain, for the time at least to which these commentaries belong. This is evidently owing to the fact that these works were originally preserved by oral tradition; their consignment to writing only took place later, and possibly in different localities at the same time, so that discrepancies of all sorts were inevitable. But besides these variations there are many alterations and additions which are obviously of a wholly arbitrary nature, partly made intentionally, and partly due to the mistakes of transcribers. In reference to this latter point, in particular, the fact must not be lost sight of that, in consequence of the destructive influence of the climate, copies had to be renewed very frequently. As a rule, the more ancient Indian manuscripts are only from three to four hundred years old; hardly any will be found to date more than five hundred years back.[198a] Little or nothing, therefore, can here be effected by means of so-called diplomatic criticism. We cannot even depend upon a text as it appears in quotations, such quotations being generally made from memory,—a practice which, of course, unavoidably entails mistakes and alterations.

The distinction in point of subject-matter between the first and second periods consists mainly in the circumstance that in the former the various subjects are only handled in their details, and almost solely in their relation to the sacrifice, whereas in the latter they are discussed in their general relations. In short, it is not so much a practical, as rather a scientific, a poetical, and artistic want that is here satisfied. The difference in the form under which the two periods present themselves is in keeping with this. In the former, a simple and compact prose had gradually been developed, but in the latter this form is abandoned, and a rhythmic one adopted in its stead, which is employed exclusively, even for strictly scientific exposition. The only exception to this occurs in the grammatical and philosophical Sútras; and these again are characterised by a form of expression so condensed and technical that it cannot fittingly be termed prose. Apart from this, we have only fragments of prose, occurring in stories which are now and then found cited in the great epic; and further, in the fable literature and in the drama; but they are uniformly interwoven with rhythmical portions. It is only in the Buddhist legends that a prose style has been retained, the

---

198a Regarding the age, manner of preparation, material, and condition of text of Indian MSS., see Ráj. Lála Mitra's excellent report, dated 15th February 1875, on the searches instituted by him in native libraries down to the end of the previous year, which is appended to No. IX. of his *Notices of Sanskrit MSS.* Quite recently some Devanágarí MSS. of Jaina texts, written on broad palm-leaves, have been discovered by Bühler, which date two centuries earlier than any previously known. A facsimile of one of these MSS. in Bühler's possession, the Ávaśyaka-Sútra, dated *Samvat* 1189 (A.D. 1132), is annexed to the above-mentioned report: "it is the oldest Sanskrit MS. that has come to notice," Ráj. L. Mitra, *Notices*, iii. 68 (1874). But a letter from Dr. Rost (19th October 1875) intimates that in one of the Sanskrit MSS. that have lately arrived in Cambridge from Nepál, he has read the date 128 of the Nepál era, *i.e.*, A.D. 1008. Further confirmation of this, of course, still remains to be given.

language of which, however, is a very peculiar one, and is, moreover, restricted to a definite field. In fact, as the result of this neglect, prose-writing was completely arrested in the course of its development, and declined altogether. Anything more clumsy than the prose of the later Indian romances, and of the Indian commentaries, can hardly be; and the same may be said of the prose of the inscriptions.

This point must not be left out of view, when we now proceed to speak of a classification of the Sanskṛit literature into works of Poetry, works of Science and Art, and works relating to Law, Custom, and Worship. All alike appear in a poetic form, and by 'Poetry' accordingly in this classification we understand merely what is usually styled *belles-lettres*, though certainly with an important modification of this sense. For while, upon the one hand, the poetic form has been extended to all branches of the literature, upon the other, as a set-off to this, a good deal of practical prose has entered into the poetry itself, imparting to it the character of poetry 'with a purpose.' Of the epic poetry this is especially true.

It has long been customary to place the Epic Poetry at the head of Sanskṛit literature; and to this custom we here conform, although its existing monuments cannot justly pretend to pass as more ancient than, for example, Páṇini's grammar, or the law-book which bears the name of Manu. We have to divide the epic poetry into two distinct groups: the *Itihása-Puráṇas* and the *Kávyas*. We have already more than once met with the name Itihása-Puráṇa in the later Bráhmaṇas, namely, in the second part of the Śatapatha-Bráhmaṇa, in the Taittiríya-Áraṇyaka, and in the Chhándogyopanishad. We have seen that the commentators uniformly understand these expressions to apply to the legendary passages in the Bráhmaṇas themselves, and not to separate works; and also that, from a passage in the thirteenth book of the Śatapatha-Bráhmaṇa, it results with tolerable certainty that distinct works of this description cannot then have existed, inasmuch as the division into *parvans*, which is usual in the extant writings of this class, is there expressly attributed to other works, and is not employed in reference to these Itihása-Puráṇas themselves. On the other hand, in the Sarpa-vidyá ('serpent-knowledge') and the Devajana-vidyá ('genealogies of the gods')—to which, in the passage in question, the distribution into *parvans*, that is to say, existence in a distinct form, is expressly assigned—we have in all probability to recognise mythological accounts, which from their nature might very well be regarded as precursors of the epic. We have likewise already specified as forerunners of the epic poetry, those myths and legends which are found interspersed throughout the Bráhmaṇas, here and there, too, in rhythmic form,* or which lived on elsewhere in the tradition regarding the origin of the songs of the Ṛik. Indeed, a few short prose legends of this sort have been actually preserved here and there in the epic itself. The Gáthás also—stanzas in the Bráhmaṇas, extolling individual deeds of prowess—have already been cited in the like connection: they were sung to the accompaniment of the lute, and were composed in honour either of the prince of the day or of the pious kings of old (see *I. St.*, i. 187). As regards the extant epic—the *Mahá-Bhárata*—specially, we have already pointed out the mention in the Taittiríya-Áraṇyaka, of Vyása Páráśarya[199] and Vaiśampáyana,[200] who are given in the poem itself as its original authors; and we have also remarked (p. 143) that the family of the

* As, for instance, the story of Hariśchandra in the second part of the Aitareya-Bráhmaṇa.

[199] Vyása Páráśarya is likewise mentioned in the *vaṅśa* of the Sáma-vidhána-Bráhmaṇa, as the disciple of Vishvaksena, and preceptor of Jaimini; see *I. St.*, iv. 377.—The Mahábháshya, again, not only contains frequent allusions to the legend of the Mahá-Bhárata, and even metrical quotations that connect themselves with it, but it also contains the name of Śuka Vaiyásaki; and from this it is clear that there was then already extant a poetical version of the Mahá-Bhárata story; see *I. St.*, xiii. 357. Among the prior births of Buddha is one (No. 436 in Westergaard's *Catalogus*, p. 40), bearing the name Kaṇha-Dípáyana, i.e., Krishṇa-Dvaipáyana!

[200] Vaiśampáyana appears elsewhere frequently, but always in special relation to the transmission of the Yajur-Veda. By Páṇini, it is true (iv. 3. 104), he is simply cited generally as a Vedic teacher, but the Mahábháshya, commenting on this passage, describes him as the teacher of Kaṭha and Kalápin. In the Calcutta Scholium, again, we find further particulars (from what source? cf. Táránátha on *Siddh. Kaum.*, i. 590), according to which (see *I. St.*, xiii. 440) nine Vedic schools, and among them two belonging to the Sáma-Veda, trace their origin to him. In the Ṛig-Gṛihya he is evidently regarded (see above, pp. 57, 58), after the manner of the Vishṇu-Puráṇa, as the special representative of the Yajur-Veda; and so he appears in the Anukr. of the Átreyí school, at the head of its list of teachers, specially as the preceptor of Yáska Paiṅgi.

Paráśaras is represented with especial frequency in the *vaṅśas* of the White Yajus.* We also find repeated allusions in the Bráhmaṇas to a Naimishíya sacrifice, and, on the authority of the Mahá-Bhárata itself, it was at such a sacrifice that the *second* recitation of the epic took place in presence of a Śaunaka. But, as has likewise been remarked above [pp. 34, 45], these two sacrifices must be kept distinct, and indeed there is no mention in the Bráhmaṇas of a Śaunaka as participating in the former. Nay, several such sacrifices may have taken place in the Naimisha forest [see p. 34]; or it is possible even that the statement as to the recitation in question may have no more foundation than the desire to give a peculiar consecration to the work. For it is utterly absurd to suppose that Vyása Páráśarya and Vaiśampáyana—teachers mentioned for the first time in the Taittiríya-Áraṇyaka—could have been anterior to the sacrifice referred to in the Bráhmaṇas. The mention of the "Bhárata" and of the "Mahá-Bhárata" itself in the Gṛihya-Sútras of Áśvaláyana [and Śáṅkháyana] we have characterised [p. 58] as an interpolation or else an indication that these Sútras are of very late date. In Páṇini the word "Mahá-Bhárata" does indeed occur; not, however, as denoting the epic of this name, but as an appellative to designate any individual of special distinction among the Bháratas, like Mahá-Jábála,-Hailihila (see *I. St.*, ii. 73). Still, we do find names mentioned in Páṇini which belong specially to the story of the Mahá-Bhárata—namely, Yudhishṭhira, Hástinapura, Vásudeva, Arjuna,† Andhaka-Vṛishṇayas, Droṇa (?); so that the legend must in any case have been current in his day, possibly even in a poetical shape; however surprising it may be that the name Páṇḍu‡ is never mentioned by him. The earliest direct

---

* This renders Lassen's reference (*I. AK.*, i. 629) of the name Páráśarya to the astronomer or chronologer Paráśara, highly questionable.

† A worshipper of Vásudeva, or of Arjuna, is styled 'Vásudevaka,' 'Árjunaka.' Or is Arjuna here still a name of Indra? [From the context he is to be understood as a Kshatriya; see on this, *I. St.*, xiii. 349, ff.; *Ind. Antiq.* iv. 246.]

‡ This name only occurs in the Mahá-Bhárata and in the works resting upon it. Yet the Buddhists mention a mountain tribe of Páṇḍavas, as alike the foes of the Śákyas (*i.e.*, the Kośalas) and of the inhabitants of Ujjayiní; see Schiefner, *Leben des Śákyamuni*, pp. 4, 40 (in the latter passage they appear to be connected with Takshaśilá?), and, further, Lassen, *I. AK.*, ii. 100, ff.; Foucaux, *Rgya Cher Rol Pa*, pp. 228, 229 (25, 26).

evidence of the existence of an epic, with the contents of the Mahá-Bhárata, comes to us from the rhetor Dion Chrysostom, who flourished in the second half of the first century A.D.; and it appears fairly probable that the information in question was then quite new, and was derived from mariners who had penetrated as far as the extreme south of India, as I have pointed out in the *Indische Studien*, ii. 161–165.* Since Megasthenes says nothing of this epic, it is not an improbable hypothesis that its origin is to be placed in the interval between his time and that of Chrysostom; for what ignorant† sailors took note of would hardly have escaped his observation; more especially if what he narrates of Herakles and his daughter Pandaia has reference really to Kṛishṇa and his sister, the wife of Arjuna, if, that is to say, the Páṇḍu legend was already actually current in his time. With respect to this latter legend, which forms the subject of the Mahá-Bhárata, we have already remarked, that although there occur, in the Yajus especially, various names and particulars having an intimate connection with it, yet on the other hand these are presented to us in essentially different relations. Thus the Kuru-Pañchálas in particular, whose internecine feud is deemed by Lassen to be the leading and central feature of the Mahá-Bhárata, appear in the Yajus on the most friendly and peaceful footing: Arjuna again, the chief hero of the Páṇḍus, is still, in the Vájasaneyi-Saṃhitá and the Śatapatha-Bráhmaṇa, a name of Indra:‡ and lastly, Janamejaya Párikshita, who in the Mahá-Bhárata is the great-grandson of Arjuna, appears, in the last part of the Śatapatha-Bráhmaṇa, to be still fresh in the memory of the people, with the rise and downfall of himself and his house. I have also already expressed the conjecture that it is perhaps in the deeds and downfall of this Janamejaya that we have to look for the original plot

* It is not, however, necessary to suppose, as I did, *l. c.*, that they brought this intelligence from the south of India itself: they might have picked it up at some other part of their voyage.

† That they were so appears from their statement as to the Great Bear, *l. c.*

‡ In the thirteenth book of the Śatapatha-Bráhmaṇa, Indra also bears the name Dharma, which in the Mahá-Bhárata is especially associated with Yudhishṭhira himself, though only in the forms *dharma-rája*, *dharma-putra*, &c.

of the story of the Mahá-Bhárata;* and, on the other hand, that, as in the epics of other nations, and notably in the Persian Epos, so too in the Mahá-Bhárata, the myths relating to the gods became linked with the popular legend. But so completely have the two been interwoven that the unravelling of the respective elements must ever remain an impossibility. One thing, however, is clearly discernible in the Mahá-Bhárata, that it has as its basis a war waged on the soil of Hindustán between Aryan tribes, and therefore belonging probably to a time when their settlement in India, and the subjugation and brahmanisation of the native inhabitants, had already been accomplished. But what it was that gave rise to the conflict—whether disputes as to territory, or it may be religious dissensions—cannot now be determined.—Of the Mahá-Bhárata in its extant form, only about one-fourth (some 20,000 *ślokas* or so) relates to this conflict and the myths that have been associated with it;[201] while the elements composing the remaining three-fourths do not belong to it at all, and have only the loosest possible connection therewith, as well as with each other. These later additions are of two kinds. Some are of an epic character, and are due to the endeavour to unite here, as in a single focus, all the ancient legends it was possible to muster,—and amongst them, as a matter of fact, are not a few that are tolerably antique even in respect of form. Others are of purely didactic import, and have been inserted with the view of imparting to the military caste, for which the work was mainly intended, all possible instruction as to its duties, and especially as to the reverence due to the priesthood. Even at the portion which is recognisable as the original basis—that relating to the war—many generations must have laboured before the text attained to an approximately settled shape. It is noteworthy that it is precisely in this part that repeated allusion is made to the Yavanas, Śakas, Pahlavas,[201a] and other peoples; and that

* Which of course stands in glaring contradiction to the statement that the Mahá-Bhárata was recited in his presence.

[201] And even of this, two-thirds will have to be sifted out as not original, since in the introduction to the work (i. 81) the express intimation is still preserved that it previously consisted of 8800 *ślokas* only.

[201a] In connection with the word *Pahlava*, Th. Nöldeke, in a communication dated 3d November

these, moreover, appear as taking an actual part in the conflict—a circumstance which necessarily presupposes that at the time when these passages were written, collisions with the Greeks, &c., had already happened.[202] But as to the period when the final redaction of the entire work in its present shape took place, no approach even to a direct conjecture is in the meantime possible; [203] but at any rate, it must have been some centuries after the commencement of our era.* An interesting discovery has

1875, mentions a point which, if confirmed, will prove of the highest importance for determining the date of composition of the Mahá-Bhárata and of the Rámáyaṇa (see my Essay on it, pp. 22, 25), as well as of Manu (see x. 44). According to this, there exists considerable doubt whether the word *Pahlav*, which is the basis of *Pahlava*, and which Olshausen (v. sup., p. 4, note) regards as having arisen out of the name of the *Parthavas*, Parthians, can have originated earlier than the first century A.D. This weakening of *th* to *h* is not found, in the case of the word *Mithra*, for example, before the commencement of our era (in the MIIPO on the coins of the Indo-Scythians, Lassen, *I. AK.*, ii. 837, and in *Meherdates* in Tacitus). As the name of a people, the word Pahlav became early foreign to the Persians, learned reminiscences excepted: in the Pahlavi texts themselves, for instance, it does not occur. The period when it passed over to the Indians, therefore, would have to be fixed for about the 2d–4th century A.D.; and we should have to understand by it, not directly the Persians, who are called Párasikas, rather, but specially the Arsacidan Parthians.

202 Of especial interest in this connection is the statement in ii. 578, 579, where the Yavana prince Bhagadatta (Apollodotus (?), according to von Gutschmid's conjecture; *reg.* after B.C. 160) appears as sovereign of Maru (Marwar) and Naraka, as ruling, Varuṇa-like, the west, and as the old friend of Yudhishṭhira's father; see *I. St.*, v. 152.—In the name of the Yavana prince Kaserumant, we appear to have a reflex of the title of the Roman Cæsars; see *Ind. Skiz.*, pp. 88, 91; cf. L. Feer on the *Kesari-náma-saṃgrámah* of the Avadána-Śataka in the *Séances de l'Acad. des Inscr.* (1871), pp. 47, 56, 60.

203 With regard to the existence, so early as the time of the Mahábháshya, of a poetical version of the Mahá-Bhárata legend, see *I. St.*, xiii. 356 ff. "Still this does not in the smallest degree prove the existence of the work in a form at all resembling the shape in which we now have it; and as the final result, we do not advance materially beyond the passage in Dion Chrysostom (*I. St.*, ii. 161 ff.), relating to the 'Indian Homer.' For the statements of the Greek writer themselves evidently date from an earlier time; and although not necessarily derived, as Lassen supposes, from Megasthenes himself, yet they at any rate take us back to a period pretty nearly coincident with that of the Bháshya."

* We have a most significant illustration of the gradual growth of the Mahá-Bhárata in an episode commented upon by Śaṃkara, which by the time of Nîlakaṇṭha (*i.e.*, in the course of 6 or 7 centuries) had become expanded by a whole chapter of 47 *ślokas*; see my *Catal. of the Sanskrit MSS. in the Berlin Lib.*, p. 108.

recently been made in the island of Bali, near Java, of the Kavi translation of several *parvans* of the Mahá-Bhárata, which in extent appear to vary considerably from their Indian form.[204] A special comparison of the two would not be without importance for the criticism of the Mahá-Bhárata. For the rest, in consequence of the utter medley it presents of passages of widely different dates, the work, in general, is only to be used with extreme caution. It has been published at Calcutta,[205] together with the *Hari-vanśa*, a poem which passes as a supplement to it.*—Respecting the *Jaimini-Bhárata*, which is ascribed, not to Vyása and Vaiśampáyana, but to Jaimini, we have as yet no very precise information: the one book of it with which I am acquainted is wholly different from the corresponding book of the ordinary Mahá-Bhárata.†

---

[204] See the observations, following R. Friederich's account, in *I. St.*, ii. 136 ff.

[205] 1834–39 in four vols.; recently also at Bombay (1863) with the commentary of Nílakaṇṭha. Hippolyte Fauche's incomplete French translation (1863–72, ten vols.) can only pass for a translation in a very qualified sense; see as to this *I. Str.*, ii. 410 ff. Individual portions of the work have been frequently handled: *e.g.*, Pavie has translated nine pieces (Paris, 1844) and Foucaux eleven (Paris, 1862). Bopp, it is well known, early made the finest episodes accessible, beginning with the *Nala* (London, 1819), whereby he at the same time laid the foundation of Sanskrit philology in Europe. For the criticism of the Mahá-Bhárata, the ground was broken and important results achieved by Lassen in his *Indische Alterthumskunde* (vol. i. 1847). For the contents of the work, see Monier Williams's *Indian Epic Poetry* (1863), and *Indian Wisdom* (1875).

* In Albírúní's time, the 11th century, it passed as a leading authority; see *Journ. Asiat.*, Aug. 1844, p. 130. [Subandhu, author of the *Vásavadattá*, had it before him, in the 7th century; see *I. Str.*, i. 380. A French translation by A. Langlois appeared in 1834.]

† See my *Catal. of the Sanskṛit MSS. in the Berl. Lib.*, pp. 111–118: according to Wilson (*Mack. Coll.*, ii. 1), this book would appear to be the only one in existence; see also Weigle in *Z. D. M. G.*, ii. 278. [This book, the *áśvamedhikam parva*, was printed at Bombay in 1863; according to its concluding statements as they appear in this edition, Jaimini's work embraced the entire epos; but up to the present, apart from this 13th book, nothing further is known of it; see as to this my paper in the *Monatsberichte der Berl. Acad.*, 1869, p. 10 ff. A Kanárese translation of this book is assigned to the beginning of the 13th century (*ibid.*, pp. 13, 35); quite recently, however, by Kittel, in his Preface to Nágavarma's Prosody, pp. vi. lxxi., it has been relegated to the middle of the 18th (!) century. The peculiar colouring of the Kṛishṇa sect, which pervades the whole book, is noteworthy; Christian legendary matter and other Western influences are unmistakably present; *Monatsb.*, *l. c.*, p. 37 ff. A good part of the contents has been communicated by

Side by side with the Itihása we find the *Puráṇa* mentioned in the Bráhmaṇas, as the designation of those cosmogonic inquiries which occur there so frequently, and which relate to the '*agra*' or 'beginning' of things. When in course of time distinct works bearing this name arose, the signification of the term was extended; and these works came to comprehend also the history of the created world, and of the families of its gods and heroes, as well as the doctrine of its various dissolutions and renovations in accordance with the theory of the mundane periods (*yugas*). As a rule, five such topics are given as forming their subject (see Lassen, *I. AK.*, i. 479), whence the epithet *Pañcha-lakshaṇa*, which is cited in Amara's lexicon as a synonym of Puráṇa. These works have perished, and those that have come down to us in their stead under the name of Puráṇas are the productions of a later time, and belong all of them to the last thousand years or so. They are written (cf. Lassen, *l. c.*) in the interests of, and for the purpose of recommending, the Śiva and Vishṇu sects; and not one of them corresponds exactly, a few correspond slightly, and others do not correspond at all, with the description of the ancient Puráṇas preserved to us in the Scholiasts of Amara, and also here and there in the works themselves. "For the old narratives, which are in part abridged, in part omitted altogether, have been substituted theological and philosophical doctrines, ritual and ascetic precepts, and especially legends recommending a particular divinity or certain shrines" (Lassen, *I. AK.*, i. 481). Yet they have unquestionably preserved much of the matter of these older works; and accordingly it is not uncommon to meet with lengthy passages, similarly worded, in several of them at the same time. Generally speaking, as regards the traditions of primitive times, they closely follow the Mahá-Bhárata as their authority; but they likewise advert, though uniformly in a prophetic tone, to the historic

Talboys Wheeler in his *History of India*, vol. i. (1867), where, too, there is a general sketch of the contents of the Mahá-Bhárata itself; see *I. Str.*, ii. 392.—It remains further to mention the re-cast of the Mahá-Bhárata by the Jaina Amarachandra, which is extant under the title *Bála-Bhárata*,—in 44 *sargas* of 6550 *anushṭubh* verses,—and which appeared in the Benares *Paṇḍit* (1869 ff.), edited by Vechana Rámaśástrin. This work belongs probably to the 11th century, see *Z. D. M. G.*, xxvii. 170.

lines of kings. Here, however, they come into the most violent conflict, not only with each other, but with chronology in general, so that their historical value in this respect is extremely small. Their number is considerable, amounting to eighteen, and is doubled if we reckon the so-called *Upapuráṇas*, in which the epic character has been thrust still more into the background, while the ritual element has come quite to the front. Up to this time only one single Puráṇa, the Bhágavata-Puráṇa, has been published—the greater part of it at least—edited [and translated] by Burnouf: but of the others we have excellent notices in Wilson's translation of the Vishṇu-Puráṇa.[246]

As the second group of Epic Poetry we designated the *Kávyas,* which are ascribed to certain definite poets (*kavis*); whereas the Itihásas and Puráṇas are attributed to a mythical personage, Vyása, who is simply *Διασκευή* (Redaction) personified.* At the head of these poems stands the *Rámáyaṇa* of Válmíki, whose name we found cited among the teachers of the Taittiríya-Prátiśákhya.† In respect of language, this work is closely related to the war-portion of the Mahá-Bhárata, although in individual cases, where the poet displays his full elegance, it bears plainly enough on its surface, in rhyme and metre, the traces of a later date. In

---

[246] As also in the separate analyses of various Puráṇas, now collected in vol. i. of Wilson's *Essays on Sanskrit Literature* (ed. Rost, 1864). Above all, we have here to mention, further, the minute accounts given of the Puráṇas by Aufrecht in his *Catal. Cod. Sansc. Bibl. Bodl.*, pp. 7–87. The *Vishṇu-Puráṇa* has been recently published at Bombay, with the commentary of Ratnagarbhabhaṭṭa (1867); Wilson's translation of it has been republished, edited by Fitzedward Hall in five vols. (1864–1870), with material additions and corrections. There are now also several editions of the *Bhágavata-Puráṇa*; amongst them, one with the comm. of Śrídharasvámin (Bombay, 1860). The *Márkaṇḍeya-Puráṇa* has been edited in the *Bibl. Indica* by K. M. Banerjea (1855–1862); and the *Agni-Puráṇa* is now appearing in the same series (begun 1870; caps. 1–214 thus far). An impression of the *Kalki-Puráṇa* appeared at Calcutta in 1873; and lithographed editions of the *Liñga-Puráṇa* (1858) and of portions of the *Padma*, *Skanda*, *Garuḍa*, *Brahma-vaivarta*, and other Puráṇas have appeared at Bombay; see *I. Str.*, ii. 245 ff., 301 ff.

* The words *kavi*, in the sense of 'singer, poet,' and *kávya*, in that of 'song, poem,' are repeatedly used in the Veda, but without any technical application; see *Vájas. Saṃh. Spec.*, ii. 187 [*trayí vai vidyá kávyaṃ chhandas*, Śat., viii. 5. 2. 4].

† Whether by this name we have to understand the same person is of course not certain, but considering the singularity of the name, it is at least not improbable.

regard to contents, on the contrary, the difference between it and this portion of the Mahá-Bhárata is an important one. In the latter human interest everywhere preponderates, and a number of well-defined personages are introduced, to whom the possibility of historical existence cannot be denied, and who were only at a later stage associated with the myths about the gods. But in the Rámáyaṇa we find ourselves from the very outset in the region of allegory; and we only move upon historical ground in so far as the allegory is applied to an historical fact, namely, to the spread of Aryan civilisation towards the south, more especially to Ceylon. The characters are not real historic figures, but merely personifications of certain occurrences and situations. Sítá, in the first place, whose abduction by a giant demon, and subsequent recovery by her husband Ráma, constitute the plot of the entire poem, is but the field-furrow, to which we find divine honours paid in the songs of the Ṛik, and still more in the Gṛihya ritual. She accordingly represents Aryan husbandry, which has to be protected by Ráma—whom I regard as originally identical with Balaráma "halabhṛit," "the plough-bearer," though the two were afterwards separated —against the attacks of the predatory aborigines. These latter appear as demons and giants; whereas those natives who were well disposed towards the Aryan civilisation are represented as monkeys,—a comparison which was doubtless not exactly intended to be flattering, and which rests on the striking ugliness of the Indian aborigines as compared with the Aryan race. Now this allegorical form of the Rámáyaṇa certainly indicates, *à priori*, that this poem is later than the war-part of the Mahá-Bhárata; and we might fairly assume, further, that the historical events upon which the two works are respectively based stand to each other in a similar relation. For the colonisation of Southern India could hardly begin until the settlement of Hindustán by the Aryans had been completed, and the feuds that arose there had been fought out. It is not, however, altogether necessary to suppose the latter; and the warfare at least which forms the basis of the Mahá-Bhárata might have been waged concurrently with expeditions of other Aryan tribes to the south. Whether it was really the Kośalas, as whose chief Ráma appears in the Rámáyaṇa, who effected the colonisation of the south,* as stated in the poem; or whether the poet merely was a Kośala, who claimed this honour for his people and royal house, is a point upon which it is not yet possible to form a judgment. He actually represents Sítá as the daughter of Janaka, king of the Videhas, a tribe contiguous to the Kośalas, and renowned for his piety. The scanty knowledge of South India displayed in the Rámáyaṇa has been urged as proving its antiquity; since in the Mahá-Bhárata this region appears as far more advanced in civilisation, and as enjoying ample direct communication with the rest of India. But in this circumstance I can only see evidence of one of two things: either that the poet did not possess the best geographical knowledge; whereas many generations have worked at the Mahá-Bhárata, and made it their aim to magnify the importance of the conflict by grouping round it as many elements as possible: or else—and this is the point I would particularly emphasise—that the poet rightly apprehended and performed the task he had set himself, and so did not mix up later conditions, although familiar to him, with the earlier state of things. The whole plan of the Rámáyaṇa favours the assumption that we have here to do with the work, the poetical creation, of one man. Considering the extent of the work, which now numbers some 24,000 *ślokas*, this is saying a great deal; and before epic poetry could have attained to such a degree of perfection, it must already have passed through many phases of development.† Still,

* It was by them also—by Bhagíratha, namely—that, according to the Rámáyaṇa, the mouths of the Ganges were discovered. Properly, they were the Eastern rather than the Southern foreposts of the Aryans.

† Of these phases we have probably traces in the *granthaḥ Siśukrandíyaḥ* [to this Goldstücker in his *Páṇini*, p. 28, takes exception, doubtless correctly; see *I. St.*, v. 27], *Yamasabhíyaḥ*, *Indrajananíyaḥ*, mentioned by Páṇini, iv. 3. 88; and in the *Ákhyánas* and *Chánaráṭas*, which, according to Páṇini, vi. 2. 103, are to be variously designated according to the different points of the compass. The term Chánaráṭa still remains unintelligible to me; see *I. St.*, i. 153. (For the rest, as stated by the Calcutta scholiast, this rule, vi. 2. 103, is not interpreted in the Bháshya of Patamjali; it may possibly therefore not be Páṇini's at all, but posterior to the time of Patamjali.)—The word *grantha* may have reference either to the outward fastening (like the German *Heft*, *Band*) or to the inner composition: which of the two we have to suppose remains still undecided, but I am inclined to pronounce for the former. [See above pp. 15, 99, 165.]

it is by no means implied that the poem was of these dimensions from the first: here, too, many parts are certainly later additions; for example, all those portions in which Ráma is represented as an incarnation of Vishṇu, all the episodes in the first book, the whole of the seventh book, &c. The poem was originally handed down orally, and was not fixed in writing until afterwards, precisely like the Mahá-Bhárata. But here we encounter the further peculiar circumstance—which has not yet been shown to apply, in the same way at all events, to the latter work—namely, that the text has come down to us in several distinct recensions, which, while they agree for the most part as to contents, yet either follow a different arrangement, or else vary throughout, and often materially, in the expression. This is hardly to be explained save on the theory that this fixing of the text in writing took place independently in different localities. We possess a complete edition of the text by G. Gorresio, containing the so-called Bengálí recension, and also two earlier editions which break off with the second book, the one published at Serampore by Carey and Marshman, the other at Bonn by A. W. von Schlegel. The manuscripts of the Berlin library contain, it would seem, a fourth recension.*

* See my Catalogue of these MSS., p. 119. [Two complete editions of the text, with Ráma's Commentary, have since appeared in India, the one at Calcutta in 1859–60, the other at Bombay in 1859; respecting the latter, see my notice in *I. Str.*, ii. 235–245. Gorresio's edition was completed by the appearance in 1867 of the text, and in 1870 of the translation, of the *Uttara-káṇḍa*. Hippolyte Fauche's French translation follows Gorresio's text, whereas Griffith's metrical English version (Benares, 1870–74, in 5 vols.) follows the Bombay edition. In my Essay, *Ueber das Rámáyaṇam*, 1870 (an English translation of which appeared in the *Indian Antiquary* for 1872, also separately at Bombay in 1873), I have attempted to show that the modifications which the story of Ráma, as known to us in its earliest shape in Buddhist legends, underwent in the hands of Válmíki, rest upon an acquaintance with the conceptions of the Trojan cycle of legend; and I have likewise endeavoured to determine more accurately the position of the work in literary history. The conclusion there arrived at is, that the date of its composition is to be placed towards the commencement of the Christian era, and at all events in an epoch when the operation of Greek influence upon India had already set in. This elicited a rejoinder from Kashinath Trimbak Telang (1873), entitled, *Was the Rámáyaṇa copied from Homer;* as to which see *Ind. Ant.*, ii. 209, *I. St.*, xiii. 336, 480. The same writer afterwards, in the *Ind. Ant.*, iii. 124, 267, pointed out a half *śloka* which occurs in the *Yuddha-káṇḍa*,

Between the Rámáyaṇa and the remaining Kávyas there exists a gap similar to that between the Mahá-Bhárata and the extant Puráṇas. Towards filling up this blank we might perhaps employ the titles of the Kávyas found in the Kavi language in the island of Bali,[207] most of which certainly come from Sanskṛit originals. In any case, the emigration of Hindús to Java, whence they subsequently passed over to Bali, must have taken place at a time when the Kávya literature was particularly flourishing; otherwise we could not well explain the peculiar use they have made of the terms *kavi* and *kávya*. Of the surviving Kávyas, the most independent in character, and on that account ranking next to the Rámáyaṇa—passably pure, too, in respect of form—are two works * bearing the name of Kálidása, namely, the *Raghu-vaṅśa* and the *Kumára-saṃbhava* (both extant in Kavi also). The other Kávyas, on the contrary, uniformly follow, as regards their subject, the Mahá-Bhárata or the Rámáyaṇa; and they are also plainly enough distinguished from the two just mentioned by their language and form of exposition. This latter abandons more and more the epic domain and passes into the erotic, lyrical, or didactic-descriptive field; while the language is more and more overlaid with turgid bombast,

---

and also twice in Patamjali's Mahábháshya. But the verse contains a mere general reflection (*eti jívantam ánando naraṃ varshaśatád api*), and need not therefore have been derived from the Rámáyaṇa. In itself, consequently, it proves nothing as to the priority of the poem to Patamjali, and this all the less, as it is expressly cited by Válmíki himself merely as a quotation. On this and some other kindred points see my letter in the *Ind. Ant.*, iv. 247 ff. (1875).]

[207] See Friederich, *l. c.*, *I. St.*, ii. 139 ff. The numerous traces which are contained in Pataṃjali's Mahábháshya of epic or narrative poems then actually extant, and which appear in that work as direct quotations therefrom, take us back to a far earlier time; see *I. St.*, xiii. 463 ff.

* They have been edited by Stenzler, text with translation [and repeatedly in India since, with or without the commentary of Mallinátha. To the seven books of the Kumára-saṃbhava, which were the only ones previously known, ten others have recently been added; on the critical questions connected with these, see, *e.g.*, *Z. D. M. G.*, xxvii. 174–182 (1873). From the astrological data contained in both works, H. Jacobi has shown, in the *Monatsber. der Berl. Acad.*, 1873, p. 556, that the date of their composition cannot be placed earlier than about the middle of the 4th century A.D. The Raghu-vaṅśa was most probably composed in honour of a Bhoja prince; see my Essay on the Rám. Táp. Up., p. 279, *I. Str.*, i. 312].

until at length, in its latest phases, this artificial epic resolves itself into a wretched jingle of words. A pretended elegance of form, and the performance of difficult tricks and feats of expression, constitute the main aim of the poet; while the subject has become a purely subordinate consideration, and merely serves as the material which enables him to display his expertness in manipulating the language.[208]

Next to the epic, as the second phase in the development of Sanskrit poetry, comes the Drama. The name for it is *Náṭaka*, and the player is styled *Naṭa*, literally 'dancer.' Etymology thus points us to the fact that the drama has developed out of dancing, which was probably accompanied, at first, with music and song only, but in course of time also with pantomimic representations, processions, and dialogue. We find dancing repeatedly mentioned in the songs of the Ṛik (*e.g.*, in i. 10. 1, 92. 4, &c.), but with special frequency in the Atharva-Saṃhitá and the Yajus,* though everywhere still under the root-form

---

[208] Six of these artificial epics are specially entitled *Mahákávyas*. These are, in addition to the *Raghuvaṅśa* and *Kumára-sambhava*:—(1) the *Bhaṭṭi-kávya*, in 22 *sargas*, composed in Valabhí under king Śrí-Dharasena (xxii. 35), in the 6th or 7th cent. therefore; it deals with the story of Ráma, and is written with a special reference to grammar: (2) the *Mágha-kávya* or *Śiśupála-badha* of Mágha, the son of Dattaka, in 22 *sargas* (Suprabhadeva, grandfather of the poet, is described as the minister of a king Śrí-Dharmanábha), and (3) the *Kirátárjuníya* of Bháravi, in 18 *sargas*,—both prior to Halâyudha (end of the 10th cent.), see *I. St.*, viii. 193, 195, 196: (4) the *Naishadhíya* of Śrí-Harsha, in 22 *sargas*, of the 12th cent. (see Bühler in the *Journal Bombay Br. R. A. S.*, x. 35). The *Rághava-paṇḍavíya* of Kavirája, in any case later than the 10th cent. (see *I. Str.*, i. 371), enjoys a high esteem; it handles, in the self-same words, at once the story of the Rámáyaṇa and that of the Mahá-Bhárata, and, like the *Nalodaya*, in 4 *sargas*, which is even ascribed to Kálidása (edited so long ago as 1830 by Ferd. Benary), is one of the most characteristically artificial pieces of this class of poetry. All these works have been frequently published in India, and to them are to be added many other similar productions. — The Prákṛit poem *Setu-bandha* or *Rávana-badha*, which relates to the story of Ráma, and is reputed to be by Kálidása, also merits special mention here. Of this Paul Goldschmidt has already published two chapters (Göttingen, 1873); and Siegfried Goldschmidt is engaged on an edition of the entire text.

* With various kinds of musical accompaniment, according to the Váj. Saṃh. xxx., where we meet with quite a number of musicians and dancers, as well as with the name Śailúsha itself, which, at a later time, at all events, belongs specially to actors; see *I. Str.*, i. 76, 83. According to the scholium on Káty., xxii. 4. 3, by those "*vrátyagaṇasya*

nṛit. The prákṛitized form *naṭ* occurs for the first time in Páṇini, who, besides, informs us of the existence of distinct Naṭa-sútras,* or manuals for the use of *naṭas*, one of which was attributed to Śilálin, and another to Kṛiśáśva, their adherents being styled Śailálinas and Kṛiśáśvinas respectively. The former of these names finds an analogue, at least, in the patronymic Śailáli, which occurs in the thirteenth *káṇḍa* of the Śatapatha-Bráhmaṇa; and it may also, perhaps, be connected with the words Śailúsha and Kuśílava, both of which denote 'actor' (?).† The latter name, on the contrary, is a very surprising one in this connection, being otherwise only known to us as the name of one of the old heroes who belong in common to the Hindús and the Parsís.‡ Beyond this allusion we have no vestige of either of these works. Páṇini further cites § the word *náṭyam* in the sense of '*naṭánáṃ dharma ámnáyo vá.*' In both cases, we have probably to understand by the term the art of dancing, and not dramatic art.—It has been uniformly held hitherto that the Indian drama arose, after the manner of our modern drama in the Middle Ages, out of religious solemnities and spectacles (so-called 'mysteries'), and also that dancing originally subserved religious purposes. But in support of this latter assumption, I have not met with one single instance in the Śrauta- or Gṛihya-Sútras with which I am acquainted (though of the latter, I confess, I have only a very super-

---

ye sampádayeyuḥ," as the text has it, we have to understand specially teachers of dancing, music, and singing. "In the man who dances and sings, women take delight," Śat., iii. 2. 4. 6.

* The two rules in question, iv. 3. 110, 111, according to the Calcutta scholiast, are not explained in the Bháshya of Patamjali; possibly, therefore, they may not be Páṇini's at all, but posterior to the time of Patamjali. [The *Śailálino naṭáḥ* are mentioned in the Bháshya to iv. 2. 66; in the Anupada-sútra, the *Śailálinaḥ* are cited as a ritual school; see *I. St.*, xiii. 429.]

† These terms are probably derived from *śíla*, and refer to the corrupt, loose morals of those so designated; and the same must apply to Śiláta, if this be a cognate word. The derivation from Kuśa and Lava, the two sons of Ráma, at the beginning of the Rámáyaṇa, has manifestly been invented in order to escape the odium of the name '*ku-śílava.*'

‡ Ought we here to understand the name literally, as, perhaps, a kind of mocking epithet to express poverty, with at the same time, possibly, a direct ironical reference to the renowned Kṛiśáśva of old??

§ iv. 3. 129: this rule, also, is not explained in the Bháshya; perhaps therefore it is not Páṇini's, but later than Patamjali.

ficial knowledge).[209] The religious significance of dancing is thus, for the older period at least, still questionable; and since it is from dancing that the drama has evidently sprung, the original connection of the latter with religious solemnities and spectacles becomes doubtful also. Besides, there is the fact that it is precisely the most ancient dramas that draw their subjects from civil life; while the most modern, on the contrary, almost exclusively serve religious purposes. Thus the contrary, rather, would seem to be the case, namely, that the employment of dancing * and of the drama at religious solemnities was only the growth of a later age.[210] This does not imply, however, that dancing was excluded from those great sacrificial festivals which were now and then celebrated by princes; but only that it did not itself constitute part of the sacred rite or religious ceremony, and could only, and did only, find a place in the intervals. The name applied to the stage-manager in the dramas themselves, 'Sútra-dhára,' is referred, and no

---

209 Even now I am acquainted with but little from these sources bearing on this point. Amongst other things, at the *pitṛimedha* we find dancing, music, and song, which represent the three forms of *śilpa* or art (Śáṅkh. Br. 29. 5), prescribed for the whole day, Káty., 21. 3. 11. But a *Snátaka* might not participate in any such performance, either actively or passively, Pár. ii. 7. On the day preceding the departure of a bride, four or eight married women (unwidowed) performed a dance in her house, Śáṅkh. Gṛi. i. 11.

* It is known in the Megha-dúta, v. 35, 36.

210 Through the unexpected light shed by the Mahábháshya of Patamjali on the then flourishing condition of theatrical representation, this question has recently taken a form very favourable to the view of which Lassen is the principal exponent, and which regards the drama as having originated in religious spectacles resembling our mysteries. The particulars there given regarding the performance of a *Kaṅsavadha* and *Valibandha* by so-called *śaubhikas*—(comp. perhaps the *saubhikas* in Háráválí, 151, though these are explained as *indrajálikas*, 'jugglers,' cf. *sobha*, *sobhanagaraka*, *I. St.*, iii. 153)—lead us directly to this conclusion; see *I. St.*, xiii. 354, 487 ff. "But between the dramatic representations known in the Bháshya, which bear more or less the character of religious festival-plays, and the earliest real dramas that have actually come down to us, we must of course suppose a very considerable interval of time, during which the drama gradually rose to the degree of perfection exhibited in these extant pieces; and here I am still disposed to assign a certain influence to the witnessing of Greek plays. The Indian drama, after having acquitted itself brilliantly in the most varied fields—notably too as a drama of civil life—finally reverted in its closing phases to essentially the same class of subjects with which it had started—to representations from the story of the gods."—*Ibid.*, pp. 491, 492.

doubt rightly, to the original sense of '(measuring) line-holder,' 'carpenter;'* since it appears to have been one of the duties of the architect at these sacrificial celebrations, over and above the erection of the buildings for the reception of those taking part in the sacrifice, likewise to conduct the various arrangements that were to serve for their amusement. (See Lassen, *I. AK.*, ii. 503.) Whether the *naṭas* and *nartakas* mentioned on such occasions are to be understood as dancers or actors, is at least doubtful; but in the absence of any distinct indication that the latter are intended, I hold in the meantime to the etymological signification of the word; and it is only where the two appear together (*e.g.*, in Rámáy. i. 12. 7 Gorr.) that *naṭa* has certainly to be taken in the sense of 'actor.' Buddhist legend seems, indeed, in one instance—in the story of the life of Maudgalyáyana and Upatishya, two disciples of Buddha—to refer to the representation of dramas in the presence of these individuals.† But here a question at once arises as to the age of the work in which this reference occurs; this is the main point to be settled before we can base any conclusion upon it. Lassen, it is true, says that "in the oldest Buddhistic writings the witnessing of plays is spoken of as something usual;" but the sole authority he adduces is the passage from the Dulva indicated in the note. The Dulva, however, that is, the Vinaya-Piṭaka, cannot, as is well known, be classed amongst the "oldest Buddhistic writings;" it contains pieces of widely different dates, in part, too, of extremely questionable antiquity. In the Lalita-Vistara, apropos of the testing of Buddha in the

---

* And therefore has probably nothing to do with the Naṭa-sútras mentioned above? For another application of the word by the Buddhists, see Lassen, *I. AK.*, ii. 81. Of a marionette theatre, at all events, we must not think, though the Javanese puppet-shows might tempt us to do so.

† Csoma Körösi, who gives an account of this in *As. Res.* xx. 50, uses these phrases: "They meet on the occasion of a festival at Rája-gṛiha: . . . their behaviour during the several *exhibitions of spectacles*—their mutual addresses after the shows are over." By 'spectacle' must we here necessarily understand 'dramatic spectacle, drama'?? [Precisely the same thing applies to the word *visúka*, which properly only signifies 'merrymaking' in the *Suttas* of the Southern Buddhists, where the witnessing of such exhibitions (*visúka-dassana*) is mentioned among the reproaches directed by Bhagavant against the worldly ways of the Brahmans; see Burnouf, *Lotus de la Bonne Loi*, p. 465; *I. St.*, iii. 152–154.]

various arts and sciences (Foucaux, p. 150), *náṭya* must, undoubtedly, be taken in the sense of 'mimetic art'—and so Foucaux translates it; but this does not suppose the existence of distinct dramas. The date, moreover, of this particular work is by no means to be regarded as settled; and, in any case, for the time of Buddha himself, this examination-legend carries no weight whatever.

With respect, now, to the surviving dramas, it has hitherto been usual to follow what is supposed to be the tradition, and to assign the most ancient of them, the Mṛichhakaṭí and Kálidása's pieces, to the first century B.C.; while the pieces next following—those of Bhavabhúti—belong to a time so late as the eighth century A.D. Between Kálidása and Bhavabhúti there would thus be a gap of some eight or nine centuries—a period from which, according to this view, not one single work of this class has come down to us. Now this is in itself in the highest degree improbable; and were it so, then surely at the very least there ought to be discernible in the dramas of the younger epoch a very different spirit, a very different manner of treatment, from that exhibited in their predecessors of an age eight or nine hundred years earlier.* But this is by no means the case; and thus we are compelled at once to reject this pretended tradition, and to refer those *soi-disant* older pieces to pretty much the same period as those of Bhavabhúti. Moreover, when we come to examine the matter more closely, we find that, so far as Kálidása is concerned, Indian tradition does not really furnish any ground whatever for the view hitherto accepted: we only find that the tradition has been radically misused. The tradition is to the effect that Kálidása lived at the court of Vikramáditya, and it is contained in a memorial verse which says that Dhanvantari, Kshapaṇaka, Amarasiñha, Śaṅku, Vetálabhaṭṭa, Ghaṭakarpara, Kálidása, Varáhamihira, and Vararuchi † were the 'nine gems' of Vikrama's

* I have here copied Holtzmann's words, referring to Amara, in his excellent little treatise, *Ueber den griechischen Ursprung des indischen Thierkreises*, Karlsruhe, 1841, p. 26.

† This is obviously the Vriracha who is mentioned by the Hindustání chronicler as the author of the Vikrama-charitra (*Journ. Asiat.* Mai, 1844, p. 356). [This recension—ascribed to Vararuchi—of the Siñhásana-dvátriñśiká is actually extant; see Aufrecht, *Cat. of Sansk. MSS. Libr. Trin. Coll. Camb.*, p. 11, and Westergaard, *Catal. Codd. Or. Bibl. Reg. Hauniensis*, p. 100.]

court. Now it is upon this one verse—a mere waif and stray, that has come, like Schiller's 'Mädchen aus der Fremde,' from nobody knows where,* and which is, in any case, of the most questionable authority—that the assumption rests that Kálidása flourished in the year 56 B.C.! For people were not satisfied with hastily accepting as genuine coin the tradition here presented—and this notwithstanding the fact that they at the same time impugned to some extent the trustworthiness of the verse embodying it †—they at once rushed to the conclusion that the Vikrama here named must be *the* Vikramáditya, whose era, still current in our own day, commences with the year 56 B.C. But then, we know of a good many different Vikramas and Vikramádityas: ‡ and, besides, a tradition which is found in some modern works,§ and which ought surely, in the first instance, to have been shown to be baseless before any such conclusion was adopted, states expressly (whether correctly or not is a question by itself) that king Bhoja, the ruler of Málava, who dwelt at Dhárá and Ujjayiní, was the Vikrama at whose court the 'nine gems' flourished; and, according to an inscription,‖ this king Bhoja lived

* It is alleged to be taken from the Vikrama-charitra; but Roth, in his analysis of this work in the *Journ. Asiat.*, Octob. 1845, p. 278 ff., says nothing of it. [And in fact it occurs neither there nor in any of the other recensions of the Siṅhásana-dvátriṅśiká to which I have access. It is, however, found embodied both in the Jyotirvid-ábharaṇa, of about the sixteenth century (22. 10, see *Z. D. M. G.*, xxii. 723, 1868), and in a Singhalese MS. of the so-called Navaratna (with Singhalese commentary) cited in Westergaard's *Catal. Codd. Or. Bibl. Reg. Haun.*, p. 14 (1846).]

† Partly on erroneous grounds. It was asserted, namely, that the word Ghaṭakarpara in the verse was only the name of a work, not of a person: this, however, is not the case, as several poems, besides, are found ascribed to him.

‡ 'Sun of might' is quite a general title, and not a name.

§ See, for instance, also Haeberlin's *Sanskrit Anthology*, pp. 483, 484.

‖ See Lassen, *Zeitsch. für die Kunde des Morg.*, vii. 294 ff.; Colebrooke, ii. 462. According to Reinaud in the *Journ. Asiat.*, Sept. 1844, p. 250, Bhoja is mentioned some years earlier by Albírúní, who wrote in A.D. 1031, as his contemporary; and Otbí alludes to him earlier still, in A.D. 1018, as then reigning; see Reinaud, *Mém. sur l'Inde*, p. 261. According to a later Hindustání chronicler, he lived 542 years after Vikramáditya (see *Journ. Asiat.* Mai, 1844, p. 354), which would make the date of the latter about A.D. 476. Upon what this very precise statement rests is unfortunately uncertain; the Vikrama-charitra does not fix in this definite way the interval of time between Bhoja and Vikrama. Roth, at all events, in his analysis of the work (*Journ. Asiat.*, Sept. 1854, p. 281) merely says, "*bien des années après* (*la mort de Vikramáditya*) *Bhoja parvint au*

about 1040–1090 A.D. On the other hand, there exists no positive ground whatever for the opinion that the Vikrama of the verse is *the* Vikramáditya whose era begins in B.C. 56. Nay, the case is stronger still; for up to the present time we have absolutely no authentic evidence * to show whether the era of Vikramáditya dates from the year of his birth, from some achievement, or from the year of his death, or whether, in fine, it may not have been simply *introduced* by him for astronomical reasons! † "To assign him to the first year of his era might be quite as great a mistake as we should commit in placing Pope Gregory XIII. in the year one of the Gregorian Calendar, or even Julius Cæsar in the first year of the Julian period to which his name has been given, *i.e.*, in the year 4713 B.C." (Holtzmann, *op. cit.*, p. 19).

---

souverain pouvoir." [The text has simply: "*bahúni varsháṇi gatáni.*" Nor does any definite statement of the kind occur in any of the various other recensions of the Siṅhásana-dvátriṅśiká, although a *considerable* interval is here regularly assumed to have elapsed between the rule of Vikrama at Avanti and that of Bhoja at Dhárá.]—To suppose two Bhojas, as Reinaud does, *l. c.*, and *Mém. sur l'Inde*, pp. 113, 114, is altogether arbitrary. We might determine the uncertain date of Vikramáditya by the certain date of Bhoja, but we cannot reverse the process. The date 3044 of Yudhishṭhira's era is, *J. As.*, *l. c.*, p. 357, assigned to the accession of Vikramáditya; but it does not appear whether this is the actual tradition of the Hindustání chronicler, or merely an addition on the part of the translator. Even in the former case, it would still only prove that the chronicler, or the tradition he followed, mixed up the common assertion as to the date of Vikrama with the special statement above referred to. [To the statements of the Hindustání chronicler, Mir Cher i Ali Afsos, no great importance, probably, need be attached. They rest substantially on the recension attributed to Vararuchi of the Siṅhásana-dvátriṅśiká, which, however, in the MS. before me (Trin. Coll., Camb.), yields no definite chronological data. — After all, the assumption of several Bhojas has since turned out to be fully warranted; see, *e.g.*, Rájendralála Mitra in *Journ. A. S. Beng.* 1863, p. 91 ff., and my *I. Str.*, i. 312.]

* See Colebrooke, ii. 475; Lassen, *I. AK.*, ii. 49, 50, 398; Reinaud, *Mém. sur l'Inde*, pp. 68 ff., 79 ff.; Bertrand in the *Journ. Asiat.*, Mai, 1844, p. 357.

† We first meet with it in the astronomer Varáha-Mihira in the fifth or sixth century, though even this is not altogether certain, and, as in the case of Brahmagupta in the seventh century, it might possibly be the era of Śáliváhana (beg. A.D. 78). Lassen does, in fact, suppose the latter (*I. AK.*, i. 508), but see Colebrooke, ii. 475.—Albírúní gives particulars (v. Reinaud, *Journ. Asiat.*, Sept. 1844, pp. 282–284) as to the origin of the *Śaka* era; but regarding the basis of the *Saṃvat* era of Vikrama he does not enlarge. [Even yet these two questions, which are of such capital importance for Indian chronology, are in an altogether unsatisfactory state. According to Kern, Introd. to his edition of the

The dramas of Kálidása—that one of the 'nine gems' with whom we are here more immediately concerned—furnish in their contents nothing that directly enables us to determine their date. Still, the mention of the Greek female slaves in attendance upon the king points at least to a time not especially early; while the form in which the popular dialects appear, and which, as compared with that of the inscriptions of Piyadasi, is extraordinarily degraded, not unfrequently coinciding with the present form of these vernaculars, brings us down to a period at any rate several centuries after Christ. But whether the tradition is right in placing Kálidása at the court of Bhoja in the middle of the eleventh century appears to me very questionable; for this reason in particular, that it assigns to the same court other poets also, whose works, compared with those of Kálidása, are so bad, that they absolutely must belong to a later stage than his—for example, Dámodara Miśra, author of the Hanuman-náṭaka. Moreover, Kálidása has allotted to him such a large number of works, in part too of wholly diverse character, that we cannot but admit the existence of several authors of this name; and, in point of fact, it is a name that has continued in constant use down to the present time. Nay, one even of the three dramas that are ascribed to Kálidása would seem, from its style, to belong to a different author from

---

Bṛihat-Saṃhitá of Varáha-Mihira, 5 ff. (1866), the use of the so-called *Saṃvat* era is not demonstrable for early times at all, while astronomers only begin to employ it after the year 1000 or so. According to Westergaard, *Om de indiske Kejserhouse* (1867), p. 164, the grant of Dantidurga, dated *Śaka* 675, *Saṃvat* 811 (A.D. 754), is the earliest certain instance of its occurrence; see also Burnell, *Elem. of South. Ind. Pal.*, p. 55. Others, on the contrary, have no hesitation in at once referring, wherever possible, every *Saṃvat-* or *Saṃvatsare*-dated inscription to the *Saṃvat* era. Thus, *e.g.*, Cunningham in his *Archæol. Survey of India*, iii. 31, 39, directly assigns an inscription dated *Saṃv.* 5 to the year B.C. 52: Dowson, too, has recently taken the same view, *J. R. A. S.*, vii. 382 (1875). According to Eggeling (Trübner's *Amer. and Or. Lit. Rec.*, special number, 1875, p. 38), one of the inscriptions found in Sir Walter Elliot's copies of grants dates as far back as the year *Śaka* 169 (A.D. 247). Burnell, however, declares it to be a forgery of the tenth century. Fergusson, too, *On the Śaka, Saṃvat, and Gupta Eras*, pp. 11–16, is of opinion that the so-called *saṃvat* era goes no farther back than the tenth century. For the present, therefore, unfortunately, where there is nothing else to guide us, it must generally remain an open question which era we have to do with in a particular inscription, and what date consequently the inscription bears.]

the other two.[211] And this view is further favoured by the circumstance, that in the introduction to this play Dhávaka, Saumilla, and Kaviputra are named as the poet's predecessors; Dhávaka being the name of a poet who flourished contemporaneously with king Śrí-Harsha of Kashmír, that is, according to Wilson, towards the beginning of the twelfth century A.D.[212] There may, it is

---

[211] In the introduction to my translation of this drama, the Málavikágnimitra, I have specially examined not only the question of its genuineness, but also that of the date of Kálidása. The result arrived at is, in the first place, that this drama also really belongs to him.—and in this view Shankar Paṇḍit, in his edition of the play (Bombay, 1869), concurs. As to the second point, internal evidence, partly derived from the language, partly connected with the phase of civilisation presented to us, leads me to assign the composition of Kálidása's three dramas to a period from the second to the fourth century of our era, the period of the Gupta princes, Chandragupta, &c., "whose reigns correspond best to the legendary tradition of the glory of Vikrama, and may perhaps be gathered up in it in one single focus." Lassen has expressed himself to essentially the same effect (*I. AK.*, ii. 457, 1158-1160); see also *I. St.*, ii. 148, 415-417. Kern, however, with special reference to the tradition which regards Kálidása and Varáha-Mihira as contemporaries, has, in his preface to Varáha's Bṛihat-Saṃhitá, p. 20, declared himself in favour of referring the 'nine gems' to the first half of the sixth century A.D. Lastly, on the ground of the astrological data in the Kumára-sambhava and Raghu-vaṅśa, Jacobi comes to the conclusion (*Monatsber. der Berl. Acad.*, 1873, p. 556) that the author of these two poems cannot have lived before about A.D. 350; but here, of course, the preliminary question remains whether he is to be identified with the dramatist. Shankar Paṇḍit, in Trübner's *Am. and Or. Lit. Rec.*, 1875, special No., p. 35, assumes this, and fixes Kálidása's date as at all events prior to the middle of the eighth century. For a definite chronological detail which is perhaps furnished by the Meghadúta, see note 219 below. By the Southern Buddhists Kálidása is placed in the sixth century; Knighton, *Hist. of Ceylon*, 105; *Z. D. M. G.*, xxii. 730. With modern astronomers, the idea of a triad of authors of this name is so fixed, that they even employ the term Kálidása to denote the number 3; see *Z. D. M. G.*, xxii. 713.

[212] The date of Śrí-Harsha, of whom Dhávaka is stated in the Kávya-prakáśa to have been the protégé—Kashmír is not here in question—has since been fixed by Hall (Introd. to the Vásavadattá) for the seventh century, rather. Hall, moreover, questions the existence of Dhávaka altogether (p. 17), and is of opinion that he "never enjoyed any more substantial existence than that of a various reading."—This conjecture of Hall's as to the name of the author of the Ratnávalí, in which Bühler also concurred, has since been brilliantly verified. According to Bühler's letter from Śrínagara (publ. in *I. St.*, xiv. 402 ff.), all the Kashmír MSS. of the Kávya-prakáśa read, in the passage in question, *Báṇa*, not Dhávaka, the latter name being altogether unknown to the Paṇḍits there: "As Mammaṭa was a native of Kashmír, this reading is undoubtedly the correct one."—Comp. note 218 below.

true, have been more Dhávakas than one; another MS., moreover, reads Bhásaka;[213] and besides, these introductions are possibly, in part, later additions. In the case of the Mṛichhakaṭí at least, this would appear to be certain, as the poet's own death is there intimated.* This last-mentioned drama, the Mṛichhakaṭí—whose author, Śúdraka, is, according to Wilson, placed by tradition prior to Vikramáditya[214] (*i.e.*, the same Vikrama at whose court the 'nine gems' flourished?)—cannot in any case have been written before the second century A.D. For it makes use of the word *nâṇaka* as the name of a coin;† and this term, according to Wilson (*Ariana Antiqua*, p. 364), is borrowed from the coins of Kanerki, a king who, by the evidence of these coins, is proved to have reigned until about the year 40 A.D. (Lassen, *I. AK.*, ii. 413). But a date long subsequent to this will have to be assigned to to the Mṛichhakaṭí, since the vernacular dialects it introduces appear in a most barbarous condition. Besides, we meet with the very same flourishing state of Buddhism which is here revealed in one of the dramas of Bhavabhúti, a poet whose date is fixed with tolerable certainty for the eighth century A.D. The Rámáyaṇa and the war-part of the Mahá-Bhárata must, to judge from the use

---

[213] The passage exhibits a great number of various readings; see Haag, *Zur Texteskritik u. Erklärung von Kálidása's Málavikágnimitra* (1872), pp. 7, 8. Hall, *l. c.*, prefers the readings *Bhásaka*, *Rámila*, and *Saumila*; Haag, on the contrary, *Bhása*, *Saumilla*, *Kaviputra*. In Báṇa's Harsha-charita, Introd., v. 15, Bhása is lauded on account of his dramas: indeed, his name is even put before that of Kálidása.

* Unless Śúdraka-rája, the reputed author, simply was the patron of the poet? It is quite a common thing in India for the actual author to substitute the name of his patron for his own.

[214] In a prophetic chapter of the Skanda-Puráṇa, for instance, he is placed in the year *Kali* 3290 (*i.e.*, A.D. 189), but at the same time only twenty years before the Nandas whom Cháṇakya is to destroy. To Vikramáditya, on the other hand, is assigned the date *Kali* 4000, *i.e.*, A.D. 899 (!); see the text in Íśvarachandra Vidyáságara's *Marriage of Hindoo Widows*, p. 63 (Calc. 1856), and in my Essay on the Rámáyaṇa, p. 43.

† According to the Viśva-kosha, quoted by Mahídhara to Váj. Saṃh. 25. 9, it is a synonym of *rúpa* (= rupee?). Yájnavalkya (see Stenzler, Introd., p. xi.) and Vṛiddha-Gautama (see Dattaka Mímáṅsá, p. 34) are also acquainted with *náṇaka* in the sense of 'coin.' [Both Lassen, *I. AK.*, ii. 575, and Müller, *A. S. L.*, p. 331, dispute the conclusions drawn from the occurrence of the word *náṇaka*, but I cannot be persuaded of the cogency of their objections.]

made of their heroes in the Mṛichhakaṭí, already have been favourite reading at the time when it was composed; while, on the other hand, from the absence of allusion to the chief figures of the present Puráṇas, we may perhaps infer with Wilson that these works were not yet in existence. This latter inference, however, is in so far doubtful as the legends dealt with in these younger Puráṇas were probably, to a large extent, already contained in the older works of the same name.* The two remaining dramas of Bhavabhúti, and the whole herd of the later dramatic literature, relate to the heroic tradition of the Rámáyaṇa and Mahá-Bhárata, or else to the history of Kṛishṇa; and the later the pieces are, the more do they resemble the so-called 'mysteries' of the Middle Ages. The comedies, which, together with a few other pieces, move in the sphere of civil life, form of course an exception to this. A peculiar class of dramas are the philosophical ones, in which abstractions and systems appear as the *dramatis personæ.* One very special peculiarity of the Hindú drama is that women, and persons of inferior rank, station, or caste, are introduced as speaking, not in Sanskṛit, but in the popular dialects. This feature is of great importance [215] for the criticism of the individual pieces; the conclusions resulting from it have already been adverted to in the course of the discussion.

---

* Besides, the slaying of Śumbha and Niśumbha by Deví, which forms the subject of the Deví-Máhátmya, v.–x., in the Márkaṇḍ.-Puráṇa, is referred to in the Mṛichhakaṭí, p. 105.22 (ed. Stenzler).—Whether, *ibid.* 104.18, *Karaṭaka* is to be referred to the jackal of this name in the Pañchatantra is uncertain.—At page 126.9 Stenzler reads *gallakka*, but Wilson (*Hindu Theatre*, i. 134) reads *mallaka*, and considers it not impossible that by it we have to understand the Arabic *málik!*—In regard to the state of manners depicted, the Mṛichhakaṭí is closely related to the Daśa-kumára, although the latter work, written in the eleventh century [rather in the sixth, see below, p. 213], belongs certainly to a later stage. Ought the Śúdraka who is mentioned in this work, p. 118, ed. Wilson, to be identified, perhaps, with the reputed author of the Mṛichhakaṭí?

[215] For example, from the relation in which the Prákṛit of the several existing recensions of the Śakuntalá stands to the rules of the Prákṛit grammarian Vararuchi, Pischel has drawn special arguments in support of the view advocated by him in conjunction with Stenzler, that of these recensions the Bengálí one is the most ancient; see Kuhn's *Beiträge zur vergl. Sprachforsch.*, viii. 129 ff. (1874), and my observations on the subject in *I. St.*, xiv. 35 ff.

From the foregoing exposition it appears that the drama meets us in an already finished form, and with its best productions. In almost all the prologues, too, the several works are represented as new, in contradistinction to the pieces of former poets; but of these pieces, that is, of the early beginnings of dramatic poetry, not the smallest remnant has been preserved.[216] Consequently the conjecture that it may possibly have been the representation of Greek dramas at the courts of the Grecian kings in Bactria, in the Panjáb, and in Gujarát (for so far did Greek supremacy for a time extend), which awakened the Hindú faculty of imitation, and so gave birth to the Indian drama, does not in the meantime admit of direct verification. But its historical possibility, at any rate, is undeniable,[217] especially as the older dramas nearly all belong to the west of India. No internal connection, however, with the Greek drama exists.[218] The fact, again, that no dramas are found either

---

[216] See Cowell in *I. St.*, v. 475; and as to the Kaṅsa-vadha and Vali-bandha, the note on p. 198 above.

[217] Cf. the Introduction to my translation of the Málaviká, p. xlvii., and the remarks on *Yavaniká* in *Z. D. M. G.*, xiv. 269; also *I. St.*, xiii. 492.

[218] The leading work on the Indian dramas is still Wilson's *Select Specimens of the Theatre of the Hindus*, 1835², 1871³. The number of dramas that have been published in India is already very considerable, and is constantly being increased. Foremost amongst them still remain: —the *Mṛichhakaṭiká* of Śúdraka, the three dramas of Kálidása (*Śakuntalá*, *Urvaśí*, and *Málaviká*), Bhavabhúti's three (*Málatí-mádhava*, *Mahá-víra-charitra*, and *Uttara-ráma-charitra*); —the *Ratnávalí* of King Srí-Harshadeva, composed, according to Wilson's view, in the twelfth century, and that not by the king himself, but by the poet Dhávaka, who lived at his court, but according to Hall, by the poet Báṇa in the beginning of the seventh century; see Hall, Introduction to the Vásavadattá, p. 15 ff. (cf. note 212 above), *I. Str.*, i. 356), *Lit. Cent. Bl.*, 1872, p. 614;—the *Nágánanda*, a Buddhistic sensational piece ascribed to the same royal author, but considered by Cowell to belong to Dhávaka (see, however, my notice of Boyd's translation in *Lit. C. B.*, 1872, p. 615);—the *Veṇí-saṃhára* of Bhaṭṭa-náráyaṇa, a piece pervaded by the colouring of the Kṛishṇa sect, written, according to Grill, who edited it in 1871, in the sixth, and in any case earlier than the tenth century (see *Lit. C. B.*, 1872, p. 612);—the *Viddha-śálabhañjiká* of Rája-Śekhara, probably prior to the tenth century (see *I. Str.*, i. 313);—the *Mudrá-rákshasa* of Viśákhadatta, a piece of political intrigue, of about the twelfth century; and lastly, the *Prabodha-chandrodaya* of Kṛishṇa-miśra, which dates, according to Goldstücker, from the end of the same century.—Two of Kálidása's dramas, the Śakuntalá and Urvaśí, are each extant in several recensions, evidently in consequence of their having enjoyed a very special popularity. Since the appearance of Pischel's pamphlet, *De Kálidásae Śakuntali Recensionibus* (Breslau,

in the literature of the Hindús, who emigrated to the island of Java about the year 500 A.D. (and thence subsequently to Bali), or among the Tibetan translations, is perhaps to be explained, in the former case, by the circumstance that the emigration took place from the east coast of India,* where dramatic literature may not as yet have been specially cultivated (?). But in the case of the Tibetans the fact is more surprising, as the Meghadúta of Kálidása and other similar works are found among their translations.

The Lyrical branch of Sanskṛit poetry divides itself, according to its subject, into the Religious and the Erotic Lyric. With respect to the former, we have already seen, when treating of the Atharva-Saṃhitá, that the hymns of this collection are no longer the expression of direct religious emotion, but are rather to be looked upon as the utterance of superstitious terror and uneasy apprehension, and that in part they bear the direct character of magic spells and incantations. This same character is found faithfully preserved in the later religious lyrics, throughout the Epic, the Puráṇas, and the Upanishads, wherever prayers of the sort occur; and it has finally, within the last few centuries, found its classical expression in the Tantra literature. It is in particular by the heaping up of titles under which the several deities are invoked that their favour is thought to be won; and the 'thousand-name-prayers' form quite a special class by themselves. To this category belong also the prayers in amulet-form, to which a prodigious virtue is ascribed, and which enjoy the very highest repute even in the present day. Besides these, we also meet with prayers, to Śiva † especially, which

1870), in which he contends, with great confidence, for the greater authenticity of the so-called Bengálí recension, the questions connected herewith have entered upon a new stage. See a full discussion of this topic in *I. St.*, xiv. 161 ff. To Pischel we are also indebted for our knowledge of the Dekhan recension of the Urvaśí: it appeared in the *Monatsber. der Berl. Acad.*, 1875, pp. 609-670.

* Yet the later emigrants might have taken some with them! [In this Kavi literature, moreover, we have actually extant, in the Smaradahana, a subsequent version of the Kumára-sambhava, and in the Sumana-santaka (?) a similar version of the Raghu-vaṅśa, *i.e.*, works which, in their originals at least, bear the name of Kálidása; see *I. St.*, iv. 133. 141.] Do the well-known Javanese puppet-shows owe their origin to the Indian drama?

† Whose worship appears, in the main, to have exercised the most favourable influence upon his followers,

for religious fervour and childlike trust will bear comparison with the best hymns of the Christian Church, though, it must be admitted, their number is very small.

The Erotic Lyric commences, for us, with certain of the poems attributed to Kálidása. One of these, the *Meghadúta*, belongs at all events to a period[219] when the temple worship of Śiva Mahákála at Ujjayiní was in its prime, as was still the case at the time of the first Muhammadan conquerors. Together with other matter of a like sort, it has been admitted, and under Kálidása's name, into the Tibetan Tandjur,* from which, however, no chronological deduction can be drawn, as the date of the final completion of this compilation is unknown. The subject of the Meghadúta is a message which an exile sends by a cloud to his distant love, together with the description of the route the cloud-messenger is to take—a form of exposition which has been imitated in a considerable number of similar poems. A peculiar class is composed of the sentences of Bhartṛihari,

---

whereas it is the worship of Kṛishṇa that has chiefly countenanced and furthered the moral degradation of the Hindús.

[219] A very definite chronological detail would be furnished by v. 14, provided Mallinátha's assertion is warranted, to the effect that this verse is to be taken in a double sense, *i.e.*, as referring at the same time to Diṅnága, a violent opponent of Kálidása. For in that case we should in all probability have to understand by Diṅnága the well-known Buddhist disputant of this name, who lived somewhere about the sixth century; see my discussion of this point in *Z. D. M. G.*, xxii. 726 ff.

* Considering the scarcity of the *Asiatic Researches*, I here give Csoma Körösi's account of the Tandjur, contained in vol. xx., 1836, in some detail. "The Bstan-Hgyur is a compilation in Tibetan of all sorts of literary works" (in all some 3900), "written mostly by ancient Indian Paṇḍits and some learned Tibetans in the first centuries after the introduction of Buddhism into Tibet, commencing with the seventh century of our era. The whole makes 225 volumes. It is divided into the Ṛgyud and the Mdo (Tantra and Sútra classes, in Sanskrit). The Ṛgyud, mostly on *tantrika* rituals and ceremonies, makes 87 volumes. The Mdo, on science and literature, occupies 136 volumes. One separate volume contains (58) hymns or praises on several deities or saints, and one volume is the index for the whole.—The Ṛgyud contains 2640 treatises of different sizes: they treat in general of the rituals and ceremonies of the mystical doctrine of the Buddhists, interspersed with many instructions, hymns, prayers, and incantations.—The Mdo treats in general of science and literature in the following order: theology, philosophy" (these two alone make 94 volumes), "logic or dialectic, philology or grammar, rhetoric, poesy, prosody, synonymics, astronomy, astrology, medicine and ethics, some hints to the mechanical arts and histories." See further, in particular, Anton Schiefner's paper, *Ueber die logischen und grammatischen Werke im Tandjur*, in the Bulletin of the St. Petersburg Academy (read 3d September 1847).

Amaru, &c., which merely portray isolated situations, without any connection as a whole. A favourite topic is the story of the loves of Kṛishṇa and the shepherdesses, the playmates of his youth. It has already been remarked that the later Kávyas are to be ranked with the erotic poems rather than with the epic. In general, this love-poetry is of the most unbridled and extravagantly sensual description; yet examples of deep and truly romantic tenderness of feeling are not wanting. It is remarkable that, in regard to some of these poems, we encounter the same phenomenon as in the case of the Song of Solomon: a mystical interpretation is put upon them, and in one instance at least, the Gíta-Govinda of Jayadeva,[219a] such a mystical reference appears really to have been intended by the poet, however incompatible this may at first sight seem with the particularly wanton exuberance of fancy which is here displayed.

Of the Ethico-Didactic Poetry—the so-called *Níti-Śástras*—but little has survived in a complete form (some pieces also in the Tibetan Tandjur), no doubt because the great epic, the Mahá-Bhárata, in consequence of the character of universality which was gradually stamped upon it, is itself to be regarded as such a Níti-Śástra. Still, relics enough of the aphoristic ethical poetry have been preserved to enable us to judge that it was a very favourite form, and achieved very excellent results.[220] Closely allied

---

[219a] Acc. to Bühler (letter Sep. 1875), Jayadeva, who does not appear in the Sarasv.-kaṇṭhábh., flourished under king Lakshmaṇasena of Gauḍa, of whom there is extant an inscription of the year 1116, and whose era, still current in Mithilá, begins, acc. to *Ind. Ant.* iv. 300, in A.D. 1170.

[220] See Böhtlingk's critical edition of these aphorisms, *Indische Sprüche*, 3 vols., 1863-65 (with 5419 vv.), 2d edition, 1870-73 (with 7613 vv.), and Aufrecht's analysis, in the *Z. D. M. G.*, xxvii. 1 ff. (1873), of the *Śárṅgadhara-Paddhati*, of the fourteenth century,—an anthology of about 6000 vv. culled from 264 different authors and works. Compare also Joh. Klatt, *De Trecentis Cháṇakyæ Sententiis* (1873), and Dr. John Muir's *Religious and Moral Sentiments from Sanskrit Writers* (1875). Regarding an anthology which, both in extent and antiquity, surpasses that of Śárṅgadhara, viz., the *Sad-ukti-karṇámṛita* of Śrídharadása, compiled *Śake* 1127 (A.D. 1205), and comprising quotations from 446 poets, see the latest number of Ráj. Lála Mitra's *Notices*, iii. 134-149. The statement at the close of the work respecting the era of king Lakshmaṇasena, in whose service the poet's father was, is both in itself obscure, and does not well harmonise with our other information on the point. On account of the numerous examples it quotes we may also here mention the *Sarasvatí-kaṇṭhábharaṇa*, a treatise on poetics attributed to king Bhoja-deva, and therefore

to it is the literature of the 'Beast-Fable,' which has a very special interest for us, as it forms a substantial link of connection with the West. We have already pointed out that the oldest animal-fables known to us at present occur in the Chhándogyopanishad. Nor are these at all limited there to the representation of the gods as assuming the forms of animals, and in this shape associating with men, of which we have even earlier illustrations,* but animals are themselves introduced as the speakers and actors. In Páṇini's time, complete cycles of fables may possibly have already existed, but this is by no means certain as yet.† The oldest fables, out of India, are those of Babrius, for some of which at least the Indian original may be pointed out.[221] But the most ancient book

---

belonging probably to the eleventh century; see on it Aufrecht, *Catalogus*, pp. 208, 209.—To this class also belongs, though its contents are almost entirely erotic, the Prákṛit anthology of Hála, consisting properly of only 700 verses (whence its name *Sapta-śataka*), which, however, by successive recensions have grown to 1100–1200. It was the prototype of the *Sapta-śati* of Govardhana, a work of about the twelfth century, which in its turn seems to have served as the model for the *Satta-sai* of the Hindí poet Bihári Lal; see my Essay on the Sapta-śataka of Hála (1870), pp. 9, 12, and *Z. D. M. G.*, xxviii. 345 ff. (1874), and also Garrez in the *Journ. Asiat.*, August 1872, p. 197 ff.

* For instance, the story of Manu and the fish, Indra's metamorphosis into the birds *markaṭa* and *kapiñjala*, his appearance in the form of a ram, &c. In the Ṛik the sun is frequently compared to a vulture or falcon hovering in the air.

† The words cited in support of this are not Páṇini's own, but his scholiast's (see p. 225). [But, at all events, they occur directly in the Mahábháshya; see *I. St.*, xiii. 486.]

[221] In my paper, *Ueber den Zusammenhang indischer Fabeln mit griechischen* (*I. St.*, iii. 327 ff.), as the result of special investigations bearing upon A. Wagener's Essay on the subject (1853), I arrived at exactly the opposite conclusion; for in nearly every instance where a Greek fable was compared with the corresponding Indian one, the marks of originality appeared to me to belong to the former. In all probability the Buddhists were here the special medium of communication, since it is upon their popular form of literary exposition that the Indian fable and fairy-tale literature is specially based. Otto Keller, it is true, in his tract, *Ueber die Geschichte der griech. Fabel* (1862), maintains, in opposition to my view, the Indian origin of the fables common to India and Greece, and suggests an ancient Assyrian channel of communication. His main argument for their Indian origin is derived from the circumstance that the relation existing in Greek fable between the fox and the lion has no real basis in the nature of the two animals, whereas the jackal does, as a matter of fact, stand to the lion in the relation portrayed in Indian fable. But are jackals, then, only found in India, and not also in countries inhabited by Semitic peoples? And is not the Greek animal-fable precisely

of fables extant is the *Pañcha-tantra.* The original text of this work has, it is true, undergone great alteration and expansion, and cannot now be restored with certainty; but its existence in the sixth century A.D. is an ascertained fact, as it was then, by command of the celebrated Sassanian king Núshírván (reg. 531–579), translated into Pahlaví. From this translation, as is well known, subsequent versions into almost all the languages of Asia Minor and Europe have been derived.[222] The recension of the extant text seems to have taken place in the Dekhan;[223] while the epitome of it known as the *Hitopadeśa* was probably drawn up at Palibothra, on the Ganges. The form of the Hindú collections of fables is a peculiar one, and is therefore everywhere easily recognisable, the leading incident which is narrated invariably forming a framework within which stories of the most diverse description are set.*—Allied to the fables are the

---

a Semitic growth? That the Indians should turn the fox of the Greek fable back again into the jackal necessarily followed from the very nature of the case. The actual state of things, namely, that the jackal prowls about after the lion, had indeed early attracted their attention; see, *e.g.*, Ṛik, x. 28. 4; but there is no evidence at all that in the older period the knowledge was turned to the use to which it is put in the fable, the only characteristics mentioned of the jackal being its howling, its devouring of carrion, and its enmity to the dog. (In Śatap., xii. 5. 2. 5, the jackal is, it is true, associated with the word *vidagdha*, and this is certainly noteworthy; but here the term simply signifies 'burnt' or 'putrid.') Keller's views as to the high antiquity of the Indian authors he cites are unfounded.

[222] See on this Benfey's translation (1859) of the Pañcha-tantra, which follows Kosegarten's edition of the text (1848). Here there is a full exposition of the whole subject of the later diffusion of the materials of Indian fable throughout the West. Kielhorn and Bühler have published a new edition of the text in the *Bombay Sanskṛit Series* (1868 ff.).

[223] From Benfey's researches, it appears that, in this recension, the original text, which presumably rested on a Buddhistic basis, underwent very important changes, so that, curiously enough, a German translation made in the last quarter of the fifteenth century from a Latin rendering, which in its turn was based upon a Hebrew version, represents the ancient text more faithfully than its existing Sanskṛit form does. Of this, for the rest, two or more other recensions are extant; see *I. Str.*, ii. 166. For the 14th chap. of the Kalíla wa Dimna, no Indian original had been known to exist; but quite recently a Tibetan translation of this original has been discovered by Anton Schiefner; see his *Bharatae Responsa*, St. Petersburg, 1875. On a newly discovered ancient Syriac translation of the groundwork of the Pañcha-tantra, made, it is supposed, either from the Pahlaví or from the Sanskṛit itself, see Benfey in the *Augsburger Allg. Zeit.* for July 12, 1871.

* Precisely the same thing takes place in the Mahá-Bhárata also.

Fairy Tales and Romances,[224] in which the luxuriant fancy of the Hindús has in the most wonderful degree put forth all its peculiar grace and charm. These too share with the fables the characteristic form of setting just referred to, and thereby, as well as by numerous points of detail, they are sufficiently marked out as the original source of most of the Arabian, Persian, and Western fairy tales and stories; although, in the meantime, very few of the corresponding Indian texts themselves can be pointed out.

As regards the last branch of Indian poetry, namely, Geography and History, it is characteristic enough that the latter can only fittingly be considered as a branch of poetry; and that not merely on account of its form—for the poetic form belongs to science also—but on account of its subject-matter as well, and the method in which this is handled. We might perhaps have introduced it as a division of the epic poetry; but it is preferable to keep the two distinct, since the works of the class now in question studiously avoid all matter of a purely mythical description. We have already remarked that the old Purāṇas contained historical portions, which, in the existing Purāṇas, are confined to the mere nomenclature of dynasties and kings; and that here they clash violently, not only with one another, but with chronology generally. We meet with the same discrepancies in all works of the class we are now considering, and especially in its leading representative, Kalhaṇa's *Rája-taraṃgiṇí*, or history of Kashmír, which belongs to the twelfth century A.D. Here, it is

---

[224] Here, before all, is to be mentioned Somadeva's *Kathá-sarit-ságara*, of the twelfth century, edited by Herm. Brockhaus (1839–66). Of the *Vṛihat-kathá* of Guṇáḍhya, belonging to about the sixth century—a work which is supposed to have been written in the *Paiśáchí bhásha*, and which is the basis of the work of Somadeva,—a recast by Kshemaṃkara has recently been discovered by Burnell and Bühler, see *Ind. Antiq.*, i. 302 ff. (Kshemaṃkara is also called Kshemendra; according to Bühler (letter from Kashmír, pub. in *I. St.*, xiv. 402 ff.) he lived under king Ananta (1028–1080), and wrote 1020–1040).—The *Daśa-kumára-charita* of Daṇḍin, belonging to about the sixth century, was edited by Wilson in 1846, and by Bühler in 1873: Subandhu's *Vásava-dattá* (seventh century ?) was edited by Hall, with an excellent critical introduction, in 1859 (*Bibl. Ind.*): Báṇa's *Kádambarí*, of about the same date, appeared at Calcutta in 1850. For an account of these last three works see my *I. Str.*, i. 308–386.

true, we have to do with something more than mere bald data; but then, as a set-off to this, we have also to do with a poet, one who is more poet than historian, and who, for the rest, appeals to a host of predecessors. It is only where the authors of these works treat of contemporary subjects that their statements possess a decided value; though, of course, precisely with respect to these, their judgment is in the highest degree biassed. But exceptions likewise appear to exist, and in particular, in some princely houses, family records, kept by the domestic priests, appear to have been preserved, which, in the main,* seem to be passably trustworthy.[225]—As for Geography, we repeatedly

* Only the family pedigree must not enter into the question, for these genealogical tables go back almost regularly to the heroic families of the epic.

[225] Certain statements in the astrological treatise *Gárgí Saṃhitá*, cap. *Yuga Puráṇa*, in which the relations of the Yavanas with India are touched upon (see Kern, Pref. to Bṛhat-Saṃhitá, p. 33 ff.), appear to have a real historical significance. Báṇa's *Harsha charita*, too, seems to be a work embodying some good information; see Hall, Pref. to the Vásava-dattá, p. 12 ff. (1859). And the same remark applies to the *Vikramáñka-charita* by Bilhaṇa of Kashmir, in 18 *sargas*, composed about A.D. 1085, just edited with a very valuable introduction by Bühler. This work supplies most important and authentic information, not only regarding the poet's native country, and the chief cities of India visited by him in the course of prolonged travels, but also as to the history of the Chálukya dynasty, whose then representative, Tribhuvana-malla, the work is intended to exalt. In Bühler's opinion, we may hope for some further accession to our historical knowledge from the still existing libraries of the Jainas, and, I might add, from their special literature also, which is peculiarly rich in legendary works (*charitra*). The *Śatrumjaya-máhátmya* of Dhaneśvara, in 14 *sargas*, composed in Valabhí, under king Śiláditya, at the end of the sixth century, yields, it is true, but scant historical material, and consists for the most part merely of popular tales and legends; see my paper on it (1858), p. 12 ff. (Bühler, *l. c.*, p. 18, places this work as late as the thirteenth century; similarly, Lassen, *I. AK.*, iv. 761, but see my Essay on the Bhagavatí, i. 369.) Still, a great variety of information has been preserved by the Jainas, which deserves attention; for example, respecting the ancient kings Vikramárka and Śáliváhana, though, to be sure, they, too, have become almost wholly mythical figures. The *Víra-charitra* of Ananta, lately analysed by H. Jacobi in *I. St.*, xiv. 97 ff., describes the feuds between the descendants of these two kings; introducing a third legendary personage, Śúdraka, who, aided by the Málava king, the son of Vikramárka, succeeds in ousting the son of Śáliváhana from Pratishṭhána. It is written in a fresh and graphic style, but, to all appearance, it has only a very slight really historical nucleus; indeed, it expressly claims to be an imitation of the Rámáyaṇa! The *Siṅhásana-dvátriṅśiká*, too, a work extant in several recensions, of which one, the *Vikrama-charitra* (see above, p. 200), is attributed to Vararuchi, is almost solely, as the *Vetála-pañ-*

find, in the various Puráṇas, jejune enumerations of mountains, rivers, peoples, and the like.[226] But modern works, also, upon this subject are quoted: these, however, are known only by name.—A leading source, besides, for history and geography, is supplied by the exceedingly numerous inscriptions and grants,* which, indeed, being often of very considerable extent, might almost pass as a special branch of the literature. They are usually drawn up in prose, though mostly with an admixture of verse. Of coins the number is comparatively small; yet they have furnished surprisingly rich information regarding a period previously quite unknown in its details, the period of the Grecian kings of Bactria.[227]

From this general view of Sanskṛit poetry, we now turn to the second division of Sanskṛit literature, to the works of Science and Art.

---

chavinśati is exclusively, made up of matter of the fairy-tale description. The stories in the *Bhoja-prabandha* of king Bhoja and his court of poets, are mere fanciful inventions. —Bühler, in his letter from Kashmír (*I. St.*, xiv. 404, 405), states that he has now also discovered the *Níla-mata* which was used by Kalhaṇa, as also the *Taraṃgiṇís* of Kshemendra and Helárája; for the Rája-taraṃgiṇí itself there is thus the prospect of important corrections.

[226] Of special interest, in this regard, are the sections styled *Kúrma-vibhága* in the astrological texts; see Kern, *Pref. to Bṛih. Saṃh.*, p. 32, and in *I. St.*, x. 209 ff. Cunningham's otherwise most meritorious work, *Ancient Geography of India* (1871), has unfortunately taken no account of these.

* On metal plates, first mentioned in Yájnavalkya's law-book and in the Pañcha-tantra: in Manu's Code they are not yet known. [See the special accounts given of these in Burnell's *Elem. of S. Ind. Palæog.*, p. 63 ff.]

[227] Wilson's *Ariana Antiqua* (1841) and Lassen's *Indische Alterthumskunde* (1847–61) still form the chief mine of information and basis of research in the field of Indian history. In the department of Numismatics and Inscriptions, Burgess, Burnell, Cunningham, Dowson, Eggeling, Fergusson, Edw. Thomas, Vaux, Bhaṇḍarkar, and Rájendra Lála Mitra have of late done eminent service. In connection with the so-called cave-inscriptions, the names of Bháu Dájí, Bird, Stevenson, E. W. and A. A. West, Westergaard, and J. Wilson, amongst others, may be mentioned.

We give the precedence to the Science of Language,[228] and take Grammar first.

We have already had frequent occasion to allude to the early beginnings and gradual development of grammatical science. It grew up in connection with the study and recitation of the Vedic texts; and those works which were specially devoted to it, protected by the sacredness of their subject, have, in part, survived. But, on the other hand, we have no records of the earlier stages of that grammatical study which was directed to and embraced the entire range of the language;* and we pass at once into the magnificent edifice which bears the name of Páṇini as its architect, and which justly commands the wonder and admiration of every one who enters.† Páṇini's grammar is distinguished above all similar works of other countries, partly by its thoroughly exhaustive investigation of the roots of the language, and the formation of words; partly by its sharp precision of expression, which indicates with an enigmatical succinctness whether forms come under the same or different rules. This is rendered possible by the employment of an algebraic terminology of arbitrary contrivance, the several parts of which stand to each other in the closest harmony, and which, by the very fact of its sufficing for all the phenomena which the language presents, bespeaks at once the marvellous ingenuity of its inventor, and his profound penetration of the entire material of the language. It is not, indeed, to be assumed that Páṇini was altogether the inventor of this method; for, in the first place, he directly presupposes, for example, a collection of primary affixes (*Uṇ-ádi*); and, in the second place, for various grammatical elements there occur in his work two sets of technical terms, the one of which is peculiar to himself, while the other, as testified by his

[228] The general assertion in the Mahábháshya to i. 1. 1 f. 44ª (*chhandovat sútráṇi bhavanti*) which ascribes Vedic usage to Sútras in general, is explained by Kaiyaṭa in the sense that, *not* the *vaiśeshika-sútráṇi*, for example, but only the *vyákaraṇa-sútráni* are here meant, since these latter belong to the Veda as *aṅga*; see *I. St.*, xiii. 453.

* Only in Yáska's Nirukti are beginnings of the kind preserved; yet here etymology and the investigation of roots and of the formation of words are still in a very crude stage.

† *E.g.*, of Père Pons so long ago as 1743, in the *Lettres Édifiantes*, 26. 224 (Paris).

commentators, is taken from the Eastern grammarians.* But at any rate, it seems to have been he who generalised the method, and extended it to the entire stock of the language. Of those of his predecessors whom he mentions directly by name, and whose names recur in part in Yáska's Nirukti, the Prátiśákhya-Sútras, or the Áraṇyakas, some may possibly have worked before him in this field; in particular, Śákaṭáyana perhaps, whose grammar is supposed (Wilson, *Mack. Coll.*, i. 160) to be still in existence, although nothing definite is known about it.[229]

The question now arises, When did Páṇini live? Böhtlingk, to whom we owe an excellent edition of the grammar, has attempted to fix his date for the middle of the fourth century B.C., but the attempt seems to be a failure. Of the reasons adduced, only one has any approach to plausibility, which is to the effect that in the Kathá-sarit-ságara, a collection of popular tales belonging to the twelfth century, Páṇini is stated to have been the disciple of one Varsha, who lived at Páṭaliputra in the reign of Nanda, the father of Chandragupta (Σανδρόκυπτος). But not only is the authority of such a work extremely questionable in reference to a period fifteen centuries earlier; the assertion is, besides, directly contradicted, both as to time and place, by a statement of the Buddhist Hiuan Thsang, who travelled through India in the first half of the seventh century. For Hiuan Thsang, as reported by Reinaud (*Mém. sur l'Inde*, p. 88), speaks of a double existence of Páṇini, the earlier one belonging to mythical times, while the second is put by him 500 years after Buddha's

---

* See Böhtlingk in the Introduction to his *Páṇini*, p. xii., and in his tract, *Ueber den Accent im Sanskrit*, p. 64.

[229] In Benfey's *Orient und Occident*, ii. 691–706 (1863), and iii. 181, 182 (1864), G. Bühler has given an account of a commentary (*chintámaṇi-vṛitti*) on the *Śabdánuśásana* of Śákaṭáyana, according to which (p. 703) Páṇini's work would appear to be simply "an improved, completed, and in part remodelled edition" of that of Śákaṭáyana. The author of this commentary, Yakshavarman, himself a Jaina, in his introduction describes Śákaṭáyana also as such—namely, as '*mahá-śramaṇa-saṃghádhipati*;' see also *I. St.*, xiii. 396, 397. In Burnell's opinion, Vaṅśa-Bráhm., p. xli., many of Śákaṭáyana's rules are, on the contrary, based upon Páṇini, or even on the *Várttikas*, nay, even on the further interpretations in the Mahábháshya. Might not these contradictions be explained by supposing that the existing form of the work combines both old and new constituents?

death, *i.e.*, 100 years later than the reign of king Kanishka, who lived, as he says, 400 years after Buddha.* As Kanishka is proved by coins to have reigned down to A.D. 40 (Lassen, *I. AK.*, ii. 413), Páṇini, according to this, would have to be placed not earlier than A.D. 140. A statement so precise, obtained by Hiuan Thsang on the spot, can hardly be a mere invention; while no significance need be attached to the earlier mythical existence, nor to the circumstance that he makes Páṇini a Buddhist.[230] As Phonini's birthplace he mentions Pholotoulo, some six miles north-west of the Indus, and this agrees with the name 'Śáláturíya,' the formation of which is explained by Páṇini, and which in later writings is an epithet applied to the grammarian himself; 'Śálátura,' the basis of the name, being phonetically identical † with the Chinese 'Pholotoulo.' That Páṇini belonged to precisely this north-western district of

* The text of Hiuan Thsang is unfortunately not yet accessible: it seems to be much more important than the description of Fa Hian's travels, and to enter considerably more into detail. [This blank has since been filled up by Stan. Julien's translation of the biography and memoirs of Hiuan Thsang (1857 ff., 3 vols.). From this it now appears that the above statement, communicated from the text by Reinaud, is not quite exact. The real existence of Páṇini is not there placed 500 years after Buddha at all: all that is said is, that at that date there still existed in his birthplace a statue erected in his honour (see *Siyuki*, i. 127); whereas he himself passed as belonging 'dans une haute antiquité.']

[230] The true state of the case is, rather, that with regard to Páṇini's date there is no direct statement at all: a legend merely is communicated of a Buddhist missionary who had taken part in the council under king Kanishka, and who came from it to Páṇini's birthplace. Here he intimated to a Brahman, whom he found chastising his son during a lesson in grammar, that the youth was Páṇini himself, who, for his heretical tendencies in his former birth, had not yet attained emancipation, and had now been born again as his son; see *I. St.*, v. 4.

† The commentators make Śálátura the residence of Páṇini's ancestors, and this is, in fact, the sense in which Páṇini's rule is to be taken. But the Chinese traveller, who obtained his information on the spot, is assuredly a better authority, especially as it has to be remarked that the rule in question (iv. 3. 94), according to the Calcutta scholiasts, is not explained in the Bháshya, and may possibly, therefore, not be Páṇini's at all, but posterior to the time of Patamjali. [The name Śáláturíya does not, in fact, occur in the Bháshya; but, on the other hand, Páṇini is there styled Dákshíputra, and the family of the Dákshis belonged to the Váhíkas in the North-West; see *I. St.*, xiii. 395, 367. The name Śálaṅki also, which is bestowed on him in later writings, and which actually occurs in the Bháshya, though it does not clearly appear that he is meant by it, leads us to the Váhíkas; see *I. St.*, xiii. 395, 375, 429. Hiuan Thsang expressly describes Páṇini as belonging to the Gandháras (Γάνδαροι).]

India, rather than to the east, results pretty plainly from the geographical data contained in his work;* still he refers often enough to the eastern parts of India as well, and, though born in the former district, he may perhaps have settled subsequently in the latter. Of the two remaining arguments by means of which Böhtlingk seeks to determine Páṇini's date, the one, based on the posteriority of Amara-siṅha, "who himself lived towards the middle of the first century B.C.," falls to the ground when the utter nullity of this latter assumption is exposed. The other is drawn from the Rája-taraṃgiṇí, a rather doubtful source, belonging to the same period as the Kathá-sarit-ságara, and rests, moreover, upon a confusion of the Northern and Southern Buddhist eras, consequently upon a very insecure foundation. In that work it is related that the Mahábháshya, or great commentary on Páṇini, which is ascribed to Pataṃjali, was, by the command of king Abhimanyu, introduced into his dominions by Chandra, who had himself composed a grammar. Now the Northern Buddhists agree in stating that Kanishka, the immediate predecessor of Abhimanyu, lived 400 years after Buddha's death. If, therefore, with the Southern Buddhists, we place this event in the year B.C. 544, then, of course, the date to be assigned to Kanishka would be B.C. 144, and to Abhimanyu B.C. 120, or thereabouts.† But upon the evidence of coins, which are at all events a sure authority,‡ Kanishka (Kanerki) reigned until A.D. 40 (Lassen, *I. AK.*, ii. 413); and Abhimanyu himself therefore must have reigned 160 years later than the date derived from the previous supposition—according to Lassen (*l. c.*), till A.D. 65. Consequently, even admitting Böhtlingk's further reasoning, we should still have to fix Páṇini's date, not for B.C. 350 or thereabouts, as his result gives, but 160 years later at any rate. But in view of

---

* The circumstance that the only two works containing legends concerning him and the commentary upon his grammar—the Kathá-sarit-ságara and the Rája-taraṃgiṇí—were both written in Kashmír, also tells in favour of this view. [On the geographical data in Páṇini, see Bhaṇḍarkar in *Ind. Antiq.*, i., 21 (1872), also *I. St.*, xiii. 302, 366.]

† As Böhtlingk, *op. cit.*, p. xvii., xviii., supposes; see also Reinaud, *Mém. sur l'Inde*, p. 79.

‡ Of these Böhtlingk could not avail himself, as they only came to our knowledge some years after his edition of Páṇini appeared.

Hiuan Thsang's assertion, no credit whatever need at present be attached to the statement in the Rája-taraṃgiṇí. If Páṇini did not really flourish until 100 years after Kanishka, *i.e.*, A.D. 140,[231] it is self-evident that the commentary upon his work cannot have been in existence, and still less have been introduced into Kashmír, under Abhimanyu, Kanishka's immediate successor!—But, apart altogether from the foregoing considerations, we have, in Páṇini's work itself, a very weighty argument which goes to show that the date to be assigned to him can by no means be so early as Böhtlingk supposes (about B.C. 350). For in it Páṇini once mentions the Yavanas, *i.e.*, Ἰάονες, Greeks,* and explains the formation of the word *yavanání*

[231] But no such inference is deducible from Hiuan Thsang's account, now that we are in possession of its exact tenor (see note 230 above): the statement of the Rája-taraṃgiṇí is thus in no way impugned by it.

* Lassen (*I. AK.*, i. 729) asserts that the most ancient meaning of the word *yavana* was probably 'Arabia,' because incense, which came from Arabia, was termed *yávana;* but this assertion is distinctly erroneous. So far as we know at present, this latter term first occurs in the Amara-kosha, and there along with *turushka*, which can scarcely be a very ancient word. It may consequently either date from the time of the commercial intercourse of the Indians with Arabia shortly before Muhammad, or even with the Muhammadan Arabs; or else—like *yavaneshṭa*, 'tin' [Hemach., 1041, according to Böhtlingk-Rieu, 'lead,' not 'tin']. and *yavana-priya*, 'pepper,' the chief articles of traffic with the Greeks of Alexandria—it may possibly have been named, not from the Arabs, but from the Greeks, who brought incense as well as tin and pepper from India (Lassen, *I. AK.*, 286 n.)! Wherever we find the Yavanas mentioned in the epic, or other similar ancient writings, only the Greeks can be meant. [The almost constant association of them with the Kambojas, Śakas, &c., is conclusive as to this; see *I. Str.*, ii. 321; *I. St.*, xiii. 371. The name Yavana was then in course of time transferred to the political successors of the Greeks in the empire of Western India, that is, to the Indo-Scythians themselves, to the Persians (Párasíkas, whose women, for example, are termed *Yavanís* by Kálidása in Raghuv., iv. 61), and, lastly, to the Arabs or Moslems; see *I. St.*, xiii. 308. Recently, it is true, Rájendra Lála Mitra, in the *Journ. As. Soc. Beng.*, 1874, p. 246 ff., has pronounced against the view that the Greeks were originally meant by the Yavanas; but his arguments are in great part of a very curious kind. Cf. further on this point my letter in the *Ind. Antiq.*, iv. 244 ff. (1875), where, in particular, I point out that the name Yavana first became popularised in India through Alexander, *i.e.*, through his Persian interpreters, although it may possibly have been known previously through the medium of the Indian auxiliaries who served in the army of Darius.]—There is a remarkable legend in the Puráṇas and the twelfth book of the Mahá-Bhárata, of the fight of Krishṇa with Kála-Yavana, 'the Black Yavana,' so called, it would appear, in contradistinction to the (White) Yavanas? Ought we here to understand African or dark Sem-

—to which, according to the *Várttika*, the word *lipi*, 'writing,' must be supplied, and which therefore signifies 'the writing of the Yavanas.'[232]—In the Pañcha-tantra, Páṇini is said to have been killed by a lion; but, independently of the question whether the particular verse containing this allusion belongs to the original text or not, no chronological inference can be drawn from it.[233]

---

itic races that had come into collision with the Indians? At the time of the Daśa-kumára, the name Kála-Yavana (as well as Yavana itself) does, in point of fact, expressly designate a seafaring people —supposed by Wilson to be the Arabs. In the legend in the Puráṇas and the Mahá-Bhárata, on the contrary, no reference to the sea is traceable; and Wilson therefore (Vishṇu-Pur., 565, 566) refers it to the Greeks, that is, those of Bactria. This view is perhaps confirmed by the circumstance that this Kála-Yavana is associated with a *Gárgya*; since it is to *Garga*, at least, who uniformly appears as one of the earliest Indian astronomers, that a verse is ascribed, in which the Yavanas (here unquestionably the Greeks) are highly extolled. Possibly this is the very reason why Gárgya is here associated with Kála-Yavana.

[232] For the different explanations that have been attempted of this word, see *I. St.*, v. 5–8, 17 ff.; Burnell, *Elem. of S. Ind. Pal.*, p. 7, 93: the latter regards it as "not unlikely that *lipi* has been introduced into Indian from the Persian *dipi*." Benfey also, in his *Geschichte der Sprachwissenschaft*, p. 48 (1869), understands by *Yavanání* 'Greek writing;' but he places the completion of Páṇini's work as early as B.C. 320. In that case, he thinks, Páṇini "had already had the opportunity during six years of becoming acquainted with Greek writing in his own immediate neighbourhood without interruption, Alexander having, as is well known, established satrapies in India itself and in the parts adjoining"—in the vicinity of the Indus, namely, near which Páṇini's birthplace was. But to me it is very doubtful indeed that a space so short as six years should have sufficed to give rise to the employment by the Indians of a special term and affix to denote Greek writing—(which surely in the first years after Alexander's invasion can hardly have attracted their attention in so very prominent a way!)—so that the mere expression 'the Greek' directly signified 'the writing of the Greeks,' and Páṇini found himself obliged to explain the formation of the term in a special rule. "The expression could only have become so very familiar through prolonged and frequent use—a thing conceivable and natural in Páṇini's native district, in those provinces of North-Western India which were so long occupied by the Greeks. But this of course presupposes that a lengthened period had intervened since the time of Alexander."—*I. St.*, iv. 89 (1857).

[233] Since the above was written the question of Páṇini's date has been frequently discussed. Max Müller first of all urged, and rightly, the real import of Hiuan Thsang's account, as opposed to my argument. Apart from this, however, I still firmly adhere to the reasoning in the text; see *I. St.*, iv. 87, v. 2 ff. To the vague external testimony we need hardly attach much importance. Páṇini's vocabulary itself (cf. *yavanání*) can alone yield us certain information. And it was upon this path that Goldstücker proceeded in his *Páṇini, his place in Sanskrit Literature* (September 1861)—a work distinguished in an eminent

Páṇini's work has continued to be the basis of grammatical research and the standard of usage in the language down even to the present time. Owing to its frequent obscurity it was early commented upon, and—a circumstance to which there is no parallel elsewhere in the literature—some of these earliest interpretations have come down to us. At their head stand the *Paribháshás*, or explanations of single rules, by unknown authors; next come the *Várttikas* (from *vritti*, 'explanation') of Kátyáyana;* and after these the *Mahábháshya* of Pataṃjali. With regard to the date of Kátyáyana, the statement of Hiuan Thsang, to the effect that 300 years after Buddha's death, *i.e.*, in B.C. 240,† "*le docteur Kia to yan na*" lived at Támasavana in the Panjáb, is by Böhtlingk referred to this Kátyáyana; but when we remember that the same traveller assigns to Páṇini's second existence a date so late as 500 years after Buddha, such a reference of course becomes highly precarious. Besides, the statement is in

---

degree by truly profound investigation of this aspect of the question as well as of the literature immediately bearing upon it. The conclusion he arrives at is that Páṇini is older than Buddha, than the Prátiśákhyas, than all the Vedic texts we possess, excepting the three Saṃhitás of the Ṛik, Sáman, and Black Yajus—older than any individual author in whatever field, with the single exception of Yáska (p. 243). In May 1861, before the separate publication of this work, which had previously (Nov. 1860) appeared as the preface to Goldstücker's photo-lithographed edition of the Mánava-Kalpa-Sútra, I endeavoured—and, as I believe, successfully—in a detailed rejoinder in *I. St.*, v. 1–176, to rebut these various deductions, point by point. For the post-Buddhistic date of Páṇini, compare in particular the evidence adduced, pp. 136–142, which is excellently supplemented by Bühler's paper on Sákaṭáyana (1863, see note 229 above). To the mention of the 'Yavanání' has to be added a peculiar circumstance which Burnell has recently noticed

(*Elem. S. Ind. Pal.*, p. 96): The denoting of numbers by the letters of the alphabet in their order (i=2), to which Goldstücker (*Páṇini*, p. 53) first drew attention, and which, according to the Bháshya, is peculiar to Páṇini, occurs in his work only, and is "precisely similar to the Greek and Semitic notation of numerals by letters of the alphabet." If, further, the Greek accounts of the confederation of the 'Οξυδράκαι and Μαλλοί be correct; if, that is to say, their alliance first took place through fear of Alexander, whereas they had up till then lived in constant enmity, then in all probability Apiśali, and *à fortiori* Páṇini also, would have to be set down as subsequent to Alexander; see *I. St.*, xiii. 375 n.

* Who there mentions several of these Paribháshás.

† That is, if we adopt the chronology of the Southern Buddhists; but, rather, only B.C. 60, since Kaniṣhka, whose date, as we saw, is fixed by coins for A.D. 40, is by Hiuan Thsang placed 400 years after Buddha's death.

itself an extremely indefinite one, the "docteur" in question not being described as a grammarian at all, but simply as a descendant of the Kátya family.[234] Even admitting, however, that the reference really is to him, it would still be in conflict with the tradition—in itself, it is true, of no particular authority—of the Kathá-sarit-ságara, which not only represents Kátyáyana as the contemporary of Páṇini, but identifies him with Vararuchi, a minister of King Nanda, the father of Chandragupta (Σανδρόκυπτος), according to which, of course, he must have flourished about B.C. 350. As regards the age of the Mahábháshya,[235] we have seen that the assertion of the Rája-taraṃgiṇí as to its introduction into Kashmír in the reign of Abhimanyu, the successor of Kanishka, *i.e.*, between A.D. 40 and 65, is, for the reasons above assigned, in the meantime discredited.[236] For the present, therefore, we are without information as to the date of those interpretations, just as we are regarding the date of Páṇini himself. But when once they are themselves in our hands, it will certainly be possible to gather from their contents, by means of the great number of words they contain, a tolerably clear image of the time when they originated,[237] in the same way as we

---

[234] It is this only that has weight; whereas no importance whatever is to be attached, as we have already seen (note 230), to the second existence of Páṇini. On the various Kátyas, Kátyáyanas, at the time of the Bháshya itself, for instance, see *I. St.*, xiii. 399.

[235] The name Pataṃjali (we should expect Pát°.) is certainly somehow connected with that of the Pataṃchala Kápya of the land of the Madras, who appears in the Yájnavalkíya-káṇḍa of the Śatap. Br. It occurs again (see below, p. 237) as the name of the author of the Yoga-Sútras. Pataṃjali appears as name of one of the prior births of Buddha (No. 242, in Westergaard's *Catalogus*, p. 39). In the *Pravarádhyáya*, § 9 (Yajuḥ-Pariś.), the Pataṃjalis are classed as belonging to the family of Viśvámitra.—According to later accounts, by Gonardíya, who is cited four times in the Bháshya, we have to understand Pataṃjali himself; and the same applies to the name Goṇikáputra; see on this *I. St.*, v. 155, xiii. 316, 323, 403.

[236] By no means; see note 231.

[237] On the basis of the lithographed edition of the Mahábháshya, published at Benares in 1872 by Rájárámaśástrin and Bálaśástrin, with Kaiyaṭa's commentary (of about the seventh century (?), see *I. St.*, v. 167), I have attempted in *I. St.*, xiii. 293–502, to sketch such an outline. The first section of the work, with Kaiyaṭa, and Nágeśa's gloss, belonging to the eighteenth century, was published so long ago as 1856 by Ballántyne. A photo-lithographed issue of the entire Bháshya, prepared under Goldstücker's supervision, at the expense of the Indian Government, has recently appeared in London, in 3 vols. (vol. i., the Bháshya; vol. ii., Bháshya with Kaiyaṭa's Comm.; vol. iii., Nágoji-

can even now attempt, although only in broad outline, a picture of the time of Páṇini.* With regard to the latter, the condition of the text, in a critical point of view, forms a main difficulty. A few of the Sútras found in it are already notoriously acknowledged not to be Páṇini's; and there is the further peculiar circumstance, that, according to the scholiasts of the Calcutta edition, fully a third of the entire Sútras are not interpreted in the Mahábháshya at all.† The question then arises whether this is merely

bhaṭṭa's Schol. on Kaiyaṭa). Goldstücker, in his *Páṇini*, p. 228 ff., mainly upon the ground of the statement in the Bháshya "*aruṇad Yavanaḥ Sáketam*," which he connects with an expedition of Menander (B.C. 144–120) against Ayodhyá, fixed the date of the composition of the work for the period of this expedition, or specially for B.C. 140–120. The objections urged by me (*I. St.*, v. 151) against this assumption were, in the first place, materially weakened by a remark of Kern's in his Preface to the Bṛih. Saṃh. of Varáha-Mihira, p. 37, according to which the statement in the same passage of the Bháshya "*aruṇad Yavano Mádhyamikán*" is not necessarily to be referred to the Buddhistic school of this name, first founded by Nágárjuna, but may possibly have reference to a tribe called Mádhyamika, mentioned elsewhere. In the next place, Bhaṇḍarkar, in the *Ind. Antiq.*, i. 299 ff, ii. 59 ff., attempted to prove that Pataṃjali wrote the particular section where he speaks in the above terms of Menander (who is assumed, on Goldstücker's authority, to be meant by 'Yavana') between A.D. 144 and 142, seeing that he there at the same time speaks of sacrifices as *still* being performed for Pushpamitra (A.D. 178–142). In my reply in *I. St.*, xiii. 305 ff., I emphasised these points: first, that the identity of the Yavana and Menander is by no means made out; next, that it does not at all necessarily follow from the passage in question that Pataṃjali and Pushyamitra (this is the correct form) were contemporaries; and, lastly, that Pataṃjali may possibly have found these examples already current, in which case they cannot be used to prove anything with regard to him, but only with regard to his predecessors—it may be, even Páṇini himself. And although I am now disposed, in presence of Bhaṇḍarkar's further objections, to admit the historical bearing of the statement referring to Pushyamitra (but see Böhtlingk's opposite view in *Z. D. M. G.*, xxix. 183 ff.), still, with respect to all the examples here in question, I must lay special stress on the possibility, just mentioned, that they may belong to the class of *múrdhábhishikta* illustrations (*ibid.*, p. 315). We must for the present rest satisfied, therefore (p. 319), with placing the date of the composition of the Bháshya between B.C. 140 and A.D. 60,—a result which, considering the wretched state of the chronology of Indian literature generally, is, despite its indefiniteness, of no mean importance.

* See *I. St.*, i. 141–157. [The beginning here made came to a standstill for want of the Mahábháshya.]

† In the case of some of these, it is remarked that they are not explained *here*, or else not separately. Acquaintance with the Mahábháshya itself will alone yield us satisfactory information on this point. [From Aufrecht's accounts in his *Catal. Codd. Sansk. Bibl. Bodl.*, it appeared that of Páṇini's 3983 rules only 1720 are directly discussed; and Gold-

because these particular Sútras are clear and intelligible of themselves, or whether we may not also here and there have to suppose cases where the Sútras did not yet form part of the text at the time when this commentary was composed. The so-called *gaṇas*, or lists of words which follow one and the same rule, and of which, uniformly, only the initial word is cited in the text itself, are for the present wholly without critical authenticity, and carry no weight, therefore, in reference to Páṇini's time. Some such lists must, of course, have been drawn up by Páṇini; but whether those now extant are the same is very problematical: indeed, to some extent it is simply impossible that they can be so. Nay, such of them even as chance to be specified singly in the Mahábháshya can, strictly speaking, prove nothing save for the time of this work itself.* Here, too, another word of caution is necessary,—one which ought, indeed, to be superfluous, but unfortunately is not, as experience shows,—namely, that care must be taken not to attribute to words and examples occurring in the scholia, composed so recently as fifty years ago, of the Calcutta edition of Páṇini, any validity in reference to the time of Páṇini himself. No doubt such examples are usually derived from the Mahábháshya; but so long as this is not actually proved to be the case, we are not at liberty at once to assume it; and besides, even when it is clear that they are actually borrowed from the Mahábháshya, they are good only for the time of this work itself, but not for that of Páṇini.[238]

---

stücker then showed that the Bháshya is not so much a commentary on Páṇini as rather a defence of him against the unjust attacks of Kátyáyana, the author of the *várttikas*; see *I. St.*, xiii. 297 ff.].

* See *I. St.*, i. 142, 143, 151. [xiii. 298, 302, 329].

[238] This is not quite strictly to the purpose. Max Müller was the first to point out that Páṇini's Sútras were evidently from the beginning accompanied by a definite interpretation, whether oral or written, and that a considerable proportion of the examples in the Bháshya must have come from this source; nay, the Bháshya has itself a special name for these, such examples being styled *múrdhábhishikta*; see *I. St.*, xiii. 315. Unfortunately, however, we have not the slightest clue (*I. Str.*, ii. 167) to enable us to decide, in individual instances, whether an example belongs to this class of *múrdh.* or not.—On the other hand—as results not only from the data in the Rája-taraṃgiṇí, but also, in particular, from the statements at the close of the second book of Hari's Vákyapadíya, which were first cited by Goldstücker, and have lately been published in a corrected form by Kielhorn in the *Ind. Antiq.*, iii. 285–

In addition to Páṇini's system, there grew up in course of time several other grammatical systems, having their own peculiar terminology; and grammatical literature in general attained to a most remarkably rich and extensive development.[239] The Tibetan Tandjur likewise embraces

---

237—the Bháshya has undergone manifold vicissitudes of fortune, has been more than once *vichhinna*, and arranged afresh, so that the possibility of considerable changes, additions, and interpolations cannot be denied. Strictly speaking, therefore, in each individual case it remains, *à priori*, uncertain whether the example is to be credited to Patamjali himself, or to these subsequent remodellings of the text (or, reversely, to Patamjali's predecessors, or even to Páṇini himself); see *I. St.*, xiii. 320, 329; *Ind. Antiq.*, iv. 247. Kielhorn, it is true, in *Ind. Antiq.*, iv. 108, has protested very strongly against the view "that at some time or other the text of the Mahábháshya had been lost, that it had to be reconstructed," &c. He will only "perhaps allow a break so far as regards its traditional interpretation," while we are for the time being bound "to regard the text of the Mahábháshya as given by our MSS. to be the same as it existed about 2000 years ago." Let us, then, await the arguments he has to offer in support of this; for his protest alone will hardly suffice in the face of the statements on the subject that are still preserved in the tradition itself. On three separate occasions, the epithets *vipl'ávita*, *bhrashṭa*, *vichhinna* are employed of the work. And there is the further circumstance that, according to Burnell's testimony (Pref. to Vaṅśa-Bráh., p. xxii. n.), the South Indian MSS. of the text appear to vary materially: see also Burnell's *Elem. S. Ind. Pal.*, pp. 7, 32.

239 The *Vákyapadíya* of Hari, the editing of which has now been undertaken by Kielhorn, connects itself specially with the Mahábháshya.—The *Káśiká* of Vámana, a direct commentary on Páṇini, is at present being edited by Bála-śástrin in the Benares *Paṇḍit*. According to him, it was composed in the thirteenth century, as Goldstücker had already hinted; whereas the date previously assigned to it, in accordance with Böhtlingk's view, was towards the eighth century; see *I. St.*, v. 67; Cappeller's Introd. to Vámana's *Kávyálaṃkáravṛitti*, pp. vii., viii.—To Aufrecht we owe an edition (Bonn, 1859) of Ujjvaladatta's Commentary (of the thirteenth century or so) on the *Uṇádi-Sútras*, which are perhaps (see *I. Str.*, ii. 322) to be ascribed to Śákaṭáyana; and Jul. Eggeling is engaged on an edition of the *Gaṇa-ratna-mahodadhi* of Vardhamána.—Of Bhaṭṭoji-Díkshita's *Siddhánta-kaumudí* (seventeenth century) we have now a new and good edition by Táránátha Váchaspati (Calc., 1864–1865).—A highly meritorious work is the edition, with English version, &c., of Varadarája's *Laghu-kaumudí* by J. R. Ballantyne (originally published at Mirzapore, 1849).—Śántanava's *Phiṭ-Sútras* were edited by Kielhorn in 1866; and to him we also owe an excellent edition of Nágoji-bhaṭṭa's *Paribháshendu-śekhara*, a work of the last century (Bombay, 1868–74).—Of grammatical systems which proceed on their own lines, departing from Páṇini, we have Vopadeva's *Mugdha-bodha*, of the thirteenth century, in an edition, amongst others, by Böhtlingk (St. Petersburg, 1847): the *Sárasvata* of Anubhúti-svarúpáchárya appeared at Bombay in 1861 in a lithographed edition; the *Kátantra* of Sarvavarman, with Durgasiṅha's Commentary, is being edited by Eggeling in the *Bibl. Indica* (in

a tolerable number of grammatical writings, and these for the most part works that have been lost in India itself.[240]

As regards Lexicography—the second branch of the science of language—we have already pointed out its first beginnings in the Nighaṇṭus, collections of synonyms, &c., for the elucidation of the Vedic texts. But these were of a practical character, and wholly confined to the Veda: the need of collections towards a dictionary of Sanskṛit, being, on the contrary, more a scientific one, was naturally only awakened at a much later time. Here, too, the earliest attempts in this direction have perished, and the work of Amara-siṅha, the oldest of the kind that has come down to us, appeals expressly in the introduction to other Tantras, from which it was itself compiled. Its commentators also expressly mention by name as such Tantras the Trikáṇḍa, the Utpaliní, and the works of Rabhasa, Kátyáyana, Vyáḍi,* and Vararuchi, the two latter as authorities for the gender of words.

1874 it had reached to iv. 4. 50). The system of this grammar is of peculiar interest on this account, that a special connection appears to exist between it and the Páli grammar of Kachchdyana, particularly in regard to the terminology employed. According to Bühler's letter from Kashmír (pub. in *I. St.*, xiv. 402 ff.), the Kátantra is the special grammar of the Káśmíras, and was there frequently commented upon in the 12th-16th centuries. Of older grammatical texts, he has further discovered the *Paribháshás* of Vyáḍi and Chandra, as also the *Varṇa-Sútras* and *Shaḍ-bháshá-chandriká* of the latter; likewise an *Avyaya-vṛitti* and *Dhátu-taraṃgiṇí* by Kshíra (Jayápíḍa's preceptor), and a very beautiful *bhúrja*-MS. of the Káśiká. In one of these MSS. this last-named work is ascribed to Vámana and Jayáditya (Jayápíḍa?), whereby the earlier view as to its date again gains credit.—For a list of "Sanscrit-Grammars," &c., see Colebrooke's *Misc. Ess.*, ii. 38 ff., ed. Cowell.—It remains still to mention here Cowell's edition of the *Prákṛita-prakáśa* of Vararuchi (1854, 1868); further, an edition recently (1873) published at Bombay of Hemachandra's (according to Bháu Dáji, A.D. 1088-1172, see *Journ. Bombay Br. R. A. S.*, ix. 224) Prákṛit Grammar, which forms the eighth book of his great treatise on Sanskṛit grammar, the *Śabdánuśásana*; and lastly, Pischel's valuable dissertation *De Grammaticis Pracriticis* (1874), which supplements the accounts in Lassen's *Institut. Linguæ Pracriticæ* (Bonn, 1837) with very important material.

[240] See Schiefner's paper on the logical and grammatical writings in the Tandjur, p. 25, from the *Bulletin de la Classe hist. phil. de l'Acad. Imp. des Sc. de St. Petersbourg*, iv., Nos. 18, 19 (1847), from which it appears that the *Chandra-Vyákaraṇa-Sútra*, the *Kalápa-Sútra*, and the *Sarasvatí-Vyákaraṇa-Sútra*, in particular, are represented there.

* A Vyáḍi is cited in the Ṛik-Prátiśákhya [and in Goldstücker's *Páṇini* he plays a very special part. The *Saṃgraha*, several times mentioned in the Bháshya, and there assigned to *Dákshdyaṇa*, is by Nágeśa—who describes it as a work in

The question now is to determine the age of Amarasiṁha—a question which, in the first instance, exactly coincides with the one already discussed as to the date of Kálidása, for, like the latter, Amara is specified by tradition among the 'nine gems' of the court of Vikrama—that Vikrama whom Indian tradition identifies with king Bhoja (A.D. 1050), but to whom European criticism has assigned the date B.C. 56, because—an era bearing this name commences with that year. The utter groundlessness of this last assumption has been already exposed in the case of Kálidása, though we do not here, any more than there, enter the lists in defence of the Indian tradition. This tradition is distinctly contradicted, in particular, by a temple-inscription discovered at Buddhagayá, which is dated 1005 of the era of Vikramáditya (*i.e.*, A.D. 949), and in which Amara-deva is mentioned as one of the 'nine jewels' of Vikrama's court, and as builder of the temple in question. This inscription had been turned to special account by European criticism in support of its view; but Holtzmann's researches (*op. cit.*, pp. 26–32) have made it not improbable that it was put there in the same age in which Amara-siṁha's dictionary was written, seeing that both give expression to precisely the same form of belief, a combination, namely, of Buddhism with Vishnuism—a form of faith which cannot possibly have continued very long in vogue, resting as it does on a union of directly opposite systems. At all events, inscription and dictionary cannot lie so much as 1000 years apart,—that is a sheer impossibility. Unfortunately this inscription is not known to us in the original, and has only survived in the English translation made by Ch. Wilkins in 1785 (a time when he can hardly have been very proficient in Sanskṛit!): the text itself is lost,

100,000 *ślokas*—attributed to a Vyáḍi, meaning in all likelihood the same Vyáḍi who is elsewhere mentioned in the Bháshya. Now upon the strength of this, Goldstücker sets up a direct relation of kinship between Páṇini, who is designated *Dákshíputra* in the Bháshya, and this (Vyáḍi) *Dákshâyaṇa*; only the former must be "at least two generations" prior to the latter. And on this he grounds a specific "historical argument" for the determination of Páṇini's date; for if Vyáḍi, Páṇini's descendant collaterally, is cited in the Ṛik-Pr., then of course this work must be later than Páṇini; see against all this *I. St.*, v. 41, 127–133, xiii. 401].

with the stone on which it was incised. That the dictionary belongs, in any case, to a period considerably later than the first century B.C.—the date commonly assigned to it—is sufficiently indicated by data furnished by the work itself. For, in the first place, it enumerates the signs of the zodiac, which were unquestionably borrowed by the Hindús from the Greeks; and, according to Letronne's investigations, the completion of the zodiac did not take place among the Greeks themselves before the first century A.D.; so that, of course, it cannot have become known to the Hindús till one or several centuries later. Again, in the Amara-kosha, the lunar mansions are enumerated in their new order, the fixing of which was due to the fresh life infused into Indian astronomy under Greek influence, the exact date being uncertain, but hardly earlier than A.D. 400. Lastly, the word *dínára* occurs here,* which, as pointed out by Prinsep, is simply the Latin *denarius* (see Lassen, *I. AK.*, ii. 261, 348). The use of the term *tantra* in the sense of 'text-book' may perhaps also be cited in this connection, as it belongs only to a definite period, which is probably the fifth or sixth century, the Hindús who emigrated to Java having taken the word with them in this sense.[241]—All this, of course, yields us no direct date. If it be correct, as stated by Reinaud (*Mém. sur l'Inde*, p. 114), that there existed a Chinese translation of the work, "rédigée au vi^e siècle," this would give us something tolerably definite to go by. But Stan. Julien does not, it would seem, in the passage cited by Reinaud as his authority, express himself in quite such definite terms; as he merely speaks of the "traduction chinoise de l'Amarakocha, qui paraît avoir été publiée . . .":† nor are the positive grounds he adduces in support of this view directly before us, so that we might test

---

* It also occurs in the Pañchatantra, in a legend of Buddhistic origin.—I may here also remark in passing, that the word *dramma*, *i.e.*, *δραχμή*, is employed in the twelfth century by Bháskara, as well as in inscriptions [cf. *Z. D. M. G.*, vi. 420].

241 Of special interest also is the Arabico-Persian word *pílu* for elephant; cf. Kumárila on Jaim., i. 3. 5, cited by Colebrooke, *Misc. Ess.*, i. 314[1] (339[2]); Gildemeister in *Z. D. M. G.*, xxviii. 697.

† The meaning of *paraître*, however, is doubtful; it can signify either 'seem' or 'be clear' (according to all evidence),—in the latter sense like the Latin *apparere*, and the English '*appear*,' being indeed derived from *apparescere*.

them. Of the Tibetan translation of the work in the Tandjur no particulars are known. How great the difficulty is of arriving at any sort of decision in this matter is shown by the example of one of the most celebrated of living Indianists, H. H. Wilson. For while, in the preface to the first edition of his Sanskṛit Dictionary (1819), he rather inclined to the view that Amara-siṅha flourished in the fifth century A.D., and while again, in the second edition of the work (1832), under the word 'Vararuchi,' he expressly transfers the 'nine gems' to the court of Bhoja (A.D. 1050),—in the preface (p. vi.) to his translation of the Vishṇu-Puráṇa (1840), on the contrary, he makes Amara-siṅha live "in the century prior to Christianity!"—But, independently of all that has hitherto been advanced, the mere circumstance that the other dictionaries we possess, besides the Amara-kosha, all belong to the eleventh, twelfth, and following centuries, constrains us to come to a conclusion similar to that which was forced upon us in regard to the drama—namely, that as the Amara-kosha is in no way specifically distinguished in character from these other productions, so it cannot be separated from them by a very wide interval of time. (Holtzmann, p. 26.)[242]

Besides the dictionaries, we have also to mention a class of lexical works quite peculiar to the Hindús—namely, the lists of roots styled *Dhátu-páráyaṇas* or *Dhátu-páṭhas:* * though these belong rather to the province of grammar. They are written partly in prose and partly in *ślokas*. The latter is the form adopted in all the dictionaries, and it supplies, of course, a strong guarantee of the integrity of the text, the interlacing of the different verses rendering interpolation well-nigh impossible.†

242 Since the above was written, nothing new has appeared on this question. To the editions of the Amara-kosha then already published, those, namely, of Colebrooke (1808) and of Loiseleur Deslongchamps (Paris, 1839, 1845), various new ones have since been added in India. Of other vocabularies we may mention the editions, by Böhtlingk and Rieu (1847) of Hemachandra's *Abhidhána-chintámaṇi*, and by Aufrecht (London, 1861) of Halâyudha's *Abhidhána-ratna-málá*, belonging to about the end of the eleventh century. A Páli redaction of the Amara-kosha by Moggallána belongs to the close of the twelfth century; see *I. Str.*, ii. 330.

* For the literature of these, see Westergaard's preface to his excellent *Radices Linguæ Sanscritæ* (Bonn, 1841).

† See Holtzmann, *op. cit.*, p. 17.

Lastly, as a third phase of the science of language, we have to consider Metric, Poetics, and Rhetoric.

With the beginnings of Prosody we have already become acquainted in connection with the Veda (see p. 23). The treatise ascribed to Piñgala even appears as an appendage to the Veda itself, however little claim it has to such a position, specifying as it does the most highly elaborated metres, such as were only used in later times (see p. 60). The tradition which identifies Piñgala with Patamjali, the author of the Mahábháshya and the Yoga-Śástra, must answer for itself; for us there exists no cogent reason for accepting it.[243] The other existing treatises on metre are likewise all modern: they superseded the more ancient works; and the same is the case, in an equal degree, with the writings on poetics and rhetoric. Of the *Alamkára-Śástra* of Bharata, which is often cited as the leading authority on these subjects, only the few quoted passages would seem to have survived, although, according to one commentary,* the work was itself but an extract from the Agni-Puráṇa. A. W. von Schlegel in his *Réflexions sur l'Étude des Langues Asiat.*, p. 111, speaks of a manuscript, preserved in Paris, of the *Sáhitya-darpaṇa*, another leading work on this subject, as dated *śake* 949, *i.e.*, A.D. 1027; and this, if correct, would naturally be of the highest importance for the age of the works therein quoted. But *à priori* I am firmly persuaded that this statement rests on a mistake or misunderstanding;[244] for the oldest manuscripts with which I have had any opportunity of becoming acquainted are, as already mentioned (p. 182), not so much

---

[243] Cf. on this *I. St.*, viii. 158 ff.

* See my *Catal. of the Sansk. MSS. in the Berl. Lib.*, p. 227. [Respecting the *Náṭya-Śástra* of Bharata fuller information was first supplied by Hall in his edition of the *Daśa-rúpa* (1865), at the close of which he has given the text of four chapters of the work (18-20, 34); see also W. Heymann's account of it in the *Göttinger Gel. Anzeigen*, 1874, p. 86 ff.]

[244] The Sáhitya-darpaṇa was only composed towards the middle of the fifteenth century in E. Bengal, on the banks of the Brahmaputra; see Jagan-mohana-śarman in the preface to his edition of the drama *Chaṇḍa-Kauśika*, p. 2. It has already been edited several times in India, amongst others by Roer in the *Bibl. Indica* (1851, vol. x.). Ballantyne's translation, *ibid.*, is unfortunately not yet entirely printed, and reaches only to Rule 575; for the close of the work, however, from Rule 631, we have a translation by Pramadá Dása Mitra, which appeared in the *Paṇḍit*, Nos. 4–28.

as 500 years old, and it will be difficult to find any of a yet greater age.—For the rest, in the field of rhetoric and poetics, the Hindú mind, so fertile in nice distinctions, has had free scope, and has put forth all its power, not seldom in an extremely subtle and ingenious fashion.[245]

We now come to the consideration of Philosophy, as the second branch of the scientific Sanskṛit literature.

I rank it here after the science of language, not because I regard it as of later origin, but because the existing text-books of the philosophical systems seem to me to be posterior to the text-book of grammar, the Sútra of Páṇini, since they appear, to some extent, to presuppose the existence of Upanishads, writings which, in their extant form, manifestly belong to a very late period, comparatively speaking.

The beginnings of philosophical speculation go back, as we have already more than once seen (see especially pp. 26, 27), to a very remote age. Even in the Saṃhitá of the Ṛik, although only in its later portions, we find hymns that bespeak a high degree of reflection. Here, too, as with all other peoples, it was especially the question as to the origin of the world that more imme-

---

[245] Daṇḍin's *Kávyádarśa*, of the sixth century, and Dhanaṃjaya's *Daśa-rúpa*, of the middle of the tenth century, have been published in the *Bibl. Indica*, the former edited by Premachandra Tarkavágíśa (1863), the latter by Hall (1865). From these we learn, amongst other things, the very important fact that in Daṇḍin's day two definite, provincially distinguished, varieties of style (*ríti*) were already recognised, namely, the *Gauḍa* style and the *Vaidarbha* style, to which in course of time four others, the *Páñchálí*, *Láṭí*, *Ávantiká*, and *Mágadhí*, were added; cf. my Essay on the Rámáyaṇa, p. 76, and *I. St.*, xiv. 65 ff. Báṇa passes for the special representative of the Pañchála style; see Aufrecht in *Z. D. M. G.*, xxvii. 93; whereas the Káśmíra Bilhaṇa, for example, adopted the Vaidarbha-ríti; see Bühler, Vikramáñka-char., i. 9.—Vámana's *Kávyálaṃkára-vṛitti* has lately been edited by Cappeller (Jena, 1875), and belongs, he thinks, to the twelfth century. Mammaṭa's *Kávya-prakáśa*, several times published in India, belongs, in Bühler's opinion, to the same date, since Mammaṭa, according to Hall (*Introd. to Vásava.*, p. 55), was the maternal uncle of the author of the Naishadhíya; see Bühler in *Journ. Bomb. Br. R. A. S.*, x. 37, my *I. Str.*, i. 356, and my Essay on Hála's Sapta-śataka, p. 11. Cf. here also Aufrecht's account of the Sarasvatí-kaṇṭhábharaṇa (note 220 above).—A rich accession to the Alaṃkára literature also will result from Bühler's journey to Kashmir: the works range from the ninth to the thirteenth century.

diately gave rise to philosophical contemplation. The mystery of existence, of being, and of life forces itself directly upon the soul, and along with this comes the question, how the riddle is to be solved, and what is its cause. The idea that most readily presents itself, and which is therefore, in fact, everywhere recognisable as the earliest one, is that of an eternal matter, a chaotic mass, into which order and system are gradually introduced, whether—and here we have two distinct views, each of which has its intrinsic warrant, and which must therefore have been early opposed to each other—by virtue of an indwelling capacity of development, or by impulse from without, whereby of course an object or Being existing outside of this chaotic mass is *eo ipso* postulated. This point reached, the idea is then a very natural one to regard this Being, whence the impulse proceeds, as higher and more exalted than the primary chaotic matter itself; and, as speculation advances, this primary matter continues to sink to a more and more subordinate position, till at length its very existence appears as dependent upon the will of this Being, and so the idea of a creation arises. The steps of this gradation may actually be followed with tolerable distinctness in the Vedic texts. In the more ancient portions the notion everywhere still is that the worlds were but 'fixed,' 'arranged' (*stabhita, skabhita* *), by the aid of the *metres* (it is thus that the harmony of the universe is explained); only at a later stage is the idea developed of their *sarjana*, 'emission' or creation. As time goes on, the creative Being is conceived as more and more transcendental and supernatural, so that as a means of communication between him and the real universe intermediate grades of beings, demiurges, are required, by classifying and systematising whom speculation strives

* It is interesting that the German word *schaffen* is derived from this root *stabh, skabh*, 'establish;' originally therefore it had not the sense in which it is now used. The idea of the 'establishment,' 'arrangement' of the worlds may possibly therefore date from the epoch when Teutons and Indians still dwelt together: or has the same use of the word grown up independently with both peoples? Perhaps the 'yawning gulf' of chaos, '*gahanaṃ gambhîraṃ*,' '*ginunga gap*,' might also be instanced as a similar primitive notion? [The connection here supposed between *schaffen* and *stabh, skabh, σκήπτειν*, is very questionable; the word seems rather to belong to *schaben, scabere, σκάπτειν*.]

to introduce order, but naturally only with the result of producing greater confusion. We have thus three distinct views as to the origin of the world — that of its 'development,' that of its 'arrangement,' and that of its 'creation.' The two former agree in so far as the theory of development requires an 'arranger' also; they are, however, sufficiently distinguished by the circumstance that in the former this Power is regarded as the first production of the capacity of development residing in primary matter; in the latter, on the contrary, as an independent Being existing outside of it. The theory of a creation starts generally with a desire on the part of the Creator to be no longer alone, the expression of which desire is immediately followed by the emanation itself. Either it is a female being that first proceeds from the Creator, in connection with whom, by a process of begetting,* he then accomplishes the further work of creation; or it is the breath of life that first of all emanates, and in its turn produces all the rest; or again, the mere expression of the desire itself involves creation, *vách* or speech here appearing as its immediate source; or the process is conceived in a variety of other ways. The notion that the world is but Illusion only belongs to the latest phase of this emanation theory.—It is impossible at present to attempt even an approximate sketch of the gradual growth of these three different theories into complete philosophical systems; the Bráhmaṇas and Upanishads must first be thoroughly studied. Nor until this has been done will it be possible to decide the question whether for the beginnings of Greek philosophy any connection with Hindú speculation can be established—with reference to the five elements in particular,† a point which for the present is doubtful.‡ I have already stated generally (p. 29) the reasons which lead me to assign a comparatively late date to the existing text-books (Sútras) of the Hindú philosophical systems.[246]

---

* By incest therefore: the story in Megasthenes of the incest of the Indian Herakles with his daughter refers to this.

† And the doctrine of metempsychosis!

‡ See Max Müller in *Z. D. M. G.*, vi. 18 ff. [Cf. my review of Schlüter's book, *Aristoteles' Metaphysik eine Tochter der Sánkhyalehre* in *Lit. Cent. Bl.*, 1874, p. 294.]

[246] Cf. Cowell's note to Colebrooke's *Misc. Ess.*, i. 354. "The Sútras as we have them cannot be the original

Unfortunately we are not yet in possession of the treatises themselves; * and for what follows I have had to depend mainly upon Colebrooke's Essays on the subject.[247]

The most ancient philosophical system appears to be the *Sámkhya* theory, which sets up a primordial matter as the basis of the universe, out of which the latter is by successive stages evolved. The word *Sámkhya* itself occurs first in the later Upanishads; † while in the earlier Upanishads and Bráhmaṇas the doctrines afterwards belonging to the Sáṃkhya system still appear in incongruous combination with doctrines of opposite tendency, and are cited along with these under the equivalent designations of *Mímáṅsá* (√ *man*, speculation), *Ádeśa* (doctrine), *Upanishad* (sitting), &c. I am especially induced to regard the Sáṃkhya as the oldest of the existing systems by the names of those who are mentioned as its leading representatives: Kapila, Pañchaśikha, and Ásuri. The last of these names occurs very frequently in the Śatapatha-Bráhmaṇa as that of an important authority for sacrificial ritual and the like, and also in the lists of teachers contained in that work (namely,

form of the doctrines of the several schools. They are rather a recapitulation of a series of preceding developments which had gone on in the works of successive teachers."

* Only two of them have thus far appeared in India; but of the edition of the Vedánta-Sútra with Śaṃkara's commentary I have not yet been able to see a copy; only the edition of the Nyáya-Sútra is known to me. The whole of these texts are at present being edited in India by Dr. Ballantyne, with English translation. [These editions, entitled *Aphorisms of the Sánkhya, Vedánta, Yoga*, &c., extend to all the six systems, each *sútra* being regularly followed by translation and commentary; but unfortunately only a few numbers of each have appeared.]

[247] In the new edition of Colebrooke's Essays (1873), these are accompanied with excellent notes by Professor Cowell. Since the above was written, much new material has been added by the labours of Roer, Ballantye, Hall, Cowell, Müller, Gough, K. M. Banerjea, Barth. St. Hilaire. In the *Bibl. Indica* and the Benares *Paṇḍit* many highly important editions of texts have appeared, and we are now in possession of the Sútras of all the six systems, together with their leading commentaries, three of them in translation also. See also in particular the *Sarva-darśana-saṃgraha* of Mádhava in the *Bibl. Ind.* (1853–58), edited by Íśvarachandra Vidyáságara, and Hall's *Bibliographical Index to the Ind. Phil. Syst.* (1859).

† Of the Taittiríya and Atharvan, as also in the fourteenth book of the Nirukti, and in the Bhagavad-gítá. As regards its sense, the term is rather obscure and not very significant; can its use have been in any way influenced and determined by its association with the doctrine of *Sákya?* or has it reference purely and solely to the twenty-five principles? [The latter is really the case; see *I. St.*, ix. 17 ff. Kapilas tattva-*saṃkhyátá*, Bhág. Pur., iii. 25. 1.]

as disciple of Yájnavalkya, and as only one or a few generations prior to Yáska). Kapila, again, can hardly be unconnected with the Kápya Pataṃchala whom we find mentioned in the Yájnavalkíya-káṇḍa of the Vṛihad-Áraṇyaka as a zealous representative of the Brahmanical learning. Kapila, too—what is not recorded of any other of these reputed authors of Sútras—was himself afterwards elevated to divine rank; and in this quality we meet with him, for example, in the Śvetáśvataropanishad.* But it is above all the close connection of his tenets with Buddhism[248]—the legends of which, moreover, uniformly speak both of him and of Pañchaśikha as long anterior to Buddha—which proves conclusively that the system bearing his name is to be regarded as the oldest.[249] The question as to the possible date of Kapila is thus closely linked with that of the origin of Buddhism generally, a point to which we shall revert in the sequel, in connection with our survey of the Buddhistic literature. Two other leading doctors of the Sáṃkhya school as such appear towards the sixth century of our era, Íśvara-Krishṇa and Gauḍapáda: the former (according to Colebrooke, i. 103) is expressly stated

* In the invocations of the Pitṛis which (see above, pp. 55, 56) form part of the ordinary ceremonial, Kapila, Ásuri, Pañchaśikha (and with them a Voḍha or Boḍha), uniformly occupy a very honourable place in later times; whereas notice is more rarely taken of the remaining authors of philosophical Sútras, &c. This too proves that the former are more ancient than the latter.

248 This relates, according to Wilson, to the community of the fundamental propositions of both in regard to "the eternity of matter, the principles of things, and the final extinction" (Wilson, *Works*, ii. 346, ed. Rost.). In opposition to this, it is true, Max Müller expressly denies any special connection whatever between Kapila's system, as embodied in the Sútras, and Buddhist metaphysics (*Chips from a German Workshop*, i. 226, 1870); yet he himself immediately afterwards gives the correct explanation of this, when he says that the existing Sútras of Kapila are "of later date, posterior, not anterior, to Buddha." On the subject itself, see specially *I. St.*, iii. 132, 133.

249 In the sacred texts of the Jainas also, not only is the *Saṭṭhi-tanta* (*Shashṭi-tantra*, explained by the comm. as *Kápila-Śástra*) specified along with the four Vedas and their Añgas, but in another passage the name Kávila appears along with it, the only other Brahmanical system here mentioned being the Baïsesiya (Vaiśeshika). (The order in which they are given is Baïsesiya, Buddha-sásaṇa, Kávila, Logáyaṭa, Saṭṭhi-tanta.) So also in a similar enumeration in the Lalitavistara, after Sáṃkhya Yoga, only Vaiśeshika is further specified. See my paper on the Bhagavatí of the Jainas, ii. 246-248.

to be the author of the existing Sámkhya-Sútra, while the latter embodied its doctrine in several Upanishads.[250]

Connected with the Sámkhya school, as a further development of it, is the Yoga system of Patamjali,[251] whose name describes him as in all probability a descendant of the Kápya Patamchala of the Vṛihad-Áraṇyaka. Along with him (or prior to him) Yájnavalkya, the leading authority of the Śatapatha-Bráhmaṇa, is also regarded as a main originator of the Yoga doctrine, but this only in later writings.* Whether Patamjali is to be identified with the

---

250 The Sútras of Kapila, the so-called *Sámkhya-pravachana*, are now published, with the commentary of Vijnána-bhikshu in the *Bibl. Ind.*, edited by Hall (1854-56); a translation by Ballantyne also appeared in the same series, 1862-65. In his preface to the S. Prav., as well as in the preface some years later to his edition of Vijnána-bhikshu's *Sámkhya-sára*, Hall gives a special account, with which, however, he is himself by no means satisfied (see his note to Wilson's Vishṇu-Pur., iii. 301), of Kapila and the leading works extant of the Sámkhya system. He regards the Sámkhya-pravachana as a very late production, which may here and there even "be suspected of occasional obligation to the Kárikás of Íśvarakṛishṇa" (Sámkhya-sára, Preface, p. 12). Of course this does not affect either the antiquity of Kapila himself or his "alleged connection with the Sámkhya" (p. 20). Cowell, too (Colebrooke, *Misc. Ess.*, i. 354, note), regards the Sámkhya school itself "as one of the earliest," while the Sútras, on the contrary, are of late origin, inasmuch as they not only "refer distinctly to Vedánta texts," but also "expressly mention the Vaiśeshika in i. 25, v. 85; for the Nyáya, cf. v. 27, 86, and for the Yoga, i. 90." Besides the Vaiśeshikas (i. 25), only Pañchaśikha (v. 32, vi. 68) and Sanandanácharya (vi. 69) are actually mentioned by name. An interesting detail is the opposing of the names Srughna and Páṭaliputra (i. 28) as an illustration of separate locality (similarly in the Mahábháshya, see *I. St.*, xiii. 378).

251 The Yoga-Sútra ascribed to Patamjali (likewise called *Sámkhya-pravachana-Sútra*), with extracts from Bhoja's commentary upon it, was edited, text with translation, to the extent of one-half, by Ballantyne in his *Aphorisms;* the second half appeared in the *Paṇḍit*, Nos. 28-68, edited by Govinda-deva-śástrin.—An *Áryá-pañchásíti* by Śesha (whom the editor identifies with Patamjali), in which the relation of *prakṛiti* and *purusha* is elucidated in a Vaishṇava sense, was edited by Bálaśástrin in No. 56 of the Paṇḍit; there exists also a Śaiva adaptation of it by Abhinavagupta; see *Z. D. M. G.*, xxvii. 167. According to Bühler's letter (*I. St.*, xiv. 402 ff.), Abhinavagupta is supposed to have died in A.D. 982; but Bühler has not himself verified the date, which is stated to occur in the hymn written by Abhinava on his deathbed.

* Particularly in the twelfth book of the Mahá-Bhárata, where, with Janaka, he is virtually described as a Buddhist teacher, the chief outward badge of these teachers being precisely the *káshâya-dhâraṇam mauṇḍyam* (M.-Bh., xii. 11898, 566). It appears, at all events, from the Yájnavalkíya-káṇḍa that both gave a powerful impulse to the practice of religious mendicancy: in the Atharvopanishads, too, this is clearly shown (see p. 163). [In the Yájna-

author of the Mahábháshya remains for the present a question. The word *yoga* in the sense of 'union with the Supreme Being,' 'absorption therein by virtue of meditation,' first occurs in the later Upanishads, especially in the tenth book of the Taittiríya-Áraṇyaka and in the Káṭhakopanishad, where this very doctrine is itself enunciated.[252] As there presented, it seems to rest substantially upon a dualism, that is, upon the 'arrangement' theory of the universe; in this sense, however, that in the Káṭhakopanishad at least, *purusha*, primeval soul, is conceived as existing prior to *avyakta*, primordial matter, from the union of which two principles the *mahán átmá*, or spirit of life, is evolved. For the rest, its special connection with the Sáṃkhya system is still, in its details, somewhat obscure, however well attested it is externally by the constant juxtaposition of 'Sáṃkhya-Yoga,' generally as a compound. Both systems appear, in particular, to have countenanced a confounding of their *purusha*, *íśvara* with the chief divinities of the popular religion, Rudra and Kṛishṇa, as may be gathered from the Śvetáśvataropanishad,[252a] the Bhagavad-gítá, and many passages in the twelfth book of the Mahá-Bhárata.* One very peculiar side of the Yoga

---

valkya-Smṛiti, iii. 110, Y. describes himself ostensibly as the author of the Áraṇyaka as well as of the Yoga-Śástra.]

[252] It is in these and similar Upanishads, as also in Manu's Dharma-Śástra (cf. Johäntgen's Essay on the Law-Book of Manu, 1863), that we have to look for the earliest germs and records of the atheistic Sáṃkhya and the deistic Yoga systems.

[252a] In my paper on the Śvetáśvataropanishad I had to leave the point undetermined whether, for the period to which this work belongs, and specially as regards the monotheistic Yoga system it embodies, an acquaintance with the corresponding doctrines of Christianity is to be assumed or not; see *I. St.*, i. 423. Lorinser, on the other hand, in his translation of the Bhagavad-gítá (Breslau, 1869), unreservedly assumes such an acquaintance in the case of this poem. From the point of view of literary chronology no forcible objection can be brought against this; some of the points, too, which he urges are not without importance; but on the whole he has greatly over-estimated the scope of his argument: the question is still *sub judice*.

* More particularly with regard to the Bhágavata, Páñcharátra, and Páśupata doctrines. [A Sútra of the Páñcharátra school, that, namely, of Śáṇḍilya (ed. by Ballantyne in the *Bibl. Indica*, 1861), is apparently mentioned by Śaṃkara, Vedánta-S. Bh. ii. 2. 45. It rests, seemingly, upon the Bhagavad-gítá, and lays special stress upon faith in the Supreme Being (*bhaktir íśvare*); see on it Cowell's note in Colebrooke's *Misc. Ess.*, i. 438. On the development of the doctrine of *bhakti*, Wilson surmises Christian conceptions to have had some influence; see my paper on the Rám. Táp. Up., pp. 277, 360. The

doctrine—and one which was more and more exclusively developed as time went on—is the Yoga practice; that is, the outward means, such as penances, mortifications, and the like, whereby this absorption into the supreme Godhead is sought to be attained. In the epic poems, but especially in the Atharvopanishads, we encounter it in full force: Páṇini, too, teaches the formation of the term *yogin*.

The most flourishing epoch of the Sáṃkhya-Yoga belongs most probably to the first centuries of our era, the influence it exercised upon the development of Gnosticism in Asia Minor being unmistakable; while further, both through this channel and afterwards directly also, it had an important influence upon the growth of the Śúfí philosophy.* Albírúní translated Pataṃjali's work into Arabic at the beginning of the eleventh century, and also, it would appear, the Sáṃkhya-Sútra,† though the information we have as to the contents of these works does not harmonise with the Sanskṛit originals.

The doctrines of the two *Mímáṅsás* appear to have been reduced to their present systematic shape at a later period than those of the Sáṃkhya;[253] and, as indicated by their respective names, in the case of the *Púrva-Mímáṅsá* earlier than in the case of the *Uttara-Mímáṅsá*. The essential purpose of both Mímáṅsás is to bring the doctrines enunciated in the Bráhmaṇas or sacred revelation into harmony and accord with each other. Precepts relating to practice form the subject of the Púrva-Mímáṅsá, which is hence also styled *Karma-Mímáṅsá*; while doctrines regarding the essence of the creative principle and its relation to the

---

Nárada-Pañcharátra (edited in *Bibl. Ind.* by K. M. Banerjea, 1861-65) is a ritual, not a philosophical, Vaishṇava text-book.]

* See [Lassen, *I. AK.*, iii. 379 ff.] Gildemeister, *Script. Arab. de reb. Ind.*, p. 112 ff.

† Reinaud in the *Journ. Asiat.*, 1844, pp. 121-124; H. M. Elliot, *Bibl. Index to the Hist. of Muhammedan India*, i. 100.

253 Now that the antiquity of the *extant* form of the Sáṃkhya-Sútras, according to Hall, has become so exceedingly doubtful, the view above expressed also becomes in its turn very questionable. Besides, as we shall presently see, in both the Mímáṅsá-Sútras teachers are repeatedly cited who are known to us from the Vedic Sútra literature; while nothing of the kind occurs in either of the Sáṃkhya-pravachana-Sútras. This does not of course touch the point of the higher antiquity of the doctrines in question; for the names Kapila, Pataṃjali, and Yájnavalkya distinctly carry us back to a far earlier time than do the names Jaimini and Bádaráyaṇa—namely, into the closing phases of the Bráhmaṇa literature itself.

universe form the subject of the Uttara-Mímáṅsá, which is hence also designated *Brahma-Mímáṅsá*, *Śáríraka-Mímáṅsá* ('doctrine of embodied spirit'), or also *Vedánta* ('end of the Veda'). The term 'Mímáṅsá' originally denotes merely speculation in general; it occurs frequently in this sense in the Bráhmaṇas, and only became a technical expression later,[254] as is probably the case also with 'Vedánta,' a word first occurring in the later Upanishads, in the tenth book of the Taittiríya-Áraṇyaka, the Káṭhakopanishad, Muṇḍakopanishad, &c.

The *Karma-Mímáṅsá-Sútra* is ascribed to Jaimini, who is mentioned in the Puráṇas as the revealer of the Sámaveda, though we search in vain in Vedic literature for any hint of his name.* Still, of the teachers who

---

[254] In the Mahábháshya, *mímáṅsaka*, according to Kaiyaṭa, is to be taken in the sense of *mímáṅsám adhíte;* and as the term also occurs therein contradistinction to *aukthika*, it might, in point of fact, refer to the subject of the Púrva-Mímáṅsá. Still the proper word here for one specially devoted to such studies would rather seem to be *yájnika;* see *I. St.*, xiii. 455, 466.

* With the exception of two probably interpolated passages in the Gṛihya-Sútras of the Ṛik (see pp. 56–58).—Nor is there anything bearing on it in the Gaṇapáṭha of Páṇini—of which, indeed, for the present, only a negative use can be made, and even this only with proper caution. But as the word is irregularly formed (from Jeman we should expect Jaimani), this circumstance may here, perhaps, carry some weight. [Apparently it is not found in the Mahábháshya either; see *I. St.*, xiii. 455. On the other hand, the name Jaimini occurs in the concluding *vaṅśa* of the Sáma-vidhána-Bráhm. (v. *I. St.*, iv. 377), and here the bearer of it is described as the disciple of Vyása Páráśarya, and preceptor of a Paushpiṇḍya, which answers exactly to the statement in the Vishṇu-Pur., iii. 6. 1, 4, where he appears as the teacher of Paushpiṇji (cf. also Raghuv., 18. 32, 33). The special relation of Jaimini to the Sáma-Veda appears also from the statements in the Ṛig-Gṛihyas (see note 49 above), which agree with Vishṇu-Pur., iii. 4. 8, 9. Indeed, the Charaṇa-vyúha specifies a Jaiminíya recension of the Sáman; and this recension appears to be still in existence (see note 60 above). In the Pravara section of the Áśval.-Śrauta-S., xii. 10, the Jaiminis are classed as belonging to the Bhṛigus.—All this, however, does not afford us any direct clue to the date of our Jaimini above, whose work, besides, is properly more related to the Yajur- than to the Sáma-Veda. According to the Pañchatantra, the 'Mímáṅsákṛit' Jaimini was killed by an elephant—a statement which, considering the antiquity of this work, is always of some value; although, on the other hand, unfortunately, in consequence of the many changes its text has undergone, we have no guarantee that this particular notice formed part of the original text which found its way to Persia in the sixth century (cf. *I. St.*, viii. 159).—There is also an astrological (Játaka) treatise which goes by the name of Jaimini-Sútra; see *Catal. of Skr. MSS. N. W. Pro.* (1874), pp. 508, 510, 514, 532.]

are cited in this Sútra — Átreya, Bádari, Bádaráyaṇa, Lábukáyana (?),[255] Aitiśáyana—the names of the first and second, at all events, may be pointed out in the Taittiríya-Prátiśákhya and the Śrauta-Sútra of Kátyáyana respectively; while we meet with the family of the Aitaśáyanas in the Kaushítaki-Bráhmaṇa.* Bádaráyaṇa is the name of the author of the Brahma-Mímáṅsá-Sútra; but it by no means follows from the mention of him here that his Sútra is older than the Sútra of Jaimini; for not only may the name, as a patronymic, have designated other persons besides, but in the Sútra of the Brahma-Mímáṅsá the case is exactly reversed, and Jaimini in his turn is mentioned there. All that results from this, as well as from the fact of each Sútra frequently citing its own reputed author, is rather that these Sútras were not really composed by these teachers themselves, but only by their respective schools.† The name Bádaráyaṇa is *not* to be found "in Páṇini," as has recently been erroneously asserted,‡ but only in the *gaṇa-páṭha* to Páṇini, not a very sure authority for the present.—As leading expounders of the Jaimini-Sútra we have mention of Śabara-svámin,[256] and, after him, of Kumárila-bhaṭṭa;[256a] the latter is said to have flourished prior to Śaṃkara.§

---

[255] In the passage in question (vi. 7. 37) ought we not to read Lámakáyana? This is the name of a teacher who is several times mentioned in the Sáma-Sútras; see *I. St.*, iv. 384, 373.—The apparent mention of Buddha in i. 2. 33 (*buddha-śástrát*) is only apparent: here the word 'buddha' has nothing whatever to do with the name 'Buddha.'—To the above names must, however, be added Kárshṇájini (iv. 3. 17, vi. 7. 35) and Kámukáyana (xi. 1. 51); the former of these is found also in Kátyáyana and in the Vedánta-Sútra, the latter only in the *gaṇa* 'Naḍa.'

* xxx. 5, where they are characterised as the scum of the Bhṛigu line, "*pápishṭhá Bhṛigúṇám.*"

† See Colebrooke, i. 102, 103, 328, and above p. 49.

‡ By Max Müller in his otherwise most valuable contributions to our knowledge of Indian philosophy in the *Z. D. M. G.*, vi. 9.

[256] This commentary of Śabara-svámin, which is even cited by Śaṃkara (*Vedánta-Sútra-bh.*, iii. 3. 53), with the text of Jaimini itself, is at present still in course of publication in the *Bibl. Ind.*, ed. by Maheśachandra Nyáyaratna (begun in 1863; the last part, 1871, brings it down to ix. 1. 5).—Mádhava's Jaiminíya-nyáya-málá-vistara, edited by Goldstücker (1865 ff.), is also still unfinished; see my *I. Str.*, ii. 376 ff.

[256a] Who appears also to have borne the odd name of Tutáta or even Tutátita. At all events, Tautátika, or Tautátita, is interpreted by the scholiast of the Prabodha-chandrodaya, 20. 9, ed. Brockhaus, to mean Kumárila; and the same explanation is given by Aufrecht in his *Catalogus*, p. 247, in the case of the Tautátitas mentioned in Mádhava's Sarva-darśana-saṃgraha.

§ See Colebrooke, i. 298: yet the tolerably modern title *bhaṭṭa* awakens some doubt as to this: it may

The *Brahma-Sútra* * belongs, as we have just seen, to Bádaráyaṇa. The notion that creation is but Illusion, and that the transcendental Brahman is alone the Real, but throning in absolute infinitude without any personal existence, is the fundamental doctrine of this system. The attempt is here made to demonstrate that this doctrine is the end and aim of the Veda itself, by bringing all Vedic passages into harmony with this monotheistic pantheism, and by refuting the various views of the Sáṃkhya, or atheistic, the Yoga, or theistic, and the Nyáya, or deistic schools, &c. The notice thus taken of the other systems would of itself seem to prove the posteriority of the Brahma-Sútra; still, it is for the present uncertain whether its polemic is in fact directed against these systems in the form in which we now have them, or merely perhaps against the original tenets out of which these systems have sprung. The teachers' names, at least, which are mentioned in the Brahma-Sútra recur to a large extent in the Śrauta-Sútras; for example, Áśmarathya in Áśvaláyana; † Bádari, Kárshṇájini and Káśakṛitsni in Kátyáyana [see above, p. 139], and, lastly, Átreya in the Taittiríya-Prátiśákhya. The name Auḍulomi belongs exclusively to the Brahma-Sútra.[257] The mention of Jaimini and of Bádaráyaṇa himself has been already touched upon.—Windischmann in his excellent "Śaṃkara" (Bonn, 1832)

---

not have belonged to him originally perhaps? [According to Cowell, note to Colebrooke's *Misc. Ess.*, i. 323, there actually occur in Śaṃkara "allusions to Kumárila-bhaṭṭa, if no direct mention of him;" the title *bhaṭṭa* belongs quite specially to him: "he is emphatically designed by his title Bhaṭṭa." For the rest, this title belongs likewise to Bhaṭṭa-Bháskara-Miśra and Bhaṭṭotpala, and therefore is not by any means 'tolerably modern.']

* This name itself occurs in the Bhagavad-gítá, xiii. 4, but here it may be taken as an appellative rather than as a proper name.

† We have already seen (p. 53) that the Áśmarathaḥ Kalpaḥ is instanced by Páṇini's scholiast as an example of the new Kalpas, in contradistinction to the earlier ones, and so is regarded as of the same age with Páṇini. If, as is likely, the scholiast took this illustration from the Mahábháshya [but this is not the case; v. *I. St.*, xiii. 455], then this statement is important. I may mention in passing that Áśmarathya occurs in the *gaṇa* 'Garga;' Auḍulomi in the *gaṇa* 'Báhu;' Kṛishṇájina in the *gaṇas* 'Tika' and 'Upaka;' in the latter also Káśakṛitsna. The Gaṇa-páṭha, however, is a most uncertain authority, and for Páṇini's time without weight.

[257] It is found in the Mahábháshya also, on Páṇini, iv. 1. 85, 78; see *I. St.*, xiii. 415.

has attempted directly to fix the age of the Brahma-Sútra. For Bádaráyaṇa bears also the additional title of Vyása, whence, too, the Brahma-Sútra is expressly styled Vyása-Sútra. Now, in the Śaṃkara-vijaya—a biography of the celebrated Vedánta commentator Śaṃkara, reputed to be by one of his disciples—we find it stated (see Windischmann, p. 85; Colebrooke, i. 104) that Vyása was the name of the father of Śuka, one of whose disciples was Gauḍapáda, the teacher of Govindanátha, who again was the preceptor of Śaṃkara;[258] so that the date of this Vyása might be conjecturally set down as from two to three centuries prior to Śaṃkara, that is, between 400 and 500 A.D. But the point must remain for the present undetermined,* since it is open to question whether this Vyása ought really to be identified with Vyása Bádaráyaṇa, though this appears to me at least very probable.[259]

---

258 See now in Aufrecht's *Catalogus*, p. 255ᵇ, the passage in question from Mádhava's (!) Śaṃkara-vijaya, v. 5 (rather v. 105, according to the ed. of the work published at Bombay in 1864 with Dhanapati-súri's commentary), and *ibid.*, p. 227ᵇ, the same statements from another work. The Śaṃkara-vijaya of Ánandagiri, on the contrary, Aufrecht, p. 247 ff. (now also in the *Bibl. Ind.*, edited by Jayanáráyaṇa, 1864–1868), contains nothing of this.

* Śaṃkara, on Brahma-Sútra, iii. 3. 32, mentions that Apántaratamas lived as Kṛishṇa-Dvaipáyana at the time of the transition from the Kali to the Dvápara *yuga;* and from the fact of his not at the same time expressly stating that this was Vyása Bádaráyaṇa, author of the Brahma-Sútra, Windischmann concludes, and justly, that in Śaṃkara's eyes the two personages were distinct. In the Mahá-Bhárata, on the contrary, xii. 12158 ff., Śuka is expressly given as the son of Kṛishṇa Dvaipáyana (Vyása Páráśarya). But the episode in question is certainly one of the very latest insertions, as is clear from the allusion to the Chínas and Húṇas, the Chinese and Huns.

259 In the meantime, the name Bádaráyaṇa is only known to occur, besides, in the closing *vaṃśa* of the Sáma-Vidhána-Br.: see *I. St.*, iv. 377; and here the bearer of it appears as the disciple of Páráśaryáyaṇa, four steps later than Vyása Páráśarya, and three later than Jaimini, but, on the other hand, as the teacher (!) of Táṇḍin and Śáṭyáyanin. Besides being mentioned in Jaimini, he is also cited in the Śáṇḍilya-Sútra. In Varáha-Mihira and Bhaṭṭotpala an astronomer of this name is referred to; and he, in his turn, according to Aufrecht (*Catalogus*, p. 329ᵃ), alludes, in a passage quoted from him by Utpala, to the '*Yavana-vṛiddhás*,' and, according to Kern, Pref. to Bṛih. Saṃh., p. 51, "exhibits many Greek words."—The text of the Brahma-Sútra, with Śaṃkara's commentary, has now been published in the *Bibl. Ind.*, edited by Roer and (from part 3) Ráma Náráyaṇa Vidyáratna (1854–1863): of the translation of both by K. M. Banerjea, as of that in Ballantyne's *Aphorisms*, only one part has appeared (1870).

In respect of their reduction to systematic shape, the logical Sútras of Kaṇáda and Gotama appear to rank last. But this by no means indicates that these logical inquiries are themselves of later origin—on the contrary, the other Sútras almost uniformly begin with such—but merely that the formal development of logic into two philosophical schools took place comparatively late. Neither of the schools restricts itself to logic alone; each embraces, rather, a complete philosophical system, built up, however, upon a purely dialectical method. But as yet little has been done to elucidate the points of difference between the two in this regard.[260] The origin of the world is in both derived from atoms, which combine by the will of an arranging Power.[261]—Whether the name of the *Πράμναι*, who are described by Strabo as contentious dialecticians, is to be traced to the word *pramáṇa*, 'proof,' as Lassen supposes, is doubtful. The word *tarka*, 'doubt,' again, in the Káṭhakopanishad, ought rather, from the context, to be referred to the Sáṃkhya doctrines, and should not be taken in the sense, which at a later period is its usual one, of 'logic.' In Manu too (see Lassen, *I. AK.*, i. 835), according to the traditional interpretation, *tarkin* still denotes 'one versed in the Mímáṅsá logic.'[262] Yet Manu is also acquainted with logic as a distinct

---

[260] In this respect, Roer in particular has done excellent service: in the copious notes to his translation of the Vaiśeshika-Sútra he has throughout special regard to this very point (in *Z. D. M. G.*, vols. xxi. xxii. 1867, 1868). Before him, Müller, with some of Ballantyne's writings as a basis, had already taken the same line (in vols. vi. and vii. of the same Journal, 1852, 1853). The text of the Vaiśeshika-Sútras, with the commentary, called Upaskára, of Śaṃkara-miśra, appeared in *Bibl. Ind.* in 1860, 1861, edited, with a gloss of his own, by Jaya Náráyaṇa Tarkapañchánana. In the *Paṇḍit* (Nos. 32–69) there is a complete translation of both text and commentary by A. E. Gough.—Jaya Náráyaṇa has also since then (1864–65) edited, in the *Bibl. Ind.*, the Nyáya-darśana of Gotama with the commentary of Vátsyáyana (Pakshila-svámin). The earlier edition (1828) was accompanied with the commentary of Viśvanátha. The first four books have been translated by Ballantyne in his *Aphorisms.*

[261] We find the atomic theory especially developed among the Jainas, and that in a materialistic form, yet so, that the atomic matter and the vital principle are conceived to be in eternal intimate connection; see my Essay on the Bhagavatí of the Jainas, ii. 168, 176, 190, 236. We have a mythological application of it in the assumption of a prajápati Maríchi; see *I. St.*, ix. 9.

[262] In Párask., ii. 6 ("*vidhir vidheyas tarkaś cha vedaḥ*"), *tarka* is equivalent to *arthaváda, mímáṅsá.*

science, as well as with the three leading methods of proof which it teaches, though not under the names that were afterwards usual. According to the most recent investigations on the subject,* "the terms *naiyáyika* and *kevala-naiyáyika* (Páṇ., ii. 1. 49) would point to the Nyáya system as antecedent to Páṇini:" these words, however, do not occur in the text of Páṇini at all (which has merely the word *kevala!*), but only in his scholiast.†—Kaṇáda's system bears the name *Vaiśeshika-Sútra*, because its adherents assert that *viśesha*, 'particularity,' is predicable of atoms; the system of Gotama, on the other hand, is styled *Nyáya-Sútra*, κατ' ἐξοχήν. Which of the two is the older is still uncertain. The circumstance that the doctrines of the Vaiśeshikas are frequently the subject of refutation in the Vedánta-Sútra,—whereas Gotama's teaching is nowhere noticed, either in the text or in the commentaries upon it, as stated by Colebrooke (i. 352),—tells *à priori* in favour of the higher antiquity of the former;[263] but whether the author of the Vedánta had these 'doctrines of Kaṇáda' before him in their systematised form, as has recently been assumed‡ is a point still requiring investigation.[264]—For the rest, these two systems are at

---

* By Max Müller, *l. c.*, p. 9.

† This is one of the cases of which I have already spoken (p. 225).

[263] In the Sáṃkhya-Sútra they are even expressly mentioned by name (see p. 237); also in the sacred texts of the Jainas (v. note 249).—The circumstance that the Gotama-Sútra does not, like the other five philosophical text-books, begin with the customary Sútra-formula, '*athá 'taḥ*,' may perhaps also be regarded as a sign of later composition.

‡ M. Müller, *l. c.*, p. 9: "Whereas Kaṇáda's doctrines are there frequently discussed."

[264] In neither of the Sútras are there references to older teachers whose names might supply some chronological guidance. As regards the names of their authors themselves, Kaṇáda or Kaṇabhuj (Kaṇabhaksha) is mentioned by Varáha-Mihira and Śaṃkara, while Akshapáda, so far as we know at present, is first mentioned by Mádhava. Their patronymics, Káśyapa and Gautama (this form is preferable to Gotama) date, it is true, from a very early time, but, beyond this, they tell us nothing. Of interest, certainly, although without decisive weight, is the identification—occurring in a late commentator (Anantayajvan) on the Pitṛimedha-Sútra of Gautama, belonging to the Sáma-Veda—of this latter Gautama with Akshapáda; see Burnell's *Catalogue*, p. 57.—From Cowell's preface to his edition of the Kusumáñjali (1864) it appears that the commentary of Pakshila-svámin, whom he directly identifies with Vátsyáyana, was composed prior to Diṅnága, that is to say (see note 219 above), somewhere about the beginning of the sixth century. Uddyotakara, who is mentioned by Subandhu in the seventh century, wrote against Diṅnága, and

present, and have been for a long time past, those most in favour in India; and it would also appear that among the philosophical writings contained in the Tibetan Tandjur, logical works are the most numerously represented.

Besides these six systems, all of which won for themselves a general currency, and which on the whole are regarded as orthodox—however slight is the title of the Sáṃkhya theory, for instance, to be so esteemed—we have frequent mention of certain heterodox views, as those of the Chárvákas, Laukáyatikas,[265] Bárhaspatyas. Of this last-mentioned school there must also have existed a complete system, the Bárhaspatya-Sútra; but of all this nothing has survived save occasional quotations, introduced with a view to their refutation, in the commentaries of the orthodox systems.

We now come to the third branch of the scientific literature, Astronomy, with its auxiliary sciences.* We have already seen (pp. 112, 113) that astronomy was cultivated to a considerable extent even in Vedic times; and we found it expressly specified by Strabo (see pp. 29, 30) as a favourite pursuit of the Brahmans. It was at the same time remarked, however, that this astronomy was still in a very elementary stage, the observations of the heavens being still wholly confined to a few fixed stars, more especially to the twenty-seven or twenty-eight lunar asterisms, and to the various phases of the moon itself.[266] The circumstance that the Vedic year is a solar year of 360 days,

---

so did Vácharpati-miśra in the tenth, and Udayana, the author of the Kusumáñjali, in the twelfth century; see also Cowell's note to Colebrooke's *Misc. Ess.*, i. 282. Gangeśa's Nyáya-chintámaṇi, the most important work of the later Nyáya literature, is also placed in the twelfth century; see *Z. D. M. G.*, xxvii. 168. Aulúkya, given by Mádhava as a name for the tenets of Kaṇáda, rests on a play upon the word *káṇáda*, 'crow-eater' = *ulúka*.

[265] In the Mahábháshya there is mention of a "*varṇiká Bhágurí lokáyatasya;*" see *I. St.*, xiii. 343. A Bháguri appears among the teachers cited in the Bṛihad-devatá. The Lokáyatas are also repudiated by the Buddhists, Northern as well as Southern; v. Burnouf, *Lotus de la bonne Loi*, pp. 409, 470. The Jainas, too, rank their system only with *loiya-* (*laukika*) knowledge; see above, note 249.—On the Chárvákas, see the introduction of the Sarva-darśana-saṃgraha.

* See *I. St.*, ii. 236–287.

[266] The cosmical or astronomical data met with in the Bráhmaṇas are all of an extremely childish and naïve description; see *I. St.*, ix. 358 ff.

and not a lunar year, does indeed presuppose a tolerably accurate observation and computation of the sun's course; but, agreeably to what has just been stated, we can hardly imagine that this computation proceeded upon the phenomena of the nocturnal heavens, and we must rather assume it to have been based upon the phenomena of the length or shortness of the day, &c. To the elaboration of a quinquennial cycle with an intercalary month a pretty early date must be assigned, since the latter is mentioned in the Ṛik-Saṃhitá. The idea of the four mundane ages, on the contrary—although its origin, from observation of the moon's phases, may possibly be of extreme antiquity[267]—can only have attained to its complete development towards the close of the Vedic period: Megasthenes, as we know, found the Yuga system flourishing in full perfection. That the Hindú division of the moon's path into twenty-seven (or twenty-eight) lunar mansions is of Chinese origin, as asserted by Biot (*Journal des Savants*, 1840, 1845; see Lassen, *I. AK.*, i. 742 ff.), can hardly be admitted.[268] Notwithstanding the accounts of Chinese writers, the contrary might equally well be the case, and the system might possibly have been introduced into China through the medium of Buddhism, especially as Buddhist writings adhere to the ancient order of the asterisms—commencing with *Kṛittiká*—precisely as we find it among the Chinese.[269]

---

[267] Roth disputes this origin in his Essay, *Die Lehre von den vier Weltaltern* (1860, Tübingen).

[268] On the questions dealt with in what follows, a special discussion was raised between J. B. Biot, myself, and Whitney, in which A. Sédillot, Steinschneider, E. Burgess, and Max Müller also took part. Cf. the *Journal des Savants* for 1859, and Biot's posthumous *Études sur l'Astronomie Indienne et Chinoise* (1862); my two papers, *Die Vedischen Nachrichten von den Nakshatra* (1860, 1862), as also *I. Str.*, ii. 172, 173; *I. St.*, ix. 424 ff. (1865), x. 213 ff. (1866); Whitney in *Journ. Am. Or. Soc.*, vols. vi. and viii. (1860, 1864, 1865); Burgess, *ibid.*; Steinschneider in *Z. D. M. G.*, xviii. (1863); Müller in Pref. to vol. iv. of his edition of the Ṛik (1862); Sédillot, *Courtes Observations sur quelques Points de l'Histoire de l'Astronomie* (1863); and, lastly, Whitney in the second vol. of his *Oriental and Linguistic Studies* (1874). To the views expressed above I still essentially adhere; Whitney, too, inclines towards them. In favour of Chaldæa having been the mother-country of the system, one circumstance, amongst others, tells with especial force, viz., that from China, India, and Babylon we have precisely the same accounts of the length of the longest day; whilst the statements, *e.g.*, in the Bundehesch, on this head, exhibit a total divergence; see Windischmann (*Zoroastrische Studien*, p. 105).

[269] This assertion of Biot's has not been confirmed; the Chinese list commences with Chitrá (*i.e.*, the autumnal equinox), or Uttaráshádhás

To me, however, the most probable view is that these lunar mansions are of Chaldæan origin, and that from the Chaldæans they passed to the Hindús as well as to the Chinese. For the מַזָּלוֹת of the Book of Kings, and the מַזָּרוֹת of the Book of Job,[270] which the Biblical commentators erroneously refer to the zodiac, are just the Arabic منازل, 'mansions;' and here even Biot will hardly suppose a Chinese origin. The Indians may either have brought the knowledge of these lunar mansions with them into India, or else have obtained it at a later time through the commercial relations of the Phœnicians with the Panjáb. At all events, they were known to the Indians from a very early period, and as communication with China is altogether inconceivable at a time when the Hindús were perhaps not even acquainted with the mouths of the Ganges, Chinese influence is here quite out of the question. The names of some of these asterisms occur even in the Ṛik-Saṃhitá (and that under peculiar forms); for example, the *Aghás, i.e., Maghás*, and the *Arjunyau, i.e., Phalgunyau*—a name also applied to them in the Śatapatha-Bráhmaṇa—in the nuptial hymn, *maṇḍala* x. 85. 13; further, *Tishya* in *maṇḍala* v. 54. 13, which, however, is referred by Sáyaṇa to the sun (see also x. 64. 8). The earliest complete enumeration of them, with their respective regents, is found in the Taittiríya-Saṃ-

(the winter solstice), both of which rather correspond to an arrangement in which Revatí passes as the sign of the vernal equinox; see my first Essay on the Nakshatras, p. 300.—Cf. here also the account of the twenty-eight lunar asterisms, contained in a letter from Wassiljew to Schiefner (see the latter's German translation of the Preface to Wassiljew's Russian rendering of Táranátha's history of Buddhism, pp. 30-32, 1869), and communicated, according to the commentary on the Buddhistic Lexicon Mahávyutpatti, from the book Sannipáta (Chinese Ta-tsi-king). According to this account, it was the astronomer Kharoshṭha (ass's-lip)—a name which, as well as that of Xarustr, who, as Armenian authorities state, originated the science of astronomy in Chaldæa, Wassiljew compares with Zoroaster, but in which I am inclined rather to look for the Kraushṭuki whose acquaintance we make in the Atharva-Pariś. (see *Lit. C. Bl.*, 1869, p. 1497)—who arranged the constellations in the order quoted in the Dictionary in question, that is, beginning with *Kṛittiká*. Afterwards there came another Ṛishi, Kála (Time!), who set up a new theory in regard to the motion of the constellations, and so in course of time Chitrá came to be named as the first asterism. To all appearance, this actually proves the late, and Buddhistic, origin of the Chinese Kio-list; see *Nakshatras*, i. 306.

[270] On this point see specially *I. St.*, x. 217.

hitá; a second, which exhibits considerable variation in the names, betokening a later date, occurs in the Atharva-Saṃhitá and the Taittiríya-Bráhmaṇa; the majority of the names are also given in Páṇini. This latter list contains for the most part the names employed by the later astronomers; and it is precisely these later ones that are enumerated in the so-called Jyotisha or Vedic Calendar (along with the zodiacal signs too!). To this latter treatise an importance has hitherto been attributed to which its contents do not entitle it. Should my conjecture be confirmed that the Lagadha, Lagata, whose system it embodies, is identical with the Lát who is mentioned by Albírúní as the author of the ancient Súrya-Siddhánta [see, however, p. 258 n.], then it would fall in the fourth or fifth century of our era; and even this might almost seem too high an antiquity for this somewhat insignificant tract, which has only had a certain significance attached to it on account of its being ranked with the Veda.*

A decided advance in astronomical science was made through the discovery of the planets. The earliest mention of these occurs, perhaps, in the Taittiríya-Áraṇyaka, though this is still uncertain;[271] beyond this, they are not noticed in any other work of the Vedic period.[272] Manu's

* This is why it adheres to the old order of the lunar asterisms, as is done even at the present day in writings that bear upon the Veda. [According to the special examination of the various points here involved, in the introduction to my Essay on the Jyotisha (1862), a somewhat earlier term is possible; assuming, of course, as I there do, that those verses which betoken Greek influence do not really belong to the text as it originally stood. The author appears occasionally also under the name Lagaḍáchárya; see above, p. 61, note.]

[271] The passages referred to are, in fact, to be understood in a totally different sense; see *I. St.*, ix. 363, x. 271.

[272] The Maitráyaṇí-Up. forms the single exception, but that only in its last two books, described as *khila*; see above, notes 103, 104. On the subject itself, see further my Essay on the Jyotisha, p. 10, *I. St.*, ix. 363, 442, x. 239, 240.—The two Ṛik passages which are thought by Alf. Ludwig, in his recently published *Nachrichten des Ṛig- und Atharva-Veda über Geographie, &c., des alten Indiens*, to contain an allusion to the planets (i. 105. 10, x. 55. 3), can hardly have any such reference. Neither the Śáṭyáyanaka, cited by Sáyaṇa to i. 105. 10, nor Sáyaṇa himself, has any thought of the planets here (see *I. St.*, ix. 363 n.). For the '*divichará grahâḥ*' of Ath. S., 19. 9. 7, the Ath. Pariśishṭas offer other parallels, showing that here too the planets are not to be thought of, especially as immediately afterwards, in v. 10, the '*grahâś chândramasâḥ . . âdityâḥ . . râhuṇâ*' are enumerated, where, distinctly, the allusion is only to eclipses. This particular section of the Ath. S. (19. 7) is, moreover, quite a late production; see *I. St.*, iv. 433 n.

law-book is unacquainted with them; Yájnavalkya's Code, however—and this is significant as to the difference in age of these two works—inculcates their worship; in the dramas of Kálidása, in the Mṛichhakaṭí and the Mahá-Bhárata, as well as the Rámáyaṇa, they are repeatedly referred to.* Their names are peculiar, and of purely Indian origin; three of them are thereby designated as sons respectively of the Sun (Saturn), of the Earth (Mars), and of the Moon (Mercury); and the remaining two as representatives of the two oldest families of Ṛishis,—Añgiras (Jupiter) and Bhṛigu (Venus). The last two names are probably connected with the fact that it was the adherents of the Atharva-Veda—which was likewise specially associated with the Ṛishis Añgiras and Bhṛigu—who at this time took the lead in the cultivation of astronomy and astrology.† Besides these names others are also common; Mars, for example, is termed 'the Red;' Venus, 'the White' or 'Beaming;' Saturn, 'the Slow-travelling;' this last being the only one of the names that testifies to any real astronomical observation. To these seven planets (sun and moon being included) the Indians added two others, Ráhu and Ketu, the 'head' and 'tail' respectively of the monster who is conceived to be the cause of the solar and lunar eclipses. The name of the former, Ráhu, first occurs in the Chhándogyopanishad,[273] though here it can hardly be taken in the sense of 'planet;' the latter, on the contrary, is first mentioned in Yájnavalkya. But this number nine is not the original number,—if indeed it be to the planets that the passage of the Taittiríya-Áraṇyaka, above instanced, refers—as only seven (*sapta súryáḥ*) are there mentioned. The term for planet, *graha*, 'the seizer,' is evidently of astrological origin; indeed, astrology was the focus in which astronomical inquiries generally converged, and from which they drew light and animation after the practical exigencies of worship had been once for all satisfied. Whether the Hindús discovered the planets inde-

* In Páṇ., iv. 2. 26, *śukra* might be referred to the planet Śukra, but it is preferable to take it in the sense of Soma-juice.

† Whence Bhárgava came to signify 'an astrologer;' see Daśakumára, ed. Wilson, p. 162. 11.

[273] Cf. also Ráhula as the name of Buddha's son, who, however, also appears as Lághula; see *I. St.*, iii. 130, 149.

pendently, or whether the knowledge came to them from without, cannot as yet be determined; but the systematic peculiarity of the nomenclature points in the meantime to the former view.[274]

It was, however, Greek influence that first infused a real life into Indian astronomy. This occupies a much more important position in relation to it than has hitherto been supposed; and the fact that this is so, *eo ipso* implies that Greek influence affected other branches of the literature as well, even though we may be unable at present directly to trace it elsewhere.[275] Here it is necessary to insert a few particulars as to the relations of the Greeks with the Indians.

The invasion of the Panjáb by Alexander was followed by the establishment of the Greek monarchies of Bactria, whose sway, in the period of their prime, extended, although only for a brief season, over the Panjáb as far as Gujarát.[276] Concurrently therewith, the first Seleucidæ, as well as the Ptolemies, frequently maintained direct relations, by means of ambassadors, with the court of Páṭaliputra;* and thus it comes that in the inscriptions

---

[274] Still it has to be remarked that in the Atharva-Pariśishṭas, which, with the Jyotisha, represent the oldest remains of Indian astrology, the sphere of influence of the planets appears in special connection with their Greek names; see *I. St.*, viii. 413, x. 319.

[275] Cf. my paper, *Indische Beiträge zur Geschichte der Aussprache des Griechischen* in the *Monatsberichte der Berl. Acad.*, 1871, p. 613, translated in *Ind. Antiq.*, ii. 143 ff., 1873.

[276] According to Goldstücker, the statement in the Mahábháshya as to a then recent siege of Sáketa (Oude) by a Yavana prince has reference to Menander; while the accounts in the Yuga-Puráṇa of the Gárgí Saṃhitá even speak of an expedition of the Yavanas as far as Páṭaliputra. But then the question arises, whether by the Yavanas it is really the Greeks who are meant (see *I. Str.*, ii. 348), or possibly merely their Indo-Scythian or other successors, to whom the name was afterwards transferred; see *I. St.*, xiii. 306, 307; also note 202 above.

* Thus Megasthenes was sent by Seleucus to Chandragupta (d. B.C. 291); Deimachus, again, by Antiochus, and Dionysius, and most probably Basilis also, by Ptolemy II. to Ἀμιτροχάτης, Amitraghâta, son of Chandragupta. [Antiochus concluded an alliance with Σωφαγασήνας, Subhagasena (?). Seleucus even gave Chandragupta his daughter to wife; Lassen, *I. AK.*, ii. 208; Talboys Wheeler, *History of India* (1874), p. 177. In the retinue of this Greek princess there of course came to Páṭaliputra Greek damsels as her waiting-maids, and these must have found particular favour in the eyes of the Indians, especially of their princes. For not only are παρθένοι εὐειδεῖς πρὸς παλλακίαν mentioned as an article of traffic for India, but in Indian inscriptions also we find Yavana girls

of Piyadasi we find mention of the names of Antigonus, Magas, Antiochus, Ptolemy, perhaps even of Alexander himself (cf. p. 179), ostensibly as vassals of the king, which is of course mere empty boasting. As the result of these embassies, the commercial intercourse between Alexandria and the west coast of India became particularly brisk; and the city of Ujjayiní, 'Οζηνή, rose in consequence to a high pitch of prosperity. Philostratus, in his life of Apollonius of Tyana—a work written in the second century A.D., and based mainly on the accounts of Damis, a disciple of Apollonius, who accompanied the latter in his travels through India about the year 50 A.D.—mentions the high esteem in which Greek literature was held by the Brahmans, and that it was studied by almost all persons of the higher ranks. (Reinaud, *Mém. sur l'Inde*, pp. 85, 87.) This is not very high authority, it is true [cf. Lassen, *I. AK.*, iii. 358 ff.]; the statement may be an exaggeration, but still it accords with the data which we have now to adduce, and which can only be explained upon the supposition of a very lively intellectual interchange. For the Indian astronomers regularly speak of the Yavanas as their teachers: but whether this also applies to Paráśara, who is reputed to be the oldest Indian astronomer, is still uncertain. To judge from the quotations, he computes by the lunar mansions, and would seem, accordingly, to stand upon an independent footing. But of Garga,* who passes for the next oldest astronomer,

specified as tribute; while in Indian literature, and especially in Kálidása, we are informed that Indian princes were waited upon by Yavanís; Lassen, *I. AK.*, ii. 551. 957, 1159, and my Preface to the Málaviká, p. xlvii. The *métier* of these damsels being devoted to Eros, it is not a very far-fetched conjecture that it may have been owing to their influence that the Hindú god of Love, like the Greek Eros, bears a dolphin (*makara*) on his banner, and, like him, is the son of the goddess of Beauty; see *Z. D. M. G.*, xiv. 269. (For *makara* = dolphin, see *Journ. Bomb. Br. R. A. S.*, v. 33, 34; *I. Str.*, ii. 169); and cf. further *I. St.*, ix. 380.]

* The name of Paráśara, as well as that of Garga, belongs only to the last stage of Vedic literature, to the Áraṇyakas and the Sútras: in the earlier works neither of the two names is mentioned. The family of the Paráśaras is represented with particular frequency in the later members of the *vaṁśas* of the Śatapatha-Bráhmaṇa: a Garga and a Paráśara are also named in the Anukramaṇí as Ṛishis of several hymns of the Ṛik, and another Paráśara appears in Páṇini as author of the Bhikshu-Sútra; see pp. 143, 185. [The Gargas must have played a very important part at the time of the Mahábháshya, in the eyes of the author at all events; for on almost

an oft-quoted verse has come down to us, in which he extols the Yavanas on account of their astronomical knowledge. The epic tradition, again, gives as the earliest astronomer the Asura Maya, and asserts that to him the sun-god himself imparted the knowledge of the stars. I have already elsewhere (*I. St.*, ii. 243) expressed the conjecture that this 'Asura Maya' is identical with the 'Ptolemaios' of the Greeks; since this latter name, as we see from the inscriptions of Piyadasi, became in Indian 'Turamaya,' out of which the name 'Asura Maya' might very easily grow; and since, by the later tradition (that of the Jnána-bháskara, for instance) this Maya is distinctly assigned to Romaka-pura* in the West. Lastly, of the five Siddhántas named as the earliest astronomical systems, one—the Romaka-Siddhánta—is denoted, by its very name, as of Greek origin; while a second—the Pauliśa-Siddhánta—is expressly stated by Albírúní † to have been composed by Paulus al Yúnání, and is accordingly, perhaps, to be regarded as a translation of the *Εἰσαγωγή* of Paulus Alexandrinus.[277] The astronomers

---

every occasion when it is a question of a patronymic or other similar affix, their name is introduced among those given as examples; see *I. St.*, xiii. 410 ff. In the Atharva-Pariśishṭas, also, we find Garga, Gárgya, Vṛiddha-Garga cited: these latter Gargas are manifestly very closely related to the above-mentioned Garga the astronomer. See further Kern, Pref. to Varáha-Mihira's Bṛih. Saṃh., p. 31 ff.; *I. Str.*, ii. 347.]

* See my *Catal. of the Sansk. MSS. in the Berl. Lib.*, p. 288. In reference to the name Romaka, I may make an observation in passing. Whereas, in Mahá-Bhárata xii. 10308, the Raumyas are said to have been created from the *roma-kúpas* ('hair-pores') of Vírabhadra, at the destruction of Daksha's sacrifice, at the time of Rámáyaṇa i. 55. 3, their name must have been still unknown, since other tribes are there represented, on a like occasion, as springing from the *roma-kúpas*. Had the author been acquainted with the name, he would scarcely have failed to make a similar use of it to that found in the Mahá-Bhárata. [Cf. my Essay on the Rámáyaṇa, p. 23 ff.]

† Albírúní resided a considerable time in India, in the following of Mahmúd of Ghasna, and acquired there a very accurate knowledge of Sanskṛit and of Indian literature, of which he has left us a very valuable account, written A.D. 1031. Extracts from this highly important work were communicated by Reinaud in the *Journ. Asiat.* for 1844, and in his *Mém. sur l'Inde* in 1849 [also by Woepcke, *ibid.*, 1863]: the text, promised so long ago as 1843, and most eagerly looked for ever since, has, unfortunately, not as yet appeared. [Ed. Sachau, of Vienna, is at present engaged in editing it; and, from his energy, we may now at length expect that this grievous want will be speedily supplied.]

277 Such a direct connection of the Puliśa-Siddhanta with the *Εἰσαγωγή* is attended with difficulty,

and astronomical works just instanced—Garga, Maya, the Romaka-Siddhánta, and the Pauliśa-Siddhánta—are, it is true, known to us only through isolated quotations; and it might still be open to doubt, perhaps, whether in their case the presence of Greek influence can really be established; although the assertion, for instance, that Puliśa, in opposition to Áryabhaṭa,[278] began the day at midnight, is of itself pretty conclusive as to his Western origin. But all doubt disappears when we look at the great mass of Greek words employed in his writings by Varáha-Mihira, to whom Indian astronomers assigned, in Albírúní's day, as they still do in our own,* the date 504 A.D.—employed, too, in a way which clearly indicates that they had long been in current use. Nay, one of his works—the Horá-Śástra—even bears a Greek title (from ὥρη); and in it he not only gives the entire list of the Greek names of the zodiacal signs and planets,† but he also directly employs several of the latter—namely, *Ára*, *Ásphujit*, and *Koṇa*—side by side with the Indian names, and just as frequently as he does these. The signs of the

---

from the fact that the quotations from Puliśa do not accord with it, being rather of an astronomical than an astrological description. That the Εἰσαγωγή, however, was itself known to the Hindús, in some form or other, finds support in the circumstance that it alone contains nearly the whole of the technical terms adopted by Indian astronomy from the Greek; see Kern's Preface to his edition of Varáha-Mihira's Bṛihat-Saṃh., p. 49.—Considerable interest attaches to the argument put forward by H. Jacobi in his tract, *De Astrologiæ Indicæ Horá Appellatæ Originibus* (Bonn, 1872), to the effect that the system of the twelve mansions occurs first in Firmicus Maternus (A.D. 336–354), and that consequently the Indian Horá-texts, in which these are of such fundamental significance, can only have been composed at a still later date.

[278] This, and not Áryabhaṭṭa, is the proper spelling of his name, as is shown by the metre in his own work (*Gaṇita-páda*, v. 1). This was pointed out by Bháu Dájí in *J. R. A. S.*, i. 392 (1864).

* See Colebrooke, ii. 461 (415 ed. Cowell).

† These are the following: *Kriya* κριός, *Távuri* ταῦρος, *Jituma* δίδυμος, *Kulíra* κόλουρος (?), *Leya* λέων, *Páthona* παρθένος, Júka ζυγόν, *Kaurpya* σκορπίος, *Taukshika* τοξότης, Ákokera αἰγόκερως, Hṛidroga ὑδροχόος, *Ittha* ἰχθύς; further, *Heli* Ἥλιος, *Himna* Ἑρμῆς, *Ára* Ἄρης, Koṇa Κρόνος, *Jyau* Ζεύς, Ásphujit Ἀφροδίτη. These names were made known so long ago as 1827 by C. M. Whish, in the first part of the *Transactions of the Literary Society of Madras*, and have since been frequently published; see in particular Lassen, in *Zeitsch. f. d. Kunde des Morg.*, iv. 306, 318 (1842); lately again in my Catal. of the Sansk. MSS. in the Berl. Lib., p. 238.—*Horá* and *kendra* had long previously been identified by Père Pons with ὥρη and κέντρον; see *Lettres Édif.*, 26. 236, 237, Paris, 1743.

zodiac, on the contrary, he usually designates by their Sanskṛit names, which are translated from the Greek. He has in constant use, too, the following technical terms, all of which are found employed in the same sense in the **Εἰσαγωγή** of Paulus Alexandrinus, viz.,* *dṛikáṇa* = **δεκανός**, *liptá* = **λεπτή**, *anaphá* = **ἀναφή**, *sunaphá* = **συναφή**, *durudhará* = **δορυφορία**, *kemadruma* (for *kremaduma*) = **χρηματισμός**,[279] *veśi* = **φάσις**, *kendra* = **κέντρον**, *ápoklima* = **ἀπόκλιμα**, *panaphará* = **ἐπαναφορά**, *trikoṇa* = **τρίγωνος**, *hibuka* = **ὑπόγειον**, *jámitra* = **διάμετρον**, *dyutam* = **δυτόν**, *meshúraṇa* = **μεσουράνημα**.

Although most of these names denote astrological relations, still, on the other hand, in the division of the heavens into zodiacal signs, *decani*, and degrees, they comprise all that the Hindús lacked, and that was necessary to enable them to cultivate astronomy in a scientific spirit. And accordingly we find that they turned these Greek aids to good account; rectifying, in the first place, the order of their lunar asterisms, which was no longer in accordance with reality, so that the two which came last in the old order occupy the two first places in the new; and even, it would seem, in some points independently advancing astronomical science further than the Greeks themselves did. Their fame spread in turn to the West; and the Andubarius (or, probably, Ardubarius), whom the *Chronicon Paschale* † places in primeval times as the earliest Indian astronomer, is doubtless none other than Áryabhaṭa, the rival of Puliśa, who is likewise extolled by the Arabs under the name Arjabahr. For, during the eighth and ninth centuries, the Arabs were in astronomy the disciples of the Hindús, from whom they borrowed the lunar mansions in their new order, and whose Siddhántas (Sindhends) they frequently worked up and translated,—in part under the supervision of Indian astronomers themselves, whom the Khalifs of Bagdad, &c., invited to their courts. The same thing took place also

---

* See *I. St.*, ii. 254.

[279] Rather = *κενόδρομος*, according to Jacobi, *l. c.* To this list belongs, further, the word *harija* = *ὁρίζων*; Kern, *l. c.*, p. 29.

† The *Chronicon Paschale* nominally dates from the time of Constantius (330); it underwent, however, a fresh recension under Heraclius (610–641), and the name Andubarius may have been introduced then.

in regard to Algebra and Arithmetic in particular, in both of which, it appears, the Hindús attained, quite independently,[280] to a high degree of proficiency.[281] It is to them also that we owe the ingenious invention of the numerical symbols,* which in like manner passed from them to the

[280] But cf. Colebrooke in his famous paper *On the Algebra of the Hindus* (1817) in *Misc. Ess.*, ii. 446, 401 ed. Cowell. Woepcke, indeed (*Mém. sur la propagation des Chiffres Indiens*, Paris, 1863, pp. 75-91), is of opinion that the account in the Lalita-Vistara of the problem solved by Buddha on the occasion of his marriage-examination, relative to the number of atoms in the length of a *yojana*, is the basis of the 'Arenarius' of Archimedes (B.C. 287-212). But the age of the Lalita-Vistara is by no means so well ascertained that the reverse might not equally well be the case; see *I. St.*, viii. 325, 326; Reinaud, *Mém. sur l'Inde*, p. 303.

[281] The oldest known trace of these occurs, curiously, in Piñgala's Treatise on Prosody, in the last chapter of which (presumably a later addition), the permutations of longs and shorts possible in a metre with a fixed number of syllables are set forth in an enigmatical form; see *I. St.*, viii. 425 ff., 324-326.—On geometry the Śulva-Sútras, appertaining to the Śrauta ritual, furnish highly remarkable information; see Thibaut's Address to the Aryan Section of the London International Congress of Orientalists, in the special number of *Trübner's American and Oriental Literary Record*, 1874, pp. 27, 28, according to which these Sútras even contain attempts at squaring the circle.

* The Indian figures from 1-9 are abbreviated forms of the initial letters of the numerals themselves [cf. the similar notation of the musical tones]: the zero, too, has arisen out of the first letter of the word *śúnya*, 'empty' [it occurs even in Piñgala, *l. c.* It is the decimal place-value of these figures which gives them their special significance. Woepcke, in his above-quoted *Mém. sur la propag. des Chiffres Indiens* (*Journ. Asiat.*, 1863), is of opinion that even prior to their adoption by the Arabs they had been obtained from India by the Neo-Pythagoreans of Alexandria, and that the so-called Gobar figures are traceable to them. But against this it has to be remarked that the figures in question are only one of the latest stages of Indian numerical notation, and that a great many other notations preceded them. According to Edward Thomas, in the *Journ. Asiat.* for the same year (1863), the earliest instances of the use of these figures belong to the middle of the seventh century; whereas the employment of the older numerical symbols is demonstrable from the fourth century downwards. See also *I. St.*, viii. 165, 256. The character of the Valabhî Plates seems to be that whose letters most closely approach the forms of the figures. Burnell has quite recently, in his *Elem. S. Ind. Pal.*, p. 46 ff., questioned altogether the connection of the figures with the first letters of the numerals; and he supposes them, or rather the older 'Cave Numerals,' from which he directly derives them, to have been introduced from Alexandria, "together with Greek Astrology." In this I cannot in the meantime agree with him; see my remarks in the *Jenaer Lit. Z.*, 1875, No. 24, p. 419. Amongst other things, I there call special attention to the circumstance that Hermann Hankel, in his excellent work (posthumous, unfortunately), *Zur Geschichte der Mathematik* (1874), p. 329 ff., declares Woepcke's opinion

Arabs, and from these again to European scholars.[282] By these latter, who were the disciples of the Arabs, frequent allusion is made to the Indians, and uniformly in terms of high esteem; and one Sanskṛit word even—*uchcha*, signifying the apex of a planet's orbit—has passed, though in a form somewhat difficult to recognise (*aux*, genit. *augis*), into the Latin translations of Arabian astronomers [283] (see Reinaud, p. 325).

As regards the age and order of sequence of the various Indian astronomers, of whom works or fragments of works still survive, we do not even here escape from the uncertainty which everywhere throughout Indian literature attends questions of the kind. At their head stands the Áryabhaṭa already mentioned, of whose writings we possess at present only a few sorry scraps, though possibly fuller fragments may yet in course of time be recovered.[284] He appears to have been a contemporary of Puliśa; and, in any case, he was indebted to Greek influence, since he reckons by the zodiacal signs. According to Albírúní, he

---

to the effect that the Neo-Pythagoreans were acquainted with the new figures having place-value, and with the zero, to be erroneous, and the entire passage in Boethius on which this opinion is grounded to be an interpolation of the tenth or eleventh century].

[282] See also Woepcke, *Sur l'Introduction de l'Arithmétique Indienne en Occident* (Rome, 1859).

[283] As also, according to Reinaud's ingenious conjecture (p. 373 ff.), the name of Ujjayiní itself—through a misreading, namely, of the Arabic ازين as *Arín*, *Arim*, whereby the 'meridian of Ujjayiní' became the '*coupole d'Arin*.'

[284] The researches of Whitney in *Jour. Am. Or. Soc.*, vi. 560 ff. (1860), and of Bháu Dájí in *J. R. A. S.*, i. 392 ff. (1865), have brought us full light upon this point. From these it appears that of Áryabhaṭa there are still extant the *Daśagíti-Sútra* and the *Áryáshṭaśata*, both of which have been already edited by Kern (1874) under the title *Áryabhaṭíya*, together with the commentary of Paramádíśvara; cf. A. Barth in the *Revue Critique*, 1875, pp. 241–253. According to his own account therein given, Áryabhaṭa was born A.D. 476, lived in Eastern India at Kusumapura (Palibothra), and composed this work at the early age of twenty-three. In it he teaches, amongst other things, a quite peculiar numerical notation by means of letters.—The larger work extant under the title *Árya-Siddhánta* in eighteen *adhyáyas* is evidently a subsequent production; see Hall in *Journ. Am. Or. Soc.*, vi. 556 (1860), and Aufrecht, *Catalogus*, pp. 325, 326: Bentley thinks it was not composed until A.D. 1322, and Bháu Dájí, *l. c.*, pp. 393, 394, believes Bentley "was here for once correct."—Wilson, *Mack. Coll.*, i. 119, and Lassen, *I. AK.*, ii. 1136, speak also of a commentary by Áryabhaṭa on the Súrya-Siddhánta: this is doubtless to be ascribed to *Laghu-Áryabhaṭa* (Bháu Dájí, p. 405). See also Kern, Pref. to Bṛih. Saṃh., p. 59 ff.

was a native of Kusumapura, *i.e.*, Páṭaliputra, and belonged consequently to the east of India. Together with him, the authors of the following five Siddhántas are looked upon as ancient astronomers—namely, the unknown * author of the *Brahma-Siddhánta* or *Paitámaha-Siddhánta*; next, the author of the *Saura-Siddhánta*, who is called Lát by Albírúní, and may possibly be identical with the Lagata, Lagadha mentioned as author of the Vedáñga treatise Jyotisha, as well as with Láḍha, a writer occasionally quoted by Brahmagupta; † further, Puliśa, author of the *Pauliśa-Siddhánta*; and lastly, Śrísheṇa and Vishṇuchandra, to whom the *Romaka-Siddhánta* and the *Vasishṭha-Siddhánta*—works said to be based upon Áryabhaṭa's system [285]—are respectively attributed. Of these five Siddhántas, not one seems to have survived. There exist works, it is true, bearing the names Brahma-Siddhánta, Vasishṭha-Siddhánta, Súrya-Siddhánta and Romaka-Siddhánta; but that these are not the ancient works so entitled appears from the fact that the quotations from the latter, preserved to us by the scholiasts, are not contained in them.[286] In point of fact, three distinct Vasishṭha-Siddhántas, and, similarly, three distinct Brahma-Siddhántas,

---

* Albírúní names Brahmagupta as the author of this Brahma-Siddhánta; but this is erroneous. Perhaps Reinaud has misunderstood the passage (p. 332).

† Láḍha may very well have arisen out of Lagadha; [the form Láṭa, however, see Kern, Pref. to Bṛih. Saṃh., p. 53, points rather to Λαρική].

285 As also upon Láṭa, Vasishṭha, and Vijayanandin, according to Bháu Dájí, *l. c.*, p. 408. In the latter's opinion the Romaka-Siddhánta is to be assigned to *Śake* 427 (A.D. 505), and was "composed in accordance with the work of some Roman or Greek author." Bhaṭṭotpala likewise mentions, amongst others, a Yavaneśvara Sphujidhvaja (or Áspho), a name in which Bháu Dájí looks for a Speusippus, but Kern (Pref. to Bṛih. Saṃh., p. 48) for an Aphrodisius.

286 See on this point Kern, Pref. to Bṛih. Saṃh., pp. 43–50. Up to the present only the Súrya-Siddhánta has been published, with Rañganátha's commentary, in the *Bibl. Ind.* (1854–59), ed. by Fitzedward Hall and Bápú Deva Śástrin; also a translation by the latter, *ibid.* (1860, 1861). Simultaneously there appeared in the *Journ. Am. Or. Soc.*, vol. vi., a translation, nominally by Eb. Burgess, with an excellent and very thorough commentary by W. D. Whitney, who has recently (see *Oriental and Linguistic Studies*, ii. 360) assumed "the entire responsibility for that publication in all its parts." In his view, p. 326, the Súrya-Siddhánta is "one of the most ancient and original of the works which present the modern astronomical science of the Hindus;" but how far the existing text "is identical in substance and extent with that of the original Súrya-Siddhánta" is for the present doubtful. Cf. Kern, *l. c.*, pp. 44–46.

are cited. One of these last, which expressly purports to be a recast* of an earlier work, has for its author Brahmagupta, whose date, according to Albírúní, is the year A.D. 664, which corresponds pretty closely with the date assigned to him by the modern astronomers of Ujjayiní, A.D. 628.[287] To him also belongs, according to Albírúní,† a work named *Ahargaṇa*, corrupted by the Arabs into *Arkand*. This Arkand, the Sindhends (*i.e.*, the five Siddhántas), and the system of Arjabahr (Áryabhaṭa) were the works which, as already remarked, were principally studied and in part translated by the Arabs in the eighth and ninth centuries. —On the other hand, the Arabs do not mention Varáha-Mihira, although he was prior to Brahmagupta, as the latter repeatedly alludes to him, and although he gathered up the teaching of these five Siddhántas in a work which is hence styled by the commentators *Pañchasiddhántiká*, but which he himself calls by the name *Karaṇa*. This work seems to have perished,[288] and only the astrological works of Varáha-Mihira have come down to us—namely, the *Saṃhitá* ‡ and the *Horá-Śástra*. The latter, however, is

* Albírúní gives a notice of the contents of this recast: it and the Pauliśa-Siddhánta were the only two of these Siddhántas he was able to procure.

[287] This latter date is based on his own words in the Bráhma Sphuṭa-Siddhánta, 24. 7, 8, which, as there stated, he composed 550 years after the *Śaka-nṛipála* (°*ánta?*), at the age of thirty. He here calls himself the son of Jishṇu, and he lived under Śrí-Vyághramukha of the Śrí-Chápa dynasty; Bháu Dájí, *l. c.*, p. 410. Pṛithúdakasvámin, his scholiast, describes him, curiously, as Bhilla-Málavakáchárya; see *Z. D. M. G.*, xxv. 659; *I. St.*, xiii. 316. Chaps. xii. (*gaṇita*, arithmetic) and xxviii. (*kuṭṭaka*, algebra) of his work have, it is well known, been translated by Colebrooke (1817).

† Reinaud, *Mém. sur l'Inde*, p. 322.

[288] "Yesterday I heard of a second MS. of the Pañchasiddhántiká." Bühler's letter of 1st April 1875. See now Bühler's special report on the Pañchasiddhántiká in *Ind. Antiq.*, iv. 316.

‡ In a double edition, as *Bṛihat-Saṃhitá* and as *Samása-Saṃhitá*. Of the former Albírúní gives us some extracts; see also my *Catal. of the Sansk. MSS. in the Berl. Lib.*, pp. 238–254. [For an excellent edition of the Bṛihat-Saṃhitá (*Bibl. Ind.*, 1864–65), we are indebted to Kern, who is also publishing a translation of it (chaps. i.–lxxxiv. thus far) in the *Journ. R. A. S.*, iv.–vi. (1870–74). There also exists an excellent commentary on it by Bhaṭṭotpala, drawn up *Śake* 888 (A.D. 966), and distinguished by its exceedingly copious quotations of parallel passages from Varáha-Mihira's predecessors. In the Bṛihaj-Játaka, 26. 5, the latter calls himself the son of Ádityadása, and an Ávantika or native of Avanti, *i.e.*, Ujjayiní.]

incomplete, only one-third of it being extant.* He mentions a great number of predecessors, whose names are in part only known to us through him; for instance, Maya and the Yavanas (frequently), Paráśara, Manittha,[289] Śaktipúrva, Vishṇugupta,† Devasvámin, Siddhasena, Vajra, Jívaśarman, Satya,[290] &c. Of Áryabhaṭa no direct mention is made, possibly for the reason that he did nothing for astrology: in the Karaṇa he would naturally be mentioned.[291] While Áryabhaṭa still computes by the era of Yudhishṭhira, Varáha-Mihira employs the *Śaka-kála*, *Śaka-bhúpa-kála*, or *Śakendra-kála*, the era of the Śaka king, which is referred by his scholiast to Vikrama's era.[292] Brahmagupta, on the contrary, reckons by the *Śaka-nṛipánta*—which, according to him, took place in the year 3179 of the Kali age—that is to say, by the era of Śáliváhana.—The tradition as to the date of Varáha-Mihira has already been given: as the statements of the astronomers of to-day correspond with those current in Albírúní's time, we may reasonably take them as trustworthy, and accord-

---

* Namely, the Játaka portion (that relating to nativities) alone; and this in a double arrangement, as *Laghu-Játaka* and as *Bṛihaj-Játaka*: the former was translated by Albírúní into Arabic. [The text of the first two chaps. was published by me, with translation, in *I. St.*, ii. 277: the remainder was edited by Jacobi in his degree dissertation (1872). It was also published at Bombay in 1867 with Bhaṭṭotpala's commentary; similarly, the Bṛihaj-Játaka at Benares and Bombay; Kern's Pref., p. 26. The text of the first three chaps. of the *Yátrá* appeared, with translation, in *I. St.*, x. 161 ff. The third part of the Horá-Śástra, the *Viváha-paṭala*, is still inedited.]

[289] This name I conjecture to represent Manetho, author of the Apotelesmata, and in this Kern agrees with me (Pref. to Bṛih. Saṃh., p. 52).

† This is also a name of Cháṇakya; Daśakum. 183. 5, ed. Wilson. [For a complete list and examination of the names of teachers quoted in the Bṛihat-Saṃhitá, among whom are Bádaráyaṇa and Kaṇabhuj, see Kern's Preface, p. 29 ff.]

[290] Kern, Preface, p. 51, remarks that, according to Utpala, he was also called Bhadatta; but Aufrecht in his *Catalogus*, p. 329ᵃ, has Bhadanta. In the Jyotirvid-ábharaṇa, Satya stands at the head of the sages at Vikrama's court; see *Z. D. M. G.*, xxii. 722, xxiv. 400.

[291] And as a matter of fact we find in Bhaṭṭotpala a quotation from this work in which he is mentioned; see Kern, *J. R. A. S.*, xx. 383 (1863); Bháu Dájí, *l. c.*, 406. In another such quotation Varáha-Mihira refers to the year 427 of the Śaka-kála, and also to the Romaka-Siddhánta and Pauliśa; Bháu Dájí, p. 407.

[292] This statement of Colebrooke's, ii. 475 (428 ed. Cowell), cf. also Lassen, *I. AK.*, ii. 50, is unfounded. According to Kern, Preface, p. 6 ff., both in Varáha-Mihira and Utpala, only the so-called era of Śáliváhana is meant.

ing to these he flourished in A.D. 504.[293] Now this is at variance, on the one hand, with the tradition which regards him as one of the 'nine gems' of Vikrama's court, and which identifies the latter with king Bhoja,[294] who reigned about A.D. 1050;[295] and, on the other hand, also with the assertion of the astronomer Śatánanda, who, in the introduction to his Bhásvatí-karaṇa, seemingly acknowledges himself to be the disciple of Mihira, and at the same time states that he composed this work *Śake* 1021 (= A.D. 1099). This passage, however, is obscure, and may perhaps refer merely to the instruction drawn by the author from Mihira's writings;* otherwise we should have to admit the existence of a second Varáha-Mihira, who flourished in the middle of the eleventh century, that is, contemporaneously with Albírúní. Strange in that case that the latter should not have mentioned him!

After Varáha-Mihira and Brahmagupta various other astronomers distinguished themselves. Of these, the most eminent is Bháskara, to the question of whose age, however, a peculiar difficulty attaches. According to his own account, he was born *Śake* 1036 (A.D. 1114), and completed the Siddhánta-śiromaṇi *Śake* 1072 (A.D. 1150), and the Karaṇa-kutúhala *Śake* 1105 (A.D. 1183); and with this the modern astronomers agree, who assign to him the date *Śake* 1072 (A.D. 1150).[296] But Albírúní, who wrote in A.D.

---

[293] Kern, Preface, p. 3, thinks this is perhaps his birth year: the year of his death being given by Ámarája, a scholiast on Brahmagupta, as *Śake* 509 (A.D. 587).

[294] This identification fails of course. If Varáha-Mihira really was one of the 'nine gems' of Vikrama's court, then this particular Vikrama must simply have reigned in the sixth century. But the preliminary question is whether he was one of these 'gems.' See the statements of the Jyotirvid-ábharaṇa, *l. c.*

[295] See, *e.g.*, Aufrecht, *Catalogus*, p. 327[b], 328[a].

* Moreover, Śatánanda, at the close of his work—in a fragment of it in the Chambers collection (see my *Catal. of the Sansk. MSS. Berl. Lib.*, p. 234)—seems to speak of himself as living *Śake* 917 (A.D. 995). How is this contradiction to be explained? See Colebrooke, ii. 390 [341 ed. Cowell. The passage in question probably does not refer to the author's lifetime; unfortunately it is so uncertain that I do not understand its real meaning. As, however, there is mention immediately before of Kali 4200 = A.D. 1099, exactly as in Colebrooke, this date is pretty well established.—The allusion to Mihira might possibly, as indicated by the scholiast Balabhadra, not refer to Varáha-Mihira at all, but merely to *mihira*, the sun!]

[296] This also agrees with an inscription dated *Śake* 1128, and relating to a grandson of Bháskara, whose Siddhánta-śiromaṇi is here

1031 (that is, 83 years before Bháskara's birth !), not merely mentions him, but places his work—here called Karaṇa-sára—132 years earlier, namely, in A.D. 899; so that there is a discrepancy of 284 years between the two accounts. I confess my inability to solve the riddle; so close is the coincidence as to the personage, that the بشقر of Albírúní is expressly described, like the real Bháskara, as the son of Mahádeva.* But notwithstanding this, we have scarcely any alternative save to separate Albírúní's *Bashkar*, son of *Mahdeb*, and author of the *Karaṇa-sára*, from *Bháskara*, son of *Mahádeva*, and author of the *Karaṇa-kutúhala!*[297]—more especially as, in addition to the discrepancy of date, there is this peculiar circumstance, that whereas Albírúní usually represents the Indian *bh* by *b-h*

also mentioned in terms of high honour; see Bháu Dájí, *l. c.*, pp. 411, 416. Again, in a passage from the Siddhánta-śiromaṇi, which is cited by Mádhava in the Kála-nirṇaya, and which treats of the years having three intercalary months, the year of this description which fell *Śaka-kále* 974 (A.D. 1052) is placed in the past; the year 1115, on the contrary (and also 1256, 1378), in the future.—Bháskara's Lílávatí (arithmetic) and Víja-gaṇita (algebra) have, it is well known, been translated by Colebrooke (1817); the former also by Taylor (1816), the latter by Strachey (1818). The Gaṇitádhyáya has been translated by Roer in the *Journ. As. S. Bengal*, ix. 153 ff. (Lassen, *I. AK.*, iv. 849); of the Goládhyáya there is a translation by Lancelot Wilkinson in the *Bibl. Ind.* (1861–62). To Wilkinson we also owe an edition of the text of the Goládhyáya and Gaṇitádhyáya (1842). The Lílávatí and Víja-gaṇita appeared in 1832, 1834, likewise at Calcutta. Bápú Deva Śástrin has also issued a complete edition (?) of the Siddhánta-śiromaṇi (Benares, 1866). Cf. also Herm. Brockhaus, *Ueber die Algebra des Bháskara*, Leipzig, 1852, vol. iv. of the *Berichte der Kön. Sächs. Ges. der Wissensch.*, pp. 1–45.

* Reinaud, it is true, reads Mahádatta with ت instead of ب; but in Sanskrit this is an impossible form of name, as it gives no sense. [At the close of the Goládhyáya, xiii. 61, as well as of the Karaṇa-kutúhala, Bháskara calls his father, not Mahádeva, but Maheśvara (which of course is in substance identical); and he is likewise so styled by Bháskara's scholiast Lakshmídhara; see my *Catal. of the Berl. Sansk. MSS.*, pp. 235, 237.]

[297] This is really the only possible way out of the dilemma. Either, therefore, we have to think of that elder Bháskara "who was at the head of the commentators of Áryabhaṭa, and is repeatedly cited by Pṛithúdakasvámin, who was himself anterior to the author of the Śiromaṇi," Colebrooke, ii. 470 (423 ed. Cowell); or else under Reinaud's بشقر (pp. 335, 337) there lurks not a Bháskara at all, but perhaps a Pushkara. It is certainly strange, however, that he should be styled بن مهدث and author of a Karaṇa-sára. Can it be that we have here to do with an interpolation in Albírúní?

(*e.g.*, *b-huj* = *bhúrja*, *balb-hadr* = *balabhadra*), and for the most part faithfully preserves the length of the vowels, neither of these is here done in the case of Bashkar, where, moreover, the *s* is changed into *sh*.

Bháskara is the last star of Indian astronomy and arithmetic. After his day no further progress was made, and the astronomical science of the Hindús became once more wholly centred in astrology, out of which it had originally sprung. In this last period, under the influence of their Moslem rulers, the Hindús, in their turn, became the disciples of the Arabs, whose masters they had formerly been.* The same Alkindi who, in the ninth century, had written largely upon Indian astronomy and arithmetic (see Colebrooke, ii. 513; Reinaud, p. 23) now in turn became an authority in the eyes of the Hindús, who studied and translated his writings and those of his successors. This results indisputably from the numerous Arabic technical expressions which now appear side by side with the Greek terms dating from the earlier period. These latter, it is true, still retain their old position, and it is only for new ideas that new words are introduced, particularly in connection with the doctrine of the constellations, which had been developed by the Arabs to a high degree of perfection. Much about the same time, though in some cases perhaps rather earlier, these Arabic works were also translated into another language, namely, into Latin, for the benefit of the European astrologers of the Middle Ages; and thus it comes that in their writings a number of the very same Arabic technical terms may be pointed out which occur in Indian works. Such *termini technici* of Indian astrology at this period are the following:† *mukáriṇá* مُقارنة ☌ conjunction, *mukávilá* مُقابلة ☍ opposition, *taraví* تربيع □ quartile aspect, *tasdí* تسديس

---

* Thence is even taken the name for astrology itself in this period,—namely, *tájika*, *tájika-śástra*, which is to be traced to the Persian تازی = 'Arabic.'

† See *I. St.*, ii. 263 ff. Most of these Arabic terms I know in the meantime only from mediæval Latin translations, as no Arabic texts on astrology have been printed, and the lexicons are very meagre in this respect. [Cf. now Otto Loth's meritorious paper, *Al-Kindi als Astrolog* in the *Morgenländische Forschungen*, 1874, pp. 263–309, published in honour of Fleischer's jubilee.]

* sextile aspect, *taślí* تثليث △ trine aspect; further, *hadda* هدّ *fractio*, *muśallaha* مصالحة, *ikkavála* اقبال *perfectio*, *induvára*, ادبار *deterioratio*, *itthiśála* and *muthaśila* اتصال and متّصل *conjunctio*, *ísarapha* and *músarípha* اصراف and مصرف *disjunctio*, *nakta* (for *nakla*) نقل *translatio*, *yamayá* جمعة *congregatio*, *manaú* منع *prohibitio*, *kamvúla* قبول *receptio*, *gairikamvúla* غير قبول *inreceptio*, *sahama* سهم *sors*, *inthihá* and *munthahá* انتهاء and منتهى *terminus*, and several others that cannot yet be certainly identified.

The doctrine of Omens and Portents was, with the Indians, intimately linked with astrology from the earliest times. Its origin may likewise be traced back to the ancient Vedic, nay, probably to some extent even to the primitive Indo-Germanic period. It is found embodied, in particular, in the literature of the Atharva-Veda, as also in the Gṛihya-Sútras of the other Vedas.[208] A prominent place is also accorded to it in the Saṃhitás of Varáha-Mihira, Nárada, &c.; and it has, besides, produced an independent literature of its own. The same fate has been shared in all respects by another branch of superstition—the arts, namely, of magic and conjuration. As the religious development of the Hindús progressed, these found a more and more fruitful soil, so that they now, in fact, reign almost supreme. On these subjects, too, general treatises exist, as well as tracts on single topics belonging to them. Many of their notions have long been naturalised in the West, through the medium of the Indian fables and fairy tales which were so popular in the Middle Ages—those, for instance, of the purse (of Fortunatus), the league-boots, the magic mirror, the magic ointment, the invisible cap, &c.[209]

---

[208] Cf. my paper, *Zwei Vedische Texte über Omina und Portenta* (1859), containing the Adbhuta-Bráhmaṇa and *adhy.* xiii. of the Kauśika-Sútra.

[209] Some of these, the invisible cap, for instance, are probably to be traced to old mythological superstitious notions of the primitive Indo-Germanic time. In the Sáma-Vidhána-Bráhmaṇa (cf. Burnell, Pref., p. xxv.), we have the purse of Fortu-

We have now to notice Medicine, as the fourth branch of the scientific literature.

The beginnings of the healing art in Vedic times have been already glanced at (pp. 29, 30). Here, again, it is the Atharva-Veda that occupies a special position in relation to it, and in whose literature its oldest fragments are found—fragments, however, of a rather sorry description, and limited mostly to spells and incantations.[300] The Indians themselves consider medicine as an Upaveda, whence they expressly entitle it *Áyur-Veda*,—by which term they do not understand any special work, as has been supposed. They derive it, as they do the Veda itself, immediately from the gods: as the oldest of human writers upon it they mention, first, Átreya, then Agniveśa, then Charaka,[301] then Dhanvantari, and, lastly, his disciple

---

natus, p. 94; see *Lit. C. Bl.*, 1874, pp. 423, 424.—Magic, further, stands in a special relation to the sectarian Tantra texts, as well as to the Yoga doctrine. A work of some extent on this subject bears the name of Nágárjuna, a name of high renown among the Buddhists; see my *Catal. of the Berl. Sansk. MSS.*, p. 270.

[300] See Virgil Grohmann's paper, *Medicinisches aus dem Atharva-Veda mit besonderem Bezug auf den Takman* in *I. St.*, ix. 381 ff. (1865).—*Sarpa-vidyá* (serpent-science) is mentioned in Śatap. Br. xiii., as a separate Veda, with sections entitled *parvan*; may it not have treated of medical matters also? At all events, in the Áśval. Śr., *Visha-vidyá* (science of poisons) is directly coupled with it. As to the contents of the *Vayo-vidyá* (bird-science), mentioned in the same passage of the Śat. Br., it is difficult to form a conjecture. These *Vidyá*-texts are referred to elsewhere also in the Śat. Br. (in xi. xiv.), and appear there, like the *Vaidyaka* in the Mahábháshya, as ranking beside the Veda. A *Várttika* to Pán. iv. 2. 60, teaches a special affix to denote the study of texts, the names of which end in *-vidyá* or *-lakshaṇa*; and we might almost suppose that Páṇini himself was acquainted with texts of this description. From what Patamjali states, besides birds and serpents, cattle and horses also formed the subject of such works. All the special data of this sort in the Mahábháshya point to practical observations from the life; and out of these, in course of time, a literature of natural history could have been developed; see *I. St.*, xiii. 459–461. The *lakshaṇa* sections in the Atharva-Pariśishṭas are either of a ceremonial or astrological-meteorological purport; while, on the other hand, the astrological Saṃhitá of Varáha-Mihira, for instance, contains much that may have been directly derived from the old *vidyás* and *lakshaṇas*.

[301] In the Charaka-Saṃhitá itself Bharadvája (Punarvasu) Kapishṭhala heads the list as the disciple of Indra. Of his six disciples—Agniveśa, Bhela, Jatúkarṇa, Paráśara, Hárita, Kshárapáṇi—Agniveśa first composed his *tantra*, then the others theirs severally, which they thereupon recited to Átreya. To him the narration of the text is expressly referred; for after the opening words of each *adhyáya* ('*athâto . . . vyákhyásyámaḥ*') there uniformly follows the phrase, "*iti ha smáha bha-*

Suśruta. The first three names belong specially to the two divisions of the Yajus, but only to the period of the Sútras and the school-development of this Veda.[302] The medical works bearing these titles can in no case therefore be of older date than this. How much later they ought to be placed is a point for the determination of which we have at present only the limit of the eighth century A.D., at the close of which, according to Ibn Beithar and Albírúní (Reinaud, p. 316), the work of Charaka, and, according to Ibn Abi Uśaibiah, the work of Suśruta also, were translated into Arabic. That Indian medicine had in Páṇini's time already attained a certain degree of cultivation appears from the names of various diseases specified by him (iii. 3. 108, v. 2. 129, &c.), though nothing definite results from this. In the *gaṇa* 'Kártakaujapa' (to Páṇini, vi. 2. 37) we find the 'Sauśrutapárthavás' instanced among the last members; but it is uncertain what we have to understand by this expression. The *gaṇas*, moreover, prove nothing in regard to Páṇini's time; and besides, it is quite possible that this particular Sútra may not be Páṇini's at all, but posterior to Pataṃjali, in whose Mahábháshya, according to the statement of the Calcutta scholiast, it is not interpreted.[303] Dhanvantari is named in Manu's law-book and in the epic, but as the mythical physician of the gods, not as a human personage.[304] In the Pañchatantra two physicians, Śálihotra and Vátsyá-

gaván Átreyaḥ." Quite as uniformly, however, it is stated in a closing verse at the end of each *adhyáya* that the work is a *tantra* composed by Agniveśa and rearranged (*pratisaṃskṛita*) by Charaka.

[302] The same thing applies substantially to the names mentioned in Charaka (see last note)—Bharadvája, Agniveśa (Hutáśaveśa !), Jatúkarṇa, Paráśara, Hárita. And amongst the names of the sages who there appear as the associates of Bharadvája, we find, besides those of the old Ṛishis, special mention, amongst others, of Áśvaláyana, Bádaráyaṇa, Kátyáyana, Baijavápi, &c. As medical authorities are further cited, amongst others (see the St. Petersburg Dict. Supplement, vol. vii.), Kṛiśa, Sáṃkṛityáyana, Káñkáyana, Kṛishṇátreya.

[303] '*Sauśruta*' occurs in the Bháshya; is, however, expressly derived from *suśrut*, not from Suśruta. Consequently neither this name nor the Kutapa-Sauśruta mentioned in another passage has anything to do with the Suśruta of medical writers; see *I. St.*, xiii. 462, 407. For the time of the author of the Várttikas we have the fact of the three humours, *váta*, *pitta*, *śleshman*, being already ranked together, *l. c.*, p. 462.

[304] As such he appears in the verse so often mentioned already, which specifies him as one of the 'nine gems' at Vikrama's court, together with Kálidása and Varáha-Mihira; see Jyotirvid-ábharaṇa, *l. c.*

yana,* whose names are still cited even in our own day, are repeatedly mentioned:[305] but although this work was translated into Pahlaví in the sixth century, it does not at all follow that everything now contained in it formed part of it then, unless we actually find it in this translation (that is, in the versions derived from it).† I am not aware of any other references to medical teachers or works; I may only add, that the chapter of the Amarakosha (ii. 6) on the human body and its diseases certainly presupposes an advanced cultivation of medical science.

An approximate determination of the dates of the existing works[305a] will only be possible when these have been subjected to a critical examination both in respect of their contents and language.‡ But we may even now dis-

---

* This form of name points us to the time of the production of the Sútras, to Vátsya. [It is found in Taitt. Ár., i. 7. 2, as patronymic of a Pañchaparṇa.]

[305] Śálihotra's specialty is here veterinary medicine (his name itself signifies 'horse'); that of Vátsyáyana the *ars amandi.* Of the former's work there are in London two different recensions; see Dietz, *Analecta Medica*, p. 153 (No. 63) and p. 156 (No. 70). According to Sir H. M. Elliot's *Bibl. Index to the Hist. of Muh. Ind.*, p. 263, a work of the kind by this author was translated into Arabic in A.D. 1361. The Káma-Sútra, also, of Vátsyáyana, which by Madhusúdana Sarasvatí in the Prasthána-bheda is expressly classed with Áyur-Veda, is still extant. This work, which, judging from the account of its contents given by Aufrecht in his *Catalogus*, p. 215 ff., is of an extremely interesting character, appeals, *in majorem gloriam*, to most imposing ancient authorities—namely, Auddálaki, Śvetaketu, Bábhravya Páñchála, Gonardíya (*i.e.*, Patamjali, author of the Mahábháshya?), Goṇikáputra, &c. It is also cited by Subandhu, and Śaṃkara himself is said to have written a commentary on it; see Aufrecht, *Catalogus*, p. 256a.

† This was rightly insisted upon by Bentley in opposition to Colebrooke, who had adduced, as an argument to prove the age of Varáha-Mihira, the circumstance that he is mentioned in the Pañchatantra (this is the same passage which is also referred to in the Vikrama-Charitra; see Roth, *Journ. Asiat.*, Oct. 1845, p. 304.) [Kern, it is true, in his Pref. to the Bṛih. Saṃhitá, pp. 19, 20, pronounces very decidedly against this objection of Bentley's, but wrongly, as it seems to me; for, according to Benfey's researches, the present text of the Pañchatantra is a very late production; cf. pp. 221, 240, above.]

[305a] According to Turnour, *Mahávaṅsa*, p. 254, note, the medical work there named in the text, by the Singhalese king Buddhadása (A.D. 339), entitled Sáratthа-Saṃgaha, is still in existence (in Sanskṛit too) in Ceylon, and is used by the native medical practitioners; see on this Davids in the *Transactions of the Philol. Society*, 1875, pp. 76, 78.

‡ The Tibetan Tandjur, according to the accounts given of it, contains a considerable number of medical writings, a circumstance not without importance for their chronology. Thus, Csoma Körösi in the *Journ. As. Soc. Beng.*, January 1825, gives

miss, as belonging to the realm of dreams, the naïve views that have quite recently been advanced as to the age, for example, of the work bearing Suśruta's name.* In language and style, it and the works resembling it with which I am acquainted manifestly exhibit a certain affinity to the writings of Varáha-Mihira.[306] "If then"—here I make use of Stenzler's† words—"internal grounds should render it probable that the system of medicine expounded in Suśruta has borrowed largely from the Greeks, there would be nothing at all surprising in such a circumstance so far as chronology is affected by it."[307] But in the meantime, no such internal grounds whatever appear to exist: on the contrary, there is much that seems to tell against the idea of any such Greek influence. In the first place, the Yavanas are never referred to as authorities; and amongst the individuals enumerated in the introduction as contemporaries of Suśruta,‡ there is not one whose name has a foreign sound.§ Again, the cultivation of medicine

---

the contents of a Tibetan work on medicine, which is put into the mouth of Śákyamuni, and, to all appearance, is a translation of Suśruta or some similar work.

* To wit, by Vullers and Hessler; by the former in an essay on Indian medicine in the periodical *Janus*, edited by Henschel; by the latter in the preface to his so-called translation of Suśruta [1844–50].

306 The Charaka-Saṃhitá has rather higher pretensions to antiquity; its prose here and there reminds us of the style of the Śrauta-Sútras.

† From his examination of Vullers's view in the following number of *Janus*, ii. 453. I may remark here that Wilson's words, also quoted by Wise in the Preface to his *System of Hindu Medicine* (Calc. 1845), p. xvii., have been utterly misunderstood by Vullers. Wilson fixes "as the most modern limit of our conjecture" the ninth or tenth century, *i.e.*, A.D., but Vullers takes it to be B.C.!! [Cf. now Wilson's *Works*, iii. 273, ed. Rost.]

307 This is evidently Roth's opinion also (see *Z. D. M. G.*, xxvi. 441, 1872). Here, after expressing a wish that Indian medicine might be thoroughly dealt with by competent scholars, he adds the remark, that "only a comparison of the principles of Indian with those of Greek medicine can enable us to judge of the origin, age, and value of the former;" and then further on (p. 448), apropos of Charaka's injunctions as to the duties of the physician to his patient, he cites some remarkably coincident expressions from the oath of the Asklepiads.

‡ Hessler, indeed, does not perceive that they are proper names, but translates the words straight off.

§ With the single exception perhaps of Paushkalávata, a name which at least seems to point to the North-West, to Πευκελαῶτις. [We are further pointed to the North-West of India (cf. the Καμβισθολοι) by the name of Bharadvája Kapiṣṭhala in the Charaka-Saṃhitá, which, moreover, assigns to the neighbourhood of the Himavant (*párśve Himavataḥ śubhe*) that gathering of sages, out of which came the

is by Suśruta himself, as well as by other writers, expressly assigned to the city of Káśí (Benares)—in the period, to be sure, of the mythical king Divodása Dhanvantari,* an incarnation of Dhanvantari, the physician of the gods. And lastly, the weights and measures to be used by the physician are expressly enjoined to be either those employed in Magadha or those current in Kaliñga; whence we may fairly presume that it was in these eastern provinces, which never came into close contact with the Greeks, that medicine received its special cultivation.

Moreover, considerable critical doubts arise as to the authenticity of the existing texts, since in the case of some of them we find several recensions cited. Thus Atri, whose work appears to have altogether perished, is also cited as *laghv*-Atri, *bṛihad*-Atri; Átreya, similarly, as *bṛihad*-Átreya, *vṛiddha*-Átreya, *madhyama*-Átreya, *kanishṭha*-Átreya; Suśruta, also as *vṛiddha*-Suśruta; Vágbhaṭa, also as *vṛiddha*-Vágbhaṭa; Hárîta, also as *vṛiddha*-Hárîta; Bhoja, also as *vṛiddha*-Bhoja—a state of things to which we have an exact parallel in the case of the astronomical Siddhántas (see pp. 258, 259, and Colebrooke ii. 391, 392), and also of the legal literature. The number of medical works and authors is extraordinarily large. The former are either systems embracing the whole domain of the science, or highly special investigations of single topics, or, lastly, vast compilations prepared in modern times under the patronage of kings and princes. The sum of knowledge embodied in their contents appears really to be most respectable. Many of the statements on dietetics and on the origin and diagnosis of diseases bespeak a very keen observation. In surgery, too, the Indians seem to have attained a special

---

instruction of Bharadvája by Indra. Again, Agniveśa is himself, *ibid.*, i. 13 comm., described as Chándrabhágin, and so, probably (cf. *gaṇa* '*bahvádi*' to Páṇini, iv. 1. 45) associated with the Chandrabhágá, one of the great rivers of the Panjáb. And lastly, there is also mentioned, *ibid.*, i. 12, iv. 6, an ancient physician, Káñkáyana, probably the Kankah or Katka of the Arabs (see Reinaud, *Mém. sur l'Inde*, p. 314 ff.), who is expressly termed Váhîka-bhishaj. We have already met with his name (p. 153 above) amongst the teachers of the Atharva-Pariśishṭas.]

* Suśruta is himself said, in the introduction, to have been a disciple of his. This assertion may, however, rest simply on a confusion of this Dhanvantari with *the* Dhanvantari who is given as one of the 'nine gems' of Vikrama's court.

proficiency,[308] and in this department European surgeons might perhaps even at the present day still learn something from them, as indeed they have already borrowed from them the operation of rhinoplasty. The information, again, regarding the medicinal properties of minerals (especially precious stones and metals), of plants, and animal substances, and the chemical analysis and decomposition of these, covers certainly much that is valuable. Indeed, the branch of Materia Medica generally appears to be handled with great predilection, and this makes up to us in some measure at least for the absence of investigations in the field of natural science.[309] On the diseases, &c., of horses and elephants also there exist very special monographs. For the rest, during the last few centuries medical science has suffered great detriment from the increasing prevalence of the notion, in itself a very ancient one, that diseases are but the result of transgressions and sins committed, and from the consequent very general substitution of fastings, alms, and gifts to the Brahmans, for real remedies.—An excellent general sketch of Indian medical science is given in Dr. Wise's work, *Commentary on the Hindu System of Medicine*, which appeared at Calcutta in 1845.[310]

The influence, which has been already glanced at, of Hindú medicine upon the Arabs in the first centuries of the Hijra was one of the very highest significance; and the Khalifs of Bagdad caused a considerable number of works upon the subject to be translated.* Now, as Ara-

---

[308] See now as to this Wilson, *Works*, iii. 380 ff., ed. Rost.

[309] Cf. the remarks in note 300 on the *vidyás* and the *vaidyaka*.

[310] New ed. 1860 (London). Cf. also two, unfortunately short, papers by Wilson *On the Medical and Surgical Science of the Hindus*, in vol. i. of his *Essays on Sanskrit Literature*, collected by Dr. Rost (1864, *Works*, vol. iii.). Up to the present only Suśruta has been published, by Madhusúdana Gupta (Calc. 1835–36, new ed. 1868) and by Jivánanda Vidyásagara (1873). An edition of Charaka has been begun by Gangádhara Kavirája (Calc. 1868–69), but unfortunately, being weighted with a very prolix commentary by the editor, it makes but slow progress. (Part 2, 1871, breaks off at *adhy.* 5.) It furnished the occasion for Roth's already mentioned monograph on Charaka, in which he communicates a few sections of the work, iii. 8 ('How to become a doctor') and i. 29 ('The Bungler') in translation. From the Bhela-Samhitá (see note 301 above), Burnell, in his *Elem. of S. Ind. Pal.*, p. 94, quotes a verse in a way (namely, as 31. 4) which clearly indicates that he had access to an entire work of this name.

* See Gildemeister, *Script. Arab. de rebus Indicis*, pp. 94–97. [Flügel, following the *Fihrist al-ulúm* in *Z. D. M. G.*, xi. 148 ff., 325 ff. (1857).]

bian medicine constituted the chief authority and guiding principle of European physicians down to the seventeenth century, it directly follows—just as in the case of astronomy—that the Indians must have been held in high esteem by these latter; and indeed Charaka is repeatedly mentioned in the Latin translations of Avicenna (Ibn Sina), Rhazes (Al Rasi), and Serapion (Ibn Serabi).*

Besides Áyur-veda, medicine, the Hindús specify three other so-called Upavedas—*Dhanur-veda, Gándharva-veda,* and *Artha-śástra, i.e.,* the Art of War, Music, and the Formative Arts or Technical Arts generally; and, like Áyur-veda, these terms designate the respective branches of literature at large, not particular works.

As teacher of the art of war, Viśvámitra is mentioned, and the contents of his work are fully indicated;[311] the name Bharadvája also occurs.[312] But of this branch of literature hardly any direct monuments seem to have been preserved.† Still, the Níti-Śástras and the Epic comprise many sections bearing quite specially upon the science of war;[313] and the Agni-Puráṇa, in particular, is distinguished by its very copious treatment of the subject.[314]

Music was from the very earliest times a favourite pursuit of the Hindús, as we may gather from the numerous allusions to musical instruments in the Vedic literature; but its reduction to a methodical system is, of course, of later date. Possibly the Naṭa-Sútras mentioned in Páṇini (see above, p. 197) may have contained something of the

---

* See Royle *On the Antiquity of Hindu Medicine*, 1838.

311 By Madhusúdana Sarasvatí in the Prasthána-bheda, *I. St.*, i. 10, 21.

312 Where Bharadvája can appear in such a position, I am not at present aware; perhaps we ought to read Bháradvája, *i.e.*, Droṇa?

† With the exception of some works on the rearing of horses and elephants, which may perhaps be classed here, although they more properly belong to medicine.

313 The Kámandakíya Níti-Śástra in nineteen chaps., to which this especially applies, has been published by Rájendra Lála Mitra in the *Bibl. Ind.* (1849–61), with extracts, which, however, only reach as far as the ninth chap., from the commentary entitled 'Upádhyáya-nirapekshá;' in style and matter it reminds us of the Bṛihat-Saṃhitá of Varáha-Mihira. A work of like title and subject was taken to Java by the Hindús who emigrated thither, see *I. St.*, iii. 145; but whether this emigration actually took place so early as the fourth century, as Ráj. L. M. supposes, is still very questionable.

314 See Wilson '*On the Art of War*' (Works, iv. 290 ff.).

kind, since music was specially associated with dancing. The earliest mention of the names of the seven notes of the musical scale occurs, so far as we know at present, in the so-called Vedáñgas—in the Chhandas [315] and the Śikshá; [316] and they are further mentioned in one of the Atharvopanishads (the Garbha), which is, at least, not altogether modern. As author of the Gándharva-veda,* *i.e.*, of a treatise on music, Bharata is named, and, besides him, also Íśvara, Pavana, Kalinátha,[317] Nárada; [318] but of these the only existing remains appear to be the fragments cited in

[315] See on this *I. St.*, viii. 259–272. The designation of the seven notes by the initial letters of their names is also found here, in one recension of the text at least, *ibid.*, p. 256. According to Von Bohlen, *Das alte Indien*, ii. 195 (1830), and Benfey, *Indien*, p. 299 (in *Ersch and Gruber's Encyclopædie*, vol. xvii., 1840), this notation passed from the Hindús to the Persians, and from these again to the Arabs, and was introduced into European music by Guido d' Arezzo at the beginning of the eleventh century. Corresponding to the Indian *sa ri ga ma pa dha ni* we have in Persian, along with the designation of the notes by the first seven letters of the alphabet (A—G), the scale *da re mi fa sa la be*; see Richardson and Johnson's *Pers. Dict.* s. v. *Durr i mufassal.*—Does the word *gamma*, 'gamut,' Fr. *gamme*, which has been in use since the time of Guido d'Arezzo to express the musical scale, itself come from the equivalent Sanskrit term *gráma* (Prákṛ. *gáma*), and so exhibit a direct trace of the Indian origin of the seven notes? See Ludwig Geiger's precisely opposite conjecture in his *Ursprung der Sprache*, i. 458 (1868). The usual explanation of the word is, of course, that it is derived from the Γ (gamma) which designates the first of the twenty-one notes of Guido's scale, and which was "known and in common, if not universal, use for more than a century before his time;" see Ambros, *Geschichte der Musik*, ii. 151 (1864). "There being already a *G* and a *g* in the upper octaves, it was necessary to employ the equivalent Greek letter for the corresponding lowest note." The necessity for this is not, however, so very apparent; but, rather, in the selection of this term, and again in its direct employment in the sense of 'musical scale' a reminiscence of the Indian word may *originally* have had some influence, though Guido himself need not have been cognisant of it.

[316] And this not merely in the Śikshá attributed to Páṇini, but in the whole of the tracts belonging to this category; see my Essay on the Pratijñá-Sútra, pp. 107–109; Haug, *Accent*, p. 59.

* This title is derived from the Gandharvas or celestial musicians.

[317] This name is also written Kallinátha (Kapila in Lassen, *I. AK.*, iv. 832, is probably a mistake), by Sir W. Jones, *On the Musical Modes of the Hindus* in *As. Res.*, iii. 329, and by Aufrecht, *Catalogus*, p. 210ᵃ. Bühler, however, *Catal. of MSS. from Guj.*, iv. 274, has the spelling given in the text. But, at any rate, instead of Pavana, we must read 'Hanumant, son of Pavana.' For Bharata, see above, p. 231.

[318] See the data from the Nárada-śikshá in Haug, *Ueber des Wesen des Ved. Accents*, p. 58. The 'gandharva Nárada' is probably originally only Cloud personified; see *I. St.*, i. 204, 483, ix. 2.

the scholia of the dramatic literature. Some of these writings were translated into Persian, and, perhaps even earlier, into Arabic. There are also various modern works on music. The whole subject, however, has been but little investigated.[319]

As regards the third Upaveda, *Artha-Śástra*, the Hindús, as is well known, have achieved great distinction in the technical arts, but less in the so-called formative arts. The literature of the subject is but very scantily represented, and is for the most part modern.

Painting, in the first place, appears in a very rudimentary stage. Portrait-painting, for which perspective is not required, seems to have succeeded best, as it is frequently alluded to in the dramas.[319a] In Sculpture, on the contrary, no mean skill is discernible.[320] Among the reliefs carved upon stone are many of great beauty, especially those depicting scenes from Buddha's life, Buddha being uniformly represented in purely human shape, free from mythological disfigurement.—There exist various books of

---

[319] Besides Sir W. Jones, *l. c.*, see also Patterson in vol. ix. of the *As. Res.*, Lassen, *I. AK.*, iv. 832, and more particularly the special notices in Aufrecht's *Catalogus*, pp. 199–202. Śárngadeva, author of the Sangítaratnákara, cites as authorities Abhinavagupta, Kírtidhara, Kohala, Someśvara; he there treats not only of music, especially singing, but also of dancing, gesticulation, &c.

[319a] On modern painting, see my Essay, *Ueber Krishṇa's Geburtsfest*, p. 341 ff.—It is noteworthy that the accounts of 'the manner of origin of the production of likenesses' at the close of Táranátha's hist. of Buddhism (Schiefner, p. 278 ff.) expressly point to the time of Aśoka and Nágárjuna as the most flourishing epoch of the Yaksha and Nága artists. In an address recently delivered to the St. Petersburg Academy (see the Bulletin of 25th Nov. 1875), Schiefner communicated from the Kágyur some 'Anecdotes of Indian Artists,' in which, among other things, special reference is made to the Yavanas as excellent painters and craftsmen. On pictorial representations of the fight between Kaṅsa and Krishṇa, see the data in the Mahábháshya, *I. St.*, xiii. 354, 489; and on likenesses of the gods for sale in Páṇini's time, Goldstücker's *Páṇini*, p. 228 ff.; *I. St.*, v. 148, xiii. 331.

[320] Through the recent researches of Fergusson, Cunningham, and Leitner the question has been raised whether Greek influence was not here also an important factor. Highly remarkable in this regard are, for example, the parallels between an image of the sun-god in his car on a column at Buddhagayá and a well-known figure of Phœbus Apollo, as shown in Plate xxvii. of Cunningham's *Archæological Survey of India*, vol. iii. 97 (1873). The same type is also exhibited on a coin of the Bactrian king Plato, lately described by W. S. W. Vaux in the *Numism. Chronicle*, xv. 1–5 (1875).

instructions and treatises on the subject:[321] according to the accounts given of them, they deal for the most part with single topics, the construction of images of the gods, for example; but along with these are others on geometry and design in general.

A far higher degree of development was attained by Architecture, of which some most admirable monuments still remain: it received its chief cultivation at the hands of the Buddhists, as these required monasteries, topes (*stúpas*), and temples for their cult. It is not, indeed, improbable that our Western steeples owe their origin to an imitation of the Buddhist topes. But, on the other hand, in the most ancient Hindú edifices the presence of Greek influence[321a] is unmistakable.[322] (See Benfey, *Indien*, pp. 300–305.) Architecture, accordingly, was often systematically

---

[321] *E.g.*, also in Varáha-Mihira's Bṛihat - Saṃhitá, one chapter of which, on the construction of statues of the gods, is communicated from Albírúní by Reinaud in his *Mém. sur l'Inde*, p. 419 ff. See also *I. St.*, xiii. 344–346.

[321a] In the fifth vol., which has just appeared, of his *Archæological Survey of India*, p. 185 ff., Cunningham distinguishes an Indo-Persian style, the prevalence of which he assigns to the period of the Persian supremacy over the valley of the Indus (500–330), and three Indo-Grecian styles, of which the Ionic prevailed in Takshila, the Corinthian in Gandhára, and the Doric in Kashmír. Rájendra Lála Mitra, it is true, in vol. i. of his splendid work, *The Antiquities of Orissa* (1875), holds out patriotically against the idea of any Greek influence whatever on the development of Indian architecture, &c. (At p. 25, by the way, my conjecture as to the connection between the Asura Maya, Turamaya, and Ptolemaios, see above, p. 253, *I. St.*, ii. 234, is stated in a sadly distorted form.) Looking at his plates, however, we have a distinct suggestion of Greek art, for example, in the two fountain-nymphs in Plate xvi., No. 46; while the Bayadere in Plate xviii., No. 59, from the temple of Bhuvaneśvara, middle of seventh century (p. 31), seems to be resting her right hand on a dolphin, beside which a Cupid (?) is crouching, and might therefore very well be an imitation of some representation of Venus. (Cf. Ráj. L. M., p. 59.)

[322] This does not mean that the Indians were not acquainted with stone-building prior to the time of Alexander—an opinion which is confuted by Cunningham, *l. c.*, iii. 98. The painful minuteness, indeed, with which the erection of brick-altars is described in the Vedic sacrificial ritual (cf. the Śulva-Sútras) might lead us to suppose that such structures were still at that time rare. But, on the one hand, this would take us back to a much earlier time than we are here speaking of; and, on the other, this scrupulous minuteness of description may simply be due to the circumstance that a specifically sacred structure is here in question, in connection with which, therefore, every single detail was of direct consequence.

treated of,[323] and we find a considerable number of such works cited, some of which, as is customary in India, purport to proceed from the gods themselves, as from Viśvakarman,[324] Sanatkumára, &c. In the Saṃhitá of Varáha-Mihira, too, there is a tolerably long chapter devoted to architecture, though mainly in an astrological connection.

The skill of the Indians in the production of delicate woven fabrics, in the mixing of colours, the working of metals and precious stones, the preparation of essences,[325] and in all manner of technical arts, has from early times enjoyed a world-wide celebrity: and for these subjects also we have the names of various treatises and monographs. Mention is likewise made of writings on cookery and every kind of requirement of domestic life, as dress, ornaments, the table; on games of every description, dice,* for ex-

---

[323] See Lassen, *I. AK.*, iv. 877. Rám Ráz's *Essay on the Architecture of the Hindus* (1834) is specially based on the Mánasára in fifty-eight *adhyáyas*, presumably composed in S. India (p. 9). Máyamata (Maya's system, on which see Ráj. L. M., *Notices*, ii. 306), Káśyapa, Vaikhánasa, and the Sakaládhikára ascribed to Agastya, were only secondarily consulted. The portion of the Agni-Puráṇa published in the *Bibl. Ind.* treats, *int. al.*, of the building of houses, temples, &c. The Ratha-Sútra and the Vástu-Vidyá are given by Śankha (Schol. on Káty., i. 1. 11) as the special rules for the *rathakára*. The word *Sútra-dhára*, 'measuring-line holder,' 'builder,' signifies at the same time 'stage-manager;' and here perhaps we have to think of the temporary erections that were required for the actors, spectators, &c., during the performance of dramas at the more important festivals. In this latter acceptation, indeed, the word might also possibly refer to the Naṭa-*Sútras*, the observance of which had to be provided for by the *Sútra-dhára*? See above, pp. 198, 199.

[324] On a Viśva-karma-prakáśa and a Viśvakarmíya-Śilpa, see Rájendra Lála Mitra, *Notices of Sansk. MSS.*, ii. 17, 142.

[325] The art of perfumery appears to have been already taught in a special Sútra at the time of the Bháshya; cf. the observations in *I. St.*, xiii. 462, on *chándanagandhika*, Páṇ. iv. 2. 65; perhaps the *Sámastam* ('*náma śástram*,' Kaiyaṭa) Bháshya to Páṇ. iv. 2. 104, belongs to this class also.

* In *I. St.*, i. 10, I have translated, doubtless incorrectly, the expression *chatuḥshashṭi-kalá-śástra* (cited in the Prasthána-bheda as part of the Artha-śástra) by 'treatise on chess,' referring the 64 *kalás* to the 64 squares of the chess-board; whereas, according to *As. Res.* i. 341 (Schlegel, *Réflex. sur l'Étude des Langues Asiat.*, p. 112), it signifies 'treatise on the 64 arts'? In the Daśakumára, however (p. 140, ed. Wilson), the *chatuḥshashṭi-kalágama* is expressly distinguished from the Artha-śástra. —See an enumeration of the 64 *kalás*, from the Śiva-tantra in Rádhákántadeva's *Śabda-kalpa-druma*, s. v. [On the game of *Chatur-aṅga* see now my papers in the *Monatsber. der Berl. Acad.*, 1872, pp. 60 ff., 502 ff.; 1873, p. 705 ff.; 1874, p. 21 ff.; and also Dr. Ant. van der Linde's beautiful work, *Geschichte des Schachspiels* (1874, 2 vols.).

ample; nay, even on the art of stealing—an art which, in fact, was reduced to a regular and complete system [cf. Wilson, Daśakum., p. 69, on Karṇísuta, and *Hindu Theatre*, i. 63]. A few of these writings have also been admitted into the Tibetan Tandjur.

From Poetry, Science, and Art, we now pass to Law, Custom, and Religious Worship, which are all three comprehended in the term 'Dharma,' and whose literature is presented to us in the *Dharma-Śástras* or *Smṛiti-Śástras*. The connection of these works with the Gṛihya-Sútras of Vedic literature has already been adverted to in the introduction (see pp. 19, 20), where, too, the conjecture is expressed that the consignment of the principles of law to writing may perhaps have been called forth by the growth of Buddhism, with the view of rigidly and securely fixing the system of caste distinctions rejected by the new faith, and of shielding the Brahmanical polity generally from innovation or decay. In the most ancient of these works, accordingly—the Law-Book of *Manu*—we encounter this Brahmanical constitution in its full perfection. The Brahman has now completely attained the goal from which, in the Bráhmaṇas, he is not very far distant, and stands as the born representative of Deity itself; while, upon the other hand, the condition of the Śúdra is one of the utmost wretchedness and hardship. The circumstance that the Vaidehas and the Lichhavis (as Lassen, no doubt rightly, conjectures for Nichhivis) are here numbered among the impure castes, is — as regards the former — certainly a sign that this work is long posterior to the Śatapatha-Bráhmaṇa, where the Vaidehas appear as the leading representatives of Brahmanism. The position allotted to this tribe, as well as to the Lichhavis, may, perhaps, further be connected with the fact that, according to Buddhist legends, the Vaidehas, and especially this Lichhavi family of them, exercised a material influence upon the growth of Buddhism. The posteriority of Manu to the whole body of Vedic literature appears, besides, from many other special indications; as, for instance, from the repeated mention of the several divisions of this literature; from the connection which subsists with some passages in the Upanishads; from the completion of the Yuga system and the triad of deities; as well as, generally, from the minute and nicely elaborated distribution and regulation of the whole of life, which are here presented to us.

I have likewise already remarked, that for judicial procedure proper, for the forms of justice, the connecting link is wanting between the Dharma-Śástra of Manu and Vedic literature. That this code, however, is not to be regarded as the earliest work of its kind, is apparent from the very nature of the case, since the degree of perfection of the judicial procedure it describes justifies the assumption that this topic had been frequently handled before.* The same conclusion seems, moreover, to follow from the fact of occasional direct reference being made to the views of predecessors, from the word 'Dharma-Śástra' itself being familiar,† as also from the circumstance that Patamjali, in his Mahábháshya on Páṇini, is acquainted with works bearing the name of Dharma-Sútras.[326] Whether remains of these connecting links may yet be recovered, is, for the present at least, doubtful.‡ For the domestic relations of the Hindús, on the contrary—for education, marriage, household economy, &c.—it is manifestly in the Gṛihya-Sútras that we must look for the sources of the Dharma-Śástras; and this, as I have also had frequent occasion

* See Stenzler in *I. St.*, i. 244 ff.

† Yet neither circumstance is strictly conclusive, as, considering the peculiar composition of the work, the several passages in question might perhaps be later additions.

[326] See now on this *I. St.*, xiii. 458, 459.

‡ Allusions to judicial cases are of very rare occurrence within the range of Vedic literature; but where they do occur, they mostly agree with the precepts of Manu. So also, for example, a verse in Yáska's Nirukti, iii. 4, concerning the disability of women to inherit, which, besides, directly appeals to 'Manuḥ Sváyambhuvaḥ.' This is the first time that the latter is mentioned as a lawgiver. [See also Śáṅkh. Gṛih., ii. 16; Ápast., ii. 16. 1, ed. Bühler. On Vedic phases of criminal law, see Burnell, Pref. to Sáma-vidhána-Br., p. xv.; *Lit. C. Bl.*, 1874, p. 423.]

to observe (pp. 58, 84, 102, 143), is the explanation of the circumstance that most of the names current as authors of Gṛihya-Sútras are at the same time given as authors of Dharma-Śástras.* The distinction, as a commentator † remarks, is simply this, that the Gṛihya-Sútras confine themselves to the points of difference of the various schools, whereas the Dharma-Śástras embody the precepts and obligations common to all.[327]

* In the case of Manu, too, there would seem to have existed a Mánava Gṛihya-Sútra as its basis (?), and the reference to the great ancestor Manu would thus appear to be only a subsequent one (?). [This surmise of mine, expressed with diffidence here, above at pp. 19, 102, and in *I. St.*, i. 69, has since been generally accepted, and will, it is hoped, find full confirmation in the text of the Mán. Gṛihyas., which has meanwhile actually come to light. I have already pointed out one instance of agreement in language with the Yajus texts, in the word *abhinimrukta*; see *I. Str.*, ii. 209, 210.]

† Áśárka on the Karma-pradípa of Kátyáyana.

[327] In his *Hist. of Anc. Sansk. Lit.* (1859), Max Müller gave some account of the Dharma-Sútra of Ápastamba, which is extant under the title Sámayácharika-Sútra. He also characterised three of the Dharma-Śástras printed at Calcutta (the Gautama, Vishṇu, and Vasishṭha) as being Dharma-Sútras of a similar kind; expressing himself generally to the effect (p. 134) that all the metrical Dharma-Śástras we possess are but "more modern texts of earlier Sútra-works or Kula-dharmas belonging originally to certain Vedic Charaṇas." (The only authority cited by him is Stenzler in *I. St.*, i. 232, who, however, in his turn, refers to my own earlier account, *ibid.* pp. 57, 69, 143). Johäntgen, in his tract, *Ueber das Gesetzbuch des Manu* (1863), adopted precisely the same view (see, *e.g.*, p. 113). Bühler, finally, in the Introduction to the *Digest of Hindu Law*, edited by him, jointly with R. West (vol. i., 1867), furnished us for the first time with more specific information as to these Dharma-Sútras, which connect themselves with, and in part directly belong to, the Vedic Sútra stage. In the appendix to this work he likewise communicated various sections on the law of inheritance from the four Dharma-Sútras above mentioned, and that of Baudháyana. He also published separately, in 1868, the entire Sútra of Ápastamba, with extracts from Haradatta's commentary and an index of words (1871). This Sútra, in point of fact, forms (see above, notes 108 and 109) two *praśnas* of the Áp. Śrauta-Sútra; and a similar remark applies to the Sútra of Baudháyana. According to Bühler's exposition, to the five Sútras just named have to be added the small texts of this class, consisting of prose and verse intermingled, which are ascribed to Uśanas, Kaśyapa, and Budha; and, perhaps, also the Smṛitis of Hárita and Śaṅkha. All the other existing Smṛitis, on the contrary, bear a more modern character, and are either (1) metrical redactions of ancient Dharma-Sútras, or fragments of such redactions (to these belong our Manu and Yájnavalkya, as well as the Smṛitis of Nárada, Paráśara, Bṛihaspati, Saṃvarta),—or (2) secondary redactions of metrical Dharma-Śástras,—or (3) metrical versions of the Gṛihya-Sútras,—or lastly, (4) forgeries of the Hindú sects.—The material in vol. i. of Bühler and West's work has been

As regards the existing text of Manu, it cannot, apparently, have been extant in its present shape even at the period to which the later portions of the Mahá-Bhárata belong. For although Manu is often cited in the epic in literal accordance with the text as we now have it, on the other hand, passages of Manu are just as often quoted there which, while they appear in our text, yet do so with considerable variations. Again, passages are there ascribed to Manu which are nowhere found in our collection, and even passages composed in a totally different metre. And, lastly, passages also occur frequently in the Mahá-Bhárata which are not attributed to Manu at all, but which may nevertheless be read *verbatim* in our text.* Though we may doubtless here assign a large share of the blame to the writers making the quotations (we know from the commentaries how often mistakes have crept in through the habit of citing from memory), still, the fact that our text attained its present shape only after having been, perhaps repeatedly, recast, is patent from the numerous inconsistencies, additions, and repetitions it contains. In support of this conclusion, we have, further, not only the fabulous tradition to the effect that the text of Manu consisted originally of 100,000 *ślokas*, and was abridged, first to 12,000, and eventually to 4000 *ślokas* †—a tradition which at least clearly displays a reminiscence of various remodellings of the text—but also the decisive fact that in the legal commentaries, in addition to Manu, a *Vṛiddha*-Manu and a *Bṛihan*-Manu are directly quoted,‡ and must therefore have been still extant at the time of these commentaries. But although we cannot determine, even approximately, the date when our text of Manu received its present shape,[328] there is little doubt that its contents,

utilised critically, in its legal bearing, by Aurel Mayr, in his work, *Das indische Erbrecht* (Vienna, 1873); see on it *Lit. C. Bl.*, 1874, p. 340 ff.

* See Holtzmann, *Ueber den griechischen Ursprung des indischen Thierkreises*, p. 14. [As to Manu's position in Varáha-Mihira, see Kern, Pref. to Bṛih. Saṃh., pp. 42, 43, and on a Páli edition of Manu, Rost in *I. St.*, i. 315 ff.]

† Our present text contains only 2684 *ślokas*.

‡ See Stenzler, *l. c.*, p. 235.

[328] Johäntgen (pp. 86, 95) assumes as the latest limit for its composition the year B.C. 350, and as the earliest limit the fifth century. But this rests in great part upon his further assumption (p. 77) that the Bráhmaṇas, Upanishads, &c., known to us are all of later date—an assumption which is rendered in

compared with those of the other Dharma-Śástras, are, on the whole, the most ancient, and that, consequently, it has been rightly placed by general tradition * at the head of this class of literature. The number of these other Dharma-Śástras is considerable, amounting to fifty-six, and is raised to a much higher figure—namely, eighty—if we reckon the several redactions of the individual works that have so far come to our knowledge, and which are designated by the epithets *laghu*, *madhyama*, *bṛihat*, *vṛiddha*.[329] When once the various texts are before us, their relative age will admit of being determined without great difficulty. It will be possible,† in particular, to characterise them according to the preponderance, or the entire absence, of one or other of the three constituent elements which make up the substance of Indian law, that is to say, according as they chiefly treat of domestic and civil duties, of the administration of justice, or of the regulations as to purification and penance. In Manu these three constituents are pretty much mixed up, but upon the whole they are discussed with equal fulness. The code of Yájnavalkya is divided into three books, according to the three topics, each book being of about the same extent. The other works of the class vary.

With regard to the code of Yájnavalkya, just mentioned—the only one of these works which, with Manu, is as yet generally accessible—its posteriority to Manu follows plainly enough, not only from this methodical distribution of its contents, but also from the circumstance ‡ that

---

the highest degree doubtful by the remarks he himself makes, in agreement with Müller and myself, upon the probable origin of the work from a Gṛihya-Sútra of the Mánava school of the Black Yajus, as well as upon the various redactions it has undergone, and the relation of the work itself and the various schools of the Yajus to Buddhism (pp. 112, 113); see *I. Str.*, ii. 278, 279.

* Which those Hindús who emigrated to Java also took with them.

329 Bühler, *l. c.*, p. 13 ff., enumerates 78 Smṛitis and 36 different redactions of individual Smṛitis,—in all, a total of 114 such texts. To these, however, we have still to add, for example, from his *Catalogue of MSS. from Gujarát*, vol. iii., the Smṛitis of Kokila, Gobhila, Súryáruṇa, *laghu*- and *vṛiddha*-Parásara, *laghu*-Bṛihaspati, *laghu*-Śaunaka; while to the collective titles purposely omitted by him from his list—Chaturviṅśati, Shaṭtriṅśat (extracts from 24 and 36 Smṛitis), and Saptarshi—we have probably to add, from the same source, the Shaḍaśíti and Shaṇṇavati? The Aruṇa-Smṛiti is also specified in the *Catal. Sans. MSS., N. W. Prov.*, 1874, p. 122.

† See Stenzler, *l. c.*, p. 236.

‡ See Stenzler in the Pref. to his edition of Yájnavalkya, pp. ix.–xi.

it teaches the worship of Gaṇeśa and the planets, the execution, upon metal plates, of deeds relating to grants of land, and the organisation of monasteries—all subjects which do not occur in Manu; while polemical references to the Buddhists, which in Manu are at least doubtful,[330] are here unmistakable.[331] In the subjects, too, which are common to both, we note in Yájnavalkya an advance towards greater precision and stringency; and in individual instances, where the two present a substantial divergence, Yájnavalkya's standpoint is distinctly the later one. The earliest limit we can fix for this work is somewhere about the second century A.D., seeing that the word *náṇaka* occurs in it to denote 'coin,' and this term, according to Wilson's conjecture, is taken from the coins of Kanerki, who reigned until A.D. 40.* Its latest limit, on the other hand, may be fixed about the sixth or seventh century, as, according to Wilson, passages from it are found in inscriptions of the tenth century in various parts of India, and the work itself must therefore date considerably earlier. Its second book reappears literally in the Agni-Puráṇa; whether adopted into the latter, or borrowed from it, cannot as yet be determined. Of this work also two recensions are distinguished, the one as *bṛihad*-Yájnavalkya, the other as *vṛiddha*-Yájnavalkya (see also Colebrooke, i. 103). As to its relation to the remaining

---

[330] If by the *pravrajitás* in viii. 363, Buddhist *brahmachárinis* be really meant, as asserted by Kullúka, then this particular precept—which puts the violation of their persons on the same footing with violence done to "other public women," and punishes the offence with a small fine only—is to be taken not merely, as Talboys Wheeler takes it (*Hist. of India*, ii. 583), as a bitter sarcasm, but also as evidence that the work was composed at a time when the Buddhist nuns had already really deteriorated; cf. the remarks in a similar instance in regard to Páṇini, *I. St.*, v. 141.

[331] Cf. Johäntgen, pp. 112, 113.

* See above, p. 205: the same applies also to the Vṛiddha-Gautama law-book. [According to Jacobi, *De Astrologiæ Indicæ Originibus*, p. 14, the statement in Yájnavalkya, i. 80, that *coitus* must take place '*susthe indau*,' rests upon an acquaintance with the Greek astrological doctrine of the 'twelve houses' (and, in fact, this is the sense in which the Mitákshará understands the passage); so that, in his opinion, Yájnavalkya cannot be placed earlier than the fourth century of our era. This interpretation, however, is not absolutely forced upon us, as *sustha* might equally well refer to one of the lunar phases or mansions which from an early period were regarded as auspicious for procreation and birth; see *Lit. C. Bl.*, 1873, p. 787.]

codes, Stenzler, from the preface to whose edition the foregoing information is taken, is of opinion that it is antecedent to all of them,[332] and that, therefore, it marks the next stage after Manu.*

But in addition to the Dharma-Śástras, which form the basis and chief part of the literature dealing with Law, Custom, and Worship, we have also to rank the great bulk of the epic poetry—the Mahá-Bhárata, as well as the Rámáyaṇa—as belonging to this branch of literature, since in these works, as I remarked when discussing them, the didactic element far outweighs the epic. The Mahá-Bhárata chiefly embraces instruction as to the duties of kings and of the military class, instruction which is given elsewhere also, namely, in the Níti-Śástras and (apparently) in the Dhanur-Veda; but besides this, manifold other topics of the Hindú law are there discussed and expounded. The Puráṇas, on the contrary, chiefly contain regulations as to the worship of the gods by means of prayers, vows, fastings, votive offerings, gifts, pious foundations, pilgrimages, festivals, conformably to the shape which this worship successively assumed; and in this they are extensively supported by the Upapuráṇas and the Tantras.

Within the last few centuries there has further grown up a modern system of jurisprudence, or scientific legal literature, which compares and weighs, one against another, the different views of the authors of the Dharma-Śástras. In particular, extensive compilations have been prepared, in great measure by the authority and under the auspices of various kings and princes, with a view to meet the prac-

[332] Müller has, it is true, claimed (see above, note 327) for the Dharma-Śástras of Vishṇu, Gautama, and Vaśishṭha the character of Dharma-Sútras; and Bühler (pp. xxi.–xxv.) expressly adds to the list the similar texts attributed to Uśanas, Kaśyapa, and Budha, and also, though with a reservation, those of Hárita and Sañkha (Vaśishṭha belongs probably to the Dráhyáyaṇa school of the Sáma-Veda, see pp. 79, 85—the Veda with which Gautama is likewise associated). Still, in Bühler's opinion (p. xxvii.), Manu and Yájnavalkya, although only "versifications of older Sútras," may yet very well be of higher antiquity "than some of the Sútra works which have come down to our times."

* This, to be sure, is at variance with i. 4, 5, where twenty different Dharma-Śástra authors are enumerated (amongst them Yájnavalkya himself): these two verses are perhaps a later addition (?).

tical want of a sufficient legal code.[333] The English themselves, also, have had a digest of this sort compiled, from which, as is well known, the commencement of Sanskṛit studies dates. These compilations were mostly drawn up in the Dekhan, which from the eleventh century was the refuge and centre of literary activity generally. In Hindustán it had been substantially arrested by the inroads and ravages of the Muhammadans;* and it is only within the last three centuries that it has again returned thither, especially to Káśí (Benares) and Bengal. Some of the Mogul emperors, notably the great Akbar and his two successors, Jehángír and Sháh Jehán†—who together reigned 1556–1656—were great patrons of Hindú literature.

This brings us to the close of our general survey of Sanskṛit literature; but we have still to speak of a very peculiar branch of it, whose existence only became known some twenty or thirty years ago, namely, the Buddhistic Sanskṛit works. To this end, it is necessary, in the first place, to premise some account of the origin of Buddhism itself.[334]

---

[333] See Colebrooke's account of these in his two prefaces to the *Digest of Hindu Law* (1798) and the *Two Treatises on the Hindu Law of Inheritance* (1810), now in Cowell's edition of the *Misc. Ess.*, i. 461 ff.; also Bühler's *Introduction*, *l. c.*, p. iii. ff.

* This finds expression, *e.g.*, in the following *śloka* of Vyása: "*Samprápte tu kalau kále Vindhyádrer uttare sthitáḥ | bráhmaṇá yajnarahitá jyotiḥ-śástra-paráñmukháḥ.*" || "In the Kali age, the Brahmans dwelling north of the Vindhya are deprived of the sacrifice and averse from Jyotiḥ-śástra:" and in this verse from another Dharma-śástra: "*Vindhyasya dakshiṇe bhága yatra Godávarí sthitá | tatra vedáś cha yajnáś cha bhavishyanti kalau yuge.*" || "In the Kali age the Vedas and sacrifices will have their home to the south of the Vindhya, in the region where flows the Godávarí." Similar expressions occur in the Law-book of Atri and in the Jaganmohana.

† As well as the latter's son, Dára Shakoh.

[334] Cf. C. F. Köppen's excellent work, *Die Religion des Buddha* (1857, 1859, 2 vols.).

Of the original signification of the word *buddha*, 'awakened' (sc. from error), 'enlightened,' as a complimentary title given to sages in general,* I have already more than once spoken (pp. 27, 167). I have also already remarked that the Buddhist doctrine was originally of purely philosophical tenor, identical with the system afterwards denominated the Sáṃkhya, and that it only gradually grew up into a religion in consequence of one of its representatives having turned with it to the people.† Buddhist tradition has itself preserved in individual traits a reminiscence of this origin of Buddha's doctrine, and of its posteriority to and dependence upon the Sáṃkhya philosophy.[335] Thus it describes Buddha as born at Kapila-vastu, 'the abode of Kapila,' and uniformly assigns to Kapila, the reputed founder of the Sáṃkhya system, a far earlier date. Again, it gives Máyá-dévi as the mother of Buddha, and here we have an unmistakable reference to the Máyá of the Sáṃkhya.[335a] Further, it makes Buddha, in his prior birth among the gods, bear the name Śvetaketu [336]—a name which, in the Śatapatha-Bráhmaṇa, is borne by one of the contemporaries of Káṇya Pataṃchala, with whom Kapila ought probably to be connected. And, lastly, it distinctly ranks Pañchaśikha, one of the main propagators of Kapila's doctrine, as a demigod or Gandharva. Of the names belonging to the teachers mentioned in Buddhist legend as contemporaries of Buddha, several also occur in Vedic

---

* The name *bhagavant*, which is also applied to Buddha in particular, is likewise a general title of honour, still preserved among the Brahmans to designate Ṛishis of every kind, and is bestowed very specially on Vishṇu or Krishṇa; while in the contracted form, *bhavant*, it actually supplies the place of the pronoun of the second person [*I. St.*, ii. 231, xiii. 351, 352].

† See *I. St.*, i. 435, 436, and above, pp.

[335] In the list of ancient sages at the beginning of the Charaka-Saṃhitá, we find mention, amongst others, of a "Gautamaḥ Sáṃkhyaḥ"—an expression which the modern editor interprets, "Bauddhaviśesha-Gautama-vyávrittaye!" But in truth there might perhaps actually be here an early complimentary allusion to Buddha! A "Párikshir (!) bhikshur Átreyaḥ" is named shortly after.

[335a] Máyá, however, belongs not to the Sáṃkhya, but specially to the Vedánta doctrine.

[336] Can the legend in the Mahá-Bhárata, xii. 2056, have any connection herewith—to the effect that Śvetaketu was disowned by his father Uddálaka because of his being "*mithyá viprán upacharan*"?—The name Śvetaketu further occurs among the prior births of Buddha, No. 370 in Westergaard's *Catalogus*, p. 40; but amongst these 539 *játakas* pretty nearly everything appears to be mentioned!

literature, but only in its third or Sútra stage, *e.g.*, Kátyáyana, Kátyáyaníputra, Kauṇḍinya, Ágniveśya, Maitráyaṇíputra, Vátsíputra,* Paushkarasádi; but no names of teachers belonging to the Bráhmaṇa period are found in these legends.[337] This is all the more significant, as Buddhism originated in the same region and district to which we have to allot the Śatapatha-Bráhmaṇa, for instance—the country, namely, of the Kosalas and Videhas, among the Śákyas and Lichhavis. The Sákyas are the family of which Buddha himself came: according to the legend,† they had immigrated from the west, from Potala, a city on the Indus. Whether this tradition be well founded or not, I am, at all events, disposed to connect them with the Śákáyanins who are referred to in the tenth book of the Śatapatha-Bráhmaṇa, and also with the Śákáyanyas of the Maitráyaṇa-Upanishad, which latter work propounds precisely the Buddhistic doctrine of the vanity of the world, &c. (see above, pp. 97, 137).[338] Among the Kosala-Videhas this doctrine, and in connection with it the practice of subsistence upon alms as Pravrájaka or Bhikshu, had been thoroughly disseminated by Yájnavalkya and their king Janaka; and a fruitful soil had thereby been prepared for Buddhism (see pp. 137, 147, 237). The doctrines promulgated by Yájnavalkya in the Vṛihad-Áraṇyaka are in fact completely Buddhistic, as also are those of the later Atharvopanishads belonging to the Yoga system. Nay, it would even seem as if Buddhist legend itself assigned Bud-

---

* To these names in *-putra*, which are peculiar to Buddhist legend and the *vaṅśa* of the Śatapatha-Bráhmaṇa, belongs also, in the former, the name Śáriputra, Śárikáputra.

[337] Unless Buddha's preceptor Áráḍa may have something to do with the Árálhi Saujáta of the Ait. Br., vii. 22 (?). The special conclusion to be based upon these name-synchronisms is that the advent of Buddha is to be set down as contemporaneous with the latest offsets of the Bráhmaṇa literature, *i.e.*, with the Áraṇyakas and older Sútras; *I. St.*, iii. 158 ff.

† See Csoma Körösi, *Journ. As. Soc. Beng.*, Aug. 1833; Wilson, *Ariana Antiq.*, p. 212: "The truth of the legend may be questioned, but it not improbably intimates some connection with the Śakas or Indo-Scythians, who were masters of Pattalene subsequent to the Greek princes of Bactria." The legend may possibly have been invented in the time of Kanerki, one of these Śaka kings, with a view to flatter him for the zeal he displayed on behalf of Buddhism.

[338] So, too, Johäntgen, *Ueber das Gesetzbuch des Manu*, p. 112, refers the traces of Buddhistic notions exhibited in that work specially to the school of the Mánavas, from which it sprang.

dha to a period exactly coincident with that of Janaka, and consequently of Yájnavalkya also; for it specifies a king Ajátaśatru as a contemporary of Buddha, and a prince of this name appears in the Vṛihad-Áraṇyaka and the Kaushítaki-Upanishad as the contemporary and rival of Janaka.[339] The other particulars given in Buddhist legend as to the princes of that epoch have, it is true, nothing analogous to them in the works just mentioned; the Ajataśatru of the Buddhists, moreover, is styled prince of Magadha, whereas he of the Vṛihad-Áraṇyaka and the Kaushítaki-Upanishad appears as the sovereign of the Káśis. (The name Ajátaśatru occurs elsewhere also, *e.g.*, as a title of Yudhishṭhira.) Still, there is the further circumstance that, in the fifth *káṇḍa* of the Śatapatha-Bráhmaṇa, Bhadrasena, the son of Ajátaśatru, is cursed by Áruṇi, the contemporary of Janaka and Yájnavalkya (see *I. St.*, i. 213); and, as the Buddhists likewise cite a Bhadrasena—at least, as the sixth successor of Ajátaśatru—we might almost be tempted to suppose that the curse in question may have been called forth by the heterodox anti-brahmanical opinions of this Bhadrasena. Nothing more precise can at present be made out; and it is possible that the two Ajátaśatrus and the two Bhadrasenas may simply be namesakes, and nothing more—as may be the case also with the Brahmadatta of the Vṛihad-Áraṇyaka and the two kings of the same name of Buddhist legend.—It is, at any rate, significant enough that in these legends the name of the Kuru-Pañchálas no longer occurs, either as a compound or separately;[340] whilst the Páṇḍavas are placed in Buddha's time, and appear as a wild mountain tribe, living by marauding and plunder.* Buddha's teaching was mainly fostered in the district of Magadha, which, as an extreme border province, was perhaps never completely

---

339 Highly noteworthy also is the peculiar agreement between Buddhist legends and those of the Vṛihad-Áraṇyaka in regard to the six teachers whom Ajátaśatru and Janaka had before they were instructed by Buddha and Yájnavalkya respectively; see *I. St.*, iii. 156, 157.

340 The Kurus are repeatedly mentioned by the Southern Buddhists; see *I. St.*, iii. 160, 161.

* The allusion to the five Páṇḍus in the introduction of the Lalita-Vistara (Foucaux, p. 26) is probably, with the whole passage in which it occurs, an interpolation, being totally irreconcilable with the other references to the Páṇḍavas contained in the work.

brahmanised; so that the native inhabitants always retained a kind of influence, and now gladly seized the opportunity to rid themselves of the brahmanical hierarchy and the system of caste. The hostile allusions to these Mágadhas in the Atharva-Saṃhitá (see p. 147—and in the thirtieth book of the Vájasaneyi-Saṃhitá? pp. 111, 112) might indeed possibly refer to their anti-brahmanical tendencies in times antecedent to Buddhism: the similar allusions in the Sáma-Sútras, on the contrary (see p. 79),[341] are only to be explained as referring to the actual flourishing of Buddhism in Magadha.*

With reference to the tradition as to Buddha's age, the various Buddhist eras which commence with the date of his death exhibit the widest divergence from each other. Amongst the Northern Buddhists fourteen different accounts are found, ranging from B.C. 2422 to B.C. 546; the eras of the Southern Buddhists, on the contrary, mostly agree with each other, and all of them start from B.C. 544 or 543. This latter chronology has been recently adopted as the correct one, on the ground that it accords best with historical conditions, although even it displays a discrepancy of sixty-six years as regards the historically authenticated date of Chandragupta. But the Northern Buddhists, the Tibetans as well as the Chinese—independently altogether of their era, which may be of later origin than this particular tradition †—agree in placing the reign of king Kanishka, Kanerki, under whom the third (or fourth) Buddhist council was held, 400 years after Buddha's death; and on the evidence of coins, this Kanishka reigned down to A.D. 40 (see Lassen, *I. AK.*, ii. 412, 413), which would bring down the date of Buddha's death to about the year B.C. 370. Similarly, the Tibetans place Nágárjuna—who, according to the Rája-taraṃgiṇí, was contemporaneous with Kanishka—400 years after the death of Buddha; whereas the Southern Buddhists make him live 500 years after that event. Nothing like

341 And on another occasion, in the Baudháyana-Sútra also; see note 126.

* For other points of contact in the later Vedic literature, see pp. 129, 138 [98, 99, 151]. Lassen has drawn attention, in *I. AK.*, ii. 79, to the Buddhistic names of the mountains about Rájagriha, the capital of Magadha, found in Mahá-Bhárata, ii. 799.

† Which is met with so early as the seventh century A.D., in Hiuan Thsang.

positive certainty, therefore, is for the present attainable.[342] *À priori,* however, it seems probable that the council which was held in the reign of king Kanerki, and from which the existing shape of the sacred scriptures of the Northern Buddhists nominally dates, really took place 400, and not so much as 570, years after Buddha's death. It seems probable also that the Northern Buddhists, who alone possess these Scriptures complete, preserved more authentic information regarding the circumstances of the time of their redaction—and consequently also regarding the date of Nágárjuna—than did the Southern Buddhists, to whom this redaction is unknown, and whose scriptures exist only in a more ancient form which is alleged to have been brought to Ceylon so early as B.C. 245, and to have been there committed to writing about the year B.C. 80 (Lassen, *I. AK.*, ii. 435).—Of these various eras, the only one the actual employment of which at an early period can at present be proved is the Ceylonese, which, like the other Southern eras, begins in B.C. 544. Here the period indicated is the close of the fourth century A.D.; since the Dípavaṅsa, a history of Ceylon in Páli verse, which was written at that date, appears to make use of this era, whereby naturally it becomes invested with a certain authority.

If, now, we strip the accounts of Buddha's personality of all supernatural accretion, we find that he was a king's son, who, penetrated by the nothingness of earthly things, forsook his kindred in order thenceforth to live on alms, and devote himself in the first place to contemplation, and thereafter to the instruction of his fellow-men. His doctrine was,* that "men's lots in this life are conditioned and regulated by the actions of a previous existence, that no evil deed remains without punishment, and no good deed without reward. From this fate, which dominates the individual within the circle of transmigration, he can only

---

[342] Nor have the subsequent discussions of this topic by Max Müller (1859), *Hist. A. S. L.*, p. 264 ff., by Westergaard (1860), *Ueber Buddha's Todesjahr* (Breslau, 1862), and by Kern, *Over de Jaartelling der Zuidel. Buddhisten* (1874), so far yielded any definite result; cf. my *I. Str.*, ii. 216; *Lit. C. Bl.*, 1874, p. 719.

* Though it is nowhere set forth in so succinct a form: it results, however, as the sum and substance of the various legends.

escape * by directing his will towards the one thought of liberation from this circle, by remaining true to this aim, and striving with steadfast zeal after meritorious action only; whereby finally, having cast aside all passions, which are regarded as the strongest fetters in this prison-house of existence, he attains the desired goal of complete emancipation from re-birth." This teaching contains, in itself, absolutely nothing new; on the contrary, it is entirely identical with the corresponding Brahmanical doctrine; only the fashion in which Buddha proclaimed and disseminated it was something altogether novel and unwonted. For while the Bráhmans taught solely in their hermitages, and received pupils of their own caste only, he wandered about the country with his disciples, preaching his doctrine to the whole people,† and—although still recognising the existing caste-system, and explaining its origin, as the Bráhmans themselves did, by the dogma of rewards and punishments for prior actions—receiving as adherents men of every caste without distinction. To these he assigned rank in the community according to their age and understanding, thus abolishing within the community itself the social distinctions that birth entailed, and opening up to all men the prospect of emancipation from the trammels of their birth. This of itself sufficiently explains the enormous success that attended his doctrine: the oppressed all turned to him as their redeemer.‡ If by this alone he struck at the root of the Brahmanical hierarchy, he did so not less by declar-

* See Schmidt, *Dsanglun der Weise und der Thor*, Pref., p. xxxiii. ff.

† See Lassen, *I. AK.*, ii. 440, 441; Burnouf, *Introd. à l'Histoire du Buddhisme Indien*, pp. 152–212.

‡ Under these circumstances, it is indeed surprising that it should have been possible to dislodge Buddhism from India. The great numbers and influence of the Brahman caste do not alone completely account for the fact; for, in proportion to the whole people, the Brahmans were after all only a very small minority. My idea is that the strict morality required by Buddhism of its adherents became in the long run irksome to the people; the original cult, too, was probably too simple. The Brahmans knew how to turn both circumstances to the best advantage. Kṛishṇa-worship, as they organised it, offered far more satisfaction to the sensual tastes of the people; while the various cults of the Śaktis, or female deities, most likely all date from a time shortly preceding the expulsion of the Buddhists from India.

ing sacrificial worship—the performance of which was the exclusive privilege of the Brahmans—to be utterly unavailing and worthless, and a virtuous disposition and virtuous conduct, on the contrary, to be the only real means of attaining final deliverance. He did so, further, by the fact that, wholly penetrated by the truth of his opinions, he claimed to be in possession of the highest enlightenment, and so by implication rejected the validity of the Veda as the supreme source of knowledge. These two doctrines also were in no way new; till then, however, they had been the possession of a few anchorites; never before had they been freely and publicly proclaimed to all.

Immediately after Buddha's death there was held, according to the tradition, a council of his disciples in Magadha, at which the Buddhist sacred scriptures were compiled. These consist of three divisions (*Piṭakas*), the first of which—the *Sútras**—comprises utterances and discourses of Buddha himself, conversations with his hearers; while the *Vinaya* embraces rules of discipline, and the *Abhidharma*, dogmatic and philosophical discussions. A hundred years later, according to the tradition of the Southern, but a hundred and ten according to that of the Northern Buddhists, a second council took place at Páṭaliputra for the purpose of doing away with errors of discipline which had crept in. With regard to the third council, the accounts of the Northern and Southern Buddhists are at issue. (Lassen, *I. AK.*, ii. 232.) According to the former, it was held in the seventeenth year of the reign of Aśoka, a year which we have to identify with B.C. 246—which, however, is utterly at variance with the equally traditional assertion that it took place 218 years after Buddha's death, *i.e.*, in B.C. 326. At this council the precepts of the law were restored to their ancient purity, and it was at the same time resolved to send forth missionaries to propagate the doctrines of Buddha. The Northern Buddhists, on the contrary, place the third council 400 years after Buddha's death, in the reign of Kanishka, one

* This name alone might suggest that Buddha himself flourished in the Sútra, not in the Bráhmaṇa, period.

of the Turushka (Śaka) kings of Kashmír, who, as we have seen, is established, on numismatic evidence, to have reigned until A.D. 40. The sacred scriptures of the Northern Buddhists, which are alleged to have been fixed at this council, are still extant, not merely in the Sanskṛit originals themselves, which have recently been recovered in Nepál,* but also in a complete Tibetan translation, bearing the name *Kágyur*, and consisting of one hundred volumes; † as well as, partially at least, in Chinese, Mongolian, Kalmuck, and other translations. The scriptures of the Southern Buddhists, on the contrary, are not extant in Sanskṛit at all. With reference to them, it is alleged that one year after their arrangement at the third council, that of Aśoka (*i.e.*, in the year B.C. 245), they were brought by Mahendra, the apostle of Ceylon, to that island, and by him translated

---

* By the British Resident there, B. H. Hodgson, who presented MSS. of them to the Asiatic Societies of Calcutta, London, and Paris. The Paris collection was further enriched in 1837 with copies which the *Société Asiatique* caused to be made through Hodgson's agency. This led Burnouf to write his great work, *Introduction à l'Histoire du Buddhisme Indien*, Paris, 1844 [followed in the end of 1852 by his not less important production, the translation of the *Lotus de la Bonne Loi*; see *I. St.*, iii. 135 ff., 1864. The British Museum and the University Library in Cambridge are now also in possession of similar MSS. A catalogue, compiled by Cowell and Eggeling, of the Hodgson collection of Buddhist Sanskṛit MSS. in the possession of the Royal Asiatic Society has just appeared.]

† Regarding the compass and contents of this Tibetan translation, our first (and hitherto almost our sole) information was supplied by a Hungarian traveller, Csoma Körösi, the Anquetil du Perron of this century, a man of rare vigour and energy, who resided for a very long time in Tibet, and who by his Tibetan grammar and dictionary has conquered this language for European science. Two pretty extensive works from the Kágyur have already been edited and translated: the *Dsanglun* in St. Petersburg by Schmidt, and the *Rgya Cher Rol Pa* (Lalita-Vistara) in Paris by Foucaux. [Since then L. Feer, especially, has rendered valuable service in this field by his *Textes tirés du Kandjour* (1864–71, 11 parts); also Schiefner, *e.g.*, by his editions of the *Vimala-praśnottara-ratnamálá* (1858)—the Sanskṛit text of which was subsequently edited by Foucaux (cf. also *I. Str.*, i. 210 ff.)—and of the *Bharatæ Responsa* (1875). Schiefner has further just issued a translation from the Kágyur of a group of Buddhist tales, under the title, *Mahákátyáyana und König Tschanda Pradjota*. The ninth of these stories contains (see p. vii. 26 ff.) what is now probably the oldest version of the so-called 'Philosopher's Ride,' which here, as in the Pañchatantra (iv. 6), is related of the king himself; whereas in an Arabian tale of the ninth century, communicated in the appendix (p. 66) and in our own mediæval version, it is told of the king's wise counsellor.

into the native Singhalese.[343] Not until some 165 years later (*i.e.*, in B.C. 80) were they consigned to writing in that language, having been propagated in the interval by oral transmission only.[344] After a further period of 500 years (namely, between A.D. 410 and 432) they were at length rendered into the sacred Páli tongue (cf. Lassen, *I. AK.*, ii. 435), in which they are now extant, and from which in turn translations into several of the languages of Farther India were subsequently made.* As to the relation of these scriptures of the Southern Buddhists to those of their Northern co-religionists, little is at present known beyond the fact that both present in common the general division into three parts (*Sútra, Vinaya, Abhidharma*). In extent they can hardly compare with the latter,[345] nor even, according to the foregoing exposition,† in authenticity.[346] Unfortunately but little information has as yet

---

343 It was not the Páli text itself, but only the oral commentary (*atthakathá*) belonging to it, which was translated into Singhalese. (See the following notes.) So at least it is stated in the tradition in the Mahávaṅsa. For the rest, it is extremely doubtful how much of the *present* Tipiṭaka may have actually been in existence then. For if we compare the statements contained in the Bhabra missive—addressed by king Piyadasi to the synod of Magadha, which was then engaged in the accommodation of schisms that had sprung up—relative to the sacred texts (*dhamma-paliyáyáni*) as they then stood, a mighty difference becomes apparent! See Burnouf, *Lotus*, p. 724 ff.; *I. St.*, iii. 172 ff.

344 See Mahávaṅsa, chap. xxxiii. p. 207; Turnour, *Preface*, p. xxix.; Muir, *Orig. Sansk. Texts*, ii. 69, 70 (57^2); *I. St.*, v. 26.

* That is to say, translated back again(?); for this sacred language must be the same that Mahendra brought with him? [Not the texts themselves, only their interpretation (*atthakathá*) was now rendered back again into Páli, namely, by Buddhaghosha, who came from Magadha, and resided a number of years in Ceylon.]

345 The extent of the Páli Tipiṭaka is also very considerable; see the accounts in Hardy's *Eastern Monachism*, pp. 167–170. On the earliest mention of the name Tipiṭaka in a Sanskṛit inscription of Buddhaghosha at Kanheri (in the *Journ. Bombay Br. R. A. S.*, v. 14), see *I. St.*, v. 26.

† If indeed the case be as here represented! I can in the meanwhile only report. [Unfortunately, I had trusted to Lassen's account, in the passage cited in the text, instead of referring to Turnour himself (pp. xxix. xxx.); the true state of the case (see the preceding notes) I have set forth in *I. St.*, iii. 254.]

346 The question which of the two redactions, that of the Northern or that of the Southern Buddhists, is the more original has been warmly debated by Turnour and Hodgson. (The latter's articles on the subject are now collected in a convenient form in his *Essays on Languages, Lit. and Rel. of Nepal and Tibet*, 1874.) Burnouf, also, has discussed the question in his *Lotus de la Bonne Loi*, p. 862 ff., and has decided, in principle no doubt rightly, that both possess an equal title. Compare here *I. St.*, iii. 176 ff., where certain

been imparted regarding their contents, &c.* Southern Buddhism, however, supplies us with copious and possibly trustworthy accounts of the first centuries of its existence, as well as of the growth of the Buddhist faith generally, a Páli historical literature having grown up in Ceylon at a comparatively early period,[340a] one of the most important works of which—the Mahávaṅsa of Mahánáma, composed towards A.D. 480—has already been published, both in the original text and in an English version.

---

doubts are urged by me against some of his assumptions, as also specially with regard to Buddhaghosha's highly significant part in the shaping of the Páli Tipiṭaka. Kern has recently, in his Essay *Over de Jaartelling der zuidelijke Buddhisten*, gone far beyond those objections of mine; but, as it seems to me, he goes further than the case requires; see *Lit. C. Bl.*, 1874, p. 719. At any rate, even fully acknowledging the part belonging to Buddhaghosha, it appears to me now that the claim of the Páli Tipiṭaka to superior originality is, after all, far stronger than that of the Sanskṛit texts of the Northern Buddhists, from which, as from the sacred writings of the Jainas, it is distinguished, greatly to its advantage, by its comparative simplicity and brevity. Cf. also S. Beal's very pertinent observations in the *Ind. Antiq.*, iv. 90.

* The most authentic information as yet is to be found in the Introduction to G. Turnour's edition of the Mahávaṅsa (1835, Ceylon) and in the scattered essays of this scholar; also, though only in very general outline, in Westergaard's Catalogue of the Copenhagen Indian MSS. (1846, Havniæ), which comprise a tolerable number of these Páli works, purchased by the celebrated Rask in Ceylon. Clough's writings, too, contain much that bears upon this subject: also Spiegel's *Anecdota Palica*. Exceedingly copious information regarding Southern Buddhism is contained in a work that has just reached me, by R. Spence Hardy, *Eastern Monachism, an Account of the Origin, Laws, &c., of the Order of Mendicants founded by Gotama Buddha*, London, 1850, 444 pp. The author was twenty years a Wesleyan missionary in Ceylon, and appears to have employed this time to excellent purpose. [This was followed in 1853 by his *Manual of Buddhism*, also a very valuable work. —The study of Páli and its literature has recently taken a great spring, particularly through the labours of V. Fausböll (*Dhammapada*, 1855; *Five Játakas*, 1861; *Dasarathajátaka*, 1871; *Ten Játakas*, 1872; *The Játaka, together with its Commentary*, Pt. i., 1875), James de Alwis (*Introduction to Kachcháyana's Grammar*, 1863; *Attanagaluvaṅsa*, 1866), P. Grimblot (*Extraits du Paritta*, 1870), L. Feer (*Daharasutta* and others of these Páli-suttas in his *Textes tirés du Kandjour*, 1869 ff.), Joh. Minayeff (*Páṭimokkhasutta* and *Vuttodaya*, 1869; *Grammaire Palie*, 1874, Russian edition 1872), E. Kuhn (*Kachcháyanappakaraṇæ Specimen*, 1869, 1871; *Beiträge zur Páli-Grammatik*, 1875), E. Senart (*Grammaire de Kachcháyana*, 1871), R. Childers (*Khuddakapáṭha*, 1869; *Dictionary of the Páli Language*, 1872–75), M. Coomára Svámy (*Suttanipáta*, 1874); to which may be added the grammatical writings of W. Storck (1858, 1862) and Fr. Müller (1867–69).

[340a] Northern Buddhism has likewise found its historians. The Tibetan Táranátha (see note 350) cites as his precursors Bhaṭaghaṭi, Indradatta, Kshemendrabhadra.

With respect now to the scriptures of the Northern Buddhists, the Sanskṛit originals, namely—for it is these alone that concern us here—we must, in the first place, keep in view that, even according to the tradition, their existing text belongs only to the first century of our era; so that, even although there should be works among them dating from the two earlier councils, yet these were in any case subjected to revision at the third. In the next place, it is *à priori* improbable—nor is it indeed directly alleged—that the whole of the existing works owed their origin to this third council, and amongst them there must certainly be many belonging to a later period. And lastly, we must not even assume that all the works translated in the Tibetan Kágyur were already in existence at the time when translations into Tibetan began to be made (in the seventh century); for the Kágyur was not completed all at once, but was only definitively fixed after a prolonged and gradual growth.* From these considerations alone, it is abundantly plain how cautious we ought to be in making use of these works. But there is still more to be borne in mind. For even supposing the origin of the most ancient of them really to date from the first and second councils,[347] still, to assume that they were recorded in writing so early as this is not only *prima facie* questionable, but is, besides, distinctly opposed to analogy, since we are expressly informed that, with the Southern Buddhists, the consignment to writing only took place in the year B.C. 80, long subsequent to both councils. The main purpose of the third council under Kanishka may possibly just have been to draw up written records; had such records been already in existence, Buddhism could hardly have been split up thus early into eighteen different sects, as we are told was the case in Kanishka's time, only 400 years after Buddha's death. Why, during all the eighteen centuries that have since elapsed no such amount of schism has sprung up, evidently because a written basis was then secured. Lastly, one important point which must not be

---

* According to Csoma Körösi, the Tibetan translations date from the seventh to the thirteenth centuries, principally from the ninth.

[347] The data contained in the Bhabra missive as to the *dhamma-paliyáyáni* as they then stood render such a supposition extremely doubtful here, just as in the case of the Páli Tipiṭaka (see note 343).

lost sight of in estimating the authenticity of the existing Buddhist scriptures is the circumstance that the sources from which they were drawn were in a different language. True, we cannot make out with absolute certainty in what language Buddha taught and preached; but as it was to the people he addressed himself, it is in the highest degree probable that he spoke in the vernacular idiom. Again, it was in Magadha * that the first council of his disciples assembled, and it was doubtless conducted in the dialect of this country, which indeed passes as the sacred language of Buddhism. The same remark applies to the second council, as well as to the one which, according to the Southern Buddhists, is the third, both of which were likewise held in Magadha.† Mahendra, who converted Ceylon in the year following this third council, took with him to that island the Mágadhí language, afterwards called Páli: ‡ this, too, is the dialect in which the inscriptions of this period, which at least bespeak Buddhistic influence, are composed.[348] At the last council, on the contrary, which falls some 300 years later, and at which the existing scriptures of the Northern Buddhists are alleged to have

---

* In the old capital (Rájagṛiha).

† In the new capital (Páṭaliputra).

‡ That Páli could have been developed in Ceylon from an imported Sanskṛit is altogether inconceivable.

348 The edicts of Piyadasi present themselves to us in three distinct dialects. One of these, that of Dhauli, exhibits a number of the peculiarities which distinctively belong to the Ardhamágadhí of the Jainas, and the dialect designated Mágadhí by the Prákrit grammarians. It is in it that the Bhabra missive addressed to the third council is composed—a circumstance which conclusively proves that it was then the official language of Buddhism, and, in point of fact, Mágadhí (since Dhauli belongs geographically to this district); see *I. St.*, iii. 180, and my Essay on the Bhagavatí of the Jainas, i. 396. But then, on the other hand, this dialect displays a particularly marked divergence from Páli, the language which has come down to us officially under the name of Mágadhí, and which presents special features of resemblance to that dialect, rather, which is employed in the inscriptions of Girnar. The question has therefore been raised whether Páli is really entitled to the name Mágadhí, which in the Páli literature is applied to it, or whether it may not have received this title merely from motives of ecclesiastical policy, having reference to the significance of the land of Magadha in the history of Buddhism. Westergaard even surmises (*Ueber den ältesten Zeitraum der indischen Geschichte*, p. 87 n., 1862) that Páli is identical with the dialect of Ujjayiní, the mother-tongue of Mahendra, who was born there; and Ernst Kuhn (*Beiträge zur Páli-Grammatik*, p. 7, 1875) adopts this opinion. But Pischel (*Jenaer Lit. Zeit.*, 1875, p. 316) and Childers (*Páli Dict.*, Preface, p. vii.) pronounce against it.

been compiled, the language employed for this purpose was not Mágadhí, but Sanskṛit, although not the purest. The reason of this lies simply in the locality. For this concluding council was not held in Magadha, nor even in Hindustan at all, whose rulers were not then favourably disposed towards Buddhism, but in Kashmír, a district which—partly no doubt in consequence of its being peopled exclusively by Aryan tribes,* but partly also (see pp. 26, 45, 178) because, like the North-West of India generally, it has to be regarded as a chief seat of the cultivation of Indian grammar—had preserved its language purer than those Aryans had been able to do who had emigrated to India, and there mingled with the native inhabitants. Those priests,† therefore, who here undertook the compilation and recording in writing of the sacred scriptures were, if not accomplished grammarians, yet in all probability sufficiently conversant with grammar to be able to write passable Sanskṛit.‡

Agreeably to what has just been set forth,[349] it is in the highest degree risky to regard, as has hitherto been done,

---

* The Greeks and Scythians were both too scanty in numbers, and too short a time in close contact with the natives, to exercise any influence in the way of modifying the language.

† And it was evidently priests, educated men therefore, who formed the third council. In the first two, laymen may have taken part, but the Buddhistic hierarchy had had time to develop sufficiently in the interval.

‡ Burnouf thinks differently, *Hist. du Buddh.*, pp. 105, 106, as also Lassen, *I. AK.*, ii. 9, 491–493 [but see *I. St.*, iii. 139, 179 ff.].

349 Beside the two branches of Buddhistic literature discussed in the foregoing pages—the Páli texts of the Southern and the Sanskṛit texts of the Northern Buddhists—there stands a third group, occupying, from its original constitution, a kind of intermediate place between the other two—namely, the Ardhamágadhí texts of the Jainas. The sect of the Jainas is in all probability to be regarded as one of the schismatic sects that branched off from Buddhism in the first centuries of its existence. The legendary narratives of the personal activity of its founder, Mahávíra, not only refer it exclusively to the same district which Buddhism also recognises as its holy land, but they, moreover, display so close an affinity to the accounts of Buddha's ministry that we cannot but recognise in the two groups of narratives merely varying forms of common reminiscences. Another indication that the Jaina sect arose in this way out of Buddhism—although by some it has even been regarded as of pre-Buddhistic origin—is afforded by the circumstance, amongst others, that its sacred texts are styled, not *Sútras*, but *Añgas*, and consequently, in contradistinction to the oldest Buddhist texts, which date from the Vedic *Sútra* period, belong rather to the *Añga* stage, that is to say, to the period when the Añgas or Vedáñgas, works posterior to the Vedic Sútras,

the data yielded by a Buddhistic literature fashioned in this way as valid for the epoch of Buddha himself, which is removed from the last council by an interval of four, or, if we accept the Southern chronology, of nearly six, centuries. Oral traditions, committed to writing in a different language, after such a series of years, and moreover only extant in a mass of writings that lie several centuries apart, and of which the oldest portions have still to be critically sifted out, can only be used with extreme caution; and *à priori* the data they furnish serve, not so much to characterise the epoch about which they tell, as rather the epoch, in particular, in which they received their present shape. But however doubtful, according to

were produced. But there is a further circumstance which is quite conclusive as to this point—namely, that the language in which these texts are composed, and which, according to the scholiasts, is Ardha-mágadhí, exhibits a more developed and considerably later phase than the language of the Páli texts, to which, in its turn, the Páli scholia expressly apply the designation Mágadhí. (At the same time, there are also dialectic differences between the two.) See my paper on the Bhagavatí of the Jainas, pp. 441, 373, 396 ff., 416. To the eleven principal Angas have to be added a large number of other writings, styled *Upánga*, *Múla-Sútra*, *Kalpa-Sútra*, &c. An enumeration of the entire set, showing a total of fifty works, consisting of about 600,000 *ślokas*, may be seen in Rájendra Lála Mitra's *Notices of Sanskrit MSS.*, iii. 67 ff., 1874. Of these texts—our knowledge of the Jainas is otherwise derived from Brahmanic sources only—all that has hitherto been published is a fragment of the fifth Anga or Bhagavatí-Sútra, dating perhaps from the first centuries of our era, edited by myself (1866–67). In *I. St.*, x. 254 ff. (1867), I have also given an account of the *Súrya-prajnapti*, or seventh Upánga-Sútra, a commentary on which is said to have been composed by Bhadrabáhusvámin, author of the Kalpa-Sútra, a work seemingly written in the seventh century. Lastly, there is a translation by Stevenson (1848) of this Kalpa-Sútra itself, which stands thirtieth in the list of the sacred texts. Cf. also S. J. Warren, *Over de godsdienstige en wijsgeerige Begrippen der Jainas*, 1875. Thanks to G. Bühler's friendly exertions, the Royal Library in Berlin has lately acquired possession of nearly all these fifty sacred texts, with or without commentaries, and in good old MSS., so that we may hope soon to be better informed regarding them.—But the Jainas have also a great significance in connection with Sanskrit literature, more especially for grammar and lexicography, as well as on account of the historical and legendary matter which they have preserved (see above, p. 214, and cf. my paper on the Śatrumjaya Máhátmya, 1858). One of their most honoured names is that of Hemachandra, who flourished in the time of the Gurjara prince Kumárapála (1088–1172). Under the title Yoga-Śástra he composed a compendium of the Jaina doctrines in twelve *prakáśas*, the first four of which, treating of their ethics, have recently been edited and translated by Ernst Windisch (*Z. D. M. G.*, xxviii., 185 ff., 1874).

this view, are the validity and authority of these writings in reference to the subjects which they have hitherto been taken to illustrate, they are nevertheless important, on the other hand, for the history of the inner development of Buddhism itself; though even here, of course, their trustworthiness is altogether relative. For the many marvellous stories they recount both of Buddha himself and of his disciples and other adherents, as well as the extravagant mythology gradually developed in them, produce upon the whole the impression of a wild and formless chaos of fantastic inventions.

Our chief object must now, of course, be to establish a relative chronology and order of sequence amongst these various writings—a task which Burnouf, whose researches are our sole authority on the subject,* also set himself, and which he has executed with great judgment and tolerable conclusiveness. And, first, of the *Sútras*, or accounts of Buddha himself. Burnouf divides these into two classes: the *simple Sútras*, and the so-called *Mahávaipulya-* or *Maháyána-Sútras*, which he declares to be the more modern of the two in point of language, form, and doctrine. As far as the latter point is concerned, he is no doubt right. For, in the first place, in the Mahávaipulya-Sútras Buddha appears almost exclusively surrounded by gods and Bodhisattvas (beings peculiar to the Buddhistic mythology); whereas in the simple Sútras it is human beings who mostly form his following, with whom gods are only now and then associated. And, in the second place, the simple Sútras do not exhibit any trace of those doctrines which are not common Buddhistic property, but belong to the Northern Buddhists only, as, for example, the worship of Amitábha, Mañjuśrí, Avalokiteśvara, Ádibuddha,† and the Dhyánibuddhas; and further, do not contain any trace of mystic spells and magic formulas, all of which are found, and in abundance, in the

* I cannot refrain from expressing here, in a few words at least, my sincere and profound sorrow that now, as these sheets, which I would so gladly have submitted to his judgment, are passing through the press, Eugène Burnouf has been taken from among us. His premature death is an irreparable loss to learning, as well as to all who knew him, and, which is the same thing, revered and loved him.

† The word is found in a totally different sense in those portions of the Máṇḍúkyopanishad which are due to Gauḍapáda.

Mahávaipulya-Sútras only. But whether the circumstance that the language of the lengthy poetical pieces, which are inserted with special frequency in these last, appears in a much more degenerated form—to wit, a medley of Sanskṛit, Prákṛit, and Páli—than is the case with the prose portions, is to be taken as a proof of the posteriority of the Mahávaipulya-Sútras, does not seem to be quite so certain as yet. Do these poetical portions, then, really agree so completely, in form and substance, with the prose text in respect to the several points just instanced, that they may be regarded as merely an amplification or recapitulation of it? Or are they not rather distinguished from it precisely in these points, so that we might regard them as fragments of older traditions handed down in verse, exactly like the analogous pieces which occur so often in the Bráhmaṇas?* In the latter case we should have to regard them as proof, rather, that the Buddhist legends, &c., were not originally composed in Sanskṛit, but in vernacular dialects. From the account of the

* We must be content with simply putting the question, as we are still unfortunately without the Sanskṛit text of even a single one of these Sútras; the sole exception being an insignificant fragment from the *Lalita-vistara*, one of the Mahávaipulya-Sútras, communicated by Foucaux at the end of his edition of the Tibetan translation of this work. [The entire text of the Lalita-vistara, in twenty-seven chapters, has since appeared in the *Bibl. Ind.*, edited by Rájendra Lála Mitra (1853 ff.); the translation breaks off at chapter iii. Foucaux published the fourth chapter of the *Sad-dharma-puṇḍaríka* in 1852, and Leon Feer an Avadána, named *Pratihárya*, in 1867. Lastly, the *Káraṇḍa-vyúha*, a terribly inflated Mahâyána-Sútra, in honour of Avalokiteśvara, has been edited by Satyavrata Sámáśrami (Calc., 1873). A translation of the Lalita-vistara, begun by S. Lefmann in 1874, embraces, so far, the first five chapters, and is accompanied with very copious notes.—The conjecture expressed above as to the poetical portions had previously been advanced—although when I wrote I was not aware of the fact—in the *Journ. As. Soc. Beng.*, 1851, p. 283, see *I. St.*, iii. 140. It was subsequently worked out in greater detail by Rájendra L. Mitra, in a special essay on the dialect of these Gáthás, likewise in *Journ. As. Soc. Beng.* (1854, No. 6). Here the date of their composition is even carried back to the period immediately succeeding Buddha's death, see Muir, *Orig. S. Texts*, ii.[2] 115 ff. Kern, *Over de Jaartelling*, p. 108 ff., does not see in these Gáthás any peculiar dialect, but merely later versions of stanzas originally composed in pure Prákṛit. Lastly, Edward Müller, in his tract, *Der Dialekt der Gáthá des Lalita-vistara* (Weimar, 1874) perceives in them the work of poets who were not quite at home in Sanskṛit, and who extended to it the laxness of their own vernacular.

Chinese traveller, Fa Hian, who made a pilgrimage from China to India and back in A.D. 399–414, it would appear that the Mahávaipulya-Sútras were then already pretty widely diffused, since he mentions several of the doctrines peculiar to them as extensively studied.[350]

Of the *simple* Sútras, it is at least possible, in the absence of evidence, that such as are concerned solely with Buddha's personality may be more ancient than those relating also to persons who lived some hundreds of years later; but beyond this we cannot at present determine anything. Their contents are of a somewhat multifarious description, and for the several divisions we also find special technical designations.* They contain either simple legends, styled *Ityukta* and *Vyákaraṇa* (corresponding to

---

[350] The accounts of Fa Hian are far surpassed in moment by those of Hiuan Thsang, who travelled over India in the years 629–645 A.D. Of special importance also are the Chinese translations of Buddhistic works, which are nearly all based upon the texts of the Northern Buddhists, and some of which profess to be very ancient. Of four such translations of the Lalitavistara, the first is said to have been made at a date so early as A.D. 70–76, the second in A.D. 308, and the third in 652; see on this *I. St.*, iii. 140, viii. 326. Similarly, the Sad-dharma-puṇḍarîka is said to have been thrice translated; first in A.D. 280, next in A.D. 397–402, and again in A.D. 601–605. Beal, in the *Indian Antiq.*, iv. 90, 91, mentions not only a translation of the *Brahmajála-Sútra* of the year A.D. 420, but also a whole set of fifty Sútras (amongst them, *e.g.*, the *Sámajátaka*) "translated at different dates, from A.D. 70 to 600, and by various scholars, all of them from Sanskṛit or Páli,"—all, therefore, from the Indian original,—whereas the translations of later times were mostly derived through the medium of the Tibetan. For the criticism of the respective texts, fuller particulars of these, in part so ancient, translations, would of course be of great importance. Of one of these works, a version of the *Abhinishkramaṇa-Sútra*, a complete translation has recently been published by Beal, under the title, *The Romantic Legend of Śákya Buddha*, 1875. The special points of relation here found to Christian legends are very striking. The question which party was the borrower Beal properly leaves undetermined, yet in all likelihood we have here simply a similar case to that of the appropriation of Christian legends by the worshippers of Kṛishṇa.—Highly important for the history of Northern Buddhism is W. Wassiljew's work, drawn from Tibeto-Chinese sources, *Der Buddhismus*, 1860, as also Táranátha's History of Buddhism in India, a work composed so late as 1608, but resting upon older, and in part Sanskṛit, authorities: rendered into Russian by Wassiljew, — Tibetan text, with German version, by Schiefner, 1869; cf. also Lassen, *I. AK.*, ii. 6, note.

* According to Spiegel, in his review, of which I have frequently availed myself here, of Burnouf's work, in the *Jahrb. für wiss. Kritik*, 1845, p. 547, most of these names are also found among the Southern Buddhists.

the Itihása-Puráṇas in the Bráhmaṇas); or legends in the form of parables, styled *Avadána*, in which we find many elements of the later animal-fables;[351] or further, tales of presages and wonders, *Adbhuta-dharma;* or again, single stanzas or songs of several stanzas (*Geya* and *Gáthá*) serving to corroborate previous statements; or lastly, special instruction in, and discussion of, definite topics, denominated *Upadeśa* and *Nidána*. All these reappear in a similar way, only in a much more antique guise and under different names,* in the Bráhmaṇas and Áraṇyakas, as well as in the prose legends interspersed here and there throughout the Mahá-Bhárata, which in style also (though not in language) offer the greatest resemblance to these Buddhistic Sútras. Quite peculiar to these latter,† however, are the passages called *Játakas*, which treat of the prior births of Buddha and the Bodhisattvas.

Now those data in the Sútras which have hitherto been taken as valid for Buddha's time, but which we can only consider as valid, primarily, for the time when the Sútras were composed, are chiefly of a kind bearing upon the history of the Indian religion. For just as Buddha recognised the existence of caste, so, too, he naturally recognised the then existing Hindú Pantheon.‡ But it must not by any means be imagined that in Buddha's time this Pantheon had attained to that phase of development which we here find in the Sútras, assuming that we follow the

---

[351] From the Chinese translation Stan. Julien has published quite a collection of such stories, for the most part very short (*Les Avadánas, Contes et Apologues Indiens*, 1859). The high importance of these, as well as of the Buddhistic Játaka and other stories generally, in the literature of the fable and fairy-tale, is shown in full relief by Benfey in the introduction to his translation of the Pañchatantra.

* Only Gáthá and Upadeśa (Ádeśa at least) occur also in the Bráhmaṇas.

† Although connecting links are found here and there in the Mahá-Bhárata also, especially in the twelfth book. Indeed, many of the Buddhist legends stand distinctly related to corresponding Brahmanic popular tales and legends, which they have simply transformed [or conversely, into which they have themselves been transformed] to suit the object in view.

‡ Lassen's assertion (*I. AK.*, ii. 453) that "Buddha recognised no gods" refers only to the circumstance that they too are regarded by him as subjected to the eternal succession of existence; their existence itself he in no way denied, for in the doctrines put into his mouth there is constant reference to them. [He abolished their significance, however, as he did that of caste.]

Southern chronology and place Buddha in the sixth century B.C., that is, doubtless, in the period of the Bráhmaṇas,—works in which a totally different Pantheon prevails. But if, on the other hand, he did not teach until the fourth century B.C., as must be the case if the assertion of the Tibetans and Chinese be correct, to the effect that the third council took place under Kanishka (who lived A.D. 40), four hundred years after Buddha's death—and this view is favoured by the circumstance that of the names of teachers who are mentioned as contemporaries of Buddha, such as reappear in the Brahmanical writings all belong to the literature of the Vedic Sútras, not to that of the Bráhmaṇas—there would at least be a greater possibility, *à priori*, that the Pantheon found in the Buddhistic Sútras, together with similar data, might have some validity for the time of Buddha, which on this supposition would be much nearer to them. The details of the subject are briefly these. The Yakshas, Garuḍas, Kinnaras,[352] so often mentioned in these Sútras, are still quite unknown in the Bráhmaṇas: the name Dánava, too, occurs but seldom (once as an epithet of Vṛitra, a second time as an epithet of Śushṇa), and never in the plural to designate the Asuras generally;[353] nor are the gods ever styled Suras there.[354] The names of the Nágas and Mahoragas are never mentioned,* although serpent-worship itself (*sarpa-vidyá*) is repeatedly referred to;† the Kumbháṇ-

[352] Where the Kinnaras and their wives appear as 'heavenly choristers,' as, *e.g.*, in the Meghadúta, Raghuvaṅśa, and Mahá-Bhárata, I conjecture the word to be a popular etymological adaptation from the Greek *κινυρά*, although the latter is properly only used of mournful, plaintive tones: *kiṃnara* itself is formed after the model of *kiṃpurusha*.

[353] This is a mistake: the Dánus, Dánavas, appear even in the Ṛik; nay, the former in the Avesta as well; see *Ábán Yesht*, § 73; *Farvard. Y.*, § 37, 38 (here as earthly foes?)

[354] *Sura* is a bastard formation from *asura*, resting on a misunderstanding of the word, which was wrongly analysed into *a-sura*. The mention of the term in Nir., iii. 8, is patently an interpolation, as it is quite foreign to the Vedic texts.

* "In the sense of elephant the word *nága* occurs once in the Vṛihad-Áraṇyaka, Mádhy., i. 1. 24" (Errata, first German ed.). [Also in the Ait. Br., viii. 22; whereas in the Śat. Br., xi. 2. 7. 12, *mahánága* is better interpreted, with Sáyaṇa, as 'serpent.' The antiquity of this latter meaning is favoured by etymology, cf. Engl. *snake*; see Kuhn's *Zeitschrift*, ix. 233, 234.]

† In the Atharva-Saṃhitá, in particular, many prayers are addressed to the *Sarpas*; in the Śat. Br. they are once identified with the *lokas*: can the term have originally denoted 'the stars' and other spirits

das,* too, are absent. This lack of allusion in the Bráhmaṇas to any of these *genii* might be explained by supposing them to have been principally the divinities of the inferior classes of the people, to which classes Buddha specially addressed himself, and to whose conceptions and range of ideas he was therefore obliged to have particular regard. In this there may be a great deal of truth, but the remaining cycle of deities, also, which appears in the Buddhistic Sútras, is completely that belonging to the epic poetry. In the Bráhmaṇas, on the contrary, the name of Kuvera, for instance, is only mentioned once † (and that in the Bráhmaṇa of the White Yajus); [355] Śiva and Śaṃkara only occur along with other appellative epithets of Rudra, and are never employed alone as proper names to denote him; the name of Náráyaṇa, again, is of extremely rare occurrence, whilst Śakra,[356] Vásava,[357] Hari, Upendra, Janárdana, Pitámaha, are totally unknown. We thus perceive that the Buddhistic Sútras, in all of which these names are prevalent, represent precisely the same stage as the Epic literature.‡ The

---

of the air? [Serpent-worship has unquestionably mythological, symbolical relations; but, on the other hand, it has also a thoroughly realistic background.] The Maitráyaṇí-Upanishad does, indeed, mention the Suras, Yakshas, and Uragas; but this Upanishad belongs (see p. 98) altogether to the later period. It is allied to these Buddhistic Sútras in contents, and probably also in age.

* A kind of dwarfs with 'testicles as large as jars' (?). In the later Brahmanical writings they are styled *Kushmáṇḍas*, *Kúshmáṇḍas* ('gourd'?); see also Mahídhara on Váj. Saṃh., xx. 14. [Cf. the *Kumbha-mushkas* in Ath., viii. 6. 15, xi. 9. 17, and perhaps also the *śiśna-devas* in Ṛik, vii. 21. 5, x. 99. 3; Roth on Nir., p. 47.]

† The Taittiríya-Áraṇyaka, which contains several of these names, cannot exactly be ranked with the Bráhmaṇa literature.

355 Also in the parallel passages in the Ṛik Sútras, and once besides in the Áth. S. (viii. 10. 28).

356 As an appellative epithet of Indra, Śakra occurs in the Ṛik even, but it is there employed of other gods as well.

357 As an epithet of Indra (but not as a name for him) Vásava occurs once in Ath. S., vi. 82. 1. In the Nirukti also, xii. 41, it appears in direct connection with him, but at the same time also with Agni; indeed, it is with Agni and not with Indra that the Vasus are chiefly associated in the Bráhmaṇas; see *I. St.*, v. 240, 241.

‡ The Mára so frequently mentioned would almost appear to be a purely Buddhistic invention; in Bráhmaṇical writings I have nowhere met with him. [Minayeff's conjecture, in the introduction to his *Grammaire Pálie, trad. par* Stan. Guyard, p. viii., that the name Mára is directly related to *Mairya*, an epithet of Ahriman in the Avesta, and in such a way that both "*remontent à une époque antérieure à la séparation des Iraniens et des Hindous*," is rendered extremely doubtful by the mere circumstance that nothing of the sort occurs anywhere in the Vedic

non-mention of Kṛishṇa[358] proves nothing to the contrary, the worship of Kṛishṇa as a divinity being of altogether uncertain date:[359] besides, it is still a question whether we have not really to understand him by the Asura Kṛishṇa who is repeatedly referred to in these Sútras (see p. 148).—Although—to notice other points besides the Pantheon—the lunar asterisms in the Sútras begin with *Kṛittiká*, that is to say, still retain their old order, we cannot adduce this as proof that a comparatively high antiquity ought to be assigned to these writings, for the new order of the asterisms probably only dates from the fourth or fifth century A.D.; all that results from this is, that the particular passages are earlier than this last-mentioned date. As an indication, on the contrary, of a date not specially ancient, we must certainly regard the mention of the planets, as also the occurrence of the word *dínára* (from *denarius*), which Burnouf (p. 424, n.) has twice met with in the *older* Sútras (see Lassen, *I. AK.*, ii. 348).

As regards the second division of the Buddhist scriptures, the *Vinaya-Piṭaka*, or precepts concerning discipline and worship, these are almost entirely wanting in the Paris collection, doubtless because they are looked upon as peculiarly holy, and are therefore kept as secret as possible by the priests, being indeed specially intended for

---

(Gopatha-Br., i. 28, see note 166, is only an apparent exception, due probably to Buddhistic influence). If, therefore, a direct connection really exists between Mára and Aṅra Mainyu, it can only have come about in historic times; and for this there is nowhere any analogy.

358 Whether the Southern Buddhists are acquainted with Kṛishṇa is not yet clear. Buddha's prior birth as Kaṇha has, according to the text published in Fausböll's edition, p. 194, nothing to do with Kṛishṇa; the Játaka as Mahákaṇha (No. 461 in Westergaard's *Catal.*, p. 41), can hardly have any reference to him either; but what of the Játaka as *Kesava?* (No. 341 in Westergaard's *Catal.*, p. 40). The expression in Hardy, *East. Mon.*, p. 41, "You are yet a youth, your hair is like that of Kṛishṇa" (*I. St.*, iii. 161), is unfortunately not before us in the original text: might not the passage simply mean, "Your hair is yet black?" The fact of Kṛishṇa appearing in the Abhidhánappadípiká as a name of Vishṇu proves, of course, just as little for the ancient texts as the patronymics Kaṇhi, Kaṇháyana in the schol. on Kachch., v. 2. 4 (Senart, pp. 185, 186), which have necessarily to be referred to the epic or divine personality of Kṛishṇa.

359 On the significance of the data contained in the Mahábháshya on this point, see *I. St.*, xiii. 349: for the earliest occurrence of Kṛishṇa in an inscription, see Bayley in *Journ. As. Soc. Beng.*, 1854, p. 51 ff., with which cf. *I. Str.*, ii. 81, and my Essay *Ueber Kṛishṇa's Geburtsfest*, p. 318.

the clergy.—Like the Buddhist mythology, the Buddhist hierarchy was a thing of gradual growth. Buddha, as we have seen, received all without distinction as disciples, and when ere long, in consequence of the great numbers, and of the practice of living constantly together, except in the winter season, some kind of distribution of rank was required, it was upon the principle of age * or merit † that this took place. As the Buddhist faith spread more and more, it became necessary to distinguish between those who devoted themselves entirely to the priestly calling, the *bhikshus*,‡ monks, and *bhikshuṇís*, nuns, on the one

* The aged were called *sthavira*, a word not unfrequently added to a proper name in the Brahmanical Sútras to distinguish a particular person from younger namesakes: points of connection herewith are to be found in the Bráhmaṇas also. [Regarding the winter season, see Childers, *Páli Dict., s. v. vasso.*]

† The venerable were styled *arhant* (ἄρχων), also a title bestowed upon teachers in the Bráhmaṇas.

‡ When Páṇini speaks of Bhikshu-Sútras, and gives as their authors Páráśarya and Karmanda, teaching (iv. 3. 110, 111) that their respective adherents are to be styled Páráśariṇas and Karmandinas, and (iv. 2. 80) that the Sútra of the former is called Páráśariya, the allusion must be to Brahmanical mendicants, since these names are not mentioned in Buddhistic writings. By Wilson, too, in the second edition of his Dictionary, *karmandin* is given as 'beggar, religious mendicant, member of the fourth order.' [According to the St. Petersburg Dictionary, from Amara, ii. 7. 41, and Hemachandra, 809.] But the circumstance must not be overlooked that, according to the Calcutta scholiasts, neither of these two rules of Páṇini is explained in the Mahábháshya, and that possibly, therefore, they may not be Páṇini's at all, but posterior to the time of Patamjali. [The 'Páráśariṇo bhikshavaḥ,' at least, are really mentioned in the Bháshya to iv. 2. 66; see *I. St.*, xiii. 340.]—That mendicant monks must, as a matter of fact, have been particularly numerous in Páṇini's time is apparent from the many rules he gives for the formation of words in this connection, *e.g.*, *bhikshácharа*, iii. 2. 17; *bhikshāka*, iii. 2. 155; *bhikshu*, iii. 2. 168; *bhaiksha* from *bhikshá* in the sense of *bhikshāṇáṃ samúhas*, iv. 2. 38. Compare, in particular, also ii. 1. 70, where the formation of the name for female mendicants (*śramaṇá*, and, in the *gaṇa, pravrájitá*) is treated of, which can only refer to Buddhistic female mendicants. [This last rule, which gives the epithet 'virgin' as a special (not as an indispensable) quality of the *śramaṇá*, taken in connection with iv. 1. 127, can hardly be said to throw a very favourable light on the 'virginity' of the class generally; cf. Manu, viii. 363, note 330 above. The words *sarvánnína*, v. 2. 9, and *kaukkuṭika*, iv. 4. 6, likewise exhibit a very distinct Buddhistic colouring; on this see *I. St.*, v. 140 ff. On Buddhistic mendicants at the time of the Bháshya, see the data collected in *I. St.*, xiii. 340 ff.]—The entire institution of the fourth order rests essentially on the Sáṃkhya doctrine, and its extension was certainly due to a large extent to Buddhism. The red or reddish-yellow garment (*kasháyavasana*) and the tonsure (*mauṇḍya*) are the principal badges of the Buddhist *bhikshus*; see above, pp. 78, 237. On a commentary, extant in India, on a Bhikshu-Sútra, see *I. St.*, i. 470.

hand, and the Buddhist laity on the other, *upásakas* and *upásikás.** Within the priesthood itself, again, numerous shades of distinction in course of time grew up, until at length the existing hierarchy arose, a hierarchy which differs very essentially from the Brahmanical one, inasmuch as admission to the priestly order is still, as in Buddha's time, allowed to members of the lowest castes on the same conditions as to any one else. Among the laity the Indian castes still continue to exist wherever they existed in the past; it is only the Bráhman caste, or priesthood by birth, that has been abolished, and in its place a clergy by choice of vocation substituted. The Buddhist cult, too, which now is second to none in the world for solemnity, dignity, pomp, and specialities, was originally exceedingly simple, consisting mainly in the adoration of the image of Buddha and of his relics. Of the latter point we are first informed by Clemens Alexandrinus. Afterwards the same honour was paid to the relics of his most eminent disciples also, and likewise to princes who had deserved specially well of Buddhism. The story of the ashes of Menander, related by Plutarch (see Wilson, *Ariana*, p. 283), is doubtless to be understood in this sense.† Now this relic-worship, the building of steeples—traceable, perhaps, to the topes (*stúpas*) which

* Or specially *buddhopásaka*, *buddhopásiká*, as we find it several times in the Mṛichhakaṭí.

† For I regard Menander, who on his coins is called Minanda, as identical with Milinda, king of Ságala (Śákala), respecting whom see Turnour in the *Journ. As. Soc. Beng.*, v. 530 ff.; Burnouf, *l. c.*, p. 621; and *Catal. MSS. Or. Bibl. Haun.*, p. 50. (From an article by Spiegel in the *Kieler Allgemeine Monatsschrift*, July 1852, p. 561, which has just reached me while correcting these sheets, I see that Benfey has already identified Menander with Milinda [see the Berlin *Jahrbücher für wissensch. Kritik*, 1842. p. 87ᵇ].)—Schiefner in his notice, *Ueber Indra's Donnerkeil*, p. 4 of the separate impression, 1848, has expressed the conjecture that the Buddha Amitábha, who is uniformly placed in the western country Sukhavatí, may be identical with Amyntas, whose name appears as Amita on his coins; in the name Basili, too (in Schmidt's *Dsanglun*, p. 331), he discovers the word βασιλεύς. [But Schiefner calls my attention to the circumstance, that as far back as 1852, in his *Ergänzungen und Berichtigungen zu Schmidt's Ausgabe des Dsanglun*, p. 56, to p. 256, l. 3 of the Tibetan text, he withdrew the identification of Basili with βασιλεύς: his connection, too, of Amita with Amyntas, which had been questioned by Köppen, ii. 28, note 4, he now regards as doubtful.] The legend of the Western origin of the Śákyas I have already characterised (p. 285) as perhaps invented as a compliment to Kanishka.

owe their origin to this relic-worship—the system of monachism, the use of bells and rosaries,* and many other details, offer such numerous features of resemblance to Christian ritual, that the question whether Christianity may not perhaps have been here the borrowing party is by no means to be summarily negatived, particularly as it is known that Buddhist missionaries penetrated at an early period, possibly even in the two centuries preceding our era, into Western countries as far as Asia Minor. This is still, however, an entirely open question, and requires investigation.[360]

The third division of the Buddhist sacred scriptures, the *Abhidharma-Piṭaka*, contains philosophical, and especially metaphysical, discussions. It is hardly to be imagined that Buddha himself was not clearly cognisant of the philosophical basis of his teaching, and that he simply adopted this latter from his predecessors, so that the courage and energy pertaining to its public promulgation † constituted his sole merit. But it seems just as certain that he was not concerned to propagate a philosophical system, and that his aim was purely a practical one, to

* Afterwards adopted by the Bráhmans also. [The very name *rosary* has possibly arisen from a confusion of the two Indian words *japamálá* and *japámálá*; see my paper, *Ueber Kṛishṇa's Geburtsfest*, pp. 340, 341; Köppen, *Die Religion des Buddha*, ii. 319; and also my letter in the *Indian Antiq.*. iv. 250.]

360 See *Ind. Skiz.*, p. 64 (1857), and the data from the Abbé Huc's Travels in Tibet in Köppen, i. 561, ii. 116. According to the interesting discovery made by Laboulaye (see Müller, *Chips*, iv. 185) and F. Liebrecht with regard to Barlaam and Josaphat, one of the saints of the Catholic Church stands at length revealed as Bodhisattva himself—a discovery to which Reinaud's ingenious identification of Yúasaf, Yúdasf, with Búdsatf (*Mém. sur l'Inde*, p. 91) might alone have led; see *Z. D. M. G.*, xxiv. 480.—But neither is the contrary supposition, namely, that Christian influences may have affected the growth of Buddhist ritual and worship, as they did that of the Buddhist legends, by any means to be dismissed out of hand. Indeed, quite apart from the oft-ventilated question as to the significance of such influences in the further development of Kṛishṇa-worship, there are legends connected with the Śiva cult also, as to which it is not at all a far-fetched hypothesis that they have reference to scattered Christian missionaries; see *I. St.*, i. 421, ii. 398; *Z. D. M. G.*, xxvii. 166 (v. 263).—That Western influence has played a part in Tibet, finds support in a letter of Schiefner's, according to which, in a work of Dsaja Paṇḍita, Galen is mentioned as the physician of the Persians, and is said to have been consulted by the first Tibetan king, along with a celebrated Indian and a celebrated Chinese physician.

† In this courage the circumstance that he belonged by birth to the military caste finds expression.

awaken virtuous actions and dispositions. This is in accord with the circumstance, that, whereas the Buddhists allege of the Sútra-Piṭaka and the Vinaya-Piṭaka that they were delivered by Buddha himself, in the case of the Abhidharma-Piṭaka, on the contrary, they start with the admission that it is the production of his disciples. According to Burnouf, the doctrines of the Abhidharma are in reality only a further development or continuation of the views here and there propounded in the Sútras; indeed, the writings in question often merely add single words to the thoughts expressed in the Sútras: "but in any case there exists an interval of several centuries between the two, and that difference which distinguishes a doctrine still in its earliest beginnings from a philosophy which has arrived at its furthest development." * In the Brahma-Sútra of Bádaráyaṇa doctrines are repeatedly combated which, on Śaṃkara's testimony, belong to two distinct schools of Buddhist philosophy, and consequently both of these, and perhaps also the other two schools which are ranked with them, belong to a period preceding the composition of this Brahma-Sútra.—The doctrines themselves cannot be recognised with perfect distinctness, and their affinity, although undeniable, to the doctrines of the Sáṃkhya system is still enveloped in some obscurity.[361] On this point, however, so much is clear, that, although Buddha himself may actually have been in full harmony with the doctrines of Kapila, as they then existed,† yet his adherents developed these in their own fashion; in the

---

* Whether now, after these words of Burnouf's, *loc. cit.*, p. 522, Lassen's view (*I. AK.*, ii. 458) is tenable—to the effect that "although, in the collection bearing the name of Abhidharma, there are writings of various dates, yet they must all be assigned to the period preceding the third council" (this third council in B.C. 275 being here expressly distinguished from the fourth under Kanishka)—appears to me in the very highest degree doubtful.

[361] Cf. for this *I. St.*, iii. 132; Max Duncker, *Geschichte der Arier*, p. 234 ff. (1867); Köppen, i. 214 ff.—"The extinction, the 'blowing out' of individual existence was certainly the goal to which Buddha aspired; hardly, however, the resolving of this existence into nothing, but only its return to the same state of *avidyá*, or unconsciousness which belonged to primeval matter before it attained to development at all," *Lit. C. Bl.*, 1857, p. 770 (*I. Str.*, ii. 132). Childers thinks differently, *Páli Dict.*, *s. v. nirváṇa.*

† Were he really to be identified with the Śákáyanya of the Maitráyaṇí Upanishad (see p. 97), we should have in this work tolerably direct evidence to the above effect.

same way as the followers of Kapila also pursued their own path, and so eventually that system arose which is now extant under the name Sáṃkhya, and which differs essentially from the Buddhist philosophy.* To the four schools into which, as we have just seen, this philosophy was split up at a comparatively early period, four others were afterwards added—or perhaps these superseded the former—but neither have the doctrines of these later schools been as yet set forth with anything like sufficient certainty.[362] The question, too, whether Buddhistic conceptions may not perhaps have exercised a direct influence on the development of Gnostic doctrines,† particularly those of Basilides, Valentinian, and Bardesanes, as well as of Manes, must for the present be regarded as wholly undetermined;[363] it is most intimately bound up with the question as to the amount of influence to be ascribed to Indian philosophy generally in the shaping of these doctrines. The main channel of communication in the case of the latter was through Alexandria; the Buddhist missionaries, on the contrary, probably mostly came from the Panjáb through Persia.

Besides the three Piṭakas, the Sanskrit manuscripts that have been procured from Nepál contain other works also, consisting, in part, of a large number of commentaries on and elucidations of the Piṭakas, in part, of a

---

* Whether vv. 9–11 of the Íśopanishad are to be taken, with the commentator, as specially referring to the Buddhists, as I assume in *I. St.*, i. 298, 299, appears to me doubtful now: the polemic may simply be directed against the Sáṃkhya tenets in general.

[362] Our information regarding them is derived exclusively from Hodgson's Essays (now collected, see note 345). Their names, Svábhávika, Aiśvarika, Kármika, Yátnika, are so far unsupported by any other literary evidence. Only for the names Sautrántika, Vaibháshika, Mádhyamika, Yogáchára, is such testimony found. Táranátha, for example, is acquainted with these latter only, and they are also the only ones known to Wassiljew in his special work on Tibetan and Chinese Buddhism. See on this point *Lit. C. Bl.*, 1875, p. 550.

† See F. Nève, *L'Antiquité Chrétienne en Orient*, p. 90, Louvain, 1852.

[363] Cf. now Lassen, *I. AK.*, iii. 387–416; my *Ind. Skiz.*, p. 64; Renan, *Hist. des Lang. Sém.*, 2d ed., 1858, pp. 274, 275. That their influence upon the growth of the doctrines of Manes in particular was a most important one is shown, for example, by this circumstance alone, that the formula of abjuration for those who renounced these doctrines expressly specifies **Βοδδα** and the **Σκυθιανος** (seemingly a separation of 'Buddha Śákyamuni' into two)—Lassen, iii. 415.—Cf. also Beal, *J. R. A. S.*, ii. 424 (1866).

most peculiar class of writings, the so-called Tantras, which are looked upon as especially sacred, and which stand precisely upon a level with the Brahmanical works of the same name. Their contents are made up of invocations of various Buddhas and Bodhisattvas, as also of their Śaktis, or female energies, with a motley admixture of Śivaïtic deities; to which are added longer or shorter prayers addressed to these beings, and directions how to draw the mystic diagrams and magic circles that secure their favour and protection.[364]

---

[364] Cf. Emil Schlagintweit's *Buddhism in Tibet* (1863, with a folio atlas of twenty plates).—Recently there have also come from Nepál Sanskrit MSS. containing works of poetry; as to which see Klatt in the preface to his edition of the sentences of Cháṇakya, taken therefrom (1873).

SUPPLEMENTARY NOTES.

SUPPLEMENTARY NOTES.

P. 9, 36 ff. (and 64, 29 ff.). Burnell, in his preface to the Ársheya-Br. (Mangalore, 1876), p. xvi. ff., and Aufrecht, *Hymnen des Ṛigveda* (Bonn, 1877), Pref. pp. xvi., xvii., dispute the superior antiquity of the readings of the Sáma-Saṃhitá, as compared with those of the Ṛik-Saṃhitá.

P. 25, note [17], and p. 67, note [56]. On the Śikshás see Kielhorn's paper in the *Ind. Antiq.*, v. 141 ff., 193 ff., and my comments thereon, *ibid.*, p. 253.

P. 32, note [21]. On the Váshkalas somewhat more light has now been cast. In the first place, from a comparison of the *káriká* quoted in my Catal. of the Berlin Sansk. MSS., p. 314, '*Śákalánáṃ samání va ity ṛichá 'ntyá "hutir bhavet | Báshkalánáṃ tu tachhamyor ity ṛichá 'ntyáhutir bhavet*,' it results that the citation in the forty-eighth Atharva-pariśishṭa (see *I. St.*, iv. 431) of the *śamyuváka* as the concluding verse of the Ṛik-Saṃhitá has reference to the Váshkala-recension of the latter. Next, it becomes evident that this recension stood in a special relation to the Śáñkháyana texts, since in the Śáñkh. Gṛih., 4. 5. 9, the same verse is cited as the concluding one of the Saṃhitá, and this expressly as the view of Kaushítaki. In addition to this we have the fact that the *pratíka* of the whole section to which this verse belongs, and which forms the last *khila*—*saṃjnána*—in the vulgate recension of the Ṛik-Saṃhitá, is found cited in the Śáñkháy.-Śrauta-Sútra, 3. 6. 4, but is wanting in the parallel passage, Áśval., 2, 11. And, lastly, we shall probably also have to allot to the Váshkalas the eleven hymns—ten *Áśvináni* and one *Aindrávaruṇam súktam*—which, as Rud. Meyer has recently pointed out (Ṛigvidhána, Praef., p. xxiv.), are cited in the Bṛihaddevatá, 3. 24, between Ṛik-Saṃh., i. 73 and 74. For, according to Meyer, their *pratíkas* prove to be identical with those given by the scholiast on Śáṅkh. Śr., 9. 20. 14, for the '*triśatam suparṇam*' there mentioned in the text, which again is specified under this name in the Śáṅkh. Br. itself (18. 4) as part of the Áśvina-śastra. Probably, too, the other portions of text, which, as stated by Meyer (*l. c.*, p. xxv. ff.), appear in the Bṛihaddevatá as well as in the Ṛigvidhána, as belonging to the Ṛik-Saṃhitá, whereas they are found neither in the vulgate—the Śákala-Saṃhitá—itself, nor in its *khila* portions, will have to be assigned to the Váshkalas. In point of fact, the *saṃjnána khila* also, to which (see above) the concluding verse of the Váshkala-Saṃhitá belongs, is mentioned in both texts (Meyer, p. xxii.). An exact comparison of the Ṛik-verses cited in the Śáṅkháyana texts will probably throw full light upon this point.—In Bühler's letter from Kashmír (published in *I. St.*, xiv. 402 ff.) the interesting information was given that he had there discovered an excellent *bhúrja*-MS., some five to six hundred years old, of the Ṛik-Saṃhitá in the Śákala recension. This MS. is accentuated, whereas the Kashmír Vedic MSS. are not wont to be so, but the accent is denoted in a totally different manner from that customary in India, the *udátta* alone being marked by a perpendicular line, precisely as, according to Haug, is usual in one of the two schools of the Maitráyaṇí Saṃhitá, and as we ourselves do; cf. my remarks in the *Jenaer Lit. Zeit.*, 1875, p. 315. On this MS. see now the detailed report of Bühler's journey in the *Journal Bomb. Br. R. A. S.*, 1877, extra No., pp. 35, 36.

Pp. 35, 36, note §. See also Myriantheus, *Die Aśvins* (Munich, 1876), and James Darmesteter, *Ormazd et Ahriman* (Paris, 1877).

P. 41, note [29]. See Alfred Hillebrandt, *Varuṇa und Mitra, ein Beitrag zur Exegese des Veda* (Breslau, 1877).

P. 43, note [32]. Max Müller's issue of the text alone of the Ṛik has now appeared in a second edition (London, 1877). *Saṃhitá-páṭha* and *pada-páṭha* are here printed on opposite pages. Respecting the latter it has to be remarked that, as in Müller's previous editions, so again in this one the so-called *galitas* are in no way marked, the text which a particular passage shows the first time it occurs being uniformly simply repeated, without any reference to what is done in the MSS. themselves in these cases. This is all the more surprising as, after I had pointed out this defect, in my review of the last volume of his large edition in the *Lit. Cent. Blatt*, 17th April 1875, Müller himself, in an article which appeared in the same periodical a year and a half later (16th December 1876) fully recognised the critical importance of the *galitas.*—Aufrecht's edition has also been reprinted (Bonn, 1877): the preface (comp. desideratum at note 28) contains a variety of critical remarks.—Complete translations of the Ṛik-Saṃhitá, by Alfred Ludwig (Prag, 1876) and Hermann Grassmann (Leipzig, 1876–77) have appeared.—Very meritorious, also, is the edition of the Ṛik-Saṃhitá which is appearing in monthly numbers at Bombay, under the title 'Vedárthayatna,' with English and Mahráṭhí translation, as well as with Mahráṭhí commentary: the latest No. brings it down to i. 100. The name of the excellent editor, Shankar Paṇḍit, is an open secret.—Lastly, there remains to be mentioned M. Haug's *Vedische Räthselfragen und Räthselsprüche* (Ṛik, i. 164, 1876).

P. 48, note 33b. Rájendra Lála Mitra's edition, in the *Bibl. Indica*, of the Áitareya-Áraṇyaka with Sáyaṇa's commentary, has now been completed. A MS. acquired by Bühler in Kashmír shows a number of variations; see his Report of Journey, *l. c.*, p. 34.

P. 50, 6 (cf. p. 285). Pañchálachaṇḍa appears in a Páli Sutta among the *mahásenápatis* of the Yakkhas; for the conclusions to be drawn from this see *Jenaer Lit. Zeit.*, 7th April 1877, p. 221.

P. 56, 8. The Śáñkh. Gṛih. (4. 10. 3) inserts between Viśvámitra and Vámadeva, the two representatives of the third and fourth *maṇḍalas*, the name of Jamadagni, to whom in the Anukramaṇí to the Śákala-Saṃhitá only the last three verses of the third *maṇḍala* (iii. 62, 16–18) are in this place ascribed,—but in addition to these, also five entire hymns and four separate verses in the last three *maṇḍalas*. Have we here also to do with a divergence of the Váshkala school? (In Śáñkh. Gṛih., 4. 5. 8, however, there is no trace of this variation from the vulgate; rather, the verse iii. 62. 18 appears there as the concluding verse of the third *maṇḍala*.)

P. 58, note [50]. The Śáñkh. Gṛihya has been published, with translation and notes, by Herm. Oldenberg; see *I. St.*, xv. 1–166. There exists also another recension of it, which is designated as Kaushítaka-Gṛihya, but which, according to Oldenberg, is rather to be understood as Śámbavya-Gṛihya. Its text is 'nowise identical' with the Śáñkh. Gṛih., 'but it has borrowed from the latter by far the greatest part both of its matter and form.' The last two books of the Śáñkh. Gṛih. are not used in it, and a great deal is lacking besides.

P. 61, note *. On the Jyotisha a very meritorious work has just appeared by G. Thibaut.

P. 62, 6, 26 ff. On the Bṛihaddevatá and Ṛigvidhána see R. Meyer's edition of the latter work (Berlin, 1877).

P. 65, 28. The forty-eighth Atharva-pariśishṭa, see *I. St.*, iv. 432, gives indeed the same beginning, but a different concluding verse to the Sáma-Saṃhitá, namely, the last verse but one of the *first* part of the vulgate; accordingly, it did not reckon the second part as belonging to the Saṃhitá at all, while for the first part also it presents the discrepancy stated.

P. 65, note [60]. The Áraṇya-Saṃhitá, with Sáyaṇa's commentary, has been edited by Satyavrata Sámáśramin, and that in a double form, namely, separately (Calcutta, 1873), and also in the second part of his large edition of the Sáma-Saṃhitá, p. 244 ff.

P. 66, note [61]. This edition of the Sáma-Saṃhitá, in the *Bibl. Indica*, has now reached, in its fifth volume, as far as 2. 8. 2. 5.

Pp. 73, 74. The Talavakára- or Jaiminíya-Bráhmaṇa, to which the Kenopan. belongs, has been recovered by Burnell (letter of 19th April). Also a Sámaveda-Prátiśákhya.

Pp. 74, 75, notes [71], [72]. The Ársheya-Bráhmaṇa and Saṃhitopanishad-Bráhmaṇa have also been edited by Burnell (Mangalore, 1876, 1877); the former with a lengthy introduction containing an inquiry into the Gánas, the secondary origin of the Saṃhitá from these, the chanting of the *sámans*, &c. On this compare A. Barth's detailed notice in the *Revue Critique*, 21st July 1877, pp. 17–27. The Ársheya-Bráhmaṇa has, further, just been issued a second time by Burnell, namely, in the text of the Jaiminíya school, which he had meanwhile recovered (Mangalore, 1878).

Pp. 99–101. According to the catalogue (1876) of M. Haug's collection of MSS., there are now in the Royal Library at Munich, with which this collection was incorporated in the spring of 1877, not only two MSS. of the Maitráyaṇí Saṃhitá, but also several more or less complete, but, unfortunately, in great part modern, copies of Ápastamba, Mánava, Bháradvája, Baudháyana, Vaikhánasa, Hiraṇyakeśin.—The description (in notes 108, 109) of the Dharma-Sútras as part of the Śrauta-Sútras is not quite correct; rather both are portions, possessing an equal title, of a collective Sútra-whole, to which in each case there also belonged a Gṛihya- and a Śulva-Sútra, and which we might perhaps designate by the name of Kalpa-Sútra. —[The North-Western origin of the Kaṭha school (cf. *Κάθαιοι*, *I. St.*, xiii. 439) is also, in a certain measure, attested by the fact that, according to Bühler's letter from Kashmír (dated September 1875, published in *I. St.*, xiv. 402 ff.) on the results of his search for MSS. in that province, this school is still in the present day the prevailing one in Kashmír. The Brahmans there call themselves, it is true, *chaturvedi*, but they follow the rules of the Káṭhaka-Gṛihya-Sútra of Laugákshi. Besides portions of all the Vedas, the Bhaṭṭas learn by heart the Paddhati of Devapála, the commentary and *prayoga* to the Káthaka-Gṛihya. 'Of these Gṛihyas I have acquired several MSS., among them an old one on *bhúrja*. To the Káṭhaka-Sútra are attached a Pravarádhyáya, an Ársha, the Cháráyaṇíyá Śikshá, and several other Pariśishṭas.'—*Additional note in second German edition.*] According to Bühler, *Z. D. M. G.*, xxii. 327, the Dharma-Sútra of the Káṭhaka school is identical with the Vishṇu-Smṛiti. On this, and on the Káṭhaka school in Kashmír generally, see now Bühler, Report of Journey, *l. c.*, pp. 20, 36, 37.

P. 103, note [116]. The Taitt. Prátiśákhya has also been edited in the *Bibl. Indica* by Rájendra Lála Mitra (1872).

Pp. 117, 118. The forty-eighth Atharva-Pariśishṭa specifies a recension of the Váj. Saṃh., which begins with 1. 1, but which ends with 23. 32! See *I. St.*, iv. 432.

P. 114. For the formula *Ambe ambike 'mbálike*, which differs in all three Yajus texts, Páṇini (vi. 7. 118) has a fourth reading; on this and the other points of connection between Páṇini and the vocabulary of the Yajus texts, see *I. St.*, iv. 432.

P. 138, 23. According to Mahávaṅsa, p. 9. 12, 15, the name of Buddha's wife was Bhadda- or Subhadda-Kachcháná!

P. 139, note [147]. Śatap., 3. 1, 1–2. 2, is translated in Bruno Lindner's dissertation, *Ueber die Díkshá* (Leipzig, 1878); other portions in Delbrück's *Altind. Wortfolge* (1878).

P. 142, note [155]. The Páraskara has been edited by Stenzler (1876).

P. 150, note [165]. In the forty-eighth Atharva-Pariśishṭa, the commencement of the Atharva-Saṃhitá is given just as in the published recension, but it ends there with Book xvi.; see *I. St.*, iv. 432.

P. 151, note [166]. With the *doshapati* compare the *pápman ásura* in the Nṛisiṅhop.; see *I. St.*, ix. 149, 150.

P. 153 ff. Cf. Paul Regnaud, *Matériaux pour servir à l'Histoire de la Philosophie de l'Inde*, 1876, and my review of this work in the *Jenaer Lit. Zeit.* of 9th February 1878.

P. 182, note [193]. The dates of the Nepálese MSS. apparently reach back as far as A.D. 883! See Dan. Wright, *History of Nepal*, 1877, *Jenaer Lit. Zeit.*, 1877, p. 412.

Pp. 187, 188, note [201a]. On Olshausen's explanation of the word *Pahlav*—the basis of the Indian *Pahlava*—from *Parthava*, 'Parthians,' see now also Th. Nöldeke in *Z. D. M. G.*, xxxi. 557 ff.

P. 189, note [204]. According to Kern, *Over de oud-Javaansche Vertaling van't Mahábhárata* (Amsterdam, 1877), p. 7 ff., the Kavi translation of the Adi-parvan, from which he there communicates the text of the Paushyacharita, dates from the beginning of the eleventh century.

P. 189, note [205]. For the criticism of the Mahá-Bhárata, Holtzmann's researches (*Indische Sagen*, Preface, Stuttgart, 1854) are also of great importance.

P. 191, note [206]. The Index to Hall's edition of Wilson's translation of the Vishṇu-Puráṇa (vol. v. part ii.) appeared in 1877. The edition of the Agni-Puráṇa in the *Bibl. Ind.* has now reached *adhy.* 294.

P. 195, 15. The identity of the author of the Raghuvaṅśa and Kumára-sambhava with the dramatist Kálidása is contended for by Shankar Paṇḍit in the *Transactions* of the *London Congress of Orientalists* (London, 1876), p. 227 ff.

P. 196, note 208. Bháravi and Kálidása are mentioned together in an inscription of Pulakeśi II., 'in the Śaka year 507 (A.D. 585–6);' at that date, therefore, they must have been already famous. See Bháu Dájí in *Journ. Bomb. Br. R. A. S.*, ix. 315, and J. F. Fleet in *Ind. Antiq.*, v. 68.—On the Kashmír poets Chandraka and Meṇṭha, of about the fifth (?) century, Ratnákara of the ninth, Kshemendra and Bilhaṇa of the eleventh, Somadeva, Mañkha, Kalhaṇa, &c., of the twelfth century, see Bühler, Report of Journey, *l. c.*, p. 42 ff.

P. 199, note †. For the text of these Suttas see now Grimblot, *Sept suttas Pális* (Paris, 1876), p. 89; '*nachcham gítaṃ váditaṃ pekkham akkháṇam . . iti vá iti evarúpá vísúkadassaná*' (exhibitions, p. 65, spectacles, pp. 179, 215). From this it appears that the word here properly in question is not so much the general term *vísúka* as rather, specially, *pekkha* (*prekshya*), 'exhibition,' 'spectacle,' translated by 'theatricals,' pp. 65, 179, 'représentations dramatiques,' p. 215; comp. *prekshaṇaka* as the name of a species of drama in Bharata (Hall, Daśarúpa, p. 6), and *dṛiśya* in the Sáhitya-darpaṇa as the name of dramatic poetry in general.

Pp. 200, 12, 205, 20. According to Hall, Vásavad., Introd., p. 27, Bhavabhúti would have to be placed earlier than Subandhu, and if so, of course, *à fortiori*, earlier than Báṇa: the latter, however, does not allude to him in the classic passage in the introduction to the Harsha-charita, where he enumerates his predecessors (Hall, *ibid.*, pp. 13, 14). See also *Ind. Streifen*, i. 355.

P. 201, note ‖. According to Lassen, *I. AK.*, iii. 855, 1163, Bhoja died in 1053. An inscription of his in the *Ind. Antiq.*, 1877, p. 54, is dated in the year 1022.

P. 203, note. According to Bühler, *Ind. Antiq.*, v. 112 (April, 1876), a grant of King Jayabhaṭa is 'older than the year 445 A.D., and dated in the Vikrama era.'

P. 204, note 211. In *Z. D. M. G.*, xxx. 302, Jacobi cites from the Urvaśí a (chronometrical) *datum* betokening Greek influence.

P. 207, note 213. Of new publications, &c., of Indian dramas have to be mentioned: Bhaṇḍarkar's edition of the

Málatí-mádhava (Bombay, 1876), Cappeller's edition of the Ratnávalí (1877, in the second edition of Böhtlingk's *Sanskṛit-Chrestomathie*), the Bengálí recension of the Śakuntalá, edited by Pischel (see Cappeller in the *Jenaer Lit. Zeit.*, 1877, p. 121), the two latter dramas translated by Ludw. Fritze; lastly, Regnaud's translation of the Mṛichhakaṭiká (Paris, 1876).—On the question as to the various recensions of Kálidása's Śakuntalá—discussed in *I. St.*, xiv. 161 ff.—see also Bühler's Report of Journey, *l. c.*, p. lxxxv. ff., where the first act of the Kashmír recension of this drama is printed.

P. 210, note 220. To this place also belongs Śrívara's Subháshitávalí of the fifteenth century, containing quotations from more than 350 poets; see Bühler, Report of Journey, *l. c.*, p. 61 ff.; further, the Subháshita-ratnákara by Krishna Shastri Bhátavadekar (Bombay, 1872).—Here, too, have to be mentioned the four papers *Zur Kritik und Erklärung verschiedener indischer Werke*, published by O. Böhtlingk in vols. vii. and viii. of the *Mélanges Asiatiques* of the St. Petersburg Academy (1875–76).

P. 212, note 222. Comp. Benfey's Introduction to Bickell's edition and translation of the 'Kalilag und Damnag' (Leipzig, 1876). It now appears doubtful whether the ancient Pahlaví version really rested upon one individual work as its basis, or whether it is not rather to be regarded as an epitome of several independent texts; see my notice of the above work in *Lit. C. Bl.*, 1876, No. 31, Bühler, Report of Journey, p. 47; Prym in the *Jenaer Lit. Zeit.*, 1878, Art. 118.

P. 213, note 224. Read 'recast by Kshemendra.' It is only to Kshemendra that the statements from Bühler's letter, given in the next sentence, refer. Bühler now places him in the second and third quarter of the eleventh century, Report of Journey, *l. c.*, p. 45 ff.

P. 213. On the Rája-taraṃgiṇí see now Bühler, Report of Journey, pp. 52–60, lxvi.–lxxxii. (where an amended translation of i. 1–107 is given); and on the Níla-mata, of about the sixth or seventh century, *ibid.*, p. 38 ff., lv. ff.

P. 214, note 225. The Harsha-charita appeared at Calcutta in 1876, edited by Jívánanda.—On the Siṅhásana-dvátriṅśiká see now my paper in *I. St.*, xv. 185 ff.

P. 215, note 227. In the interpretation of Indian inscriptions, Bühler and Fleet also, in particular, have of late done very active service (especially in *Ind. Antiq.*, vols. v., vi.).

P. 221, note [233]. Goldstücker's 'facsimile' (comp. note [106], p. 100) edition of the Mánavakalp. is not 'photo-lithographed,' but lithographed from a tracing.

P. 226, note [238]. Kielhorn has come forward with great vigour in defence of the Mahábháshya, first, in a lengthy article in the *Ind. Antiq.*, v. 241 (August 1876), next in his Essay, *Kátyáyana and Patamjali* (Bombay, December 1876), which deals specially with the analysis of the work into its component parts; and, lastly, in his edition of the work itself, which exhibits the text critically sifted, in direct reference thereto (the first number, Bombay, 1878, gives the *naváhnikam*). Cf., further, two articles by Bhaṇḍarkar, *On the Relation of Kátyáyana to Páṇini and of Patamjali to Kátyáyana* in *Ind. Antiq.*, v. 345 ff. (December 1876), and on *Goldstücker's Theory about Páṇini's Technical Terms* (reprint of an earlier review of G.'s *Páṇini*), *ibid.*, vi. 107 ff. To this place also belongs an article on the Mahábháshya, which was sent off by me to Bombay on 9th October 1876, but which only appeared in the *Ind. Antiq.*, vi. 301 ff., in October 1877.

P. 226, note [239]. On the antiquity of the Káśiká see now Bühler's Report of Journey, p. 72. The issue of the work in the Paṇḍit is perhaps by this time completed. It is to be hoped that it will appear in a separate edition.—Bühler's information regarding Vyáḍi, the Mahábháshya, Kátantra, &c., is given in detail in his Report of Journey.—On Burnell's essay, *On the Aindra School of Sanskrit Grammarians* (1875), which contains rich materials, see my critique in the *Jenaer Lit. Zeit.*, March 1876, p. 202 ff.—Of Hemachandra's Prákṛit-Grammar Pischel has given us a new edition (Halle, 1877, text and good index of words).

P. 229, note †. This note, according to Barth, *Revue Critique*, 3d June 1876, is to be cancelled, as *paraître* can only have the sense of 'seem' (*scheinen*).

P. 231, note [243]. On Kshemendra's Loka-prakáśa see Bühler, Report of Journey, p. 75.

P. 231, 29. See note above to p. 182.

P. 231, note [244]. The translation of the Sáhitya-darpaṇa in the *Bibl. Indica* is now finished.—For the rich information supplied by Bühler regarding the Alaṃkára literature in Kashmír, see his Report of Journey, p. 64 ff. According to this, the Alaṃkára-śástra of Bhaṭṭa Udbhaṭa dates from the time of Jayápíḍa (779–813), whose *sabhápati* the author was. Vámana, too, in Bühler's opinion, belongs to the same period. Ánandavardhana and Ratnákara belong to the ninth century, Mukula to the tenth, Abhinavagupta to the beginning, Rudraṭa to the end, of the eleventh, while Ruyyaka flourished at the commencement, and Jayaratha at the close, of the twelfth century; Mammaṭa is to be placed still later.

P. 235, note [247]. Of the Sarva-darśana-saṃgraha there is now a translation, by Cowell and Gough, in the *Paṇḍit*, 1875 ff.

P. 237, note [250]. The Sáṃkhya-tattva-pradípa has been translated by Govindadevaśástrin in the *Paṇḍit*, Nos. 98 ff.

P. 237, note [251]. Abhinavagupta was still living in A.D. 1015; Bühler, Report of Journey, p. 80.—The Śaiva-śástra in Kashmír, *ibid.*, pp. 77–82, is divided into two groups, of which the one connects itself with the Spanda-śástra of Vasugupta (854), the other with the Pratyabhijná-śástra of Sománanda (ab. 900) and Utpala (ab. 930). It is of the latter—which appears to rest upon Śaṃkara—that Abhinavagupta is the leading representative.

P. 241, note [256]. The last number of this edition of Śabarasvámin brings it down to 10. 2. 73; the edition of the Jaiminíya-nyáya-málá-vistara has just been completed by Cowell. The Jaimini-sútra is being published in the Bombay monthly periodical, 'Shaḍdarśana-chintaniká,' begun in January 1877—text and commentary with a double translation, in English and Mahráṭhí.

P. 243, note [259]. Váchaspatimiśra's Bhámatí, a gloss on Śaṃkara's commentary on the Vedánta-sútra, is in course of publication in the *Bibl. Ind.* edited by Bálaśástrin,—commenced in 1876.—In the *Paṇḍit* for 1876, p. 113, in the Preface to his edition of Srínivásadása's Yatíndramatadípiká, Rámamiśraśástrin cites a passage from Rámánuja's Brahmasútra-bháshya, in which the latter mentions the *bhagavad*-Bodháyana as his predecessor therein, and as separated from him by several generations of *púrváchâryas*. As such *púrváchâryas* Rámamiśra gives the names of Dramiḍa, Guhadeva, and Brahmánandi, at the same time designating them by the epithets *maharshi* and *suprâchînatama*. By Śrînivâsadâsa himself (p. 115) the teachers are mentioned in the following order: Vyâsa, Bodhâyana, Guhadeva, Bhâruchi, Brahmânandi, Draviḍâchârya, Śrî-Parânkuśanâtha, Yâmunamuni, Yatîśvara.—Here is also to be mentioned the edition in the *Paṇḍit*, by Vechanarâmaśâstrin, of two commentaries on the Vedânta-sûtra, viz., the Śaiva-bhâshya of Śrîkaṇṭha Śivâchârya (see *Z. D. M. G.*, xxvii. 166), and the Vedânta-kaustubha-prabhâ of Keśava Kâśmîrabhaṭṭa.—Further, in the second edition of his *Sanskṛit-Chrestomathie* (1877) Böhtlingk has given a new translation of the Vedânta-sâra; and the Vidvanmanorañjinî of Râmatîrtha, a commentary thereon, has been published, text with translation, in the *Paṇḍit* by Gough and Govindadevaśâstrin. In the same journal has also appeared the Advaita-makaranda of Lakshmîdhara.

P. 245, note [264]. A translation, by Keśavaśâstrin, of the Nyâya-darśana and of Vâtsyâyana's commentary thereon, has begun to appear in the *Paṇḍit* (new series, vol. ii.). The fourth book of Gangeśa's Nyâya-chintâmaṇi, with the commentary of Ruchidatta, has also been edited, *ibid.* (Nos. 66–93) by Bâlaśâstrin.

P. 247, note [268]. Of importance are the names, communicated to me from Albîrûnî by Ed. Sachau, of the *menâzil* in Soghd and Khvârizm, the list of which begins with *thurayyâ*, *i.e.*, with *kṛittikâ*, and that under the name *parvî;* by this is evidently meant *parvîz*, *i.e.*, the name which stands *third* in the Bundehesh, whence it necessarily follows that the list of names in the latter is the modern one, commencing with *âśvinî;* see *Jenaer Lit. Zeit.*, 1877 (7th April), p. 221. Some of the names here cited by Albîrûnî are distinctly Indian, as *frshtbâth*, *i.e.*, *proshṭhapâda*, the *ancient* form of name, consequently, (not *bhadrapadâ*). Here, too, presumably, as in the case of China, the Buddhists were the channel of communication.

Pp. 250, 251, note [274]. The proposition laid down by H. Jacobi in *Z. D. M. G.*, xxx. 306, that no Indian writings, which enumerate the planets in the order—Sun, Moon, Mars, &c.—can have been composed *earlier* than the third century A.D., has application to Yâjnavalkya, as well as to the Atharva-pariśishṭas, which in point of fact already observe this order; see *I. St.*, x. 317.

P. 253, note *. The absence of mention of the Romakas in the Rámáyaṇa may perhaps also rest upon geographical grounds, namely, on the probable origin of the poem in the east of India, in the land of the Kośalas, whereas the 'war-part' of the Mahá-Bhárata was in all likelihood composed in Central, if not in Western India.

P. 256, note [281]. Cf. Thibaut's paper 'On the Śulva-sutras' in the *Journ. As. Soc. Bengal*, 1875 (minutely discussed by Mor. Cantor in the hist. lit. div. of the *Zeitsch. für Math. und Physik*, vol. xxii.), and his edition of the Śulva-sútra of Baudháyana with the commentary of Dvárakánáthayajvan (text with translation) in the *Paṇḍit*, May, 1875–77.

P. 256, note *. The explanation of the Indian figures from the initial letters of the numerals has recently been rudely shaken, see Bühler in *Ind. Ant.*, vi. 48,—through the deciphering, namely, of the ancient 'Nágarí numerals' by Paṇḍit Bhagvánlál Indraji, *ibid.*, p. 42 ff. These, it appears, turn out to be *other* letters, yet the derivation of the later figures from them can hardly be called in question. What principle underlies these ancient numerals is, for the rest, still obscure: the zero has not yet a place among them; there are letter-symbols for 4–10 (1–3 being merely represented by strokes) for the tens up to 90, and for the hundreds up to 1000. Comp. pp. 222, note [233], and 257, note [284].

P. 260, note *. The remainder of the Yátrá has now been edited by Kern in *I. St.*, xiv. and xv.

P. 266 ff. In complete opposition to the former dreams about the high antiquity of Indian medicine, Haas has recently, in *Z. D. M. G.*, xxx. 617 ff. and xxxi. 647 ff., characterised even the most ancient of the Indian medical texts as quite modern productions, to be traced to Arabian sources. In the accounts given by the Arabs themselves of the high repute in which Indian medicine stood with them, and of the translation of works of the kind, which are specified by name, from Sanskṛit into Arabic, he recognises hardly any value. As regards the latter point, however, there exists absolutely no ground for throwing doubt upon statements of so definite a character made by the old Arab chroniclers; while, with respect to the former point, the language of Suśruta, Charaka, &c., is distinctly opposed to the assignment to them of *so* late a date. At the same time, every real proof of the presence of Greek (or even Arabian) conceptions in the works in question, will have to be thankfully received. But the early existence of medical knowledge in India would in no way be prejudiced thereby, as its beginnings are well attested by evidence from the Vedic period, especially from the Atharvaveda.

P. 270, note [310]. Charaka, as Bühler informs me, has now also been printed at Bombay, edited by Dr. Anna Mureshvar Kunte, Grant Medical College.

P. 271, note [313]. The Kavi translation of the Kámandaki-níti probably belongs, at the earliest, to about the same date as the translation of the Mahá-Bhárata; see remark above to note [204].—Progress has been made with the printing of Nirapeksha's commentary in the *Bibl. Indica.*

P. 273, note [319]. On modern Indian music, see now the numerous writings of Sourindro Mohun Tagore, Calcutta, 1875 ff., cf. *Jenaer Lit. Zeit.*, 1877, p. 487.—It is possible that the investigation of the *gánas* of the Sáma-veda, in case these are still in actual use and could be observed, might yield some practical result for the ancient *laukika* music also.

P. 274, note [321a]. For such representations of Venus, supported on the tail of a dolphin, or with a dolphin and Cupid behind her, see J. J. Bernouilli, *Aphrodite* (Leipzig, 1873), pp. 245, 370, 405. See also numerous representations of the kind in the *Musée de Sculpture par le Comte F. de Clarac* (Paris, 1836–37), vol. iv., pl. 593, 607, 610, 612, 615, 620, 622, 626–628, 634.

P. 278, note [327]. Bühler has also published a translation of Ápastamba: it is now being reprinted in the series of 'Sacred Books of the East' which is appearing under Max Müller's direction.—Gautama has been edited by Stenzler (London, 1876), and is also comprised in Jívánanda's large collection 'Dharmashastrasamgraha' (Calcutta, 1876), which, all inaccuracies notwithstanding, is yet a very meritorious publication, on account of the abundance of material it contains. It embraces 27 large and small Smṛiti-texts, namely, 3 Atris, 2 Vishṇus, 2 Háritas, Yájnavalkya, 2 Uśanas', Angiras, Yama, Ápastamba, Saṃvarta, Kátyáyana, Bṛihaspati, 2 Paráśaras, 2 Vyásas, Śaṅkha, Likhita, Daksha, 2 Gautamas, and 2 Vasishṭhas.—Nárada's Smṛiti has been translated by Jolly (London, 1876); see also his papers, *Ueber die rechtliche Stellung der Frauen bei den Indern* (Munich, 1876), and *Ueber das indische Schuldrecht* (Munich, 1877).

P. 280, note [329]. The Aruṇa-Smṛiti, Bühler informs me, is quite a late production, probably a section of a Puráṇa.

P. 281. As Yájnavalkya enumerates the planets in their Greek order (1. 295) the *earliest* date we can assign to this work is the third century A.D. (see remark above to p. 251, note [274], following Jacobi).

P. 284, 5. See remark on Pañchálachaṇḍa above, note to p. 50.

P. 288. E. Senart, in his ingenious work, *La Légende du Bouddha* (Paris, 1875), traces the various legends that are narrated of Buddha (and in part, identically, of Kṛishṇa also) to ancient solar myths which were only subsequently applied to Buddha; comp. my detailed notice and partial rejoinder in the *Jenaer Lit. Zeit.*, 1876 (29th April), p. 282 ff.

P. 291, note †. Schiefner's 'Indische Erzählungen,' from the Kágyur, in vols. vii. and viii. of the *Mélanges Asiatiques* of the St. Petersburg Academy, embrace already forty-seven such legends.

P. 292, note [345]. Whether the Buddhaghosha of this inscription is, as Stevenson assumes (p. 13), to be identified with the well-known B. must still appear very doubtful, as the princes mentioned in the rest of these inscriptions belong to a far older period; see Bhaṇḍarkar in the *Transactions of the London Congress of Orientalists* (1876), p. 306 ff.

P. 293, note *. *Sept suttas Pális, tirés du Díghanikáya*, from the papers of Paul Grimblot, were published by his widow in 1876 (Paris), text with translation.—The second part of Fausböll's edition of the Játaka appeared in 1877.—The Maháparinibbána-sutta was edited in 1874 by Childers in the *Journal R. A. S.*, vols. vii. and viii.: a separate impression of it has just appeared. The same journal also contains an edition of the Pátimokkha by Dickson. An edition of the whole Vinaya-piṭaka by Herm. Oldenberg is in the press.

P. 297, note [349]. A collected edition of the sacred Aṅgas

of the Jainas was published last year (1877) at Calcutta by Dhanapatisiṅhají: the text is accompanied with the commentary of Abhayadeva and a *bháshá*-explanation by Bhagván Vijaya.

P. 300, note [350]. On this compare also S. Beal, *The Buddhist Tripiṭaka as it is known in China and Japan* (Devonport, 1876).

P. 303, note ‡. On possible points of connection between the Avesta and Buddhism see *Jenaer Lit. Zeit.*, 1877, p. 221.

P. 305, note ‡. In Gautama the word *bhikshu* appears expressly as the name of the third of the four *áśramas;* in place of it Manu has *yati.*

BERLIN, *24th May* 1878.

SANSKRIT INDEX.

Akshapáda, 81. 245.
akshara, 'syllable,' 15. 16.
— philos., 161.
Agastya, 53. 275 (archit.).
Agni, 31. 40. 63. 159. 178. 303.
— *chayana*, 120. (274).
— *Puráṇa*, 191. 231. 271. 275. 281. 318.
— *rahasya*, 118. 120.
Agniveśa, 265. 266. 269 (med.).
Agnisvámin, 79.
agra, 190.
aghás, 248.
Añga, 25. 216 (s. *Vedáñga*). 296. 297. 326, 327 (Jain.).
Añgas, 147.
Añgir, 158.
Añgiras, 31. 53. 153. 158. 160. 162. 164. 250. 325 (*Smṛiti*).
— (Jupiter) 250.
Añgirasas, 124. 148 ff.
Ajátaśatru, 51. 127. 138. 286 (his six teachers).
— comm., 82.
atikrushṭa, 111.
atthakathá, 292.
Atri, 31. 38. 53. 102. 103. 140 Ved.
— 102. 283. 325 (jur.).
— 269 med.
— daughter of, 38. 140.
— *bṛihad°*, 269 (med.).
— *laghu°*, 269 (med.).
Atharvan, 151 (as *prajápati*). 153 (*bṛihaspati* and *bhagavant*). 158. 164.
— (= *Ath. Veda*), 78.
Atharva-Pariśishṭas, 249. 251. 253. 265.
— the forty-eighth *Ath. Par.*, 313. 316. 317. 318.
Atharva-Pariśishṭa, Greek order of the planets in the *Ath. Pariśishṭas*, 323.
— *Paippale*, 158. 169.
— *Prátiśákhya*, 146. 151.
— *Veda*, 8. 22. 29. 145 ff. 249. 265.
— *śikhare*, 164.
— *śikhá*, 164. 167.
Atharvaśiras, 154. 166. 169. 170.
Atharva-Saṃhitá, 11. 208. 318.
Atharváñgirasas, 11. 72. 93. 121. 127. 149. 150 (°*rasa* sing.)
Atharváṇas, 113. 124. 148. 149.
Atharvopanishads, 28. 153 ff. 239.
athá 'taḥ, 245. 265.
Adbhutadharma, 301 (Buddh.).
Adbhuta-Bráhmaṇa, 69. 152.
advaita, 171.
Advaita-makaranda, 323.
adhidevatam, 121.
adhiyajnam, 121.
adhyayana, 8.
adhyátmam, 121.
Adhyátmarámáyaṇa, 168.
adhyáya, 14. 31. 32. 107. 117.
adhyáyádín, 66.
adhvaryu, 14. 80. 149.
adhvaryus (pl.), 8. 80. 86. 87. 121.
Ananta, 141 (comm.).
Anantadeva, 101
Anantayajvan, 85. 245.
anaphá, 255 (Greek).
Anukramaṇís, 24. 32. 33. 61. 64. 65. 74. 83. 85. 87. 88. 90. 103. 104. 107. 143. 144. 145. 152.
Anupada-Sútra, 80. 81. 84. 88. 95.
Anubráhmaṇa, 12. 82.
anubráhmaṇin, 82.
Anubhútiprakáśa, 97.
Anubhútisvarúpácbárya, 226.

anulamba, 68.
anuváka, 31. 33. 88. 94. 107. 109. 124. 145.
— °*kánukramaṇí*, 32. 61.
anuvyákhyána, 122. 127.
anuśásana, 121. 122. 127.
anustotra, 84.
anúchána, 78.
Andhaka-Vṛishṇayas, 185.
Andhomatí, 106.
anvadhyáya, 57. 176.
anvákhyána, 122.
Apántaratamas, 243.
Apsaras, 125.
Abhayadeva, 327.
Abhichára-Kalpa, 153.
Abhidharma (Buddh.). 290. 292. 307 ff.
Abhidhána-chintámaṇi, 230.
— *ratnamálá*, 230.
Abhinavagupta, 237. 273. 322.
abhinimrukta, 278.
Abhinishkramaṇa-Sútra, 300.
Abhimanyu, 219. 220. 223.
abhiyajna-gáthás, 45.
Abhíra, 3.
abhyanúkta, 122.
Amarakosha, 220. 229 ff. 267.
Amarachandra, 190.
Amaradeva, 228.
Amarasiṅha, 200. 219. 227 ff.
Amaru, 210.
Amita, 306.
Amitábha, 298. 306.
Amitragháta, 251.
Amṛitanádopanishad, 154. 165. 171.
Amṛitavindúpanishad, 99. 154. 165.
Ambá, 114. 134. 317.
Ambiká, 39. 114. 134. 317.
Ambáliká, 39. 114. 134. 317.
ayana, 66.
ayogú, 111.
Ayodhyá, 89. 178. 224.
Aruṇa, 133. °ṇas, 93.
— *Smṛiti*, 280. 326.
Aruṇi, 93 (and plur.)
Arkalinas, 33.
arjuna, Arjuna (and Indra), 37. 50. 114. 115. 134. 135. 136. 137. 185. 186.
arjunyau, 248.
Arthaśástra, 271. 273. 275.
ardha, 73 (inhabited place).
ardhamágadhí, 295. 296. 297.
arhant, 78. 138. 305.
Alaṃkáraśástra, 231. 322.
Avadána, 299. 301 (Buddh.).
Avalokiteśvara, 298. 299.
avyakta, 238.
Avyayavṛitti, 227.
aśítipatha, 119.
Aśoka, 179. 273. 290. 291.
Aśvaghosha, 161. 162.
Aśvapati, 71. 120.
aśvamedha, 54. 114. 126.
— °*káṇḍa*, 118.
Aśvala, 53. 129.
Asháḍha, 133.
ashṭaka, 31. 32. 42. 43. 89.
ashṭádhyáyí, 118.
asura, 302 (*sura* formed from).
— language of the A.'s, 180.
— Kṛishṇa, 148. 304.
— Maya, 253, 274.
ahargaṇa, 258.
ahi, 36.
ahína, 66. 76. 79. 80. 139.
Ahobalasúri, 101.
ákáśa, 128.
ákokera, 254.
ákhyána, 122. 193.
— *vidas*, 45.
Ágamaśástra, 161.
Ágniveśya, 102. 285.
Ágniveśyáyana, 49. 53. 102.
ágneyam parva, 66.
Áṅgirasa, 71. 148. 153.
Áṅgirasakalpa, 153.
áchárya, 73. 77. 81. 121.
Áṭṇára, 68. 125.
áṇava, 171.
átman, 97. 156. 161 ff.
— (*mahán*), 238.
Átmaprabodhopanishad, 166. 167. 169.
Átmánanda, 42.
Átmopanishad, 158. 162.
Átreya, 87–89. 91. 92. 93. 102. 103. *Taitt.*, 153. *Áth.*, 241. 242. (phil.). 265. 269. (med.).
— *kanishṭha*°, 269. (med.).
— *bṛihad*°, 269. (med.).
— *madhyama*°, 269. (med.).
— *vṛiddha*°, 269. (med.).
— (*bhikshu*), 284.
Átharvaṇa, 128. 149.
— *Gṛihya*, 152.
Átharvaṇikas, 82. 149.
Átharvaṇíyarudropanishad, 154. 170.
áditya, 131.
ádityáni, 131.
Ádityadása, 259.

Ádibuddha, 298.
ádeśa, 73. 121. 149. 235. 301.
Ánanda-giri, 51. 243.
— jnána, 51.
— tírtha, 42. 51.
— vana, 168.
— vardhana, 322.
Ánandavallí, 94. 154. 156. 157.
Ánarttíya, 55.
Ándhras, 94.
Ápastamba, 88, 89 ff. 100. 101. 102. 317. 325.
— *Dharmasútra*, 101. 102. 106. 278. 325.
Ápiśali, 222.
ápoklima, 255 (Greek).
Áptavajrasúchí, 161.
Ábhipratáriṇa, 136.
Ámarája, 261.
áyana, names in, 53. 120.
Áyaḥsthúṇa, 130.
Áyurveda, 265. 267. 271.
ára, 254 (Greek).
Áraṇyaka, 8. 28. 29. 48. 92.
— *káṇḍa*, 118.
— *jyotisha*, 153.
— *saṃhitá*, 65.
Áraṇyagána, 64. 65.
Áraṇya-Saṃhitá, 316.
Áráḍa, Árálhi, 285.
Áruṇa, 93.
Áruṇi, 51. 69. 71. 123. 130. 132. 133. 157. 286.
Áruṇikopanishad, 163. 164.
Áruṇins, 93.
Áruṇeya, 133. 157.
árchika, 63. 65. 66.
Árjunaka, 185.
Áryas, 3. 79. 178.
Áryabhaṭa, 61. 254. 255. 257 ff.
Áryabhaṭíya, 61. 257.
Áryasiddhánta, 257.
Áryápañchásíti, 237.
Áryáshṭaśata, 257.
Ársha, 85.
Árshikopanishad, 162.
Ársheya-Kalpa, 75. 77.
Ársheya-Bráhmaṇa, 74. 313. 316.
Álambáyana, 53.
Ávantika, 259.
Ávantiká, *ríti*, 232.
Áśárka, 84. 278.
Áśmarathaḥ, *kalpaḥ*, 46. 53. 242.
Áśmarathya, 53. 242.
áśrama, °*mopanishad*, 164.
— (*bhikshu*), 327.
Áśvatarásvi, 133.
Áśvaláyana, 32. 34. 49. 52 ff. 59. 62. 80. 85. 101. 106. 169. 266.
— Kauśalya, 159.
— *Pariśishṭa*, 62.
— *Bráhmaṇa*, 49.
Áśvina-śastra, 314.
áśviní series, 323.
Ásuráyaṇa, 128. 140.
Ásuri, 128. 131. 133. 137. 235. 236.
áskanda, 113.
ásphujit, 254 (Greek).
Ásphuji(d)dhvaja (?), 258.
ikkavála, 264 (Arabic).
iṭhimiká, 89.
Itará, 48.
Itihásas, 24. 72. 93. 122. 124. 127. 159. 190. 191.
Itihásapuráṇa, 121. 183. 301.
ittha, 254 (Greek).
itthiśála, 264 (Arabic).
ityukta, 300.
inthihá, 264 (Arabic).
induvára, 264 (Arab.)
Indra, 32. 40. 52. 63. 123. 127. 176 (gramm.). 186. 211. 265 (med.). 303.
— and Arjuna, 37. 50. 115. 136. 185. 186.
Indrajananíya, 193.
Indradatta, 293.
Indradyumna, 133.
Indraprastha, 178.
Indrota, 34. 125.
Irávatí, 178.
iś, 108.
Íśána, 45. 110.
Íśopanishad, 116. 155. 309.
íśvara, 238.
Íśvara, 272 mus.
Íśvarakṛishṇa, 236. 237.
isaràpha, 264 (Arabic).
uktapratyuktam, 122.
uktha, 67. 81.
ukthártha, 83.
Ukha, 91.
Ugrasena, 125. 135.
uchcha, 257.
Ujjayiní, 185. 201. 209. 252. 257 259. 295.
Ujjvaladatta, 226.
uṇádi, 216. 226.
Uttaratápiní, 169.
Uttaramímáṅsá, 239 ff.
Uttararámacharita, 207.
Uttaravallí, 157.

uttará, *uttarárchika*, 63. 65.
uttaráshádhás, 247.
Utpala, 243. 260. 322.
Utpaliní, 227.
Udayana, 246.
udátta, 314.
udíchyas, 132. 178.
udgátar, 14. 67. 149.
Uddálaka, 69. 71. 123. 130. 131. 157. 284.
Uddyotakara, 245.
Udbhaṭa, 322.
Upagrantha-Sútra, 83. 84.
Upatishya, 199.
upadeśa, 301 (Buddh.).
upadhá, 144.
Upanishads, 28. 29. 42. 48. 73. 74. 121. 127. 153 ff. 235. 277.
— number of, 154. 155.
— (*Up. Bráhmaṇa*), 34. 74.
Upapuráṇas, 171. 191. 282.
Upalekha, 40. 59.
Upaveda, 265. 271. 273.
upavyákhyána, 122.
upaskára, 244.
upastha, 114.
upákhyána, 73, 122.
Upáñgas, 297 (Jain.).
upádhyáya, 82.
— *nirapekshá*, 271.
upásaka, °*siká*, 306.
Upendra, 303.
ubhayam antareṇa, 49.
Umá, 74. 156.
uraga, 98. 303.
Urvaśí, 134. 207 (drama). 208.
ulúka, 246.
Uvaṭṭa, 42.
Uśanas (Kávya), 36. 153.
— 278. 282. 325 (jur.).
Uśíṇara, 45.
Ushasti, 71.
ushṭra, 3.
Ūhaṭa, 34. 42. 59. 116.
Ūvaṭa, 144.
Úhagána, *Úhyagána*, 64.
Ṛik-Saṃhitá, 9. 10. 11. 14. 31 ff.
— and *Sáma-S.*, readings of, 313.
— concluding verse of, in the forty-eighth *Ath. Par.*, 313.
— Kashmír MS., 314.
— *galitas* in, 314, 315.
Ṛigvidhána, 62. 74. (33). 313. 314. 316.
Ṛigveda, 8. 33 (*ṛigvedayuptaye*). 45. 121. 123. 127.
ṛichas, 8. 9. 14. 31. 33. 63. 64. 65. 74. 75.
— number of, 121. 153.
Ṛishi, 8 (= *Veda*). 122. 145.
— *Bráhmaṇa*, 64.
— *mukháni*, 66.
Ṛishy-Anukramaṇí, 88.
Ekachúrṇi, 42. 91.
ekapádiká, 117.
ekavachana, 124.
ekahaṅsa, 129.
ekáha, 66. 76. 79. 80. 139.
eke, 134. 140.
Aikshváka, 125.
Aitareya, 48. 49. 56. 70. 85.
— *Bráhmaṇa*, 16. 44 ff. 72.
— °*yaka*, 34. 62.
— °*yáraṇyaka*, 32. 48 ff. 75. 315.
— °yins, 49. 81. 85.
— °*opanishad*, 48. 155.
Aitiśáyana, 53. 241 (Aita°).
Aindra (School), 321.
aindram parva, 66.
aiśvarika, 309.
om, 158. 160. 161. 163. 164.
orimiká, 89.
aukthika, 83. 240.
Aukhíyas, 88.
Auḍulomi, 242.
Audanya, 134.
audíchya, 34.
Audumbaráyaṇa, 53.
Auddálaki, 157 (Ved.). 267 (erot.).
Audbhári, 88.
Aupatasvini, 134.
Aupamanyava, 75.
Aupaveśi, 133.
Aupaśivi, 143.
Aupoditeya, 133.
Aulúkya, 246.
Aushṭrákshi, 75.
Kaṅsavadha, 198. 207.
Kachcháná (Buddha's wife), 318.
Kachcháyana, 227. 293.
Kaṭha, 89. 92. 184; plur. 88. 89. 317.
— Kálápas, 89.
— *vallí*, 157.
— *śákhá*, 89.
— *śrutyupanishad*, 163. 164.
— *Sútra*, 99. 100.
Kaṇabhaksha, Kaṇabhuj, 245. 260.
Kaṇáda, 244. 245. 246.
kaṇḍiká, 59. 89. 107. 117. 118–120.
kaṇva, 140 (deaf).

Kaṇva, 3. 31. 52. 106. 105 (plur.). 140.
—*Smṛiti-Śástra*, 143.
Kaṇha, 304.
Kaṇhi, Kaṇháyana, 304.
Katas, 138.
Kathásaritságara, 213. 217. 219. 223.
Kadrú, 134.
Kanishka, Kanerki, 205. 218. 219. 220. 222. 223. 281. 285. 287. 288. 290. 294. 302. 306. 308.
kanishṭha, 269 (treya).
kanyákumárí, 157.
Kapardigiri, 179.
Kapardisvámin, 42. 101.
kapiñjala, 211.
Kapila, 96. 137. 162. 235 ff. 272. 284. 308.
Kapilavastu, 33. 137. 284.
Kapishṭhala, 265. 268 (med.).
— Kaṭhas, 88.
Kapishṭhala-Saṃhitá, 88.
Kabandha, 149.
Kabandhin, 159.
Kambojas, 178. 220.
kamvúla, 264 Arab.
karaṭaka, 206.
karaṇa, 259 (astr.).
— *kutúhala*, 261. 262.
— *sára*, 262.
Karavindasvámin, 101.
karálí, 159.
Karka, 141.
Karṇátakas, 94.
Karṇísuta, 276.
Karmanda, °dinas, 305.
Karmapradípa, 84. 85. 278.
Karmamímáṅsá, 239 ff.
Karmargha, 153.
kalás (the sixty-four), 275.
Kalápa-Sútra, 227 (gramm.).
Kalápin, 184.
kali, 113. 283 *yuga*.
— era, 205. 260. 261.
Kaliñga, 269.
Kalinátha, 272.
kaliyuga, 243.
Kalki-Puráṇa, 191.
Kalpa, 16. 46. 53. 75. 93. 153 (*Ath.*). 176. 242.
— *kára*, 144.
— *Sútras*, 16. 34. 75. 100. 102 (Ved.). 297 (Jain.) 317.
Kalpánupada, 84.
Kalhaṇa, 213. 215. 319.
Kavasha, 120.
Kavi, 153 (Uśanas). 191. 195.
Kaviputra, 204. 205.
Kavirája, 196.
kaśyapa, 140 (having black teeth).
Kaśyapa, 53. 140.
— 278. 282 jur.
kasháya, 78. 306.
Kaserumant, 188.
Kahola, 129. 133.
Káñkáyana, 153 (Ath.). 266. 269 (med.)
Káṭhaka, 41. 81. 85. 88. 89 ff. 103. 317.
— *Gṛihya*, 101. 317.
Káṭhakopanishad, 93. 156, 238. 240.
káṇáda, 246.
káṇḍa, 59. 89. 91. 92. 117 ff. 145.
Káṇḍamáyana, 53.
Káṇva, 103. 106. 113 ff. 142. 143. 144 (gramm.).
Káṇvaka, 105.
Káṇvíputra, 105.
Káṇvyáyana, 105.
Kátantra, 226. 227. 321.
Kátíya-Gṛihya, 142.
Kátíya-Sútra, 91. 99. 100. 142.
Kátya, 138. 223.
Kátyáyana, 53. 61. 80. 83. 84. 107. 138 ff. (Ved.) 222. 321. (gramm.), 227 lex. 266 med. 285 (Buddh.).
— *Smṛiti-Śástra* of, 143. 326.
— Kabandhin, 159.
Kátyáyaní, 127. 138; = Durgá, 138. 157.
— putra, 71. 138. 285.
Kádambarí, 213.
Kápila-Śástra, 236.
Kápya, 126. 137. 223. 236. 237. 284.
Kámandakíya (*Níti-Śástra*), 271. 325.
Káma-Sútra, 267.
Kámukáyana, 241.
Kámpíla, 114. 115; °lya, 115. 138.
Kámboja, 75.
Káraṇḍavyúha, 299.
Kárttakaujapa, 266.
Kárttikeya, 103 (comm.).
kármika, 309.
Kárshṇájini, 140. 241. 242.
Kála, 248.
Kálanirṇaya, 262.
Kálabavins, 14. 81. 83. 96.
Kálayavana, 220. 221.
Kálágnirudropanishad, 171.
Kálápa, 89. 96.

Kálidása, 195. 196. 200 ff. 209. 228. 250. 252. 266. 318 f.
-- three Kálidásas, 204.
káli, 159.
Kávasheya, 120. 131.
Kávila, 236.
kávyas, 183. 191. 195. 210.
Kávya 36 (Uśanas). 153.
Kávyaprakáśa, 204. 232.
Kávyádarśa, 232.
Kávyálaṃkáravṛitti, 226. 232.
Káśakṛitsna, 42. 91. 140. 242.
Káśakṛitsni, 139. 140. 242.
Káśis, 125. 286.
Káśiká, 106. 130. 226. 227. 321.
Káśí, 269. 283.
Káśmíras, 227.
Káśyapa, 143 (gramm.). 245 (phil.). 275 (archit.).
káshádyadháraṇa, 237.
kitava, 111.
kiṃnara, 302.
Kirátárjuníya, 196.
Kíkaṭas, 79.
Kírtidhara, 273.
kuṭṭaka, 259.
Kuṭhumi, 84.
Kuṇḍina, 91.
— (town), 168.
Kutapa-Sauśruta, 266.
kuntápasúkta, 146.
Kuntí, 90.
Kubhá, 3.
Kumárapála, 297.
Kumárasambhava, 195. 196. 208. 318.
Kumárilabhaṭṭa, 68. 74. 241. 242.
Kumárilasvámin, 100.
Kumbhamushkas, 303.
Kumbháṇḍas, 302. 303.
Kurus, 114. 123. 135. 136. 137. 138 (and Katas). 286.
Kurukshetra, 68. 136.
Kuru-Pañchálas, 10. 34. 39. 45. 68. 90. 114. 129. 132. 135. 186. 286.
kuladharma, 278.
kulíra, 254.
Kullúka, 281.
Kuvera, 124. 303.
Kuśa and Lava, 197.
kuśílava, 197.
Kushmáṇḍas, 303.
Kusumapura, 257. 258.
Kusumáñjali, 245. 246.
kúrmavibhága, 215.
Kúshmáṇḍas, 303.
kṛit, 144.
kṛita, 113 (*yuga*).
kṛittiká, 2. 148. 247. 248. 304. 323.
— series, date of, 2.
Kṛityachintámaṇi, 80.
Kṛiśa, 266 med.
Kṛiśáśva, °śvinas, 197.
kṛishṇa (black), 304.
Kṛishṇa Devakíputra, 71. 104. 148. 169. 186. 238. 284. 304.
— and Kálayavana, 220. 221.
— and the Páṇḍavas, 136.
— and the shepherdesses, 210.
— worship of, 71. 189. 209. 238. 289. 300. 304. 307. 326.
— Áñgirasa, 71. 148.
— Dvaipáyana, 184. 243.
— Asura Kṛishṇa, 148. 304.
— Kṛishṇa Hárita, 50.
Kṛishṇajit, 54. 58.
Kṛishṇamiśra, 207.
Kṛishṇájina, 242.
Kṛishṇátreya, 266 med.
Kekayas, 120. 132.
ketu, 250.
Kenopanishad, 73. 74. 75. 156 ff. 171. 316.
kemadruma, 255.
kerala, 245.
— *naiyáyika*, 245.
Keśava Káśmírabhaṭṭa, 323.
Keśin (Asura), 148.
Keśi-súdana, °han, 148.
'*Kesarí*' *saṃgrámaḥ*, 188.
keśava, 304.
Kaikeya, 120.
Kaiyaṭa, 56. 83. 93. 95. 223. 224.
Kaivalyopanishad, 155. 163. 169 f.
Kokila, 280.
koṇa, 254.
Kośala, 160. 185. 192. 193. 324.
Kosala, 33. 68. 137. 285.
— Videhas, 34. 39. 132. 134. 135. 285.
Kohala, 273.
Kaukústa, 134.
kaukkuṭika, 305.
Kauṇḍinya, 102. 285.
Kautsa, 77. 140.
Kautsáyana, 97.
Kauthumas, 47. 65. 76. 83. 84. 89. 96. 106.
Kaudreyas, 140.
Kaumárila, 241.
Kauravya, 39. 123. 135. 136.

Kaurupañchála, 123.
kaurpya, 254 (Greek).
Kaulopanishad, 171.
Kauśalya (Áśvaláyana), 159.
Kauśámbeya, 123.
Kauśika, 149. 152. 153 (*Ath.*).
— (Comm.), 42. 91.
Kaushítaka, 56.
Kaushítaka, 46. 81.
— °*káraṇyaka*, 50. 54.
Kaushítaki, °kin, 46. 68. 82. 133. 134. 313.
— *Bráhmaṇa*, 26. 44 ff. 71.
— *Upanishad*, 50. 73. 127. 155. 286.
Kaushítakeya, 129.
Kausalya, 125. 159 (ś).
Kausurubindi, 123.
Kauhala, 75.
kramapáṭha, 34. 49. 60.
kríya, 254 (Greek).
Krivi, Kraivya, 125.
Krauñcha, 93.
Kraushṭuki, 61 metr. 153. 248 *Ath.*
klíba, 111.
kshatrapati, 68.
Kshapaṇaka, 200.
Kshárapáṇi, 265 med.
Kshírasvámin, 79. 227.
Kshudras, 84.
Kshurikopanishad, 165.
Kshemaṃkara, 213.
Kshemendra, 213. 215. 319. 320. 321.
Kshemendrabhadra, 293.
Kshairakalambhi, 77.
Kshaudra, 84.
Khaṇḍika, 88.
Khadirasvámin, 79.
Kharoshṭha, 248.
Kháḍáyana, 53, °nins 14. 81.
Kháṇḍikíyas, 87. 88.
Kháḍiragṛihya, 84.
khila, 92. 97. 107. 130. 144. 249. 313 f.
— *káṇḍa*, 127. 128. 130. 131.
khuddakapáṭha, 293.
Gaṅgá, 51. 168. 193. 248.
Gaṅgádhara, 142.
Gaṅgeśa, 246. 323.
gaṇas, 225. 266 gramm.
gaṇaka, 113.
Gaṇapatipúrvatápiní, 170.
Gaṇapatyupanishad, 154. 170.
gaṇapáṭha, 138. 225. 240. 241. 242.
Gaṇaratnamahodadhi, 226.
gaṇita, 159.
gaṇitádhyáya, 262.
Gaṇeśa, 281.
— *tápiní*, 170.
Gadádhara, 142.
Gandharva, 272 (Nárada). 284 (Pañchaśikha).
— possessed by a, 126.
Gandhára, 70. 132. 218, °ris, 147.
Garuḍa, 171. 302 (plur.).
— *Puráṇa*, 191.
Garuḍopanishad, 171.
Garga, 153 *Ath.* 221. 252 ff. (astr.).
— plur. 252. 253.
— Vṛiddhagarga, 153. 253.
Garbhopanishad, 160. 167. 272.
galitas, 314. 315.
gallakka, 206.
gahanaṃ gambhíram, 233.
Gáṅgyáyani, 51.
Gáṇapatyapúrvatápaníya, 170.
gáthás, 24. 33. 45. 72. 73. 93. 121. 122. 124. 125. 127. 132. 184.
— 299. 301 Buddh.
Gánas, 63. 64. 81. 316. 325.
Gándharvaveda, 271. 272.
gáyatrísampanna, 140.
Gárgí Váchaknaví, 56. 129.
— *Saṃhitá*, 214. 251.
Gárgya, 56 (*Gṛihya*). 63 (*Sámav.*). 75 (Maśaka). 143 (gramm.). 153 (*Ath.*).
— and Kálayavana, 221.
— Báláki, 51.
Gítagovinda, 210.
— (time of composition), 210.
Guṇáḍhya, 213.
Gupta (dynasty), 204.
Gurudevasvámin, 101.
Gurjara, 297.
Guhadeva, 42. 323.
guhya ádeśa, 73.
guhyaṃ náma, 115.
Gúḍhárthar atnamálá, 42.
Gṛitsamada, 31.
gṛihastha, 28. 164.
Gṛihya-Sútras, 15. 17. 19. 20. 69. 84. 101. 152. 153. 264. 276. 278.
geya, 301 Buddh.
Geyagána, 66.
gairikamvúla, 264 Arab.
Gairikshita, 41.
Goṇikáputra, 223 gr. 267 (erot.).
Gotama, 244 ff. (log.).
— *Sútra*, 245.

Godávarí, 283.
Gonardíya, 223 gr. 267 (erot.).
Gopatha-Bráhmaṇa, 106. 150. 151. 152. 304.
Gopavanas, 140.
Gopálatápaníyopanishad, 169.
gopí, 169.
Gopíchandanopanishad, 169.
Gobhila, 80. 82. 83. 84.
— *Smṛiti*, 280.
goládhyáya, 262.
Govardhana, 211.
Govinda, comm., 55. 62.
— teacher of Śaṃkara, 161. 243.
— svámin, 101 comm.
Gauḍa (style), 232.
Gauḍapáda, 161. 167. 236. 243. 298.
Gautama, 77 (two G.'s).
— 84. 143 (jur.).
— 153. 162 (*Ath.*).
— 245 (phil.).
— 162 (Ṛishi).
— *Dharma* (-*Sútra*), 85. 278. 281. 282. 325. 326. 327.
— (*Pitṛimedha-Sútra*), 84. 245.
Gautamaḥ Sáṃkhyaḥ, 284.
Gautamas, 137.
grantha, 15. 99. 165. 193.
— (*nidánasaṃjnaka*), 81.
graha, 67 (Soma-vessel).
— eclipse, 249.
— planet, 98. 249. 250.
— (*bálagraha*), 98.
gráma, 64. 77.
Grámageyagána, 64. 65.
Ghaṭakarpara, 200. 201.
Ghora Áṅgirasa, 71.
Chatuḥshashṭikaláśástra, 275 (°*lágama*).
chaturaṅga, game of, 275.
Chatur-adhyáyiká, 151 (°*ádhyáyiká*).
Chaturviṅśatismṛiti, 280.
Chandra, 219. 227.
Chandraka, 319.
Chandragupta, 4. 204. 217. 223. 251. 287.
— (Gupta dynasty), 204.
Chandrabhágá, 269.
Chandra-Vyákaraṇa, 227.
Champá, 178.
charaka, 87.
Charaka, 265. 266. 268. 270. 284. 324. 325 med.
Charaka-Śákhá, 89.
Charakas, 87. 88. 164.
Charakáchárya, 87. 113.
Charakádhvaryus, 87. 133. 134.
Charaṇa-vyúha, 95. 142. 153 (*Ath.*).
°*charitra*, 214.
Chákra, 123.
Chákráyaṇa, 71.
Cháṇakya, 205. 210. 260. 310.
cháṇḍála, 129.
Chánaráṭas, 193.
chándanagandhika, 275.
Chándrabhágin, 269.
Śrí-Chápa, 259.
Cháráyaṇíya, 88. 103. 317 (*Śikshá*).
Chárvákas, 246.
Chálukya, 214.
Chitra, 51.
Chitraratha, 68 (Báhlíkam).
chitrá, 247. 248 (series).
Chintámaṇivṛitti, 217.
Chínas, 243.
Chúḍa, 130.
Chúlikopanishad, 165.
chela, 138.
Chelaka, 138.
Chaikitáneya, 138.
Chaikitáyana, 138.
Chaitrarathi, 68.
Chailaki, 133.
Chyavana, 134.
Chhagalin, 96. 99.
chhandas (Vedic text), 8. 14. 57. 60. 103. 176.
— (*Sáma-Saṃhitá*), 63.
— metr., 25. 60. 145. 272.
Chhandasiká, 63.
Chhandogas, 8. 66. 81. 86. 121.
chhandobháshá, 103.
chhandovat, 216.
Chhagaleya, 96. 102. 155, °yins, 96.
Chhágeyas, 96.
Chhándogya-Bráhmaṇa, 69.
Chhándogyopanishad, 70 ff. 155.
Jaganmohana, 283.
Jaṭápaṭala, 60.
Jatúkarṇa, 265 med.
Janaka, 33. 53. 68. 76. 123. 124. 127. 129. 132. 135. 193. 237. 285. 286 (his six teachers).
janaka (*prajápati*), 76.
— *saptarátra*, 76.
Janamejaya, 34. 123. 125. 131. 134. 135. 136. 186.
Janárdana, 303.
japamálá, 307.

Jamadagni, 162, 315.
Jayatírtha, 42.
Jayadeva, 210 (date of).
Jayabhaṭa, 319.
Jayaratha, 322.
Jayaráma, 143.
Jayáditya, Jayápíḍa, 227. 322.
Jarásaṃdha, 98.
Jalada, 150.
Játaka, astr., 240. 260.
Játakas, Buddh., 284. 293. 301. 326.
játakarman, 19. 102. 142.
játi, 161.
Játúkarṇya, 138. 139. 140. 143.
Jánaki, 130.
Jábála, 71. 130. 132. 134. 163. 185.
Jábáli, 143 (*Smṛiti*).
Jábálopanishad, 163. 164. 168.
jámitra, 255 (Greek).
jituma, 254 (Greek).
Jishṇu, 259.
jíva, 162.
Jívagosvámin, 169.
Jívala, 133.
Jívaśarman, 260.
júka, 254 (Greek).
jeman, 240.
Jainas, 214. 217. 236. 244. 293. 295 ff.
Jaimini, 56-58 (*Gṛihya*). 65 (*Sámav.*). 184. 189. 239 ff. (phil.).
— *Bhárata*, 57. 189.
— *Sútra*, 240 (astr.). 322.
Jaiminíya, 65. 240. 316. 317.
— *nyáyamálávistara*, 241. 322.
Jaivali, 71.
Jnánabháskara, 253.
Jnánayajna, 91. 94.
Jyotirvid-ábharaṇa, 201. 260. 261. 266.
Jyotisha, 25. 30. 60. 61. 153 (*Áraṇyaka°*). 249. 258. 316.
jyau, 254 (Greek).
Takshan, 133.
Takshaśilá, 185.
Taṇḍálakshaṇa-Sútra, 83. 84.
tad and *tvam*, 162.
Tadevopanishad, 108. 155.
taddhita, 144.
tantra ceremonial, 167. 208. 209. 265. 282. 310.
— gramm., 227. 229.
— 'text-book,' 229 (term taken to Java). 265. 266.
taravi, 263 (Arabic).
tarka, 158. 244.
tarkin, 244.
Talavakára-Bráhmaṇa, 316.
Talavakáras, 74.
taśíl, *tasdí*, 263. 264 (Arabic).
Tájika (*-Śástra*), 263 (Arabic).
Táṇḍam (*puráṇam*), 76.
Táṇḍin, 61 (gr.), 243.
Táṇḍins, 70.
Táṇḍya, 66 ff. 74. 133.
tápasa, 129. 138.
°tápaníya, *°tápiní*, 167 ff.
Tárakopanishad, 163. 164. 168.
Táranátha, 248. 293. 300. 309.
Tálavṛintanivásin, 101.
távuri, 254 (Greek).
tiñ, 144.
tittiri, 87 (partridge).
Tittiri, 41. 87. 88. 90. 91.
Tipiṭaka, 292. 293. 294.
Tirimdira, 3.
tishya, 248.
tíkshṇadaṅshṭra, 167.
Tutáta, °tita, 241.
Tura, 120. 131 (Kávasheya).
Turanmya, 253. 274.
turushka, Turushka, 220. 291.
tulyakála, 12. 129.
Tejovindúpanishad, 165. 171.
Taittiríya, 81. 87, °yakas 102. 162 (°yake). 317 (*Prát.*).
— *Saṃhitá*, 88 ff. 108. 248.
— *°yáraṇyaka*, 92–94. 238. 240. 249. 303.
— *°yopanishad*, 93. 94.
taukshika, 254 (Greek).
Tautátika, °tita, 241.
Taulvali, 53.
trayí vidyá, 8. 45. 121. 191.
Trasadasyu, 68.
Trikáṇḍa, 227.
trikoṇa, 255 (Greek).
Tripiṭaka, 292.
tripuṇḍravidhi, 171.
Tripuropanishad, 171.
Tripuryupanishad, 161. 162.
Tribháshyaratna, 103.
Tribhuvanamalla, 214.
Triśúlaṅka, 62.
tretá, 113. 159.
Traitana, 36.
tvam and *tad*, 162.
Daksha, 326 (*Smṛiti*).
Daṇḍin, 213. 232.
Dattaka, 196.
Dadhyañch, 128. 149.
Dantidurga, 203.

dampati, 38.
Darśanopanishad, 171.
darśapúrṇamásau, 101.
Daśakumára, °*charita*, 206. 213. 250. 276.
daśat, 63. 124. 149.
Daśatayí, 83 (comm.).
daśatayí, plur. *daśatayyas*, 32. 82.
Daśapurusham-rájya, 123.
Daśarúpa, 231, 232.
Dasarathajátaka, 293.
Daharasutta, 293.
Dáksháyaṇa, 227. 228.
Dákshi, Dákshíputra, 218. 228.
Dánava, Dánu, 302.
Dálbhya, 85 (*Pariśishṭa*). 143 (gr.).
dásaka, 36.
Dásaśarman, 55.
digvijayas, 141.
Diñnága, 209. 245.
Divodása, 269.
dínára, 229. 304 (*denarius*).
Dípavaṅsa, 288.
Duḥshanta, 125.
durudhará, 255 (Greek).
Durga, 33. 41. 42. 63.
Durgasiṅha, 226.
Durgá, 138, 159.
dushkṛita, 87.
Dushṭarítu, 123.
dṛikáṇa, 255 (Greek).
dṛiśya, 319.
Dṛishadvatí, 67. 102.
Deva, Devayájnika, Srí Deva, 141. 142.
Devakí, 71.
Devakíputra, 71. 148. 166. 169.
devajanavidas, 121.
devajanavidyá, 124. 183.
Devatádhyáya, 74. 75.
Devatráta, 54.
Devadatta, 160.
Devapála, 317.
Devarájayajvan, 41. 42.
Devasvámin, 260 (astr.).
Devápi, 39.
Devyupanishad, 154. 170. 171.
°*deśíya*, 79.
Daivata, 85.
Daivápa, 125.
doshapati, 151. 318.
dyuta, 255 (Greek).
Dyaushpitar, 35.
Dramiḍa, Dravidáchárya, 322. 323.
dramma, 229 (Greek).
draha, 79.
Dráviḍas, 94.
Dráhyáyaṇa, 53. 79. 84. 282.
Droṇa, 185. 271.
dvápara, 113. 151. 243.
Dvárakánáthayajvan, 324.
Dvivedagaṅga, 72. 104. 139.
Dvaipáyana, s. Kṛishṇa.
Dhanaṃjaya, 232.
Dhanapatisúri, 243.
Dhanurveda, 271, 282.
Dhaneśvara, 214.
Dhanvantari, 200. 265. 266. 269.
Dhanvin, 80.
Dhammapada, 293.
dhammapaliyáyáni, 292. 294.
Dharma, 176. 276 ff.
— *Śástras*, 159. 276–283.
— *Śástra-saṃgraha*, 325. 326.
— *Sútras*, 19. 85. 101. 277 ff. 317.
dharmas, 101.
Dharma, °putra, °rája, 186.
dharmáchárya, 56.
Dhátu-taraṃgiṇí, 227.
Dhátu-páṭha, -*páráyaṇa*, 230.
Dhánaṃjayya, 76. 77. 82.
Dhárá, 201. 202.
Dhávaka, 204. 205. 207.
Dhúmráyaṇa, 141.
Dhúrtasvámin, 79. 101.
Dhṛitaráshṭra (Vaichitravírya), 39. 90. 114.
— king of the Káśis, 125.
Dhyánavindúpanishad, 165.
Dhyánibuddhas, 298.
dhruvasya prachalanam, 98.
nakta (*nakla*), 264, Arab.
nakshatras, 2. 90.
Nakshatra-Kalpa, 153.
nakshatradarśa, 112.
Nagnajit, 132. 134.
Nachiketas, 157.
naṭa, 196. 197. 199.
— *Sútras*, 197. 199. 271. 275.
Nanda, 205. 117. 223.
Nandikeśvara-Upapuráṇa, 171.
Namin, 68.
Naraka, 188.
nartaka, 199.
Nala, 132. 189.
Nalodaya, 196.
Navaratna, 201.
Navahasta, 101.
Náka, 123.
Nágas (*nága*), 273. 302.

Nágánanda, 207.
Nágárjuna, 224. 265. 287. 288 (date of).
Nágeśa, 223. 227.
Nágojibhaṭṭa, 223. 224. 226.
Náṭakas, 196.
náṭya, 197. 200.
— *Śástra*, 231.
náṇaka, 205. 281.
Nádavindúpanishad, 165.
Nárada, 72 (Ved.). 153 (*Áth. Par.*). 264 (astr.). 272 (etym. and mus.).
— *pañcharátra*, 239.
— *Śikshá*, 61. 272.
— (-*Smṛiti*), 278. 326.
Nárasiṅha, 167, °*mantra* 167. 168.
Náráyaṇa, 94. 123 (*purusha*). 160. 166. 167. 303.
Náráyaṇa, 54 (comm., several N.'s). 58 (do.). 141. 158 ff. (*Upan.*).
Náráyaṇíyopanishad, 93. 157. 166. 167. 169. 171.
Náráyaṇopanishad, 166. 170.
náráśaṅsís, 93. 121. 122. 127.
nigama, 8.
Nigama-Pariśishṭa, 25. 142. 153.
Nighaṇṭus, 25. 41. 153 (*Áth.*). 227.
nitya, 167.
Nichhivis, 276.
nidána, 81 (Ved.). 301 (Buddh.).
Nidána-Sútra, 24. 62. 77. 81. 82.
Nimi, 68.
Nirapeksha, 325.
Nirálambopanishad, 162.
Nirukta, °*kti*, 25. 26. 41. 42. 44. 59. 62. 88. 160. 167. 216. 217. 235.
Nirṛiti, 152.
nirbhuja, 49.
nirváṇam, 161 (*bráhma*). 308 (Buddh.).
Niśumbha, 206.
Nishadhas, 132.
Nishádas, 77.
Níti-Śástras, 210. 271. 282.
Nílakaṇṭha, 188. 189.
Nílamata, 320.
Nílarudropanishad, 171.
Nṛisiṅha, 167. 168.
— *tápaníyopanishad*, 167. 168.
Nṛisiṅha, 101 comm., 168.
Negas, Naigeyas, 65. 85.
Naigeya-Sútra, 84.
Naighaṇṭukas, 25. 85.
Naidánas, 81.
Naimiśíya, 70.
Naimisha, °shíya, 34. 45. 54. 59. 68. 185.
naiyáyika, 245.
Nairuktas, 26. 85.
Naishadhíya, 196. 232.
Naishidha, 132.
Nyáya, 159. 237. 242. 245. 246.
— *chintámaṇi*, 246. 323.
— *darśana*, 244. 323.
— *Sútra*, 85. 235. 245.
Pakshilasvámin, 244. 245.
Pañchatantra, 206. 212. 215. 221. 229. 240. 266. 267. 291. 301.
pañchadaśarcha, 122.
Pañchaparṇa, 267.
pañchamáśrama, 164.
pañchalakshaṇa, 190.
Pañchaviṅśa-Bráhmaṇa, 66 ff.
Pañchavidhi-Sútra, 83. 84.
Pañchavidheya, 83. 84.
Pañchaśikha, 235. 236. 237. 284.
Pañchasiddhántiká, 259.
Pañchálas, 10. 90. 114. 115. 125. 135. 136.
Pañchálachaṇḍa, 50. 315. 326.
pañchálapadavṛitti, 34.
Pañchála Bábhravya, 10. 34. (erot. Páñch°).
pañchiká, 44.
paṭala, 59. 82. 84.
Pataṃchala, 126. 137. 223. 236. 237. 284.
Pataṃjali, 87. 219 ff. 231. 277. 321 (gr.).
— 137. 223. 231. 237 ff. (phil.).
°*patha*, 117.
padakára, 91.
padapáṭha, 23. 33. 43. 49. 60. 63.
padavṛitti, 34.
Paddhatis, 55. 59. 85. 102. 141. 142. 143. 145. 317.
Padma-Puráṇa, 191.
Padmayoni, 153.
panaphará, 255 (Greek).
Para, 68. 125.
Paramahaṅsa, °*haṅsopanishad*, 163. 164.
Paramádíśvara, 257.
parameśvara, 162.
Paráśara, 44. 143. 185. 252. 260 (astr.). 265. 266 (med.).
— (-*Smṛiti*), 278. 280 (*laghu* and *vṛiddha*). 326.
Parikshit, 136.

Paritta, 293 (Buddh.).
paribhâshâs, 101. 140. 144. 222. 227.
Paribhâshendusekhara, 226.
parivrâjaka, 112. 147. 164.
Parisishṭas, 60. 62. 69. 75. 84. 85. 101. 107. 142. 146. 149. 150. 151. 153. 317.
Parisesha, 119 (*Satap. Br.*).
Parthavas, 4. 188. 318.
parvan, 66 (*Sâmav.*). 124 (*Atharvan*, &c.). 146. 149. 183. 184.
Parśu, 3 (.4).
°*paliyâyâni*, 292. 294.
Pavana, 272.
Paśupatiśarman, 54.
Pahlavas, 187. 188. 318.
Pâñcharâtra, 238.
Pâñchavidhya, 83.
Pâñchâla, 267.
pâñchâlî, 34 (gr.). 232 (*rîti*).
Pâñchâlya, 138.
Pâñchi, 133.
Pâṭaliputra, 217. 237. 251. 258. 290. 295.
Pâṭimokkhasutta, 293. 326.
pâṭha, 22. 49. 103.
Pâṇini, 3. 8. 12. 15. 26. 41. 57. 59. 61. 77. 82. 87. 216–222. 232. 239. 241. 242. 245. 249. 266. 281. 318. 321.
— posterior to Buddha, 222. 305.
— posterior to Alexander, 221. 222.
Pâṇinîyâ Sikshâ, 61. 272.
Pâṇḍavas, Pâṇḍus, 39. 98. 114. 115. 126. 135. 136. 137. 185. 186. 286.
pâṇḍitya, 129. 161.
pâthona, 254 (Greek).
pâdas, 161 (the four).
pâpman âsura, 318.
Pâraśavya, 3.
Pârasîkas, 188. 220.
Pâraskara, 66. 142. 143. 318.
Pârâśariṇas, 143. 305.
Pârâśarîya, 305.
Pârâśarya, 143. 305 (*Bhikshu-Sûtra*).
— (Vyâsa), 93. 184. 185. 240. 243.
Pârâśaryâyaṇa, 243.
Pârikshi, 284.
Pârikshitas, °tîyas, 34. 125. 126. 135. 136. 186.
Pârikshita, 136.
Pâli, 288. 292. 293. 295.
Pâśupata, 238.
Piṅgala, 46. 60. 231. 256.
piṭaka, 290. 304. 309.
piṇḍapitṛiyajna, 19. 55.
Piṇḍopanishad, 171.
pitâmaha, 303.
pitṛitarpaṇa, 55.
Pitṛibhûti, 141.
pitṛimedha, 108. 198.
— *Sûtra*, 84. 245.
pitta, 266.
Pippalâda, 153. 159. 160. 164.
Piyadasi, edicts of, 6. 76. 178. 203. 252. 253. 292. 295.
pîlu, 229 (Persian).
puṁśchalî, °*lû*, 111. 112.
°*putra*, 71. 131. 285.
Punarvasu, 265.
Purâṇas (Ved.), 24. 72. 93. 121. 122. 124. 127. 159. 190.
— 190. 191. 195. 206. 207, 213. 215. 282.
purâṇaṃ Tâṇḍam, 76.
purâṇaprokta, 12. 129.
Purukutsa, 68. 125.
purusha, 162 (the three *p.*'s, phil.). 237. 238.
— Nârâyaṇa, 123. 124.
— *medha*, 54. 87. 90. 108. 111.
— *sûkta*, 65. 108. 155.
purushottama, 168.
Purûravas, 134.
purohita, 150.
Puliśa, 253. 254. 255. 257. 258.
Pushkara (?), 262.
Pushpa-Sûtra, 82. 84.
Pushyamitra, 224.
pûtâ (filthy) *vâch*, 180.
Pûrṇa, 98.
Pûrvamîmâṅsâ, 239 ff.
Pṛithûdakasvâmin, 259. 262.
pṛishṭha, 67.
pekkha, 319.
Paiṅgalopanishad, 171.
Paiṅgi, Paiṅgin, Paiṅgya, 14. 41. 46. 56. 81. 90. 130. 134. 184.
Paiṅgya, the, 46.
Paitâmahasiddhânta, 258.
°*paippale*, 158. 169.
Paippalâda, 146. 150. 152. 160.
Paila, 56. 57. 58.
Paiśâchabhâshya, 91.
paiśâchî bhâshâ, 213.
Potala, 285.
Pauliśasiddhânta, 253. 254. 258. 259. 260.

paulkasa, 129.
Paushkarasádi, 102. 285.
Paushkalávata, 268.
Paushpiṇḍya, °piñji, 240.
Paushyacharita, 318.
prakṛiti, 177. 237.
prachalanam, 98.
Prajápati, 76. 97. 137. 151. 244.
prajnapti, s. *Súrya°*, 297.
Praṇavopanishad, 154. 165.
Pratijná-Pariśishṭa, 102. 106. 115. 119.
Pratithi, 56.
pratibuddha, 129. 138.
Pratishṭhána, 214.
Pratihára-Sútra, 83.
Pratihárya, 299 (Buddh.).
pratṛiṇṇa, 49.
Pratyabhijñáśástra, 322.
prapáṭhaka, 63. 64. 65. 66. 76. 79. 80. 81. 82. 83. 84. 89. 97. 117. 145. 151.
Prabodhachandrodaya, 207. 241.
Pramagaṃda, 79.
pramáṇa, 28. 244.
prayogas, 102.
pravachana, 12. 83. 85. 131.
pravarakhaṇḍa, 101. 240.
pravaráḍhyáya, 142. 317 (*Káṭh.*).
pravargya, 108. 119. 139.
Praváhaṇa, 71.
pravrájaka, 285.
pravrájitá, 281. 305.
pravrájin, 129.
Praśántarága, 141.
praśna, 89. 100. 101. 102.
Praśnopanishad, 58. 158 ff.
Prasthánabheda, 267. 271. 275.
prákṛita, 177.
— *prakáśa*, 227.
Práchyas, 34. 132. 178.
Práchya-Kaṭhas, 88.
— *Páñchálíshu*, 34.
Práṇágnihotropanishad, 154. 162.
Prátipíya, 123.
Prátibodhíputra, 112.
Prátiśákhya-Sútras, 23. 26. 59 (*Ṛigv.*). 83 (*Sámav.*). 102 (*Taitt.*). 143 (*Vájas.*). 151 (*Ath.*).
Prátítheyí, 56.
prámáṇas, 28.
práyaśchitta, 84. 118. 139.
prekshaṇaka, 319.
Proti, 123.
Prauḍha-Bráhmaṇa, 74.
Plákshayaṇa, 53.
phalguna, 115. 134. 136.
phálgunyas, 248.
Phiṭ-Sútras, 226.
Phulla-Sútra, 83.
baïseriya, 236.
°*badha*, °*vadha*, 196. 198.
bandhu, 12. 124.
Babhru, 56.
Barku, 133.
Balabhadra, 261. 263 (schol.).
Balaráma, 192.
bahuvachana, 124.
Bahvṛichas, 8. 66. 86. 89. 121. 122.
Bahvṛicha-Pariśishṭa, 62.
Bahvṛicha-Bráhmaṇa, 100.
Báṇa, 99. 204. 205. 207. 213. 214. 232. 319.
Bádaráyaṇa, 53. 140. 239 ff. (phil.). 266 (med.).
— (astr.), 260.
— *Sútra*, 163.
Bádari, 139–140. 241. 242.
Bábhravya, 10. 34 (Ved.). 267 (erot.).
Bárhaddaivata, 72.
Bárhaspatya, °*Sútra*, 246.
Bálakṛishṇa, 91.
bálakhilyas (s. *vála°*), 97.
Bála-Bhárata, 190.
Báláki, 51.
Báverujátaka, 3.
Báshkala, 313.
Báhíkabhishaj, 269.
Báhíkas, 33. 96. 132. 178. 218.
Báhlíka, 68.
Bilhaṇa, 214. 232. 319.
Bukka, 42.
Buḍila, 133. 134.
buddha (awakened, enlightened), 27. 167. 241. 284.
— *śástra*, 241.
Buddha, 3. 56. 98. 102. 138. 184. 199. 200. 217 ff. 236. 241. 256. 273. 283 ff.
— date of Buddha's death, 217–220. 287–288. 302.
— posterior (?), or prior, to Páṇini, 3. 222. 305.
— lived in the *Sútra* period, 290. 301 f.
— wife of, 318.
— and Kṛishṇa, 326.
Buddhagayá, 228. 273.
Buddhaghosha, 292. 293. 326.
Buddhadása, 267.
Buddhaśásana, 236.

buddhopâsaka, °*sikâ*, 305.
√*budh*, 27.
— with *prati*, 129.
Budha, 278. 282 (jur.).
Bṛihaj-jâtaka, 259. 260.
— *jâbâla*, 163.
Bṛihat-Kathâ, 213.
— *Saṃhitâ*, 203. 204. 259 ff. 271. 274.
Bṛihad-Atri, 269.
— *Âtreya*, 269.
— *Âraṇyaka*, 70. 71. 72. 73. 100. 119. 127 ff. 139. 155. 285. 286.
— *uttaratâpinî*, 169.
— *devatâ*, 24. 33. 41. 62. 81. 88. 314. 316.
— *Yâjnavalkya*, 281.
Bṛihadratha, 97. 98.
bṛihant, 280.
Bṛihan-nârâyaṇopanishad, 156. 157. 166.
— *Manu*, 279.
Bṛihaspati, 153 (Atharvan).
— *Smṛiti*, 278. 280 (*laghu*). 326.
Baijavâpi, 266 (med.)., s. Vaijavâpa.
Boḍha, 236.
Bodhâyana, 322. 323.
Bodhisattvas, 298. 301. 307. 310.
Bauddhas, 108. 158.
Baudhâyana, 100. 101. 102. 112. 114. 317. 324.
— *Dharma*, 101. 102. 278.
Brahmagupta, 61. 202. 258 ff.
brahma-chârin, 28. 112. 123. 164.
— *jâlasûtra*, 300.
brahmaṇya, 166.
Brahmadatta, king, 138. 286 (three).
— 55 (comm.).
brahman, etymology of, 11.
— neut., prayer, formula, 11. 149.
— — Divine Power, 6. 127. 161. 171. 242.
— masc., Supreme God, 6. 97. 151. 158. 161. 166. 167. 170, together with Vishṇu and Rudra, 97. 161, with Vishṇu and Śiva, 167. 180.
— — chief priest, 123. 149.
Brahma-pura, 169.
— bandhu, 78. 79. 112. 141.
— *mîmâṃsâ*, 240. 241 ff.
— *vid*, 161.
— *vidyopanishad*, 164.
— *vindûpanishad*, 99. 158. 165.
— *veda*, 149. 150.
Brahmavaivarta-Purâṇa, 191.
— *Siddhânta*, 258.
— *Sûtra*, 70. 96. 242 ff. 308. 322.
— *hatyâ*, 125. 126.
Brahmânandi, 322. 323.
Brahmopanishad, 160 ff.
brâhma Sphuṭasiddhânta, 259.
brâhmaṇa, neut. (appellative: 'explanation,' 'section of a text'), 76. 93. 117. 124. 152.
— — work, 8. 11–15. 76. 159. 176. 239. 240.
— masc., 111. 161 (nature of a Br.), 176 (two languages), 180 (*na mlechhet*), 276.
— *svara*, 176.
bhakti, 238.
Bhagadatta, 188.
Bhagavatî-Sûtra, 297.
Bhagavadgîtâ, 169. 235. 238. 242.
bhagavant, 121. 153 (Atharvan), 160 (Añgiras), 169 (*mahâdevaḥ*, 284 (Buddha, &c.).
Bhagîratha, 193.
Bhaṭaghaṭî, 293.
Bhaṭṭa, 42. 90. 91. 241; s. Bhâskaramiśra.
Bhaṭṭa-nârâyaṇa, 207.
Bhaṭṭi-kâvya, 196.
Bhaṭṭoji Dîkshita, 89. 226.
Bhaṭṭotpala, 242. 243. 258. 259 ff.
Bhadatta, Bhadanta, 260.
Bhadrabâhusvâmin, 297.
Bhadrasena, 286.
Bharata, son of Duḥshanta, 125.
— plur. 114. 125.
— 231 (rhet.). 272 (mus.).
Bharatasvâmin, 42. 65. 79.
Bharadvâja, 31. 162. 163 (*Upan.*).
— (Kapishṭhala), 265. 268 (med.).
Bhartṛiyajna, 141.
Bhartṛihari, 209. 210.
Bhallu, 95.
Bhava, 178.
bhavant, 121. 284.
Bhavabhûti, 159. 200. 205. 206. 207. 319.
Bhavasvâmin, 42. 79. 91. 101.
Bhasmajâbâla, 163.
Bhâgavata, 238.
— *Purâṇa*, 191.
Bhâgavitti, 130.
Bhâguri, 62. 246.
Bhâṇḍitâyana, 77.
Bhâmatî, 322.
Bhârata, 56. 176. 185.

Bháradvája, 100–102 (*Taitt.*). 139. 140. 158 (*Ath.*). 271 (Droṇa ?).
Bháradvájíya-Sútra, 100. 317.
Bháravi, 196. 319.
Bháruchi, 323.
Bháruṇḍáni sámáni, 170.
Bhárgava, 150. 153. 159 (Vaidarbhi).
bhárgava, 250 (astrologer).
Bhállavins, 14. 62. 81. 95. 134.
Bhállaveya, 95. 126. 134.
Bhállavyupanishad, 95. 154. 164.
bháshá, 57. 103. 144. 176. 177. 180.
Bháshika-Sútra, 68. 95.
bháshika-svara, 176.
Bháshya, 56. 57. 144. 176.
Bhása, Bhásaka, 205.
Bháskara, 229. 261 ff.
— miśra, 42. 90. 91. 94. 101. 103. 171.
Bhásvatíkaraṇa, 261.
bhikshá, 123. 305.
bhikshdka, 305.
bhikshdchara, °*charya*, 129. 305.
bhikshu, °*kshuṇí*, 284. 285. 305. 306. 327.
— *Sútra*, 143. 252. 305. 306.
Bhilla, 259.
Bhímasena, 125. 135.
Bhíshma, 39.
bhútagaṇa, 98.
bhúrja, 227. 263. 314. 317.
Bhṛigu, 53. 153. 241.
— plur., 148. 240. 241.
— *vallí*, 94. 154. 156. 157.
Bhela, 265. 270 (med.).
bhaiksha, 305.
bhaishajyas, 152.
bhogandtha, 42.
Bhoja, 195. 202 (more than one).
— king of Dhárá, 201. 202. 203. 215. 228. 230. 261. 319.
— 269 med.
— *vṛiddha*°, 269 (med.).
Bhojadeva (reputed author of the *Sarasvatíkaṇṭhábharaṇa*), 210.
Bhojaprabandha, 215.
bhrashṭa, 226.
makara, dolphin, 252.
makha, 127.
Magadha, 79, 98. 112. 147. 269 (weights). 286. 287. 290. 292. 295. 296.
— vásin, 112.
Magas, 148.
Maghasvámin, 80.
maghás, 248.
Maṅkha, 319.
Mañjuśrí, 298.
maṇi, 140.
Maṇikarṇiká, 168.
maṇḍala, 31. 32. 34. 43. 64. 82.
Maṇḍúka, 49.
Matsya, 95.
Mathurá, 169.
Madras, 126. 137. 223.
Madragára, 75.
madhu, 128.
Madhu-káṇḍa, 15. 127 ff. 138.
— *Bráhmaṇa*, 128.
Madhuka, 130.
Madhusúdana, 166.
— Sarasvatí, 267. 271.
Madhyatápiní, 167. 169.
Madhyadeśa, 102. 106. 115. 133.
madhyama, 269 (Atri). 280.
— *káṇḍa*, 118. 119.
madhyamiká, 89.
Madhyavallí, 157.
manaú, 264 Arabic.
Manittha, 260 (also with *ṇ*).
Manu, 134. 211 (and the fish). 277 (*sváyambhuva*).
— Code of, 20. 73. 102. 143. 183. 188. 238. 244. 249. 266. 276 ff.
— *Sútra*, 99.
mantra, 8 (= *Veda*). 176.
— *rája*, 167. 168.
Mammaṭa, 204. 232. 322.
(*asura*) Maya, 253. 254. 260. 275.
Maríchi, 244.
Maru, 188.
Maruts, 40. 43.
markaṭa, 211.
Malayadeśa, 55.
mallaka, 206.
Mallinátha, 195. 209.
Maśaka, 75. 76. 83. 84.
Mahákauha, 304.
Mahákála, 209.
Mahákaushítaki-Bráhmaṇa, 47.
mahájábála, 163. 185 (Maháj.).
Mahádeva, 45. 123. 169.
Mahádeva, 100. 101 141 (comm.). 262 (astr.).
mahán átmá, 238.
— *devaḥ*, 110. 123.
mahándga, 302.
Mahánáma, 293.
Mahánárdyaṇopanishad, 154.
Mahdparinibbána, 326.
Mahá-Bráhmaṇa, 74. 138.

Mahá-Bhárata, 4. 24. 34. 37. 39. 45. 56. 57. 72. 98. 114. 135. 136. 176. 184–190. 205. 206. 210. 243. 250. 279. 282. 301. 318. 324. 325.
Mahábháshya, 219–226. 231. 238. 321.
Mahámeru, 93.
Maháyána-Sútras, 98. 299.
mahárája, 138.
Mahávańsa, 292. 293.
Mahávákyamuktávalí, 155.
mahávishṇu, 167.
Mahávíra, 296 (Jain.).
Mahávíracharitra, 207.
Mahávṛishas, 70. 147.
Mahávaipulya-Sútras, 298 ff.
Mahávyutpatti, 248 (Buddh.).
mahásála, 161.
mahásramaṇa, 217.
Mahidása, 48. 70.
mahishí, 114.
Mahídhara, 104. 107 ff., 116. 141.
Mahendra, 291. 292. 295.
Maheśvara, 262 (astr.).
Mahopanishad, 154. 166.
Mahoragas, 302.
Mágadha, 79.
— deśíya, 79. 112. 141.
mágadha, 111. 112. 138. 147. 287.
mágadhí, 232 (*ríti*).
— language, 295. 296. 297.
Mágha-kávya, 196.
Máṇḍavya, 61.
Máṇḍúkáyana, 53.
Máṇḍúkí-Śikshá, 49. 61.
Máṇḍúkeya, 49. 56. 112.
Máṇḍúkyopanishad, 161. 164. 167. 168. 298.
Mátṛidatta, 101.
Mátṛimodaka, 144.
mátrá, 160 (*om*). 161.
Máthava, 134.
Mádravatí, 126.
Mádrí, 126.
Mádhava, 41. 42. 47. 116. 235. 241. 243. 245. 246. 262.
— deva, 42.
Mádhavas, 95. 166.
Mádhuki, 133. 134.
mádhurí, 91.
mádhyaṃdina, southern, 106.
Mádhyaṃdinas, 10. 11. 105 ff. 134. 139. 144.
Mádhyaṃdináyana, 105.
Mádhyaṃdini, 106.
Mádhyamika, 309.
Mádhyamikas, 224.
Mánava, 134 (Śaryáta).
Mánava, Mánavas, 91. 102. 280. 285.
Mánava-Gṛihya, 20. 102. 278. 317.
Mánava-Dharmaśástra, 20. 277 ff.
Mánasára, 275.
Mánutantavyau, 134.
Máya-mata, 275.
máyá, 284.
Máyádeví, 284.
Mára, 151. 303. 304.
Márkaṇḍeya-Puráṇa, 191. 206.
Málatí-mádhava, 207. 320.
Málava, 201. 214.
Málavakácharya, 259.
Málaviká, *Málavikágnimitra*, 204. 207.
málámantra, 167.
Máhaki, 153.
Máhitthi, 134.
Máhisheya, 103.
Mitákshará, 107. 281.
Minanda, 306.
Milinda, 306.
Mihira, 261.
mímáńsaka, 102. 240.
Mímáńsá, 121. 159. 235. 239 ff.
mímáńsá-kṛit, 240.
— *Sútra*, 140. 239.
mukáriná, 263 (Arabic).
mukávilá, 263 (Arabic).
Mukula, 322.
mukta, 167. 34 (and *ámukta*).
Muktikopanishad, 155.
Mugdhabodha, 226.
Muñjasúnu, 55.
Muṭibhas, 134.
Muḍimbha, 134.
Muṇḍakopanishad, 58. 158 ff. 240.
Muṇḍopanishad, 164.
muthaśila, 264 (Arabic).
Mudrárákshasa, 207.
muni, 129.
munthahá, 264 (Arabic).
muhúrta, 151.
Mújavants, 147.
múrdhábhishikta, 224. 225.
Múla-Sútra, 297 (Jain.).
músaripha, 26; (Arabic).
Mṛichhakaṭí, 200, 205, 206. 207. 250. 305. 320.
mṛityumṛityu, 167.
Mṛityulāñghanopanishad (?), 170.
Mṛityuláñgala, °láñgúla, 170.
Meghadúta, 198. 204. 208. 209. 302.

Meṇṭha, 319.
Medhâtithi, 52.
Meru, 93.
meshûraṇa, 255 (Greek).
Maitra, 91. 97.
Maitra-Sûtra, 99.
Maitrâyaṇîputra, 71. 98. 285.
Maitrâyaṇîyas, 88. 91. 99. 102.
Maitrâyaṇî-Saṃhitâ, 314. 317.
Maitrâyaṇopanishad, 52. 96 ff. 155. 165. 285.
Maitreya, 97. 98. 99.
Maitreyî, 56. 99.
— Yâjnavalkya's wife, 127.
Mainâga, 93.
moksha, 161.
Moggallâna, 230.
mauṇḍya, 237. 306.
Mauda, 150.
Maudgalya, 123.
Maudgalyâyana, 199.
mauna, 129.
√*mlechh*, 180.
Yakshas, 98. 273. 302. 303.
Yakshavarman, 217.
Yajuḥ-Saṃhitâ, 9. 10.
Yajurveda, 8. 45. 85 ff. 121. 123. 127. 164. 184.
— °*dâmnâye*, 144.
yajus, 8. 9 s. *śukla*.
yajus-verses, number of the, 121.
yajnâvakîrṇa, 68.
yajnopavîta, 161.
yati, 327 (*âśrama*).
Yatîndramatadîpikâ, 322.
Yatîśvara, 323.
Yama, 36.
— *Smṛiti*, 325.
Yamasabhîya, 193.
yamayâ, 264 (Arabic).
Yamunâ, 68.
Yavana, 178. 187. 188. 214. 220 ff. 251. 252. 253. 260 (astr.). 268.
— *priya*, 220.
— vṛiddhâs, 243.
yavanânî, 220 ff.
yavanikâ, 207.
Yavanî, 220. 252.
Yavaneśvara, 258.
yavaneshṭa, 220.
Yaśoga (!), Yaśogopi, 141.
Yaśomitra, 111.
Yaskâḥ, 41.
yâjushî, 163.
Yâjnavalkîya-kâṇḍa, 127. 129 ff. 137. 138.
Yâjnavalkâni brâhmaṇâni, 95. 129. 130.
Yâjnavalkya, 33. 104. 120. 123. 124. 126. 127. 128. 129. 130. 131. 132. 138. 143. 144. 163. 168. 236. 237 ff. 285.
— 's Code, 107. 122. 143. 205. 215. 250. 278. 280 ff. 323. 325. 326.
yâjnika, 240.
Yâjnikadeva, 141.
Yâjnikî-Upanishad, 93. 94.
yâtuvidas, 121.
yâtnika, 309.
yâtrâ, 260 (astr.). 324.
Yâdvas, 3.
Yâmunamuni, 323.
Yâvana, 220.
Yâska, 25. 26. 32. 33. 39. 41. 42. 44. 46. 57. 59. 61. 62. 81. 82. 85. 88. 90. 91. 128. 140. 142. 176. 184. 216. 217. 236. 277.
yugas (the four), 70. 113. 151. 159. 190. 243. 247. 277.
— quinquennial, 113. 247.
Yuga-Purâṇa, 214. 251.
Yudhishṭhira, 185. 186. 188. 286.
— 's era, 202. 260.
Yoga, 96. 137. 156. 158. 160. 162. 163. 165. 166. 235. 236 ff. 265. 285.
— s. *Sâṃkhyayoga*.
— *tattva*, 165.
— *Śâstra*, 297 (Jain.).
— *śikhâ*, 165.
— *Sûtra*, 223. 237.
Yogâchâra, 309.
yogin, 161. 239.
yaudha, 78.
rakta, 78.
Raghuvaṃśa, 195. 196. 208. 302. 318.
Raṅganâtha, 258.
ratnas (the nine), 200. 228. 261.
Ratnâkara, 319. 322.
Ratha-Sûtra, 275.
Rabhasa, 227.
Ratnâvalî, 204. 320.
Rahasya, 119 (*Śatap. Br.*).
Râjagṛiha, 199. 287. 295.
Râjataraṃgiṇî, 213. 215. 219. 220. 223. 225. 287. 320.
râjaputra, 95.
râjasûya, 54.
Râjastambâyana, 120.
Râjaśekhara, 207.
Râṇâyana, 53.

Ráṇáyaníputra, 71. 77. 79.
Ráṇáyaníyas, 65. 79. 84.
Ráta, 61.
Ráma, 135. 168. 192.
— as incarn. of Vishṇu, 194.
— Aupatasvini, 134.
Rámakṛishṇa, 85. 143.
Rámachandra, 59.
Rámatápaníyopanishad, 168.
Rámatírtha, 323.
Rámánuja, 168. 322.
Rámánanda, 168.
Rámáyaṇa, 4. 37. 89. 98. 135. 188. 191 ff. 205. 206. 214. 250. 324.
Rámila, 205.
Rávaṇa (comm.). 42. 66.
Rávanabadha, 196.
Ráhu, 73. 249. 250.
Ráhula, 250.
rítis (varieties of style), 232.
Ruchidatta, 323.
Rudra, 6. 40. 97. 110. 123. 159. 170. 171. 238. 303.
— by the side of Brahman and Vishṇu, 97. 161.
— *jábála*, 163.
Rudraṭa, 322.
Rudradatta, 101.
Rudraskanda, 80. 84.
Rudrákshajábála, 163.
Rudropanishad, 154. 170.
rúpa (coin), 205.
Ruyyaka, 322.
Reṇudíkshita, 142.
revatí, 248.
Revá, 123.
Romaka, 253. 324.
— *pura*, 253.
— *siddhánta*, 253. 254. 258. 260.
romakúpa, 253.
Raumyas, 253.
Rauhiṇáyana, 120.
°*lakshaṇa*, 265.
Lakshmaṇasena, 210.
— era of, 210.
Lakshmídhara, 262 (astr.). 323.
Lagaḍáchárya, 61. 249.
Lagata, °dha, 61. 249. 258.
laghu, 280.
— *Atri*, 269 (med.).
— *Áryabhaṭa*, 257.
— *Kaumudí*, 226.
— *Játaka*, 78. 260.
— *Jábála*, 163.
— *Paráśara*, 280 (jur.).
— *Bṛihaspati*, 280 (jur.).
— *Śaunaka*, 280 (jur.).
Laṃká, 78.
Lalita-Vistara, 199. 236. 256. 286. 291. 299. 300.
Lágbula, 250.
Láṭa, 76. 258.
Láṭika, 76.
Láṭí (*ríti*), 232.
Láṭyáyana, 53. 68. 76–79. 84. 105.
Láḍhácbárya, 61. 258.
Lábukáyana, 53. 241.
Lámakáyana, 53. 77. 241.
— °nins, 14. 99.
Likhita, 326 (*Smṛiti*).
Liñga-Puráṇa, 191.
Lichhavis, 276. 277. 285.
lipi, 221.
liptá, 255 (Greek).
Líláratí, 262 (astr.).
leya, 254 (Greek).
loiya (*laukika*), 246.
Lokaprakáśa, 321.
Lokáyatas, 246.
Logáyata, 236.
lohita, 78.
Laukákshas, 96.
Laukáyatikas, 246.
Laugákshi, 99. 102. 103. 139. 317.
— *Sútra*, 99.
Vaiśesiya, 236.
vaṅśa, 41. 71. 120. 127. 128. 129 ff. 184.
— *nartin*, 113.
— *Bráhmaṇa*, 42. 74. 75. 79. 84.
Vajra, 260.
vajranakha, 167.
Vajrasúchyupanishad, 162.
Vaḍavá, 56.
Vatsa, 3.
Vada (?), 148.
vaditar, 180.
Vayovidyá, 265.
Varadatta, 55.
Varadarája, 76. 83 (Ved.). 226 (gr.).
Vararuchi, 200. 202. 230 (Vikrama); 83 (*Phulla-Sútra*), 103 (*Taitt. Prát.*), 206. 227 (*Prákṛita-prakáśa*), 223 (*vártt.*), 227. 230 (lex.).
Varáhamihira, 78. 160. 200. 202. 203. 204. 243. 254. 259 ff. 268. 275. 279.
Varuṇa, 35. 188.
varga, 31.
varṇa, 18. 161.
— *Sútras*, 227.
varṇiká, 246.

Vardhamána, 226.
Varsha, 217.
Valabhí, 196. 214. 256.
Valibandha, 198. 207.
°valli, 93. 157.
Valhika, 123. 134.
Valhikas, 147.
Vaśa (-Uśînaras), 45.
Vasishṭha, 31. 37. 53. 79. 123. 162.
— *siddhánta*, 258.
— *Smṛiti*, 326.
Vasugupta, 322.
Vasus, 303.
vákovákya, 121. 122. 127.
Vákyapadîya, 225. 226.
Vágbhaṭa, 269 (med.).
— *vṛiddha*°, 269.
vách, 74. 176. 234.
— (*pútá*), 180.
Váchaknaví, 56. 129.
Váchaspatimiśra, 246. 322.
vája, 104.
vájapeya, 54.
Vájaśravasa, 157.
vájasani, 104.
Vájasaneya, 104. 128. 130. 131.
Vájasaneyaka, 100. 105. 144.
Vájasaneyi-Saṃhitá, 317 (conclusion in the forty-eighth *Ath. Par*).
Vájasaneyins, 81. 105.
vájin, 104.
Váñcheśvara (?), 101.
váta, 266.
Vátsîputra, 71. 138. 285.
— °tríyas, 138.
Vátsya, 139. 140. 267.
Vátsyáyana, 244. 245 (phil.), 266. 267 (erot.), 323.
— Pañchaparṇa, 267.
Vádhúna (?), 100.
vánaprastha, 28. 164.
Vámakakshấyaṇa, 120.
Vámadeva, 31. 315.
Vámana, 84 (*Sámav.*), 226. 227 (gr.), 232 (rhet.), 322.
Vámarathyas, 140.
Váráṇasí, 162. 163.
várdhamantra, 168.
Váruṇyupanishad, 94.
Várkali, 33. 123.
Várkalinas, 33.
várttikas, 222. 225.
Várshagaṇya, 77.
Várshṇa, 133.
Várshṇya, 133.
Várshyáyaṇi, 53.
válakhilya-súktas, 31, 32.
Váleyas, 140.
Válmíki, 102 (*Taitt.*). 191. 194.
Váshkala, 14. 32. 52. 56. 62. 313 f.
— *Śruti*, 52.
Váshkalopanishad, 52. 155.
Vásava, 303.
Vásavadattá, 213. 214.
Vásishṭha, 123.
Vásishṭhas, 123.
Vásishṭha-Sútra, 79. 278. 282 (*Dharma*).
Vásudeva, 51. 137. 166. 168. 169. 185.
Vásudeva, 143 (comm.).
vásudevaka, 185.
Vástuvidyá, 275.
váhîka, s. *báh*°.
Vikrama, 200. 201. 202. 204. 205. 228. 260. 261. 266. 269.
— era of, 201 ff. 260. 319.
— *charitra*, 200. 201. 214. 267.
Vikramáñkacharita, 214.
Vikramáditya, 200. 201. 202. 205. 228.
Vikramárka, 214.
Vichitravírya, 39.
vichhinna, 226.
vijaya, 140. 141.
Vijayanagara, 42.
Vijayanandin, 258.
vijita, 141.
Vijnánabhikshu, 237.
Vitána-Kalpa, 153.
°*vid*, 121.
vidagdha, 33. 212.
Vidagdha, 33. 129.
Vidut (!), 148.
Videgha, 134.
Videha (s. Kosala-Videhas), 10. 33. 53. 68. 123. 129. 137. 193. 285.
Viddhaśálabhañjiká, 207.
Vidyá, 121. 122. 127. 265. 270.
— (*trayî*), 8. 45. 121. 191.
Vidyánagara, 42.
Vidyáraṇya, 42. 54. 97. 170.
Vidvanmanorañjinî, 323.
vidhi (*Sáma*°), 74. 83 (five *vidhis*).
— (Ved.), 244.
vidhána, 33, s. *Ṛig*°, *Sáma*°.
vidheya, 244.
Vinaya (Buddh.), 199. 290. 292. 304. 308. 326.
Vináyaka, 47 (comm.), 62 (do.).
Vindhya, 51. 99. 283.
viplávita, 226.

Vimalapraśnottaramálá, 291.
Vivasvant, 144.
Viváhapaṭala, 260.
viś, *viśas*, 18. 38.
— *pati*, 38.
Viśákhadatta, 207.
Viśála, 48.
viśesha, 245.
Viśvakarman, 275 (°rmíyaśilpa).
Viśvakarmaprakáśa, 275.
Viśvakosha, 205.
Viśvanátha, 244 (phil.).
Viśvavada, 148.
Viśvámitra, 31. 37. 38. 53. 315. 162 (*Upan.*). 271 (*Dhanurveda*).
Viśveśvara, 169 (comm.).
Vishavidyá, 265.
Vishṇu, 6. 42. 97. 126. 127. 156. 165. 166. 167. 168. 171. 190. 194. 284.
— with Rudra and Brahman, 97. 161.
— with Śiva and Brahman, 167. 180.
— Code of, 170. 278. 282. 317. 325.
Vishṇugupta, 260.
Vishṇuchandra, 258.
Vishṇuputra, 59.
Vishṇu-Puráṇa, 58. 142. 191. 230. 318.
Vishṇuyaśas, 82.
Vishvaksena, 184.
víjagaṇita, 262.
Víracharitra, 214.
Vírabhadra, 253.
vísúka, 199. 319.
Vuttodaya, 293.
vṛitti, °*kára*, 91. 222.
Vṛitra, 302.
vṛiddha, 280.
— *Átreya*, 269 (med.).
— *Garga*, 153. 253.
— *Gautama*, 205. 281 (jur.).
— dyumna, 136.
— *Paráśara*, 280 (jur.).
— *Bhoja*, 269 (med.).
— *Manu*, 279.
— *Yájnavalkya*, 281.
— *Vágbhaṭa*, 269 (med.).
— *Suśruta*, 269 (med.).
— *Hárita*, 269 (med.).
vṛihant, s. *bṛihant*.
Vṛishṇi, 185.
Veṇísaṃhára, 207.
Vetálabhaṭṭa, 200.
Vetálapañchaviṅśati, 214. 215.
Veda, 8. 23. 58. 144. 176. 244 (triple).
— *śákhá*, 93.
Vedáṅgas, 25. 60. 145. 159. 258. 272.
vedátharva, 149.
Vedánta, 48. 51. 158. 161. 162. 240. 245.
— *kaustubhaprabhá*, 323.
— *sára*, 323.
— *Sútra*, 51. 158. 159. 235. 241. 245. 322 f.
Vedárthayatna, 315.
Veyagána (!), 64.
veśi, 255 (Greek).
vaikṛita, 177.
Vaikhánasa, 100. 275. 317.
Vaichitravírya, 90.
Vaijavápa, °páyana, 142.
Vaitána-Sútra, 152.
vaidarbha (*ríti*), 232.
Vaidarbhi, 159 (Bhárgava).
Vaideha, 276.
Vaidyaka, 265. 270.
Vaibháshika, 309.
vaiyákaraṇas, 26.
Vaiyághrapadíputra, 106.
Vaiyághrapadya, 106.
Vaiyásaki, 184.
Vaiśampáyana, 34. 41. 56. 57. 58. 87. 89. 93. 135. 184.
Vaiśeshika, Vaiśeshikas, 236. 237. 245.
Vaiśeshika-Sútra, 216. 244. 245.
Vaiśravaṇa, 124.
Vaishṇava (Makha), 127.
Voḍha, 236.
Vopadeva, 226.
Vyákaraṇa, 25 (*Aṅga*). 83.
— *sútráṇi*, 216.
— Buddh., 300.
vyákṛi, 176.
vyákhyána, 122. 127.
Vyághrapád, 106.
Vyághramukha, 259.
Vyáḍi, Vyáli, 227. 228. 321.
vyávahárikí, 176.
Vyása, Páráśarya, 93. 184. 185. 240. 243.
— Bádaráyaṇa, 243.
— father of Śuka, 243.
— author of the *Śatarudriya* (!), 111.
— 62 (teacher of Shaḍguruśishya).
— (*Smṛiti*), 283. 326.
— *Sútra*, 243.
Vraja, 169.

vrâtînas, 78. 147.
vrâtya, 68. 78. 110. 112. 141. 146. 147. 180.
— gaṇa, 196.
— stoma, 67. 78. 80.
Śaka, 187. 220. 260. 285. 291.
— era, 202. 203. 260 (°kâla, °bhûpakâla, Śakendrakâla). 261. 262.
— nṛipânta, 259. 260.
Śakuntalâ, 125.
— (drama), 206. 207. 320.
Śakti, 171. 289. 310.
Śaktipûrva, 260 (astr.).
śakra, 303.
śaṃkara, 303 (epithet of Rudra).
Śaṃkara, 42. 48. 51. 56. 58. 70. 72. 73. 74. 94. 96. 116. 119, 127. 131. 139. 157. 159. 160 ff. 188. 241. 242. 243. 267 (erot.). 308.
— miśra, 244.
— vijaya, 243.
Śaṃkarânanda, 52. 163. 164. 170.
Śaṅku, 200.
Śaṅkha, 58. 275. 278. 282 (*Dharma*). 326 (*Smṛiti*).
śatapatha, 117. 119.
Śatapatha-Brâhmaṇa, 116 ff. 276. 284. 318.
Śatarudriya, 108. 111. 155. 169. 170.
Śatânanda, 261.
Śatânîka, 125.
Śatrumjaya Mâhâtmya, 214. 297.
śani, 98.
Śaṃtanu, 39.
Śabarasvâmin, 241. 322.
Śabala, 35.
Śabdânuśâsana, 217. 227.
Śambûputra, 71.
śamyuvâka, 313.
Śaryâta, 134.
Śarva, 178.
Śarvavarman, 226,
Śalâtura, 218.
śastra, canon, 14. 32. 67. 121.
Śâkaṭâyana, 53. 143. 151. 152. 217. 222. 226.
Śâkapûṇi, 85.
Śâkala, 32. 33. 62. 313. 314. 315.
— (Sâgala), 306.
Śâkalya, 10. 32. 33. 34. 50 (two Śâkalyas). 56. 143 (gramm.). 163.
— Vidagdha, 33. 129.
Śâkalyopanishad, 163. 167.
Śâkâyanins, 33. 96. 120. 133. 137. 285.
Śâkâyanya, 97. 98. 133. 137. 285. 308.
śâkta, 171.
Śâkya, 33. 133. 137. 185. 235. 285. 306.
śâkyabhikshu, 78.
Śâkyamuni, 56. 98. 137. 268. 309.
Śâkhâ, 10. 91. 158. 162. 181.
Śâṅkhâyana, 32. 52 ff., 80. 313. 314.
— *Gṛihya*, 176. 313. 315. 316.
— *Pariśishṭa*, 62.
— *Brâhmaṇa*, 44-47.
— *Sûtra*, 44.
— *Âraṇyaka*, 50. 132.
Śâṭyâyana, 53, 95. 102. 128.
— °naka 100. 249.
— °ni, °nins, 14. 77. 81. 83. 95. 96. 120. 243.
Śâṇḍilya, 71. 76. 77. 78. 80. 82. 120. 131. 132.
— 143 (*Smṛiti*).
— *Sûtra*, 238. 243.
— °lyâyana, 53. 76. 120.
śâtapathikas, 85.
Śâṃtanava, 226.
Śânti-Kalpa, 153.
Śâmbavyagṛihya, 316.
Śâmbuvis, 14. 81.
śâmbhava, 171.
Śâriputra, 285.
Śârîraka-Mîmâṅsâ, 240.
Śârṅgadeva, 273.
Śârṅgadhara(-*Paddhati*), 210.
Śâlaṃkâyana, 53. 75.
Śâlaṃkâyanajâ, 96.
Śâlaṃkâyanins, 14. 77. 96
Śâlaṃki, 96. 218.
Śâlâturîya, 218.
Śâlivâhana, 202. 214. 260.
Śâlihotra, 266. 267.
Śikshâ, 25. 60. 61. 145. 272. 313. 317.
— *valli*, 93. 94. 155.
Śiras (*Upanishad*), 170.
Śilâditya, 214.
Śilâlin, 197.
śilpa, 198.
Śiva, worship of, 4. 45. 110. 111. 156. 157. 165. 169. 190. 208. 209. 303. 307.
— developed out of Agni (and Rudra), 159.
— beside Brahman and Vishṇu, 167. 180.
Śivatantra, 275.
Śivayogin, 62.
Śivasaṃkalpopanishad, 108. 155.
Śiśukrandîya, 193.

Śiśupálabadha, 196.
śiśna, 114.
śiśnadevas, 303.
√*śu*, 178.
Śuka, son of Vyása, 184. 243.
śukra (Venus?), 98. 250.
— *yajúñshi*, 104.
śukriya, 104. 107. 144.
— *káṇḍa*, 104.
śukláni yajúñshi, 104. 131. 144.
Śuñgas, 33.
śuddha, 167.
Śunakas, 33. 34.
Śunaḥśepa, 47. 48. 55.
Śumbha, 206.
Śulva-Sútra, 101. 256. 274. 317. 324.
śushṇa, 302.
Śúdra, 18. 77. 111. 112. 276.
Śudras, 147.
Śúdraka, 205. 206. 207. 214.
śúnya (zero), 256.
Śúlapáṇi, 166.
Śesha, 101 (comm.). 237 (phil.).
Śaityáyana, 53.
Śailáli, 134. 197.
Śailálinas, 197.
śailúsha, 111. 196. 197.
Śaivabháshya, 323.
Śaivaśástra, 322.
Śaiśiris, 33.
Śaiśiríya, 32. 33.
Śauñgáyani, 75.
Śauchivṛikshi, 77. 82.
Śaunaka (*Ṛigv.*), 24. 32–34. 49. 54. 56. 59. 62. 85. 143.
— (*Ath.*), 150. 151. 158. 161. 162. 165.
— (*Mahá-Bhárata*), 185.
— Indrota, 34. 125.
— Svaidáyana, 34.
— *Gṛihya*, 55 (*Ṛigv.*).
— *vartita*, 158. 162 (*Ath.*).
— *laghu°*, 280 (*Smṛiti*).
Śaunakíyas, 158. 162.
Śaunakíyá, 151.
Śaunakopanishad (?), 164. 165.
śaubhikas, 198; s. *saubhikas*.
Śaubhreyas, 140.
Śaulváyana, 53.
Śyáparṇas, 180.
śyena, 78.
√*śram*, 27.
śramaṇa, 27. 129. 138.
śramaṇá, 305.
Śrí Ananta, 141.
Śríkaṇṭha Śiváchárya, 323.
Śrí Chápa, 259.
Śrídatta, 141.
Śrídharadása, 210.
Śrídharasena, 196.
Śrínivása, 42.
Śrínivásadása, 322. 323.
Śrí Dharmanábha, 196.
Śrípati, 54. 58.
Śríparáñkuśanátha, 323.
Śrímaddattopanishad, 164.
Śrívara, 320.
Śrí Vyághramukha, 259.
Śríshena, 258.
Śrí Harsha, king, 204. 207.
— 196 (*Naishadhachar.*).
Śrí Hala, 145.
√*śru*, 15.
Śrutasena, 125. 135.
Śruti, 15. 17. 68. 81. 96. 149 (plur.). 159. 164.
śreshṭha, 126.
Śrauta-Sútras, 16. 17. 19. 52.
śleshman, 266.
śloka, 24. 69. 70. 72. 73. 74. 83. 87. 97. 99. 103. 121. 122. 123. 125. 127.
Śviknas, 132.
Śvetaketu, 51. 71. 123. 132. 133. 137. 267 (erot.). 284.
Śvetáśvatara, 96. 99.
— *°ropanishad*, 96. 155. 156. 161. 165. 169.-236. 238.
Shaṭchakropanishad, 168.
Shaṭtriñśat (*Smṛiti*), 280.
Shaḍaśíti (*Smṛiti*), 280.
Shaḍguruśishya, 33. 61. 62. 83.
Shaḍdarśanachintaniká, 322.
Shaḍbháshácháchandriká, 227.
Shaḍviñśa-Bráhmaṇa, 69. 70.
Shaṇṇavati (*Smṛiti*), 280.
Shashṭitantra, 236.
shashṭipatha, 117. 119.
saṃ = *saṃvat* (but of what era?), 141. 202. 203.
saṃvat era, 182. 202. 203.
Saṃvarta (*Smṛiti*), 278. 326.
Saṃvartaśrutyupanishad, 154. 164.
saṃskára, 102 (the sixteen *s.*).
— (gramm.), 144.
— *gaṇapati*, 143.
saṃskṛitabháshá, 177.
saṃsthá, 66. 67.
Saṃhitá (Ved.), 8. 9. 10. 14. 22–24. 60.
— (phil.), 75.

Saṃhitá (astr.), 259. 264. 265. 275.
— *Kalpa*, 153.
— *páṭha*, 43. 49.
— *°topanishad*, 34 (*Bráhmaṇa*). 74. 75 (*Sámav.*). 93. 155 (*Taitt.*). 316 (*Sámav.*).
Sakaládhikára, 275 (arch.).
saṃkhyátar, 235.
Saṃgítaratnákara, 273.
saṃgraha, 119 (*Śatapatha-Bráhmaṇa*). 227 (gramm.).
saṃjnána, 313. 314.
Saṭṭhitanta, 236.
sattra, 66. 76. 79. 80. 139.
sattráyaṇa, 101.
Satya, 260 astr.
Satyakáma, 71. 130. 132. 134.
Satyaváha, 158.
Satyáshádha, 100. 101. 102.
Sadánírá, 134.
Saduktikarṇámṛita, 210.
Saddharmapuṇḍaríka, 299. 300.
Sanatkumára, 72. 164;—275 (archit.).
Sanandanácbárya, 237.
saṃdhi, 23.
saṃnipáta, 248 (Buddh.).
Saṃnyásopanishad, 164.
Saptarshi (*Smṛiti*), 280.
Saptaśataka, *Saptaśati*, 83. 211. 232.
sapta súryáḥ, 250 (249).
samánam á, 131.
Samása-Saṃhitá, 259.
sampradáya, 152.
samráj, 123.
Sarasvatí, 74 (Vách).
— *vyákaraṇa*, 227.
Sarasvatí, 4. 38. 44 (Indus). 53. 67. 80. 102. 120. 134. 141.
— *kaṇṭhábharaṇa*, 210. 232.
sarga, 190. 196. 214.
sarjuna, 233.
sarpa, 302.
sarpavidas, 121.
Sarpavidyá, 124. 183. 265. 302.
Sarvadarśanusaṃgraha, 235. 241. 322.
sarvamedha, 54.
Sarvánukramaṇí, 61.
sarvánnína, 305.
Sarvopanishatsáropanishad, 162.
Salvas, 120. 132. 180.
sahama, 264 (Arabic).
Ságala, 306.
Sáketa, 224. 251.
Sáṃkṛityáyana, 266 (med.).
Sáṃkhya, 96. 97. 108. 137 (*Śatap.*). 158. 160. 165–167. 235–239. 242. 244. 246. 284. ff. 306. 308. 309.
— *tattva-pradípa*, 322.
— *pravachana*, 237.
— *pravachana-Sútra*, 237. 239.
— *bhikshu*, 78.
— *yoga*, 160. 166. 238. 239.
— *sára*, 237.
— *Sútra*, 237. 239. 245.
Sáṃkhyaḥ (Gautamaḥ), 284.
Sáṃkhyáyana, 47.
Sáṃjívíputra, 131.
Sáti, 75.
Sátyayajna, °jni, 133.
Sátrájita, 125.
Sápya, 68.
Sámajátaka, 300 (Buddh.).
Sámatantra, 83.
sáman, 8. 9. 64. 66. 121.
— number of the *sámans*, 121.
Sámayácharika-Sútra, 19. 278.
Sámalakshaṇa, 83.
Sámavidhi, °*vidhána*, 72. 74. 277.
Sámaveda, 45. 63 ff. 121. 316. 325 (*Gánas* of).
— *Prátiśákhya*, 316.
Sáma-Saṃhitá, 9. 10. 32. 63 ff. 313 (readings). 316.
Sámastam, 275.
Sáyakáyana, 96. 120.
Sáyakáyanins, 96.
Sáyaṇa, 32. 41. 42. 43. 46. 47. 48. 52. 65. 66. 68. 69. 72. 74. 91. 92. 94. 101. 139. 150.
Sáratthasaṃgaha, 267 (med.).
Sárameya, 35.
Sárasvata, 226 (gramm.).
Sárasvata páṭha, 103.
Sávayasa, 133.
Sáhityadarpaṇa, 231. 321.
Siṅhásanadvátriṅśiká, 200–202. 214. 320.
Siddhasena, 260 (astr.).
Siddhánta, 253. 255. 258 ff. 269 (astr.).
— *kaumudí*, 89. 226.
— *śiromaṇi*, 261. 262.
Sítá, 135. 192. 193.
Sukanyá, 134.
Sukhavatí, 306.
Suttanipáta, 293.
sutyá, 66. 67.
Sudáman, 68.
Sudyumna, 125.

sunaphá, 255 (Greek).
Sundarítápaníyopanishad, 171.
suparṇa, 314.
Suparṇádhyáya, 171.
Suparṇí, 134.
Suprabhadeva, 196.
Subandhu, 189. 213. 245. 267. 319.
Subhagasena, 251.
Subhadrá, 114. 115. 134.
Subháshitaratnákara, 320.
Subháshitávalí, 320.
Sumanasantaka (?), 208.
Sumantu, 56. 57. 58. 149.
sura, 98. 302. 303.
Suráshṭra, 76.
Sulabha, 56.
Sulabhá, 56.
Suśravas, 36.
suśrut, 266.
Suśruta, 266 ff. 324.
— *vṛiddha*, 269.
súkta, 31. 32. 124. 149.
súta, 111.
Sútras, 8. 15 (etymol.; *chhandovat*); 29. 56. 57. 216. 285. 290.
— 127. 128 (passages in the *Bráhmaṇas*).
— 290. 292. 296. 298 ff. (Buddh.).
— 128. 161 (*s.* = Brahman).
sútradhára, 198. 275.
Súrya, 62 (comm.).
Súrya, 40 (god).
— *prajnapti*, 297 (Jain.).
— *Siddhánta*, 61. 249. 257. 258.
— °*opanishad*, 154. 170.
(*sapta*) *súryáḥ*, 250 (249).
Súryáruṇa (*Smṛiti*), 280.
Sṛiñjayas, 123. 132.
Setubandha, 196.
Saitava, 61.
Saindhavas, °váyanas, 147.
sobha, °*nagaraka*, 198.
Soma, 6. 63 (god).
— (sacrifice), 66. 107.
Somadeva, 213. 319.
Sománanda, 322.
Someśvara, 273 (mus.).
Saujáta, 285.
Sauti, 34.
Sautrántika, 309.
sautrámaṇí, 107. 108. 118. 139.
saubhikas, 198; s. *śaubhikas*.
Saumápau, 134.
Saumilla, 204. 205.
Saurasiddhánta, 258.
saulabháni Bráhmaṇáni, 56. 95.
Sauśravasa, 105.
Sauśrutapárthavás, 266.
Skanda, 72.
— *Puráṇa*, 191. 205.
Skandasvámin, 41. 42. 79.
Skandopanishad, 171.
√*skabh*, *stabh*, 233.
stúpa, 274. 307.
stotra, 67.
stoma, 67. 81.
staubhika, 63.
sthavira, 77. 102. 305.
stánaka, 89.
Spandaśástra, 322.
Sphujidhvaja (?), 258.
Sphuṭa-Siddhánta, 259.
Smaradahana, 208.
Smárta-Sútras, 17. 19. 34 (*Śaun.*). 101.
Smṛiti, 17. 19. 20. 81.
— *Śástras*, 20. 84. 143. 276.
Srughna, 237.
Svaraparibháshá, 83.
svádhyáya, 8. 93. 144.
svábhávika, 309.
°*svámin*, 79.
Sváyambhuva, 277.
Svaidáyana, 34.
Haṅsanádopanishad, 165.
Haṅsopanishad, 164. 165.
hadda, 264 Arabic.
Hanumant, 272.
Hanumannáṭaka, 203.
Haradatta, 89. 278.
Hari, 166 (Vishṇu). 303 (Indra).
Hari, 225. 226 gramm.
harija, 255 (Greek).
Harivaṅśa, 34. 189.
Hariśchandra, 184.
Harisvámin, 72. 79. 139.
Hariharamiśra, 142.
Śrí Harsha (king), 204. 207.
— 196 (*Naishadhachar.*).
— *charita*, 205. 214. 319 f.
Śrí Hala, 145.
halabhṛit, 192.
Halàyudha, 60 (metr.). 196. 230 (lex.).
hasa, 112.
hastighaṭa, 117.
Háridravika, 88.
Hárita (Kṛishṇa), 50.
— 269 med.
— *vṛiddha*°, 269 (med.).
— (*Dharma*), 278. 282. 325.
Hála, 83. 211. 232.

Háleyas, 140.
Hástinapura, 185.
Hitopadeśa, 212.
hibuka, 255 (Greek).
Himavant, 51. 268.
himna, 254 (Greek).
Hiraṇyakeśi, 100–102. 317.
— *śákhíya-Bráhmaṇa*, 92.
Hiraṇyanábha, 160.
Hutáśaveśa, 266.
Húṇas, 243.
hṛidroga, 254 (Greek).
heṭṭhá, 89.
helayas, *helavas*, 180.
Hemachandra, 227. 321 (gr.). 230 (lex.). 297 (Jain.).
Helárája, 215.
heli, 254 (Greek).
Haimavatí, 74. 156.
Hairaṇyanábha, 125.
Hailihila, 185.
hotar, 14. 53. 67. 80. 86. 89. 109. 129. 149.
horá, 254 (Greek).
— *Śástra*, 254. 259. 260.
hautraka, 101,
Hrasva, 112.

INDEX OF MATTERS, ETC.

Αἰγόκερως, 254.
Ahriman (and Mára), 303. 304.
Akbar, 283.
Albírúní, 60. 189. 201. 239. 249. 253. 254. 257–262. 266. 274. 323.
Alexander, 4. 6. 27. 28. 30. 179. 221. 222. 251.
Alexandria, 256. 309.
Alexandrinus (Paulus), 253.
Algebra, 256. 259.
Alkindi, 263.
Ἀμιτροχάτης, 251.
Amulet-prayers, 208.
Amyntas, 306.
Ἀναφή, 255.
Andubarius, 255.
Animal fables, 70. 211 ff., 301.
Antigonus, 179. 252.
Antiochus, 179. 252.
Aphrodisius (?), 258.
Ἀφροδίτη, 254.
Ἀπόκλιμα, 255.
Apollodotus, 188.
Apollonius of Tyana, 252.
Apotelesmata, 289.
Arabs: Arabian astronomy, 255–257. 263. 264.
— Arabic astronomical terms, 263–264.
— commercial intercourse of the Indians with Arabia, 220.
— Arabian figures, 256.
Arabs: medicine, 266. 270, 271.
— music, 273.
— philosophy, 239.
Archimedes, 256.
Arenarius, 256.
Ἄρης, 254.
Arim, Arin, coupole d', 257.
Aristoteles, 234.
Arithmetic, 256. 259.
Arjabahr, 255. 259.
Arkand, 259.
Arrian, 4. 106. 136.
Arsacidan Parthians, 188.
Ars amandi, 267.
Asklepiads, oath of the, 268.
Ἀστρονομία of the Indians, 30.
Atoms, 244.
Aux, augis, 257.
Avesta, 6. 36. 148 (Indian names of its parts), 302.
— and Buddhism, 327.
Avicenna, 271.
Babrius, 211.
Babylon, 2. 247.
Bactria, 207; s. Valhika.
Bagdad, 255. 270.
Bali, island of, 189. 195. 208.
Bardesanes, 309.
Barlaam, 307.
Bashkar, 262. 263.
Βασιλεύς, Basili, 306.
Basilides, 309.

Basilis, 251.
Beast-fable, 211 ff. 301.
Bells, 307.
Bengálí recensions, 194. 206. 208.
Bhabra missive, 292. 294, 295.
Bihári Lál, 211.
Blessed, world of the, 50. (73).
Βόδδα, 309.
Boethius, 257.
Βραχμᾶνες, 28. 30.
Buddhism, Buddhists, 3. 4. 20. 22. 27. 78. 79. 99. 111. 138. 151. 165. 205. 229. 236. 247. 276. 277. 280. 283 ff.
Buddhist nuns, 281.
Bundehesh, 247. 323.
Cæsar, 188.
Castes, 10. 18. 78. 79. 110. 111. 161. 178. 287. 289. 290. 301. 306.
Ceylon, 192. 288. 291. 293. 295.
— medicine in, 267.
Chaldæans, astronomy, 248 (Xarustr).
Chaos, 233.
Chess, 275.
Chinese lunar asterisms, 247. 248 (Kio-list).
— statements on the date of Kanishka, 287.
— translations, 229 (Amara). 291. 300. 301 (Buddh.).
— travellers, s. Fa Hian, Hiuan Thsang.
Χρηματισμός (! κενόδρομος), 255.
Christian influences, 71. 189. 238. 300. 307.
— ritual, influence of Buddhist ritual and worship on (and *vice versa*), 307.
— sects, Indian influence on, 239. 309.
Chronicon Paschale, 255.
Clemens Alexandrinus, 306.
Coin, 205 (náṇaka), 229 (dínára).
Coins, Indian, 215. 218. 219.
Commentaries, text secured by means of, 181.
Comparative mythology, 35, 36.
Constantius, 255.
Creation, 233, 234.
Creed-formulas, 166.
Curtius, 136.
Cycles, quinquennial and sexennial, 113. 247.
Damis, 252.
Dancing, 196 ff.
Dára Shakoh, 283.
Day, beginning of the, at midnight, 254.
Decimal place-value of the figures, 256.
Deeds of gift, *v.* Grants.
Degrees of the heavens, 255.
Deimachus, 251.
Δεκανός, 255.
Dekhan, 4. 6. 192. 283.
Dekhan recension (of the Urvaśí), 208.
Δημήτηρ, 35.
Demiurges, 233.
Denarius, 229. 304.
Dhauli, 179. 295.
Diagrams, mystic, 310.
Dialects, 6. 175 ff. 295. 296. 299.
Διάμετρον, 255.
Δίδυμος, 254.
Diespiter, 35.
Dion Chrysostom, 186. 188.
Dionysius, 251.
Διόνυσος, 6.
Districts, division of Vedic schools according to, 65. 94. 132. 133.
— — of other text-recensions, 195. 206–208.
— Varieties of style distinguished by names of, 232.
Dolphin, emblem of the God of Love, 252. 274. 325 (Cupid and Venus).
Δορυφορία, 255.
Δραχμή, 229.
Dravidian words, 3.
Dsanglun, 289. 291. 306.
Dulva, 199.
Durr i mufassal, 272.
Δυτόν, 255.
Egypt, commercial relations between India and, 3.
Εἰσαγωγή, 253–255.
Elements, the five, 234.
Embryo, 160.
Ἐπαναφορά, 255.
Eras, Indian, 202. 203. 210. 260.
Fa Hian, 218. 300.
Farther India, geographical names in, 178.
Ferédún, 36.
Festival-plays, religious, 197. 198.
Figures, 256. 324.
— expressed by words, 60. 140.
Firdúsí, 37.
Firmicus Maternus, 254.

Fortunatus, purse of, 264–265.
Fox, in Fable, 211, 212.
Gamma, gamme, 272 (mus.).
Ganges, 4. 38.
— mouths of the, 193. 248.
Galen, 307.
Geometry, 256.
Ginunga gap, 233.
Girnar, 179. 295.
Gnosticism, 239. 309.
Gobar figures, 256.
Gods, images, statues of, 273. 274.
— language of the, 176.
— triad of: Agni, Indra, and Súrya, 40. 63 (A., I., and Soma);—Brahman, Rudra, and Vishṇu, 97. 161. 167 (Śiva), 180 (Śiva), 277.
Grants, 203. 215. 281.
Greek female slaves, 203. 251, 252.
— monarchies of Bactria, 188. 207. 215. 221. 251. 285.
— words, 254, 255.
Greeks: Greek Architecture, 274 (three styles in India).
— Astronomy, 153. 243. 249. 251 ff.
— Commerce with India, 252.
— Drama, 207.
— Fables, 211.
— God of Love, 252. 274 (?).
— Influence upon India generally, 251 ff.
— Medicine, 268. 324. 325.
— Philosophy, 220. 221. 234.
— Sculpture, 273.
— Writing, 221.
Guido d'Arezzo, 272.
Gujarát, 139. 179. 207. 251.
Gymnosophists, 27.
Ἥλιος, 254.
Ἡρακλῆς, 6. 136. 186. 234.
Heraclius, 255.
Heretics, 98.
Ἑρμῆς, 254.
Homer, Indian, 186. 188.
— Homeric cycle of legend, 194.
Ὥρη, 254.
Ὁρίζων, 255.
Hindustán, 4. 6. 10. 18. 38. 39. 70. 187. 192. 283. 296.
Hiuan Thsang, 217 ff., 287. 300.
Humours, the three, 266.
Huśravaṅh, 36.
Ὑδροχόος, 254.
Ὑλόβιοι, 28. 48.
Ὑπόγειον, 255.
Ibn Abi Uśaibiah, 266.
Ibn Baithar, 266.
Ἰχθύς, 254.
Immigration of the Áryas into Hindustán, 38. 39.
Indo-Scythians, 220. 285.
Indus, 10. 37. 38. 218. 285.
Inheritance, law of, 278, 279.
Initial letters of names employed to denote numbers, 256; to mark the seven musical notes, 272.
Inscriptions, 183. 215. 228.
Intercalary month, 247. 262 (three in the year!).
Invisible cap, 264.
Jackal and lion in Fable, 211, 212.
Java, island of, 189. 195. 208. 229. 171. 280.
Jehán, 283.
Jehángir, 283.
Jemshíd, 36.
Josaphat, 307.
Kabul, 3. 179.
Kafu (kapi), 3.
Kágyur, 291. 294. 326.
Κάθαια, 317.
Kaikavús, 36.
Kai Khosrú, 36.
Kalilag and Damnag, 320.
Kalíla wa Dimna, 212.
Kalmuck translations, 291.
Καμβισθολοι, 88. 268.
Kambojas, 178.
Καμβύσης, 178.
Kanárese translation, 189.
Kanerki, s. Kanishka.
Kanheri, 292.
Kankah, 269.
Kapur di Giri, 179; s. Kapardigiri.
Kashmír, 204. 213. 215. 220. 223. 227. 232. 291. 296.
Kava Uś, 36.
Kavi languages, origin of name, 195.
— translations, 318 (date of). 325.
Keeping secret of doctrines, 49.
Κενόδρομος, 255.
Κέντρον, 254. 255.
Κῆπος, 3.
Κέρβερος, 35.
Κινυρά, 302.
Kio-list, 248.
Κόλουρος, 254.
Κωφήν, 3.
Κριός, 254.

Κρόνος, 254.
Λαρική, 76. 258.
Lát, 249. 258.
League-boots, 264.
Λέων, 254.
Λεπτή, 255.
Lion and jackal (fox), 211, 212.
Longest day, length of the, 247.
Love, God of, 252. 274.
Lunar mansions, 2. 30. 90. 92. 148. 229. 246–249. 252. 255. 281. 304.
— phases, 281.
Μαδιανδινοί, 10. 106.
Magas, 179. 252.
Magic, art of, 264, 265.
Magic mirror, 264.
— ointment, 264.
Mahmúd of Ghasna, 253.
Mairya (and Mára?), 303.
Μαλλοί, 222.
Manes, 309.
Manes, sacrifice to the, 55. 93. 100. 108. 118.
Manetho, 260.
Mansions, twelve, 254. 281 (astr.).
Manuscripts, late date of, 181. 182 (oldest).
Μάσσαγα, 75.
Mazzaloth, Mazzaroth, 248.
Medicine in Ceylon, 267; in India, 324, 325.
Megasthenes, 4. 6. 10. 20. 27. 48. 70. 88. 106. 136. 137. 186. 234. 251.
Meherdates, 188.
Menander, 224. 251. 306.
Menázil, 323 (in Soghd).
Mendicancy, religious, 237.
Μεσουράνημα, 255.
Metempsychosis, 234.
Metrical form of literature, 182, 183.
Missionaries, Buddhist, 290. 307. 309.
— Christian, 307.
Μνήμη, ἀπὸ μνήμης, 20.
Monachism, system of, 307.
Monasteries, 274. 281.
Mongolian translations, 291.
Mundane ages (four), 247; s. Yuga.
Music, modern Indian, 325.
Musical scale, 272.
Mysteries, 197. 198.
Mythology, Comparative, 35. 36.
Names, chronology from, 29. 53. 71. 120. 239. 284. 285 (s. also Añga, Kavi, Tantra, Sútra).
Nearchus, 15.
Neo-Pythagoreans, 256, 257.
Nepál, 291. 309, 310.
Nepálese MSS., date of, 318.
Nerengs, 56.
North of India, purity of language in the, 26. 45. 296.
Notes, the seven musical, 160. 272.
Numbers, denoting of, by the letters of the alphabet in their order, 222.
Numerical notation by means of letters, 257. 324.
— Symbols, 256.
Núshírván, 212.
Omens, 69. 152. 264.
Ophir, 3.
Oral tradition, 12 ff, 22. 48.
Ordeal, 73.
Orissa, 179. 274.
Otbí, 201.
Οὐρανός, 35.
'Οζηνή, 252 (s. Arin).
'Οξυδράκαι, 222.
Pahlav, 188.
Pahlaví, translation of Pañchatantra into, 212. 267.
Páli redaction of the Amarakosha, 230.
— of Manu's Code, 279.
Πανδαία, 136. 137. 186.
Panjáb, 2. 3. 4. 88. 207. 248. 251. 309.
Pantheism, 242.
Παρθένος, 254.
Parthians, 4. 188. 318.
Parví, parvíz, 323.
Pattalene, 285.
Paulus Alexandrinus, 253. 255.
— al Yúnání, 253.
Peacocks, exportation of, to Báveru, 2, 3.
Periplus, 4. 6.
Permutations, 256.
Persa-Aryans, 6. 133. 148, 178.
Persians, 3. 4. 188;—273 (mus.). 274 (arch.).
Persian Epos, 36. 37. 187.
— translation of the Upanishads, 155.
— Veda, 36. 148.
Personal deity, 165, 166.
Πευκελαῶτις, 268.
Φάσις, 255.

'Philosopher's Ride,' 291.
Philostratus, 252.
Phœbus Apollo, 273 (type of).
Phœnicians, their commercial relations with India, 2, 3. 248.
Pholotoulo, 218.
Phonini, 218.
Planets, 98. 153. 249–251. 254, 255. 281. 304.
— Greek order of the, 319. 323. 326.
Plato (Bactrian king), 273.
Pliny, 136.
Plutarch, 306.
Polar star, 98.
Popular dialects, 6. 175–180.
Πράμναι, 28. 244.
Prose-writing arrested in its development, 183.
Ptolemaios, 253. 274 (astr.).
Ptolemy, 179. 251. 252 (two).
— 130 (geogr.).
Quinquennial cycle, 113. 247.
Quotations, text as given in, 182. 279.
Relic-worship, 306. 307.
Rgya Cher Rol Pa, 185. 291.
Rhazes, 271.
Rock-inscriptions, 179.
Rosary, 307.
Σανδρόκυπτος, 217. 223.
Σαρμάναι, 28.
Scale, musical, 272.
Schools, great number of Vedic, 142.
Seleucus, 4.
Semitic origin of Indian writing, 15.
— — of the Beast-fable, 211, 212.
Serapion, 271.
Seven musical notes, 160. 272.
Sindhend, 255. 259.
Singhalese translations, 292.
Σκορπίος, 254.
Σκυθιανός, 309.
Snake, 302.
Solar year, 246, 247.
Solomon's time, trade with India in, 3.
Σωφαγασήνας, 251.
Speusippus (?), 258.
Squaring of the circle, 256.
Steeples, 274. 306.
Stone-building, 274.
Strabo, 6. 27. 28. 30. 244. 246.
Style, varieties of, distinguished by names of provinces, 232.
Succession of existence, 289. 301.
Śúfí philosophy, 239.
Συναφή 255.
Sun's two journeys, stellar limits of the, 98.
Συραστρηνή, 76.
Surgery, 269. 270.
Tandjur, 209. 210. 226. 230. 246. 267. 276.
Ταῦρος, 254.
Teachers, many, quoted, 50. 77.
Texts, uncertainty of the, 181, 182. 224, 225.
Thousand-name-prayers, 208.
Tibetans, translations of the, 208. 212. 291. 294. 300; s. Dsanglun, Kágyur, Rgya Cher Rol Pa, Tandjur.
Tiridates, 3, 4.
Τοξότης, 254.
Transcribers, mistakes of, 181.
Translations, s. Arabs, Chinese, Kalmuck, Kanárese, Kavi, Mongolian, Pahlaví, Páli, Persian, Singhalese.
Transmigration of souls, 73. 288.
Τρίγωνος, 255.
Trojan cycle of legend, 194.
Tukhiim, peacocks, 3.
Valentinian, 309.
Venus with dolphin (and Cupid), 325.
Vernaculars, 175–180. 203.
Veterinary medicine, 267.
Weights, 160. 269.
Writing, 10. 13. 15;—of the Yavanas, 221.
— consignment to, 22. 144. 181. 292. 296.
Written language, 178 ff.
Yeshts, 56. 302.
Yima, 36.
Yúasaf, Yúdasf, Búdsatf, 307.
Zero, 256.
Ζεύς, 35.
— planet, 254.
Zodiacal signs, 98, 229. 249. 254. 255. 257.
Zohak, 36.
Ζυγόν, 254.

INDEX OF AUTHORS.

Ambros, 272.
Anandachandra, 58. 68. 79.
Anquetil du Perron, 52. 96. 154, 155. 162.
Aufrecht, 16. 32. 43. 59. 80. 84. 112. 150. 191. 200. 210. 211. 224. 226. 230. 232. 243. 257. 260. 261. 267. 272. 313. 315.
Bálaśástrin, 223. 226. 237. 322, 323.
Ballantyne, 223. 226. 235. 237. 244.
Banerjea, 191. 235. 238. 243.
Bápú Deva Śástrin, 258. 262.
Barth, 257. 316. 321.
Barthelemy St. Hilaire, 235.
Bayley, 304.
Beal, 293. 300. 309. 327.
Benary, F., 196.
Benfey, 15. 22. 43. 44. 64. 66. 117. 157. 212. 221. 267. 272. 274. 301. 306. 320.
Bentley, 257. 267.
Bergaigne, 44.
Bernouilli, 325.
Bertrand, 202.
Bhagvánlál Indraji, 324.
Bhagván Vijaya, 327.
Bhaṇḍarkar, 60. 150. 215. 219. 224. 319. 321. 326.
Bháu Dájí, 215. 227. 254–262. 319.
Bibliotheca Indica, s. Ballantyne, Banerjea, Cowell, Hall, Rájendra L. M., Roer, &c.
Bickell, 320.
Biot, 247, 248.
Bird, 215.
Böhtlingk, 22. 106. 210. 217–220. 222. 226. 230. 320. 323.
Von Bohlen, 272.
Bollensen, 44.
Bopp, 178. 189.
Boyd, 207.
Bréal, 4. 36.
Brockhaus, 213. 262.
Browning, 84.
Bühler, 50. 54. 92. 97. 101. 152. 155. 164. 170. 182. 196. 204. 210. 212, 213. 214, 215. 217. 222. 227. 232. 237. 259. 272. 277, 278. 280. 282, 283. 297. 314. 315. 317. 319–322. 324–326.
Burgess, Eb., 247. 258;—Jas., 215.
Burnell, 3. 13. 15. 20. 22. 42. 61. 65. 69. 74. 83. 90. 91. 94. 101. 102. 103. 150. 155. 163, 164. 170, 171. 178. 203. 213. 215. 217. 221, 222. 226. 245. 256. 270. 313. 316. 321.
Burnouf, 81. 111. 162. 179. 191. 199. 246. 289. 291, 292. 296. 298. 300. 306. 308.
Cantor, 324.
Cappeller, 226. 232. 320.
Carey, 194.
Chandrakánta Tarkálaṃkára, 84.
Childers, 178. 293. 295. 305. 308. 326.
Clarac, Comte de, 325.
Clough, 293.
Colebrooke, 42. 43. 61. 97. 148. 151. 154, 157, 158. 163. 201. 202. 227. 229. 230. 234. 235. 236. 238. 241, 242. 243. 245. 256. 259–263. 267. 269. 281. 283.
Coomára Swámy, 293.
Cowell, 42. 43. 50. 52. 91. 97. 98. 99. 207. 227. 234. 235. 237, 238. 242. 256. 283. 291. 322.
Cox, 36.
Csoma Körösi, 199. 209. 267. 285. 291. 294.
Cunningham, 178. 203. 215. 273, 274.
D'Alwis, 293.
Darmesteter, J., 314.
Davids, 267.
De Gubernatis, 36.
Delbrück, 31. 44. 318.
Gerard de Rialle, 3.
Dhanapati Siṅhají, 327.
Dickson, 326.
Dietz, 267.
Donner, 19. 44.
Dowson, 141. 203. 215.
Dümichen, 3.
Duncker, 308.
D'Eckstein, 97.
Eggeling, 203. 215. 226. 291.
Elliot, H. M., 239. 267.
Elliot, W., 154, 155.
Fauche, 189. 194.
Fausböll, 293. 304. 326.
Feer, 188. 291. 293. 299.
Fergusson, 203. 215. 273.
Fleet, 319. 321.
Flügel, 270.

Foucaux, 185. 189. 200. 286. 291. 299.
Friederich, 189. 195.
Fritze, 320.
Gangádhara Kavirája, 270.
Garrez, 211.
Geiger, L., 272.
Geldner, 44.
Gildemeister, 161. 229. 239. 270.
Giriprasádavarman, 116.
Goldschmidt, Paul, 196.
Goldschmidt, Siegfried, 65. 196.
Goldstücker, 12. 15. 22. 87. 100. 130. 144. 193. 207. 221, 222. 223. 224, 225. 227. 241. 251. 273. 321.
Gorresio, 194.
Gough, 235. 244. 322. 323.
Govindadevaśástrin, 237. 322. 323.
Grassmann, 44. 315.
Griffith, 194.
Grill, 207.
Grimblot, 293. 319. 326.
Grohmann, 265.
Grube, 171.
Von Gutschmid, 188.
Haag, 205.
Haas, 19. 58. 84. 142. 152. 324.
Haeberlin, 201.
Hall, 106. 191. 204. 207. 213. 214. 231. 232. 235. 237. 257. 258. 318. 319.
Haukel, 256.
Harachandra Vidyábhúshaṇa, 151.
Hardy, 292, 293. 304.
Haug, 22. 25. 32. 47. 60. 61. 91. 93. 100. 150. 152. 153. 155. 162. 314, 315. 317.
Hessler, 268.
Heymann, 231.
Hillebrandt, 44. 314.
Hodgson, 291. 292. 309.
Holtzmann, 200. 228. 230. 279. 318.
Huc, 307.
Íśvarachandra Vidyáságara, 205. 235.
Jacobi, 195. 204. 214. 254. 255. 260. 281. 319. 323. 326.
Jaganmohanaśarman, 231.
Jayanáráyaṇa, 243, 244.
Jívánanda Vidyáságara, 270. 320. 325.
Johäntgen, 102. 238. 278, 279. 281. 285.
Jolly, 326.
Jones, Sir W., 272.
Julien, Stan., 218. 301.
Kaegi, 44.
Kashinath Trimbak Telang, 194.
Keller, O., 211, 212.
Kennedy, Vans, 170.
Kern, 61. 179. 202. 204. 215. 224. 243. 257–261. 267. 279. 288. 293. 299. 318. 324.
Keśavaśástriu, 323.
Kielhorn, 25. 61. 68. 95. 101. 155. 170. 212. 225, 226. 313. 321.
Kittel, 189.
Klatt, 210. 310.
Knighton, 204.
Köppen, 283. 306. 307. 308.
Kosegarten, 212.
Kṛishṇashastri, 320.
Kuhn, Ad., 25. 32. 35, 36. 62.
Kuhn, E., 293. 295.
Kunte, 325 (Mureshvar).
Laboulaye, 307.
Langlois, 43. 189.
Lassen, 4. 28. 75. 176. 179. 185. 188. 189. 190. 198. 199. 201. 202. 204. 205. 214, 218–220. 227. 229. 239. 244. 247. 251, 252. 254. 257. 260. 273. 275, 276. 287–290. 292. 296. 301. 308. 309. 319.
Lefmann, 299.
Leitner, 273.
Letronne, 229.
Liebrecht, 307.
Linde, Van der, 275.
Lindner, 318.
Loiseleur Deslongchamps, 230.
Lorinser, 238.
Loth, O., 263.
Ludwig, A., 44. 249. 315.
Madhusúdana Gupta, 270.
Maheśachandra Nyáyaratna, 91. 241.
Marshman, 194.
Mayr, 279.
Meyer, Rud., 313, 314. 316.
Minayeff, 3. 293. 303.
Müller, E., 299.
Müller, Fr., 293.
Müller, M., 15. 16. 19. 22. 31. 32. 35. 36. 42. 43. 48. 49. 55. 58. 59. 61. 63. 69. 93. 101. 106. 116. 142. 151. 155. 176. 180. 205. 221. 225. 234–236. 241. 244, 245. 247. 278. 282. 288. 307. 314. 315. 325.
Muir, 41. 44. 210. 292. 299.
Myriantheus, 314.
Nève, 309.
Nöldeke, 187. 318.
Oldenberg, 316. 326.

Olshausen, 4. 188. 318.
Patterson, 273.
Pavie, 189.
Pertsch, 40, 60.
St. Petersburg Dictionary, 16. 104. 108. 112. 141. 266. 305.
Pischel, 206–208. 227. 295. 320. 321.
Poley, 50. 139.
Pons, Père, 216. 254.
Pramadá Dása Mitra, 231.
Premachandra Tarkavágíśa, 232.
Prinsep, 179. 229.
Prym, 320.
Rádhákánta Deva, 275.
Rájárámaśástrin, 223.
Rájendra Lála Mitra, 48. 61. 65. 73. 84. 94. 142. 151. 155. 158. 162–164. 166, 167. 169–171, 182. 202. 210. 215. 220. 271. 274. 275. 297. 299. 315. 317.
Rámamaya Tarkaratna, 158. 168.
Rámamiśraśástrin, 322.
Rámanáráyaṇa, 58. 91. 243.
Rám Ráz, 275.
Rask, 293.
Regnaud, 318. 320.
Regnier, 34. 59.
Reinaud, 61. 148. 201. 202. 217. 219. 229. 239. 252, 253. 256–259. 262, 263. 266. 269. 274. 307.
Renan, 309.
Rieu, 230.
Roer, 43. 48. 51. 54. 73. 74. 91. 94. 96. 116. 139. 154. 157. 160. 161. 231. 235. 244. 262.
Rosen, 43.
Rost, 66. 182. 191. 236. 268. 270. 279.
Roth, 8. 22. 23. 25. 33. 36. 38. 42 43. 44. 48. 63. 70. 80. 102. 112. 146. 147. 150. 152. 178. 201. 247. 267, 268. 270. 303.
Royle, 271.
Sachau, 253. 323.
Satyavrata Sámáśrami, 66. 299. 316.
Schiefner, 56. 185. 209. 212. 227. 248. 291. 300. 306. 307. 326.
Schlagintweit, E., 310.
Schlegel, A. W. von, 194. 231. 275.
Schlüter, 234.
Schmidt, 289. 291. 306.
Schönborn, 48.
Schwanbeck, 20.
Sédillot, 247.
Senart, 293. 304. 326.
Shankar Paṇḍit, 204. 315. 318.
Sourindra Mohan Tagore, 325.
Speijer, 19. 102. 142.
Spiegel, 293. 300. 306.
Steinschneider, 247.
Stenzler, 34. 55. 58. 142; 195. 206. 268. 277–280. 318. 325.
Stevenson, 43. 65. 215. 297. 326.
Storck, 293.
Strachey, 262.
Streiter, 55.
Táránátha Tarkaváchaspati, 89. 184. 226.
Taylor, J., 262.
Taylor, W., 155. 162. 164, 165. 167. 169–171.
Thibaut, 60. 256. 316. 324.
Thomas, 215. 256.
Turnour, 267. 292, 293. 306.
Vaux, 215. 273.
Vechanarámaśástrin, 190. 323.
Vinson, 3.
Viśvanáthaśástrin, 60.
Vullers, 268.
Wagener, A., 211.
Warren, 297.
Wassiljew, 248. 300. 309.
Weigle, 189.
West, A. A., 215.
West, R., 278.
West, E. W., 215.
Westergaard, 22. 184. 201. 203. 215. 223. 230. 284. 288. 293. 295. 304.
Wheeler, T., 190. 251. 281.
Whish, 254.
Whitney, 2. 23. 64. 103. 150. 152. 247. 257, 258.
Wilkins, 228.
Wilkinson, 262.
Williams, 189.
Wilson, H. H., 43. 148. 179. 189. 191. 204–207. 213. 215. 221. 230. 236, 237. 250. 268. 270, 271. 281. 285. 305. 306. 318.
Wilson, J., 215.
Windisch, 297.
Windischmann, 73. 243.
Wise, 270.
Woepcke, 253. 256, 257.
Wright, Dan., 318.
Zimmer, 44.

PRINTED BY BALLANTYNE, HANSON AND CO.
EDINBURGH AND LONDON

TRÜBNER'S ORIENTAL SERIES.

"A knowledge of the commonplace, at least, of Oriental literature, philosophy, and religion is as necessary to the general reader of the present day as an acquaintance with the Latin and Greek classics was a generation or so ago. Immense strides have been made within the present century in these branches of learning; Sanskrit has been brought within the range of accurate philology, and its invaluable ancient literature thoroughly investigated; the language and sacred books of the Zoroastrians have been laid bare; Egyptian, Assyrian, and other records of the remote past have been deciphered, and a group of scholars speak of still more recondite Accadian and Hittite monuments; but the results of all the scholarship that has been devoted to these subjects have been almost inaccessible to the public because they were contained for the most part in learned or expensive works, or scattered throughout the numbers of scientific periodicals. Messrs. TRÜBNER & Co., in a spirit of enterprise which does them infinite credit, have determined to supply the constantly-increasing want, and to give in a popular, or, at least, a comprehensive form, all this mass of knowledge to the world."—*Times*.

Second Edition, post 8vo, pp. xxxii.—748, with Map, cloth, price 21s.

THE INDIAN EMPIRE: ITS PEOPLE, HISTORY, AND PRODUCTS.

By the HON. SIR W. W. HUNTER, K.C.S.I., C.S.I., C.I.E., LL.D.,
Member of the Viceroy's Legislative Council,
Director-General of Statistics to the Government of India.

Being a Revised Edition, brought up to date, and incorporating the general results of the Census of 1881.

"It forms a volume of more than 700 pages, and is a marvellous combination of literary condensation and research. It gives a complete account of the Indian Empire, its history, peoples, and products, and forms the worthy outcome of seventeen years of labour with exceptional opportunities for rendering that labour fruitful. Nothing could be more lucid than Sir William Hunter's expositions of the economic and political condition of India at the present time, or more interesting than his scholarly history of the India of the past."—*The Times*.

THE FOLLOWING WORKS HAVE ALREADY APPEARED:—

Third Edition, post 8vo, cloth, pp. xvi.—428, price 16s.

ESSAYS ON THE SACRED LANGUAGE, WRITINGS, AND RELIGION OF THE PARSIS.

BY MARTIN HAUG, PH.D.,

Late of the Universities of Tübingen, Göttingen, and Bonn; Superintendent of Sanskrit Studies, and Professor of Sanskrit in the Poona College.

EDITED AND ENLARGED BY DR. E. W. WEST.

To which is added a Biographical Memoir of the late Dr. HAUG by Prof. E. P. EVANS.

I. History of the Researches into the Sacred Writings and Religion of the Parsis, from the Earliest Times down to the Present.
II. Languages of the Parsi Scriptures.
III. The Zend-Avesta, or the Scripture of the Parsis.
IV. The Zoroastrian Religion, as to its Origin and Development.

"'Essays on the Sacred Language, Writings, and Religion of the Parsis,' by the late Dr. Martin Haug, edited by Dr. E. W. West. The author intended, on his return from India, to expand the materials contained in this work into a comprehensive account of the Zoroastrian religion, but the design was frustrated by his untimely death. We have, however, in a concise and readable form, a history of the researches into the sacred writings and religion of the Parsis from the earliest times down to the present—a dissertation on the languages of the Parsi Scriptures, a translation of the Zend-Avesta, or the Scripture of the Parsis, and a dissertation on the Zoroastrian religion, with especial reference to its origin and development."—*Times.*

Post 8vo, cloth, pp. viii.—176, price 7s. 6d.

TEXTS FROM THE BUDDHIST CANON

COMMONLY KNOWN AS "DHAMMAPADA."

With Accompanying Narratives.

Translated from the Chinese by S. BEAL, B.A., Professor of Chinese, University College, London.

The Dhammapada, as hitherto known by the Pali Text Edition, as edited by Fausböll, by Max Müller's English, and Albrecht Weber's German translations, consists only of twenty-six chapters or sections, whilst the Chinese version, or rather recension, as now translated by Mr. Beal, consists of thirty-nine sections. The students of Pali who possess Fausböll's text, or either of the above named translations, will therefore needs want Mr. Beal's English rendering of the Chinese version; the thirteen above-named additional sections not being accessible to them in any other form; for, even if they understand Chinese, the Chinese original would be unobtainable by them.

"Mr. Beal's rendering of the Chinese translation is a most valuable aid to the critical study of the work. It contains authentic texts gathered from ancient canonical books, and generally connected with some incident in the history of Buddha. Their great interest, however, consists in the light which they throw upon everyday life in India at the remote period at which they were written, and upon the method of teaching adopted by the founder of the religion. The method employed was principally parable, and the simplicity of the tales and the excellence of the morals inculcated, as well as the strange hold which they have retained upon the minds of millions of people, make them a very remarkable study."—*Times.*

"Mr. Beal, by making it accessible in an English dress, has added to the great services he has already rendered to the comparative study of religious history."—*Academy.*

"Valuable as exhibiting the doctrine of the Buddhists in its purest, least adulterated form, it brings the modern reader face to face with that simple creed and rule of conduct which won its way over the minds of myriads, and which is now nominally professed by 145 millions, who have overlaid its austere simplicity with innumerable ceremonies, forgotten its maxims, perverted its teaching, and so inverted its leading principle that a religion whose founder denied a God, now worships that founder as a god himself."—*Scotsman.*

Third Edition, post 8vo, cloth, pp. xxiv.—360, price 10s. 6d.

THE HISTORY OF INDIAN LITERATURE.

By ALBRECHT WEBER.

Translated from the Second German Edition by JOHN MANN, M.A., and THÉODOR ZACHARIAE, Ph.D., with the sanction of the Author.

Dr. BUHLER, Inspector of Schools in India, writes:—"When I was Professor of Oriental Languages in Elphinstone College, I frequently felt the want of such a work to which I could refer the students."

Professor COWELL, of Cambridge, writes:—"It will be especially useful to the students in our Indian colleges and universities. I used to long for such a book when I was teaching in Calcutta. Hindu students are intensely interested in the history of Sanskrit literature, and this volume will supply them with all they want on the subject."

Professor WHITNEY, Yale College, Newhaven, Conn., U.S.A., writes:—"I was one of the class to whom the work was originally given in the form of academic lectures. At their first appearance they were by far the most learned and able treatment of their subject; and with their recent additions they still maintain decidedly the same rank."

"Is perhaps the most comprehensive and lucid survey of Sanskrit literature extant. The essays contained in the volume were originally delivered as academic lectures, and at the time of their first publication were acknowledged to be by far the most learned and able treatment of the subject. They have now been brought up to date by the addition of all the most important results of recent research."—*Times.*

Post 8vo, cloth, pp. xii.—198, accompanied by Two Language Maps, price 7s. 6d.

A SKETCH OF THE MODERN LANGUAGES OF THE EAST INDIES.

By ROBERT N. CUST.

The Author has attempted to fill up a vacuum, the inconvenience of which pressed itself on his notice. Much had been written about the languages of the East Indies, but the extent of our present knowledge had not even been brought to a focus. It occurred to him that it might be of use to others to publish in an arranged form the notes which he had collected for his own edification.

"Supplies a deficiency which has long been felt."—*Times.*

"The book before us is then a valuable contribution to philological science. It passes under review a vast number of languages, and it gives, or professes to give, in every case the sum and substance of the opinions and judgments of the best-informed writers."—*Saturday Review.*

Second Corrected Edition, post 8vo, pp. xii.—116, cloth, price 5s.

THE BIRTH OF THE WAR-GOD.

A Poem. By KALIDASA.

Translated from the Sanskrit into English Verse by RALPH T. H. GRIFFITH, M.A.

"A very spirited rendering of the *Kumárasambhava*, which was first published twenty-six years ago, and which we are glad to see made once more accessible."—*Times.*

"Mr. Griffith's very spirited rendering is well known to most who are at all interested in Indian literature, or enjoy the tenderness of feeling and rich creative imagination of its author."—*Indian Antiquary.*

"We are very glad to welcome a second edition of Professor Griffith's admirable translation. Few translations deserve a second edition better."—*Athenæum.*

Post 8vo, pp. xii.—228, cloth, price 7s. 6d.

THE CLASSICAL POETRY OF THE JAPANESE.

BY BASIL HALL CHAMBERLAIN,
Author of "Yeigo Heñkaku Shirañ."

"A very curious volume. The author has manifestly devoted much labour to the task of studying the poetical literature of the Japanese, and rendering characteristic specimens into English verse."—*Daily News.*

"Mr. Chamberlain's volume is, so far as we are aware, the first attempt which has been made to interpret the literature of the Japanese to the Western world. It is to the classical poetry of Old Japan that we must turn for indigenous Japanese thought, and in the volume before us we have a selection from that poetry rendered into graceful English verse."—*Tablet.*

"It is undoubtedly one of the best translations of lyric literature which has appeared during the close of the last year."—*Celestial Empire.*

"Mr. Chamberlain set himself a difficult task when he undertook to reproduce Japanese poetry in an English form. But he has evidently laboured *con amore*, and his efforts are successful to a degree."—*London and China Express.*

Post 8vo, pp. xii.—164, cloth, price 10s. 6d.

THE HISTORY OF ESARHADDON (Son of Sennacherib), KING OF ASSYRIA, B.C. 681-668.

Translated from the Cuneiform Inscriptions upon Cylinders and Tablets in the British Museum Collection; together with a Grammatical Analysis of each Word, Explanations of the Ideographs by Extracts from the Bi-Lingual Syllabaries, and List of Eponyms, &c.

BY ERNEST A. BUDGE, B.A., M.R.A.S.,
Assyrian Exhibitioner, Christ's College, Cambridge.

"Students of scriptural archæology will also appreciate the 'History of Esarhaddon.'"—*Times.*

"There is much to attract the scholar in this volume. It does not pretend to popularise studies which are yet in their infancy. Its primary object is to translate, but it does not assume to be more than tentative, and it offers both to the professed Assyriologist and to the ordinary non-Assyriological Semitic scholar the means of controlling its results."—*Academy.*

"Mr. Budge's book is, of course, mainly addressed to Assyrian scholars and students. They are not, it is to be feared, a very numerous class. But the more thanks are due to him on that account for the way in which he has acquitted himself in his laborious task."—*Tablet.*

Post 8vo, pp. 448, cloth, price 21s.

THE MESNEVI

(Usually known as THE MESNEVIYI SHERIF, or HOLY MESNEVI)

OF

MEVLANA (OUR LORD) JELALU 'D-DIN MUHAMMED ER-RUMI.

Book the First.

Together with some Account of the Life and Acts of the Author, of his Ancestors, and of his Descendants.

Illustrated by a Selection of Characteristic Anecdotes, as Collected by their Historian,

MEVLANA SHEMSU-'D-DIN AHMED, EL EFLAKI, EL 'ARIFI.

Translated, and the Poetry Versified, in English,

BY JAMES W. REDHOUSE, M.R.A.S., &c.

"A complete treasury of occult Oriental lore."—*Saturday Review.*

"This book will be a very valuable help to the reader ignorant of Persia, who is desirous of obtaining an insight into a very important department of the literature extant in that language."—*Tablet.*

Post 8vo, pp. xvi.—280, cloth, price 6s.

EASTERN PROVERBS AND EMBLEMS

ILLUSTRATING OLD TRUTHS.

BY REV. J. LONG,

Member of the Bengal Asiatic Society, F.R.G.S.

"We regard the book as valuable, and wish for it a wide circulation and attentive reading."—*Record.*

"Altogether, it is quite a feast of good things."—*Globe.*

"It is full of interesting matter."—*Antiquary.*

Post 8vo, pp. viii.—270, cloth, price 7s. 6d.

INDIAN POETRY;

Containing a New Edition of the "Indian Song of Songs," from the Sanscrit of the "Gita Govinda" of Jayadeva; Two Books from "The Iliad of India" (Mahabharata), "Proverbial Wisdom" from the Shlokas of the Hitopadesa, and other Oriental Poems.

BY EDWIN ARNOLD, C.S.I., Author of "The Light of Asia."

"In this new volume of Messrs. Trübner's Oriental Series, Mr. Edwin Arnold does good service by illustrating, through the medium of his musical English melodies, the power of Indian poetry to stir European emotions. The 'Indian Song of Songs' is not unknown to scholars. Mr. Arnold will have introduced it among popular English poems. Nothing could be more graceful and delicate than the shades by which Krishna is portrayed in the gradual process of being weaned by the love of

'Beautiful Radha, jasmine-bosomed Radha,'

from the allurements of the forest nymphs, in whom the five senses are typified."—*Times.*

"No other English poet has ever thrown his genius and his art so thoroughly into the work of translating Eastern ideas as Mr. Arnold has done in his splendid paraphrases of language contained in these mighty epics."—*Daily Telegraph.*

"The poem abounds with imagery of Eastern luxuriousness and sensuousness; the air seems laden with the spicy odours of the tropics, and the verse has a richness and a melody sufficient to captivate the senses of the dullest."—*Standard.*

"The translator, while producing a very enjoyable poem, has adhered with tolerable fidelity to the original text."—*Overland Mail.*

"We certainly wish Mr. Arnold success in his attempt 'to popularise Indian classics,' that being, as his preface tells us, the goal towards which he bends his efforts."—*Allen's Indian Mail.*

Post 8vo, pp. xvi.—296, cloth, price 10s. 6d.

THE MIND OF MENCIUS;

OR, POLITICAL ECONOMY FOUNDED UPON MORAL PHILOSOPHY.

A SYSTEMATIC DIGEST OF THE DOCTRINES OF THE CHINESE PHILOSOPHER MENCIUS.

Translated from the Original Text and Classified, with Comments and Explanations,

By the REV. ERNST FABER, Rhenish Mission Society.

Translated from the German, with Additional Notes,

By the REV. A. B. HUTCHINSON, C.M.S., Church Mission, Hong Kong.

"Mr. Faber is already well known in the field of Chinese studies by his digest of the doctrines of Confucius. The value of this work will be perceived when it is remembered that at no time since relations commenced between China and the West has the former been so powerful—we had almost said aggressive—as now. For those who will give it careful study, Mr. Faber's work is one of the most valuable of the excellent series to which it belongs."—*Nature.*

Post 8vo, pp. 336, cloth, price 16s.

THE RELIGIONS OF INDIA.

By A. BARTH.

Second Edition.

Translated from the French with the authority and assistance of the Author.

The author has, at the request of the publishers, considerably enlarged the work for the translator, and has added the literature of the subject to date; the translation may, therefore, be looked upon as an equivalent of a new and improved edition of the original.

"Is not only a valuable manual of the religions of India, which marks a distinct step in the treatment of the subject, but also a useful work of reference."—*Academy.*

"This volume is a reproduction, with corrections and additions, of an article contributed by the learned author two years ago to the 'Encyclopédie des Sciences Religieuses.' It attracted much notice when it first appeared, and is generally admitted to present the best summary extant of the vast subject with which it deals."—*Tablet.*

"This is not only on the whole the best but the only manual of the religions of India, apart from Buddhism, which we have in English. The present work . . . shows not only great knowledge of the facts and power of clear exposition, but also great insight into the inner history and the deeper meaning of the great religion, for it is in reality only one, which it proposes to describe."—*Modern Review.*

"The merit of the work has been emphatically recognised by the most authoritative Orientalists, both in this country and on the continent of Europe, But probably there are few Indianists (if we may use the word) who would not derive a good deal of information from it, and especially from the extensive bibliography provided in the notes."—*Dublin Review.*

"Such a sketch M. Barth has drawn with a master-hand."—*Critic (New York).*

Post 8vo, pp. viii.—152, cloth, price 6s.

HINDU PHILOSOPHY.

THE SĀNKHYA KĀRIKA OF IS'WARA KRISHNA.

An Exposition of the System of Kapila, with an Appendix on the Nyāya and Vais'eshika Systems.

By JOHN DAVIES, M.A. (Cantab.), M.R.A.S.

The system of Kapila contains nearly all that India has produced in the department of pure philosophy.

"The non Orientalist . . . finds in Mr. Davies a patient and learned guide who leads him into the intricacies of the philosophy of India, and supplies him with a clue, that he may not be lost in them. In the preface he states that the system of Kapila is the 'earliest attempt on record to give an answer, from reason alone, to the mysterious questions which arise in every thoughtful mind about the origin of the world, the nature and relations of man and his future destiny,' and in his learned and able notes he exhibits 'the connection of the Sankhya system with the philosophy of Spinoza,' and 'the connection of the system of Kapila with that of Schopenhauer and Von Hartmann.'"—*Foreign Church Chronicle.*

"Mr. Davies's volume on Hindu Philosophy is an undoubted gain to all students of the development of thought. The system of Kapila, which is here given in a translation from the Sānkhya Kārikā, is the only contribution of India to pure philosophy. . . . Presents many points of deep interest to the student of comparative philosophy, and without Mr. Davies's lucid interpretation it would be difficult to appreciate these points in any adequate manner."—*Saturday Review.*

"We welcome Mr. Davies's book as a valuable addition to our philosophical library."—*Notes and Queries.*

Second Edition. Post 8vo, pp. vi.—208, cloth, price 8s. 6d.

THE BHAGAVAD-GÎTÂ.

Translated, with Introduction and Notes.

BY JOHN DAVIES, M.A. (Cantab.)

"Let us add that his translation of the Bhagavad Gîtâ is, as we judge, the best that has as yet appeared in English, and that his Philological Notes are of quite peculiar value."—*Dublin Review.*

Post 8vo, pp. 96, cloth, price 5s.

THE QUATRAINS OF OMAR KHAYYAM.

Translated by E. H. WHINFIELD, M.A.,

Barrister-at-Law, late H.M. Bengal Civil Service.

Post 8vo, pp. xxxii.—336, cloth, price 10s. 6d.

THE QUATRAINS OF OMAR KHAYYAM.

The Persian Text, with an English Verse Translation.

By E. H. WHINFIELD, late of the Bengal Civil Service.

"Mr. Whinfield has executed a difficult task with considerable success, and his version contains much that will be new to those who only know Mr. Fitzgerald's delightful selection."—*Academy.*

"The most prominent features in the Quatrains are their profound agnosticism, combined with a fatalism based more on philosophic than religious grounds, their Epicureanism and the spirit of universal tolerance and charity which animates them."—*Calcutta Review.*

Post 8vo, pp. xxiv.—268, cloth, price 9s.

THE PHILOSOPHY OF THE UPANISHADS AND ANCIENT INDIAN METAPHYSICS.

As exhibited in a series of Articles contributed to the *Calcutta Review.*

By ARCHIBALD EDWARD GOUGH, M.A., Lincoln College, Oxford; Principal of the Calcutta Madrasa.

"For practical purposes this is perhaps the most important of the works that have thus far appeared in 'Trübner's Oriental Series.' . . . We cannot doubt that for all who may take it up the work must be one of profound interest."—*Saturday Review.*

In Two Volumes. Vol. I., post 8vo, pp. xxiv.—230, cloth, price 7s. 6d.

A COMPARATIVE HISTORY OF THE EGYPTIAN AND MESOPOTAMIAN RELIGIONS.

By DR. C. P. TIELE.

Vol. I.—HISTORY OF THE EGYPTIAN RELIGION.

Translated from the Dutch with the Assistance of the Author.

By JAMES BALLINGAL.

"It places in the hands of the English readers a history of Egyptian Religion which is very complete, which is based on the best materials, and which has been illustrated by the latest results of research. In this volume there is a great deal of information, as well as independent investigation, for the trustworthiness of which Dr. Tiele's name is in itself a guarantee; and the description of the successive religions under the Old Kingdom, the Middle Kingdom, and the New Kingdom, is given in a manner which is scholarly and minute."—*Scotsman.*

Post 8vo, pp. xii.—302, cloth, price 8s. 6d.

YUSUF AND ZULAIKHA.

A Poem by JAMI.

Translated from the Persian into English Verse.

By RALPH T. H. GRIFFITH.

"Mr. Griffith, who has done already good service as translator into verse from the Sanskrit, has done further good work in this translation from the Persian, and he has evidently shown not a little skill in his rendering the quaint and very oriental style of his author into our more prosaic, less figurative, language. . . . The work, besides its intrinsic merits, is of importance as being one of the most popular and famous poems of Persia, and that which is read in all the independent native schools of India where Persian is taught."—*Scotsman.*

Post 8vo, pp. viii.—266, cloth, price 9s.

LINGUISTIC ESSAYS.

By CARL ABEL.

"An entirely novel method of dealing with philosophical questions and impart a real human interest to the otherwise dry technicalities of the science."—*Standard.*

"Dr. Abel is an opponent from whom it is pleasant to differ, for he writes with enthusiasm and temper, and his mastery over the English language fits him to be a champion of unpopular doctrines."—*Athenæum.*

Post 8vo, pp. ix.—281, cloth, price 10s. 6d.

THE SARVA-DARSANA-SAMGRAHA;

OR, REVIEW OF THE DIFFERENT SYSTEMS OF HINDU PHILOSOPHY.

By MADHAVA ACHARYA.

Translated by E. B. COWELL, M.A., Professor of Sanskrit in the University of Cambridge, and A. E. GOUGH, M.A., Professor of Philosophy in the Presidency College, Calcutta.

This work is an interesting specimen of Hindu critical ability. The author successively passes in review the sixteen philosophical systems current in the fourteenth century in the South of India; and he gives what appears to him to be their most important tenets.

"The translation is trustworthy throughout. A protracted sojourn in India, where there is a living tradition, has familiarised the translators with Indian thought."—*Athenæum.*

Post 8vo, pp. lxv.—368, cloth, price 14s.

TIBETAN TALES DERIVED FROM INDIAN SOURCES.

Translated from the Tibetan of the Kah-Gyur.

By F. ANTON VON SCHIEFNER.

Done into English from the German, with an Introduction,

By W. R. S. RALSTON, M.A.

"Mr. Ralston, whose name is so familiar to all lovers of Russian folk-lore, has supplied some interesting Western analogies and parallels, drawn, for the most part, from Slavonic sources, to the Eastern folk-tales, culled from the Kahgyur, one of the divisions of the Tibetan sacred books."—*Academy.*

"The translation . . . could scarcely have fallen into better hands. An Introduction . . . gives the leading facts in the lives of those scholars who have given their attention to gaining a knowledge of the Tibetan literature and language."—*Calcutta Review.*

"Ought to interest all who care for the East, for amusing stories, or for comparative folk-lore."—*Pall Mall Gazette.*

In Two Volumes, post 8vo, pp. cviii.-242, and viii.-370, cloth, price 24s.
Dedicated by permission to H.R.H. the Prince of Wales.

BUDDHIST RECORDS OF THE WESTERN WORLD,

Translated from the Chinese of Hiuen Tsiang (A.D. 629).

By SAMUEL BEAL, B.A.,

(Trin. Coll., Camb.); R.N. (Retired Chaplain and N.I.); Professor of Chinese, University College, London; Rector of Wark, Northumberland, &c.

An eminent Indian authority writes respecting this work:—"Nothing more can be done in elucidating the History of India until Mr. Beal's translation of the 'Si-yu-ki' appears."

"It is a strange freak of historical preservation that the best account of the condition of India at that ancient period has come down to us in the books of travel written by the Chinese pilgrims, of whom Hwen Thsang is the best known."—*Times.*

Post 8vo, pp. xlviii.-398, cloth, price 12s.

THE ORDINANCES OF MANU.

Translated from the Sanskrit, with an Introduction.

By the late A. C. BURNELL, Ph.D., C.I.E.

Completed and Edited by E. W. HOPKINS, Ph.D., of Columbia College, N.Y.

"This work is full of interest; while for the student of sociology and the science of religion it is full of importance. It is a great boon to get so notable a work in so accessible a form, admirably edited, and competently translated."—*Scotsman.*

"Few men were more competent than Burnell to give us a really good translation of this well-known law book, first rendered into English by Sir William Jones. Burnell was not only an independent Sanskrit scholar, but an experienced lawyer, and he joined to these two important qualifications the rare faculty of being able to express his thoughts in clear and trenchant English. . . . We ought to feel very grateful to Dr. Hopkins for having given us all that could be published of the translation left by Burnell."—F. MAX MÜLLER in the *Academy.*

Post 8vo, pp. xii.-234, cloth, price 9s.

THE LIFE AND WORKS OF ALEXANDER CSOMA DE KOROS,

Between 1819 and 1842. With a Short Notice of all his Published and Unpublished Works and Essays. From Original and for most part Unpublished Documents.

By THEODORE DUKA, M.D., F.R.C.S. (Eng.), Surgeon-Major H.M.'s Bengal Medical Service, Retired, &c.

"Not too soon have Messrs. Trübner added to their valuable Oriental Series a history of the life and works of one of the most gifted and devoted of Oriental students, Alexander Csoma de Koros. It is forty-three years since his death, and though an account of his career was demanded soon after his decease, it has only now appeared in the important memoir of his compatriot, Dr. Duka."—*Bookseller.*

In Two Volumes, post 8vo, pp. xii.-318 and vi.-312, cloth, price 21s.

MISCELLANEOUS PAPERS RELATING TO INDO-CHINA.

Reprinted from "Dalrymple's Oriental Repertory," "Asiatic Researches," and the "Journal of the Asiatic Society of Bengal."

CONTENTS OF VOL. I.

I.—Some Accounts of Quedah. By Michael Topping.

II.—Report made to the Chief and Council of Balambangan, by Lieut. James Barton, of his several Surveys.

III.—Substance of a Letter to the Court of Directors from Mr. John Jesse, date July 20, 1775, at Borneo Proper.

IV.—Formation of the Establishment of Poolo Peenang.

V.—The Gold of Limong. By John Macdonald.

VI.—On Three Natural Productions of Sumatra. By John Macdonald.

VII.—On the Traces of the Hindu Language and Literature extant amongst the Malays. By William Marsden.

VIII.—Some Account of the Elastic Gum Vine of Prince-Wales Island. By James Howison.

IX.—A Botanical Description of Urceola Elastica, or Caoutchouc Vine of Sumatra and Pulo-Pinang. By William Roxburgh, M.D.

X.—An Account of the Inhabitants of the Poggy, or Nassau Islands, lying off Sumatra. By John Crisp.

XI.—Remarks on the Species of Pepper which are found on Prince-Wales Island. By William Hunter, M.D.

XII.—On the Languages and Literature of the Indo-Chinese Nations. By J. Leyden, M.D.

XIII.—Some Account of an Orang-Outang of remarkable height found on the Island of Sumatra. By Clarke Abel, M.D.

XIV.—Observations on the Geological Appearances and General Features of Portions of the Malayan Peninsula. By Captain James Low.

XV.—Short Sketch of the Geology of Pulo-Pinang and the Neighbouring Islands. By T. Ware.

XVI.—Climate of Singapore.

XVII.—Inscription on the Jetty at Singapore.

XVIII.—Extract of a Letter from Colonel J. Low.

XIX.—Inscription at Singapore.

XX.—An Account of Several Inscriptions found in Province Wellesley. By Lieut.-Col. James Low.

XXI.—Note on the Inscriptions from Singapore and Province Wellesley. By J. W. Laidlay.

XXII.—On an Inscription from Keddah. By Lieut.-Col. Low.

XXIII.—A Notice of the Alphabets of the Philippine Islands.

XXIV.—Succinct Review of the Observations of the Tides in the Indian Archipelago.

XXV.—Report on the Tin of the Province of Mergui. By Capt. G. B. Tremenheere.

XXVI.—Report on the Manganese of Mergui Province. By Capt. G. B. Tremenheere.

XXVII.—Paragraphs to be added to Capt. G. B. Tremenheere's Report.

XXVIII.—Second Report on the Tin of Mergui. By Capt. G. B. Tremenheere.

XXIX.—Analysis of Iron Ores from Tavoy and Mergui, and of Limestone from Mergui. By Dr. A. Ure.

XXX.—Report of a Visit to the Pakchan River, and of some Tin Localities in the Southern Portion of the Tenasserim Provinces. By Capt. G. B. Tremenheere.

XXXI.—Report on a Route from the Mouth of the Pakchan to Krau, and thence across the Isthmus of Krau to the Gulf of Siam. By Capt. Al. Fraser and Capt. J. G. Forlong.

XXXII.—Report, &c., from Capt. G. B. Tremenheere on the Price of Mergui Tin Ore.

XXXIII.—Remarks on the Different Species of Orang-utan. By E. Blyth.

XXXIV.—Further Remarks. By E. Blyth.

MISCELLANEOUS PAPERS RELATING TO INDO-CHINA—continued.

CONTENTS OF VOL. II.

XXXV.—Catalogue of Mammalia inhabiting the Malayan Peninsula and Islands. By Theodore Cantor, M.D.

XXXVI.—On the Local and Relative Geology of Singapore. By J. R. Logan.

XXXVII.—Catalogue of Reptiles inhabiting the Malayan Peninsula and Islands. By Theodore Cantor, M.D.

XXXVIII.—Some Account of the Botanical Collection brought from the Eastward, in 1841, by Dr. Cantor. By the late W. Griffith.

XXXIX.—On the Flat-Horned Taurine Cattle of S.E. Asia. By E. Blyth.

XL.—Note, by Major-General G. B. Tremenheere.

General Index.

Index of Vernacular Terms.

Index of Zoological Genera and Sub-Genera occurring in Vol. II.

"The papers treat of almost every aspect of Indo-China – its philology, economy, geography, geology—and constitute a very material and important contribution to our accessible information regarding that country and its people."—*Contemporary Review.*

Post 8vo, pp. xii.–72, cloth, price 5s.

THE SATAKAS OF BHARTRIHARI.

Translated from the Sanskrit

By the Rev. B. HALE WORTHAM, M.R.A.S.,

Rector of Eggesford, North Devon.

"A very interesting addition to Trübner's Oriental Series."—*Saturday Review.*

"Many of the Maxims in the book have a Biblical ring and beauty of expression." —*St. James' Gazette.*

Post 8vo, pp. xii.–180, cloth, price 6s.

ANCIENT PROVERBS AND MAXIMS FROM BURMESE SOURCES;

OR, THE NITI LITERATURE OF BURMA.

BY JAMES GRAY,

Author of "Elements of Pali Grammar," "Translation of the Dhammapada," &c.

The Sanscrit-Pâli word Niti is equivalent to "conduct" in its abstract, and "guide" in its concrete signification. As applied to books, it is a general term for a treatise which includes maxims, pithy sayings, and didactic stories, intended as a guide to such matters of every-day life as form the character of an individual and influence him in his relations to his fellow-men. Treatises of this kind have been popular in all ages, and have served as a most effective medium of instruction.

Post 8vo, pp. xxxii. and 330, cloth, price 7s. 6d.

MASNAVI I MA' NAVI:

THE SPIRITUAL COUPLETS OF MAULANA JALALU-'D-DIN MUHAMMAD I RUMI.

Translated and Abridged by E. H. WHINFIELD, M.A.

Late of H.M. Bengal Civil Service.

1000—17/10/92.

www.ingramcontent.com/pod-product-compliance
Lightning Source LLC
Chambersburg PA
CBHW030425300426
44112CB00009B/855